READINGS ON THE MANAGEMENT OF WORKING CAPITAL

Second Edition

KEITH V. SMITH

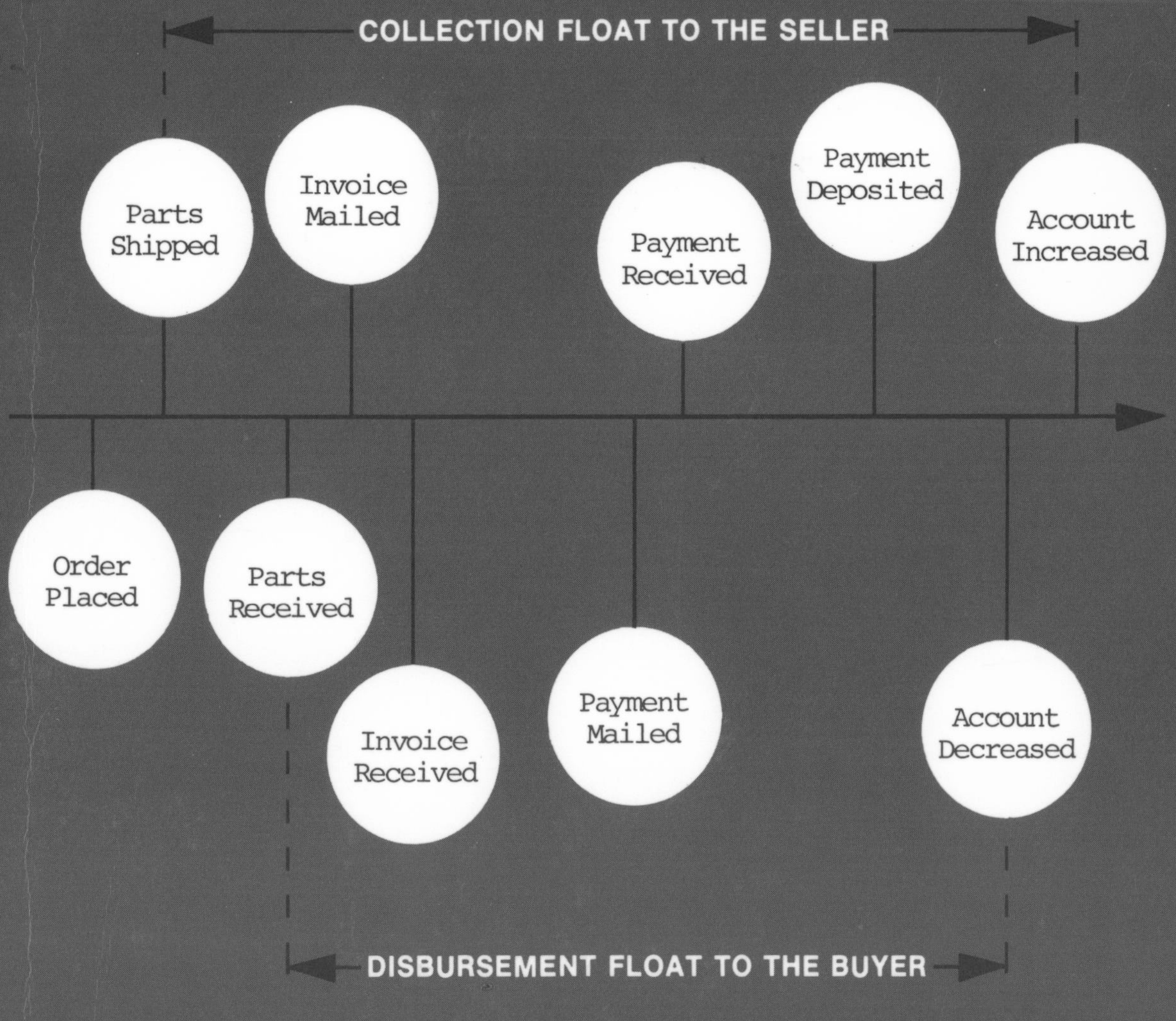

READINGS ON THE MANAGEMENT OF WORKING CAPITAL

Second Edition

READINGS ON THE MANAGEMENT OF WORKING CAPITAL

Second Edition

Keith V. Smith
Purdue University

WEST PUBLISHING COMPANY
St. Paul New York Los Angeles San Francisco

By WEST PUBLISHING CO.
50 West Kellogg Boulevard
P. O. Box 3526
St. Paul, Minnesota 55165

Printed in the United States of America
3rd Reprint—1982

Library of Congress Cataloging in Publication Data
Main entry under title:

Readings on the management of working capital.

Previous ed. complied by K. V. Smith published under title: Management of working capital.
1. Working capital—Addresses, essays, lectures.
I. Smith, Keith V. II. Smith Keith V. Management of of working capital.
HG4028.W65R4 1980 658.1'52 79-28357
ISBN 0-8299-0296-1

Contents

Preface

The first edition of READINGS ON THE MANAGEMENT OF WORKING CAPITAL was published in 1974. It consisted of 34 readings devoted to individual current assets and current liabilities, or to the overall management of working capital. In the preface to READINGS, I suggested that financial theory and guidelines for the management of working capital had not been well developed, despite the practical need for better decision making with respect to the current assets and current liabilities of the firm.

Response to the first edition has far exceeded the expectations of both the author and the publisher. The book has been adopted at a large number of colleges and universities as a supplemental text, either in an introductory or advanced course on financial management. Surprisingly, the book also has been adopted at a growing number of courses devoted solely to the management of working capital. That positive response, coupled with a continued outpouring of excellent papers on various facets of working capital management, led to a decision that a second edition of READINGS was appropriate.

During the Spring of 1978, a questionnaire on various aspects of READINGS was sent to fifteen professors who had used the first edition. Helpful responses were received from the following nine: Raj Aggarwal (University of Toledo), Amir Barnea (Cornell University), Tom Bean (Fairleigh Dickinson University), John Dran (University of Alabama, Birmingham), Christopher Hessel (Long Island University), Frederick Kelly (Montclair State College), Douglas Patterson (University of Michigan), Bernell Stone (Georgia Institute of Technology), and Timothy Sullivan (Northeastern University).

Based in part on these responses, the second edition of READINGS was developed. It consists of 46 papers, 23 of which were contained in the first edition, and 23 of which are new. The expanded number of readings and the turnover of readings from the first edition is indicative of the increased awareness that is being given to the top portion of the balance sheet of the organization. Twelve of the papers are unpublished, while 34 readings have been published in the journals of finance or management science. A balance sheet organization for READINGS is continued. My own contributions include two continued readings from the first edition (one slightly updated), the findings of a recent survey on working capital management in practice, and a final paper which develops my arguments on how the several topics of working capital can be logically integrated into overall financial theory.

I would like to acknowledge the contributions of several individuals that led to the second edition of READINGS. The finance editor of West Publishing Company, Mr. Clyde Perlee, has been a continuing source of expertise and encouragement through both editions. The constructive suggestions of nine professors were noted above. In addition, Professor Bernell Stone of Georgia Institute of Technology provided a penetrating and critical review of all aspects of the book. Professor Stone's important contributions to the field of working capital management are reflected in part by his three papers that are contained herein. Ms. Leslie Duncan competently handled a myriad of secretarial matters concerning the second edition. Finally, I again acknowledge the many capable students and business executives who continue to convince me that working capital management is an important subject that should receive increased attention, both within the curricula of academia and the executive suites of corporate management.

April 1979

Keith V. Smith

SECTION I
Introduction and Overview

The introductory section of the book consists of five papers which constitute an overview of the management of working capital. The first paper by Smith (Reading 1) includes definitions of working capital, as well as financial statistics which portray the changing importance of working capital accounts over time. Goals of the organization are reviewed, and responsibilities for various working capital decisions are identified. Also included is a review of alternative approaches to working capital management which have appeared in the financial literature. A major theme developed in the paper is that proper treatment of working capital management should reflect the several interrelationships that inevitably exist between working capital accounts of the firm.

Walker (Reading 2) recognized early that working capital is an important area for further study. He develops three propositions which comprise a basis for a theory of working capital management. The first proposition relates working capital levels to overall firm risk, the second proposition involves the type of long-term financing used to finance working capital, while the third proposition deals with the relationship between the firm's debt structure and the cash flow generated within the firm. While many of the points Walker makes are considered further in later readings, his paper should be recognized as one of the pioneering efforts in the working capital area.

Cohn and Pringle (Reading 3) attempt to integrate working capital management into an overall theory of corporate finance. They begin by reviewing briefly the capital asset pricing model which during the last decade has become a central proposition in the theory of finance. Under certain assumptions, the capital asset pricing model provides an equilibrium theory relating expected return and risk. The authors go on to explain that the assumption of perfect financial markets precludes consideration of many aspects of working capital, and that further extensions of the model under less restrictive assumptions are necessary if working capital is to be integrated into overall financial theory. Despite formidable difficulties which must be faced, Cohn and Pringle provide a useful direction for further efforts in developing a theory of working capital.

Bierman, Chopra, and Thomas (Reading 4) view working capital as a necessary determinant of firm sales and profit, but also as a buffer against ruin when profits are not realized. Using a dynamic programming approach, the authors attempt to interrelate the working capital and capital structure decisions of the firm. Their first formulation is the standard discounted cash flow approach, and their second formulation adds a risk adjustment based on the capital asset pricing model. Although there are both theoretical and practical limitations to the approach used, the paper is useful in trying to link the short-run problems of working capital to the long-run problems of financial management, and therein to avoid the difficulties of suboptimization that frequently characterize papers on working capital.

In contrast to these three theoretical papers on working capital, Smith and Sell (Reading 5) present the findings of a nationwide survey of how firms actually go about managing their current assets and current liabilities. Included are questions on working capital policy, responsibilities for different working capital accounts, and various technologies for managing float, credit, inventory, and short-term financing. In addition to reporting for the entire sample of 210 responding firms, subsample comparisons are made based on size, profitability, formality of policy, and aggressiveness of policy. The survey findings provide a real-world perspective on how many of the techniques discussed throughout the rest of the book are actually used in practice.

READING 1

An Overview of Working Capital Management

Keith V. Smith
Purdue University

I. INTRODUCTION

Financial decision-making by organizations is an important and popular topic for study, both in college classrooms and in the executive suites where corporate affairs are managed. College professors and financial executives alike, have worked to improve their understanding of how organizations raise and allocate financial resources, as well as how the organizations ought to manage these resources. The importance of financial decision-making within business is readily exemplified by the presence of financially-trained and experienced executives on boards of directors and in key positions at or near the top of the organizational hierarchy. The rising proportions of business students interested in finance, or in finance combined with managerial accounting or other related disciplines attest to its significance on college campuses.

Important theoretical developments in finance during the past decade or so have provided the potential for improved decision-making, especially within business organizations. Better understanding of return-risk relationships and the pricing of capital assets are shown to have important implications to the asset expansion and long-term financial decisions of the firm. While some of these theoretical developments await further empirical testing, others have already been reflected in the decision-making process of business firms.

Unfortunately, useful theoretical developments have not been uniform across all areas of financial decision-making within the organization. Of interest in this book is the area of "working capital management" which generally encompasses the short-term investment and financial decisions of the firm. Although certain aspects of working capital are not unrelated to longer-term financial decisions, working capital management appears to have been relatively neglected in the literature of finance. This neglect exists in spite of the fact that a high proportion of business failures are due to poor decisions concerning the working capital of the firm.

Portions of this paper, which was included in the first edition of READINGS, have been updated for the second edition.

This paper is intended as an overview of working capital management and as a survey of the existing literature dealing with the management of working capital. Some pertinent definitions are presented in Section II, and the scope of working capital management is explored in Section III. Section IV includes a review of the goals of the organization and its management, plus a comparison of the responsibilities for various working capital decisions. A series of different approaches to working capital management are reviewed in Section V together with their strong points and limitations. Section VI explores possible directions for future research.

II. DEFINITIONS

In order to place working capital management in proper perspective alongside other decision-making areas within finance, it is useful to trace briefly the evolution of the finance function during the past few decades. As the industrial revolution unfolded near the beginning of this century, the finance function was primarily concerned with making sure that the bills of the organization were paid. In other words, finance dealt almost exclusively with managing the current liabilities of the firm. But as the magnitude of assets under management grew, and as competition intensified, the finance function tended to expand in many firms to the extent that financial management was necessarily concerned not only with paying bills, but also with worrying about the entire range of financial sources. That is, finance expanded so that attention was given to the origin of all financial sources included on the right hand side of the firm's balance sheet.

As the size of business firms continued to grow and as competition continued to intensify, the finance function again tended to expand to the degree that it was concerned not only with paying bills and with all sources of financing, but also with how the total financial resources of the firm would be invested. This meant that the finance function had finally reached the point of being involved with the entire balance sheet of the firm. This expanded focus has continued, and today most textbooks in finance and many business finance courses are organized around the balance sheet of the firm. Interestingly enough, this means that while many managers in executive suites would probably give first priority to the income statement of the firm, the balance sheet has become a focal point for organizing the teaching of finance within college classrooms.

The first definitions are thus based on a representative balance sheet of the firm such as appears in Figure 1. Although there is by no means a standard format or set of accounts used by all firms, the items on both sides of Figure 1 are probably as representative as any. Balance sheet accounts are grouped into five categories: Current assets Σa_j, fixed assets ΣA_j, current liabilities $\Sigma \ell_j$, long-term liabilities ΣL_j, and equity ΣE_j.[1] The familiar balance sheet equation shows that assets $\Sigma a_j + \Sigma A_j$ equal total financing sources $\Sigma \ell_j + \Sigma L_j + \Sigma E_j$. *Working capital* is sometimes defined as the current assets of the firm--notably cash and marketable securities, accounts receivable, and inventory. In a broader and perhaps more useful sense, working capital refers to both the current assets and the current liabilities, the latter including accounts payable, short-term bank loans, and other payables and accruals becoming due within a year. *Net working capital* is defined specifically as current assets minus current liabilities, $\Sigma a_j - \Sigma \ell_j$, and is thus a single dollar value. *Working capital management* is concerned with the problems

[1] A subscript j on each balance sheet category indicates that there may be several specific accounts within that category. Summation signs refer to totals within categories.

Figure 1

REPRESENTATIVE BALANCE SHEET

ASSETS		LIABILITIES AND EQUITY	
Cash	Σa_j	Accounts Payable	$\Sigma \ell_j$
Marketable Securities		Wages and Salaries Payable	
Accounts Receivable		Taxes Payable	
Inventory		Bank Loans	
		Other Accruals	
Equipment and Fixtures	ΣA_j	Long Term Debt	ΣL_j
Buildings		Preferred Stock	
Land		Common Stock and Surplus	ΣE_j
Goodwill		Retained Earnings	
Other Intangibles			
Total Assets $\Sigma a_j + \Sigma A_j$		Total Financial Sources $\Sigma \ell_j + \Sigma L_j + \Sigma E_j$	

that arise in attempting to manage the current assets, the current liabilities, and the interrelationships that exist between them.

Figure 2, which is a schematic diagram of the flow of dollars within the firm, provides further perspective on working capital. Because this diagram is intended as an internal document, it is possible to include leased assets which usually do not appear on financial statements prepared for the public. Its similarity with the representative balance sheet should be noted along with several other points. First, the heavy arrows in Figure 2 represent the supply of non-cash assets. Suppliers provide material resources of all types used in generating products and services, and employees provide their labor resources. Leasing companies often provide some of the fixed assets of the firm. The remaining arrows in Figure 2 represent the flow of dollars to and from the various sources of financing with solid arrows indicating investment of cash, and dashed arrows indicating a return of cash to the supplier. Second, the importance of employees, government, and leasing companies as particular sources of financing that normally do not receive explicit attention on the published balance sheet of a firm is noted.

Third, Figure 2 can be divided into an upper-half and a lower-half. The lower-half is referred to as *long-term financial management* because it represents the long-term decisions that have to be made by the management of a firm. On the asset side, decisions must be made about fixed assets, while on the right-hand side, decisions must be made about the capital structure of the firm, including leasing decisions and dividend policy. In contrast, the upper-half of Figure 2 is referred to as *working capital management* since it consists of the interactions between current assets and current liabilities. The large circle, in Figure 2, emphasizes the important role of cash, even though the dollar investment in cash, typically, is less than for any of the other assets of the firm. Cash also appears both as part of working capital management and long-term financial management for the reason that dollars must be available

Figure 2

SCHEMATIC DIAGRAM OF FIRM CASH FLOW

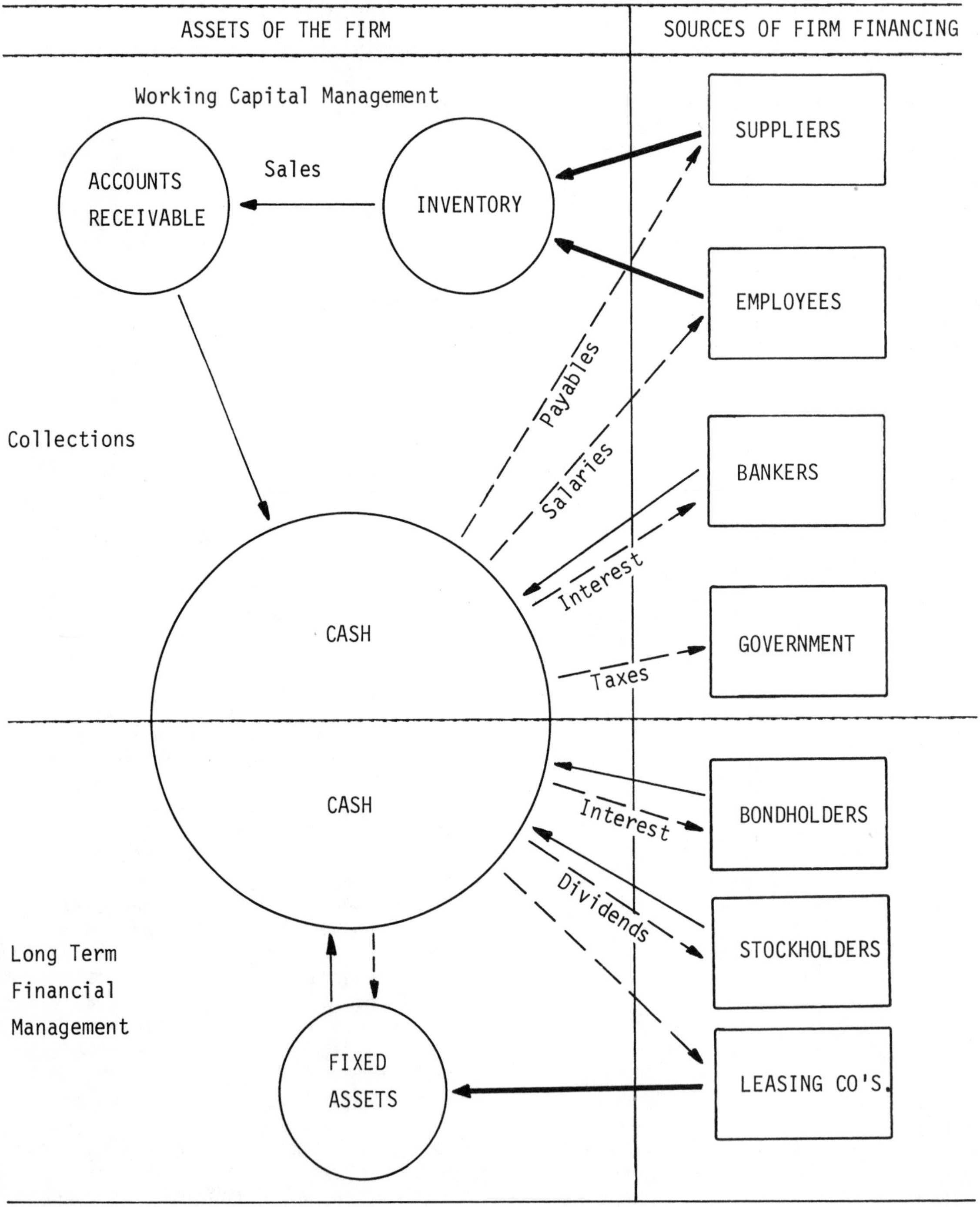

for paying all suppliers and sources of financing. The continuing flow from cash to suppliers to inventory to accounts receivable and back into cash is sometimes referred to as the *cash cycle* or the *operating cycle* of a firm. This is the main set of relationships that are at the heart of working capital management. But at the same time, working capital management involves more than just those particular current assets and current liabilities.

Based on Figure 2, it is thus useful to define *cash flow* as being closely related to working capital. A specific definition is that cash flow equals cash revenue minus cash expenses. Alternatively, cash flow for a particular period is obtained by adding depreciation expense plus any other non-cash charges to the earnings generated by the firm. This specific definition is often used by analysts as a means of tracing the progress of a given firm over time. At a more general and more useful level, however, cash flow refers to all of the cash flows into and out of the firm, together with the interrelationships that are designated in Figure 2.

Related to cash flow is *float*, which has to do with delays in the flow of cash between buyer and seller. Figure 3 is a float calendar that shows how a given firm is affected—both as a buyer and a seller—for a transition involving the purchase of electronic parts to be used in manufacturing certain industrial products. Key steps in the transaction, beginning with the placing of an order by the buying firm and ending with cash actually removed from the buyer's bank account, are identified along a time line. Float is defined in terms of value received and value given. *Collection float* to the seller is the value of the parts between the time they are shipped and the time that payment for the parts is actually available to the firm. *Disbursement float* to the buyer is the value of the parts between the time the parts are received and the time cash actually leaves the account of the buyer. As indicated in Figure 3, collection float and disbursement float for a given transaction are not necessarily equal.

A final definition has to do with the *statement of changes in financial position* which, since 1971, must be presented alongside the balance sheet and income statement as part of any audited annual reports of a business corporation. To many analysts, the statement of changes in financial position (formerly, the sources and uses of funds statement) presents the single best picture of what happened to the firm for the period in question. The residual or balancing item in a funds statement, typically, is changes in net working capital during the period. As such, *funds* is synonymous with net working capital. In more detailed breakdowns, funds is sometimes taken to be spendable cash. In any event, funds are clearly related both to working capital and cash flow. While the title of this book reflects the management of working capital, the subject matter of the readings thus also deals with funds as well as with cash flow.

In a subsequent section, we shall have occasion to illustrate the management of working capital for a specific firm. Toward this end, Figure 3 presents financial statements for Jamjul Enterprises. From the balance sheet at the top of Figure 4, we observe that current assets amount to \$80,000 + \$400,000 + \$380,000 = \$860,000 at the end of the year. Current liabilities, on the other hand, amount to \$120,000 + \$100,000 + \$60,000 = \$280,000. Net working capital thus is equal to \$860,000 - \$280,000 = \$580,000. From the income statement at the bottom of Figure 4, we note that earnings available to common shareholders (either as dividends or as retained earnings) were \$101,600 for the year. Adding depreciation, we see that cash flow for the year was \$101,600 + \$30,000 = \$131,600.

Exhibit 3. SCHEMATIC FLOAT CALENDER

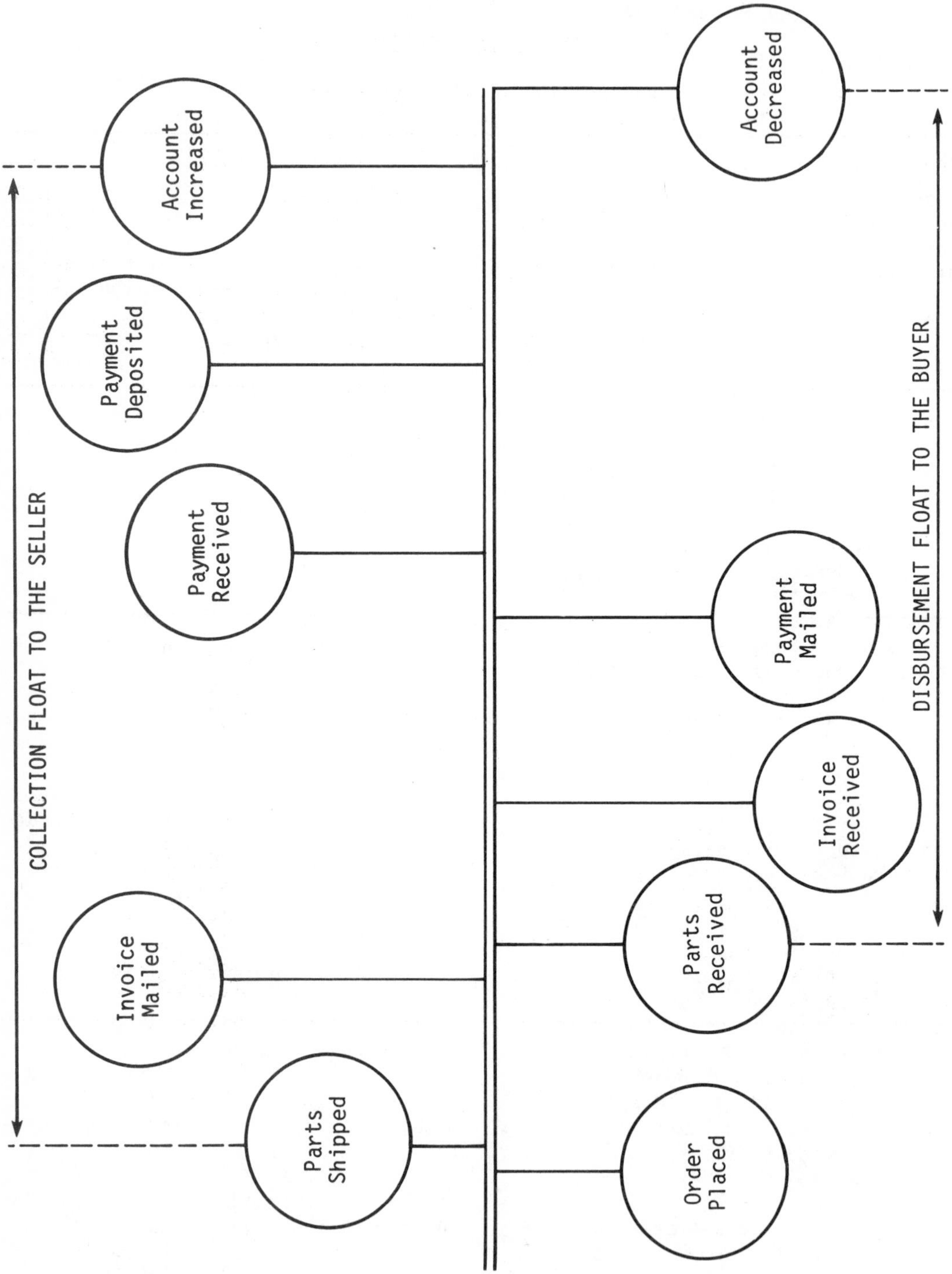

Figure 4

JAMJUL ENTERPRISES

BALANCE SHEET (as of year end)

ASSETS		LIABILITIES AND EQUITY	
Cash	$ 80,000	Accounts Payable	$ 120,000
Accounts Receivable	400,000	Bank Loans	100,000
Inventory	380,000	Other Accounts	60,000
Net Fixed	840,000	Long Term Debt	400,000
		Preferred Stock (5%)	200,000
		Equity (20,000 shares)	820,000
Total	$1,700,000	Total	$1,700,000

JAMJUL ENTERPRISES

INCOME STATEMENT (for the year)

Net Sales		$1,760,000
Cost of Goods Sold		1,340,000
Gross Income		$ 420,000
Operating and Financial Expenses:		
Rent	$37,400	
Advertising	30,000	
Depreciation	30,000	
Interest (7%)	35,000	
Salaries	64,400	196,800
Net Income Before Taxes		$ 223,200
Federal Taxes (50%)		111,600
Net Income After Taxes		$ 111,600
Preferred Dividend (5%)		10,000
Earnings Available to Equity		$ 101,600

Figure 5

AGGREGATE NET WORKING CAPITAL OF NON-FINANCIAL CORPORATIONS, 1963-1977
(In Billions of Dollars)

Year	Cash And Equivalent	Accounts Receivable	Inventory	Other	Current Assets	Accounts Payable	Taxes Payable	Other Accruals	Current Liabilities	Net Working Capital
1963	$66.7	$160.4	$107.0	$17.8	$351.7	$133.0	$16.5	$38.7	$188.2	$163.5
1965	66.9	194.1	126.9	22.3	410.2	163.5	19.1	46.9	229.6	180.7
1967	63.6	219.7	152.3	27.6	463.1	192.2	14.6	57.4	264.3	198.2
1969	58.5	197.0	186.4	31.6	473.3	204.2	12.6	76.0	287.9	185.7
1971	65.7	211.0	203.1	36.8	516.7	207.7	14.5	89.7	311.8	204.9
1973	72.6	269.6	246.7	54.4	643.2	265.9	18.1	117.0	401.0	242.3
1975	87.5	298.2	285.8	60.0	731.6	288.0	20.7	148.8	457.5	274.1
1977	115.1	325.7	375.0	84.3	900.1	306.8	26.5	209.8	543.2	357.0
Annual % Increase	3.9%	5.2%	9.3%	11.7%	6.9%	6.1%	3.4%	12.8%	7.9%	5.7%

Source: *Federal Reserve Bulletin*, selected issues.

III. SCOPE

The scope of working capital management for an individual firm, such as Jamjul Enterprises, is reflected in its financial statements. It is also of interest to examine briefly the scope of working capital management in the aggregate in order to gain additional perspective on the importance of this aspect of financial decision-making.

The increasing size of the decision-making task over a recent decade and a half is clearly evident in Figure 5, which includes all United States non-financial corporations. With minor exceptions, we see that all of the current asset accounts increased steadily over time and totalled $900.1 billion at the end of 1977. Accounts receivable and inventory constituted by far the largest dollar investments in current assets by business firms. Interestingly, cash remained virtually constant until 1973, reflecting higher interest costs, the increase of credit in our economy, and the greater concern and ability of financial managers to manage the firm with less cash. Because a firm can be managed with less cash does not mean that cash is less important. Rather, it means that the cash which is available is most important for ensuring the continued liquidity of the firm.

The current liability accounts also grew steadily over the period and totalled $543.2 billion at the end of 1977. Smallest growth was exhibited in taxes payable, while other accruals increased at 12.8% annually. Net working capital at the end of 1977 was $357.0 billion, in contrast to $163.5 billion at the end of 1963. This represents in the aggregate an annual increase of 5.7% in the net working capital position of non-financial corporations.

In contrast to these absolute values, the importance of working capital relative to the entire balance sheet is portrayed in Figure 6. For selected samples of firms in each of four economic sectors (manufacturing, wholesaling, retailing, and services), percentage breakdown of current assets and current liabilities is presented. The number of firms in each sample also is indicated.

The percentages in Figure 6 again underscore the relative importance of investment in accounts receivable and inventory, vis-a-vis investment in cash. One major exception to this occurs for service organizations that typically have little if any investment in inventory. Accounts receivable, on the other hand, was fairly even in importance across the four sectors.

Fewer differences occurred among the four sectors on the financing side of the balance sheet. Accounts payable as a source of financing was larger relative to long-term financing for wholesalers than the other three sectors. As for notes payable, the percentages ranged from 23.0% (legal services) to 8.8% (department stores).

IV. GOALS AND RESPONSIBILITIES

As in any area of decision-making, it is imperative to specify the appropriate goals for decisions concerning the management of working capital. In the case of a business firm, there are a number of different goals that have received attention. First, are those that have to do with the organization being in business to produce some product or generate some service. Producing a quality product or generating a useful service at appropriate prices is often mentioned as being the foremost goal of a firm. Other goals of a firm discussed by students of management and economics are to provide job opportunities for individuals and to allocate resources in some efficient manner. Attention has also been given to certain society-oriented goals. For instance, goals which somehow have to do with protecting the environment or conserving energy have become popular in recent years.

While such diverse goals may or may not receive prime attention, profitability

Figure 6. Working Capital Accounts as a Percentage of Total Assets of Selected Sectors and Industries, 1978

Sector and Industry	No. of Firms	Cash and Equivalent	Accounts Receivable	Inventories	Other	Current Assets	Accounts Payable	Notes Payable	Other Accruals	Current Liabilities	Net Working Capital
Manufacturing											
Soap and Detergent	36	8.5%	31.0%	24.7%	2.1%	66.3%	18.9%	11.6%	9.6%	40.2%	26.1%
Meat Packing	120	6.0	31.8	20.4	1.0	59.3	14.6	17.0	9.1	40.7	18.6
Publishing/Printing	60	6.9	28.9	29.7	3.2	68.7	15.0	10.7	17.0	42.7	26.0
Wholesaling											
Furniture	111	7.5	38.6	37.1	1.6	84.7	24.2	14.7	13.3	52.2	32.5
Jewelry	229	8.2	32.7	49.0	1.7	91.6	29.1	16.8	8.3	54.2	37.4
Sporting Goods	195	6.6	26.7	51.9	1.3	86.5	22.7	17.0	9.4	49.2	37.3
Retailing											
Office Supplies	256	7.3	30.8	41.0	1.1	80.2	21.1	14.1	10.7	45.8	34.4
Hardware	212	6.2	16.1	51.4	2.1	75.8	15.3	11.6	8.2	35.0	40.8
Department Stores	195	7.0	17.5	50.6	1.9	77.0	15.2	8.8	9.9	33.9	43.1
Services											
Data Processing	107	10.9	31.8	4.6	5.3	52.5	11.3	14.8	13.8	40.0	12.5
Legal Services	83	23.6	22.3	1.1	7.4	54.4	4.2	23.0	13.1	40.3	14.1
Travel Agencies	85	17.2	49.3	1.8	5.9	74.2	26.7	15.7	18.4	60.7	13.5

Note: Percentage values are based on total assets for the firm.

Source: Robert Morris Associates *Annual Statement Studies*, 1978.

is seldom far from the forefront of management thinking. One difficulty with profitability as a firm's goal is that it can be measured in a number of different ways. For example, profitability may be taken in an absolute sense as the bottom line of the income statement ($101,600 for Jamjul Enterprises), it can be return on sales ($101,600 ÷ $1,760,000 = 5.8%), it can be a return on equity investment using accounting data ($101,600 ÷ $820,000 = 12.4%), it can be earnings per share ($101,600 ÷ 20,000 = $5.08), or it can simply be the increase in market price of the common stock. Among these possibilities, maximizing shareholder wealth (as measured by the dividends which shareholders receive plus the increase in market price of their common stock) typically is mentioned in college classrooms as the single most important goal of the firm.

It also should be noted that the goals of the organization, whatever they are, may not be the same as the goals of management of the firm. Many managers will perhaps, in a truthful moment, admit that their major personal goal within the organization is simply to survive, or possibly to attain some higher level of achievement or status within the organization. The increased attention given to stock options, profit-sharing plans, and executive bonuses in recent years well reflects a recognition that the goals of management hopefully can be made consistent with the overall goals of the organization itself.

Financial management of a firm may consist of one or more individuals within the firm who are particularly concerned about financial decision-making within the organization. The financial manager may be the treasurer, the comptroller, the credit manager, the finance committee, the president, or other officers and directors of the firm. Because the finance function tends to be conducted at a high level within an organization, much of the top level control of the firm is likely to be financial control. As mentioned in the introductory section, often boards of directors include many individuals who have had training and experience in finance.

Management positions in the organization which are likely to bear responsibility for the various working capital accounts that appear as either current assets and current liabilities can be identified. The treasurer of an organization, for example, typically is concerned with management of cash, while the credit manager is likely to manage the level of accounts receivable within the organization. It is more difficult to generalize about inventory, for many individuals within the organization may be engaged in managing it. The purchasing manager buys raw materials needed for production or inventory acquired for resale. The production manager supervises the manufacture of finished goods inventory. The sales manager is responsible for selling inventory. The financial manager of the firm watches over the level of investment for all types of inventory.

Among the current liabilities, purchasing managers determine the levels of financing provided by suppliers, while the treasurer or other financial managers maintain the banking relationships of the firm. Because of these diverse responsibilities, practical approaches to management of working capital are, not surprisingly varied both in focus and scope. Also for that reason, many models from academia have been proposed for the management of working capital which may well turn out to be suboptimal relative to the higher level goals of the organization.

The goals of financial managers in relation to working capital decision-making also need to be identified. Remembering our earlier review of the finance function, it is no surprise that many writers talk about the dual goals of profitability and liquidity when discussing financial management of the firm. *Profitability* has to do with the overall firm goal of shareholder wealth, while *liquidity* has to do with ensuring that the firm is able to satisfy all of its current financial obligations and possesses adequate funding to carry on the longer-range activities of the organization. Thus, the liquidity goal is closely aligned with working capital management, while the profitability goal reflects both short-term and long-term decision-making.

One difficulty with the dual objectives of profitability and liquidity, is that one tends to be a trade-off against the other. In other words, decisions that tend to maximize profitability tend not to maximize the chances of adequate liquidity. Conversely, focusing almost entirely on liquidity will tend to reduce the potential profitability of the firm. Moreover, the way in which working capital is managed can have a significant impact on both the profitability and liquidity goals of the firm. Figure 7 illustrates these points for the hypothetical firm, Jamjul Enterprises.

The first column is simply a recap of the financial statements that were presented in Figure 4. For simplicity, interest is paid on the total of short-term bank loans plus long-term debt at the rate of 7% per annum. At the bottom of Figure 7, two ratios are presented. The first ratio, return on common stockholders' equity investment, was already shown to be 12.4% for the year. The current ratio of the firm, 3.1, is calculated by dividing current assets ($860,000) by current liabilities ($280,000). Rate of return on equity investment and current ratio are single measures of profitability and liquidity,

Figure 7

COMPARISON OF THREE APPROACHES TO WORKING CAPITAL MANAGEMENT

	JAMJUL ENTERPRISES	ALTERNATIVE FIRM A	ALTERNATIVE FIRM B
Cash	$ 80,000	$ 120,000	$ 40,000
Accounts Receivable	400,000	600,000	200,000
Inventory	380,000	480,000	160,000
Net Fixed	840,000	840,000	840,000
Total Assets	$1,700,000	$2,040,000	$1,240,000
Accounts Payable	$ 120,000	$ 120,000	$ 120,000
Bank Loans	100,000	0	320,000
Other Accounts	60,000	60,000	60,000
Long-Term Debt	400,000	600,000	112,000
Preferred Stock	200,000	200,000	200,000
Equity	820,000	1,060,000	428,000
Total Sources	$1,700,000	$2,040,000	$1,240,000
Net Sales	$1,760,000	$1,760,000	$1,760,000
Cost of Goods Sold	1,340,000	1,340,000	1,340,000
Gross Income	$ 420,000	$ 420,000	$ 420,000
Other Operating Expenses	161,800	161,800	161,800
Interest (7%)	35,000	42,000	30,200
Net Income Before Taxes	$ 223,200	$ 216,200	$ 228,000
Net Income After Taxes (50%)	$ 111,600	$ 108,000	$ 114,000
Preferred Dividends (5%)	10,000	10,000	10,000
Earnings Available to Equity	$ 101,600	$ 98,000	$ 104,000
Rate-of-Return on Equity Investment	12.4%	9.2%	24.3%
Current Ratio	3.1	6.7	0.8
Net Working Capital	$ 580,000	$1,020,000	($ 100,000)

respectively. Net working capital is also presented. Note that net working capital is $\Sigma a_j - \Sigma \ell_j$, while the current ratio is $\Sigma a_j \div \Sigma \ell_j$.

The second and third columns in Figure 7 refer to similar firms whose financial managers take a different stance toward the management of working capital. All other variables such as preferred stock and the debt-equity mix are held as nearly constant as possible. In the case of Alternative Firm A, larger investments in cash, accounts receivable, and inventory, together with less reliance on short-term bank loans, are reflected in the balance sheet. Larger investment in cash and inventory reflects a cautious attitude toward those current assets, while larger investment in accounts receivable indicates an attempt to increase profitability via a relaxed credit policy. Smaller use of short-term bank financing also shows a more cautious attitude since longer-term financing, though more costly, places less cash payment obligations on the firm in the next period. As a result, Alternative Firm A is larger in terms of total assets. A move down the income statement to the ratios at the bottom of the page points out that return on equity investment drops to 9.7%, while current ratio more than doubles to 6.7. Net working capital increases from $580,000 to $1,020,000. In other words, this firm is much stronger in terms of meeting its liquidity objective, but it has achieved its strength at the expense of profitability.

In contrast, Alternative Firm B is managed with less investments in current assets and with greater reliance on short-term bank borrowing as a major source of financing. For this firm, which is thus smaller, return on equity investment soars to 24.3% while the current ratio drops to 0.8. Net working capital is negative for Alternative Firm B. While one might quarrel somewhat with the assumptions that were necessary in order to make the comparisons in Figure 7, a cursory examination of the two summary ratios, together with net working capital as a dollar measure, clearly emphasizes that profitability increases while liquidity decreases, and conversely. The comparison also serves to underscore the importance of working capital management within the business firm.

V. SOME APPROACHES[2]

Having provided some perspective for working capital management within the business firm, the financial literature can be examined for various approaches to this important aspect of decision-making. Apart from the standard coverage of three or four chapters in business finance textbooks, there appear to be only three books devoted solely to working capital. Of these, Park and Gladson (1963) approach the subject with an accounting orientation emphasizing flow-of-funds, Beranek (1966) presents a series of linear models for use in optimizing the management of one or more of the working capital accounts, while Howard (1971), a British publication, presents a readable overview of the subject.

A number of financial journals and other books have included papers dealing with various aspects of working capital management. The authors, including economists, financial theorists, management scientists, and practicing business executives, have approached working capital management in different ways and in varying levels of analysis. Using the notational scheme introduced in the representative balance sheet of Figure 1, eight somewhat distinct approaches to the subject are now summarized.

A first approach consists of *aggregate guidelines* which have been

[2] Portions of the remainder of this paper were presented by the author as "Working Capital Management: Summary and Synthesis" at a meeting of the Financial Management Association in Atlanta on October 12, 1973.

used in several leading financial textbooks to introduce or to overview sections on working capital management. The important relationship, usually presented in graphical form, is

$$b \equiv (\Sigma a_j^* + \Sigma A_j - \Sigma \ell_j^*) - (\Sigma E_j + \Sigma L_j)$$

where Σa_j^* here excludes short-term marketable securities, and $\Sigma \ell_j^*$ excludes short-term bank borrowing. If net asset requirements (first bracketed term) exceeds long-term sources of financing (second bracketed term), then short-term bank borrowing is needed. For the converse, excess funds should be invested in short-term marketable securities. In other words, short-term borrowing (b positive) or lending (b negative) should be used to balance the available sources with contemplated needs. An assumption of this approach is that a business firm would never hold short-term marketable securities while also incurring short-term debt. Weston and Brigham (1972) further suggest that current asset holdings should be expanded to the point where marginal returns on increases in those assets would just equal the cost of capital required to finance such increases; moreover, current liabilities should be used in place of long-term debt whenever their use would lower the average cost of capital to the firm. Walker (1964) suggests additional propositions concerning working capital and risk in an earlier paper dealing with a theory of working capital. While correct in principle, such aggregate guidelines and propositions probably offer little help to financial managers in making and implementing specific working capital decisions.

A second approach, which has perhaps received more attention than any of the others being reviewed, is *cost balancing*. When applied to a specific current asset, this approach can be represented as the minimization problem,

$$\underset{a_j}{\text{Minimize}} \; [C_1(a_j) + C_2(a_j)]$$

where the decision variable is a particular a_j, and where $C_1(a_j)$ and $C_2(a_j)$ are two distinct types of costs associated with the dollar level of that current asset. Typically, the two types of costs move in opposite directions as the level a_j is varied. For the case of inventory in the familiar economic order quantity model, $C_1(a_j)$ represents either the ordering or set-up cost associated with accumulating inventory, while $C_2(a_j)$ represents inventory holding costs. For accounts receivable, $C_1(a_j)$ represents foregone profits as credit policy is relaxed (and sales and receivables increase), while $C_2(a_j)$ represents bad debt expenses and the opportunity costs of higher investments in receivables. For determining an appropriate cash balance, $C_1(a_j)$ includes order costs and brokerage fees for security investments, while $C_2(a_j)$ reflects the opportunity costs of higher investment in cash balances. While one might question the usefulness of cost balancing models in making working capital decisions, especially for cash and accounts receivable, they do constitute a useful framework for conceptualizing the tradeoffs inherent in managing particular current assets. One noteworthy limitation of cost balancing approaches is that they usually focus on only a single current asset, without due consideration of important interrelationships between several current assets or with current liabilities.

A third approach is to view working capital as a *constraint set* for the larger problem of maximizing the value of the firm. The constraint set may take the general form of $g[\Sigma a_j]$ or $g[\Sigma a_j - \Sigma \ell_j]$ depending on the exact specification of the model. For example, in his treatise on production and investment, Vernon Smith (1961) proposes minimizing total production cost subject to money capital requirements which include both fixed assets and net working capital. The latter is given as

$$\Sigma a_j - \Sigma \ell_j = \alpha S - \Sigma_i \beta_i W_i X_i$$

where S is firm sales, X_i is the number of units or resource i used in production, W_i is the unit price of that resource, and α and β_i are appropriate constants. In his classic synthesis of production, investment, and finance, Vickers (1968) introduces a net working capital requirement

$$\Sigma a_j - \Sigma \ell_j = g(Q)$$

where Q represents firm output as part of the money capital constraint which accompanies his objective function of maximizing the equity value of the firm. While these two excellent works are representative of how many writers have acknowledged the importance of working capital in financial decision-making, they are limited because net working capital is treated as a single entity, rather than as a series of interacting accounts on both sides of the balance sheet.

A fourth approach is to attack working capital directly with *mathematical programming*. Several authors have discussed and illustrated programming approaches. Beranek (1963) presents a series of models dealing with accounts receivable and cash balances. Mao (1969) formulates cash management into a dynamic programming context. Robichek, Teichroew, and Jones (1965) formulate a linear programming model for short-term financing of the firm as follows:

$$\underset{\ell_j}{\text{Minimize}} \quad \Sigma_k C_k(\ell_j)$$

$$\text{Subject to } f_i(\ell_j) \leq \ell_i^*.$$

In this interesting model, the decision variables are different types of borrowing ℓ_j, the objective function includes a number of relevant costs $C_k(\ell_j)$ associated with that borrowing, and constraints $f_i(\ell_j)$ are used to place limits ℓ_i^* on certain types of borrowing. An important feature of this formulation is that is necessitates consideration of other working capital accounts such as cash, accounts receivable, and accounts payable. Various mathematical programming approaches and cost balancing models are specific examples of a more general approach to financial decision-making that might be described as *operations research* or *management science*.

In contrast to the first four approaches to working capital which are deterministic, the fifth approach consists of *probability models*. These models reflect the same sorts of variables already encountered, except that certain variables are considered probablistically. For example, Beranek (1963) extends certain of his deterministic models for analyzing credit policy to include random rates of sales and random collection patterns. The incorporation of risk and uncertainty in working capital models also necessitates a different type of objective function, such as expected cost $\Sigma_i P_i C_i(a_j, \ell_j)$ where P_i represents probability, or expected profit $\Sigma_i P_i \pi_i(a_j, \ell_j)$ where π_i represents profitability. In either case, an expected value operation is used to summarize the uncertainty inherent in the cost and/or profit relationship.

A sixth approach uses *portfolio theory* because of its focus on both uncertainty and interrelationships between entities. Friedland (1966) suggests that the assets of a firm could be viewed in a portfolio context. In terms of current assets, this would amount to

$$\underset{a_j}{\text{Maximize}} \; [\Sigma a_j e_j - \lambda \Sigma\Sigma a_i a_j \sigma_{ij}]$$

where e_j is expected profitability per dollar of current asset, σ_{ij} is the covariance between current assets a_i and a_j, and λ is an appropriate return-risk parameter. Friedland also suggests an indexing scheme based on sales to imply the mutual interrelationships between current asset accounts. While Friedland's framework is useful for conceptualizing the management of firm assets, it would seem to offer little help in controlling specific asset levels over time.

Capital asset pricing theory, which builds on normative portfolio theory, also provides a powerful means of analyzing return-risk relationships for a number of important financial decisions. Recently, Weston (1973) showed that the capital asset pricing model can be used to provide guidelines for asset expansion decisions. In expansion decisions, which normally reflect longer horizons, the focus is on fixed assets, but clearly appropriate levels of working capital are needed to support these fixed investments. Excepting recent papers by Cohn and Pringle (1973), Breiman, Chopra, and Thomas (1975), and Copeland and Khoury (1979), little has been done to extend capital asset pricing theory to working capital decisions. This is somewhat surprising since the capital asset pricing model is a single period model which is closer to the horizon of working capital decisions than to that of longer-range expansion decisions which cover several future periods. One implication of capital asset pricing is that diversification by investors may be more effective than diversification by firms themselves, thus diluting somewhat the potential value of a portfolio approach to working capital.

A seventh approach is somehow to include *multiple goals* in the objective function of the firm. While the usual programming approach includes a single goal (e.g. cost or profit) as an objective function, the decision-making problem may be formulated as

$$\underset{b,\pi}{\text{Maximize}} \quad u[b(a_j,\ell_j),\ \pi(a_j,\ell_j)]$$

where the preference function π summarizes management's feelings about the relative importance of the liquidity $b(a_j,\ell_j)$ and profitability $\pi(a_j,\ell_j)$ goals. The locus of feasible combinations of b and π will depend on the nature of the firm, its investment opportunities, and its possible sources of financing. If the shape of u is specified, the shape of indifference contours and the nature of specific solutions in profitability-liquidity space may be determined.

Another planning approach by Krouse (1973) to handling multiple goals involves hierarchial optimization of a set of goals ranked in order of their relative importance to the firm. Although approaches to working capital involving multiple goals may be difficult to implement in an operational sense, they probably come closer than alternative approaches to capturing the decision-making process employed by financial managers.

The eighth approach to be reviewed is *financial simulation*. It allows one to incorporate both the uncertainty of the future and the many interrelationships between current assets, current liabilities, and other balance sheet accounts. A good illustration of simulation relative to a single current asset or liability is in the final chapter of Mao (1969). Based on 1,000 iterations of the financing requirements associated with normally distributed sales, a frequency distribution of total interest cost $C_k(\ell_j)$ is generated for each of three financing strategies. The final decision can then be made from summary measures such as mean and standard deviation from the three simulated distributions.

Two other papers proposing a simulation approach should be noted. Lerner (1968) explains how cash budgeting can be extended to reflect the uncertainty inherent in future sales, the uncertainty in collecting accounts receivable, and the firm's flexibility in paying its accounts payable. By calculating both expected values and standard deviations of forecasted cash balances, the financial manager can trace the full impact of his decision-making. At about the same time, Van Horne (1969) proposed a probabilistic forecast of the cash flows of the firm as a way of making return-risk tradeoffs. He also proposed that different assumptions about sales, receivables, payables and other related variables could be evaluated in terms of the forecasted cash flows of the firm.

It is also possible to simulate future financial statements of a firm, based on a set of simultaneous equations. For example, Warren and Shelton (1971) present a model in which both current assets and current liabilities are directly related to firm sales. That is, $\Sigma a_j = f_1(S)$ and $\Sigma \ell_j = f_2(S)$ represent two out of a total system of twenty simultaneous equations that are used to forecast future balance sheets of the firm, including forecasted current assets $\hat{\Sigma} a_j$ and forecasted current liabilities $\hat{\Sigma} \ell_j$. Although these forecasts are in the aggregate, the individual working capital accounts can be treated separately in a larger simulation system. And by simulating future financial statements over a range of different assumptions, the inherent uncertainty of the future thus can be portrayed.

The remainder of this book consists of a series of readings which are considered to be representative of the existing literature on working capital management. Rather than being organized by type of approach, however, the readings are organized according to the balance sheet account with which they deal. Following the other four papers in this introductory section, readings on current assets (cash, marketable securities, accounts receivable, and inventory) are presented. Then, readings on current liabilities (trade credit and bank credit) are included. The final section of readings includes papers on planning and controlling which have somehow captured certain of the important interrelationships between current assets and current liabilities—and thus truly deal with the management of working capital. Although a balance sheet breakdown is believed to be a preferable way of treating the subject of working capital management overall, it may be useful for readers to be aware of different methodological approaches such as have been summarized here.

VI. FUTURE DIRECTIONS

From the foregoing review of different approaches to working capital, one might conclude that working capital management has received adequate attention as an area of inquiry within the broader field of finance. Approaches to working capital management have varied from aggregate guidelines to detailed formulations into a mathematical programming context, to consideration of multiple firm goals, and to simulation. Some of the approaches provide a useful perspective for conceptualizing the problem of managing one or more working capital accounts, while others are designed to yield optimal answers to specific decision problems.

On the other hand, a careful study of the financial literature concerned with working capital may lead some readers to the conclusion that richer extensions or novel approaches may be necessary in order to reach better solutions, or to provide guidelines for assisting financial managers in decision-making concerned with current assets and current liabilities. This viewpoint is easily confirmed in conversations with practicing financial managers.

Certain features of the foregoing summary should be reiterated as essential to more useful approaches to the management or working capital. *First*, the dual financial goals of profitability and liquidity must continually be weighed and tradeoffs studied. *Second*, liquidity (not unlike profitability) more properly reflects the dynamic flow of dollars into and out of the firm over time, rather than just a static balance sheet picture at a point in time. *Third*, the several interrelationships between the management of current assets and current liabilities should be properly reflected. *Fourth*, the inherent uncertainty of the future must somehow be treated.

It would seem that a powerful means of reflecting such features, and thus better understanding the working capital situation of a particular firm, is through parallel forecasts (at least monthly) of net borrowing requirements $\hat{b}_t(a_{jt}, \ell_{jt})$ and resulting after-tax profitability $\hat{\pi}_t(a_{jt}, \ell_{jt})$ over some planning horizon t=1,2, ..., T. These dual forecasts are triggered by a forecasted sales schedule $\hat{S}_t$ and also by parameters which reflect the receivables, payables, inventory, and other policies of the firm. Because of concern here with working capital management, current assets a_j and current liabilities ℓ_j are included as arguments of both variables to be forecasted.

Simulation is a powerful method of reflecting future uncertainty. A *first* way to use simulation is to examine for each period t the distribution of net borrowing $\hat{b}_t$ and after-tax profitability $\hat{\pi}_t$ that would result from simulated sales $\hat{S}_t$ or other random variables for which probability distributions are specified. A *second* way to use simulation is to alter the various receivables, inventory, and payables policies of the firm and examine their individual or collective impacts on the profitability and liquidity goals of the firm.

Such approaches do not lead to an optimal solution per se, but instead to a series of tradeoffs between the liquidity and profitability positions of the firm. The relevant objects of choice in attempting to determine optimal tradeoffs are thus not the levels of current assets a_j and current liabilities ℓ_j, but rather the management policies whereby such levels are determined. Thus, future efforts on examining individual working capital accounts, such as inventory or accounts receivable, should be made with an eye toward how their treatment will ultimately affect both $\hat{b}_j(a_{jt}, \ell_{jt})$ and $\hat{\pi}_t(a_{jt}, \ell_{jt})$.

Inevitably, some authors have suggested that what is needed is a *systems approach* to working capital management. Cash budgeting would appear to be nothing more nor less than a systems approach to the liquidity goal of the firm—provided that all relevant cash flows are reflected. In such a spirit, parallel projections of $\hat{b}_j$ and $\hat{\pi}_j$ can thus be viewed as a systems approach to the two central goals of interest to the financial manager and of course to the firm. An illustration of such an approach is presented as Reading 42 in this book. In contrast, Reading 46 focuses on changes in working capital as investment projects that ought to be evaluated as part of the capital budgeting process of the firm.

Finally, note should be taken that the approaches to working capital management suggested here are perfectly consistent with financial simulation wherein the entire financial planning of the firm is considered. This is particularly true if the total system of equations includes working capital as a series of accounts rather than as just an aggregate variable. Financial simulation of the firm in such a manner also allows for better understanding of how working capital decisions are related to longer-term investment and longer-term financial decision-making by firm management. Reading 45 in this book deals with the interfaces between working capital management and long-term financial decision-making.

Fortunately, one may predict that improved methods reflecting these and perhaps other improved features are likely to be forthcoming. Competition among organizations in many industries and business sectors is likely to intensify as will the need for better decision-making in order to properly allocate resources. Increased costs of money have placed additional pressure on firm managers to provide products and services without using excessive investments in working capital. Better data bases and improved computer capability will add to the potential for better methods and guidelines toward this end. Above all, one may predict that closer ties between college classrooms and corporate executive suites will provide motivation for simultaneous assault on both the short-range and the long-range financial problems of the organization.

REFERENCES

1. W. Beranek, *Analysis for Financial Decisions* (Irwin, 1963).
2. W. Beranek, *Working Capital Management* (Wadsworth, 1966).
3. H. Bierman, K. Chopra, and J. Thomas, "Ruin Considerations: Optimal Working Capital and Capital Structure," *Journal of Financial and Quantitative Analysis*, 10:119-128, March, 1975.
4. T.E. Copeland and N.T. Khoury, "Analysis of Credit Extensions in a World With Uncertainty," Unpublished Manuscript (1979).
5. S. Friedland, *The Economics of Corporate Finance* (Prentice-Hall, 1966).
6. L.R. Howard, *Working Capital: Its Management and Control* (MacDonald and Evans, Ltd., 1971).
7. C.G. Krouse, "Programming Working Capital Management," Unpublished Manuscript (1973).
8. E.M. Lerner, "Simulating a Cash Budget," *California Management Review*, 11:79-86, Winter, 1968.
9. J.C.T. Mao, *Quantitative Analysis of Financial Decisions* (Macmillan, 1969).
10. C. Park and J.W. Gladson, *Working Capital* (Macmillan, 1963).
11. R.A. Cohn and J.J. Pringle, "Steps Toward An Integration of Corporate Financial Theory," Unpublished Manuscript (1973).
12. A.A. Robicheck, D. Teichroew, and J.M. Jones, "Optimal Short Term Financing Decision," *Management Science*, 12:1-36, September, 1965.
13. V.L. Smith, *Investment and Production* (Harvard University Press, 1961).
14. J.C. Van Horne, "A Risk-Return Analysis of a Firm's Working Capital Position," *Engineering Economist*, 14:71-88, Winter, 1969.
15. D. Vickers, *The Theory of the Firm: Production, Capital, and Finance* (McGraw-Hill, 1968).
16. E.W. Walker, "Toward a Theory of Working Capital," *Engineering Economist*, 10:21-35, Winter, 1964.
17. J.M. Warren and J.P. Shelton, "A Simultaneous Equation Approach to Financial Planning," *Journal of Finance*, 26:1123-1142, December, 1971.
18. J.F. Weston and E.F. Brigham, *Managerial Finance* (Holt, Rinehart and Winston, 4th edition, 1972).
19. J.F. Weston, "Investment Decisions Using the Capital Asset Pricing Model," *Financial Management* 2:25-33, Spring, 1973.

READING 2

Toward a Theory of Working Capital

Ernest W. Walker
University of Texas, Austin

Is it possible to develop a theory of working capital? This question has been the subject of considerable discussion among both academicians and practitioners of finance, but little has been written on the subject. Because of this dearth of pertinent literature, it might be concluded that students of finance generally agree that such a theory of working capital is not possible, or, perhaps, that such a theory, if developed, could not be practicably applied, and therefore would be useless.

Probably the strongest argument that might be used in denial of the formation of a theory is that business is an art and not a science, and, as such, the various business decisions cannot be guided by theory. Carl Dauten made the following observation concerning the feasibility of developing a theory of business finance:

"Another difficulty in developing a theory of business finance is that in any social science there is not only the question of what is being done in practice, but also of what can or should be done. A theory of business finance cannot be developed solely from a study of what has occurred in the past, an analysis of such data, and the drawing of generalizations. For example, a study of the working-capital policies of corporations over a period of time will not necessarily provide the data for developing a theory of working capital. In the first place, in any such series studied over a period of time each figure is in a real sense unique since business fluctuations do not repeat themselves in any determinable pattern and this makes generalization difficult and unreliable."[1]

While admitting the difficulties involved, Dauten did not altogether rule out the possibility that a theory could be developed; however, he did point out that previous experiences which are collected by empirical investigation should

[1] Carl A. Dauten, "The Necessary Ingredients of a Theory of Business Finance," *The Journal of Finance*, Vol. X, No. 2 (May 1955), p. 108.

Reprinted from THE ENGINEERING ECONOMIST (Winter 1964), Vol. 9, No. 2, pp. 21-35, by permission of the publisher, copyright The American Institute of Industrial Engineers and the American Society for Engineering Education, 25 Technology Park/Atlanta, Norcross, GA 30092.

not be used as the basis for a theory. In other words, a theory, in order to meet the needs of the business community, should be developed by proceeding logically from general propositions or principles, i.e., the deductive rather than the inductive process should be used. Although past operational data need not serve as a basis for the theory, they are of primary importance since they may be used to test and, hopefully, to support the theory once it has been developed.

An examination of the literature reveals that economists and businessmen have, in a manner of speaking, gone their separate ways in developing "theories" that may be used as guides in making business decisions. To illustrate, in establishing the conditions of success, marketing students theorize that a firm will achieve success in the long run if its average revenue equals average cost, but they have not attempted to any great extent to establish sound "guides" that management should use in equating average revenue and average cost. Businessmen, on the other hand, in striving for success have largely ignored theoretical concepts and based their decisions on past experiences as depicted by empirical studies. Considerable effort has been expended in developing rules-of-thumb and ratios to be used to guide management in formulating policies, but little or no effort has been directed toward the formulation of a theory or theories that would serve as the basis for financial policies, regardless of whether the firm is large or small, whether it operates in one industry or another, or whether in a recession or at the peak of the business cycle, etc.

Although Dauten's comments are not the final word on the subject, they do, in my opinion, support the contention that a theory of finance can be developed. It is therefore the purpose of this paper to develop several propositions that will serve as the foundation of a theory of working capital which in turn may be used in the formulation of sound policies and procedures.

Success as measured by the amount of rate of profit to owners is almost unanimously the primary objective of business firms. The policies affecting the amount of profit are predicated on theories regarding sales volume and/or costs, whereas the policies which affect the rate of profit are influenced primarily by the amount of risk that management assumes. Usually, when management adopts distribution and production policies which affect cost or sales, the change in the degree of risk assumed is relatively small in comparison with the gain that is realized. While risk should not be ignored, it is not the determining element in deciding whether to adopt a policy designed to increase sales volume or reduce costs. This is not true where changes are contemplated in policies which determine financial practices affecting either volume of profit or rate of return. It is the thesis of this writer that the amount of risk which a firm can assume is of paramount importance and should serve as a major determinant of any theory relative to finance.

The establishment of a theory requires the development of a set of propositions or hypotheses which, when proved either inductively or deductively, will serve as the basis or foundation of that theory. The theory then may be used by management as a guide in formulating the firm's policies. Once it has been developed, the theory must be tested to ascertain whether it is adaptable to the changing conditions of a dynamic economy. This paper will not attempt to test the theory in actual practice nor will each proposition be tested empirically. In the main, the method of proof used will be deduction; however, a minimum amount of financial data are employed to illustrate certain concepts.

PROPOSITION NUMBER ONE

Total capital in a business enterprise consists of fixed and working capital, and the firm's profitability is influenced by the ratio of working capital to fixed capital. Our first proposition is directly concerned with this concept; it may be stated as follows: *If the amount of working capital is varied relative to fixed capital, the amount of risk that a firm assumes is also varied and the opportunity for gain or loss is increased.* This principle implies that a definite relationship exists between the degree of risk that management assumes and the rate of return. Moreover, the principle assumes that this relationship can be changed by changing the level of working capital.[2] Up to this point in our discussion there is no proof that such a relationship exists, but for the time being let us assume that this is the case. It is believed that the following arguments not only prove this to be true, but also prove that the principle is valid and should serve as one "leg" of a theory of working capital management.

In supporting the concept that the ratio of working capital to fixed capital affects the level of risk as well as profitability, it is essential that we explore first the factors that influence the level of fixed and working capital.

A firm's volume of fixed capital is determined by its scale of production, which has been defined as the "aggregate of fixed assets with which the enterprise operates and that is not subject to alteration in the short period."[3] On the other hand, working capital is employed only when actual production is undertaken; therefore, if output is increased the need for working capital is increased and vice versa. Although the volume of production determines generally the amount of working capital that a firm needs, the precise amount is dependent upon (1) those factors which influence the amount of cash, inventories, receivables, and other current assets required to support a given volume of output and (2) management's philosophy concerning risk. Incidentally, rather than evaluating the factors which influence the amount of each component of working capital, many businessmen rely almost entirely on empirical studies or rules-of-thumb to determine working capital requirements, e.g., cash should equal five percent of sales, inventory should equal sales for two months, etc. When such techniques are used, it would be pure accident if the firm's (1) ratio of working capital to fixed capital, (2) risk, and (3) profitability were correct for the firm's level of output. It is true that the factors which influence the amount of working capital required are difficult to evaluate in a dynamic economy but informed management has been reasonably successful in making these evaluations.[4]

Although a problem exists because of management's inability to evaluate working capital determinants, a much more serious problem of management is that of determining objectively the amount of risk that should be assumed at each level of output. An examination of Figure I, which shows the various levels of working capital utilized by a hypothetical firm with an output capacity of 1,000 units, reveals that the firm's investment in

---

[2] Risk as used here means (1) risk of not maintaining adequate liquidity; (2) the risk of having too much or too little inventory to maintain production and sales; and (3) the risk of not granting adequate credit to support the proper level of sales.

[3] Norman S. Buchanan, *The Economics of Corporate Enterprise*, (New York: Holt, Rinehart and Winston, 1940), p. 146.

[4] Although a discussion of the factors which affect working capital is completely outside the scope of this paper, the following partial list of factors that management must evaluate in order to determine the level of its normal cash requirements illustrates the complexity of management's job of determining the correct level of working capital that should be maintained for each level of output: (1) the nature of the business enterprise, (2) the size of sales in relation to fixed assets, (3) the credit position of the firm, (4) the status of the firm's receivables, and (5) the status of the inventory account.

Figure I

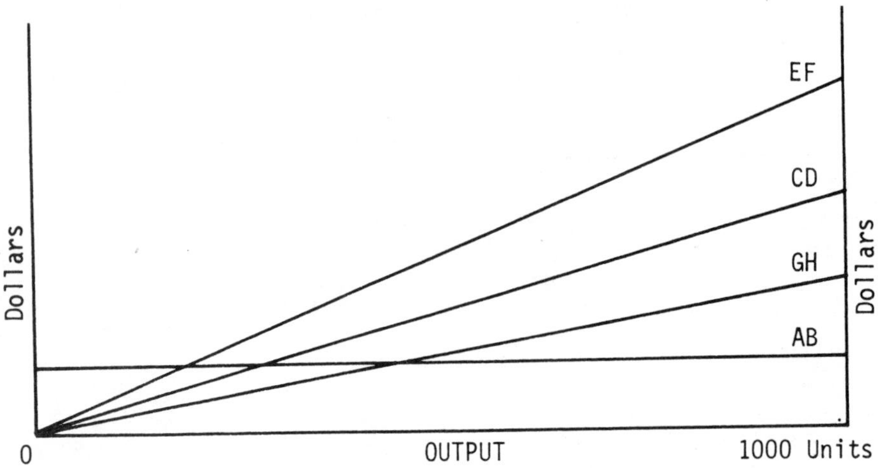

fixed assets remains constant as long as output does not exceed 100 percent capacity, as represented by the horizontal curve AB. While fixed capital remains unchanged between zero and 1,000 units of output, working capital investment varies directly with output. As mentioned before, not only does the volume of working capital required depend upon the level of output but it also varies directly with management's attitude toward risk; that is to say, a more conservative management will employ more working capital for a given volume of sales than one which can and is willing to assume more risk. Curves EF, GH, and CD represent various shades of conservatism on the part of management, e.g., the level of working capital depicted by curve EF represents a conservative policy concerning risk while the GH curve represents just the opposite. On the other hand, the level of working capital depicted by curve CD represents a management policy whose objective is to equate risk with the rate of return. Stated differently, the curve represents a level of working capital which allows the largest rate of return, but at the same time the risk assumed will not exceed the firm's capacity to assume risk. It is presumed that by correctly analyzing the factors determining the levels of working capital as well as predicting the state of the economy during the next several months, management can determine a level of working capital that will equilibrate its rate of return with its ability to assume risk; however, if adverse forces that will affect this equilibrium appear in the economy, management will be called upon to change to a policy that will bring these two elements back into balance.

It is easy to see the effect that each policy has on the firm's efficiency of capital. Other things being equal, the rate of return resulting from the policy which is represented by curve EF will be lower than that received when the policy which is depicted by curve GH is followed, but it should be emphasized that the firm is subjecting itself to more risk in the latter case. The financial data included in Table I connote the thesis that a firm's rate of return varies inversely with the level of working capital that it maintains. This presumes that there are no changes in "other" capital turnover and earnings as a percent of sales. The more *conservative* policy which is depicted in column two of Table I shows that the firm will have a greater de-

Table I

XYZ MANUFACTURING COMPANY

Financial Data

Working Capital	$ 90,000	$120,000	$ 50,000
Fixed Capital	10,000	10,000	10,000
Liabilities	30,000	30,000	30,000
Net Worth	70,000	100,000	30,000
Sales	100,000	100,000	100,000
Fixed Capital Turnover	10.0	10.0	10.0
Working Capital Turnover	1.1	.833	2.0
Total Capital Turnover	1.0	.761	1.66
Earnings as a Percent of Sales	10.0	10.0	10.0
Rate of Return Expressed as a Percent	10.0	7.6	16.6

gree of liquidity, more inventory to assure continued production, and more credit outstanding which aids the sales efforts; however, by following such policy, the firm's rate of return is less than it would be if a less conservative working capital policy were followed--see columns one and three.

The primary problem facing management is the determination of the ideal level of working capital. The analysis of the factors affecting cash, inventories, and trade credit is relatively easy to make, but the development of such a technique is outside the scope of this paper and no further attention is given to this point.

Up to this time we have used hypothetical examples to demonstrate certain points. The financial data in Table II not only substantiate these conclusions but also point up several interesting characteristics that aid the financial manager in making working capital policy.

First, it is interesting to note that changes in working capital in certain industries cause the rate of return on investment to react more favorably than in others. For example, gains and losses resulting from changes in working capital of the chemical, retail trade (department stores), tire and rubber, drug, food products and building materials industries are far greater than gains or losses which occur in the steel and paper products industries. Although these data support Proposition Number One, a much more significant fact is revealed and that is that financial management in certain industries has more to gain or lose by following aggressive working capital policies than do financial managers in other industries. That is to say, management of an average chemical firm can increase the rate of return on investment by 100 percent if it decreases its working capital by 50 percent, but management of an average steel firm can increase its rate of return on investment only 24 percent when working capital is decreased 50 percent. This shows that aggressive working capital policies pay greater "dividends" in firms of certain industries than in others. The conclusion to be drawn here is that financial management should ascertain the category to which its firm belongs before definite policies are formulated.

A second point that these data show is that a decrease in working capital results in a larger "gain" than the "loss" that results from a like increase in working capital. To illustrate this point, a decrease of 10 percent in the

Table II

CHANGES IN RATE OF RETURN WHEN WORKING CAPITAL LEVELS ARE VARIED

By Selected Industries*

Level of Working Capital	Building Materials	Drugs	Paper & Paper Products	Food Products	Tire & Rubber	Metal & Mining (Copper)	Steel	Retail Trade Dept.	Chemicals
50 %[1]	17.59	32.74	13.64	21.86	17.32	13.66	9.75	20.58	29.68
60 %[1]	16.45	30.12	13.11	20.13	15.84	13.08	9.31	18.69	24.73
70 %[1]	15.44	27.89	12.61	18.79	14.60	12.56	8.91	17.12	21.20
80 %[1]	14.55	25.97	12.15	17.62	13.53	12.07	8.54	15.79	18.55
90 %[1]	13.76	24.30	11.73	16.59	12.62	11.62	8.20	14.65	16.49
100 %[1]	13.04	22.83	11.33	15.67	11.81	10.86	7.88	13.66	14.84
110 %[1]	12.41	21.52	10.96	14.84	11.11	10.45	7.59	12.80	13.49
120 %[1]	11.83	20.36	10.61	14.10	10.48	10.11	7.32	12.05	12.37
130 %[1]	11.30	19.32	10.28	13.43	9.92	9.79	7.07	11.37	11.42
140 %[1]	10.81	18.38	9.98	12.82	9.42	9.50	6.83	10.77	10.60
150 %[1]	10.37	17.52	9.69	12.27	8.96	9.21	6.61	10.23	9.89

* Computations based on financial data taken from Studley-Shupert Industrial Composites for 1961.

[1] Expressed as a percent of the 100 percent row. The incremental change is 10 percent.

average working capital in the chemical industry results in a 10.98 percent increase in the rate of return on investment; but an increase of 10 percent, on the other hand, brings about a decrease in the rate of return on investment of only 9.1 percent. A significant fact is that each subsequent decrease in working capital brings about a greater "gain" than the "loss" which results from a corresponding increase in working capital--see Table III. This is important to the finance manager since it shows that the opportunity for gain is present if he should decide to take the risk; on the other hand, if conditions warrant a highly conservative policy, the financial manager knows that for each additional increase in working capital, the resultant loss will be smaller than the loss resulting from the previous increase.

PROPOSITION NUMBER TWO

Proposition Number One dealt primarily with the risk associated with the amount of working capital that a firm employs whereas Proposition Number Two is concerned with the risk that is directly related to the type of capital the firm uses when financing its working capital requirements. The proposition may be stated as follows: *The type of capital used to finance working capital directly affects the amount of risk that a firm assumes as well as the opportunity for gain or loss.* If a firm wishes to reduce its risk to the minimum, it would employ only equity capital; however, in so doing, the firm reduces its opportunity for higher gains or losses on equity capital since it would not be taking advantage of the leverage that results from "trading on its equity." Conversely, if a firm wishes to take advantage of leverage, it would increase the amount of debt capital employed in the financing of current assets; in so doing it must be prepared to accept more risk.

If this proposition is valid, and there seems to be no reason to believe otherwise, the problem is not whether to use debt capital but how much debt capital to use. An answer requires that management determine how much risk it can assume at any given time. Once this has been ascertained, management will know what debt-equity ratio it should use when planning its capital structure. Rather than approaching the problem in this way, there is evidence that many businessmen use certain rules-of-thumb to determine the amount of debt and equity capital employed in the financing process.

One of the more commonly applied rules-of-thumb is the debt-equity ratio. That is, one type of business will use one ratio while a different type of business will feel perfectly safe in using twice as much debt. Two principal criticisms may be lodged against this method of risk determination. The first relates to the manner by which the firm determines the ratio. In many cases management will accept a ratio that has been recommended for its particular type of business, i.e., a certain ratio may be used if the firm is a public utility while an entirely different ratio is used if the firm is classified as an industrial firm. There would be no problem if the ratio specifically reflected the amount of risk the firm could assume; unfortunately, this is not the case. There are several reasons why the conclusion that the selected ratio is not related to risk is valid. First, the ratio that is used as a guide is an average ratio and is not applicable to a particular firm. That is to say, the empirical study which produces the ratio includes many firms which may not possess the same characteristics of the firm which proposes to use the ratio. Second, as a general rule, the data supporting the ratio are obtained over several years. The financial data for these years change since the variables which influence these data are constantly changing; yet the ratio is an average which depicts a composite of all years under

Table III

MARGINAL INCREMENT (DECREMENT) OF THE RATE OF RETURN WHEN WORKING CAPITAL IS MANIPULATED

By Selected Industries--Expressed as Percent

Percentage Change +/-%	Building Materials	Drugs	Paper & Paper Products	Food Products	Tire & Rubber	Steel	Retail Trade Dept.	Chemicals
50 %	6.93	8.70	4.40	7.70	9.34	4.73	10.11	20.02
60 %	6.54	7.80	3.97	7.13	8.49	4.49	9.17	16.65
70 %	6.12	7.39	3.79	6.64	7.91	4.33	8.42	14.29
80 %	5.74	6.87	3.58	6.21	7.21	4.15	7.78	12.49
90 %	5.52	6.44	3.53	5.87	6.86	4.06	7.25	10.98
100 %	0	0	0	0	0	0	0	0
110 %	-4.84	-5.74	-3.27	-5.30	-5.93	-3.68	-6.30	-9.10
120 %	-4.68	-5.39	-3.20	-4.99	-5.67	-3.56	-5.86	-8.31
130 %	-4.42	-5.11	-3.11	-4.75	-5.34	-3.42	-5.64	-7.68
140 %	-4.34	-4.87	-2.92	-4.54	-5.04	-3.39	-5.28	-7.18
150 %	-4.07	-4.68	-2.91	-4.29	-4.89	-3.22	-5.01	-6.70

study. Since risk is associated with the future, there is no assurance whatever that the variables that influenced the average ratio will prevail in the future. In other words, the wrong criteria are used to predict the amount and degree of risk that the firm will encounter. Finally, an average ratio is not applicable to a specific firm within an industry since it is impossible to classify a firm accurately. Industries are not easily divided into homogenous categories since modern-day businesses produce products which may be classified in several different categories. For example, many firms may be classified in several different categories and their operations will be influenced by several different sets of variables. The average ratio will not reflect these risks.

The second principal criticism that may be levied against the use of the debt-equity ratio as a method of risk determination relates to the method of debt-equity ratio calculations. In the majority of cases, management does not include short-term debt in its calculations yet risk is inherent in all forms of debt.

In summary then it may be said that for the most part management resorts to rules-of-thumb which are based on empirical data when ascertaining the amount and type of capital to be used to finance working capital rather than first analyzing the amount and kind of risk that the firm can assume and then selecting the type of capital that will best satisfy the situation.

PROPOSITION NUMBER THREE

If all debt contracts possessed the same risk characteristics, it would be sufficient to say that a certain part of the working capital assets should be financed with debt and a certain part with equity capital. The proportion secured from each would depend entirely upon management's attitude toward risk and its desire for a higher return. Unfortunately the answer as to how much debt capital to employ is not that simple, since one debt instrument may be more risky than another. It is entirely possible for two firms to finance the same percentage of their working capital with debt capital and yet one could be assuming more risk than the other.

The degree of risk inherent in each debt contract is influenced by the nature of the debt contract. Although there are many characteristics of debt contracts which affect a firm's solvency, it is believed that the maturity of the debt contract is one of the most important and should be considered when developing a theory of working capital. This concept serves as the basis for the third proposition which may be stated as follows: *The greater the disparity between the maturities of a firm's debt instruments and its flow of internally generated funds, the greater the risk, and vice versa.*

The degree of risk that a firm assumes is influenced by its ability to pay its obligations as they become due; therefore, in order to determine how much risk a firm can take, it is necessary to ascertain the firm's ability to liquidate its obligations. At one time, it was believed that a firm's liquidity, and thus its ability to meet its obligations, could be measured by comparing current assets to current liabilities. For example, if the ratio of current assets to current liabilities exceeded some magic number such as two, the firm would receive a clean bill of health. Financial officers soon decided that this type of analysis failed to answer the question of whether the firm would have sufficient funds to meet its obligations *at the time* they became due and payable. In determining liquidity from this point of view, financial analysts recognize that a firm's success in the long run is dependent on its earnings, but they are also aware that its ability to meet its short-term obligations bears little or no relationship to earnings. That is to say, a firm may have good earnings but still be unable to meet its obligations due to a shortage of cash. On the other hand, a firm may experience a deficit in a particular year and still have sufficient cash to meet its obligations. In the short run a firm's debt-paying ability is predicated largely upon the receipt of internally generated funds, i.e., turnover of working capital rather than earnings that are reported on the profit and loss statement.[5]

It is a well-known fact that most business firms employ some form of debt to finance at least a part of their working capital requirements. Now the principle under consideration states that unless the maturities of these debt contracts tend to coincide with the flow of internally generated funds, the firm may experience a disruption of its financing process. Let us pursue this concept.

As working capital moves from one process to another, it changes form, i.e., cash changes to inventories to receivables and finally back to cash. Now if the original "cash" was obtained from equity sources, the firm would not be required to return these funds at a particular time; in other words, the capital is completely without risk. If debt capital is used to supply a part or all of these funds, the firm would be faced with a definite repayment schedule. It is this schedule with which management must be concerned. Generally the longer the maturity the less risk the firm would assume since management would have adequate opportunity to acquire funds from operations to satisfy the debt, or it will have sufficient opportunity to refinance the obligation. On the other hand, the shorter the maturity the greater the risk since the firm will have less time to accumulate sufficient funds to liquidate the debt, or, if the debt is to be refinanced, the firm will have less time to refund the loan. A simple example illustrates this idea. Assume a firm is just beginning and it requires $50,000 to acquire fixed assets and $25,000 to finance working capital requirements.[6] Assume that the firm obtains $60,000 from equity sources and borrows $15,000 from a bank for 12 months. Further assume that the firm completely turns its working capital every 60 days and its profit margin after taxes is ten percent per sales dollar. In this particular case the firm generates sufficient funds to repay the loan at the time it matures, e.g., it will have $20,000 available to liquidate the note ($15,000 from profits and $5,000 from depreciation). However, adequate funds would not have been available had the firm borrowed the $15,000 for 90 days unless provisions had been made to refinance the debt because in this example the firm would have accumulated only $5,000 during the 90 day period.

In the latter situation the firm would face a financial crisis even though the business was a profitable one because the financial officer failed to allow the firm sufficient time to generate adequate "cash" to liquidate the debt. Had the finance officer followed the principle set forth in Proposition Number Three, he could have reduced the amount of risk that the firm had to assume.

It should be pointed out that due to the many variables that influence the size, smoothness, and speed of a firm's cash flow, financial officers should not "tie" debt maturities precisely to cash flow. That is, in a dynamic economy such as the one in which we operate, it is difficult to predict cash flows; therefore, adequate time should be allowed between the time the funds are generated and the time the debt comes due.

---

[5] The proposition that a firm's credit position is enhanced by earnings is not ignored. That is to say, the firm can resort to external sources for funds to repay its obligations. In this case, a refunding process has been undertaken, not a liquidation of debt.

[6] Depreciation is computed on a straight-line basis and the economic life of the asset is five years with no scrap value.

SUMMARY AND CONCLUSIONS

It has been concluded that it is possible to develop a theory of working capital which will serve as a basis for working capital policies. The fundamental basis for the theory is risk; that is, in most cases the opportunity for gain or loss varies directly with the amount of risk that management assumes. The theory briefly stated is that the policies governing the amount and type of working capital are determined by the *amount of risk* that management is prepared to assume. To illustrate, by increasing the amount of risk that it is willing to assume, management can reduce the amount of working capital required and thus increase the efficiency of capital, resulting in an increase in total profits. Further, by employing more risk capital, management can increase the rate that is earned on equity capital; and finally, management can employ more debt capital provided it can accurately determine the firm's ability to repay its obligations and schedule its maturity dates accordingly.

READING 3

Steps Toward an Integration of Corporate Financial Theory

Richard A. Cohn
University of Illinois, Chicago Circle

John J. Pringle
University of North Carolina, Chapel-Hill

INTRODUCTION

Over the past fifteen years there has been a concerted effort by theoretical economists to analyze the financial decisions of business firms within the context of equilibrium models of financial markets. The two positive models with the most success to date have been the capital asset pricing model (CAPM) of Sharpe [25], Lintner [14], and Mossin [19] and the state-preference approach developed by Arrow [1] and Debreu [6].

While these models have been employed to analyze long-term corporate investment and financing decisions, virutally no research has been conducted in an attempt to apply them to working capital decisions. Generally in finance texts and in papers in professional journals the management of the firm's current assets and liabilities[1] has been treated separately from the management of long-term assets and capital structure. Normative approaches to decision-making in the realm of the current section of the balance sheet often are *ad hoc* in nature[2] and usually have been developed outside the generally accepted theory of (long-term) business finance with valuation as the guiding principle. While such approaches are operationally useful, their separate development and *ad hoc* nature leaves a feeling of incompleteness in the theory of business finance.

A second reason for attempting to unify the theory of working capital management with that of long-term decisions lies in the permanence of current assets and liabilities on the balance sheets of firms. While individual current assets and liabilities may be of short maturity, because of continuous "rolling over" there always exists a portfolio of current assets and liabilities. Short-term liabilities in the aggregate constitute a

[1] Assets and liabilities which can reasonably be expected to produce, respectively, cash receipts and payments within a year.

[2] Examples of such approaches include budgeting and inventory models for management of cash, discriminant analysis for accounts receivable, and economic-order-quantity models for inventories. See Van Horne [32] or any recent finance textbook for discussions of such approaches.

This paper has not been previously published. Reprinted by permission of the authors.

continuous source of financing for the firm, and short-term assets become "permanent" investments. It seems appropriate, therefore, to incorporate working capital cash flows into a long-term decision framework.

Two principal reasons for the separate development of short-term and long-term finance have been (1) the lack until recently of a theory of market determination of risk premia and (2) the assumption of perfect and complete financial markets on which the basic theory of long-term finance has been constructed. We argue that the CAPM and its extensions provide a theoretical basis for an integrated single-period theory that could accommodate virtually all types of financial management decisions. The CAPM represents a positive foundation of the nature of security market equilibrium on which a normative model of working capital management could be constructed.

CORPORATE FINANCIAL THEORY

The theory of long-term business finance has addressed three general questions: (1) the investment decision, i.e., the volume and composition of the firm's long-term assets, (2) the financing or capital structure decision, normally restricted to the choice between long-term debt and equity, and (3) the dividend decision, i.e., the proportion of net income paid to shareholders.[3] Valuation has provided the unifying theme for theories addressing these questions, with wealth-maximization the normative criterion.

The CAPM, put forward in the mid-sixties, filled a major gap in the theory of business finance by providing an empirically testable positive theory of the determination of stock prices, a contribution of no small importance to a normative theory based on valuation as a criterion. The CAPM provided a theory of market risk premia, giving guidance both with respect to appropriate measures of the risk of securities and to the terms of the risk-return trade-off. Mossin [20] and Hamada [8] extended the CAPM to the capital budgeting decision and showed that it provided a rigorous theoretical basis for dealing with investment projects of varying degrees of risk.[4] Hamada also applied the CAPM to the capital structure decision and in so doing provided a proof of the Modigliani-Miller propositions I and II [18] that did not require their homogeneous risk-class assumption and thus was more general than the original Modigliani-Miller proof.[5]

The CAPM also had important implications for working capital decisions. Investments by a given firm in cash, marketable securities, receivables and inventories long had been viewed as involving, in general, less risk than investments by the same firm in plant and equipment. A "cost of capital" approach, using a discount rate appropriate to the firm's "risk-class" therefore seemed distincly inappropriate in the case of investments in current assets. By providing a basis for dealing with differences in risk, the CAPM removed a major roadblock in the development of a more rigorous theoretical framework for decisions involving current assets and liabilities.

PERFECT FINANCIAL MARKETS

Common to nearly all of the theoretical work in corporate finance from Modigliani-Miller through the extensions of Mossin and Hamada was an assumption of perfect financial markets (though *not* perfect markets for real assets).[6] Assumed away were transac-

[3] See Solomon [27] for an historical development of the scope of financial management.

[4] Tuttle and Litzenberger [31], though not relying directly on the CAPM, derived investment criteria essentially equivalent to those of Mossin and Hamada.

[5] See Rubinstein [24] for a discussion of the implications of the CAPM for corporate investment and capital structure decisions.

[6] Tuttle and Litzenberger introduce certain imperfections into the equity market via an assumption that investors are prevented from diversifying. They examine the implications of the assumption for measures of project risk but restrict the analysis to real assets.

tions costs of all types, including bankruptcy penalties (some analyses simply ruled out the possibility of bankruptcy); information costs, including costs of search, acquisition and processing; indivisibilities; divergence of borrowing and lending rates; and sometimes taxes. The "perfect financial markets" assumption also implied perfect competition in financial markets and therefore a Pareto-efficient allocation of risk.[7] This assumption facilitated analysis of factors believed critical to the investment and capital structure decisions of the firm, but effectively precluded any consideration of most questions normally falling under the heading of "short-term" finance. Under the assumed conditions, the firm has no incentive to hold financial assets of any type, and distinctions between financial claims issued by the firm disappear.[8]

Where value-maximization is the objective, the incentive for investment is a return in excess of that required given the riskiness of the investment (and, in a world with taxes, taking account of the financing mix). In the CAPM, "excess" returns are defined as returns in excess of the risk-free rate plus a premium for risk, i.e., the pre-existing equilibrium expected return in perfect financial markets.

Since markets for real assets are not assumed perfect, opportunities exist to earn "excess" returns. Real assets are employed to yield outputs of greater value. The models of Tuttle and Litzenberger, Mossin and Hamada are aimed at identifying such opportunities. In the case of financial assets, however, no such opportunities exist if financial markets are assumed perfect. In the absence of transaction costs, no motive exists for holding cash. Assuming perfect competition (in financial markets), marketable securities provide no excess return; they provide a certainty-equivalent return exactly equal to the risk-free rate of interest (R_f). The perfect markets assumption also implies that the firm can borrow at any time at a certainty-equivalent cost of R_f. Under such circumstances, there would be no incentive for the firm to hold marketable securities, which promise no excess return, at the expense of forgoing excess returns on investments in real assets.[9] Hence, in perfect financial markets, liquidity is of no importance, even in the presence of uncertainty.[10] Rather than holding liquid assets that promise no excess returns, the firm simply borrows as needs arise.

The problems of managing accounts receivable also disappear under perfect financial markets. If the assumption is interpreted literally, then competitive markets for receivables would exist, and receivables would yield a certainty-equivalent return of R_f. The firm would be indifferent with respect to a decision to retain or sell receivables.

On the liability side, the assump-

[7] Within the context of the state-preference model, financial markets must be complete as well as perfect. On this point see Hirshleifer [9].

[8] With all market inperfections assumed away, the firm is indifferent even with respect to the choice between debt and equity. Taxes were recognized at the outset as being important and were incorporated explicitly into analysis of the debt/equity decision. Arguments ensued in the literature over the importance of imperfections of other types, but only recently have efforts begun to deal with imperfections such as bankruptcy penalties. Stiglitz [29, 30] and Rubinstein [24] mention the likely importance of bankruptcy penalties, but neither incorporates them explicitly. Kraus and Litzenberger [13] deal rigorously with bankruptcy costs in a state-preference approach to the capital structure decision.

[9] See Pringle [21] for an analysis and proof of this point in the case of commercial banks, in which case excess returns are earned on loans made in imperfectly competitive markets.

[10] Under certainty, a liquidity motive normally is referred to as a *transaction* motive, and under uncertainty, a *precautionary* motive. In both cases, market imperfections are necessary for existence of the motive for liquidity. Whereas a precautionary motive implies only uncertainty as to the future value of a random variable, a *speculative* motive implies an expectation that the value of the variable will change in a particular direction. The existence of market imperfections is not required to rationalize a speculative motive.

tion of perfect markets for all financial claims implies in a single-period model that there would be little distinction between claims of different types. All would have a certainty-equivalent cost to the firm of R_f.

In short, because of the perfect financial markets assumption, wealth-maximizing models designed to address the investment and capital structure decisions of the firm were incapable of dealing with decisions involving current assets (except inventories) and current liabilities. The perfect markets assumption also ruled out application of such models to financial intermediaries, which in perfect financial markets have little reason to exist.[11] Working capital decisions in firms and financial management of financial intermediaries are analogous in many ways, since both involve acquisition and issuance of financial claims (inventories excepted). In both cases, assumptions regarding imperfections and degree of competition in financial markets are critical. It is worth noting also that a major alternative to the wealth maximization model, the Markowitz [16] mean-variance model, while well suited for decision-making in the case of financial claims traded in competitive markets, is incapable of dealing with liquidity except by means of constraints (see [21]).

RECOGNITION OF MARKET IMPERFECTIONS

Where transaction costs exist, cash yields an implicit return that is a function of transaction costs avoided by its holding. Transaction costs and other imperfections such as credit rationing by banks also may cause the certainty-equivalent cost of borrowing to exceed the risk-free rate. Potential "excess" costs due to such factors can be avoided in future periods by the holding of liquid assets, and the costs so avoided can be viewed as a component of the expected return on the liquid asset. The return to the holder of the liquid asset now exceeds that consistent with CAPM equilibrium, even though the asset itself may be traded in a competitive market. Thus, in the presence of transactions costs, both a transaction and a precautionary motive for liquidity may operate. Given uncertainty with respect to future stochastic cash demands, the greater the potential excess borrowing costs in the next or future periods (due to the possibility of credit rationing or other reasons), the stronger the precautionary motive for liquidity (see [21]).

Given market imperfections, the firm also has incentive to hold receivables, as they now may yield "excess" returns. On the liability side, differences may appear in the certainty-equivalent costs of liabilities of different types, and the firm no longer is indifferent toward alternative methods of financing.

AN INTEGRATED FRAMEWORK

The objective of an integrated theory of corporate financial management would seem to be a single unified decision framework based on valuation as the normative criterion and set within the context of a positive theory of share-price determination.[12] The CAPM provides the necessary vehicle. However, it is clear that the assumption of perfect financial markets must be dropped and market imperfections introduced explicitly into the analysis.

Recent extensions of the CAPM provide the necessary groundwork.

[11] See Pyle [23], Pringle [21], Cohn [4], and Klein [12] for discussions of the implications of the perfect-markets assumption for financial intermediaries.

[12] Unless financial markets are perfect and complete, valuation is not, in general, an appropriate normative criterion for financial management of the firm, for it need not lead to the maximization of either shareholder wealth or social welfare. In reference to this point, see Long [15], Jensen and Long [11], and Mossin [20]. It is likely, however, that financial markets are sufficiently frictionless that value maximization can be adopted as a first approximation to an appropriate normative criterion.

Work by Vasicek [33], Black [2], Fama [7] and Brennan [3] has demonstrated that the basic conclusions of the CAPM hold under divergent borrowing and lending rates.[13] In particular, the expected return on a risky asset remains a linear function of the covariance of the asset's return with that of the market portfolio.

This result opens the way to application of the CAPM to working capital decisions of firms and to other situations, such as financial intermediaries, wherein transactions costs cause net rates of return to lenders to diverge from costs net to borrowers. The CAPM equilibrium relationship under perfect markets can be used as the starting point for defining yield and cost functions for assets and liabilities. Relationships then can be modified to reflect transactions costs (e.g., search and acquisition and other information costs) and, if appropriate, the effects of imperfect competition (due to barriers to entry, etc.). Explicit incorporation of such imperfections causes yields to diverge from the basic equilibrium relationships and provides opportunities for portfolio optimization.[14]

The CAPM modified along these lines can deal simultaneously with investment decisions involving real and financial assets under various assumptions as to market imperfections and degree of competition. On the liability side, markets can be assumed segmented with differing degrees of imperfection, permitting analysis of alternative methods of financing in different markets. In a dynamic context, analysis of changes over time in the degree of imperfection in different markets may shed light on the question of maturity structure of liabilities.

WORKING CAPITAL AS A DECISION VARIABLE

It has been argued ([17], [26]) that firms should seek as a matter of policy to maintain a roughly constant level of nondiversifiable risk (the only risk deemed relevant by the CAPM) for their common shares. This argument is based on the notion that a change in the risk class of the firm's shares imposes costs on investors. These costs involve both the information costs inherent in the investor's ascertaining that a change has taken place and transactions costs involved in any portfolio rebalancing made necessary by the change.

An active working capital management policy could be employed to keep the firm's shares in a given risk class. Owing to the lumpy nature of long-term investments, stock and bond flotations, and dividend payments, the firm is continually subject to shifts in the risk of its equity. The fluid nature of working capital, on the other hand, can be exploited so as to offset or moderate such swings.

The marketable securities portfolio of the firm is typically managed so as to optimize the trade-offs among expected return, risk, and liquidity. A policy could be adopted for the management of marketable securities portfolio, for example, such that the appropriate risk level at any point in time is that which maintains the risk of the company's common stock at a constant level. The same result also could be obtained by manipulating other short-term asset and liability categories.

CONCLUSIONS

The purpose of this papaer has been (1) to clarify some of the reasons for the heretofore separate treatment in the literature of investment and capital structure decisions on the one

[13] See Jensen [10] for a review of this and other work extending the CAPM. See Stigler [28] and Cohn and Pringle [5] for discussions of imperfections in the capital markets.

[14] See [21] and [22] for applications of the CAPM, modified as described above to account for market imperfections, to financial management decisions of commercial banks. The parallel with working capital decisions of firms was noted earlier.

hand and "working capital" decisions on the other, and (2) to suggest steps to integrate the two areas. It was argued that a major reason for the development of "short-term" finance outside the mainstream of "long-term" corporate financial theory was the assumption of perfect financial markets common to nearly all theoretical work in the latter area. The perfect-financial-markets assumption was useful and probably necessary in the early stages of the development of corporate financial theory, just as an assumption of no friction may be useful as a first step in the study of physical systems. It is clear, however, that the perfect-markets assumption precludes the application of the main body of corporate financial theory to a large class of problems, including working cpaital decisions in firms and the management of financial intermediaries. Explicit treatment of market imperfections also may facilitate analysis of the maturity structure of corporate liabilities, an area largely untreated to date.

Recent extensions of the capital asset pricing model provide tools that can be used to integrate corporate financial theory into a consistent single-period framework. The difficulty of such an undertaking should not be underestimated, and the discussion here, which raises more questions than it answers, was intended to suggest directions for future research. Modified to incorporate market imperfections, the CAPM can accommodate investment decisions involving real or financial assets as well as decisions concerning the financing mix, under various assumptions regarding market imperfections and the degree of competition in markets.

Given the multiperiod nature of most corporate financial management decisions, it is evident that useful operational models in many cases must involve a multiperiod framework. The argument presented here for a unified single-period theory is made not on grounds of operational usefulness but rather on the premise that sound single-period theories are a desirable first step.

REFERENCES

1. Kenneth J. Arrow, "The Role of Securities in the Optimal Allocation of Risk-bearing," *Review of Economic Studies*, (April 1964).
2. Fischer Black, "Capital Market Equilibrium with Restricted Borrowing," *Journal of Business*, (July 1972).
3. Michael J. Brennan, "Capital Market Equilibrium with Divergent Borrowing and Lending Rates," *Journal of Financial and Quantitative Analysis*, (Dec. 1971).
4. Richard A. Cohn, "Mutual Life Insurer's Portfolio and Policyholder Utility Functions," *Journal of Risk and Insurance*, (forthcoming).
5. ______________, and John J. Pringle, "Imperfections in International Financial Markets: Implications for Risk Premia and the Cost of Capital to Firms," *Journal of Finance*, (March 1973).
6. Gerard Debreu, *Theory of Value*, John Wiley & Sons, 1959.
7. Eugene F. Fama, "Risk, Return and Equilibrium," *Journal of Political Economy*, (Jan.-Feb. 1971).
8. Robert S. Hamada, "Portfolio Analysis, Market Equilibrium and Corporation Finance," *Journal of Finance*, (March 1969).
9. J. Hirshleifer, *Investment, Interest and Capital*, Prentice-Hall, 1970.
10. Michael C. Jensen, "Capital Markets--Theory and Evidence," *Bell Journal of Economics and Management Science*, (Autumn 1972).
11. ______________, and John B. Long, Jr., "Corporate Investment under Uncertainty and Pareto Optimality in the Capital Markets," *Bell Journal of Economics and Management Science*, (Spring 1972).

12. Michael A. Klein, "The Economics of Security Divisibility and Financial Intermediation," *Journal of Finance*, (Sept. 1973).
13. Alan Kraus and Robert Litzenberger, "A State-Preference Model of Optimal Financial Leverage," *Journal of Finance*, (Sept. 1973).
14. John Lintner, "The Valuation of Risk Assets and the Selection of Risky Investments in Stock Portfolios and Capital Budgets," *Review of Economics and Statistics*, (Feb. 1965).
15. John Long, "Wealth, Welfare and the Price of Risk," *Journal of Finance*, (May 1972).
16. Harry Markowitz, *Portfolio Selection*, John Wiley and Sons, 1959.
17. Jacob. B. Michaelsen and Robert C. Goshay, "Portfolio Selection in Financial Intermediaries: A New Approach," *Journal of Financial and Quantitative Analysis*, (June 1967).
18. Franco Modigliani and Merton H. Miller, "The Cost of Capital, Corporation Finance and the Theory of Investment," *American Economic Review*, (June 1958).
19. Jan Mossin, "Equilibrium in a Capital Asset Market," *Econometrica*, (Oct. 1966).
20. __________, "Security Pricing and Investment Criteria in Competitive Markets," *American Economic Review*, (Dec. 1969).
21. John J. Pringle, "The Imperfect-Markets Model of Commercial Bank Financial Management," *Journal of Financial and Quantitative Analysis*, (forthcoming).
22. ______________, "The Capital Decision in Commercial Banks," *Journal of Finance*, (forthcoming).
23. David H. Pyle, "On the Theory of Financial Intermediation," Working Paper No. 161, University of California, Berkeley, (April 1970).
24. Mark E. Rubinstein, "A Mean-Variance Synthesis of Corporate Financial Theory," *Journal of Finance*, (March 1973).
25. William F. Sharpe, "Capital Asset Prices: A Theory of Market Equilibrium Under Conditions of Risk," *Journal of Finance*, (Sept. 1964).
26. ________________, "Discussion," *Journal of Finance*, (May 1970).
27. Ezra Solomon, *The Theory of Financial Management*, Columbia University Press, 1963.
28. George J. Stigler, "Imperfections in the Capital Market," *Journal of Political Economy*, (June 1967).
29. Joseph E. Stiglitz, "A Re-Examination of the Modigliani-Miller Theorem," *American Economic Review*, (Dec. 1969).
30. ________________, "Some Aspects of the Pure Theory of Corporate Finance: Bankruptcies and Take-Overs," *Bell Journal of Economics and Management Science*, (Autumn 1972).
31. Donald L. Tuttle, and Robert H. Litzenberger, "Leverage, Diversification and Capital Market Effects on a Risk-Adjusted Capital Budgeting Framework," *Journal of Finance*, (June 1968).
32. James C. Van Horne, *Financial Management and Policy*, 2nd ed. Prentice-Hall, 1971.
33. Oldrich A. Vasicek, "Capital Asset Pricing Model with No Riskless Borrowing," unpublished memorandum, Wells Fargo Bank, San Francisco, Calif., March 1971.

READING 4

Ruin Considerations: Optimal Working Capital and Capital Structure

Harold Bierman
Cornell University

K. Chopra
Wake Forest University

L. Joseph Thomas
Cornell University

I. INTRODUCTION AND LITERATURE REVIEW

At any point in time a firm must decide both the level of working capital consistent with its productive assets and how to finance these assets. Academic theorists in business administration have traditionally approached decision making of the firm on a segmented rather than on a global basis and have been satisfied with developing suboptimizing decision rules. Thus there has been concern about managing working capital and concern about choosing the optimum capital structure, but traditionally the two decisions have not been made jointly. And even if they were made jointly, decisions would still remain in the working capital area involving inventories, credit granting, and marketable securities. This paper is an attempt to interrelate working capital and capital structure decisions with working capital used not only as a buffer to avoid ruin but also to affect sales via changing inventory levels and credit policies. The possibility of ruin introduces a discontinuity that precludes perfect elimination of leverage effects via a market.

We would expect in the near future much more attention to be paid to the interrelationships of different functional decisions. There is a need for the models currently found in production, marketing, and finance to be linked together so that the full consequences of a set of decisions in the functional areas may be evaluated.

One aspect of the problem, the choice of an optimal dynamic working capital policy in the face of ruin, is studied by Borch [4]. He defines ruin by specifying a level of working capital below which ruin ensues. His dynamic models provide useful insights into the problem, but we believe his definition of ruin can be improved. There are also two papers by Eppen and Fama, [6] and [7], that provide excellent background into dynamic models of working capital management. Eppen and Fama do not, however, include ruin in their models. A risk-return analysis of working capital, where the risk is of running out of cash, is given by Van Horne [12], but the consequences are not spelled out.

Reprinted from the JOURNAL OF FINANCIAL AND QUANTITATIVE ANALYSIS (March 1975), pp. 119-128, by permission of the publisher.

An approach by Fama [5] to an individual's multi-period wealth-consumption decisions in the face of uncertain life bears some similarities to our work.

Another side of the problem, the amount of debt and stock equity to issue when ruin is a possibility, is studied by Bierman and Thomas [3], without their discussing the importance of the level of working capital decision. They study the optimal initial debt-equity mix as well as the optimal debt retirement (if any) policy. Ruin is defined in terms of a given level of equity. In the current paper we define ruin in terms of given levels of working capital and borrowing capacity. We assume that the debt holders will force reorganization if the firm is unable to meet contractual obligations because working capital is too low *and* the firm cannot obtain more debt.

The optimal debt-equity mix in the face of ruin is also studied by Baxter [2], from the point of view of the firm. Both the research reflected in [3] and the current research focus on the effect on initial stockholders of the firm. The impact of this difference is discussed further in [3]. The general question of finding optimal debt-equity ratios is studied by many authors. We will not discuss that literature here, except to note that the commonly held idea that in the presence of taxes debt is a cheaper source of capital than stock (see Baumol and Malkiel [1], pp. 561-562) may be untrue when a possibility of ruin exists.

In this paper the acquired working capital serves as a buffer against ruin, as well as a means of increasing earnings, while the debt used to finance the working capital increases the size of the fixed payment obligations, and the cost of debt tends to reduce the total earnings of stockholders.

We assume that earnings before interest increase monotonically with increases in working capital. The increase arises for two reasons. Larger inventories enable the firm to have fewer stock-outs, thus increased sales and earnings. Also the firm can carry a larger amount of receivables, and a less restrictive credit policy is assumed to lead to higher expected profits before interest and a larger variance.

The models use dynamic programming in Markov chains, due to Howard [10], and ruin is defined using a linear combination of working capital and the level of stock equity. The justification for this is based on the assumption that if a firm has cash, it can operate; if it has equity, it can borrow.

The recognition of the dual factors affecting ruin and the assumption that the working capital level affects both the expected earnings and the variance of earnings are the main differences from previously published work. The model, of course, is still less complicated than reality where bankruptcy usually means reorganization rather than a cessation of activities. However, the initial stockholders, whose view we take, may be ruined by a reorganization arising from a condition of bankruptcy.

First, in Section II, we consider a formulation where debt retirement is not allowed (a firm may wish to maintain its initial capital structure). In Section III we use revenues to retire long-term debt where revenues are a function of the amount of working capital. In Section IV risk considerations are discussed with the possibility for risk diversification via a market, and Section V presents possible extensions and conclusions.

II. FORMULATION—WORKING CAPITAL AS A "BUFFER" WITH NO DEBT RETIREMENT

The notation we will use is:

A = amount of fixed (productive) assets. We assume a firm has a plant of value A, and its revenues derive from that plant. The firm will not be allowed to invest in other operations in this paper.

S = amount of equity at any point in time. S_o is the initial amount of equity, held by initial stockholders. We assume initially that S_o is known and is not a decision variable. This is later modified.

D = amount of debt (D_o is the initial debt). The interest payment per period is k_dD.

W = amount of working capital. W^* is the optimal level of W.

C = the total amount we can borrow, short term, to use as a buffer against ruin when working capital goes to zero. C can be made to be a function of the amount of stock equity and the amount of debt. This emergency borrowing capacity is assumed to have zero cost (it can be assumed that trade creditors are supplying the funds).

k_e = time value of money to the initial stockholders, and the discount factor for their cash flows is $\beta = 1/1(1+k_e)$.

k_d = annual cost of long-term debt; k_e and k_d are assumed to be independent of the capital structure to simplify the presentation. This assumption can be changed without difficulty.

R = a random variable for the periodic return (before interest) on fixed assets, A; it is conditional on working capital, W.

$p(r|W)$ = the probability mass function for realization, r, of the random variable, R, given a working capital W. Negative values of r are possible. However, ruin can occur in the presence of debt even if r is not negative, because of interest expense.

$f(W)$ = expected discounted return to the stockholders, when the firm's working capital is W.

If the firm has borrowed up to its capacity, ruin occurs whenever working capital goes below zero. Assume a firm can borrow $\alpha \cdot S$ where α is a constant between 0 and 1. If a firm starts with $W = W^*$ and a loss of W^* occurs first, reducing equity to $S_o - W^*$ and working capital to zero, we assume the firm can borrow $\alpha(S_o - W^*)$ and that ruin now occurs if working capital goes negative. If $W^* \geq S_o$, ruin occurs if the working capital goes negative since the firm is defined as having no debt capacity.

We assume that the firm returns to W^* in each period, if this can be done given the level of revenues.[1] Only after paying k_dD interest and reaching W^* can dividends be paid. All the excess revenue goes to dividends; that is, growth is not considered. Our goal is to maximize the expected dividend stream, discounted at $\beta = 1/(1+k_e)$, initially assuming an absence of risk aversion.

Based on the above assumptions and starting with W of working capital, the expected discounted return is defined by equation (1). The two terms of (1) are for the case where the value of r is such that we reach W^*, pay interest and dividends, and where r is insufficient to reach W^* after payment of interest. If the return is less than b, we are ruined. We assume the value of the stock equity after ruin is zero.

$$(1) \quad f(W) = \sum_{r=a}^{\infty} [(r-a) + \beta f(W^*)]p(r|W) + \beta \sum_{r=b}^{r<a} f(W + r - k_dD)p(r|W) ,$$

where

$$a = W^* - W + k_dD ,$$

[1] This is different from the work of Eppen and Fama [6]; essentially it is an assumption of zero cost to replenish W up to W^*. Since we do so only with current revenues, a zero cost seems appropriate.

$$b = -[C + W] + k_d D$$

and $(r - a)$ is the cash dividend. Assume $\alpha \cdot S_o$ is the initial borrowing capacity. If we start with W^* of working capital, and have losses of W^*, after $\alpha(S_o - W^*)$ has been borrowed and not repaid, no further borrowing is possible. C is defined as $\alpha(S_o - W^*)$ and ruin is defined as total losses equal to $W^* + C$. Equation (1) can be thought of as a Markov chain with rewards (see [10]). It is an infinite horizon model, where the firm is ruined (with probability one) at some finite time. (See Feller [8] for a discussion of general Gambler's Ruin games, to which this problem is similar.) The set of equations, one for each W value, can be evaluated for any W^*. The optimal W^* can be obtained by finding the value of W^* that maximizes the expected present value. If new common stock cannot be issued and debt cannot be retired, the optimal amount of debt is defined as being equal to $A + W^* - S_o$.

Equation (1) can be used to consider a stock issue in lieu of debt by finding the optimal W^* for different S_o values. If S_o exceeds the amount available to the initial stockholder, the issuance of the stock must dilute their percentage of ownership. The optimal size of issue (if any) is the one where the initial stockholders' fraction of ownership, determined by the price of the supplemental issue, times $f(W^*)$ is maximized. This "optimal" solution does not take account of the owners' desire to maintain control, and in actuality it would be just an input to the decision makers.

If $\alpha = 0$ or if $W^* > S_o$, a loss of W^* causes ruin because we assume the firm cannot borrow, and the problem is the same as in [4]. If $\alpha = 1$, the problem is that of [3]. If, as seems realistic, short-term credit could be arranged equal to a fraction of the value of assets financed by equity, then $0 < \alpha < 1$ and the above formulations are reasonably realistic.[2]

III. FORMULATION—ALLOWING DEBT RETIREMENT

We continue to assume that the return, r, is a function of the level of working capital, but now we allow the use of positive returns to reduce debt. The reduction of debt reduces the initial dividends, but since it increases equity and reduces fixed debt outlays, debt retirement may significantly reduce the probability of ruin and increase expected return. Debt retirement is more likely to be advantageous when k_e (the stockholders' time value of money) is low.

In this section, we allow the decision maker to choose an initial level of debt and a target level. For example, $(D_o = 10,\ D^* = 6)$ implies an initial debt level of 10, and the firm will retire debt to a level of 6 as soon as possible after reaching W^* and before paying dividends.[3] After a debt level of 6 has been reached, all excess returns are paid in dividends. The problem is to choose W^* (implying an initial value of D_o) and D^* optimally.

The new formulation must have both W and D in the state space, since in this section, one does not imply

[2] We have used the formulation to obtain solutions to simple examples. These examples demonstrate that working capital, in addition to its use in operations, can be a buffer against ruin. The examples also show that the optimal amount of working capital to have as a buffer is not intuitively obvious, but it does appear to be a nonincreasing function of k_e, the stockholders' time value of money. W^* also depends on $p(r|W)$, α, S_o, D_o, and A.

[3] This "retire down to" form of policy is intuitive, but the form of optimal policy has not been proved mathematically for the case with ruin. The problem can be formulated to consider a different amount of debt retirement for each W and r, but the computational cost is high.

the other after the initial stage. As debt is retired, S is increased and D is decreased by the amount of debt retirement. For any specified W^* we can find D^* as follows.

$$(2)\ f(W,D) = \sum_{r=a_1}^{\infty} [(r-a_1)+\beta f(W^*,D^*)]p(r|W) + \sum_{r=a_2}^{r<a_1} \beta[f(W^*,D-r+a_2)]p(r|W) + \sum_{r=a_3}^{r<a_2} \beta f[W+r-k_dD,D]p(r|W),$$

where

$a_1 = W^* + k_dD - W + D - D^*$, and $r - a_1$, is the dividend,

$a_2 = W^* + k_dD - W$,

$a_3 = -C - W + k_dD$, and other variables are as before.

The three terms are for the situations where (1) we first reach W^* and D^* using a_1 dollars of return and then pay dividends of $r - a_1$; (2) we reach W^* but not D^*; and (3) we reach neither one. The implied fourth term is ruin. If we cannot meet our debt expense even by borrowing an amount C, then $f(\cdot) = 0$.

Given the initial stockholder investment (S_o), the optimal pair (W^*,D^*) is found by trying different D^* for the W^* value under consideration, and choosing the combination of W^* and D^* that maximizes $f(W^*,D_o)$. If desired we can also consider the issuance at time zero of common stock to new investors, and then the objective would be to maximize the initial stockholders' share of $f(W^*,D_o)$.

IV. RISK AND THE CAPITAL ASSET PRICING MODEL

We now assume a capital market and the possibility of diversified portfolios. The market has perfect information about the firm and uses it to value the different alternatives in accordance with the mean variance capital asset pricing model. In this section we make use of Hamada's [9] work on the use of the capital asset pricing model for evaluating alternative capital structures. Using Hamada's symbols:

$E(R_B)$ is the expected rate of return on the stockholders' investment if debt is used,

$E(R_A)$ is the expected rate of return on the stockholders' investment if no debt is used,

$E(R_m)$ equals the expected return from investing in the market portfolio, and

R_F equals the risk-free return.

Now, if D = dollars of debt and S_o = the equity investment (so that the value of the firm is $V = S_o + D$), we can define $E(R_B)$ as the expected rate of return in equilibrium with this financing.

Hamada demonstrates (see [9], p. 19) that in equilibrium

$$(3)\quad E(R_A) = R_F + \gamma \operatorname{cov}(R_A,R_m), \text{ and}$$

$$(4)\quad E(R_B) = R_F + \gamma \operatorname{cov}(R_B,R_m), \text{ where}$$

$$\gamma = \frac{E(R_m) - R_F}{\sigma^2(R_m)}, \text{ and } \gamma \text{ is the same for all assets.}$$

Building on a paper by Smidt and Bierman [11], the risk-adjusted present value at time t for one period will be defined as $f_t(W)$ and is equal to

$$(5)\quad f_t(W) = \bar{f}_t(W) - \gamma \operatorname{cov}(\tilde{f}_t(W),R_m)$$

where $\bar{f}_t(W)$ is the expected present value using R_F as the rate of discount and $\tilde{f}_t(W)$ is a random variable. The term $\gamma \operatorname{cov}(\tilde{f}_t(W),R_m)$ is a dollar adjustment for risk required by the market and is different for every

TABLE 1

DATA REQUIREMENTS FOR THE tth PERIOD

States of the World (e_i)	Probability of e_i	Values of the Two Random Variables: Market Return	Values of the Two Random Variables: Investment Return
e_i	$p(e_1)$	R_{m1}	$f_{t,1}(W)$
e_2	$p(e_2)$	R_{m2}	$f_{t,2}(W)$
⋮	⋮	⋮	⋮
e_n	$p(e_n)$	R_{mn}	$f_{t,n}(W)$

debt-equity financing pair. If the model had only one period, the firm could proceed by collecting the information shown in Table 1. Table 1 assumes that both the market return and the investment return are conditional on the state of the world, e_i.

From Table 1 the firm could compute $\text{cov}(\tilde{f}_t(W),R_m)$ for the debt equity combination under consideration, and the risk adjusted present value $f_t(W)$ could be computed.

For the multiperiod problem we will use a dynamic programming approach similar to that used previously with some modifications as outlined below.

Modification 1: We now assume a finite horizon. In equations (1) and (2) this is accomplished by subscripting the f values, f_t on the left-hand side and f_{t-1} on the right. Then $t=1,...N$ defines the number of periods remaining. The horizon should be long enough so that realism is not lost.

Modification 2: Now instead of using $(1+k_e)^{-1}$, the discounting is accomplished using a risk-free rate of interest and subtracting a risk premium. If a positive risk-adjusted net present value is obtained, the investment is an acceptable one, and, further, the sequence of decisions that maximize the risk-adjusted net present value can be chosen as the "optimal" decisions. The risk premium required by the market may change through time due to the changes in the state of the firm (e.g., their working capital and debt levels). Each future return is adjusted using the risk premium for that time period.

The algorithm is, then, a dynamic programming algorithm where an additional computation is made to find the risk premium for each period. While the data problems are obviously serious, the computational problems are not, but it is clear that more research is needed to simplify the computations before actual application of this approach.

V. POSSIBLE EXTENSIONS AND CONCLUSIONS

We have indicated an approach to the complex problems posed by the effect of ruin on optimal working capital and capital structure. The model, contrary to previous work, allows emergency short-term borrowing to avoid ruin. Also, the possibility of retiring long-term debt and a method of considering stock issues are included. In addition, the earnings are a function of the level of working capital. Finally, a method for the possible application of the capital asset pricing model is discussed.

Many theoretical and practical questions remain in this area, and we will not try to list them all. The most notable question is the meaning of ruin. In fact, firms do not cease to operate; rather, they are usually reorganized, with courts setting the amount of equity to be held by various parties. Thus the implications to the initial stockholders are oversimplified by using a future value of zero once the firm is ruined. We could, of course, allow any arbitrary value for a final payment, but that is still too simplified. Empirical evidence as to the economic consequences to the stockholders of bankruptcy is needed.

A second major problem arises because after some adverse events a firm may not be sure that it will be able to borrow short-term money. Thus we could have a probabilistic replenishment of working capital. This is not difficult to include in the formulation, but estimating the probability of replenishment, which undoubtedly changes as the firm's position deteriorates, would seem difficult. Along these lines, an increasing cost of this debt, as we use more debt, is easy to include.

Finally, we have not allowed for growth of the firm. In other words, revenues should be usable for dividends, debt retirement, or investment in other productive assets. For a growing firm, maintaining working capital as a buffer (in addition to its use in operations) is still important because opportunities may be lost unless the firm has protected itself. We have also excluded the possibility of using retained earnings to add to working capital. This is a potentially important alternative when the expected revenues increase with increasing working capital. In general, if retained earnings could be used to finance working capital, then it might be desirable to build up working capital through time rather than start with W^*. Models to include that possibility can be derived, but they would require an additional state variable in the formulation. There would also be data problems in applying such models.

REFERENCES

1. W. J. Baumol and B. G. Malkiel, "The Firm's Optimal Debt-Equity Combination and the Cost of Capital." *The Quarterly Journal of Economics,* November 1967, pp. 547-578.
2. N. D. Baxter, "Coverage, Risk of Ruin and the Cost of Capital." *The Journal of Finance,* September 1967, pp. 395-403.
3. H. Bierman and J. Thomas, "Ruin Considerations and Debt Issuance." *The Journal of Financial and Quantitative Analysis,* January 1972, pp. 1361-1378.
4. K. Borch, "The Capital Structure of a Firm." *Swedish Journal of Economics,* 1969, pp. 1-13.
5. E. Fama, "Multiperiod Consumption-Investment Decisions." *American Economic Review,* March 1970.
6. G. Eppen and E. Fama, "Solutions for Cash Balance and Simple Dynamic-Portfolio Problems." *The Journal of Business,* January 1968, pp. 94-112.
7. G. Eppen and E. Fama, "Optimal Policies for Cash Balance and Simple Dynamic Portfolio Models with Proportional Costs." *International Economic Review,* June 1969, pp. 119-133.
8. W. Feller, *An Introduction to Probability Theory and Its Application.* Vol. 1. New York: John Wiley, 1957.
9. R. S. Hamada, "Portfolio Analysis, Market Equilibrium and Corporation Finance." *The Journal of Finance,* March 1969, pp. 13-31.
10. R. A. Howard, *Dynamic Programming and Markov Processes.* New York: John Wiley, 1960.
11. S. Smidt and H. Bierman, Jr., "Application of the Capital Asset Pricing Model to Multi-Period Investments." Cornell Working Paper, 1974.
12. J. Van Horne, "A Risk-Return Analysis of a Firm's Working Capital Position." *The Engineering Economist,* Winter 1969, pp. 71-89.

READING 5

Working Capital Management in Practice

Keith V. Smith
Purdue University

Shirley Blake Sell
University of California, Los Angeles

1. INTRODUCTION

Within any firm, decisions must be made about obtaining and using financial resources. A return-risk framework has been shown to be useful for many longer-range financial decisions, but there are still many considerations about the firm's current assets and current liabilities that do not easily fit that framework. Instead, the management of a firm's working capital has seemed to emerge as a series of independent technologies for handling various current assets and current liabilities.

While surveys have not been a mainstream part of financial research in recent years, survey findings occasionally have provided a useful perspective for developing and testing of financial theories and techniques. Excepting one study [4] which examined the use of quantitative decision models in different areas of finance, surveys typically have focused on only part of the total decision-making spectrum. With respect to longer-range decisions, surveys have been used to investigate the choice of techniques in capital budgeting [2,5]. For shorter-range decisions, surveys have tended to focus on the management of individual assets, such as cash [3,6] and accounts receivable [1,7].

As part of a U.C.L.A. graduate seminar on working capital management, a SURVEY of current management practices was conducted. The purpose of the SURVEY was to investigate responsibilities and practices for working capital management, both as individual balance sheet accounts, and as a total part of the firm's financial resources. This paper describes the SURVEY (Section 2), reviews our findings (Sections 3-10), and offers implications (Section 11).

2. RESEARCH DESIGN

The SURVEY was conducted using a four-page questionnaire. It included 35 questions, some of which asked the respondent to choose one answer among

This manuscript has not been previously published.

several possibilities, while the others asked the respondent to rank alternatives in terms of their relative importance to his or her firm. There also were questions where the respondent was asked to specify other alternatives than those provided on the printed questionnaire. Respondents also were encouraged to write comments, where appropriate, in the margins of the questionnaire. A copy of the questionnaire is included as an Appendix.

The 1,000 largest industrial firms, as listed by FORTUNE [8] were selected as the initial universe for the SURVEY. Because of cost considerations, we decided not to send questionnaires to all 1,000 firms, but rather to focus on a portion of the universe having selected characteristics. Two characteristics of interest, and for which data is available in FORTUNE, were size and profitability. Accordingly, we included in the universe the largest 200 firms, and the smallest 200 firms, on the basis of sales. And using average-return-on-equity over the past five years as a measure of relative profitability, the 200 most profitable and the 200 least profitable firms were added to the universe. Because of the overlap when both size and profitability characteristics were used, the result was a universe of 668 firms.

Using information from Standard and Poor's Corporation [9], we identified the highest ranking financial officer for each firm in this population. An individualized cover letter, a copy of the questionnaire, and a return envelope were mailed to each firm during September 1978. Fifteen questionnaires were returned because of an incorrect address, and thus the effective size of the universe for the SURVEY was 653 firms. Of these, there was no response from 431 firms; written regrets were received from nine firms; there were three unusable responses; and there were 210 usable responses which constitute the sample for our SURVEY.

Exhibit 0 provides further information about this sample, including the size and profitability subsamples. The average size of the larger subsample was $4.7 billion, while the average size of the smaller subsample was only $129 million. Though one might argue that all firms in the FORTUNE 1,000 are really "larger" firms, the average size of firms in the larger subsample was over 35 times larger than that of the "smaller" subsample. In terms of the profitability characteristic, the "more profitable" subsample had an average-return-on-equity of 11.6% over the past five years, while the "less profitable" subsample had a five-year average-return-on-equity of -4.8%.

In each cell of Exhibit 0, the number of responses is compared to the number of firms in the universe for that size-profitability combination. The response rate ranged from 37.2% for the larger subsample to 27.1% for the smaller subsample. In contrast, the response rate was quite uniform across the three profitability subsamples. The overall response rate for our SURVEY was a respectable 32.2%.

As will be explained in the next section, it also was possible to examine subsamples of the responding firms according to two other characteristics: the formality of working capital policy, and the aggressiveness of working capital policy as expressed by the respondents.

In the sections which follow, questions requesting only a single answer are reported in terms of the total sample of 210 firms, but also according to the four possible breakdowns: size, profitability, formality of policy, and aggressiveness of policy. For the size and profitability characteristics, we did not consider the middle categories. That is, we compared "larger" firms with "smaller" firms, and "more profitable" firms with "less profitable" firms. Because some respondents did not answer all the questions, the number of responses is reported in each instance.

The Statistical Package for the Social Sciences, which was used to analyze the responses to our SURVEY, provides a chi-square statistic which can be used to test statistically one subsample against another. That is, we test whether a particular subsample breakdown has an effect on the responses to a given question. In each exhibit which follows, the chi-square value is not presented, but rather the respective level of significance for the chi-square statistic. The smaller the "significance" that is reported for a given question and subsample comparison, the stronger the association. If one were to choose x% as the critical level, then for a significance level less than x%, we would reject the null hypothesis that the responses to a given question are independent of that subsample characteristic. For our analysis, we consider a result "significant" if the significance level of the chi-square statistic is less than 5%; we consider the result "weakly significant" if the significance level is between 5-10%.

For questions requesting a ranking of possible responses ("1" referring to the most important, etc.), we report the percentage of responses for each possible answer. Respondents were instructed *not* to assign ranks to alternatives that do not apply to their firm. While a ranking question allows for multiple responses to a given question, a ranking question does not lend itself as readily to statistical comparisons. One procedure which does allow a statistical comparison is to calculate the "mean ranking" for each possible response. But such a procedure, which was used in a recent study of cash management practices [3], infers a cardinal ranking on the part of respondents, which was not a part of the instructions accompanying our questionnaire. After analyzing the statistical results of such an inference, we decided *not* to try and force statistical comparisons among the four subsamples for the ranking questions included in the SURVEY.

3. POLICY AND RESPONSIBILITY

The first series of questions dealt with the responsibility for working capital within the firm, and the type of management policy that is utilized. As seen in Exhibit 1,* just under 30% of the sample firms have a formal policy for the management of their working capital, while about 60% of the firms have an informal policy. Ten percent of the responding firms indicated they have no working capital policy. A significantly greater number of the larger firms reported a formal policy than did the smaller firms. We found no association between profitability and formality of working capital policy. In the sections which follow, we limit our attention to a comparison of firms having a formal policy to those firms having an informal policy.

The financial vice president has responsibility for establishing the firm's overall working capital policy in almost half of the responding firms (Exhibit 2). The president and treasurer were the next most frequently mentioned. The controller was mentioned as having overall responsibility for working capital policy in only a single firm. Among the 28 respondents who selected the "other (please specify)" alternative, sixteen indicated that a management committee has responsibility for establishing the working capital policy of the firm. Quite likely, the management committee in those instances include one or more of the positions indicated in Exhibit 2, and thus working capital policy is a shared responsibility.

There was considerable variation in the frequency of review of the firm's working capital policy (Exhibit 3). Annual, quarterly, and monthly review was mentioned with about the same relative frequency. A much larger number of

---

* For convenience to the reader, all exhibits are placed at the end of the paper. Also, each exhibit number coincides with the number of that particular question on the SURVEY questionnaire.

firms indicated that they review working capital policy whenever necessary, thus indicating a flexible review practice. The subsample significance values were high, thus indicating no differences in frequency of review according to either the size or the profitability of the responding firms.

As seen in Exhibit 4, 28% of the firms indicated a "cautious" working capital policy, while 22% of the firms indicated an "aggressive" policy. The remaining respondents indicated a situational-type policy, or one that changes over time. This, again, is evidence of flexibility in working capital management. Neither size nor profitability of the firm has an effect on the aggressiveness of the working capital policy. In subsequent sections, we limit our attention to a comparison of firms having an aggressive policy to those indicating a cautious policy.

We also asked each firm to indicate who is responsible for individual working capital accounts (Exhibit 5). On the one hand, the treasurer was mentioned most frequently for cash, marketable securities, accounts receivable, and short-term loans. On the other hand, the controller was mentioned most frequently for inventory, accounts payable, and other accruals. Among the 33 "other" responses to responsibility for accounts receivable, the divisional manager was most frequently mentioned, followed by credit manager and operations manager. Among the 68 "other" responses to responsibility for inventory, the divisional manager was mentioned in almost half of the cases, followed again by the operations manager. This means that responsibility for accounts receivable and inventory—the two largest of the current assets accounts—is decentralized for many of the firms responding to our SURVEY. In contrast, the presidents of 18 firms were identified as being responsible for inventory, thus indicating the importance attributed to that particular current asset.

4. CASH

Three questions probed the use of various techniques for the management of the firm's cash. For reducing negative (i.e., deposit) float (Exhibit 6), the largest number of responses, and also the highest ranking, was for lockboxes. Cash discounts and regional banking also were mentioned prominently as being used by firms to try to speed up the collections of their accounts receivable. These findings are generally consistent with those of earlier surveys of cash management practices [3, 6].

Conversely, centralized disbursing was easily the most frequently mentioned technique for increasing positive (i.e., disbursement) float (Exhibit 7). It is interesting to note that the number of respondents indicated in the margins of their questionnaires that they believe that it is a bad idea to slow down payments to their suppliers. And while only 89 of the responding firms indicated that they utilize remote disbursing, it was highly ranked for those that have decided to use that particular technique. Overall, our investigation supports the findings of other studies [3, 6] which indicated that firms tend to decentralize cash collections and centralize cash disbursements.

In terms of the techniques for improving the internal flow of funds within the organization, wire transfer was by far the most frequently mentioned and highest ranked technique for moving funds within the organization.

5. MARKETABLE SECURITIES

Five questions were used to examine the management of marketable securities. In terms of the composition of the marketable securities portfolio, Exhibit 9 reports the frequency of use of particular types of marketable securities. Commercial paper, certificates of deposit and U.S. treasury bills were most frequently mentioned. Federal agency issues and bankers acceptances were mentioned by somewhat less than half of the responding sample. Of the 38 firms that indicated the use of "other" types of marketable securities, Eurodollar deposits to a large extent and repurchase agreements to a lesser extent were mentioned. For many of these responses, Eurodollar deposits were ranked as being the most important instrument for investing the excess funds of the organization. Again, our findings closely parallel that of a recent study of cash management practices [3].

We then asked financial managers to rank different characteristics of marketable securities in terms of their importance to the firm (Exhibit 10). Yield was mentioned most frequently, with marketability and maturity both receiving frequent mention. Among the "other" responses to this question, the vast majority mentioned safety, or some combination of safety, marketability, and stability of market price.

We also asked each financial manager to indicate the annual yield objective of the firm's marketable securities portfolio (Exhibit 11). Over three-fourths of the responding firms indicated a yield objective between 7% and 9%. Among the four subsample comparisons, only the one concerning aggressiveness of policy was weakly significant. That result occurred because four of the "aggressive" policy firms indicated a yield objective of less than 6.0%. In other words, the level of significance occurred solely as a result of the lower tail of the distribution for that question.

Firms were asked to indicate how they decide on transferring funds between the marketable securities portfolio and the firm's cash account (Exhibit 12). The largest number of responses were subjective judgments and the use of established guidelines. Cost balancing models, which have received extensive scrutiny in the financial literature, were mentioned by only ten of the responding firms. Transferring funds based on projected cash requirements, and on required bank balances, were frequently mentioned in the "other (please specify)" answer. Among the subsample comparisons in Exhibit 12, two comparisons were significant statistically. Smaller firms and firms with an informal working capital policy tend to use subjective judgments in transferring funds, while larger firms and firms with a formal policy tend to use established guidelines. Furthermore, none of the smaller firms reported use of cost balancing models in managing their marketable securities. Subjective judgments were also used more extensively by those firms having an informal working capital policy.

Among various strategies which can be used for managing marketable securities, buying and holding to maturity was mentioned most frequently and also had the highest ranking (Exhibit 13). And somewhat surprisingly, only 80 firms indicated that they "play the yield curve" as part of managing their portfolio of marketable securities. This finding would seem to be consistent with the primary concern of many firms for avoiding risk in the investment of their excess funds.

6. ACCOUNTS RECEIVABLE

Four questions were used to explore the management of accounts receivable. In terms of techniques used for granting credit to potential customers (Exhibit 14), the largest number of responding firms indicated they used the traditional four C's of credit (i.e., character, capacity, capital, and conditions) in examining credit applications. Sequential credit analysis is used by about half of the responding firms, while credit scoring was reported by only about one-third of the total sample.

For monitoring the payment behavior of those customers that are granted credit (Exhibit 15), an aging schedule was mentioned most frequently and received the highest ranking. Collection period and receivables turnover were also mentioned frequently by the responding firms. In contrast, aging schedules, and to a lesser extent average days outstanding, were mentioned in an earlier survey [7] as measures used by firms to control their accounts receivable.

We then asked the firms in our SURVEY to rank the variables which they considered in evaluating credit terms and policy (Exhibit 16). Marketing considerations were mentioned most frequently, while possibility of bad debt losses was mentioned next most frequently. All of the five variables which were provided for that question were ranked by at least one-third of the total sample, thus highlighting the complexity of consideration that is given to receivables management.

In terms of criteria used in evaluating changes in credit terms (Exhibit 17), there was fairly uniform response across the four possible answers. Effect on firm sales and effect on firm profits were mentioned the most frequently and had the highest numerical rankings. Return-on-investment was mentioned least frequently.

7. INVENTORY

The next four questions dealt with the management of inventory. Among possible techniques for replenishing inventory stocking points, computerized inventory control systems were far the most frequently mentioned (Exhibit 18). Cost balancing models, again a technique that has received considerable attention in the financial literature, were mentioned by only fourteen respondents. It may be that some firms actually utilize a cost balancing technique, but it is embodied in their inventory control system. Among the four subsample comparisons for this question, size had a significant effect. Larger firms make greater use of computerized inventory control systems, while the smaller firms rely more frequently on ad hoc decision rules. Formality of working capital policy had a weakly significant impact for this question——with firms having an informal policy utilizing ad hoc decisions to a greater extent.

We asked respondents to rank the variables which they consider important in inventory purchased by the firm (Exhibit 19). Availability was the most frequent response and received the highest ranking. Price discounts and shortage costs also were frequently mentioned. Although inflation was mentioned by 90 of the responding firms, it was not highly ranked among the possible answers. Among the few "other" answers to this question, expected requirements from the production schedule was the most prominent response.

Exhibit 20 reports on ranking the variables considered important in inventory produced by the firm. Production scheduling was mentioned most frequently, and it also was ranked first almost 60% of the time. Seasonality of demand and shortage cost also were mentioned frequently by the responding firms. As with the previous question, inflation was mentioned by a large number of firms, but it was not ranked highly among the possible answers to this question.

When asked to rank the criteria used in evaluating changes in inventory policy (Exhibit 21), the resulting response was fairly uniform across the four answers which were offered. Effect on firm profits was mentioned most frequently and also received the highest percentage ranking. Overall response to this question on inventory would seem to be consistent with that reported for accounts receivable in Exhibit 17. That is, there was no clear trend among the responding firms in terms of the criteria used for evaluating changes in the levels of these important current assets.

8. ACCOUNTS PAYABLE

Three questions were devoted to the management of accounts payable. In Exhibit 22, we report the extent to which firms have accounts receivable among their current assets, vis-a-vis accounts payable among their current liabilities. For the total sample, 85.4% had accounts payable less than accounts receivable, and thus were net suppliers of credit. Conversely, only 10.2% had accounts payable greater than accounts receivable, and thus were net users of credit. Among the subsample comparisons, only size had a significant effect. The observed effect that more larger firms tend to be net users of credit probably attests to the greater ability of larger firms to stretch their suppliers.

We asked the firms in the sample what was the annual cost of the trade credit which they obtained from their supplies (Exhibit 23). Almost 38% of the responding firms indicated that there was no cost to their trade credit, suggesting that they take advantage of the cash discounts offered by their suppliers. For most of the other firms, the cost of trade credit was somewhat between 1% and 11%. Only 4.6% indicated that their annual cost is greater than 11%—thus indicating that they probably are not taking advantage of cash discounts from their suppliers. For this question, there were no significant effects among any of the four subsample comparisons.

Probing more directly, we asked each firm about their policy or practice with respect to cash discounts (Exhibit 24). Almost 70% of the respondents indicated that they always take discounts, while another 20% indicated that they sometimes do so. For this particular question, the profitability characteristic was significant, as a much larger percentage of the more profitable firms always take discounts. A limitation of this question is that the size of available discounts was not mentioned. In an earlier survey [1], that examined the effect of cash discounts on firm profitability, responding firms reported discounts in 1973 ranging from 0.5% to 2.5%.

9. SHORT-TERM LOANS

The next four questions have to do with the use of short-term financing from commercial banks. In Exhibit 25, we see that all four of the possible responses were frequently used when firms were asked what is the primary use of their short-term bank loans. The largest percentage of firms indicated that they use short-term loans to meet nonspontaneous needs. In other words, they indicated a flexibility with respect to that component of total financing. Greater use of short-term financing for nonspontaneous needs was reported by larger firms, more profitable firms, firms having a formal working capital policy, and firms reporting a cautious policy. None of these subsample comparisons were statistically significant, however.

We then asked firms what type of short-term loans do they usually obtain from their commercial banks (Exhibit 26). Almost two-thirds indicated that they obtain a line-of-credit with compensating balances. Simple interest loans are obtained by only 12.9% of the respondents. Simple interest loans occur more frequently for both larger firms and more profitable firms.

The vast majority of firms indicated that their short-term bank loans never require collateral (Exhibit 27). We note that the profitability characteristic was significant here, as over 98% of the more profitable firms borrow without collateral, compared to only 88% of the less profitable respondents.

When asked about the annual cost of their short-term bank loans (Exhibit 28), two-thirds of the responding firms indicated that their cost was between 8% and 11%. Surprisingly, almost 20% of the responding firms indicated their annual cost is less than 8%. Unless annual cost was interpreted by respondents to be on an after-tax basis, this finding is rather remarkable in light of the interest rate structure that existed in 1978. The only significant subsample comparison on this question had to do with formality of working capital policy. We see that a larger percentage of firms having a formal working capital policy were able to obtain less expensive bank financing.

10. PLANNING AND CONTROLLING

The final seven questions in the SURVEY had to do with the planning and controlling of working capital within the firm. First, we asked firms to rank different measures which can be used to monitor the firm's overall working capital position (Exhibit 29). The largest number of respondents indicated use of the current ratio, with working capital turnover also frequently measured. Less important was to measure working capital as a percentage of the total investment (i.e., assets) of the firm. Among the "other" answers provided by respondents, working capital as a percentage of sales was mentioned most frequently.

We also asked financial managers about the interval for which they prepare their cash budgets (Exhibit 30). Almost 80% of the firms either do cash budgeting on a daily or weekly basis, while only 8% of the respondents prepare cash budgets on a quarterly basis. Among the subsample comparisons that were statistically significant, larger firms use more frequent intervals to a greater extent than do smaller firms. And firms having a formal working capital policy utilize cash budgeting on a daily basis to a greater extent —albeit weakly significant—than do responding firms who have an informal policy.

In connection with this, we asked financial managers to rank the uses of cash budgeting by their respective firms (Exhibit 31). By far, the most prominent response was to plan for shortages and surpluses of cash. This response was ranked first by over 95% of the respondents. Exploring the implications of alternative sales forecast received the next largest number of responses and was often ranked second in terms of its importance to the firm.

In Questions 17 and 21, we included "return-on-investment" as one possible answer when asking firms about the criteria which they use in evaluating changes in their credit and inventory, respectively. Here in a broader question, we asked firms about using a return-on-investment (ROI) criterion in evaluating possible changes in their working capital components (Exhibit 32). Just over one-half of the firms indicated that they use an ROI criterion sometimes, while over one-third indicated that they always utilize an ROI criterion. Although the subsample comparisons were not significant statistically, larger percentage responses to "always use ROI" were obtained for the larger, more profitable, formal policy, and aggressive policy subsamples.

The last three questions in the SURVEY were designed to explore the extent to which working capital is reflected as part of the firm's overall capital budgeting process. When asked if working capital implications are included in capital budgeting decisions (Exhibit 33), two-thirds of the firms indicated that they always do so. On this particular question, the size effect was weakly significant. The profitability characteristic also was statistically significant, but in a surprising direction. Eight of the more profitable firms never include working capital considerations in evaluating capital projects, while only one of the less profitable firms exclude working capital considerations.

When asked if changes in working capital components are included as capital budgeting projects (Exhibit 34), one-third of the respondents indicated that they always do so, with just under one-half of the firms indicating that they sometimes do so. For this question, only the formality of policy characteristic was weakly significant—as a greater proportion of firms having a formal policy always include working capital components as projects.

Finally, when asked about the hurdle rate used in evaluating changes in working capital components (Exhibit 35), just under one-half of the firms indicated that they utilize an average cost of capital. In contrast, just under 30% of the respondents indicated that they utilize the interest rate in evaluating changes in working capital components. A total of 31 firms reported that a discount rate is not needed in evaluating changes in working capital components. None of the subsample components were significant for this question.

11. SUMMARY AND IMPLICATIONS

Just as the responses to each of the thirty-five questions should be of interest to the respective managers responsible for individual current assets and current liabilities (see Exhibit 5), the aggregate pattern of findings of our SURVEY ought to be of interest to those managers who have responsibility for establishing the overall working capital policy of the firm (see Exhibit 2). In this concluding section, we summarize findings from an overall perspective, and offer implications to the total financial management of the organization. We begin with a look at the view of working capital management that is afforded by each of the four subsample comparisons which were made. In order to enrich the picture of working capital management, we base the following observations on comparisons beyond those judged to be statistically significant.

We compared larger firms (average sales of $4.7 billion) with smaller firms ($129 million). We found, for example, that the larger firms tend to have more formal and aggressive working capital policies, to be net users of credit, and to do their cash budgeting on a daily basis. Moreover, the larger firms tend to use established guidelines for transferring funds between the firm's cash account and marketable securities portfolio, to employ computerized inventory control systems, to take cash discounts offered by suppliers, to obtain simple interest loans, without collateral, and at a lower annual cost. In contrast, smaller firms tend to have informal and more cautious working capital policies, and to utilize ad hoc guidelines in managing surplus cash and inventory.

We also compared more profitable firms (average five-year return-on-equity of 11.6%) with less profitable firms (-4.8% return-on-equity). We found that the more profitable firms —vis-a-vis the smaller firms—tend to always take discounts from suppliers, to obtain simple interest loans, to borrow without collateral, and to borrow at a lower annual cost. In presenting these comparisons, the reader may note a modest degree of correlation between the working capital patterns for the larger and the more profitable firms that responded to the SURVEY.

Comparisons based on type of working capital policy resulted in somewhat mixed findings. The responses of firms having aggressive policies differed from those of firms having cautious policies for certain questions, but overall there did not seem to be any discernible pattern. For example, aggressive firms make greater use of computerized inventory control systems than do cautious firms. But a greater proportion of the cautious firms are able to obtain simple-interest bank loans without collateral.

In contrast, a comparison of responses from firms having formal working capital policies with those having informal policies leads to a more discernible pattern. A greater proportion of firms with formal working capital policies—when compared to those with informal policies—tend to use established guidelines for managing surplus cash, to employ computerized inventory control, to always take cash discounts offered by suppliers, to obtain short-term borrowing at a lower cost, to prepare cash budgets on a daily basis, to always use an ROI criterion in evaluating working capital changes, and to always evaluate changes in working capital components within a capital budgeting process. Again the reader may note some correlation between the working capital patterns for the larger firms and those having more formal policies for managing their current assets and current liabilities.

Apart from the management patterns afforded by these subsample comparisons, we also note the complexity of working capital management that is seen from responses to the several ranking questions included in the SURVEY. Multiple responses to many of the ranking questions underscore the acceptance of multiple technologies that have emerged in recent years in order to better manage individual balance sheet accounts. This was particularly apparent in the ranking questions dealing with the management of float and the investment of surplus cash, as well as in those questions which probed the variables considered in evaluating credit and inventory policies.

Responses to the last few questions in the SURVEY also suggest to us that for many firms, working capital management in practice is far more than just a series of independent technologies. An ROI criterion, which is consistent with an overall firm goal of wealth maximization, is used by a large majority of the respondents in evaluating changes in credit terms, inventory policies, and other working capital components. In particular, the more than 80% of firms that always, or at least sometimes, consider working capital changes alongside of other investment projects in their capital budgeting procedures would seem to be integrating working capital management into their overall financial management.

Finally, we were impressed with the thoughtful manner in which most of the 210 financial managers appeared to respond to our SURVEY. Numerous erasures and changes in rankings on various questions seemed to indicate that the respondents were carefully considering their response. Many narrative comments made on the questionnaires also convinced us that the management of working capital is considered very seriously. We were particularly struck by a comment made by the financial manager of a large petroleum company in a cover letter accompanying the questionnaire which he returned: *It pleases me to be reminded that business schools are continuing their research on such major concerns to industry as working capital management. We in business are always willing to be enlightened with new insights to our age-old problems.*

We hope that our findings presented and discussed in this paper are of use to him and other financial managers who responded to our SURVEY. Working capital management is an important subject, and certainly one for which the development of new concepts and techniques periodically should be contrasted with what is happening in practice.

EXHIBIT O. Responses to Working Capital Survey

PROFITABILITY (Return On Equity)	SIZE (Sales) Larger ($4,692 Million)	Middle ($514 million)	Smaller ($129 million)	TOTALS
More Profitable (11.6%)	$\frac{12}{35}$ = 22.6%	$\frac{39}{122}$ = 32.0%	$\frac{12}{33}$ = 36.3%	$\frac{63}{190}$ = 33.2%
Middle (4.4%)	$\frac{43}{118}$ = 36.4%	0	$\frac{32}{123}$ = 26.0%	$\frac{75}{241}$ = 31.1%
Less Profitable (-4.8%)	$\frac{18}{43}$ = 42.6%	$\frac{45}{140}$ = 32.1%	$\frac{9}{39}$ = 23.0%	$\frac{72}{222}$ = 32.4%
TOTALS	$\frac{73}{196}$ = 37.2%	$\frac{84}{262}$ = 32.1%	$\frac{53}{195}$ = 27.1%	$\frac{210}{653}$ = 32.2%

Note: The denominator of each fraction is the universe size for that size profitability category, while the numerator is the number of responding firms.

EXHIBIT 1

MANAGEMENT POLICY FOR WORKING CAPITAL

(In Percentage)

Policy	Total Sample	Larger Size	Smaller Size	More Profitable	Less Profitable
Formal Policy	29.7%	47.8%	18.0%	35.3%	29.7%
Informal Policy	60.3	52.2	82.0	64.7	70.3
No Policy	10.0	*	*	*	*
Number Of Responses	209	69	50	51	64
Significance		.002		.78	

* Responses not included in this comparison.

EXHIBIT 2

RESPONSIBILITY FOR ESTABLISHING

THE WORKING CAPITAL

Responsibility	Number Of Responses	Percentage Response
Board of Directors	14	7.4%
President	40	21.3
Vice President, Finance	83	44.1
Treasurer	22	11.7
Controller	1	0.5
Other	28	14.9
TOTAL	188	100.0%

EXHIBIT 3

FREQUENCY OF REVIEW OF WORKING CAPITAL POLICY

(In Percentage)

Frequency	Total Sample	Larger Size	Smaller Size	More Profitable	Less Profitable
Monthly	13.8%	14.1%	8.2%	13.7%	11.9%
Quarterly	17.5	16.9	20.4	15.7	17.9
Semi-Annually	4.2	5.6	4.1	2.0	1.5
Annually	15.9	15.5	16.3	13.7	13.4
Whenever Necessary	48.7	47.9	51.0	54.9	55.2
Number Of Responses	189	71	49	51	67
Significance		.87		.99	

EXHIBIT 4

TYPE OF WORKING CAPITAL POLICY

(In Percentage)

Type	Total Sample	Larger Size	Smaller Size	More Profitable	Less Profitable
Cautious	28.0%	45.7%	56.5%	56.0%	62.2%
Aggressive	21.8	54.3	43.5	44.0	37.8
Situational	46.1	*	*	*	*
Change Over Time	4.1	*	*	*	*
Number Of Responses	193	35	23	25	37
Significance		.22		.58	

* Responses not included in this comparison.

EXHIBIT 5

RESPONSIBILITY FOR MANAGING WORKING CAPITAL ACCOUNTS

Account	Number Of Responses	Percentage Responding				
		President	VP Finance	Treasurer	Controller	Other
Cash	210	0.0%	18.6%	74.8%	1.9%	4.8%
Marketable Securities	204	0.0	20.6	74.0	0.5	4.9
Accounts Receivable	210	0.5	12.9	51.4	19.5	15.7
Inventory	206	8.7	11.2	6.3	40.8	33.0
Accounts Payable	207	0.5	4.8	29.0	57.0	8.7
Short-Term Loans	207	0.5	23.7	71.5	0.5	3.9
Other Accruals	192	1.0	7.8	8.9	79.7	2.6

EXHIBIT 6

RANKING OF TECHNIQUES FOR REDUCING DEPOSIT FLOAT

Technique	Number Of Responses	Percentage Assigning Rank				
		1	2	3	4	5
Verbal or Written Requests	142	14.1%	21.1%	35.9%	25.4%	3.5%
Cash Discounts	146	27.4	33.6	26.7	12.3	0.0
Regional Banking	127	15.7	45.7	23.6	14.2	0.8
Lockboxes	173	66.5	26.0	5.8	1.7	0.0
Other	20	25.0	25.0	25.0	20.0	5.0

EXHIBIT 7

RANKING OF TECHNIQUES FOR INCREASING DISBURSEMENT FLOAT

Technique	Number Of Responses	Percentage Assigning Rank				
		1	2	3	4	5
Payroll via Bank Drafts	44	9.1%	36.4%	36.4%	18.2%	0.0%
Stretching Credit Terms	103	38.8	35.0	23.3	2.9	0.0
Centralized Disbursing	134	69.4	23.9	5.2	1.5	0.0
Remote Disbursing	89	43.8	39.3	7.9	9.0	0.0
Other	13	76.9	15.4	0.0	0.0	7.7

EXHIBIT 8

RANKING OF TECHNIQUES FOR IMPROVING INTERNAL FUNDS FLOW

Technique	Number Of Responses	Percentage Assigning Rank				
		1	2	3	4	5
Regular Mail	67	4.5%	32.8%	46.3%	16.4%	0.0%
Wire Transfer	182	70.9	28.0	1.1	0.0	0.0
Depository Transfer Checks	116	45.7	47.4	6.0	0.9	0.0
Professional Couriers	41	2.4	19.5	46.3	31.7	0.0
Other	14	42.9	21.4	21.4	0.0	14.3

EXHIBIT 9

RANKING OF MARKETABLE SECURITIES UTILIZED

Marketable Security	Number Of Responses	Percentage Assigning Rank					
		1	2	3	4	5	6
U.S. Treasury Bills	121	26.4%	21.5%	19.8%	17.4%	12.4%	2.5%
Federal Agency Issues	80	6.3	23.8	12.5	27.5	22.5	7.5
Commercial Paper	135	42.2	28.1	20.7	5.9	3.0	0.0
Certificates of Deposit	133	36.1	37.6	19.5	6.0	0.8	0.0
Bankers Acceptances	77	7.8	20.8	35.1	23.4	10.4	2.6
Other	38	57.9	15.8	13.2	5.3	5.3	2.6

EXHIBIT 10

RANKING OF CHARACTERISTICS OF MARKETABLE SECURITIES

Characteristic	Number Of Responses	Percentage Assigning Rank				
		1	2	3	4	5
Marketability	157	36.3%	28.0%	22.3%	11.5%	1.9%
Stability of Market Price	118	28.8	19.5	16.1	28.8	6.8
Yield	174	21.8	36.8	31.0	9.2	1.1
Maturity	154	13.0	29.9	31.1	23.4	0.6
Other	43	88.4	7.0	4.7	0.0	0.0

EXHIBIT 11

ANNUAL YIELD OBJECTIVE OF MARKETABLE SECURITIES PORTFOLIO

(In Percentage)

Yield Objective	Total Sample	Larger Size	Smaller Size	More Profitable	Less Profitable	Formal Policy	Informal Policy	Cautious Policy	Aggressive Policy
Less than 5.0%	0.7%	0.0%	0.0%	0.0%	1.9%	0.0%	1.0%	0.0%	0.0%
5.0 - 5.9%	3.3	0.0	5.0	6.0	1.9	0.0	3.1	0.0	14.3
6.0 - 6.9%	8.7	6.3	7.5	4.0	13.5	10.0	8.3	14.6	0.0
7.0 - 7.9%	38.0	35.4	50.0	30.0	42.3	40.0	37.5	31.7	28.6
8.0 - 8.9%	41.3	41.7	35.0	52.0	34.6	42.5	40.6	46.3	46.4
9.0 - 9.9%	6.0	14.6	2.5	4.0	5.8	5.0	7.3	4.9	7.1
Greater than 10.0%	2.0	2.1	0.0	4.0	0.0	2.5	2.1	2.4	3.6
Number Of Responses	150	48	40	50	52	40	96	41	28
Significance		.15		.14		.91		.07	

EXHIBIT 12

TECHNIQUES FOR TRANSFERRING FUNDS BETWEEN
MARKETABLE SECURITIES PORTFOLIO AND CASH ACCOUNT
(In Percentage)

Technique	Total Sample	Larger Size	Smaller Size	More Profitable	Less Profitable	Formal Policy	Informal Policy	Cautious Policy	Aggressive Policy
Subjective Judgments	43.2%	25.0%	61.7%	51.6%	38.1%	19.3%	52.2%	38.0%	36.8%
Established Guidelines	32.3	47.1	19.1	25.8	28.6	50.9	27.0	40.0	28.9
Cost Balancing Models	5.2	4.4	0.0	8.1	7.9	3.5	5.2	4.0	5.3
Other	19.3	23.5	19.1	14.5	25.4	26.3	15.7	18.0	28.9
Number Of Responses	192	68	47	62	63	57	115	50	38
Significance		.0005		.36		.0003		.57	

EXHIBIT 13

RANKING OF STRATEGIES FOR MANAGING MARKETABLE SECURITIES PORTFOLIO

Strategy	Number Of Responses	Percentage Assigning Rank				
		1	2	3	4	5
Buy and hold to maturity	137	72.3%	14.6%	7.3%	5.8%	0.0%
Ad hoc decisions	79	38.0	25.3	19.0	17.7	0.0
Play the yield curve	80	27.5	37.5	20.0	15.0	0.0
Portfolio perspective	78	24.4	44.9	26.9	3.8	0.0
Other	16	62.5	25.0	6.3	0.0	6.3

EXHIBIT 14

RANKING OF TECHNIQUES USED IN GRANTING CREDIT

Technique	Number Of Responses	Percentage Assigning Rank			
		1	2	3	4
"Four C's" of Credit	147	75.5%	19.0%	5.4%	0.0%
Sequential Credit Analysis	104	43.3	38.5	18.3	0.0
Credit Scoring	75	24.0	44.0	29.3	2.7
Other	20	65.0	25.0	10.0	0.0

EXHIBIT 15

RANKING OF MEASURES USED IN MONITORING PAYMENT BEHAVIOR OF CUSTOMERS

Measure	Number Of Responses	Percentage Assigning Rank			
		1	2	3	4
Accounts Receivable Turnover	123	17.1%	22.8%	56.9%	3.3%
Collection Period	156	28.2	53.8	17.9	0.0
Aging Schedule	181	68.5	25.4	6.1	0.0
Other	10	80.0	0.0	20.0	0.0

EXHIBIT 16

RANKING OF VARIABLES CONSIDERED IN EVALUATING CREDIT TERMS AND POLICY

Variable	Number Of Responses	Percentage Assigning Rank				
		1	2	3	4	5
Marketing Considerations	181	59.7%	34.8%	3.3%	2.2%	0.0%
Possible Bad Debt Losses	120	41.2	39.4	11.2	3.5	4.7
Existing Production Capacity	92	8.7	18.5	46.7	21.7	4.3
Inventory Requirements	70	0.0	17.1	27.1	42.9	12.9
Operating Leverage	69	8.7	14.5	20.3	11.6	44.9

EXHIBIT 17

RANKING OF CRITERIA USED IN EVALUATING CREDIT TERMS CHANGES

Criterion	Number Of Responses	Percentage Assigning Rank			
		1	2	3	4
Effect on Firm Sales	161	32.9%	31.1%	26.7%	9.3%
Effect on Level of AR	147	19.7	24.5	26.5	29.3
Effect on Firm Profits	159	44.7	30.8	19.5	5.0
Effect on Return on Investment	136	26.5	26.5	21.3	25.7

EXHIBIT 18

TECHNIQUES FOR REPLENISHING INVENTORY STOCKING POINTS

(In Percentage)

Technique	Total Sample	Larger Size	Smaller Size	More Profitable	Less Profitable	Formal Policy	Informal Policy	Cautious Policy	Aggressive Policy
Ad Hoc Decisions	19.8%	8.8%	40.8%	18.3%	14.9%	10.0%	26.5%	22.0%	10.0%
Industry Guidelines	3.0	0.0	0.0	5.0	4.5	3.3	2.6	4.0	2.5
Cost Balancing Models	7.1	7.4	4.1	8.3	6.0	6.7	7.7	10.0	7.5
Computerized Inventory Control	61.9	75.0	49.0	56.7	67.2	68.3	58.1	58.0	70.0
Other	8.1	8.8	6.1	11.7	7.5	11.7	5.1	6.0	10.0
Number Of Responses	197	68	49	60	67	60	117	50	40
Significance		.0007		.80		.08		.53	

EXHIBIT 19

RANKING OF VARIABLES CONSIDERED IN INVENTORY PURCHASED BY THE FIRM

Variable	Number Of Responses	Percentage Assigning Rank					
		1	2	3	4	5	6
Availability	164	62.2%	25.6%	9.8%	1.2%	1.2%	0.0%
Price Discounts	138	17.4	39.9	25.4	13.8	3.6	0.0
Credit Terms	96	5.2	13.5	27.1	26.0	26.0	2.1
Shortage Costs	117	20.5	38.5	22.2	12.0	6.8	0.0
Inflation	90	4.4	11.1	28.9	27.8	24.4	3.3
Other	28	82.1	7.1	7.1	3.6	0.0	0.0

EXHIBIT 20

RANKING OF VARIABLES CONSIDERED IN INVENTORY PRODUCED BY THE FIRM

Variable	Number Of Responses	Percentage Assigning Rank				
		1	2	3	4	5
Seasonality of Demand	146	37.7%	45.9%	13.0%	2.7%	0.7%
Production Schedule	170	59.4	34.1	5.9	0.6	0.0
Inflation	78	1.3	11.5	30.8	55.1	1.3
Shortage Cost	113	13.3	21.2	48.7	16.8	0.0
Other	15	73.3	0.0	20.0	0.0	6.7

EXHIBIT 21

RANKING OF CRITERIA USED IN EVALUATING INVENTORY POLICY CHANGES

Criterion	Number Of Responses	Percentage Assigning Rank			
		1	2	3	4
Effect on Inventory Level	148	29.1%	23.0%	24.3%	23.6%
Effect on Inventory Costs	139	17.3	28.1	36.7	18.0
Effect on Firm Profits	154	44.2	35.1	17.5	3.2
Effect on Return On Investment	142	35.2	30.3	12.0	22.5

EXHIBIT 22

ACCOUNTS PAYABLE (AP) VERSUS ACCOUNTS RECEIVABLE (AR) POSITION OF FIRM
(In Percentage)

Position	Total Sample	Larger Size	Smaller Size	More Profitable	Less Profitable	Formal Policy	Informal Policy	Cautious Policy	Aggressive Policy
AP greater than AR	10.2%	21.1%	5.8%	4.8%	11.3%	16.7%	8.1%	11.5%	7.3%
AP about equal to AR	4.4	9.9	1.9	6.5	1.4	3.3	4.0	1.9	4.9
AP less than AR	85.4	69.0	92.3	88.7	87.3	80.0	87.9	86.5	87.8
Number Of Responses	205	71	52	62	71	60	124	52	41
Significance		.007		.14		.21		.59	

EXHIBIT 23

ANNUAL COST OF TRADE CREDIT FROM SUPPLIERS
(In Percentage)

Annual Cost	Total Sample	Larger Size	Smaller Size	More Profitable	Less Profitable	Formal Policy	Informal Policy	Cautious Policy	Aggressive Policy
Zero	37.7%	37.3%	39.0%	37.0%	34.9%	35.3%	38.9%	44.4%	41.0%
1.0 - 5.9%	30.9	22.0	36.6	33.3	36.5	29.4	34.3	33.3	28.2
6.0 - 10.9%	26.9	35.6	24.4	24.1	23.8	33.3	23.1	17.8	28.2
11.0 - 14.9%	2.9	3.4	0.0	3.7	3.2	0.0	2.8	4.4	0.0
Greater than 15.0%	1.7	1.7	0.0	1.9	1.6	2.0	0.9	0.0	2.6
Number Of Responses	175	59	41	54	63	51	108	45	39
Significance		.29		.99		.48		.38	

EXHIBIT 24

POLICY/PRACTICE ON CASH DISCOUNTS OFFERED BY SUPPLIERS
(In Percentage)

Policy/Practice	Total Sample	Larger Size	Smaller Size	More Profitable	Less Profitable	Formal Policy	Informal Policy	Cautious Policy	Aggressive Policy
Always take discounts	69.4%	75.7%	61.5%	79.4%	54.9%	79.7%	65.6%	63.0%	70.7%
Sometimes take discounts	19.9	17.1	21.2	11.1	32.4	15.3	22.4	25.9	17.1
Take discounts but pay later	9.2	5.7	13.5	9.5	9.9	5.1	9.6	9.3	9.8
Never take discounts	1.5	1.4	3.8	0.0	2.8	0.0	2.4	1.9	2.4
Number Of Responses	206	70	52	63	71	59	125	54	41
Significance		.28		.009		.21		.78	

EXHIBIT 25

PRIMARY USE OF SHORT-TERM BANK LOANS
(In Percentage)

Primary Use	Total Sample	Larger Size	Smaller Size	More Profitable	Less Profitable	Formal Policy	Informal Policy	Cautious Policy	Aggressive Policy
Regular part of financing	20.4%	16.9%	23.4%	17.9%	24.6%	15.8%	22.8%	18.4%	23.7%
Cyclical part of financing	19.9	20.0	17.0	21.4	20.3	21.1	18.4	14.3	28.9
Seasonal part of financing	27.7	21.5	36.2	19.6	29.0	26.3	28.9	30.6	23.7
Nonspontaneous Need	31.9	41.5	23.4	41.1	26.1	36.8	29.8	36.7	23.7
Number of Responses	191	65	47	56	69	57	114	49	38
Significance		.14		.27		.63		.25	

EXHIBIT 26

TYPE OF SHORT-TERM LOANS FROM COMMERCIAL BANKS
(In Percentage)

Type	Total Sample	Larger Size	Smaller Size	More Profitable	Less Profitable	Formal Policy	Informal Policy	Cautious Policy	Aggressive Policy
Simple Interest Loans	12.9%	17.6%	12.8%	12.3%	8.7%	11.9%	15.5%	18.8%	12.6%
Discounted Loans	1.5	0.0	2.1	1.8	1.4	5.1	0.0	2.1	0.0
Loans with Compensating Balances	12.4	8.8	19.1	14.0	15.9	11.9	11.2	10.4	10.0
Line-of-Credit w/Compensating Balances	64.9	61.8	61.7	66.7	65.2	61.0	67.2	64.6	67.5
Other	8.2	11.8	4.3	5.3	8.7	10.2	6.0	4.2	10.0
Number Of Responses	194	68	47	57	69	59	116	48	40
Significance		.20		.91		.11		.64	

EXHIBIT 27

COLLATERAL AS PART OF SHORT-TERM BANK BORROWING
(In Percentage)

Collateral	Total Sample	Larger Size	Smaller Size	More Profitable	Less Profitable	Formal Policy	Informal Policy	Cautious Policy	Aggressive Policy
Loans never requiring collateral	92.3%	94.3%	87.2%	98.3%	88.4%	88.1%	94.9%	95.8%	85.0%
Loans occasionally requiring collateral	4.1	2.9	4.3	0.0	8.7	6.8	3.4	2.1	10.0
Loans always requiring collateral	3.6	2.9	8.5	1.7	2.9	5.1	1.7	2.1	5.0
Number Of Responses	196	70	47	58	69	59	117	48	40
Significance		.35		.06		.25		.19	

EXHIBIT 28

ANNUAL COST OF SHORT-TERM BANK CREDIT
(In Percentage)

Annual Cost	Total Sample	Larger Size	Smaller Size	More Profitable	Less Profitable	Formal Policy	Informal Policy	Cautious Policy	Aggressive Policy
Less than 5.0%	9.1%	13.2%	2.4%	12.8%	8.1%	10.6%	7.8%	11.9%	3.2%
5.0 - 7.9%	10.9	15.1	9.5	14.9	3.2	21.3	5.8	11.9	9.7
8.0 - 10.9%	66.1	62.3	76.2	59.6	69.4	57.4	70.9	57.1	74.2
11.0 - 13.9%	13.9	9.4	11.9	12.8	19.4	10.6	15.5	19.0	12.9
Number Of Responses	165	53	42	47	62	47	103	42	31
Significance		.20		.11		.03		.40	

EXHIBIT 29

RANKING OF MEASURES USED IN MONITORING FIRM WORKING CAPITAL

Measure	Number Of Responses	Percentage Assigning Rank			
		1	2	3	4
Current ratio	159	61.0%	29.6%	8.2%	1.3%
Working capital as percentage of assets	112	12.5	34.8	49.1	3.6
Working capital turnover	147	43.5	38.1	17.7	0.7
Other	28	67.9	28.6	0.0	3.6

EXHIBIT 30

INTERVAL OF TIME FOR PREPARING CASH BUDGET
(In Percentage)

Time Interval	Total Sample	Larger Size	Smaller Size	More Profitable	Less Profitable	Formal Policy	Informal Policy	Cautious Policy	Aggressive Policy
Daily	47.8%	63.0%	37.7%	48.4%	40.3%	55.7%	43.7%	56.6%	40.5%
Weekly	32.1	23.3	37.7	27.4	41.7	19.7	38.1	28.3	31.0
Monthly	11.9	10.9	13.2	8.0	12.5	18.0	10.3	9.4	21.4
Quarterly	8.1	2.7	11.3	16.1	5.6	6.6	7.9	5.7	7.1
Number Of Responses	209	73	53	62	72	61	126	53	42
Significance		.009		.11		.08		.26	

EXHIBIT 31

RANKING OF USES OF CASH BUDGETING BY THE FIRM

Use Of Cash Budget	Number Of Responses	Percentage Assigning Rank 1	2	3	4	5
Plan for shortages and surpluses of cash	101	95.5%	3.0%	0.0%	1.5%	0.0%
Explore implications of alternative sales forecasts	85	5.9	55.3	27.1	10.6	1.2
Explore implications of alternative credit terms	68	2.9	33.8	26.5	36.8	0.0
Explore implications of alternative inventory policies	77	0.0	39.0	42.9	18.2	0.0
Other	11	54.5	45.5	0.0	0.0	0.0

EXHIBIT 32

THE USE OF RETURN-ON-INVESTMENT CRITERION IN EVALUATING POSSIBLE CHANGES IN WORKING CAPITAL COMPONENTS
(In Percentage)

Usage	Total Sample	Larger Size	Smaller Size	More Profitable	Less Profitable	Formal Policy	Informal Policy	Cautious Policy	Aggressive Policy
Never	12.5%	12.5%	19.2%	14.5%	11.1%	8.2%	11.2%	7.4%	9.8%
Sometimes	51.0	54.2	50.0	45.2	51.4	45.9	56.8	53.7	43.9
Always	36.5	33.3	30.8	40.3	37.5	45.9	32.0	38.9	46.3
Number Of Responses	208	72	52	62	72	62	125	54	42
Significance		.59		.73		.17		.63	

EXHIBIT 33

WORKING CAPITAL IMPLICATIONS IN CAPITAL BUDGETING DECISIONS
(In Percentage)

Implication	Total Sample	Larger Size	Smaller Size	More Profitable	Less Profitable	Formal Policy	Informal Policy	Cautious Policy	Aggressive Policy
Never	5.7%	2.7%	11.3%	12.7%	1.4%	4.8%	4.0%	7.4%	4.8%
Sometimes	27.6	27.4	32.1	25.4	33.3	22.6	27.0	31.5	26.2
Always	66.7	69.9	56.6	61.9	65.3	72.6	69.0	61.1	69.0
Number Of Responses	210	73	53	63	72	63	126	54	42
Significance		.09		.03		.79		.69	

EXHIBIT 34

CHANGES IN WORKING CAPITAL COMPONENTS AS PROJECTS
IN CAPITAL BUDGETING DECISIONS
(In Percentage)

Projects	Total Sample	Larger Size	Smaller Size	More Profitable	Less Profitable	Formal Policy	Informal Policy	Cautious Policy	Aggressive Policy
Never	19.1%	12.5%	20.8%	47.5%	30.0%	13.1%	18.3%	22.6%	16.7%
Sometimes	47.8	55.6	47.2	39.7	46.5	41.0	52.4	50.9	38.1
Always	33.0	31.9	32.1	30.2	36.6	45.9	29.4	26.4	45.2
Number Of Responses	209	72	53	63	71	61	126	53	42
Significance		.42		.19		.08		.16	

EXHIBIT 35

DISCOUNT RATE USED IN EVALUATING
CHANGES IN WORKING CAPITAL COMPONENTS
(In Percentage)

Discount Rate	Total Sample	Larger Size	Smaller Size	More Profitable	Less Profitable	Formal Policy	Informal Policy	Cautious Policy	Aggressive Policy
Interest Rate	29.3%	33.3%	28.8%	21.7%	31.8%	35.6%	27.3%	23.5%	32.5%
Cost of Equity Capital	7.1	8.7	5.8	6.7	3.0	8.5	6.6	9.8	10.0
Ave. Cost of Capital	48.0	43.5	44.2	55.0	48.5	44.1	47.9	51.0	35.0
Hurdle Rate Not Needed	15.7	14.5	21.2	16.7	16.7	11.9	18.2	15.7	22.5
Number Of Responses	198	69	52	60	66	59	121	51	40
Significance		.73		.51		.53		.47	

APPENDIX

QUESTIONNAIRE ON THE MANAGEMENT OF WORKING CAPITAL

DIRECTIONS: For certain questions, you are asked to *choose* one answer among the alternatives. For other questions, you are asked to *rank* the alternatives in terms of their relative importance to your firm. Use "1" to refer to the most important, "2" for the second most important, and so forth. Please do *not* assign ranks to alternatives that do not apply to your firm—just leave the spaces blank. For some questions, you are encouraged to specify *other* alternatives in the space provided. Also feel free to write helpful comments, where appropriate, in the margins.

PART I. PORTFOLIO POLICY

1. Does your firm have an overall policy for the management of its working capital?

   Choose one
   - a. Formal policy . . . . . . ( )
   - b. Informal policy . . . . . ( )
   - c. No policy . . . . ( )

2. Who sets the management policy for working capital (if there is one) for your firm?

   Choose one
   - a. Board of Directors. . . . ( )
   - b. President . . . . ( )
   - c. Vice President, Finance . ( )
   - d. Treasurer . . . . ( )
   - e. Controller. . . . . ( )
   - f. Other (please specify). . ( )

   ____

3. How often is the management policy for working capital (if there is one) reviewed?

   Choose one
   - a. Monthly . . . . ( )
   - b. Quarterly . . . . ( )
   - c. Semi-annually . . . . . . ( )
   - d. Annually. . . . . ( )
   - e. Whenever necessary. . . . ( )

4. How would you describe your policy (if there is one) for the management of working capital?

   Choose one
   - a. Cautious. . . . . ( )
   - b. Aggressive. . . . . ( )
   - c. Situational . . . . ( )
   - d. Change over time. . . . . . ( )

PART II. MANAGING WORKING CAPITAL COMPONENTS

5. Please indicate who has the primary responsibility for managing the following components of your firm's working capital.

   P = President
   VPF = Vice President, Finance
   T = Treasurer
   C = Controller
   O—Spec. = Other (Please Specify)

	P	VPF	T	C	O—Spec.	
a. Cash	( )	( )	( )	( )	( )	____
b. Marketable securities	( )	( )	( )	( )	( )	____
c. Accounts receivable	( )	( )	( )	( )	( )	____
d. Inventory	( )	( )	( )	( )	( )	____
e. Accounts payable	( )	( )	( )	( )	( )	____
f. Short-term loans	( )	( )	( )	( )	( )	____
g. Other Accruals	( )	( )	( )	( )	( )	____

6. With respect to the management of CASH, which of the following techniques do you utilize to reduce the negative float (i.e., value of the length of time until your customers' payments are received)? Rank in order of importance.

   Rank
   - a. Verbal or written requests ( )
   - b. Cash discounts . . . . . . ( )
   - c. Regional banking . . . . . ( )
   - d. Lockboxes. . . . . ( )
   - e. Other (please specify) . . ( )

   ____

7. In trying to increase the positive float (i.e., value of the length of time until your employees and suppliers are paid), which of the following do you utilize?

Rank

a. Payroll via bank drafts . ( )
b. "Stretching" the credit terms offered by your suppliers . . . . ( )
c. Centralized disbursing. . ( )
d. Disbursing from "remote" geographic locations. . . ( )
e. Other (please specify). . ( )

____

8. In trying to improve the effective flow of funds between various divisions or facilities of your firm, which of the following techniques do you utilize to move funds from one point to another?

Rank

a. Regular mail. . . . . . . ( )
b. Wire transfer . . . . . . ( )
c. Depository transfer checks ( )
d. Professional couriers . . ( )
e. Other (please specify). . ( )

____

9. With respect to managing MARKETABLE SECURITIES, which of the following investments are used regularly by your firm?

Rank

a. U.S. Treasury bills . . . ( )
b. Federal agency issues . . ( )
c. Commercial paper. . . . . ( )
d. Certificates of deposit . ( )
e. Bankers acceptances . . . ( )
f. Other (please specify). . ( )

10. What characteristics of marketable securities are important to you in your planning?

Rank

a. Marketability . . . . . . ( )
b. Stability of market price ( )
c. Yield . . . . ( )
d. Maturity. . . . . ( )
e. Other (please specify). . ( )

____

11. What is the annualized yield objective of your marketable securities portfolio?

Choose one

a. Less than 5.0%. . . . . . ( )
b. 5.0 - 5.9% . . . . ( )
c. 6.0 - 6.9% . . . . ( )
d. 7.0 - 7.9% . . . . ( )
e. 8.0 - 8.9% . . . . ( )
f. 9.0 - 9.9% . . . . ( )
g. Greater than 10.0%. . . . ( )

12. In transferring funds between the marketable securities portfolio and your firm's cash account, how do you decide on the appropriate amounts?

Choose one

a. Subjective judgments. . . ( )
b. Established guidelines. . ( )
c. Cost balancing models . . ( )
d. Other (please specify). . ( )

____

13. What overall strategy does your firm utilize with respect to managing your firm's portfolio of marketable securities?

Rank

a. Buy and hold to maturity.( )
b. Ad hoc decisions. . . . .( )
c. Play the yield curve. . .( )
d. Portfolio perspective . .( )
e. Other (please specify). .( )

____

14. With respect to managing ACCOUNTS RECEIVABLE, which of the following techniques do you use to decide on granting credit?

Rank

a. The "four C's" of credit ( )
b. Sequential credit analysis. . . . .( )
c. Credit scoring. . . . . .( )
d. Other (please specify). .( )

____

15. In monitoring the payment behavior of your credit customers, which of the following measures do you find most useful?

	Rank
a. Account receivable turnover.	( )
b. Collection period	( )
c. Aging schedule.	( )
d. Other (please specify). .	( )

____

16. In evaluating the credit terms and policy of your firm, which of the following parameters are considered?

	Rank
a. Marketing considerations.	( )
b. Possible bad debt losses.	( )
c. Existing production capacity.	( )
d. Potential implications to the inventory requirements	( )
e. Degree of operating leverage (fixed costs to variable costs)	( )

17. What criteria do you utilize in evaluating proposed changes in the credit terms of your firm?

	Rank
a. Effect on firm sales. . .	( )
b. Effect on level of accounts receivable . . .	( )
c. Effect on level of firm profits	( )
d. Effect on return on investment.	( )

18. With respect to managing INVENTORY, how do you decide on the appropriate amounts to replenish your warehouses or other inventory storage points?

	Choose one
a. Ad hoc decisions.	( )
b. Industry guidelines . . .	( )
c. Cost balancing models . .	( )
d. Computerized inventory control systems	( )
e. Other (please specify). .	( )

____

19. In deciding on replenishment quantities for inventory *purchased* by your firm, which of the following parameters are considered?

	Rank
a. Availability of parts and materials.	( )
b. Possible price discounts on purchases	( )
c. Credit terms offered by your suppliers	( )
d. Shortage costs	( )
e. Inflationary effects . .	( )
f. Other (please specify) .	( )

____

20. In deciding on replenishment quantities for inventory *produced* by your firm, which of the following parameters are considered?

	Rank
a. Seasonality of demand. .	( )
b. Production schedules . .	( )
c. Inflationary effects . .	( )
d. Shortage costs	( )
e. Other (please specify) .	( )

____

21. What criteria do you utilize in evaluating proposed changes in the inventory policy of your firm?

	Rank
a. Effect on level of inventory.	( )
b. Effect on inventory costs	( )
c. Effect on firm profits .	( )
d. Effect on return on investment	( )

22. Which of the following conditions typically occurs on the periodic balance sheets of your firm?

	Choose one
a. Accounts payable is greater than accounts receivable	( )
b. Accounts payable is less than accounts receivable	( )
c. Accounts payable is approximately equal to accounts receivable. . .	( )

23. With respect to managing ACCOUNTS PAYABLE, what do you estimate to be the annualized cost to your firm of the trade credit obtained from your suppliers?

Choose one

a. zero. . . . . ( )
b. 1.0 - 5.9% . . . . ( )
c. 6.0 - 10.9%. . . . . ( )
d. 11.0 - 14.9% . . . . ( )
e. Greater than 15.0%. . . . ( )

24. What is your policy/practice with respect to cash discounts offered by your supplier?

Choose one

a. Always take the discount by paying on the discount date. . . . . ( )
b. Sometimes take the discount by paying on the discount date . . . . . . ( )
c. Pay later than the discount date, but still take the discount . . . . ( )
d. Never take the discount . ( )

25. With respect to managing SHORT-TERM LOANS from commercial banks, what is your *primary* use for those funds?

Choose one

a. Regular and constant part of total firm financing . ( )
b. Cyclical part of total firm financing. . . . . . ( )
c. Seasonal part of total firm financing. . . . . . ( )
d. Nonspontaneous need as it arises. . . . . ( )

26. Which of the following best describes overall the short-term loans which you obtain from commercial banks?

Choose one

a. Simple interest loans . . ( )
b. Discounted loans. . . . . ( )
c. Loans with compensating balances. . . . . ( )
d. Line of credit with compensating balances . . ( )
e. Other (please specify). . ( )

____

27. To what extent is collateral a part of your short-term loans?

Choose one

a. Loans never require collateral. . . . . ( )
b. Loans occasionally require collateral. . . . ( )
c. Loans always require collateral. . . . . ( )

28. What do you estimate to be the annualized cost of the short-term credit obtained from your commercial banks?

Choose one

a. Less than 5.0%. . . . . . ( )
b. 5.0 - 7.9% . . . . ( )
c. 8.0 - 10.9%. . . . . ( )
d. 11.0 - 13.9% . . . . ( )
e. Greater than 14.0%. . . . ( )

PART III. CONTROLLING WORKING CAPITAL

29. In monitoring the working capital of your firm over time, which of the following measures do you find useful?

Rank

a. Current ratio . . . . . . ( )
b. Working capital as a percentage of total assets ( )
c. Working capital turnover. ( )
d. Other (please specify). . ( )

____

30. What is the shortest interval of time for which your firm utilizes cash budgeting?

Choose one

a. Daily . . . . ( )
b. Weekly. . . . . ( )
c. Monthly . . . . ( )
d. Quarterly . . . . ( )
e. Other (please specify). . ( )

____

31. Which of the following describe your use of cash budgeting?

Rank

a. To plan for shortages and surpluses of cash. . ( )
b. To explore the implications of alternative sales forecasts. . . . . ( )
c. To explore the implications of alternative credit terms . . . . . . ( )
d. To explore the implications of alternative inventory policies . . . ( )
e. Other (please specify) . ( )

____

32. In considering possible changes in the management of certain working capital components, do you utilize a return on investment criterion?

Choose one

a. Never. . . . . ( )
b. Sometimes. . . . . ( )
c. Always . . . . ( )

33. Are working capital implications included in the evaluation of each capital budgeting project for your firm?

Choose one

a. Never. . . . . ( )
b. Sometimes. . . . . ( )
c. Always . . . . ( )

34. Are changes in the management of working capital components (e.g., easier credit terms, lower inventory levels) considered along with other projects in the firm's capital budgeting process?

Choose one

a. Never. . . . . ( )
b. Sometimes. . . . . ( )
c. Always . . . . ( )

35. What discount or hurdle rate is used in evaluating changes in the management of working capital components?

Choose one

a. Interest rate. . . . . . ( )
b. Cost of equity capital . ( )
c. Average cost of capital. ( )
d. Hurdle rate not needed . ( )

REFERENCES

1. K. E. Frantz and J. A. Viscione, "What Should You Do About Cash Discounts?" *Credit and Financial Management,* 78:30-37, May 1976.
2. L. J. Gitman and J. R. Forrester, "A Survey of Capital Budgeting Techniques Used by Major U.S. Firms," *Financial Management,* 6:66-71, Fall 1977.
3. L. J. Gitman, E. A. Moses, and I. T. White, "An Assessment of Corporate Cash Management Practices," *Financial Management,* 8:32-41, Spring 1979.
4. J. W. Petty and O. D. Bowlin, "The Financial Manager and Quantitative Decision Models," *Financial Management,* 5:32-41, Winter 1976.
5. J. W. Petty, D. F. Scott, and M. M. Bird, "The Capital Expenditure Decision-Making Process of Large Corporations," *Engineering Economist,* 20:159-172, Spring 1975.
6. W. L. Reed, "Profits From Better Cash Management," *Financial Executive,* 40:40-56, May 1972.
7. B. K. Stone, "The Payments-Pattern Approach to the Forecasting and Control of Accounts Receivable," *Financial Management,* 5:65-82, Autumn 1976.
8. "Directory of the 1,000 Largest Industrial Corporations," *Fortune,* May 8 and June 19, 1978.
9. *Register of Corporations, Directors and Executives,* Standard & Poor's Corporation, 1978, Volume 2.

SECTION II
Cash Management

Cash is the lifeblood of a business firm. Cash is needed to acquire supplies, resources, equipment, and other assets used in generating the products and services provided by the firm. Cash is also needed to pay wages and salaries to workers and managers, taxes to governments, interest and principal to creditors, and dividends to stockholders. More fundamentally, cash is the medium of exchange which allows management to carry on the various activities of the business firm from day to day. This section contains six readings which in varying ways deal with the management of cash.

Searby (Reading 6) reviews and illustrates a series of procedures whereby financial managers can improve the utilization of cash within their firms and thereby release funds for more profitable opportunities. The procedures cover cash collections, cash disbursements, and the synchronization of cash inflows and outflows over time. Searby also discusses the temporary availability of funds to a firm, despite a zero bank balance. Several examples are presented of how firms have used such procedures to reduce their average cash balances.

DeSalvo (Reading 7) explains how similar procedures are used by a commercial finance company to better manage its cash flows. Cash management is viewed from an overall systems viewpoint. In order to illustrate a particular cash management system in operation, the author explains what the treasurer of the company would do from hour to hour on a typical day. It becomes clear that the effectiveness of a cash management system depends heavily on a timely information system, as well as accurate forecasts of future cash flows.

The next two readings have to do with methods for improved planning of cash flows within the firm. Lerner (Reading 8) focuses on the question of determining an appropriate monthly cash balance for the firm. He explains the power of simulation to reflect jointly via a cash budget the uncertainty inherent in future sales, the uncertainty in collecting outstanding receivables, and the flexibility of the firm in paying its accounts payable. Reflecting multiple uncertainties from month to month over the planning horizon is simplified considerably if monthly cash balances are assumed to be independent. By calculating both expected values and standard deviations of forecasted cash balances, the financial manager can trace the full impact of his/her decision making as related to the liquidity position of the firm.

In order to properly manage the cash balance and flows of a large firm, it is necessary to have daily forecasts. Stone and Wood (Reading 9) explain how each component in the firm's monthly cash budget can be broken down into a daily forecast. The methodology employed is dummy-variable regression analysis. It can be applied at different levels of sophistication depending on the particular problems of the firm. The authors point out the need for a proper balance between increased accuracy of daily cash forecasts, and the costs of providing that accuracy.

Pogue, Faucette, and Bussard (Reading 10) formulate a linear programming approach to minimizing the total of service fees to the firm's commercial banks, plus the opportunity costs of holding idle cash balances. Their programming model is necessarily based on a careful review of tangible and intangible services provided to a firm by its commercial banks, and the various means whereby those banks are paid for such services. Decision variables are the number of checks, deposits, and tax payments assigned to each bank. A series of constraints places limits on the decision variables as a result of banking requirements. The authors also present a case study wherein total costs were significantly reduced as a result of such a programming approach. The case study illustrates well the complexity of the firm's bank relationship. It also serves to emphasize the important linkage between one current asset (cash) and one current liability (bank balance) that is determined by the nature of the banking relationship.

The paper by Benton (Reading 11) on electronic funds transfer is a timely reminder that cash management is not a static subject. The author explains that EFTS is a payments system in which funds are transferred electronically. In varying degree, EFTS can affect cash inflows, cash outflows, and all aspects of the firm's float. EFTS is a nationwide development involving consumers, merchants, depository institutions, producers of electronic hardware and software, and government. Benton discusses benefit-cost tradeoffs in the development of electronic transfer systems, the importance of consumer acceptance, and the many legal and regulatory issues that are yet to be answered.

READING 6

Use Your Hidden Cash Resources

Frederick W. Searby
McKinsey and Company, Inc.

Mystery story buffs and Humphrey Bogart fans alike will remember Dashiell Hammett's superb tale *The Maltese Falcon*, later made into a suspenseful movie. The title object in Hammett's story was a foot-high statue of a bird, encrusted from head to foot with precious stones. Painted over with black enamel to disguise its value, the falcon had been passed from hand to hand for centuries. Few of its possessors even guessed its true value, and none was perceptive enough to scratch its enameled surface to bare the treasure underneath.

Hammett's story provides a moral for today's top management and senior financial officers. For most companies have in their own possession a treasure of which they are unaware. They have failed to look beneath the surface of a familiar, everyday reality--the company's own cash gathering and disbursing system--little suspecting the wealth it may conceal.

To be sure, the high interest rates of the past two years have stimulated many companies to whittle down some of their cash balances or take another look at the length of their receivables. By and large, however, these belt-tightening efforts have been carried out piecemeal by individual departments. Only in rare cases has a chief executive, perceiving the profit potential in reducing his company's fallow cash assets, set in motion an across-the-board, multidepartmental review of cash gathering and dispursing processes. Yet, where this has happened, the results have often been astonishing. Consider these recent examples:

✓ A major oil company reduced the cash in its gathering and disbursing system by 75%, providing over $25 million for marketing and refining expansion.

✓ A large railroad that showed cash balances of only $9 million drew a total of $17 million out of its cash gathering and disbursing system to help finance a major equipment acquisition program.

✓ A leading insurance company that

Reprinted from the HARVARD BUSINESS REVIEW, Vol. 46, No. 2 (March-April 1968), pp. 71-80, by permission of the publisher.

showed cash balances of $8 million discovered an additional $18 million which could be profitably extracted and put to work.

Solely by tapping the previously unrecognized potential in its cash gathering and disbursing systems, each of the first two companies avoided substantial outside financing at an unfavorable time, without weakening its working capital position or its relationships with outside financial institutions, and saved approximately $1 million in interest charges. The insurance company in the third example profited by a sizable expansion of its loan portfolio.

The recurring savings to manufacturing companies with $100 million or more in assets from much less spectacular cash balance reductions--say, 20% of cash deposits held at year-end 1967 --would be about $144 million annually, assuming that the $2.4 billion thus released was invested at 6%.

REASONS FOR DORMANCY

Why has such a substantial resource lain dormant, like the treasure of the Maltese falcon, in so many companies? There are at least three reasons.

1. *Accounting treatments usually understate the size of cash balances.* A substantial portion of the cash available seldom appears as cash on a company's balance sheet, if indeed it appears at all. The two principal sources of this hidden cash are (a) receipts by an agency of the company that have not yet reached a dispersing bank (cash-in-transit), and (b) cash in a bank on which checks have been drawn but not charged to a company bank account (float). Such items thus understate the true amount of money to be managed and explain the paradox of the railroad and the insurance company mentioned above that were able to withdraw more cash than their cash balances showed.

2. *Scorekeeping practices of the financial function hinder imaginative cash management.* Frequently, the treasurer or other financial officer most able to improve cash management processes is evaluated primarily by his ability to produce funds on short call and to obtain the prime rate on commercial bank loans. Obviously, both of these factors are important to the financial health of a company. However, the first measurement can encourage money managers to maintain unnecessarily large reserve balances or excessive standby lines of credit which require

---

CLUES TO IMPROVEMENT OPPORTUNITY

Decentralized responsibility for processing cash receipts, disbursing funds, and maintaining relationships with banks.

Absence of a reasonably accurate, daily cash forecasting system.

Use of gathering or concentration banks in cities which are non-Federal Reserve or have no bank wire facilities.

Lack of current figures on:
Float in major disbursing accounts.
Cash-in-transit in parts of cash gathering system.

No record for individual accounts showing purpose, activity, tangible and intangible services, and average bank ledger balance.

No current analysis of the cost to the company, and the profitability to the bank, of each major banking relationship.

Limited use of the administrative services provided by banks, such as draft payment plans, lockboxes, depository transfer checks, zero balance accounts, and automatic wire transfers.

Maintenance of balances in a large number of banks and/or accounts for disbursing purposes.

---

sizable compensating balances with commercial banks. As for the second measurement--the rate at which money can be borrowed--it is almost always calculated at the simple interest rate, masking the true cost of borrowing when compensating balances are required by the lending bank, as they usually are.

For example, if the treasurer must maintain a 20% compensating balance to obtain the current prime rate of, let us say, 6% on a commercial bank line of credit, then the company's true cost is not 6%, but 7.5%.

3. *Corporate management has not come to grips with the substance of its cash gathering and disbursing processes.* Frequently in the past, top management has shied away from examining the company's cash processes because of their assumed complexity, preferring to leave "technical details" to the bank officers and the company's accountants--none of whom is concerned with more than a fraction of the total picture. Instead of using a cash management system designed to free cash resources for other uses, such a company is operating with a conglomeration of processes and procedures that have evolved piecemeal in response to various historical circumstances, practices, and pressures. Today, however, more and more companies are reclaiming the initiative in cash management and applying the same systematic, problem-solving approaches here that they use elsewhere in their businesses.

Basically, the process of "finding" interest-free funds within the company merely entails thorough fact gathering and analysis. But the opportunities thus identified almost always involve making tradeoffs among mutually related variables. This calls for careful analysis of the overall, interrelated, long-term profit impact of alternative decisions on the system as a whole. Moreover, some of the improvement opportunities fall in the controller's domain, while others are in the province of the treasurer--a split of responsibility that underscores the need for top management attention. Effective cash management, therefore, requires the concerted attention of talented personnel whose top management sponsorship and direction gives them the authority to cross organization lines.

INTERWOVEN OPPORTUNITIES

In real life, a company's cash gathering and cash disbursing activities are two sides of an interwoven system in which changes to one must be evaluated for their impact on the other. For the purposes of this article, however, it will be useful to consider cash gathering and cash disbursing opportunities separately.

Exhibit 1 illustrates a total cash management control system covering 85% to 90% of the expected cash flow for a typical company and shows in visual form how the various facets of cash management fit together.

Cash Gathering

An obvious but easily overlooked way to speed incoming cash is getting bills to customers earlier. Consider these examples.

✓ Simply by installing and enforcing standards, a Midwestern oil company cut several days off the time branch offices were taking to process retail customers' credit card invoices and forward them to the home office. In the home office further time was saved by mechanizing the invoice-processing operation and eliminating an auditing step that turned out to be costing more than the errors it was intended to uncover. Altogether, the company has saved $150,000 annually by taking these steps to speed up the mailing of its bills.

✓ American Telephone & Telegraph Company is working on two ways of speeding its billing processes: computerized processing of receivables and billing through customers' banks. For most of the 350,000,000 collect and credit calls handled annually by the Bell System's

Exhibit 1. SCHEMATIC DIAGRAM OF TOTAL CASH MANAGEMENT CONTROL SYSTEM

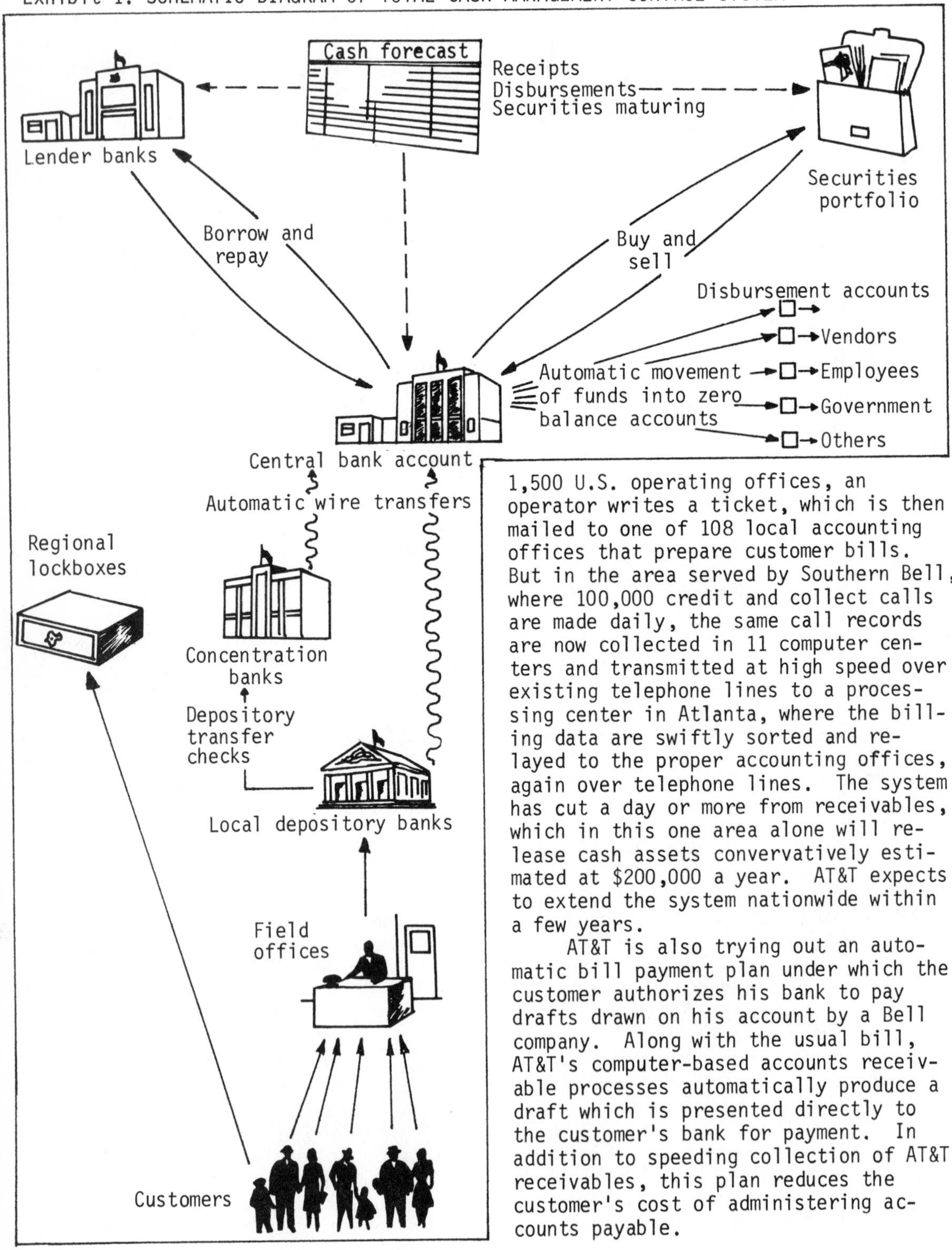

1,500 U.S. operating offices, an operator writes a ticket, which is then mailed to one of 108 local accounting offices that prepare customer bills. But in the area served by Southern Bell, where 100,000 credit and collect calls are made daily, the same call records are now collected in 11 computer centers and transmitted at high speed over existing telephone lines to a processing center in Atlanta, where the billing data are swiftly sorted and relayed to the proper accounting offices, again over telephone lines. The system has cut a day or more from receivables, which in this one area alone will release cash assets convervatively estimated at $200,000 a year. AT&T expects to extend the system nationwide within a few years.

AT&T is also trying out an automatic bill payment plan under which the customer authorizes his bank to pay drafts drawn on his account by a Bell company. Along with the usual bill, AT&T's computer-based accounts receivable processes automatically produce a draft which is presented directly to the customer's bank for payment. In addition to speeding collection of AT&T receivables, this plan reduces the customer's cost of administering accounts payable.

Exhibit 2. USE OF DEPOSITORY TRANSFER CHECKS

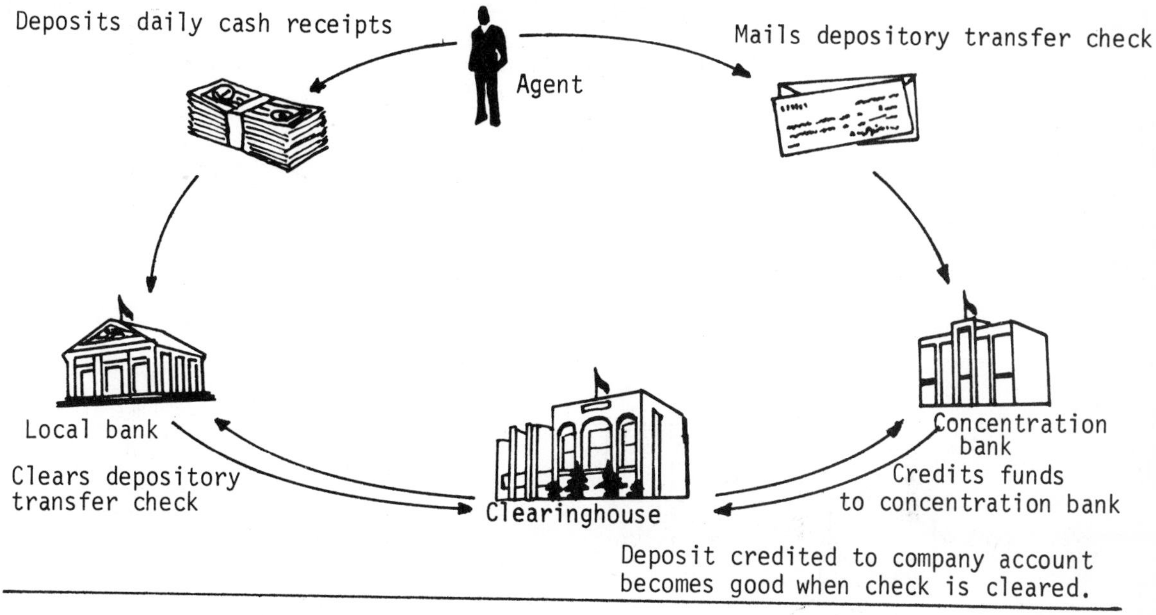

✓ Smaller companies have speeded up their billing in simpler, but no less effective, ways. A well-known shipping company found it had been losing from 2 to 13 working days in billing to various classes of customers, partly because data required for bill preparation were received unnecessarily late, and partly because a few accounting supervisors did not appreciate the time value of money. By improving the flow of data and installing elementary controls, the company was able to free $400,000 that had been tied up in receivables.

From the time the customer puts his check in the mail, the financial manager has four important opportunities: (a) to cut down cash-in-transit time; (b) to minimize "uncollected funds"--that is, recently deposited checks drawn on other banks and not yet credited to the company's account; (c) to reduce balances in collection banks and speed the movement of funds to disbursing locations; and (d) to optimize the balances necessary to compensate banks for depository and movement services.

The financial manager can avail himself of four principal devices for accelerating his company's inward cash flow: (1) depository transfer checks, (2) wire transfers, (3) lockboxes, and (4) relocation of gathering banks.

Depository transfer checks: Used to move funds to concentration or disbursing banks, depository transfer checks are nonnegotiable, usually unsigned, and payable only to a single company account in a specific bank.

In a representative situation shown in Exhibit 2, the company's local agent deposits his day's receipts in a locak bank and immediately mails a depository transfer check for the same amount to a designated concentration bank. Receiving the depository transfer check in the next day's mail, the concentration bank puts it into collection that same day, either through the Federal Reserve System or by forwarding it directly to the local depository bank.

By use of this device, funds received at field points are moved directly into concentration banks

Exhibit 3. ALTERNATIVE RETAIL CASH GATHERING SYSTEMS, COMPANY X

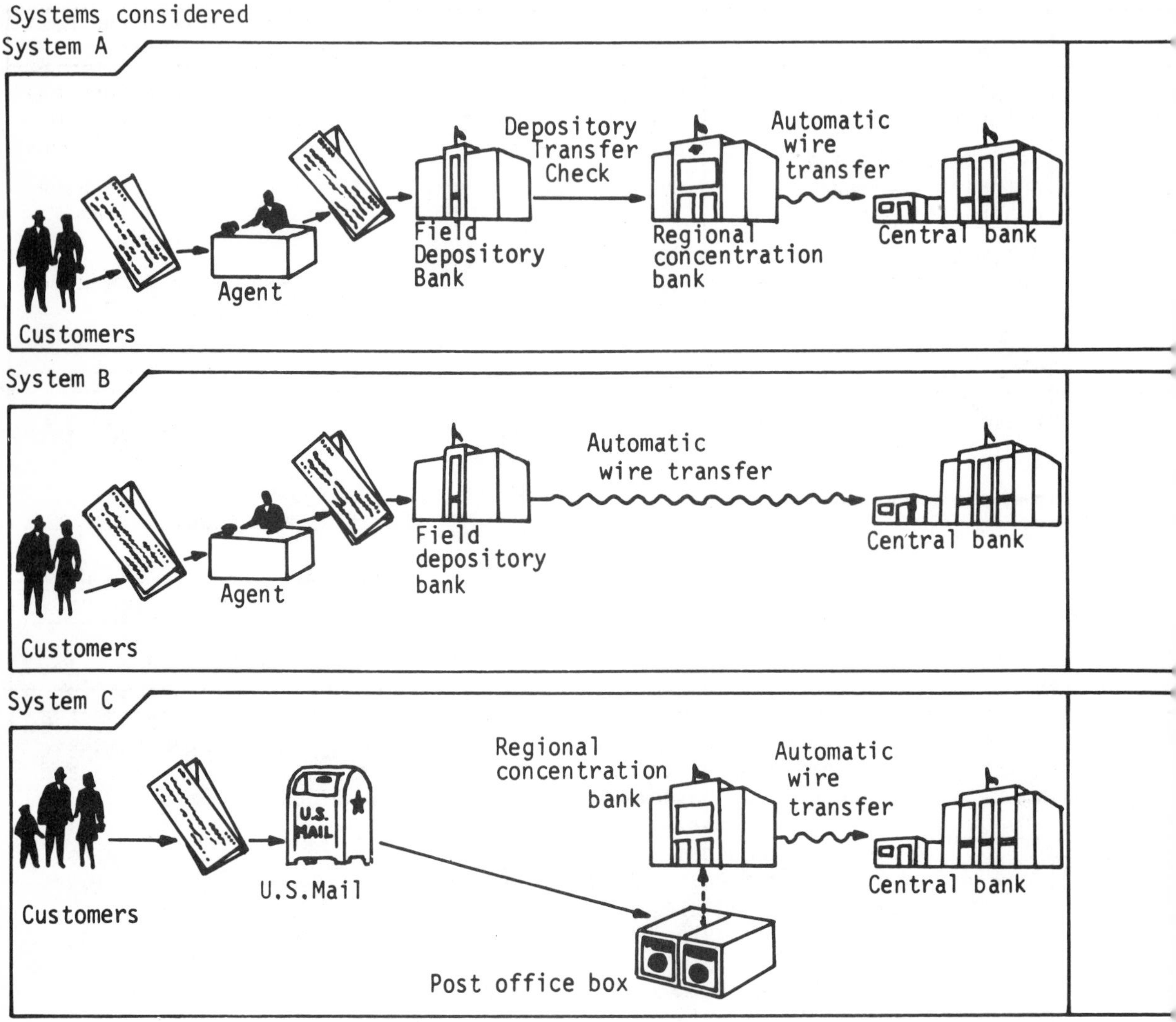

without requiring action first by headquarters' financial officers. And, although anyone in the local organization may issue a depository transfer check, since the check is nonnegotiable, it cannot be misapplied.

Depository transfer checks cost only 5 to 10 cents apiece, but they are not so fast as wire transfers and may offer no advantage when more than a day is required for mailing or clearing.

Wire transfers: Available in approximately 60 U.S. cities, wire transfers are the fastest way to move money between banks. On order, a bank will transfer a specified amount of a customer's funds by telegram to a designated bank. The funds are considered collected on receipt of the wire notice.

Frequently, a bank is given standing instructions to wire transfer routinely any funds above a stated bank balance to a specified bank. In this case the movement of funds is automatic, while balances are held at

Systems Chosen

	Description	Used where	Effect on field and home office operations
	Local cash receipt and deposit Depository transfer check to regional concentration bank Automatic wire transfer to disbursing bank	Payments made on locally maintained accounts receivable Average local receipts less than $2,500 per day or ... Wire transfer not available	200 field locations mail their deposits to new, relocated regional banks Regional banks receive mail overnight from 90% of locations Intransit cash reduced by $750,000
	Local cash receipt and ceposit Automatic wire transfer to central bank	Payments made on locally maintained accounts receivable Average local receipts exceed $2,500	Can be used in 20 field locations controlling 50% of deposits Intransit cash reduced by $1,250,000
	Direct mailing of checks to regional post office box cleared by concentration bank Automatic wire transfer to central bank	Payments made on centrally maintained credit card receivables	2 regional lockboxes established Intransit cash reduced by $800,000 Home office clerical costs reduced by $25,000 per year

the level necessary to compensate the bank fairly for its services.

Wire transfers require that both the sending and the receiving banks have access to the bank wire system. And, of course, they are uneconomical unless the value of having money available as early as possible exceeds the extra cost of the wire transfer (the price is generally about $1.50 a transfer). In general, wire transfers for amounts under $2,000 are not practical.

Lockboxes: Cash gathering can often be expedited by having remittances mailed directly to a post office box that is opened by a bank. The use of lockboxes speeds the collection of checks as well as the movement of remittances, since the checks are deposited before, rather than after, the accounting is done. On occasion, however--especially where only checks for small amounts are involved--the cost of a lockbox may outweigh its benefits. One company, for example, found that by using a lockbox it could speed up remittances from its customers by an average of 3 days. But the average remittance was only \$5, while the additional per-check cost of a lockbox was 2¢, or 8 times the incremental value of receiving the money 3 days early--\$0.0025 (i.e., $\$5 \times .06 \times 3 \div 365$, where 6% represents the value of money). Wisely, the company kept on making local deposits. But it did start using depository transfer checks to move customer remittances to gathering banks.

Installing lockboxes can also require major changes in accounting and control systems if cash receipts have to be processed at different locations.

Selection of gathering banks: Frequently, the cash gathering system can be made more effective by selecting more advantageously located banks for use as local depositories or concentration points.

A concentration bank--as well as the local depository bank, if possible --should meet five criteria:

1. The bank should be in the Federal Rexerve city which is serving the collection area.
2. It should be on the bank wire system.
3. It should receive 90% of deposited checks one day after they are mailed.
4. Its check availability schedule should average less than one and a half days for normal deposits.
5. Its service charge, earnings allowance rate, and reserve requirements should be competitive.

Many large industrial companies use several cash gathering systems, depending on the size, regularity, type, and origin of their receipts, as well as on the availability of bank services. They may use, for example, alternative combinations of the four devices just mentioned, tailoring the appropriate cash gathering system for each area in the light of such factors as mailing time statistics for the area, and local bank availability schedules, service charges, earnings allowances, and reserve requirements. Exhibit 3 shows how one company selected appropriate cash gathering systems for different areas.

Cash Disbursing

The principal opportunities available to the financial manager for improving his company's disbursing procedures and freeing more funds for investment include: (1) synchronizing transfers with clearings, (2) delaying check mailings, and (3) eliminating field working funds.

Synchronizing transfers with clearings: Financial managers recognize that the funds actually available in banks are generally greater than the balances shown on the company's books. This difference (float) is caused by the delay between the time a check is written and its clearing by the bank--due to mailing time, handling by payee, and normal collection time. Exhibit 4 shows the sizable amount of float which built up in one oil company's royalty disbursing account.

If a financial manager can accurately estimate the size of float and predict when checks will clear, he can maintain a negative book balance and invest the float. He does not have to reimburse the disbursement account until shortly before the checks are presented for payment. Often, he can synchronize transfers into disbursement accounts with check clearings if an accurate clearing projection has been developed.

One device that may help the financial manager forecast and control float is the zero balance account. Under this system, no balance is maintained in the disbursing accounts. Instead, all funds are held in a single general account, and the bank is authorized to transfer funds from the general account into each zero balance account as disbursement checks actually clear. In this way the forecasting and control

Exhibit 4. ACTUAL FUNDS AVAILABLE WHILE COMPANY Y'S BOOKS SHOWED ZERO BALANCES

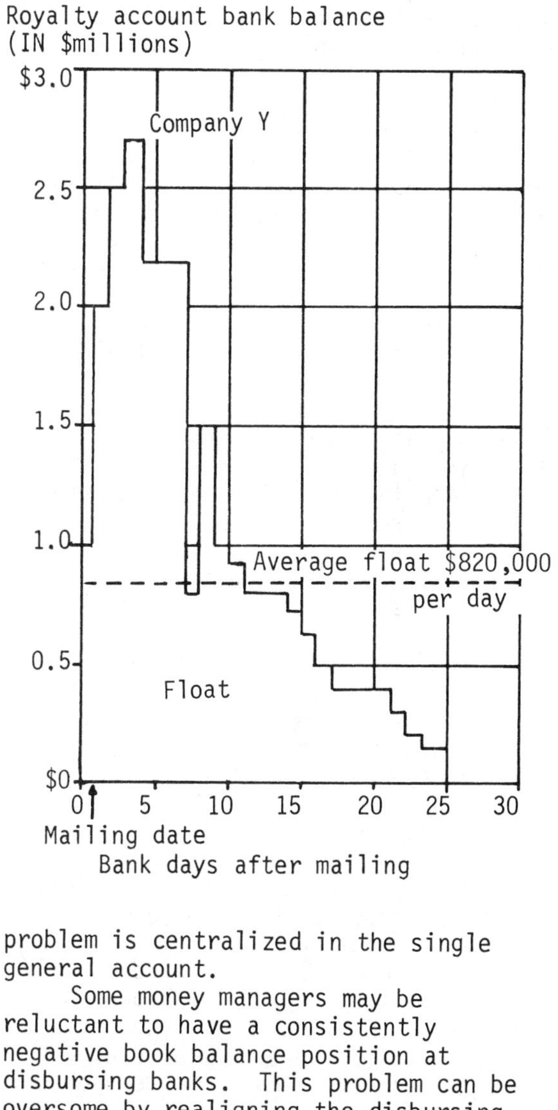

problem is centralized in the single general account.

Some money managers may be reluctant to have a consistently negative book balance position at disbursing banks. This problem can be oversome by realigning the disbursing system so that major portions of the check float are generated at the banks that require the largest compensating balances. When this is done, the float balances at these important banks usually are sufficient to cover the compensation needs, while the book balances can be held at a small positive figure.

Delaying check mailings: Without the loss of prompt-payment discounts, credit rating, or supplier goodwill, substantial free credit and cost savings can often be realized from better timing of accounts payable. For example, input data can be date-coded to trigger printing by computer and mailing on the latest possible date. (In many states, payments mailed on the discount expiration date legally qualify for the discount.) Nondiscount suppliers, such as transportation companies or joint venture partners, can be paid at the latest possible date which is consistent with legal and competitive conditions.

The oil company referred to in Exhibit 4 not only found ways to minimize its royalty payment float, but was also able to delay its royalty check mailings each month. Following a thorough study, this company discovered that it was sending out $10 million in oil royalty payments each month 12 days ahead of industry practice and 15 days ahead of legal requirements in most states. On the basis of an analysis of mailing times, the company began coding its oil royalty accounts so as to release computer-printed checks an average of 12 days later than before. The recurring savings to the company from this relatively easy change were $237,000 a year (i.e., $10,000,000 x 12/365 x 12 x .06, with the first 12 representing the number of days; the second 12, the number of months; and 6%, the value of money).

Eliminating field working funds: Many companies maintain small bank balances in field locations for convenience in paying small local bills. In total these funds frequently create unnecessarily large cash balances because of "cushions" maintained for contingencies. For example, one company with a large marketing organization in 25 states reduced its cash balances $3 million by substituting draft payments and a centralized disbursement account for field working funds.

Draft payment plans and centralized field disbursement accounts are two devices which can be used to improve field disbursing procedures. Payments to local vendors can be made with drafts drawn by themselves on a designated bank. Limits can be set on the amount of drafts, and payment may be refused. Among the advantages of drafts are that cushions are eliminated, since funds are not needed until the draft is presented; one reimbursement per day covers all drafts; bank service charges for cashing drafts are lower than for checks; and clerical costs of preparing checks and maintaining individual working funds are eliminated.

However, some of the disadvantages are that many smaller banks do not accept drafts; their use requires the cooperation of suppliers; and drafts may reduce the company's float. Alternatively, a centralized, zero-balance account can be maintained to pay local vendors. Checks are issued locally but drawn on the central account. The checks can be coded to show the disbursing location and purpose, and the bank can provide periodic listings, by code and amount, of the checks that have cleared.

This system also eliminates working fund cushions and the clerical costs of maintaining individual working funds. Furthermore, check float is centralized in a single account, simplifying the control problem.

IMPACT ON BANKS

Better corporate cash management has obvious portents for commercial banks. Sometimes, such as in the case of a receivables reduction, its effects are confined to a shifting of deposits from one company to another. At other times, say, when a company begins using automatic wire transfers to reduce cash-in-transit, the result is a shift of deposits from one bank to another bank. Overall, however, there can be no doubt that the systematic analysis and over hauling of cash management systems as described in this article will reduce (and, in fact, are currently reducing) the amount of interest-free demand deposits available to commercial banks.

How are the banks reacting to all this? Naturally enough, many are reluctant to initiate a process that in the short run results in a partial drying up of their traditional source of raw material, and in the long run may well require substantial changes in "product line" and pricing policies.

Positive View

Increasingly, however, most of the nation's biggest and most farsighted banks are taking a positive approach. Recognizing the legitimacy of their customers' concern with the profit improvement opportunities concealed in their cash management systems, these banks are taking the view--a real sign, perhaps, of the much-heralded marketing revolution in banking--that the long-term health of their institutions depends on how well they serve the best interests of their customers. And they know that this means more than simply adding new services. It means being willing to drop old services--and to look for new and more flexible pricing practices.

In fact, many banks are working actively with large corporate customers to help them design more effective cash gathering and disbursing systems--thereby, not surprisingly, strengthening greatly their working relationships with these customers. In at least one case, the bank in question inherited some of the customers' deposits from other banks less eager to assist in improving cash management, emerging with only slightly lower overall deposits. But even those whose deposits have been substantially drawn down have found themselves, thanks to their new and deeper knowledge of their customers' businesses, in a far better competitive position to develop profitable new business.

SUMMARY

Companies searching for additional cash sources or profit improvement would do well to remember Dashiell Hammett's Maltese falcon and first take a look close to home.

The opportunities for capital generation or for profit improvement in cash management are often impressive. For a company representing the mean of *Fortune*'s "500," for example, even a day's reduction in cash-in-transit would be worth well over $100,000 in recurring annual savings. For a small company, the dollar figure will be smaller but relatively no less significant. (Company managers can estimate, on a rough basis, the value of reducing a day's cash-in-transit by dividing their sales by 365 and multiplying the result by 6%. The resulting figure, of course, represents not the cash freed up, but the savings recurring annually from the cash freed up.) And this, as we have seen, is only one of a number of ways of freeing idle funds. In other words, it is only a fraction of the total opportunity.

To take advantage of the total opportunity, all that is needed to begin with is a systematic, tough-minded examination of cash processes to uncover profit opportunities such as those indicated by the symptoms listed in the ruled insert on page 24.

Once these opportunities are identified and the savings targets are established, the financial manager can proceed, with top management's support and encouragement, to implement the changes needed to reduce costs and free corporate cash reserves for profitable uses. Some of these may be independent, such as closing out inactive accounts; others may be interdependent, such as modifying cash collection procedures and setting cash balance minimums at concentration banks.

A company can expect both immediate and long-range benefits from appraising its cash handling practices and capitalizing on the unveiled potential. Not only can clerical costs in cash gathering and disbursing be minimized, but, more important, large sources of funds can be tapped for business growth.

READING 7

Cash Management Converts Dollars into Working Assets

Alfred DeSalvo
C.I.T. Financial Corporation

Cash, someone once said, is one of the most misunderstood, misidentified, and wasted commodities in the business world. While this observation may overstate the case, it has more than a little merit. There still are executives who firmly believe that a cash-rich company is a profitable company, that cash is equivalent to profits, and that a strong cash position is a primary form of financial insurance.

But perhaps the most misleading belief is the notion that cash is a working asset. Cash is indeed an asset, but only when it is used. Accounting principles to the contrary, cash is a frozen asset just like any unused piece of machinery. Indeed, cash that is idle or underused penalizes a company either with lost income from unmade investments or in interest charges on funds it borrows to take up the slack.

But even if a company's management does not fully subscribe to the concept that idle cash is a liability, it still is more than casually concerned with such questions as: Where is the money coming from? How much will it cost? How will it be employed for the full term of the loan? These questions will persist in the face of rising capital needs in what is—and is likely to remain—a capital-scarce economy.

The hard fact is that cash can be a large operating expense for any company that goes to the money markets regularly. To borrow $1 million just for a day at a prime rate of 6% costs $166.67. But of course this is only part of the cost; the borrower usually must maintain a compensating balance of at least 10% of the principal. So his true interest rate varies from 6-2/3% to 7-1/2%, depending on whether the bank demands another 10% compensating balance on granting the loan.

Over the course of a year, interest charges can amount to a tidy sum. My

---

Reprinted from the HARVARD BUSINESS REVIEW (May 1972), pp. 92-100, by permission of the publisher.

Author's note: I wish to acknowledge with thanks the contribution made in the preparation of this article by my associate, J.R. Simons, Assistant Treasurer of C.I.T. Financial Corporation.

company, C.I.T. Financial Corporation, for example, pays out as much as $105 million a year in interest on its borrowings.

The point is obvious: a company must work its cash as hard as possible. This requires an attitude and an approach that impose tight cash discipline on the entire company. Ideally, every cash dollar is at work or in transit at the close of each business day.

However, such a policy, while attractive in theory, sometimes proves unworkable or unrealistic in practice. Even the most diligent company treasurer, armed with the most elaborate forecasting and cash management methods, finds the task of keeping a lid on idle cash difficult and vexing—and the goal of reducing short-term borrowing virtually unattainable. The job is even tougher if the company has a number of more or less autonomous operations scattered across the country, or if it has major clusters of important customers in wide-ranging locations.

AN EFFICIENT SYSTEM

The cash management system we have developed and refined at C.I.T. in the last five years is a practical way of tackling this challenge. Our approach will interest—and I hope benefit—those in management who are concerned with financial performance or cash operations.

Our system is not cumbersome or expensive. More important, it works. Indeed, it works so well that the company can borrow from $25 million to $100 million a day for its 925 branches and subsidiaries and at the same time maintain unused cash at an extremely low level. In fact, C.I.T., which uses about $1 billion in short-term funds to run its business, usually concludes a working day with no cash in its banks above the compensating balances needed to maintain credit lines. The remainder of the company's short-term money is at work or enroute to work.

The procedure I describe in this article is perhaps best suited to a company with large cash inflows and outflows in many locations (C.I.T.'s daily cash needs are in excess of $50 million). But the system is applicable to any medium-sized or large company that uses borrowed funds to meet the fluctuating demands of dispersed operations, or that has a sizable number of customers in other sections of the country.

I should say a word about the conceptual framework of the C.I.T. system. As a diversified financial services enterprise, C.I.T. employs cash as its raw material. This means that the treasurer is, in effect, the company's purchasing agent; he considers and handles cash the way a steel producer does iron ore. Like the steel producer, the finance company treasurer must maintain an adequate inventory of raw material to meet the demands of the company's operations, many of which are hundreds and even thousands of miles away.

As a rule, we keep only enough cash on hand to take care of our immediate needs, plus a relatively small amount for contingencies. Like any manufacturer, we avoid tying up the company's resources in heavy inventories and instead earmark as much cash as we can for more profitable purposes. We prefer having ample sources of funds to maintaining large stocks of cash.

Any good cash management system is guided by four cardinal principles:

1. Develop and use sources of short-term money that are flexible and readily available.
2. Constantly search for ways of speeding the flow of cash from all financial sources to and through the company.
3. Never permit usable funds—borrowed or customer receipts—to stand idle for as much as a day.
4. Banks are an important part of the cash system; always treat them fairly.

The components of the system are flexible and competitive sources of short-term money, centralized control of cash, procedures that speed up the flow of funds, a simple and reliable method of keeping track of cash supplies and movements, and the vigorous investment of cash surpluses. I shall consider each component in the course of this article.

HOW IT WORKS

Of a company's sources of capital—stock offerings, retained earnings, cash flow, long-term borrowing, and short-term borrowing—the last is the most important for purposes of cash management. Short-term money (bank loans or other advances) generally is cheaper than other kinds of available capital and, most important, offers greater flexibility. Needless to say, such funds must be used within the limits of safety. (A prudent company will avoid relying on short-term funds to finance long-term commitments.)

So, depending on the nature and needs of his company, the treasurer should consider moves that increase his access to and reliance on short-term capital. As a start, he may review his ratio of long- to short-term capital, particularly if his current ratio favors the former.

C.I.T., for example, nowadays maintains an almost equal balance between long- and short-term debt—about $1 billion outstanding on each side, supported by about $600 million in equity. However, the ratio between the two is always subject to adjustment in light of significant changes in the composition of maturities of our receivables outstanding. A lengthening of average maturities might dictate a higher proportion of long-term debt. On the other hand, a notable trend toward shorter maturities might indicate greater stress on short-term borrowing.

In this connection, it should be noted that unlike many other companies, C.I.T. depends heavily for its cash needs on the commercial paper market rather than on banks and bank credit. I do not think, however, that C.I.T.'s unusual reliance on commercial paper makes the cash management system invalid for companies using more typical financing channels.

As a direct issuer of these promissory notes with a prime credit rating, C.I.T. can borrow large sums of short-term money at rates below the prime and without the burden of having to maintain noninterest-bearing compensating balances. During 1971, the company sold more than 10,000 notes of varying denominations ranging from $100,000 into the millions.

BANKING NETWORK

In C.I.T.'s system, the treasurer's office at headquarters is not a staff service but a line operation—in effect, a genuine profit center. It has full control and coordination of working capital, which relieves line operations of the burden of cash management. Exhibit I presents the interlocking elements of the system in a schematic form.

The treasurer designates a key regional bank as his major depository in each geographical area where the company has a large operation, a cluster of smaller operations, or a significant number of customers. The regional bank (sometimes called "concentration bank") should be in a Federal Reserve city and should have bank wire facilities.

A test of an acceptable strategic location for the regional bank is whether mail from all company operations or customers in that area can be expected to arrive at the bank overnight. Even allowing for the state of today's mail service, this test is a useful standard. (Other means—most likely electronic—eventually will be used to ensure overnight transmittal of funds to the regional bank. Later I shall discuss one method now being field tested by C.I.T.)

EXHIBIT 1
C.I.T.'s Funds Flow Between Field Operations and Banks

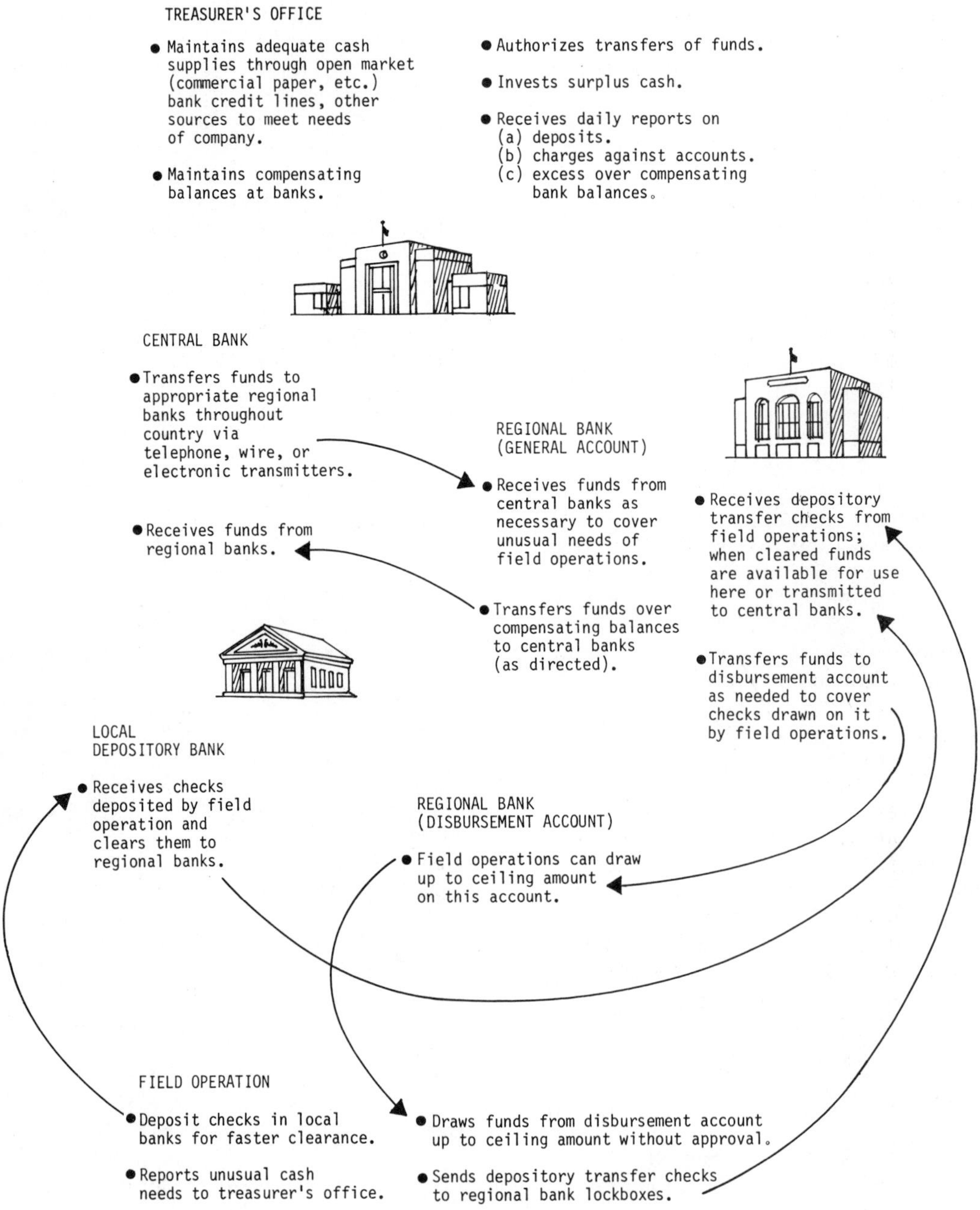

TREASURER'S OFFICE
• Maintains adequate cash supplies through open market (commercial paper, etc.) bank credit lines, other sources to meet needs of company.
• Maintains compensating balances at banks.
• Authorizes transfers of funds.
• Invests surplus cash.
• Receives daily reports on (a) deposits. (b) charges against accounts. (c) excess over compensating bank balances.
CENTRAL BANK
• Transfers funds to appropriate regional banks throughout country via telephone, wire, or electronic transmitters.
• Receives funds from regional banks.
REGIONAL BANK (GENERAL ACCOUNT)
• Receives funds from central banks as necessary to cover unusual needs of field operations.
• Transfers funds over compensating balances to central banks (as directed).
• Receives depository transfer checks from field operations; when cleared funds are available for use here or transmitted to central banks.
• Transfers funds to disbursement account as needed to cover checks drawn on it by field operations.
LOCAL DEPOSITORY BANK
• Receives checks deposited by field operation and clears them to regional banks.
REGIONAL BANK (DISBURSEMENT ACCOUNT)
• Field operations can draw up to ceiling amount on this account.
FIELD OPERATION
• Deposit checks in local banks for faster clearance.
• Reports unusual cash needs to treasurer's office.
• Draws funds from disbursement account up to ceiling amount without approval.
• Sends depository transfer checks to regional bank lockboxes.

In each regional bank we establish "zero balance" disbursing accounts to receive drafts from company operations in that area. With this type of account a field operation can write routine checks locally, but the required funds are drawn on a central account at the regional bank.

Field operations are expected to mail funds to lockboxes at the appropriate regional bank by a certain hour each day to ensure their arrival on the next business day. The time, of course, depends on local conditions.

To speed up the availability of money, field operations use the depository transfer check, which is a preprinted check requiring no signature—only the cash amount and date. This feature eliminates a potential source of delays.

When a field operation receives funds in the course of business, it deposits the checks immediately in a local depository bank and sends a depository transfer check in the total amount of the checks to a lockbox in its regional bank. In this manner funds are made available days earlier than would be the case if the checks were sent directly to the regional bank or held in the local bank for clearance and then transmitted to the regional bank.

After all the checks clear, amounts above the required compensating balances are wired to a central bank in the company's headquarters city (New York). Since the treasurer's office knows these funds are available, usually the money is already committed to another use and put to work the same day.

AUTOMATIC PROCEDURES

Field operations are authorized to spend up to a specified amount without advising the treasurer's office. At any company using such a system the upper limit depends, of course, on how much money is needed for normal business transactions. At C.I.T. the ceiling is $250,000.

When a field operation asks the treasurer's office for additional funds to handle a transaction, the money is sent only when it is actually needed. This reduces the possibility of incurring unnecessary interest charges should the money not be used on the scheduled day for some reason. Extra precautions should be taken on Fridays to avoid bank interest charges on idle cash over the weekend.

If the company has limited operations in a certain region but a significant number of customers there—and particularly if collections involve large numbers of small payments—the treasurer can hasten the flow of incoming receipts by asking customers to send payments to the designated bank in their area rather than to company headquarters. When they clear, these collections can be wired, or put to work in other ways, days earlier than otherwise would be the case.

To make the system function automatically, a company must form an administrative structure that spells out its policies and procedures. In addition, there must be standing instructions for the participating banks. Procedures should be comprehensive—that is, including all actions that help the system operate with a minimum of day-to-day supervision by the treasurer's office. Also, the treasurer or one of his executives must visit each bank to explain the procedures required of it and, if necessary, make whatever adjustments that local conditions or practices may dictate.

Since few systems are foolproof, the treasurer's office should be prepared to head off occasional lapses—say, a field operation does not mail a check in time or a bank fails to report a cash transmittal promptly. Unless the cash manager and his team are alert to possible slipups, they will encounter unavailability of funds at some time and place or idle cash at a bank incurring interest charges needlessly.

Stress on training: The best hedge against lapses is to have trained persons in the treasurer's office who are thoroughly versed in the system;

thus the treasurer should pay close attention to the selection and training of his cash management group. We at C.I.T. look for persons who are not only quick with details and emotionally steady but also familiar with the company's structure. In selecting executives, we also prefer that they have had some formal education in finance or business.

We train both executives and clerical persons in our system. It takes six months to a year, depending on the job, to train the clerical staff and up to two years to attune an executive to all the nuances of cash management.

This matter of training, I want to stress, should not be taken lightly. Even a young employee doing the most basic job needs more than a cursory indoctrination before he can confidently handle telephone calls involving extremely large sums—often in the millions of dollars. We also make certain that every person involved in the system understands the total operation as well as his particular role.

To ensure a smoothly functioning system, we urge the staff to cultivate easy relationships with the appropriate persons in the company, and we insist on cordial and fair dealings with the banks. At the same time, we constantly try to refine the system in order to reduce the likelihood of errors.

A TYPICAL DAY

At this point it may be helpful if I present a more or less typical day at a company to show the cash management system in operation. This review is based on C.I.T.'s experience.

The treasurer's office starts the day with a runoff of outstanding loans maturing that day which must be paid. Based on previous reports from field operations, the office also has a forecast of the cash needed during the day throughout the organization.

The office now sizes up the immediate availability of cash. It notes customer receipts clearing at regional banks and balances at line banks. (C.I.T. levels its bank balances daily and averages its compensating balances over a six-month period. The company considers any accumulated overages and shortages in the balances as safety valves that can be used to equalize the cash flow.)

The rundown completed, the treasurer has to make a decision. If the available funds are more than ample for the day's needs, he must decide how to invest the surplus. But if money is needed, he must determine how much to borrow from his sources and for what term. The term of the money to be borrowed is important. If, for example, a particularly large sum of cash will be needed three months hence, the treasurer most likely will want no new obligations to fall due on that day.

If the treasurer must raise money that day, he turns to his normal sources of short-term funds. If, however, he has not raised the targeted amount by noon, he can elect to (a) dip into the compensating balances at his banks, (b) take advantage of the time lag (if company headquarters are in the East or Midwest) and use a West Coast source of borrowed funds, or (c) borrow the money from his line banks.

In the case of my company, daily cash needs can range from $50 million to as high as $250 million on a tax day. Because of our heavy reliance on the commercial paper market, we handle the situation somewhat differently from that which I just outlined:

After the early morning rundown of the cash picture that day, I conduct a rate meeting in my office at 10 a.m. We set the rate for the company's commercial paper—fully competitive to attract buyers if the cash need is great, or at a somewhat lower level if it is not.

Immediately after the meeting, C.I.T.'s commercial paper sales staff of nine persons calls potential customers to place the amount of paper considered necessary to meet the needs of the day's business. These calls, incidentally, can number as high as 150 on days when the rate changes.

If the commercial paper staff has not come up with the required funds by noon, I have several options. I can take advantage of the time difference to make another try for commercial paper money through our San Francisco office; I can boost the interest rate and try again; or I can use bank credit lines. The last option is usually the last resort. In fact, we find our use of bank credit a sensitive indicator of the effectiveness of the cash management system.

In this connection it is worth noting that during all of 1970, C.I.T., which has about $808 million in credit lines at more than 400 banks in the United States and 11 banks in Canada, averaged less than $1 million a day in bank loans in this country and $4.5 million a day in Canada. In 1971 that daily average dropped to zero in the United States and to practically zero in Canada.

IN CASE OF SURPLUS

Returning to the day of our hypothetical company, let us suppose it has a surplus of funds—from incoming receipts; other cash transferrals; or, in the case of a company issuing commercial paper, an oversubscription. The surplus can be invested in the commercial paper of other federal agencies, or bank certificates of deposit. Or it can be used to build up bank balances as a hedge against the day the treasurer wants to average them down.

The criteria for investing the surplus generally are security, marketability, and yield—the importance of each depending on the company's circumstances. For example, marketability is especially important if the treasurer must turn investments into cash on short notice.

However, always seeking the highest yields is hazardous, since a single bad investment can wipe out the income accumulated from other investments. For safety and liquidity, we at C.I.T. favor, in order of preference: repurchase agreements with government securities as collateral, the commercial paper of other issuers, and certificates of deposit.

Generally, profitability is a function of the size of the portfolio. Cash put to work, at no cost to the company, can return $60,000 a year for each $1 million invested at 6%. But we do not use our cash management system primarily for direct income; rather it is to provide field operations with the funds they need to run and expand their business. Our system strives to make the maximum use of all funds. So we invest cash surpluses mainly to avoid having idle funds and only secondarily to produce income.

USE OF THE COMPUTER

While records are essential, they should be kept simple and concise. The treasurer, or his cash manager, working with large sums of money on the move, must make quick analyses and accurate decisions. A complex or extensive recordkeeping system can be counterproductive. C.I.T. uses a one-page "T account" that shows the balances each day at the company's principal banks. Other records also are simple, including an "over and under" tabulation of compensating balances at various banks and a daily cash report to senior management.

A computer can be useful, but C.I.T. uses its computer primarily as a planning and bookkeeping aid, not a decision maker. For example, on each working day the computer provides the treasurer's office with certain data, including—

...borrowings by rate periods for the previous business day;

...names of lenders and the cumulative balances for each;

...where in the country debts are falling due that day and for the next four days (the latter a precaution in the event of computer failure);

...a list of scheduled transfers of funds from the company's lead bank to out-of-town banks in order to pay off maturing debts.

The computer, of course, can play a larger role in cash management. To illustrate:

A leading electrical manufacturer feeds its daily balances directly into an information system. The computer records and transmits receipts and disbursements of every operating unit. Whenever a disbursement threatens to deplete a regional account, the computer automatically orders it replenished from the central bank.

The treasurer constantly checks the balance in the central account and invests excess funds in securities, which the computer also records. The treasurer thus keeps the book balance in its payroll and disbursements accounts to a minimum, puts idle funds to work earning interest, and is kept informed of his cash position at all times.

A major chemical company links its computers with those of its regional banks so that the cash manager automatically gets a complete rundown before 10:30 each morning.

Another big electrical company, however, which must provide money to 170 autonomous operations, does not rely on a computer but keeps track of its cash balances at more than 1,000 banks across the country through a cash operations center at company headquarters. A leased wire network is used to direct shifts of cash between accounts.

USE OF FORECASTS

Forecasting is an essential part of any cash management system. C.I.T. has an annual forecast prepared by the controller on the basis of projections from the subsidiaries, and monthly forecasts made by the treasurer's department. The latter are based on such factors as the previous month's activity, the projected needs of the upcoming month as determined by requests for cash, the experience for the same period in past years, and, finally, our estimate of current trends.

For cash management, the monthly forecast is the more important of the two. It alerts us to extraordinary cash needs during the approaching month. For example, a subsidiary may advise us that it will need $12 million to finance a jet aircraft. However, because of our reliance on the commercial paper market, we are not so much concerned about obtaining the $12 million as we are about the timing in order to have that amount available at the moment the funds are required.

The more pertinent concern is the state of our outstanding debt. The forecast enables us to make our borrowing plans in light of our debt load and cash needs for the period.

A heavy demand for cash leads to a second purpose of our monthly forecast: identifying significant divergences from the annual and monthly projections. If, for example, the need for cash has been unexpectedly high for several successive months and promises to continue in that pattern, we reexamine the annual forecast and bring it into line with prevailing demands.

We also determine whether the company should raise more short-term debt or restructure its debt by obtaining long-term capital (bonds, debentures, long-term notes). This serves to reinstate the desired balance between short-term and long-term debt. (The reader will recall that C.I.T.'s ratio at present is about evenly divided between the two.)

On the operational level, we conduct our monthly forecasts in an informal matter. Usually our cash manager calls the treasurers of the subsidiaries and asks the basic question, which may be expressed in such different forms as:

"Any extra expenses coming up?"

"What's your projection for the month?"

"What are you going to need and when?"

"Are you going to give us money this month or take money?"

This information is supplemented (or confirmed) by letter, memorandum, or telegram. Note that, in line with the automatic nature of normal cash disbursements for the purposes of the forecast, the subsidiary treasurers are asked to report only unusual cash needs and surpluses.

Another point also should be made clear: C.I.T., unlike some other companies, does not use cash projections as a means of managing its funds so as to reduce or avoid borrowing later in the month. The company borrows constantly throughout the month; therefore holding up bills for payment on a particular day is not a purpose of our forecasts.

SPEEDING THE FLOW

As I have noted, every effort must be made to speed the flow of funds. Some of the procedures used by C.I.T. are applicable to other companies as well. Treasurers may want to consider these pointers:

Open incoming mail certain to contain payments first, so that the checks can be deposited the same day. At C.I.T., mail addressed to the factoring operations—Meinhard-Commercial Corporation and William Iselin & Company—is opened at 7 a.m. These funds then become available much more quickly than if handled routinely.

Maintain a skeleton staff on bank holidays—at least in the treasurer's office. This will keep cash moving through the banks even though the rest of the company has a day off.

Establish lockboxes at regional bank cities to speed up the handling of funds from field operations. They make money available up to three days earlier than if collections are made centrally. Fast collections lower cash requirements and provide surplus for investment.

Install an electronic transmitter at headquarters for authorizing the central bank to wire specified sums to banks across the country. The funds are used to support field operations and meet debt obligations. Such a device eliminates the cumbersome and time-consuming ritual of verifying authorizations over the telephone by coded security checks. With a transmitter one person can send 90 authorizations in an hour and a half. Using the verbal method, the same number takes a full day.

Use depository transfer checks to transmit daily receipts from field operations to regional banks. These make usable funds available days earlier than when receipts are sent directly to the regional bank for clearance or held in the local bank for clearance and then transmitted to the regional bank.

Pay bills only when they fall due, and instruct field operations to do the same. This conserves cash for other purposes. One method is to pay large sums by bank drafts made out to the creditor on the day the payment is due.

The treasurer should stay abreast of developments, particularly technical advances, that can speed up the flow of cash.

C.I.T., as I mentioned earlier, is now testing a system that bypasses the mails and instead transmits daily cash receipt totals over a computerized telephone network. A regional manager simply phones to a special number the amount of a deposit and all related data. The information is immediately relayed to the appropriate regional bank, which then, for rapid clearance, deposits a depository transfer check for that amount with the Federal Reserve bank in its city.

We hope that this innovation not only will accelerate the flow of cash by as much as two days, but also will alert the treasurer's office immediately if a branch does not report a check by the specified time that day. The computerized network is expected to make the cash management system nearly completely automatic and foolproof.

CONCLUSION

Cash is an asset only when it is in use. Otherwise it is a liability. The essence of effective cash management is to keep idle dollars at an absolute minimum.

To establish a system that does this, the company should keep a significant amount of its capital in short-term funds—within the limits of safety. Short-term money costs less and can be managed with greater flexibility.

The management and coordination of short-term funds should be centralized in the office of the treasurer. This not only makes the system work better but also relieves field operations of the major responsibility of handling and keeping track of cash.

The company should establish bank accounts in regions where it has significant or numerous operations. These regional banks should not be more than 24 hours by mail from any company operation. Regional banks get the company's cash into circulation faster. If the company is based in the East, it also should consider using an emergency source of short-term money on the West Coast. Should the company be pressed for cash on any day, it can take advantage of the time difference there.

The company should encourage customers to deposit payments with a designated bank in their region rather than send money to the main office. Again, the bank should be within 24-hour reach of the farthest customer. This puts receipts into the company's cash stream much faster, thus reducing the amount of borrowing.

The treasurer must watch his balances very closely. Ideally, his bank balances, exclusive of compensating balances, should be at around point zero at the close of each day. He should avoid transferring funds to field operations until he is virtually certain they will be used on the specified day.

The treasurer should strive to keep his cash records and reporting system simple. Considering the magnitude of the funds he is controlling and coordinating, complexity can be a detriment.

In sum, for a relatively modest expenditure of time and money, a company can have a cash system that makes a significant contribution to earnings. Indeed, it can be one of the best financial moves the company makes. A well-planned and practical cash management system turns cash into a true asset by making certain it is always at work.

READING 8

Simulating a Cash Budget

Eugene M. Lerner
Northwestern University

Planning a firm's near-term financial requirements, or cash budgeting, is one of the cornerstones of modern financial management. However, neither the receipts-and disbursements method nor the adjusted-net-income method of cash budgeting,[1] the two most widely used techniques, enable the financial manager to answer the important question: *How large a buffer stock of cash should the company keep on hand to protect itself from adverse cash drains?* An answer to this important question and related cash problems can be gained by simulating the cash budget.

Present practice. The cash-budgeting techniques now widely used by corporations require the financial manager to prepare a single estimate of certain values. The receipts and disbursements method of cash budgeting, for example, assumes that the company can know its specific cash inflows from sales and collection of receivables in the months to come, as well as its cash outlays for labor, materials, dividend payments, and so forth. Then, by subtracting the total of all monthly outlays from monthly inflows, the financial officer can determine the most likely change in the company's cash position for each month in the future.

In practice few firms, if any, are able to forecast their inflows and outflows with this precision. Sales forecasts are notoriously unreliable, for actual sales depend in part upon factors that lie outside the control of the firm. Changes in the styling or marketing of competitive products, as well as changes in general economic conditions, can lead to large forecasting errors. As a result, even if the company knows what the effects of its own sales efforts are, the financial officer's estimates of monthly cash inflows may miss their mark by a wide margin.

Estimates of cash outlays are equally difficult for the financial manager to prepare. The price of materials may change; production problems may arise that lead to increased labor costs; and errors in the sales estimates themselves would necessarily lead to forecasting errors in purchases

Reprinted from the CALIFORNIA MANAGEMENT REVIEW (Winter 1968), Vol. 9, No. 2, pp. 79-86, by permission of The Regents.

--hence the volume of payables that fall due each month.

In spite of the difficulties that surround the task of estimating cash inflows and outflows, modern financial management requires preparation of a cash budget. The reason is straightforward: If a firm has either a cash shortage or cash surplus, profits will be lower than they otherwise would be.

If an unanticipated cash shortage occurs, the company may delay paying some of its vendors. These suppliers in turn will become reluctant to ship goods on credit, causing production delays if shortages of necessary parts develop. Customers will receive their orders late. Rumors may begin to spread about the financial soundness of the firm, and a drop in sales and profits would inevitably follow such a series of events.

The company may borrow to meet its unanticipated cash shortage, but it is unlikely to secure the volume of funds that it needs on advantageous terms. Lenders are naturally reluctant to advance credit on favorable terms to a company whose financial planning is so poor that it does not anticipate its needs. As a consequence, they will impose higher interest rates and more onerous operating constraints upon the company than would otherwise be the case.

Profits will also be lower if the financial manager errs on the side of conservatism and holds more cash than the company needs. Holding the idle cash balances means that the interest income which can be earned on short-term assets such as Treasury bills is foregone. But even if excess funds are invested in short-term interest-bearing assets, marketing programs that should be undertaken may not be adopted because of alleged cash shortages; R&D outlays may not be incurred because they are "too costly," and expansion into new market areas may be delayed because of "inadequate funds." Yet these very activities may yield higher returns than the securities purchased with the excess funds.

AN APPROXIMATE TOOL

It is important that a financial manager prepare a cash budget and estimate his expected cash outflows and inflows with accuracy. Realism, however, demands that the financial manager think of his receipts and disbursements estimates as what they really are: *expected results subject to a margin of error*, not single valued figures known with certainty. Simulation is therefore an approximate tool which can be used for this aspect of financial management.

The power of simulation as a tool of financial analysis is that it permits the financial manager to incorporate in his planning both the most likely value of an activity and the margin of error associated with this estimate. The advantages of simulating the cash budget are threefold:

✓ The financial manager can determine the size of the buffer stock of cash, liquidity, or bank line that he needs to meet the uncertainties that surround the company's activities.

✓ He can ascertain the effect of changes in company policies upon cash. For example, the effect of a change in receivable policy, payable policy, or the timing of purchases that enter the production process can be determined.

✓ He can determine which corporate activities have the greatest influence upon cash balances. As a consequence, the financial manager can sharpen his estimate of strategic activities and ignore those that have only a minor impact upon cash balance.

Simulation. Before an example is presented of how a firm can simulate its cash budget, it may be useful to sketch out how the simulation procedure works. Suppose that the probability attached to a particular level of sales is:

Probability	Level of Sales
.25	$100
.50	150
.25	200

Figure 1

SALES		COLLECTION RATE		DOLLARS COLLECTED	PROBABILITY OF OCCURRENCE
.25	100	.50	.50	50	.125
		.40	.75	75	.100
		.10	1.00	100	.025
.50	150	.50	.50	75	.250
		.40	.75	112.50	.200
		.10	1.00	150	.050
.25	200	.50	.50	100	.125
		.40	.75	150	.100
		.10	1.00	200	.025

and that the probability attached to the percentage of receivables collected one month after a sale is:

Probability	Percentage of receivables collected
.50	.50
.40	.75
.10	1.00

Envisage now an experiment in which we have 100 different balls in an urn; 25 are white, 50 are brown, and 25 blue. These balls correspond to the probabilities of a particular level of sales.

Draw a ball at random from the urn, note its color, and return the ball to the urn. If we selected a blue ball, we can say that it corresponds to a sales level of $200. Now go to a second urn where there are 50 red balls, 40 black ones and 10 green ones. These balls correspond to the probabilities of a particular collection rate. If the black ball is chosen, we say it corresponds to the collection of 75 percent of the sales made in the previous month. Since the blue ball in our first drawing represented a sales level of $200, and the black ball represented the collection rate of 75 percent, the collections during the second month will be $150. By repeating the drawings a large number of times, the actual distribution of collections can be estimated. This particular simulation is diagrammed in Figure 1.

Following the top lines in Figure 1, we see that since there is a 25 percent chance that sales will be $100, and a 50 percent chance that one-half of these sales will be collected in the following month, there is a 12½ percent chance that collections will lie between $50 and $112.50 and that more than one-third of the time $75 will be collected.

Probability	Dollars collected
.125	$ 50
.350	75
.150	100
.200	112.50
.150	150
.025	200

As the number of steps in the process is increased and the linkages between the steps become more intricate, the final distribution of results can no longer be efficiently determined by hand. It can however, be readily simulated by a computer, for the results of a larger number of such drawings can be calculated in a fraction of a second. Since cash budgeting is a problem involving complicated linkages, it is best handled by simulation.

An example. To illustrate how simulation can help the financial manager prepare his cash budget, let us work through a hypothetical example. The assumptions made in this example are:

1. The number of units that the firm sells has a marked seasonal pattern. This seasonal pattern is known to the financial manager to be:

Jan.	.75	July	1.00
Feb.	.75	Aug.	1.00
March	.50	Sept.	1.10
April	.85	Oct.	1.15
May	.90	Nov.	1.50
June	1.00	Dec.	1.50

2. No trend is forecasted in the number of units sold and were it not for the seasonal pattern, 500 units would be sold each month. The expected number of items that will be sold each month is found by multiplying 500 units times the seasonal factor. Thus, the expected number of units that will be sold in January is 500 times .75 or 375.

3. The actual number of units that will be sold each month fluctuates around its estimated level. The standard deviations of these fluctuations is 20. This means that though the expected number of units sold in January is 375, the actual January sales will lie between 355 and 395 roughly two-thirds of the time, that is, between the mean and plus or minus one standard deviation.

4. The selling price of each item is $10.

5. Of each month's sales, 10 percent are for cash; the remaining 90 percent are for credit. In practice these percentages will vary from month to month, and the financial manager will typically want to incorporate this fact into his analysis. In our example, it could be done by assuming that cash sales are a random variable with a mean of 10 percent and some known standard deviation. To preserve simplicity in the illustration, however, these percentages will be treated as constants.

6. The receivables generated by the credit sales are collected at the following rates: first month after sale, 70 percent; second month after sale, 20 percent; and third month after sale, 10 percent. These percentages, like the distribution of sales made for cash and credit, are stochastic variables, that is, variables whose values cannot be known with precision. Properly stated, the collection rate for the first month would be $.70 + e$ where the error term, e is expected to be zero, but has a known standard deviation. Similarly, the collection rate in the second month should be stochastic, $.20 + e$, and so forth. Once more, however, the simplifying assumption is made that the collection figures are exact. (In a later section, these collection rate percentages will be altered, and the impact of a change in receivable policy upon the firm's monthly cash balances will be shown.)

7. Inventories are purchased two months in advance of sales. The inventories that will be sold in March will be purchased in January, and so forth.

8. Only enough inventory is ordered each month to cover the expected volume of sales two months hence.

9. The price of the inventories is $3 per unit.

10. Payments are made to suppliers in the month followng the purchase, and a 2 percent discount is taken.

11. Other monthly cash outlays are $1,000 for labor, $500 for other manufacturing expenses, and $1,250 for administrative expenses. Each of these values will be treated as constants, though once again these values could have been made free to vary over some range of values.

12. Dividends and taxes of $375 and $750, respectively, are paid quarterly

in March, June, September, and December.

SIMULATION RESULTS

Analysis of the simulation. One hundred simulations of a firm's cash budget were run under the twelve assumptions made above. The data in Table I show the firm's average monthly cash balances and the standard deviation about this mean.

Table I--SIMULATED CASH BALANCE
(Standard deviation of units sold = 20)

	Average Cash Balance	Standard Deviation
Jan.	$3,104	334
Feb.	1,258	375
March	-1,221	353
April	-1,104	402
May	- 363	403
June	-1,068	372
July	591	421
Aug.	566	387
Sept.	570	339
Oct.	452	383
Nov.	909	369
Dec.	2,109	345

These simulations show that the firm will experience its largest cash inflow in January ($3,104), and its most severe cash drain in March, when it can expect to lose $1,221. However, because sales are stochastic, the actual cash balances in any particular month can vary over some range. In January, for example, the standard deviation of the cash balance about its mean is $334. Hence, the firm will show a cash inflow between $2,770 and $3,438 roughly two-thirds of the time (the expected value of $3,104 plus and minus $334).

How can the financial manager use the results of this simulation? One way is the way cash budgeting has traditionally been employed. For example, three of the four months in which the firm pays a dividend, March, June, and September, it experiences a net cash drain. If the financial manager wishes to smooth the peaks and valleys of the cash balances, he could achieve this result by changing the company's quarterly dividend periods to, say, February, May, August, and November. The simulated cash budget, then, can alert the management of the company to periods when it can anticipate sharp changes in its cash balances and suggest various options for meeting these contingencies.

The results of the simulation, however, give rise to more powerful results than this. Consider, for example, the change in cash during March. We saw that the firm can expect to run a cash deficit that month of $1,221. Hence it must carry a buffer stock of cash or make provisions for a bank loan at the end of February equal to at least this amount. However, the $1,221 deficit is only an expected value: at least half of the time, the cash deficit in March will be greater than this amount.

Suppose that the firm decides that it does not want the probability that it will be caught short of cash to be larger than 1 in 1,000. To guard against such an event, it will have to carry enough cash, or secure a line of credit to protect it from an event that lies more than 3.3 standard deviations from the mean. Since the standard deviation about March's cash balance is $353, it will have to secure funds equal to 3.3 times $353 or $1,165. When this value is added to its expected shortage of $1,221, we see that a cash balance or line of credit of $2,386 is needed at the end of February to provide for March's contingencies.

But cash deficits also occur in the months of April, May, and June. Moreover, in each month, the deficits can either be smaller or larger than the expected or average value. How large a buffer stock of liquidity must the firm now hold to protect itself from possible adverse random outflows of cash throughout this entire period?

This question can be answered once it is recognized that the variance, or square of the standard deviation, of four events, A, B, C, and D, is:

$$\begin{aligned}\mathrm{Var}(A+B+C+D) = {} & \mathrm{Var}(A)+\mathrm{Var}(B)+\mathrm{Var}(C)+\mathrm{Var}(D) \\ & +2\mathrm{Cov}(AB)+2\mathrm{Cov}(AC)+2\mathrm{Cov}(AD) \\ & +2\mathrm{Cov}(BC)+2\mathrm{Cov}(BD) \\ & +2\mathrm{Cov}(CD)\end{aligned}$$

This formidable expression becomes simplified if the monthly cash balances are independent, for then all of the covariant terms will be zero. This is the case in our illustration: the fact that March's cash balance may be above its mean value gives no information about whether April's cash balance will be above or below its mean value. The variance of the cash balance over the four months will therefore be the sum of the four variances. The standard deviation for the four-month period as a whole is the square root of this value, or \$778, in our illustration. Let us now apply these results.

Suppose that the firm does not want the probability that it will run out of cash over the entire period from March through June to be larger than 1 chance in 1,000. It must then hold enough cash so that it can handle events that are as far as 3.3 standard deviations from the mean. Thus, it will want to hold a buffer stock of cash or secure a bank line equal to 3.3 times \$778 or \$2,567. Adding this buffer stock to its anticipated needs of \$3,765 (the sum of the four months cash deficit), we find that the cash requirement to cover the four-month period as a whole is \$6,323.

ADVANTAGES OF SIMULATION

To summarize our findings to this point:

✓ The financial officer of a modern corporation prepares a cash budget to anticipate the company's cash needs and to ensure that its profits are not depressed by holding either too low or too high a cash balance.

✓ The preparation of the cash expenditures and receipts estimates is a difficult task. A financial manager could, however, be expected to develop a most likely estimate for each variable in his budget and a measure of variation about that value.

✓ By using both the expected value of the elements in the budget and their standard deviation, the financial manager can simulate his cash budget. Having performed this task, he can determine both the expected change in cash during each month and the variation about this value.

✓ By utilizing both the mean and standard deviation of the firm's cash position, the financial manager can determine both the change in the firm's cash position through time and the buffer stock of cash or liquidity that the company will need to meet the variations that can arise about his estimates.

CHANGING POLICIES

Extension of the simulation. These simulations were based upon an assumption as to how fast receivables were to be collected and payables were to be met. Suppose now that the firm changes its policies in these areas. What is the effect of these actions upon the firm's cash position? While the answer to this important financial problem is both difficult and tedious to calculate by hand, it can be readily answered through simulation. Four alternative strategies in these areas are presented in Figure 2.

Receivable policy A is the one described previously, i.e., bills are collected in the first three months at the rates of .70, .20, and .10, respectively. (See Figure 3.)

Receivable policy B is a more liberal policy. The percentage of receivables collected in the three months following a sale are .50, .30, and .18, respectively. Note that the more liberal policy assumes that only 98 percent

Figure 2

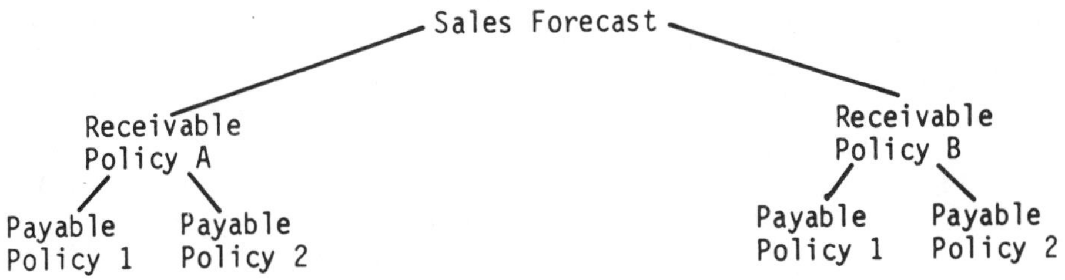

Figure 3.--MEAN CASH BALANCES: RECEIVABLE POLICY A

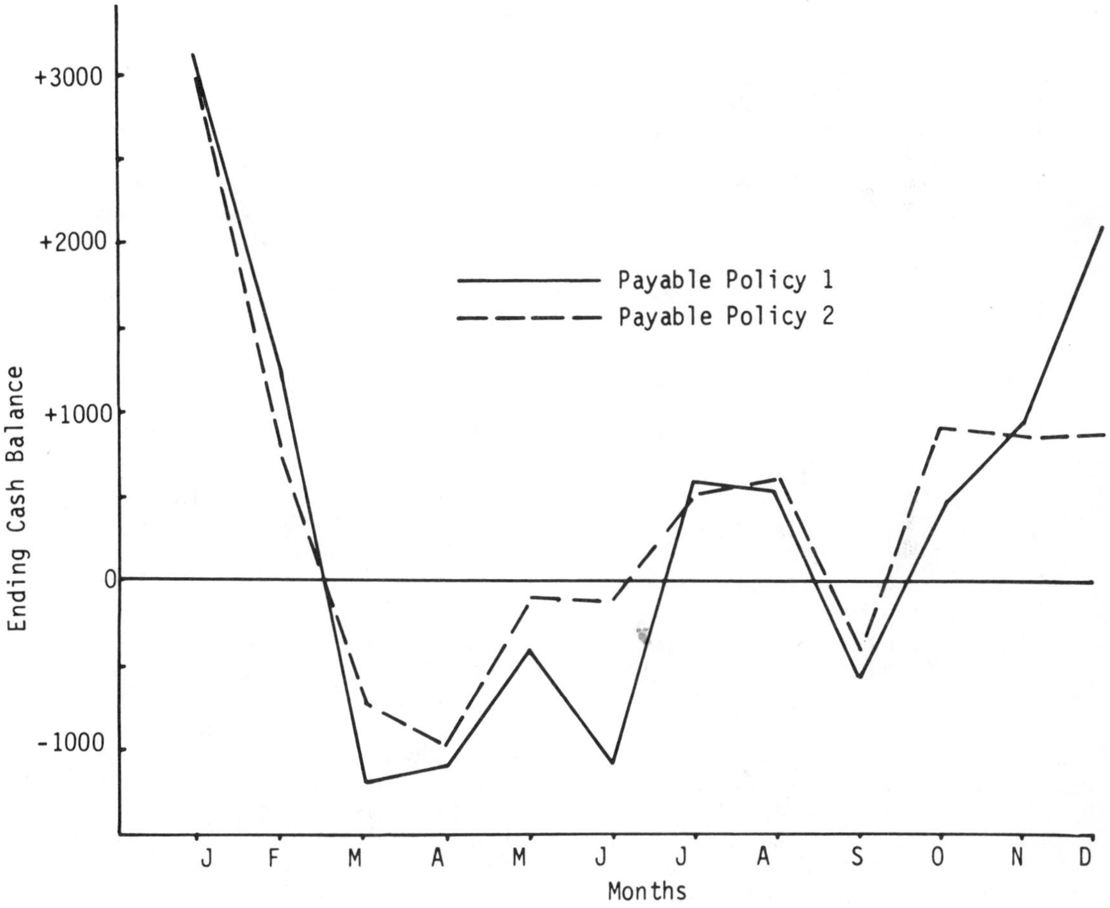

of the bills are collected; were such a policy enacted, sales would also be likely to rise. However, to make the illustrations directly comparable, we assume that no change in sales takes place. (See Figure 4.)

With payable policy 1, a 2 percent discount is taken, and the purchases are paid for in the month following the purchase. With payable policy 2, all purchases are paid for two months after they are made, and no cash dis-

Figure 4.--MEAN CASH BALANCES: RECEIVABLE POLICY B

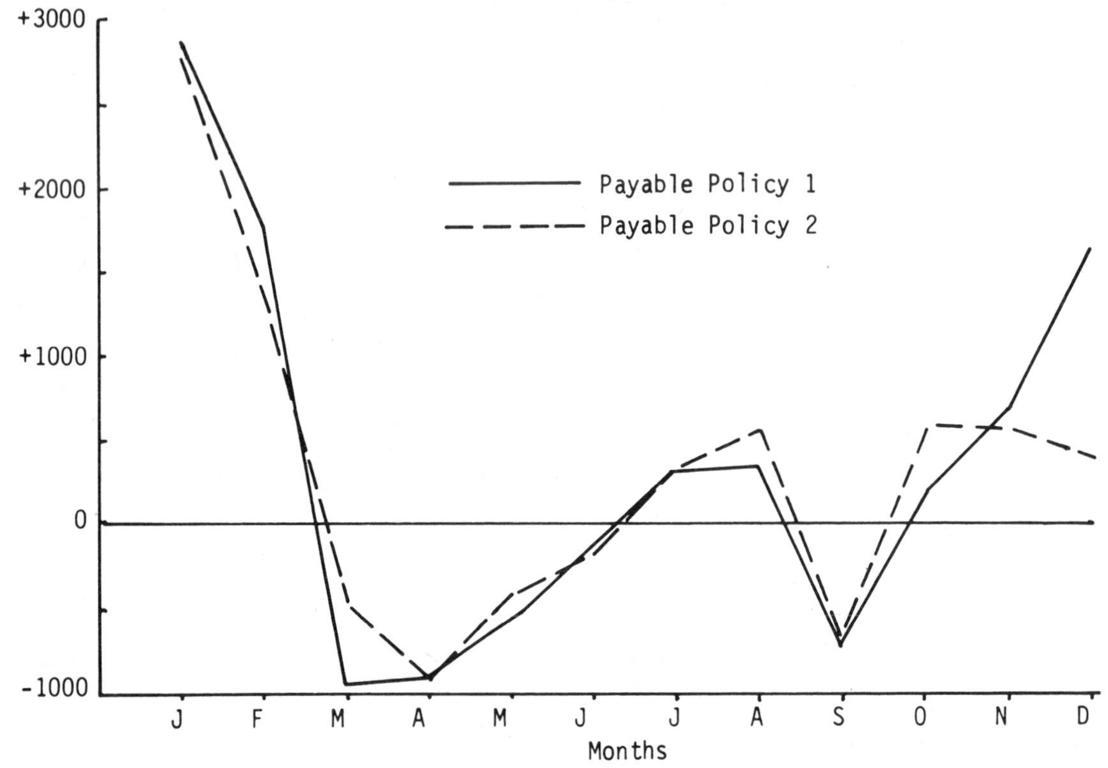

count is taken.

The results of the simulation are graphed in Figures 3 and 4. In June and December a marked difference appears in the ending cash balance with respect to the payment policy adopted under both receivable policies. In the other months of the year, the difference in ending balance is insignificant. Moreover, the pattern of cash balances appears to be the same under both receivable policies.

Through simulation then, the financial manager can ascertain what the impact of a change in corporate policy will be on the firm's cash position. Rather than adopting a specific course of action and waiting for the actual results, the financial manager can experiment with alternative feasible policies and choose the one that is most satisfactory.

The value of good information. In the simulations presented above, the financial manager was required to develop information about both the expected value and variation of the elements that entered the cash budget. A question that naturally arises is: *What benefit will accrue from spending extra time and effort to improve the forecasts that are being made?*

To answer this question, a second set of simulations was prepared. All of the assumptions made above remained as before except that the forecasting equation for the number of units sold each month was not as accurate as the one formerly used; the standard deviation of the error term was 50 rather than 20. Results are shown in Table II.

The expected monthly values of the cash balances are approximately equal for both simulations. The standard

Table II.--SIMULATED CASH BALANCE
(Standard deviation of units sold = 50)

	Average Cash Balance	Standard Deviation
Jan.	$3,098	469
Feb.	1,284	475
March	-1,160	500
April	-1,070	502
May	- 344	454
June	-1,032	484
July	582	485
Aug.	573	438
Sept.	- 533	458
Oct.	422	447
Nov.	817	459
Dec.	1,986	507

deviations in the second simulation are roughly one-third larger than in the first case.

Substantially larger buffer stocks of cash must therefore be kept on hand to provide equal amounts of protection. For example, to ensure that the probability of running out of cash in March is no larger than 1 in 1,000, 3.3 times 500 or $1,650 must be held at the end of February as the buffer stock of cash. Recall that when the better forecasting model was used, only $1,165 was needed to provide equal protection.

The loss in revenue from the increased amount of funds that must be kept on hand is then one measureable cost of the poor forecasting model. Of course, it is only one component of the total loss that results from large forecasting errors: larger inventories must be kept on hand and production costs are likely to be higher as well.

SUMMARY

Concluding remarks. The use of simulation as an analytical tool can be of great value to a financial manager seeking to estimate his future cash requirements. For with this too , he can develop an informed judgment of not only the average amount of funds he is likely to need each period, but also of the buffer stock of cash that he will need to protect his company from adverse random cash outflows.

Simulation also enables the financial manager to experiment with different financial policies in a quick and efficient manner. As a consequence, different alternatives can be evaluated in terms of their impact upon cash balances much more effectively than has heretofore been possible.

Finally, simulation can help the financial manager determine the value of information. Specifically, he can see how results would be changed if better data were available for specific inputs to the cash budget. If the results are only marginally improved and the data are expensive to collect, the financial manager can adopt a different course of action than if the improved data results in marked changes in his cash budget.

REFERENCES

1. *Managing Company Cash*, National Industrial Conference Board, Studies in Business Policy, No. 99, 1961.

READING 9

Daily Cash Forecasting: A Simple Method for Implementing the Distribution Approach

Bernell K. Stone
Georgia Institute of Technology

Robert A. Wood
Pennsylvania State University

OVERVIEW

Neither the problem of daily cash forecasting nor the state of corporate practice has received much attention in either basic finance texts or the finance literature, although a number of companies have developed successful daily forecasting procedures. This paper has two major objectives. One is simply to structure the daily cash forecasting problem. The second is to present dummy-variable regression techniques for converting data contained in the monthly cash budget into daily cash forecasts. While we focus on a particular statistical technique, the problem structuring devices we present have general applicability to statistical approaches to daily cash forecasting.

MAJOR VERSUS NONMAJOR CASH FLOWS

In most organizations, the cash flow consists of a limited number of major items and thousands of small receipts and payments. Major items such as taxes, dividends, lease payments, debt service, and even wages are easily forecastable over a horizon of 30 to 60 days in most companies, since both the amount and the timing of the payment are fairly accurately known. Other major flows, such as the receipt of payments for work on a government contract or a major cash purchase of equipment, may be almost impossible to forecast accurately. Such unforecastable major flows represent an inherently irreducible element of uncertainty in the cash flow. They are typically offset by a single financial transaction, e.g., the use of credit-line borrowing for an outflow and either the repayment of short-term borrowing or the purchase of short-term securities for an inflow.

Since most major cash flows are easily forecast and the few unforecastable major flows are simply offset by a single financial transaction, the primary focus of daily cash forecasting is the net cash flow from nonmajor items. Since the nonmajor flow consists

---

Reprinted from FINANCIAL MANAGEMENT (Fall 1977), pp. 40-50, by permission of the publisher and authors.

of many small receipts and payments, it is amenable to statistical forecasting procedures.

A CLASSIFICATION OF BASIC APPROACHES TO DAILY CASH FORECASTING

We identify two generic methodological approaches to cash forecasting—distribution and scheduling. *Distribution* refers to spreading a forecast of the total monthly flow (or its components) over the days of the month to reflect known intramonth cash flow patterns. Since measuring cash flow patterns is a problem of statistical estimation, distribution is a purely statistical approach.

Not all statistical forecasting techniques are distribution approaches. The standard procedure of projecting a time series as a moving adaptive average reflecting measured trends and cycles is not a distribution technique because it does not rely on spreading the monthly cash flow over the days of the month. In fact, such purely extrapolative techniques do not rely on the cash budget at all. Distribution can be thought of as a structuring of the cash forecasting task for the use of statistical techniques by determining the level from the cash budget and relying on statistical estimation only for the measurement of intramonth cash flow patterns, e.g., a monthly cycle and weekly subcycle. Statistically, the advantage of distribution over extrapolative techniques is less stringent stability assumptions. Distribution does not require a statistical projection of the month-to-month level of forecasts or of annual seasonals. Administratively, the advantage of distribution is that the daily cash forecast and the cash budget are logically tied together. Thus, in this paper, we only consider statistical techniques within a distribution framework.

Scheduling refers to the construction of a forecast from primitive data. For instance, the data for disbursements might be invoices, purchase authorizations, production schedules, and work plans. To illustrate the scheduling approach, consider a simplified example of a company making all purchases on credit with terms of net thirty days and following a policy of always paying on time but never early. In this situation, it is theoretically easy to specify a thirty-day disbursement schedule for payments to vendors from invoice data on hand. Developing such a schedule requires only an information system to capture and organize the invoice data. In this sense, scheduling can be viewed as information-system-based forecasting. Pure scheduling involves no statistical estimation. Pure scheduling is primarily applicable to disbursements and is generally usable only for a very short time horizon. Most sophisticated cash forecasting systems can be viewed as a combination of scheduling and distribution.

In general, distribution approaches are easier and cheaper to implement and administer than are scheduling approaches, although their success requires statistically stable cash flow patterns. This paper deals primarily with distribution approaches. In the context of presenting dummy-variable regression as a particular technique, this paper introduces a variety of problem structuring procedures that are applicable to most distribution-based approaches, including forecasting systems using a combination of distribution and scheduling.

FLOAT: THE RELATION OF BOOK BALANCES TO BANK BALANCES

For cash management purposes, the primary concern is the net collected bank balance and not the company's book balance *per se*. *Float* is the difference between the company's book balance and net collected bank balance. It consists of *disbursement float* (the dollar amount of checks written and subtracted from the company's book balance but not yet subtracted from the net collected bank balance) less *deposit float* (the dollar amount of deposits added to the company's book balance but not yet added to the net collected bank balance), i.e.,

bank balance = book balance + disbursement float - deposit float = book balance + float.

Concern with float in cash forecasting arises in the conventional two-step approach because a company first forecasts book balances and then forecasts float to obtain the net collected bank balance. In a two-step framework, a formal float forecast is necessary because day-to-day float values deviate substantially from their average value because of variations in the relative volume of disbursements and deposits and because of variations in float time arising from the effect of weekends and holidays. Most serious attempts at float forecasting focus on separate forecasts of disbursement and deposit float and take account of both day-of-the-week and holiday effects.

A SIMPLE DISTRIBUTION MODEL

ONE-STEP VERSUS TWO-STEP FORECASTS

We now describe a distribution-based forecasting system using dummy-variable regression to measure monthly and weekly cash flow patterns. This technique is amenable to forecasting both book balances and float individually. We shall present it, however, in the context of a direct, one-step forecast of net collected bank balances rather than the usual two-step procedure of first forecasting book balances and then forecasting float.

A one-step procedure has several advantages. First, the effort required to implement and administer the one-step forecast is substantially less than that required for comparable two-step procedures. Second, the data required to measure the forecast parameters are readily available from bank statements.[1] Offsetting the advantages is a possible loss in accuracy.

CASH FLOW COMPONENTS

Distribution requires intramonth cash flow patterns to be stable enough that estimates based on past data can be projected into the future with confidence. The net nonmajor flow rarely possesses such stability because disbursements (outflows) and deposits (inflows) almost always have different patterns, and their relative proportion of the total flow varies from month to month.

To obtain stability, it is necessary to divide the nonmajor flow into components with stable patterns and forecast the components. In practice, obtaining stability generally requires breaking disbursements and deposits into more detailed subcomponents; for expositional simplicity, however, we shall structure the problem with nonmajor flows divided into only disbursements and deposits.

MEASURING MONTHLY AND WEEKLY CASH FLOW PATTERNS

If there were no weekly cycles and no disturbances from holidays, a simple technique for measuring the basic monthly pattern for each component of the nonmajor flow would be to measure the average fraction of the monthly total that occurred on a given work day of the month. To structure the problem of measuring a monthly pattern in the absence of weekly cycles and holiday effects, let a_t denote an estimate of the fraction of the total monthly flow expected to occur on workday t. Assume that we have data for N past months and that f_{tn} is the fraction

[1] Most companies of any size obtain their bank statement data on magnetic tape, so it is already in computer readable form. The fact that most companies have different accounts for disbursements and deposits (and even for different subclasses of disbursements and deposits) means that the data tapes are already organized for model parameterization with the possible exception of deleting those major items included on the tape, a task easily accomplished by a single reading of the tape.

EXHIBIT 1. The Day-of-Month Effect—An Illustrative Histogram Showing the Average Fraction of the Total Monthly Flow That Occurs on a Given Workday of the Month

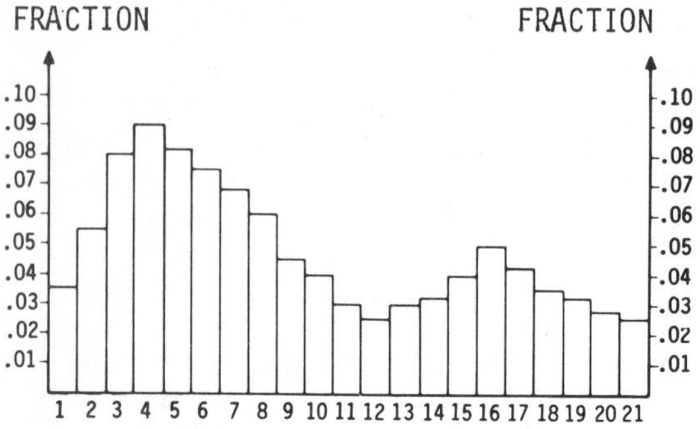

EXHIBIT 2. The Day-of-Week Effect—An Illustrative Histogram Showing the Average Fraction of Total Weekly Cash Flow Occurring on a Given Day of the Week

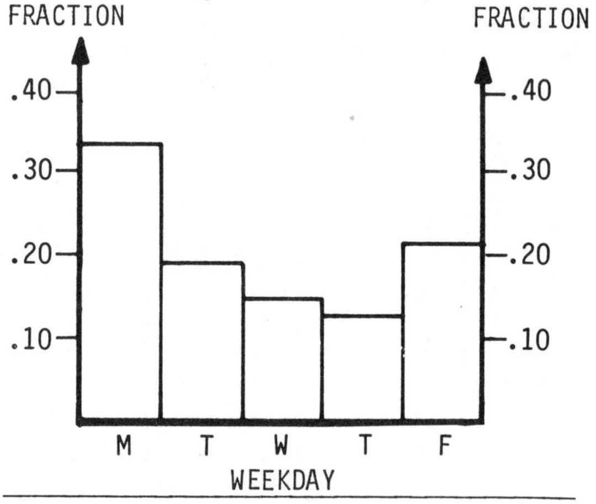

of the monthly total that occurred on workday t in month n.

If future cash flow generation is assumed to be like that of the past, then the best estimate for a_t is the average value of past fractions, i.e.,

$$(1) \quad a_t = \frac{1}{N} \sum_{n=1}^{N} f_{tn}.$$

The values of the a_t's summarize the estimate of the monthly pattern. Exhibit 1 illustrates how the estimate can be depicted graphically by a histogram showing the average proportion of the flow occurring on each work day.

If there were no monthly cycle but only a day-of-week effect, we could follow a similar procedure to measure the weekly cycle by taking an average of past values. Exhibit 2 depicts a possible distribution of weekly cash flows obtainable from such a measurement.

When there is both a monthly and weekly cycle, then we must account for their joint effect. A straightforward procedure would be to continue to measure both the monthly and weekly patterns separately as averages of past values. For instance, we might still measure a_5 as an average of the cash flow on workday 5 and hope that there is not a predominance of any one weekday occurring on day 5. A statistically superior measurement procedure, however, is to estimate both the monthly and weekly patterns simultaneously.

Dummy-variable regression[2] is a statistical device for a simultaneous

[2] The term "dummy-variable" arises from the use of artificial variables that assume the value one in a time period when a given effect is expected and zero otherwise. The reader not familiar with dummy-variable regression and its use for measuring seasonals is referred to econometrics texts, e.g., Draper and Smith [5, Chapter 5], Johnston [6, pp. 176-92], and Wonnacott and Wonnacott [16, pp. 74-76]. Econometric issues and problems pertinent to the use of dummy variables to measure seasonals are treated in Ladd [8], Lovell [9, 10], Jorgenson [7], and Suits [15]. An application of dummy variables to assess day-of-month and day-of-week effects is contained in Boyd and Mabert [2] and Mabert [12]. The reader familiar with this literature, especially Ladd [8] , Lovell [9, 10], and Jorgenson [7], is aware that there is some controversy over dummy-variable based assessment of seasonals. However, most of this pertains to statistical issues such as the consistency and interpretation of regression fits using seasonally adjusted data as input to a subsequent regression estimate of an economic relationship versus simultaneous estimation of seasonals and the economic relationship. To the extent that we are concerned only with the estimation of a seasonal pattern and do not use it as input to subsequent estimates, most of these so called "problems" are not pertinent here.

measurement of both the monthly and weekly cycle. Let the workdays of the week be numbered from 1 on Monday to 5 on Friday. Let the workdays of the month be numbered from 1 to M. The regression equation for jointly estimating the monthly and weekly patterns is

$$(2) \quad f_t = \sum_{i=1}^{M} a_i m_i + \sum_{w=1}^{5} b_w d_w$$

where m_i is a day-of-month dummy that is one when i equals t and zero otherwise, and d_w is a day-of-week dummy that is one when workday w occurs on day t and zero otherwise. The regression coefficients $a_1, a_2, \ldots, a_M$ are estimates of the monthly pattern. The regression coefficients b_1, b_2, b_3, b_4, b_5 are estimates of the day-of-week effect.[3]

If there were no day-of-week effect, then the regression equation would reduce to estimating a_t as the sample average in accord with Equation (1). If there were no day-of-month effect but only a weekly pattern, then the formula again would reduce to finding a simple average of past values. When both a day-of-month and day-of-week effect are present simultaneously, then the regression amounts to estimating a_t as an average of the past values that are corrected to reflect the weekday on which the flow occurred. Similarly, the estimate of b_w can be viewed as a refinement to averaging that corrects for day-of-month effects. Thus, the dummy-variable regression can be viewed as a sophisticated averaging procedure that estimates day-of-month and day-of-week effects simultaneously.

IMPLEMENTATION PROCEDURES

The basic activities involved in providing a one-step forecast based on dummy-variable regression are data preparation, parameter estimation, obtaining monthly totals, distribution of nonmajor flows, and combining all major and nonmajor flows to obtain the forecast of the net flow.

1. *Data Preparation.* Given bank statement data, all major items are subtracted, the nonmajor items are divided into components, and, for each component in each month, the daily totals are obtained and expressed as a fraction of the monthly total for that nonmajor component.

2. *Parameter Estimation.* For each nonmajor component, the fraction of the monthly total and the workday

---

[3] To ensure that the a's measure a pure monthly cycle and the b's measure a pure weekly cycle, we should use constrained regression. By the point-of-means property of a least-squares regression, we know that

$$1 = \sum_{t=1}^{M} a_t + \left(\frac{W}{N}\right) \sum_{w=1}^{5} b_w$$

where W is the number of weeks in the sample, and W/N is the ratio of weeks to months, a number slightly greater than four. To be a pure monthly and weekly subcycle, we would want the a's to sum to one and the b's to sum to zero. If either condition is imposed on the regression, then the other is automatically satisfied from the point-of-means property. The problem with imposing constraints on the sum of either the monthly or weekly coefficients is that one cannot simply use the typical regression package. Specialized programming is usually necessary. In the implementations known to the authors, two procedures used as substitutes to constrained regression have been: (1) to estimate the coefficients without constraint and then adjust the estimated values to give revised estimates, namely

$$a_t^* = a_t / \sum_{i=1}^{M} a_i$$

$$b_w^* = b_w - \sum_{j=1}^{5} (b_j/5);$$

(2) to use the coefficients as estimated to obtain a first-pass forecast of a nonmajor component and then renormalize the forecast so that the forecasted monthly total is correct. In the cases known to the authors, these substitutes to constrained estimation have worked reasonably well, in part because the output of the unconstrained regression has usually been close to satisfying the constraints so that adjustments of either type have been minor.

and weekday upon which it occurred is provided as input to a regression package. The regression output is a set of a's and b's for each component.

3. *Predicted Monthly Totals.* From the cash budget for the month, the total flow for each component is obtained and the major items are subtracted, leaving the forecast of the total nonmajor flow for each component.

4. *Distribution of Nonmajor Flows.* The regression coefficients are used to distribute the nonmajor flows over the workdays of the month (in accordance with procedures to be described).

5. *Overall Forecast.* The various nonmajor components are combined to obtain a forecast of the net nonmajor flow. The major components are added to obtain an overall forecast of the net daily flow.

USING THE REGRESSION COEFFICIENTS TO DISTRIBUTE THE MONTHLY FORECAST

Assume that we have been provided a forecast of the total nonmajor disbursements and deposits for a month. These forecasts of monthly totals are converted into a daily forecast of each component by distributing the total over the workdays of the month. To illustrate, let us consider disbursements. Let DIS_t denote the level of disbursements of day t. If the thirteenth workday of the month were a Friday, then the forecast for disbursements on day 13 would be

$$DIS_{13} = (a_{13} + b_5)$$

(Forecast of Total Nonmajor Disbursements for the Month).

If the forecast of total disbursements for the month were \$60 million, and if a_{13} and b_5 were .040 and .010 respectively, then the forecast for disbursements on day 13 would be

$$DIS_{13} = (.040 + .010)(\$60,000,000) = \$3,000,000.$$

Exhibit 3 provides a sample set of numerical values for the coefficients

EXHIBIT 3. Sample Calculation For Distribution of a \$60 Million Monthly Forecast of Disbursements over the Workdays of the Month

Work-day	Value of a_t	Fraction Predicted For a Given Day*	First-Pass Forecast**	Renormalized Forecast***
1	.045	$a_1 + b_3 = .025$	1,500	1,531
2	.050	$a_2 + b_4 = .030$	1,800	1,837
3	.060	$a_3 + b_5 = .070$	4,200	4,286
4	.065	$a_4 + b_1 = .095$	5,700	5,816
5	.070	$a_5 + b_2 = .070$	4,200	4,286
6	.070	$a_6 + b_3 = .050$	3,000	3,061
7	.065	$a_7 + b_4 = .045$	2,700	2,755
8	.060	$a_8 + b_5 = .070$	4,200	4,286
9	.055	$a_9 + b_1 = .085$	5,100	5,204
10	.050	$a_{10} + b_2 = .050$	3,000	3,061
11	.050	$a_{11} + b_3 = .030$	1,800	1,837
12	.045	$a_{12} + b_4 = .025$	1,500	1,531
13	.040	$a_{13} + b_5 = .050$	3,000	3,061
14	.030	$a_{14} + b_1 = .060$	3,600	3,673
15	.030	$a_{15} + b_2 = .030$	1,800	1,837
16	.025	$a_{16} + b_3 = .005$	300	306
17	.030	$a_{17} + b_4 = .010$	600	612
18	.035	$a_{18} + b_5 = .045$	2,700	2,755
19	.040	$a_{19} + b_1 = .070$	4,200	4,286
20	.040	$a_{20} + b_2 = .040$	2,400	2,449
21	.045	$a_{21} + b_3 = .025$	1,500	1,531
	1,000	+.980	58,800	60,001

* Values of b_1, b_2, b_3, b_4, b_5 were taken to be .030, .000, -.020, -.020, and .010 respectively.

** In thousands of dollars.

***In thousands of dollars, rounded to nearest thousand.

and provides a detailed example of how the model distributes the total monthly forecast over the days of the month. In this example, the total of the daily predictions from the first-pass forecast does not equal the monthly total from the cash budget. When there is not an integral number of weeks in a month, this equality is generally not guaranteed. To ensure that the sum of the daily predictions equals the appropriate monthly total, we can "renormalize" the first-pass prediction by scaling each forecast by an appropriate amount to ensure that the daily totals are consistent with the monthly total. The final column in Exhibit 3 gives the renormalized forecast.

An alternative to renormalizing is to treat the difference as a day-of-week distortion and use carry-over adjustments to reflect the day-of-week shift between months. For instance, in the example of Exhibit 3, the first-pass total is low because the month starts and ends on Wednesday, a day for which the cash flow is below average. With the carry-over adjustment, part of this month's shortage would be shifted to the start of the next month rather than being spread over the entire month. The advantage of carry-over adjustments over renormalizing is avoidance of spreading compensating errors occurring at the start and end of a month over the entire month. The disadvantage is greater complexity. Because the effect is small (usually less than 2%), most companies using the technique opt for the less accurate but simpler procedure of renormalizing.

MODEL PERFORMANCE: RESULTS FROM AN IMPLEMENTATION

Exhibits 4 and 5 plot actual and forecasted cash flows and the cumulative forecast error for an implementation of the dummy-variable approach in a company in which cash flows were divided into three components—disbursements and two classes of deposits.

EXHIBIT 4. Comparison of the Actual and Forecasted Nonmajor Cash Flows for August

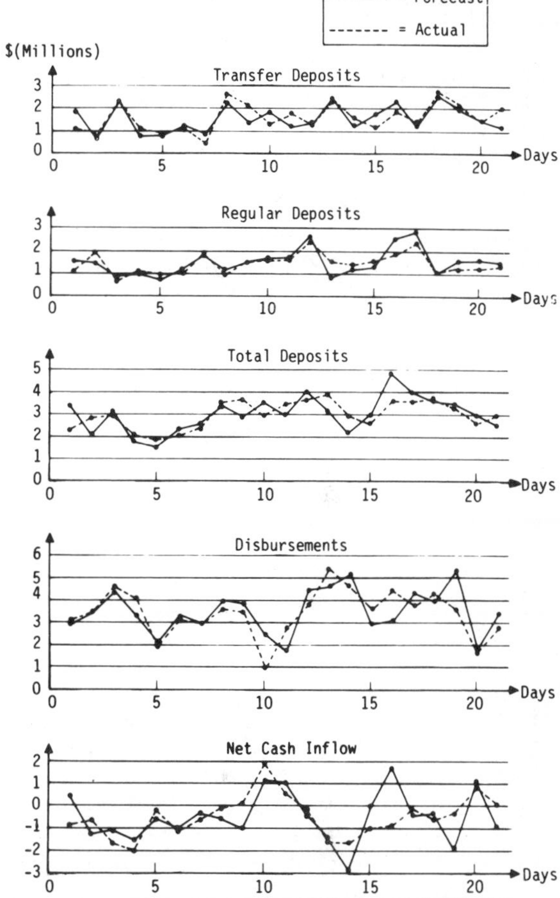

Transfer deposits were all deposits originating from gathering banks. *Regular deposits* were all the others that were processed through the company's regular deposit processing center.

The primary reason for distinguishing between the two deposit classes was different float characteristics. To see evidence of this difference in Exhibit 4, note that the peak of the weekly cycle (the high points occurring at five-day intervals) is one day later for transfer deposits than for regular deposits. If one shifts the plot for transfer deposits backward one day to reflect the delay within the banking system, then the peaks and valleys tend to line up.

EXHIBIT 5. A Plot of the Cumulative Forecast Error for Each Cash Flow Component and the Net Cash Inflow

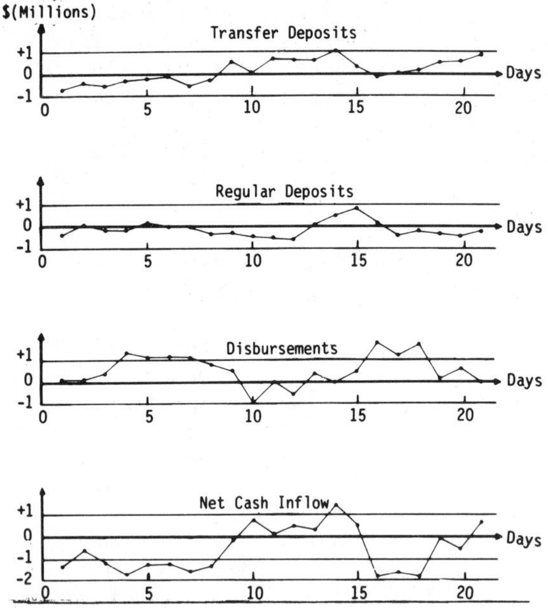

This one-day shift shows why it was necessary to divide deposits into two classes to achieve statistical stability. In fact, an attempt to use only total deposits produced very poor results with both low significance to the regression coefficients and large forecast errors.

In the forecast system illustrated in Exhibits 4 and 5, the initial measurement of the monthly and weekly cycles was based on data taken from eighteen months of past bank statements. After removing major flows, the daily fraction of each nonmajor flow and the workday and weekday on which it occurred were entered into a standard regression package. The output was a set of a's and b's for disbursements, for regular deposits, and for transfer deposits. The total nonmajor flows were then obtained from the cash budget and distributed over the workdays of the month using the procedures illustrated in Exhibit 3. The overall forecast was obtained by adding together nonmajor regular and transfer deposits, subtracting nonmajor disbursements, and adding in the major flows.

The forecast performance depicted in Exhibits 4 and 5 is typical of the model's results when the monthly cash budget is reasonably accurate. For the most part, the predicted and actual flows are close. The magnitude of the average daily error ranges from 12% to 20% in the various components. Day-to-day errors are negatively correlated, i.e., a positive error on one day tends to be followed by a negative error on the next day and vice versa. In Exhibit 4, this negative correlation is reflected by the crisscrossing of actual and forecasted flows. The primary source of error is having part of a cash flow a day or two early or late. In effect, the model provides fairly good forecasts to within a three- to four-day interval but has some large daily errors.

NECESSARY ACCURACY

The concept of necessary accuracy is an important one for evaluating the adequacy of a daily cash forecast. Conventional cash management practice is to specify a target balance and make daily adjustments to attain the target. An alternative is to use smoothing techniques such as those presented in Stone [14]. With smoothing, a company allows the balance to fluctuate around the target as long as it stays within predefined control limits, in which case no action is taken. If both the actual and projected balance exceed the limits, then the balance is adjusted by an amount that restores the expected balance to the target at the end of the smoothing interval, say five to ten business days. With smoothing, the issue is not daily accuracy but rather the accuracy over the smoothing interval. Because smoothing averages out daily errors, its use solves much of the accuracy problem by dramatically reducing the required accuracy. For instance, with a five-day smoothing period, an average daily error of 25% is less significant than one of 5% with the conventional practice of trying to hit a daily target.[4]

In Exhibit 5, the cumulative forecast error for the net nonmajor flow never deviated by more than two million from zero. Thus, with control limits of two million about this company's twenty-plus million target balance, errors in this company's nonmajor flow would not have required any adjustment in the cash balance (other than possibly a single shift in the balance level near the end of the month to make sure the average balance is on target). With smoothing, the forecast accuracy depicted in Exhibits 4 and 5 is clearly adequate.

ACHIEVABLE ACCURACY

An important concept for daily cash forecasting is "achievable accuracy." One source of uncertainty is the extent to which a cash flow can be accurately scheduled on a given day. Exhibit 4 shows a tendency for a large positive error one day to be followed by a large negative error the next. These situations represent a misplacement of a portion of the cash flow by a day. Such errors arise from variations in mail receipt, internal processing, and/or bank clearing time. Such variations shift a portion of a given day's normal flow forward or back a day. Statistical procedures can only capture the average flow on a given day. They cannot predict random fluctuations from the average although the past deviations can indicate the likelihood of such errors. While these one-day shifts in the timing of cash flows place a limit on the daily accuracy achievable for a daily forecast, they are not a problem for an attempt to place cash flows within a time interval of several days. Thus, such timing errors are inconsequential for a cash manager using smoothing techniques.

For distribution approaches, the accuracy of the cash budget places an inherent limitation on the accuracy of the daily forecast. An error in the cash budget input will be spread over the daily forecast. Over the course of the month, the cumulative error will build up to equal the total cash budget error.

ERROR DETECTION AND FORECAST CONTROL

Both predicted and actual cash flows should be monitored and the cumulative error measured for each component and for the total. If the monthly forecasts are reasonably accurate, the cumulative errors will stay near zero as in Exhibit 5. For an erroneous monthly total, however, the cumulative errors usually build up gradually. Therefore, tracking the cumulative daily error provides a control check on each nonmajor forecast component. Thus, tracking the cumulative error provides an early warning system for control checks on the monthly cash budget.

EXTENSIONS AND REFINEMENTS

HOLIDAY DISTURBANCES

Holidays disturb the normal cash flow pattern in several ways. First, on bank holidays, no disbursements or deposits are cleared at the bank; therefore, the cash flows that would normally occur on the holiday are shifted to subsequent workdays. Second, mail is delayed. Third, normal company processing is typically delayed so that some of the cash flow that would normally have occurred right after the holiday is delayed and shifted to subsequent days.

Because the essence of holiday effects is to shift flows that would normally occur on the holiday and days immediately following to subsequent

[4] This argument is based on equivalent variances. The variance of a five-day average of independent identically distributed random variables is one-fifth the daily variance. With negative correlation, it is less than one-fifth.

days, we can treat holiday effects by first predicting the normal flow that would occur in the absence of the holiday and then shifting these flows to reflect holiday delays. To illustrate this procedure quantitatively, let NF_0, NF_1, and NF_2 denote the normal flow for a cash flow component on the holiday and the two subsequent workdays, predicted on the basis of normal monthly and weekly patterns *before* adjustment for the holiday disburbance is made. Let RF_0, RF_1, and RF_2 denote the revised flow on the holiday and on the two subsequent workdays that reflect the holiday disturbances. The revised predictions can be related to the normal flows by the expressions:

$$RF_0 = 0$$

$$RF_1 = C_{10}NF_0 + C_{11}NF_1$$

$$RF_2 = C_{20}NF_0 + C_{21}NF_1 + NF_2 .$$

The C's measure holiday shifts. For instance, C_{10} and C_{20} measure the extent to which the flow that would normally occur on the holiday is shifted to the two subsequent workdays. Typical values of C_{10} and C_{20} might be .9 and .1 . Their sum should be one. Their measurement is based on the shift in normal patterns evidenced in past data. While more statistically sophisticated and accurate measures of holiday shifts are possible, this simple shift is reasonable to reflect holiday effects without becoming bogged down in unjustifiably complex measurement problems.

Holiday effects are actually more complex than the single set of holiday shifts would imply. The shift typically depends on the day of the week on which the holiday occurs, although it is generally sufficient to treat two cases—"midweek holidays" (Tuesday, Wednesday, or Thursday) and "weekend holidays" (Friday or Monday). Two-day holidays must be treated as a separate case from one-day holidays. Company holidays that are not bank holidays involve different shifts from the normal situation of a holiday for both banks and the company. Further complexity arises when there are holidays in some states and not in others.

A word of caution is in order here. We know of companies that have tried to treat all the many different holiday variations and foolishly spent more money and time on this problem than justified by any possible benefit from increased accuracy. The fact is that data are usually inadequate to measure meaningfully the parameters necessary to treat the many possible situations. As we have already indicated, such accuracy is unnecessary when cash management procedures take advantage of smoothing techniques that only require placement of the shifted cash flow within the smoothing interval. Thus, smoothing procedures solve much of the holiday problem by "dissolving it" in the sense of making a precise measurement of the holiday shift unnecessary. Smoothing allows the good cash manager to handle most of the holiday variations via judgmental adjustments to the type of holiday shift we have presented above.

ADAPTIVE PARAMETERS

As time passes, the typical company's cash flow patterns shift. Cash flow patterns must be remeasured. When the shift is gradual, an alternative to periodic updating is monthly revision to reflect the most current data. Adaptation to gradual changes can be enhanced by estimating parameters using a regression procedure (generalized least-squares) that gives greater weight to more recent data. Or, an alternative is to use sophisticated averaging techniques such as those described in references [1, 2, 4, 11]. Such refinements are theoretically interesting and promise greater accuracy in the presence of changing cash flow patterns, but all the companies that we know to be using some variant of this approach use periodic updating, generally on an annual basis.

LEVEL OF DETAIL AND DATA CAPTURE FROM BANK STATEMENTS

We have stressed the need to divide the nonmajor flows into components in order to obtain cash flows that have statistically stable patterns. Up to a point, using more components generally provides more homogeneous cash flows with more stable cash flow patterns.

Wages should almost always be separated from nonmajor payables. Wages should generally be further divided into monthly, biweekly, and weekly payments. Separating wages from nonmajor payables is usually easy because most companies use different bank accounts for wages and for regular vendor disbursements. In fact, it is common to use different accounts for different classes of wages. Hence, bank statements are usually organized to facilitate the measurement of cash flow patterns at this level of detail.

Another logical basis for division into components is operating group, subsidiary, or product line. For instance, products with different credit terms will usually have different cash flow patterns. The fact that different operating units usually have different bank accounts may mean that bank statement data is already organized into logical components, although distinctions on bases such as credit terms are rarely made in setting up bank accounts. Moreover, a company's cash budget typically does not distinguish sales by credit class.

In using dummy-variable regression, it is common to implement the model initially at a fairly coarse level of detail dictated by available data. Then, the logical cash flow components are identified and the appropriate bank accounts are set up using zero-balance accounts, which affords the informational benefits of considerable account detail at virtually no cost and no increase in cash management effort. With zero-balance accounts, the banking system can be used for data collection at very little cost.

The advantages of more component detail are greater statistical stability, less sensitivity of cash flow patterns to changes in the business environment, and the potential for close forecast control. The disadvantage is greater measurement and administrative effort. Often, a limitation to increased accuracy from more component detail is less accurate cash budget input for more detailed components. Interestingly, the motivation for more component detail is often not accuracy for cash management *per se* but rather conditional accuracy for detecting cash budget errors for control purposes.

SYNTHESIS

PROBLEM STRUCTURING

In many companies, daily cash forecasting has been viewed as an almost impossible task. Inability to obtain reasonable daily forecasts (according to most reports known to us) arises from failure to structure the problem properly. Our experience indicates that statistical procedures that are not particularly sophisticated or powerful seem to work well when the problem is properly structured.

A distribution approach is the key to structuring the problem for the use of statistical techniques. Distribution reduces the statistical task to estimating intramonth cash flow patterns. It relies on the cash budget for specifying the level of cash flows including recognizing the problem of intermonth patterns.

Key devices for providing the intramonth stability necessary to make distribution work include separating major from nonmajor flows, focusing on components of the flow rather than the total, resolving the component flows into cycles and subcycles, using workday of the month rather than calendar day as the forecast unit, and treating holiday effects as a disturbance to the basic pattern.

DUMMY-VARIABLE REGRESSION: ADVANTAGES AND LIMITATIONS

We have presented dummy-variable regression as a particular statistical technique for estimating cash flow patterns, in this case a monthly and weekly cycle. While we have illustrated the technique in the context of a one-step forecast, it can also be applied to the usual two-step procedure.

The advantages of a dummy-variable approach are simplicity, ease of implementation, low-cost administrative effort, and, when used in a one-step framework, dependence only on data available from bank statements. Crucial to the successful use of such simple techniques is recognition that smoothing procedures can greatly reduce required accuracy compared to the conventional practice of trying to hit a daily target exactly.

These advantages have associated with them some potential limitations. First, there is a trade-off between simplicity and completeness. With a simple technique, one usually gives up some of the theoretically attainable accuracy. Second, this technique (like any distribution approach) depends on the accuracy of the cash budget. Errors in the cash budget will affect the daily forecast accuracy and lead to cumulative errors. While bad for accuracy, such errors are a basis for control checks on the monthly cash budget. Third, cash flow patterns may shift over time. If the shifts are distributed over a number of months, then the use of adaptively measured parameters can mitigate forecast deterioration. But an abrupt change (such as when a company significantly alters its operating policy, credit terms, banking system, or disbursement and collection practices) typically causes a time delay before enough data are available to estimate accurately the new monthly and weekly cycles. When there is an abrupt shift, a cash forecaster is forced to rely on judgmental estimates of cash flow patterns. Then, as enough data become available, the judgment can be refined and ultimately replaced by a statistical estimate.[5]

These limitations are illustrated by the recent experience of a large multiproduct company in experimenting with variants of the dummy-variable approach. Because the company had been using a fairly sophisticated daily forecasting system for several years, there was a readily available data base and an alternative system to serve as a standard for comparison. An initial test was based on three years of past data in which two years of data were used to parameterize the model and the third year's data were used for forecast comparison.

Test results were mixed. For nonmajor vendor disbursements, the magnitude of average daily forecast error for the twelve monthly forecasts was on the order of 30% versus 5% for the actual performance of the company's own system. For deposits, the model was better—average errors of about 20% versus about 5% for the company's actual system. The poor performance on disbursements was expected since the company exercised discretionary stretching of payables to smooth its cash balance. Such discretionary stretching is a source of statistical instability that hurts the dummy-variable approach but not an information-system-based scheduling approach that does not rely on statistical

[5] We are indebted to a reviewer for pointing out that this process can be viewed in Bayesian terms as the formulation of an initial prior that is updated monthly as new data become available. Once a large number of observations are available, the data would normally dominate the prior.

projections. For deposits, about half the forecast error was imputable to the input from the monthly cash budget, an error source absent from the scheduling-based system of the company, a daily variant of the payment-pattern approach described in Stone [13]. Had the cash budget input been accurate, the comparative performance on deposits would have been roughly 10% versus 5% average daily errors.

While this company's experimentation with dummy-variable regression is still going on, it is clear that distribution based on dummy-variable regression is not competitive with the company's more sophisticated forecasting system for a thirty-day forecast. Nevertheless, dummy-variable based forecasts are a useful complement to the company's current system.

Because the accuracy of a scheduling-based approach deteriorates rapidly beyond thirty days, one use is a longer-term, weekly forecast for months three through six. A second is start-of-month cash budget control based on comparison of the distribution-based and scheduling-based forecasts. The fact that one forecast depends on the cash budget and the other does not is critical for this control comparison to work.

We cite the experience of this company for several reasons. One is to indicate the trade-off between accuracy and simplicity. A second is to note that company discretion (such as stretching payables) can produce instabilities that are difficult to measure statistically. A third is to illustrate that one forecasting system may complement another, in this case, by being better for cash-budget control and longer-term forecasts.

APPLICABILITY AND COMPANY SIZE

Daily cash forecasts in general are of limited usefulness to companies with annual sales under $20 million. The company with annual sales in the $20 million to $50 million range represents a gray area. Such companies often have average cash balances in excess of those necessary to compensate their banks. Forecast information typically reduces required transaction balances and enables such a company to reduce bank borrowing and/or to become a periodic investor in money market instruments. For such companies, the simplicity and low cost of the regression-based forecast are especially important. Simply investing an additional $100,000 over the year usually exceeds the development cost. The authors have found, however, that such companies often lack the accurate and detailed cash budget input necessary to use a distribution approach.

The regression-based forecasting methodology is probably most applicable to intermediate-sized companies, say those with annual sales of $50 million to $500 million. Very large companies can usually justify more sophisticated forecasting systems. However, as the case discussed previously indicates, even very large companies may find the approach a useful complement to more sophisticated systems. Moreover, large companies that do not now have a sophisticated daily forecasting system may find distribution approaches using this methodology a useful step toward their ultimate system.

REFERENCES

1. G.E. Box and G.M. Jenkins, *Time Series Analysis,* San Francisco, Holden-Day, Inc., 1970.
2. K. Boyd and V.A. Mabert, "A Two Stage Forecasting Approach at Chemical Bank of New York for Check Processing," *Journal of Bank Research* (Summer 1977), pp. 101-07.
3. R.G. Brown, *Smoothing, Forecasting, and Prediction of Discrete Time Series,* Englewood Cliffs, New Jersey, Prentice-Hall, Inc., 1963.
4. J.C. Chambers, S.K. Mullick, and D.D. Smith, *An Executive's Guide to Forecasting,* New York, John Wiley and Sons, Inc., 1974.

5. N.R. Draper and H. Smith, *Applied Regression Analysis,* New York, John Wiley and Sons, Inc., 1966.
6. J. Johnston, *Econometric Methods,* 2nd ed., New York, McGraw Hill Book Co., 1972.
7. D.W. Jorgenson, "Minimum Variance, Linear, Unbiased Seasonal Adjustments of Economic Time Series," *Journal of the American Statistical Association* (September 1964), pp. 681-724.
8. G.W. Ladd, "Regression Analysis of Seasonal Data," *Journal of the American Statistical Association* (June 1964), pp. 402-21.
9. M.C. Lovell, "Alternative Axiomatization of Seasonal Adjustment," *Journal of the American Statistical Association* (September 1966), pp. 800-802.
10. M.C. Lovell, "Seasonal Adjustments of Economic Time Series and Multiple Regression Analysis," *Journal of the American Statistical Association* (December 1963), pp. 993-1010.
11. J.O. McClain, "Dynamics of Exponential Smoothing with Trend and Seasonal Terms," *Management Science* (May 1974), pp. 1300-1304.
12. V.A. Mabert, "Forecast Modification Based Upon Residual Analysis: A Case Study of Check Volume Estimation," Working Paper No. 565 of the Krannert Graduate School of Industrial Administration, Purdue University (September 1976).
13. B.K. Stone, "The Payments-Pattern Approach to the Forecasting and Control of Accounts Receivable," *Financial Management* (Fall 1976), pp. 61-78.
14. B.K. Stone, "The Use of Forecasts and Smoothing in Control-Limit Models for Cash Management," *Financial Management* (Spring 1972), pp. 72-84.
15. D.B. Suits, "Use of Dummy Variables in Regression Equations," *Journal of the American Statistical Association* (March 1957), pp. 548-51.
16. R.J. Wonnacott and T.H. Wonnacott, *Econometrics,* New York, John Wiley and Sons Inc., 1970, pp. 74-76.

READING 10

Cash Management: A Systems Approach

Gerald Pogue
City University of New York

Russell Faucett
Massachusetts Institute of Technology

Ralph Bussard
Condon Computer Utilities

INTRODUCTION

Corporations maintain cash balances for essentially three reasons. First, the inflow and outflow of cash payments are not perfectly synchronized; an inventory of cash is therefore necessary to buffer these flows. Second, future cash flows and interest rates are uncertain; therefore, corporations hold cash to insure themselves against adverse events. Third, corporations use cash balances to compensate their banks for a variety of services that may be provided. This article focuses on the problem of determining the optimal level of cash balances needed to support a firm's banking system. The model described below determines the optimal level and inter-bank allocation of cash balances by which the total cost of the corporation's banking system is minimized. Total cost includes the opportunity cost of maintaining cash balances and the service fees paid directly to the banks. In addition to determining the optimal allocation of cash balances, the model specifies the best strategy for the firm's checking and deposit activity within the system. As will be discussed later, the model is also extremely useful for evaluating proposed changes in the structure of the firm's banking system (e.g., adding or deleting banks).

The general approach to this problem was developed by Robert Calman.[1] In this article, we present a brief description of an extended version of Calman's model and an application to the cash management problem of a large eastern corporation.

BANK SERVICES

The services that banks provide to corporations can be separated into two categories: tangible and intangible. Tangible services include disbursement and payroll accounts, collection of deposits, stock registration and transfer, current lines of credit or term loans, and retail and wholesale lock boxes. The latter are post office boxes maintained by banks for corporate

[1] See Calman [1], for a detailed discussion of the underlying model.

Reprinted from INDUSTRIAL MANAGEMENT REVIEW (now SLOAN MANAGEMENT REVIEW) (Winter 1970), pp. 55-74, by permission of the publisher.

customers in geographic areas where company customers are located. Customers mail their remittances to a designated lock box, rather than to a more distant company accounting center, where they are collected and processed directly by the bank responsible for the box. Essentially, lock box banking speeds up cash inflow by reducing the number of stages and days before a company sees the tangible balance-sheet benefit of its customers' payments. Three processes are reduced: the postal time between the point of mailing and the actual receipt of the check; the delay in processing the mail and depositing remittances in the bank; and the "in transit" clearing time within the banking system between the bank of deposit and the bank on which the check is drawn.

The most important intangible service is the call on future credit from the bank. By maintaining high cash balances a corporation can insure the future availability of credit from its banks. Other intangibles include special work analogous to that provided by an independent management consulting firm: advice on mergers, international business, or economic conditions, for example. Any special services that the bank provides to corporate employees would also be intangible services.

Banks are compensated for their services by cash balances, fees, and tax payments. Traditionally, banks have been compensated by the cash balances that corporations keep in their demand accounts. The bank computes a service charge credit on the demand deposit balance in order to offset part or all of the cost of services provided. Fees have commonly been the form of compensation for stock certificate registration and transfer. Recently, some banks have established fees for wholesale and retail lock box services. To a lesser extent, banks have drawn up fee schedules for intangible services such as checking, payroll processing, and deposit collection. A firm can also pay for its banking services by directing corporate tax payments into a "Tax and Loan Account" at the bank. The bank can then compute a service charge credit on these balances because the United States Treasury will generally not withdraw funds from the account for eight to 10 days after deposit.

The use of fees as compensation is generally restricted to the tangible services related to checking, deposit, stock certification, and payroll activity. Cash balances, on the other hand, compensate the bank for all services, tangible and intangible. In addition, they serve as compensation for bank credit. Tax payments, like cash balances, act as compensation for all services. Since demand deposits are a primary source of the bank's investment funds, many banks restrict the use of fees and tax payments to a small fraction of the total compensation.

Determination of the proper level of bank compensation is one of the more awkward problems of cash and bank management for a corporation. Banks have traditionally been extremely reluctant to release price schedules for their services. Increased competition between banks for lock box business however has produced full schedules for that service. In addition, some banks have released schedules for the tangible services of checking, deposits, and payroll, but more often than not, these have been "cost" schedules and not full prices. Banks continue to allow their customers to determine the proper level of compensation for services provided. Banks, however, are no different from other service organizations, especially in terms of tangible services. Consequently, there is no reason why they should not supply their customers with price schedules for the services they provide.

The general model developed by Calman and the application described here assume that management, in collaboration with its various banks, has determined prices for tangible services and estimated the approximate level of compensation for intangible services. Hence the price, not cost, of processing a check, a deposit, or a payroll are known. Furthermore, the level of compensating cash balances required by current credit agreements and the associated service charge credits are established. The value of an intangible, such as advice on international business, is estimated by determining its price as if it had been provided by another source that charged for the service.

DISBURSEMENT AND DEPOSIT FLOAT

Generally, the amount of funds available to a company in its bank account will be different from the cash balances indicated in the corporation's ledger. This difference is the cumulative result of a series of delays in the payment of the checks written by the company and the collection of checks received by the company. The difference is referred to as float. Checks written by the company will generally result in disbursement or "positive" float, which is an excess of bank net collected balances over corporate book balances. Conversely, checks received by the company and deposited in the banking system tend to result in deposit or "negative" float--an excess of book balances over bank net collected balances. These concepts will be illustrated below.

Figure I illustrates the principal sources of disbursement float. The float is caused by (1) the mailing time to the firm's creditor, (2) the creditor's delay in processing the check, and (3) the normal check collection time in the banking system. As an example of disbursement float, consider a corporation that disburses checks at a rate of one million dollars per day, and assume that a five-day delay exists before checks are presented to the firm's bank for payment. Under steady

Figure I

SOURCES OF DISBURSEMENT FLOAT

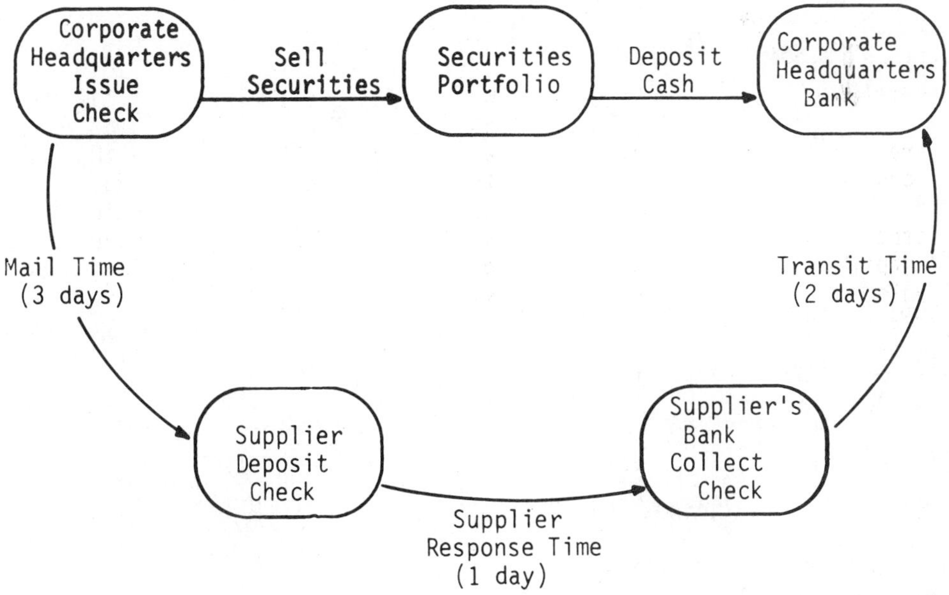

Figure II

SOURCES OF DEPOSIT FLOAT

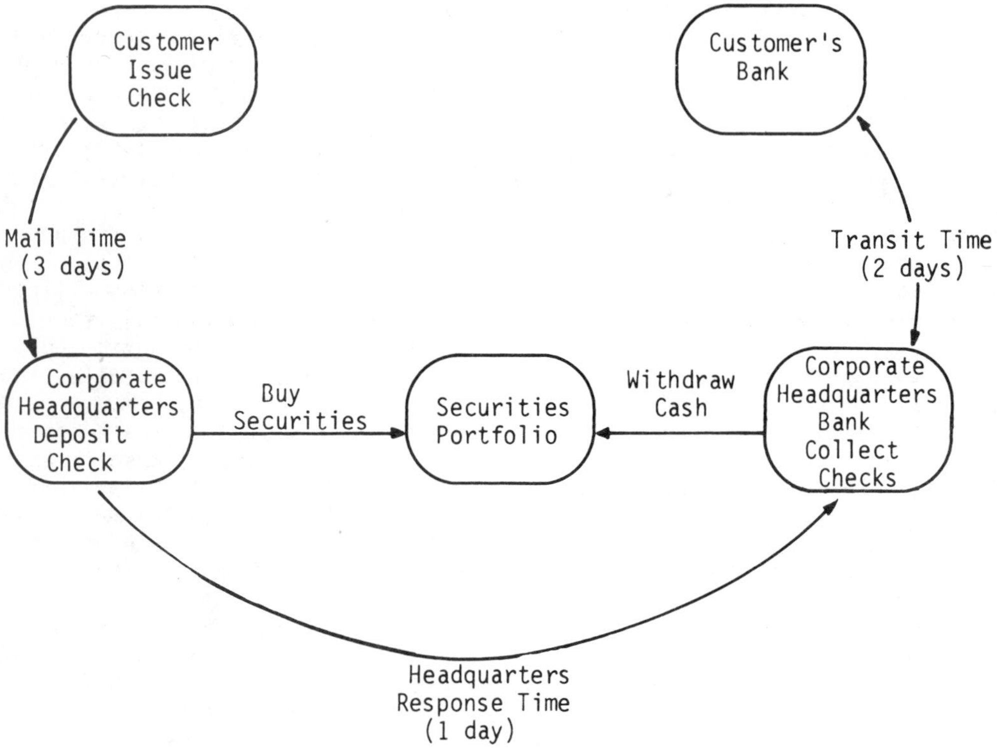

state conditions, a positive float balance of 5 million dollars will result. In other words, five days worth of checks are always in the "payment pipeline" illustrated in Figure I. Now, if the company sells some of its marketable securities at an equal rate, one million dollars per day, and deposits this amount in its bank account, the corporate book balance will always be zero. Its bank balance, however, will equal 5 million dollars. An interesting opportunity now becomes evident. By delaying the transfer of cash from the marketable securities portfolio to its bank account, the firm can continue to earn a return on those funds, while simultaneously maintaining a desired positive level of bank balances. If, for example, the firm delayed the transfer for three days, an average bank balance of 2 million dollars would result. In effect, the firm is maintaining a negative book balance by investing part of the disbursement float. Now, in an actual situation, the firm will not be able to predict the size of float balances exactly, so caution must be taken in the utilization of expected float balances. More will be said about this problem later.

As might be expected, deposit float works to the disadvantage of the corporation. Figure II illustrates the main stages involved in the cash collection process. The volume of deposit float is proportional to the interval from the time the corporation records the incoming check in its ledger to the time the funds are physically in its bank account. A further collection delay indicated in the figure is the mail time between the customer's location and the company's offices. However, this delay tends to manifest itself in accounts receivable balances rather than deposit float. Through the use of a lock box, the "in mail" and "H.Q. response" times can be reduced.

As an illustration of the relationship among book, bank, and deposit float balances, assume that a company receives customer remittances at the rate of one million dollars in checks per day and that these funds are invested in marketable securities *after* they have been collected by the firm's bank. This policy results in a zero net collected balance and a corporate book balance equal to the dollar value of deposit float. Thus, rather than being able to invest part of the float and still maintain positive bank balances, as in the disbursement case, the firm must now maintain a cash balance in excess of the amount of deposit float if it wishes to maintain a positive net collected balance. In a more normal situation, where both disbursement and deposit activities are carried on, both types of float will exist simultaneously and the net float becomes the important factor.

As evidenced in the previous discussion, the net float balance resulting from a given dollar rate of disbursements and remittances is due to the cumulative effects of various payment and collection delays, none of which can be predicted exactly. In the model described below, we have attempted to deal with this prediction problem by treating the float balances generated by different types of corporate activities as random variables. As such, it becomes necessary to evaluate the float characteristics of each major disbursement and deposit activity separately.

The probability distribution for a particular type of disbursement float can be easily estimated from the collection data stamped on the backs of processed checks. The "in transit" time for deposit items can be known with certainty if the firm's bank enters its checks into the Federal Reserve System for collection, which is the normal procedure. The funds are automatically available after a predetermined number of days (maximum of two), depending on the geographic proximity of the firm and customer banks.

The model developed below is an extension of the original Cash Alpha Model. Our extended version permits the allocation of negative book balances to banks in the system where favorable float characteristics and other considerations exist.[2] Without this extension, the firm could be in the undesirable position of having net collected balances in excess of the amounts needed to adequately compensate its system of banks. Given the possibility of negative corporate ledger balances, it becomes vital to consider the amount of uncertainty associated with projected float balances. For banks where only small average balances are to be maintained, neglect of the random nature of future float could lead to a high frequency of overdrafts (negative net collected balances). In our version of Cash Alpha, we have extended Calman's expected value treatment of float to consider the random character of the float coefficients explicitly.

DESCRIPTION OF THE MODEL

Once the prices of tangible services, the imputed value of intangible services, and the float characteristics of the firm's various checking and deposit activities have been established, the problem becomes one of determining the cash balances and activity levels that minimize the cost of the firm's banking system. This can be formulated as a linear programming problem.

The objective of the model is to minimize the sum of service fees and the opportunity costs of allocating cash balances to the banks in the system. This is achieved by assigning tangible activities (such as checks, deposits, tax payments) and cash ledger balances

---

[2] The use of negative book balances is a reasonably common industrial practice.

to banks so that each bank will be adequately compensated for its services at the lowest total cost to the firm. The cost of maintaining cash balances is the return that cash would yield if it were invested in an alternative use having the same risk. For most corporations, this alternative use would be investment in short-term securities. Hence, the cost of cash allocated to the banking system would be approximately 7 percent to 8 percent per year.

Two additional assumptions regarding company cash ledger balances are implicit in the model.

1. The firm's cash ledger balances are decreased or increased at the time when checks are issued or received by the corporation and not when the funds are paid out or collected by the banks.

2. Disbursement float is assumed to have zero direct cost to the firm. (However, as seen above, it does have an indirect opportunity cost since a dollar of ledger balances can be replaced by a dollar of disbursement float balances with no effect on the level of net collected balances.)

The primary decision variables in the model are defined below.

BAL_k = the average company ledger cash balance assigned to bank k during the period under consideration,[3] where $k = 1, \cdots, k\text{max}$, and $k$max is the number of banks in the firm's banking system.

FEE_k = the fees to be paid to bank k during the period.

X_{ijk} = disbursing activity variable, i.e., the number of checks to be issued during the period (1) by financial center i (the various company divisions, where $i = 1, \cdots, i\text{max}$; (2) of type j (vendor, payroll tax, etc.) where $j = 1, \cdots, j\text{max}$; (3) on bank k, where $k = 1, \cdots, k\text{max}$.

Y_{imk} = a deposit activity variable, i.e., the number of deposit items processed during the period (1) by financial center i, where $i = 1, \cdots, i\text{max}$; (2) of type m (customer location), where $m = 1, \cdots, m\text{max}$; (3) sent to bank k for collection, where $k = 1, \cdots, k\text{max}$.

The objective function is then given by

$$\text{Minimize } Z = \rho(T\text{BAL}) + T\text{FEE}$$

where ρ is the opportunity cost of ledger cash balances; TBAL is the total cash ledger balance of the corporation; and TFEE is the total amount of fees paid by the company.

This minimization is subject to certain constraints, which can be separated into two categories: global constraints and individual bank constraints. The global constraints are as follows:

1. The total cash ledger balance of the system is the sum of the cash ledger balances associated with each bank.

$$T\text{BAL} = \sum_{k=1}^{k\text{max}} \text{BAL}_k$$

2. The total amount of fees paid is the sum of the fees paid to each bank.

$$T\text{FEE} = \sum_{k=1}^{k\text{max}} \text{FEE}_k$$

3. The total number of checks and deposits distributed to banks by each financial center must equal the expected activity during the period. Thus, for each financial center i we have:

---

[3] In the linear programming formulation actually used, we have replaced the variable BAL_k with the pair of variables BAL_k^+ and BAL_k^- where $BAL_k = BAL_k^+ - BAL_k^-$. This substitution allows the ledger cash balance to assume negative as well as positive values.

$$\sum_{k=1}^{k\max} X_{ijk} = \hat{X}_{ij},\ j = 1, \cdots, j\max$$

$$\sum_{k=1}^{k\max} Y_{imk} = \hat{Y}_{im},\ m = 1, \cdots, m\max$$

where $\hat{X}_{ij}$ is the expected number of checks of type j that will be issued by financial center i in the next month, and $\hat{Y}_{im}$ is the expected number of deposits of type m that will be processed by financial center i in the next month.

In the application described below, the firm has four financial centers. For the month of May 1969, the activities and projected levels are shown in Table I. Consequently, the above financial center requirements result in 12 equality constraints.

The individual bank constraints describe the relationship between the company and each bank in the system. These constraints will be illustrated using one bank from the banking system in the application. This bank, New England Citizens, processes vendor disbursements, payroll checks, and deposits for two of the firm's divisions (see Tables II and III). In addition, it maintains a line of credit to the company and provides advice on international financial conditions. There is a similar set of constraints for each bank in the system.

1. Expected Float Balances Definition Constraint--The expected average disbursement float balances (positive float) during the month associated with each bank are the sum of the float balances arising from the various checks drawn on the bank.

$$\overline{PFLOAT}_k = \sum_{i=1}^{i\max} \sum_{j=1}^{j\max} \overline{PFLOAT}_{ijk},$$

$$k = 1,2, \cdots, k\max$$

In the above, $\overline{PFLOAT}_{ijk}$ is equal to the dollar value of the checks of type j issued by center i times the expected number of days (expressed as a fraction of a month) until the check arrives at the bank for payment. We can rewrite the above equation as:

$$\overline{PFLOAT}_k = \sum_{i=1}^{i\max} \sum_{j=1}^{j\max} X_{ijk} \begin{bmatrix}\text{Average} \\ \text{Check} \\ \text{Value}\end{bmatrix} \begin{bmatrix}\dfrac{\text{Expected Payment Delay}}{\text{Average Number of Days in Month}}\end{bmatrix},\ k = 1,2, \cdots, k\max.$$

For New England Citizens Bank, the expected positive float is

$$\overline{PFLOAT} = 240X_{11} + 11X_{12} + 360X_{41}.$$

Table I

EXPECTED FINANCIAL CENTER ACTIVITY LEVELS

Financial Center Number i	Vendor Checks $\hat{X}_{i1}$	Payroll Checks $\hat{X}_{i2}$	Deposit Items $\hat{Y}_{i1}$
1	2,600	8,500	475
2	600	1,900	20
3	2,400	4,300	5,800
4	1,400	2,200	20

Table II

BASIC BANK DATA

Item	Value
Net Collected balance credit per month	$ 0.002
Charge per vendor check	0.04
Charge per deposit	0.02
Charge per payroll check	0.06
Fixed charges per month	0.00
Value of intangible services per month	1,500
Line of credit	4,000,000
Compensating balance per dollar of demand deposit	0.20
Expected increase in line of credit	0.00
Supporting balance per dollar of expected credit increase	0.05

Table III

FINANCIAL CENTER/BANK DATA

	Value	
Item	Financial Center 1	Financial Center 2
Average size of vendor check	$1,100	$ 1,300
Expected days disbursement float	6.60	8.30
Desired float cushion on vendor checks	0.10	0.15
Average size of payroll check	$ 165	*
Expected days disbursement float	2.00	
Desired float cushion on payroll checks	0.60	
Average size of deposit item	$12,000	$95,000
Expected days deposit float	1.00	2.00
Desired float cushion on deposit items	0.20	0.40

* Did not issue payroll checks on New England Citizens Bank.

Similarly, the expected average monthly deposit float balance (negative float) is the sum of the deposits of type j by center i times the expected collection time. For the New England Citizens Bank, expected negative float is

$$\overline{NFLOAT} = 400Y_{11} + 6{,}300Y_{41}$$

2. Expected Net Collected Balance Definitional Constraint--By definition, the expected average net collected balance, $\overline{NCB}_k$, is given by the average monthly ledger balance plus the net positive or negative float balance.

$$\overline{NCB}_k = \overline{BAL}_k + (\overline{PFLOAT}_k - \overline{NFLOAT}_k),$$

$$k = 1,2, \cdots, k\text{max}$$

Constraints 3 and 4 below define limits of the net collected balance.

3. Net Collected Balance Constraint: Compensating Balances--The New England Citizens Bank requires the average net

collected balance to be greater than 20 percent of any existing line of credit. In addition, the company officers felt that to insure future borrowing capability, five percent of any future requirements should be maintained in current bank balances. This constraint is written:

$$\overline{NCB} \geq \begin{bmatrix}\text{Compensating}\\ \text{Balance}\\ \text{Requirement}\end{bmatrix} + \begin{bmatrix}\text{Supporting}\\ \text{Balance}\\ \text{Requirement}\end{bmatrix}$$

$$\geq 0.20(4{,}000{,}000) + 0.50(0.0)$$
$$\geq 800{,}000$$

4. Net Collected Balance Constraint: Float Variation--The expected net collected balance must also be greater than an amount which is related to the uncertainties in the float balances. To some extent, actual float balances are uncertain quantities and, during the coming period, will differ from their expected levels.[4] We can require the probability that the average net collected balance will be negative (i.e., in overdraft) to be *less* than some specified amount, say two percent. This constraint would prevent the account from being frequently overdrawn when the firm experiences an abnormally low disbursement float or a high deposit float. In the model, this desired "float cushion" for expected net collected balances is a weighed sum of the expected disbursement, payroll, and deposit floats.

For the New England Citizens Bank, the constraint is given by

$$NCB \geq 0.10\,\overline{PFLOAT}_{11} + 0.60\,\overline{PFLOAT}_{12} + 0.15\,\overline{PFLOAT}_{41} + 0.20\,\overline{NFLOAT}_{11} + 0.40\,\overline{NFLOAT}_{41}$$

The derivation of this constraint is discussed in the Appendix.

5. Cost of Expected Tangible Bank Services During the Month--The cost of processing vendor and payroll checks is given by

$$CHCST_k = \sum_{i=1}^{imax} \sum_{j=1}^{jmax} X_{ijk} d_{jk},$$

$k = 1, 2, \cdots, kmax$

where d_{jk} is the dollar cost per item of type j processed by bank k.

For the New England Citizens Bank,

$$CHCST = 0.04X_{11} + 0.06X_{12} + 0.04X_{41}$$

Similarly, the cost of processing deposits at New England Citizens is

$$DCST = 0.02Y_{11} + 0.02Y_{41}$$

6. Bank Compensation Constraint--The total compensation paid to the bank must be at least equal to the cost of expected bank services.

$$FEE_k + NCBC_k \cdot (\overline{NCB}_k) \geq CHCST_k + DCST_k + \text{Fixed Charges}_k + \text{Value Intangible Services}_k + \text{Makeup}_k,$$

$k = 1, 2, \cdots, kmax$

where $NCBC_k$ is the net collected balance credit required by bank k, and Makeup_k equals the charges resulting from any under or over compensation of the bank during previous periods.

7. FEE Limitation Constraint--The New England Citizens Bank limits the use of fees to 20 percent of the total compensation for tangible services. This is written

$$FEE_k \leq 0.20\,[CHCST + DCST + \text{Fixed Charges}_k + \text{Makeup}]$$

THE APPLICATION

The authors have applied this general model to a large corporation with sales of $100 million. The corporation is organized into five divisions, located

[4] Deposit float balances are treated as random variables, not because of any uncertainty in the collection time for a specified item, but because of uncertainty associated with item size and the mix of deposit item types.

across the country. The growth of the company has come primarily from acquisition. As each division was acquired, it added more banks to the corporate banking system. At the time of the study, each division had at least two local banks which it used for disbursements, deposits, and payroll. In addition, the corporation had a $10 million line of credit from the three largest banks in the system.

Corporate management believed that there were too many banks in the system and that their cash balances were not being used effectively. Credit agreements required that substantial compensating balances be maintained at each of the three large banks. Management was aware that substantial amounts of disbursement float were available in the system and was anxious to use these floats, to the extent possible, to generate the required compensating balances. At the same time management recognized the need to maintain local banks to serve the divisions for payroll and various intangible service needs.

By using the above approach to structure the company's banking system, the authors were able to reduce the total cash ledger balance in the system from $1.6 million to $437,000. In addition, the total monthly banking cost was decreased from $8,700 to $3,600. These reductions resulted primarily from a more effective use of disbursement float and the reassignment of tangible services to those banks requiring substantial net collected balances.

Figure III illustrates the flow of information and decisions within the cash management system. The figure describes how the various components of the cash management system are interrelated. The system is an adaptive type of feedback structure, wherein differences between planned and actual results in the previous month plus expectations regarding banking activities in future months are considered by the linear programming model in the assignment of the following month's banking activity. When used as an operating tool, the model optimally allocates activities to a predetermined banking structure according to specified corporate policies. In addition, the model is an extremely valuable planning tool for the design or modification of the corporation's banking structure and policies.

Table IV presents a comparison of how book balances, net collected balances, fees, and checking activities were allocated in the existing system during a given month according to the cash management model.

Table V is a sample printout from the computerized linear program. This printout summarizes the level of activity and the method of compensation for one bank in the system. The "BINDING NCB REQUIREMENT" refers to that constraint responsible for limiting the current level of net collected balances at the bank. If this constraint were relaxed, the linear program would be able to reduce further the book balance.

The linear programming model also computes the marginal cost of additional activity at each bank. Management can use these marginal costs as evaluation measures of banks and their services. The system approach used here is particularly useful for evaluating the results of a price renegotiation. It is important to realize that price reduction not only lowers the cost of banking at a particular bank, but can also result in a re-allocation of activities and balances away from other banks in the system. Without the systems approach of the linear programming model, most of these re-allocations and system savings could easily be overlooked.

In addition to using the marginal costs and the binding constraints as indications for negotiation, they can also be used to signal the need for structural change in the banking system. In the application discussed here, one of the three banks extending credit to the corporation was found to be quite expensive. This was not the result of an excessive fee structure but was

Figure III

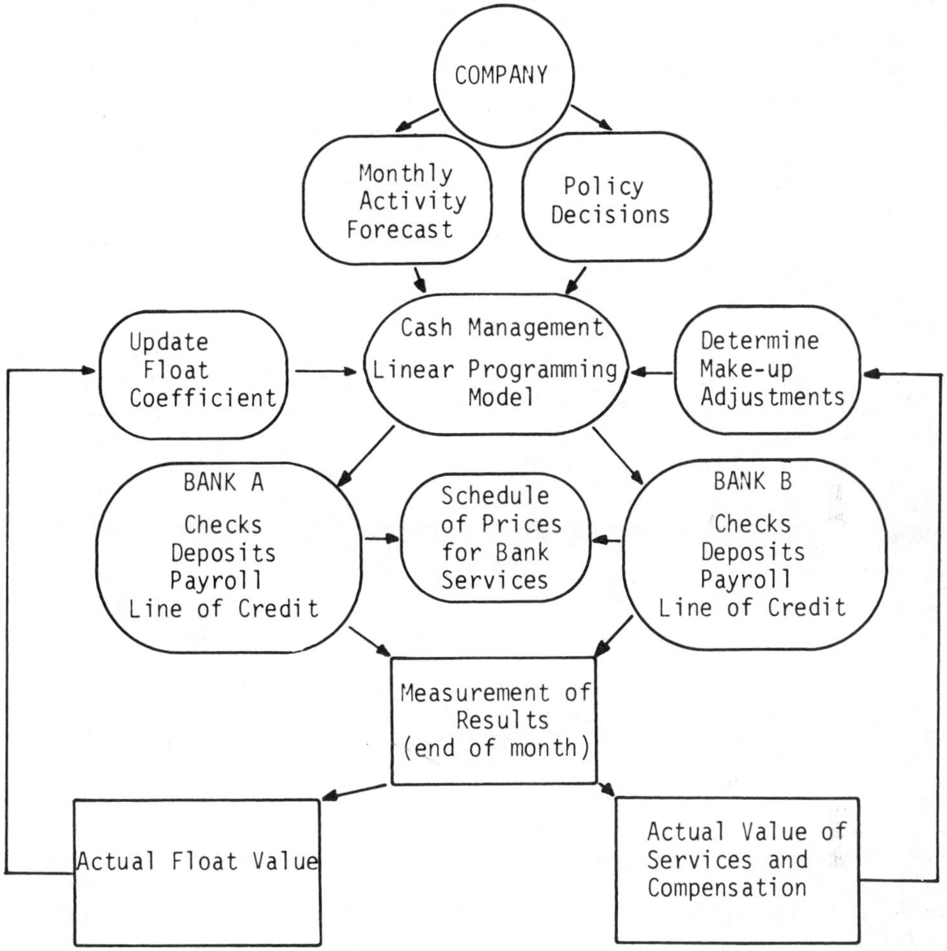
COMPANY
Monthly Activity Forecast
Policy Decisions
Update Float Coefficient
Cash Management Linear Programming Model
Determine Make-up Adjustments
BANK A
Checks
Deposits
Payroll
Line of Credit
Schedule of Prices for Bank Services
BANK B
Checks
Deposits
Payroll
Line of Credit
Measurement of Results (end of month)
Actual Float Value
Actual Value of Services and Compensation

Table IV

BANKING ACTIVITIES BEFORE (I) AND AFTER (II) APPLICATION OF MODEL

Bank	Book Balances* (I)	Book Balances* (II)	Net Collected Balances* (I)	Net Collected Balances* (II)	Fees Paid (I)	Fees Paid (II)	Check Activity Allocation* (I)	Check Activity Allocation* (II)
New England Citizens†	NA	$-276.00	$ 648	$ 800.0	$ 56	$579	$ 1,820	$ 6,214
Empire City†	NA	872.6	625	600.0	0	0	1,156	0
Pacific Southern Trust†	NA	559.4	700	600.0	0	0	2,121	580
Pilgrim State	NA	30.0	150	30.0	450	0	568	0
Steeltown Federal	NA	-608.7	160	84.7	0	281	4,440	3,170
Third National of Pittsburgh	NA	-134.4	90	14.9	0	18	183	640
First American Trust	NA	-5.7	350	5.7	0	103	480	164
Totals	$1,610	$ 437.1	$2,732	$2,135.4	$506	$981	$10,768	$10,768

*In thousands of dollars.
†A line of credit totaling $10 million is jointly provided by these banks.

Table V

BINDING NCB REQUIREMENT:			NCB REQUIRED
0.20 COMPENSATING BALANCE FOR EXISTING $4000000. LOAN PLUS			800000.
0.05 SUPPORTING BALANCE FOR FUTURE $ 0. LOAN			
NON-BINDING REQUIREMENTS:			
NET COLLECTED BALANCE GREATER THAN ZERO			0.
PAY FOR $1500./MONTH INTANGIBLE SERVICES			750000.
FLOAT RESERVED FOR FLOAT VARIATION			238388.
BOOK BALANCE	-276039.	FIXED MONTHLY CHARGE	0.
NET FLOAT	1076038.	CHECK CHARGE (0.04 EA)	160.
TOTAL NCB CREDIT (0.002/$NCB)	1600.	DEPOSIT CHARGE (0.02 EA)	9.
TOTAL FEE PAYMENT	579.	PAYROLL CHARGE (0.06 EA)	510.

	AVG DAYS FLOAT	% CUSHION	TOTAL DOLLARS
CHECK ACTIVITY : FINANCIAL CENTER 1	6.6	0.1000	2949996.
FINANCIAL CENTER 4	8.3	0.1500	1863995.
DEPOSIT ACTIVITY : FINANCIAL CENTER 1	1.0	0.2000	5600000.
FINANCIAL CENTER 4	2.0	0.4000	0.
PAYROLL ACTIVITY : FINANCIAL CENTER 1	2.0	0.6000	1399997.

primarily due to the location of the bank relative to other banks in the system and the corporate divisions which it served. The model determined that sufficient activity could not be assigned to this bank in order to use up the substantial net collected balance credits calculated on the compensating balance. The corporation's management is currently considering the possibility of replacing this bank by one which would be a more effective part of the overall system. The effect on the system is being measured by introducing various candidate banks into the linear programming model and evaluating the resulting solutions.

The linear program can also evaluate potential lock box locations. Many banks provide lock box location assistance, which generally focuses on the problem of minimizing deposit float while keeping lock box fees within reasonable limits. However, lock boxes are only one part of the banking system, and they should not be evaluated separately. The existence of compensating balances at certain banks will make it more profitable to allocate some lock box activity to those banks, even though other banks could possibly lower the deposit float. This allocation can be made correctly only in the context of the other variables in the system. By adding constraints specifying lock box fees, allocation, and float, the linear programming model can evaluate potential lock box sites.

SUMMARY

Cash management requires decision-making in several areas: the use of balances or fees for compensation; the allocation of specific activities to specific banks; the location ond optimal usage of lock boxes; and the use of disbursement float as a substitute for permanent balances. Making these decisions sequentially without considering the impact on other banks or activities can result in costly suboptimization. Linear programming can be used to optimize the cost of the total system subject to management policy and operating constraints.

APPENDIX: DEVELOPMENT OF FLOAT VARIATION CONSTRAINT

The actual average net collected balance during the future period is a random variable since it is the algebraic sum of the ledger balance and float balances, the latter of which are themselves random variables. Hence we have

$$\widetilde{NCB} = BAL + \widetilde{PFLOAT} - \widetilde{NFLOAT} \tag{1a}$$

$$= BAL + \sum_i \sum_j \widetilde{PFLOAT}_{ij} - \sum_i \sum_m \widetilde{NFLOAT}_{im} \tag{1b}$$

The required constraint on actual average net collected balances if given by

$$\text{Prob}(\widetilde{NCB} \leq 0) \leq \varepsilon \tag{2}$$

where ε is, for example, 2 percent.

Now relationship (2) is equivalent to

$$\text{Prob}\left[\frac{\widetilde{NCB} - \overline{NCB}}{\sigma(\widetilde{NCB})} \leq \frac{-\overline{NCB}}{\sigma(\widetilde{NCB})}\right] \leq \varepsilon \tag{3}$$

where $\sigma(\widetilde{NCB})$ is the standard deviation of $\widetilde{NCB}$, and $\overline{NCB}$ is the expected value of $\widetilde{NCB}$.

By Tchebyscheff's extended lemma,[5] we have

$$\text{Prob}\left(\frac{\widetilde{NCB} - \overline{NCB}}{\sigma(\widetilde{NCB})} \leq W\right) \leq \frac{1}{1 + W^2}$$

or

$$\text{Prob}\left(\widetilde{NCB} \leq \overline{NCB} + W[\sigma(\widetilde{NCB})]\right) \leq \frac{1}{1 + W^2} \tag{4}$$

where $W < 0$.

Now, if we take $\varepsilon = \dfrac{1}{1 + W^2}$

from which $W = -\left[\dfrac{1 - \varepsilon}{\varepsilon}\right]^{\frac{1}{2}}$

---

[5] See Cramer [2], Exercise 5, p. 256.

then any $\widetilde{NCB}$ satisfying

$$NCB + W(\sigma(\widetilde{NCB})) \geq 0 \tag{5}$$

where $-\dfrac{\overline{NCB}}{\sigma(\widetilde{NCB})} \leq W < 0$

will satisfy the original probability constraint. From expression (1b) and the properties of standard deviaitons, it follows that

$$\sigma(\widetilde{NCB}) \leq \sum_i \sum_j \sigma(\widetilde{\mathit{P}FLOAT_{ij}}) + \sum_i \sum_m \sigma(\widetilde{\mathit{N}FLOAT_{im}}) \tag{6}$$

Now if we replace $\sigma(\widetilde{NCB})$ in (5) by its upper bound as given by (6) and require

$$\overline{NCB} + W \sum_i \sum_j \sigma(\widetilde{\mathit{P}FLOAT_{ij}}) + W \sum_i \sum_m \sigma(\widetilde{\mathit{N}FLOAT_{im}}) \geq 0$$

or

$$NCB \geq |W| \sum_i \sum_j \sigma(\widetilde{\mathit{P}FLOAT_{ij}}) + |W| \sum_i \sum_m \sigma(\widetilde{\mathit{N}FLOAT_{im}}) \tag{7}$$

it follows that any $\overline{NCB}$ satisfying expression (7) will also satisfy the original probability constraint.

Define

$$\mathit{P}CUSH_{ij} = |W| \frac{\sigma(\widetilde{\mathit{P}FLOAT_{ij}})}{\overline{\mathit{P}FLOAT_{ij}}} \tag{8}$$

$$\mathit{N}CUSH_{im} = |W| \frac{\sigma(\widetilde{\mathit{N}FLOAT_{im}})}{\overline{\mathit{N}FLOAT_{im}}} \tag{9}$$

where the coefficient inside the bracket are simply the coefficients of variation of the float balances. They measure the standard deviation per dollar of expected float balances. These quantities can be measured from an analysis of the variations in item sizes and collection times.

Substituting (8) and (9) into (7), we obtain the desired constraint

$$NCB \geq \sum_i \sum_j (\mathit{P}CUSH_{ij})(\overline{\mathit{P}FLOAT_{ij}}) + \sum_i \sum_m (\mathit{N}CUSH_{im})(\overline{\mathit{N}FLOAT_{im}})$$

REFERENCES

1. Calman, R. *Linear Programming and Cash Management/CASH ALPHA.* Cambridge, Mass., MIT Press, 1968.

2. Cramer, H. *Mathematical Methods of Statistics.* Princeton, N.J., Princeton University Press, 1946.

READING 11

Electronic Funds Transfer: Pitfalls and Payoffs

John B. Benton
National Commission of Electronic Fund Transfers

Since 1975 the financial community has been buzzing over the prospect of an electronic system that may substitute for much of the paper-based money transfer system in this country. Already widely discussed in European nations, the electronic funds transfer system (EFTS) holds out vast promise as a means of ensuring the adequacy of payments in America's high-voltage commercial world. EFTS offers a solution to the mounting problems of a money transfer system increasingly choked with checks.

But EFTS also contains pitfalls concealed in the underbrush of capital investments and of operating expense projections. The new technology already has claimed its share of overly eager entrepreneurs.

Nevertheless, EFTS is coming, in one form or another, to one degree or another, and it behooves all prudent business people to educate themselves about this new technology and to watch developments with care. The fortunes of business—literally—may ride on EFTS in the near future. For instance:

—Companies will transmit payroll on magnetic tape to depository institutions for automatic crediting to employees' accounts.

—Retailers will accept customer cards for virtually all merchandise, debiting buyers' accounts electronically.

—Insurance companies and holders of mortgages or loans will receive automatic installment payments through their customers' banks.

—Utility companies will encourage customers to give telephone authorization to their banks to transfer payment funds automatically.

EFTS already has become significant to bankers, managers of thrift institutions, food merchandisers, and federal and state regulators of depository institutions. Lawyers, judges, and legislators, as well, are concerned with developments in this field. Also, the new technology is a subject of intense interest in the electronics industry, which annually will install a half billion dollars' worth of terminals and communications hardware in retail establishments.[1]

Congress, too, has shown interest in EFTS. Hearings and debates on the subject have been held in both the House and the Senate in recent years, and significant changes in federal law would appear to be near certainties.

To help deal with the social ramifications of EFTS, Congress established the National Commission on Electronic Fund Transfers and directed it to study developments and to explore the steps required to ensure that consumers are protected from unnecessary inconveniences, invasions of privacy, and reduced competition.

Unfortunately, business people in pursuit of profit will receive no protection from legislators. Companies will be as vulnerable as they were in the past when new technologies burst on the scene.

These situations lead to my basic warning: Business decisions about EFTS are going to depend, in a larger measure than policy makers may wish, on sound instincts. Business decisions are going to depend, to a *smaller* degree than might be wished, on an ability to collect information, to evaluate costs and benefits, and to choose on the basis of economic rationality.

The heart of the matter is: How much EFTS and when? This is a question top executives soon may have to answer for their businesses. To do so, they might examine EFTS from four standpoints: economics, technology, consumer wants, and the legal and regulatory climate. Let us examine each of these topics.

[1] This number is based on estimated growth figures for general merchandise point-of-sale terminals, automated teller machines, and bank point-of-sale terminals over the next five years and is drawn from 1977 data published by Frost & Sullivan (New York), Creative Strategies (California), and Payment Systems, Inc. (Georgia).

ECONOMIC AND TECHNOLOGICAL HURDLES

One reason for the initial growth of EFTS was the notion of cost displacement. In the late 1960's, the American Bankers Association, the Federal Reserve, and independent organizations sponsored studies that claimed that the existing paper-based payment system was becoming too expensive to be justifiable. The authors argued for a conversion to electronics, thereby substituting an inflation-hedged, machine-intensive delivery system for one that was labor-intensive and relatively unprotected from inflation.

These studies were the initial theoretical basis for EFTS. Two programs soon emerged—automated clearing houses and retail point-of-sale systems. These concepts are fully defined in the ruled insert, "What is EFTS?", on pages 154-156.

Throughout the past ten years, it has become clear that nobody is sure that these cost saving arguments can be supported. In fact, I am not aware that any empirical research on the economics of EFTS has been completed and distributed in the public domain. A study prepared by the staff of the National Commission found: "The published estimates of the costs of implementing and operating [electronic funds transfer] systems are universally based on feasibility studies that have not been tested in actual practice."[2]

Nonetheless, during the 1960's, the growth of EFTS remained tied to the cost effectiveness argument. That growth was modest and disturbed no one. During the 1970's, however, new considerations began to alter the picture. Many marketing people in banking argued that terminal-based services brought increased customer convenience, a wider variety of services, and eventually more deposits. Attention turned

[2] National Commission on Electronic Fund Transfers, *A Conceptual and Methodological Framework for the Economic Analysis of Electronic Funds Transfer Systems,* Internal Working Document 27 (Springfield, Va.: National Technical Information Service, U.S. Dept. of Commerce, November 1976), p. 2.

away from the automated clearing houses—although steady progress continued in spite of little publicity—and shifted toward the potential for retail point-of-sale systems.

Still in experimental stage: But the shift in focus to retailing did not lift EFTS out of the experimental stage. Many problems remain to be solved and, as we shall see later, experience to date has raised real questions about the practicality of EFTS.

At the same time business was experimenting with point-of-sale systems, it was also experimenting with automated teller machines. I call this experimentation because the machines certainly could not be justified during the 1971-to-1975 period on the basis of economic return. Consider the evidence:

Conservatively speaking, there was an average installed base for the four years through 1975 of 3,000 automated teller machines in about 1,000 banks—with less than 10% of them on-line. Easily $200 million worth of terminal and communications equipment, research and development, systems maintenance, telephone tariffs, and operating funds were poured into these programs.

According to industry statistics, an average total of 1,500 machines were in operation. Each of these machines processed about 1,000 transactions per month. Overall, the cost per transaction for the entire installed base must have averaged at least $2.50.

But because only a small amount of the check processing cost was displaced by the systems, the economic justification had to come almost exclusively from the revenue earned from increased deposits or new fees. Few managers of financial institutions would argue even today that market shares have moved enough to provide increased earnings sufficient to offset the high levels of costs.

A 1976 updated attempt to look at the economics of the same types of off-premise programs has been attempted by the U.S. Savings and Loan League. The league estimated the cost per transaction of all installed automated teller machines and point-of-sale programs at more than $1.50. (The drop from the earlier cost figure can be attributed almost entirely to increased operating efficiency and a large change in transaction volume per machine—from an average of 1,100 transactions per month before 1975 to almost 1,800 per month by the end of 1976.) In contrast, the highest estimates of the cost for conventional check processing are less than 50% of this number, and some giant banks claim publicly that their explicitly identifiable share of check-processing costs amounts to less than a nickel per transaction.

The lessons from such statistics are obvious: EFTS is still experimental. Only large volumes of business will ever make it economically feasible.

What explains the inability to get out of the experimental stage? One reason is that many of the pre-1976 experiments in the depository institutions failed to meet even the research and development goals. Much of what was learned soon became irrelevant. The most uncertain aspect of EFTS is the complexity of the communications systems development work involving many different types of computers, networks controllers, data records, systems interchange, and communications protocols. Most of the early systems eschewed such complexity and installed off-line machinery. New lessons are being learned in today's on-line, off-premise banking environment.

In 1977, the trends for both automated clearing house and point-of-sale programs are becoming clearer, the experiments more fruitful. The automated clearing house programs, in particular, have grown steadily behind the scenes, with cost displacement still acting as the driving motivator. For example, 32 automated clearing house associations have established 26 ongoing projects, with 6 more planned by 1978. As of December 1976, the federal government was pumping almost 6 million transactions per month through these projects, and commercial payments were comprising another half million. The government expects to reach 20 million transactions per month by 1981. Yet adding some comparative expansion estimates for commercial payments and even bumping the figures a nod, this is still less than 1% of the 40 billion checks that are expected to be drawn yearly by 1980.

Point-of-sale systems have also grown, although not as quickly as some proponents claim. Through the end of 1976, almost 2,900 depository institutions had installed about 10,000 off-premise terminals as part of approximately 200 operational projects. (Most of these are the less expensive point-of-sale terminals that today sell for about $1,500. Less than 500 of the installed base of off-premise devices are automated teller machines.) Some 150 more are on the drawing boards. But this is a modest infrastructure compared with the approximately 225,000 on-line terminals now installed in general merchandise stores throughout the United States. (About 155,000 of these are full-scale general merchandise point-of-sale terminals, and about 75,000 are credit authorization terminals.)

Although approximately 20 million transactions per year are being pumped through the systems installed by depository institutions, most of these are *not* EFTS. They are much simpler authorization/verification-type transactions. However, the infrastructure is essentially the same as that which will be required for EFTS.

High expenses up front: Let us reflect on some of the lessons that have been learned about data communications technology, and EFTS in particular.

Most important, the technology for data communications, whether it supports EFTS, credit authorization, or order entry, is expensive, much more so than was at first thought. Of the major zones of expense found in a business operation—research and development, capital investment, and annual operating—capital investment signals the scale of the operation and the downside risk. Comparatively speaking, EFTS requires more, rather than less, up-front investment than the average enterprise. For example:

> While a modest conventional credit authorization system, dedicated by a single department-store chain exclusively to the credit authorization function, may cost more than $1 million to build, the average point-of-sale system, with greatly expanded functional capability, may cost five to ten times as much. The cost of full funds transfer lies somewhere in between the cost of limited credit systems and general merchandise point-of-sale systems. The total operating cost for these kinds of systems averages from 25% to 50% of the investment value per annum.
>
> One typical check verification system today, at a bank with 350 terminals in a major metropolitan city, would cost $1.5 million to build and $350,000 per year to operate (including hardware maintenance, special software maintenance, telephone lines, systems support, and operation), or about 25% of the original investment per year. This particular system is proprietary, requires no message switching to any other bank's records, and is not even on-line to the main central processing computer.

But even in the seemingly simple systems, slight changes in the marketing strategy can cause expenses to spring out of nowhere. Suppose the bank desires to guarantee all checks passed through the system. The first thing that happens is that the data-processing cost center of the bank charges a few hundred thousand dollars against the program for what was believed to be modest batch-processing support.

Next, write-offs against bad check losses accumulate at a rate of from 0.05% to 0.07% of the gross dollar volume of checks cashed. That was planned. What was not planned was the cost of the check control program, of individual follow-ups, and of collection costs. In the examples used here, check write-offs, accumulating at 0.07%, exceeded $250,000 the first year. But it cost another $300,000 of personnel services expense to keep the number that low.

A funds transfer system, requiring more sophisticated terminals and interbank switches, would command at least another $1 million of hardware expense, create much greater management problems, and cause vastly expanded systems support expense.

What volume of activity would be required to create a 15% return on investment for a bank data communications system? To answer this, let us take the case of the bank just mentioned, assuming sensibly that:

- —The benefits derived from fee income are equal to $0.15 per transaction.
- —The displacement cost is uncertain, but it will eventually be positive (thus providing a hedge against uncertainty and making the modeled numbers even more reliable).
- —Increased income attributed solely to increased market share is not significant.
- —The model estimates cost and revenue over a five-year period.

Given such assumptions, the check verification system would require more than 600,000 transactions per month to be economically viable! Even if you doubled those transactions per month you would be doing well to break even if the checks were being guaranteed as well as being verified against a central file.

Two more points are worth noting. The first is that the up-front costs are so large that most depository institutions would have difficulty affording by themselves the expense of undertaking an EFTS. The second is that business's expectations about the time span required for next year's revenue to exceed next year's cost and for total revenue over the program's life to exceed total cost may have to be very different from the expectations that guide most business ventures. EFTS may require five years or more before it can show positive returns on even the last year's expenses.

One final point can be made. We have noted that these arguments about the positive effect of scale do not always hold firm. All cost elements are not amenable to scalar economics. If you are guaranteeing checks that average $45 per purchase in a supermarket, your bad check write-offs are probably averaging more than $0.02 for every check that you cash. And your check control costs for collection, phone calls, and other expenses are very significant and are sensitive to changes in volume.

Thus one of the key questions facing the financial manager is whether his board of directors and stockholders will tolerate capital intensive programs that take five to ten years to show net earnings on total systems cost.

Uncertainties in the cost picture: In my opinion, financial enterprises eventually will build EFTS. They sense that more than 50% of their new deposit dollars are being created by individuals. They sense, too, that the expanded services provided by data communications technology will appeal to consumers, and I think they are right. They will strive, therefore, to be first in this market.

But if you are one of those involved in this effort, beware of hidden costs. EFTS is expensive, and the people required to back up the terminals and support your program may cost you far more than you expect. There are other costs that have a way of remaining hidden until it is too late. For example:

- — The hardware or electronic equipment initially may seem expensive to obtain, but after five years the maintenance expense may be even greater.
- — The private lines leased from the telephone company are expensive and

rising in cost. About 30% of your dollars may go to Ma Bell or one of her competitors.

— The staff specialists, planners, and others who play with computers will always find new ways to use them, and expanded use means greatly expanded expense.

— If you are top management, expect to be deeply involved. EFTS is going to be expensive in terms of your time as well as that of middle management.

In the case of automated clearing houses, the Federal Reserve has all but concluded that the facilities will eventually reduce back office clearing and settlement expenses. This conclusion has not yet been tested with empirical data, but I think it is accurate.

In the case of point-of-sale systems, the facts on the cost side of the equation appear to be these: depository institutions can even now establish point-of-sale check verification systems capable of producing transactions at costs ranging from \$0.05 to \$0.30, assuming sound management, five-year amortization, and a system size having hundreds (but under a thousand) of terminals that are each transmitting a couple of thousand transactions per month. Under the same assumptions, there are funds-transfer-type automated teller machines and point-of-sale systems producing transactions at costs ranging from \$0.20 to \$0.85. An average cost per transaction of about \$0.45 for these fuller-service systems is not at all unrealistic.

I am convinced, based on my review of reasonably hard data, that future systems, made up of 5,000 to 10,000 more terminals and most transmitting about 2,500 to 5,000 transactions per month, will achieve costs per transaction of comfortably under a nickel.

However, there is also no question in my mind that during the next five years only a few systems will achieve these numbers. For some time to come, we can expect many more systems to cost a dollar or more per transaction. Obviously the question before the providers of EFTS is: How does an institution generate sufficient off-setting revenues from fees, reduced check or credit losses, reduced operating expenses, and revenues from new deposits that were attracted to the institution by EFTS-type systems?

A major caveat from all this is that the "walk first, run later" approach makes a great deal of sense. Entry through check verification is the most economical way to begin if one can avoid guaranteeing the checks. In this way, the customers of the financial institutions can become accustomed gradually to the systems that will support funds transfer, and the cost stream can be more properly aligned with the revenue derived from the benefits that are provided.

Will government follow or lead? In the preceding discussion I did not include estimates of the cost and operations of automated clearing houses. This is because the government seems to be playing by a different set of rules from those used by the private sector.

The government's analysis of EFTS benefits is not entirely guided by the same kinds of hard-cost numbers used in the private sector because of the nature of the public sector. Thus the government's support is not likely to vacillate as a function of a bad experience here and there. For example, both the Treasury and the Federal Reserve favor the expanded use of EFTS for government payments and transfers, and they can justify supporting automated clearing house developments on the basis of the benefits for the government alone.

Furthermore, the government, based on its evaluation of the public interest, supports the expansion of EFTS to point-of-sale facilities and may enter that arena as a provider of last resort if the private sector is unable or unwilling to build and operate the communications infrastructure required.

The National Commission has carefully considered what should be the government's proper role in all of this, particularly that of the Federal Reserve. It has concluded, at least in the context of today's world, that the Fed should keep its distance from point-of-sale programs. The National Commission strongly supports the use of the private sector as the primary deliverer of EFTS.

Suppose the private sector is not able to deliver? This could happen if stockholders and other providers of capital insist upon favorable earnings in the short run. Then government would become the prime mover—all signs suggest this. The private sector would default a large part of a new, and potentially viable, billion-dollar-per-year industry to the public sector.

Can industry bring the costs down? Perhaps the most important lesson to be learned from economic analysis of early EFTS experiments is that we are still focusing on the wrong systems configuration. Today we think in terms of retail systems, banking systems, supermarket systems, and so forth. Some of these systems are designed to support authorization/verification-type functions. Others control inventory. Still others do remote data processing. In the meantime, AT&T and numerous other businesses are creating competing and complementary terrestrial, microwave, or satellite-based data communications nets for prospective users. So what we have are many different systems performing seemingly different functions through different types of equipment when, in fact, the differences are more apparent than real.

In my judgment, EFTS will not become cost effective until all of these different kinds of systems are integrated into considerably more homogeneous data communications networks. There is room for regional and national approaches, different kinds of participants, and variations in style. But, more than likely, the banks will have to build future terminals and systems that can enable the data communications infrastructure established by the supermarkets, large and small retailers, gas stations, hotels, and airlines to become increasingly interdependent.

Only when these participants become interdependent will the cost per transaction for EFTS decline and become acceptable; and only in that way will the nation's relatively fixed communications resources be used effectively.

Cross currents in costs: The technology barrier has been crossed. The question is not whether the technology is available but when it will be cost effective. Advances in the last few years—mini-computers, computers built from microprocessor chips, and general advances in semiconductor technology—have cut the cost of EFTS components. Only mechanical components like printers have been stubborn. Electronic technology is clearly experiencing a declining cost curve.

However, not everything is becoming cheaper. The trend toward "distributed intelligence" (that is, computers spreading from the back office to the selling floor) means increased attempts to design unique systems, expanding needs for software, and a sure boost in the needed number of computer programmers (whose salaries are considerably higher than those of the clerical help they replace). As a result, costs will not decline as fast as might be hoped.

There are many caveats for the unwary entrant into EFTS:

—Watch out for software and consider it an unstable expense category. Its cost can outstrip that of hardware.

—Watch out for uniqueness for its own sake. Many different designs may be adopted to EFTS. There is no single perfect design.

—Watch out for overloading computer intelligence. You do not need a steam roller to crack a walnut.

—Watch out for unrealistic expectations. Every system installation will take longer than you think, and therefore it will cost more.

WHAT IS EFTS?

The National Commission has defined electronic funds transfer system as "a payments system in which the processing and communications necessary to effect economic exchange and the processing and communications necessary for the production and distribution of services incidental or related to economic exchange are dependent wholly or in large part on the use of electronics."

To put flesh and blood on this definition, consider Figure A. Here EFTS is divided into five segments: the consumers, the merchants, the communications system, the back office, and the business, government, or individual consumer of EFTS services. These segments will be tied together, in large part, by the country's existing telephone network.

The point-of-sale system is usually in a retail establishment, such as a department store, a small retailer, a supermarket, or a gas station. Point-of-sale transactions account for perhaps 25% of the checks written today. To bring in EFTS the requirements are willing consumers, business relationships between merchants and depository institutions, an EFTS communications system (including the assorted electronics wizardry and phone networks required to make it work), and access to the files of depository institutions so that a payor's records can be debited and payees can be credited for the amount of the transactions.

The telecommunications network is crucial. It connects the selling floor of a retail establishment to customer

FIGURE A. EFTS Relationships

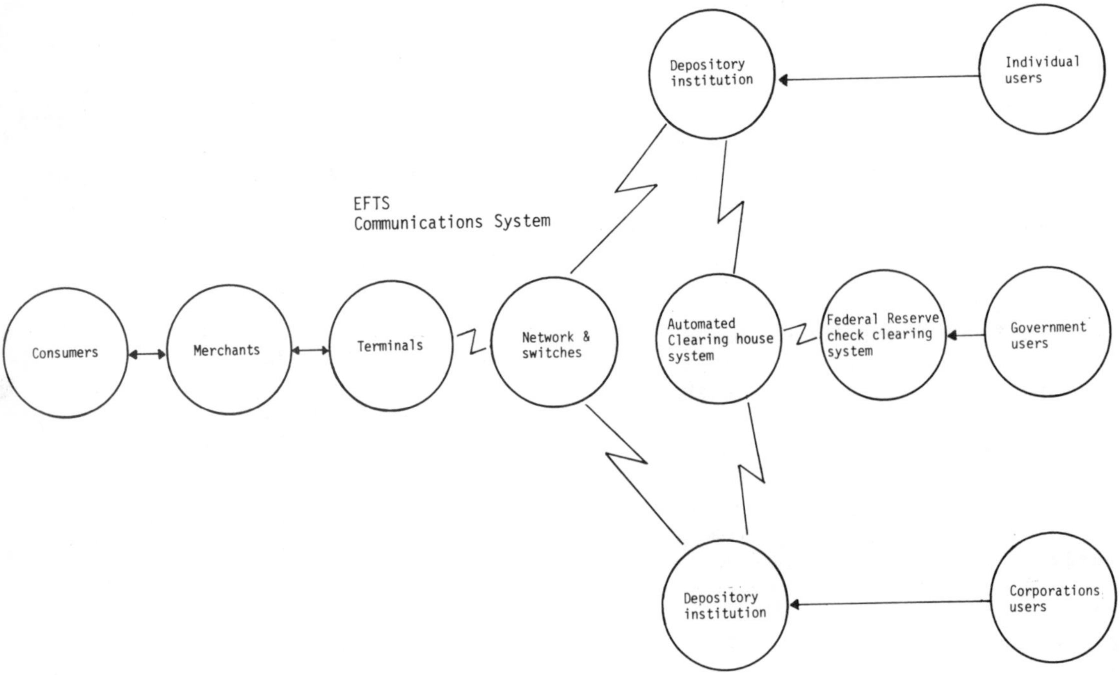

account files in financial institutions —banks, credit card suppliers, or thrift institutions. These files contain the most valid source of obtainable information about an individual's ability to pay. Bank files describe whether the individual's checking account balance is sufficient to cover the transaction; credit card files show whether he or she has maintained a satisfactory history of paying off credit purchases made possible by private label cards, bank cards, or travel and entertainment cards; thrift institution files show his or her savings account balance.

Without the use of telecommunications systems, the information described can be retrieved only with much expense and inconvenience.

During the late 1960's, large department stores began installing data communications systems and inaugurated credit authorization programs. Now these systems are being used for inventory control, sales reporting, order entry, and other related functions. From the standpoint of technological capability, they could be readily connected to the files of specific depository institutions for the purposes of verifying checks or authorizing bank-supplied credit, not to mention making electronic transfers of funds.

Also during the 1960's, savings and loans and commercial banks began to connect their tellers to customer files by telephone lines for purposes ranging from check verification to online data processing. During the past few years, these institutions have extended these data communications systems to retail and supermarket counters in many places around the country.

As for the automated clearing house, it is part of the back office clearing and settlement system. The clearing house processes payments or credits that have been arranged ahead of time, based upon an agreement between the payor and payee that specific transactions should automatically occur

FIGURE B. Potential Changes in the Consumer Payments System

Point of Change	Current Mode	EFTS Mode
Point-of-sale transaction	Cash	EFTS debit
	Cash	Check guarantee card or check
	Check	EFTS debit
	Check guarantee card	EFTS debit
Consumer bill payments	Mailed check	Preauthorized automated clearing house (ACH) debit
	Preauthorized draft	Preauthorized ACH debit
	Mailed check	Bill check
	Mailed check	Terminal credit transfer
Business and government payments to individuals	Paycheck	Preauthorized ACH credit
	Annuity check	Preauthorized ACH credit
	Pension check	Preauthorized ACH credit
Deposits to nontransaction accounts in financial institutions	Personal deposit	Preauthorized ACH credit
	Mailed deposit	Preauthorized ACH credit
Business and government payments to business	Mailed check	Terminal credit transfer
	Invoice check	Preauthorized ACH debit

according to a predetermined schedule. The key benefits are: (a) reduced volume of payroll checks, regular bill payments, and other predebitable checks and debit or credit transactions: (b) automated credits for individual consumers in the institution of their choice; (c) reduced cost of bill paying for individual consumers in cases where the payments are always made at a regular time (as in the case of home mortgages, utilities, installment loans, and insurance payments).

Some methods of payments are likely to be changed as a result of EFTS. The areas of change and the types of changes that may occur, given a continuation of existing trends, are shown in Figure B.

SUPPORTS FROM CONSUMERS

Bank marketing people are betting that consumers will be so interested in EFTS services that they will shift their deposits to institutions offering the new systems, and perhaps will even be willing to pay additional fees for them. Although merchants are also a source of banking revenue, they will not go forward with EFTS until they are fairly sure of consumer acceptance. Consequently, a key question is whether consumers are ready for EFTS. Do they want it? Or is this market being created by a technology push?

Any survey would show that consumers lack knowledge of EFTS. But these surveys are misleading. Consumers are extensively and sometimes painfully aware of the peripheral activities that are inextricably related to EFTS—credit purchase, credit reporting, check cashing, check floating, plastic card usage, opportunity costs, and even postage. The successful marketing of EFTS will depend on the consumers' desires for increased conveniences. This is the major gamble, and in my judgment, it is a pretty good one to take.

At the moment, the consumer is less concerned about EFTS benefits than about bigness per se and any potential violation of his or her rights. The majority of letters and petitions received by the National Commission simply voiced opposition to EFTS without qualifications or further clarifications. The reasons and questions given are as varied as the technology is complex:

"EFTS will invade privacy."
"It is not as reliable as paper."
"How will errors be corrected?"
"Will my money be safe?"
"EFTS is another example of jobs lost to technology!"
"What are the real motives and intentions of the American financial community?"
"EFTS is a way for government to infringe on its citizens' rights and responsibilities."
"EFTS constitutes another technological interference with human interaction."

People have even likened EFTS to the Book of Revelation's prediction of a "Mark of the Beast," the anti-Christ who would lead the world to destruction immediately preceding the second coming of Christ. Clearly the consumers need to know more about the specifics.

A number of consumer concerns will require the business executive's attention. An important area is the sanctity of information describing an individual's financial affairs. Consumers will insist that their rights and responsibilities be at least as well protected and clarified with EFTS as they are with today's paper system.

The National Commission has gone to the side of consumer rights. In doing so, it has molded a partnership between government and business to anticipate and correct potential EFTS abuses of individual rights before the abuses can become realities.

In its report to President Carter and to Congress, the National

Commission concludes that consumers benefit in a number of significant ways from EFTS.[3] Nonetheless, it strongly recommends that consumers be given a fair choice in selecting among available methods of payment. It further suggests that Congress enact a broad series of safeguards for consumers, including a procedure for contesting any government access to financial transaction information. It proposes that financial institutions be held liable for misuse of information concerning an individual's depository account as well as for fraud and computer errors that are clearly not the consumer's fault.

The National Commission's recommendations should probably be viewed as minimum protections for consumers. Consumer activists are likely to have more to say on this subject in the years ahead.

Meanwhile consumer experience with EFTS has been rather good. Credit authorization in department stores, for example, is a tremendous success. Complaints, when they are heard, are most likely to come from those who have a history of abusing their credit.

Today's EFTS volume level is limited not by consumer acceptance but by consumer awareness. Where well advertised, as by the First National Bank of Atlanta, response has lived up to predictions. The bank dubbed the check verification program "Honest Face," installed terminals in local supermarkets, and invited everyone in Atlanta to participate. The bank is claiming transactions volumes in excess of $1 million per month, quite a success in terms of consumer acceptance.

J.C. Penney, Sears, Roebuck & Company, and Montgomery Ward could hardly function without their credit authorization programs. Even Security National Bank of Alaska is operating an off-premise automated teller machine system. Almost everyone seems to be getting into the act.

On the other hand, I know of a number of cases where several million dollars were invested in EFTS hardware and almost nothing in marketing. Without exception, these programs have failed. For the present, consumers are coming out way ahead.

In many regions of the country they are receiving substantially increased services from EFTS-type programs with little change in cost.

LEGISLATIVE OBSTACLES

Political and legal realities may pose the greatest obstacle to the rapid growth of EFTS.

On the surface, the key issue is whether existing laws and regulations should be stretched, convoluted, and molded around this embryonic industry, or whether new standards and regulations should be created. The National Commission has suggested the latter course. But creating a national policy for EFTS development, as the National Commission proposed in its report in February 1977, may be far easier than executing it.

The key stumbling block is the duality of government regulation. Who will be the EFTS "guru"—the federal government or the states? Sufficient guidance is not provided by the two laws that today guide the federal and state roles in regulating and guiding the development of banking—the McFadden Act of 1927 and the Banking Act of 1933. Senator Thomas J. McIntyre's Banking Subcommittee is heading up an inquiry to reexamine these laws and test their applicability in today's world. Currently, the development of EFTS is plagued with the incongruity of having to depend on the McFadden Act as the primary source of public policy guidance.

The banking industry is in the throes of other struggles to maintain competitive balance among all types of depository institutions. The Senate

[3] *NCEFT, EFT and the Public Interest,* Report to the President and the Congress (February 23, 1977).

has debated the issues extensively since the 1970 Hunt Commission report and has developed two legislative models for reform, the proposed Financial Institutions Acts of 1973 and 1975. The House counterpart is the proposed Financial Reform Act of 1975. Some of the recommendations in these acts could decide the future form of EFTS.

In my opinion, Congress and the state legislatures must eventually make the decisions that will determine the who, where, what, and when of EFTS. The National Commission believes that the barriers to EFTS development should be lowered—that they are artificial and violate the interest of the public. EFTS development should not be tied, for example, to the laws prescribing the conditions for approving a new bank branch. Such a condition is altogether too restrictive.

Left unanswered is the question of whether the legislators will act, either in the Congress or in the states, upon various recommendations made forthrightly by the National Commission. The commission has proposed clear guidelines that cut through the rhetoric of a number of vested interests supporting mutually competing points of view. But the National Commission has no power to legislate.

What are the implications of these realities? My view is that they will not stop the *steady* growth of EFTS. However, they are likely to keep EFTS from spreading rapidly.

In conclusion, let me offer these observations and questions for businesses pondering the future of EFTS:

The cost of learning how to establish EFTS is high but, if carefully managed, worthwhile.

In spite of unfavorable short-run economics, many new commitments to EFTS are being made. This is because the long-run models look good.

Since depository institutions have never been immune to "go-go" urges, particularly during the past 15 years, their managements should beware of the "I can't afford not to" syndrome. Many of the world's great errors have been based on such thinking.

President Carter, California's Governor Brown, and other leaders talk about limited resources and lowered expectations. Does this represent the America of the future? Is EFTS consistent with such an America?

In a society with high unemployment and low energy resources, are the technological advances represented by EFTS a step forward?

From technological forecasting to future scenarios of the *Brave New World*-type, there seems to be almost unanimous opinion that EFTS is coming. Although we may have no choice about this reality, we have other choices. We can mold the shape and growth of EFTS. We can't change the answer to the question, "Whether EFTS?" but we can influence the answer to the question, "How much EFTS and when?"

SECTION III
Marketable Securities Management

Marketable securities are an important asset of the firm during times when there are excess funds available. They can be used to generate additional profits, while providing a part of overall firm liquidity. Different types of marketable securities with distinct characteristics are available to financial managers, and a number of different investment strategies can be used. This section contains five readings that discuss and evaluate some of the characteristics of marketable securities and strategies for their management.

Miller and Orr (Reading 12) discuss the problem of managing a cash balance in conjunction with a portfolio of short-term securities. They explain how a cost-balancing, inventory-type model can be extended to provide control limits on the cash balance of the firm. Cash flows are assumed to occur randomly. When the fluctuating cash balance of the firm reaches the upper (lower) control limit, securities are purchased (sold) in an amount which returns the cash balance to a specified level. Miller and Orr then describe a case study experience in which their model was used to evaluate the cash management policies of a firm characterized by frequent shifts between cash and marketable securities. Using the control model, it was possible to reduce both the number of securities transactions and the average cash balance of the firm.

Stone (Reading 13) reviews two inventory-type approaches to managing excess cash: one which assumes complete certainty in future cash flows, and one which assumes that cash flow is a random variable such as in the Miller-Orr model. Stone proposes a modification of the latter so as to better capture the realities faced by the cash manager. The idea is to use expected cash flows for the next few days in order to determine the appropriate adjustment in a control-limit model. By developing the logic on a time-shared computer, Stone suggests that the manager can usefully employ a combination of simulation and judgment to determine appropriate parameters for the model and to test alternative strategies for managing marketable securities.

A dynamic programming formulation is used by Daellenbach (Reading 14) to estimate the actual benefits that might be expected from the various models that have been proposed for managing excess cash. He compares possible benefits from each analysis with cost estimates of the development and operation of such models. Daellenbach concludes that much of the academic concern with cash management models apparently has been directed at a problem formulation and solution that offers at best only modest benefits to the firm.

Osteryoung, Roberts, and McCarty (Reading 15) investigate the possibility of a firm benefitting from "riding the yield curve," another popular strategy for managing excess cash. The authors show that selling marketable securities prior to maturity may result in a greater expected return to the firm, but only if greater risk is assumed. They present the results of an empirical test using Treasury bill prices over the period 1973-1976. Their result was that achieved returns for riskier strategies involving Treasury bills were no greater than that for the riskless strategy of simply holding Treasury bills to their maturity—and hence that riding the yield curve may be a questionable strategy for managing marketable securities.

In contrast to various conceptual strategies for managing marketable securities, Connelly (Reading 16) describes the recent practices of large firms in handling their excess cash. She reports that while most firms appear primarily interested in safety, certain firms do attempt to capture additional profits from their marketable securities portfolio. The author reports increased activity in Eurodollar deposits and certificates of deposit, a result of yield premiums amounting to 25-75 basis points. Connelly suggests that an emerging strategy for managing excess cash by many firms is to hold certificates of deposit and commercial paper to maturity, while trading Treasury bills for greater yields.

READING 12

Mathematical Models for Financial Management

Merton Miller
University of Chicago

Daniel Orr
University of California, La Jolla

One stream of current research in finance involves the extension to the field of finance of the methods and approaches that have come to be called "operations research" or "management science." Researchers working along these lines try to develop mathematical representations or "models" of typical decision-making problems in finance and, where they are given the opportunity to do so, to test and apply these models in actual decision settings. At the moment, this stream of research is still a relatively small one--really only a trickle as compared to the flood of material pouring out on the subjects of capital budgeting, or valuation. But it is a stream that can be expected to grow rapidly in the years ahead with the improvement in mathematical and computer technology and especially with the increase in the number of people who are being taught to use the tools effectively and creatively.

Rather than attempting any broad survey of work to date, this paper will present a single example of this type of research, describing both the development of the mathematical model and its application in a specific firm. Such an example can convey more graphically and more convincingly than any amount of preaching many of the important implications for management of this kind of research.

THE CASH BALANCE AS AN INVENTORY

The particular financial problem involved in our example is that of managing a cash balance in conjunction with a portfolio of short term securities. And the particular mathematical model that will be used is a type of *inventory* model that might be called a "control-limit" model.

It may be a little startling at first to think of your firm's cash balance as just another inventory--an inventory of dollars, so to speak--but is it really so farfetched? Consider, for example, some raw material item that your company stocks and ask yourself why you keep so much of it around or

Selected Paper #23, Graduate School of Business, University of Chicago, pp. 1-20. Reprinted by permission of the authors.

why you don't simply order each day's or each hour's requirement on a hand-to-mouth basis. The answer is, of course, that this would be a very wasteful policy. The clerical and other costs involved in placing orders for the material are not trivial; and there would be further costs incurred in the form of production delays or interruptions if materials were slow in arriving or if requirements on any day should happen to be higher than had been anticipated. Why, then, not eliminate these costs once and for all by placing one big order for a mountain of the stuff? Here, of course, the answer would be that there are also costs connected with *holding* inventory. These would include not just the physical costs connected with the storage space and handling, but also the cost of deterioration, or of obsolescence, or of adverse price fluctuations, and especially of the earnings foregone on capital tied up in the inventory. The inventory management problem for any physical commodity is thus one of striking a balance between these different kinds of costs; and the goal is to develop a policy in which orders will be placed on the average at just the right frequency and in just the right amounts so as to produce the smallest *combined* costs of ordering, or holding inventory, and of running out of stock.

Similarly with cash. If you want to add to or subtract from your inventory of cash by making a transfer to or from your portfolio of securities, there is an order cost involved, partly in the form of internal clerical and decision-making costs and partly in the form of brokerage fees, wire transfer costs and the like. In the other direction, if you try to cut down these in-and-out costs by holding large cash balances, there is a substantial holding cost in the form of the interest loss on the funds tied up in the balance. As for the costs connected with running out of cash, these are perhaps too obvious to require discussion before a group of this kind.

THE CONTROL-LIMIT APPROACH TO CASH MANAGEMENT

Accepting the inventory analogy as valid, what form of inventory management policy would be suitable for cash balances? Here since the typical cash balance fluctuates up and down and, in part, unpredictably, it seemed to us that the most natural approach for a wide variety of cases might be a "control-limit" policy.

How one particular kind of control-limit policy might work when applied to a cash balance is illustrated in Figure I. We say "one particular kind" since the control-limit approach is

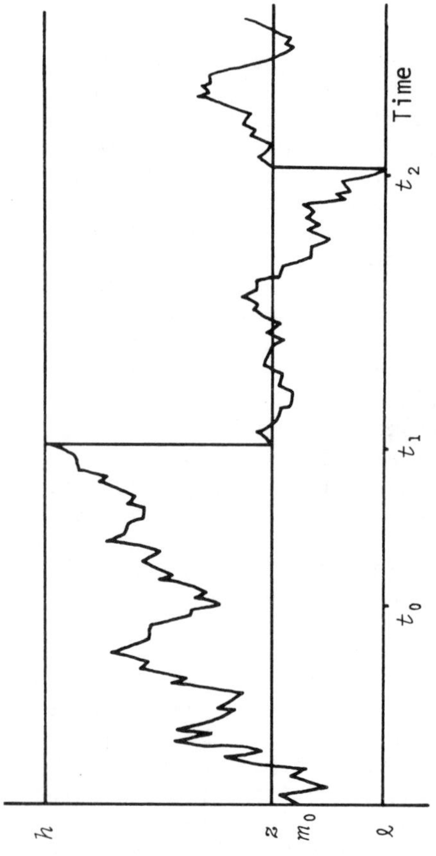

Figure I

quite flexible and many different variations can be used depending on the circumstances. The one illustrated happens to be an especially simple one and one that can be shown to be appropriate whenever the internal clerical and decision-making costs are the main costs involved in making portfolio transactions. It is also the form of policy actually used in the specific application to be described later.

The wiggly line that starts at the left at m_0 traces out the hypothetical path of a cash balance over time. As drawn, it first seems to fluctuate aimlessly until about day t_0, at which point a rising trend appears to set in. During this interval receipts are exceeding expenditures and the cash balance is building up. The buildup is allowed to continue until the day on which the cash balance first reaches or breaks through the *upper control limit* of h dollars. At this point in time--day t_1 on the graph--a portfolio purchase is made in an amount large enough to restore the cash balance to the *return point* z. Once back at z, the cash balance is allowed to wander again. No further purchases or sales are made until the balance either breaks through the upper bound at h again or until it breaks through the *lower control limit*, ℓ, as at day t_2. When the lower control limit is reached, a sale of securities from the portfolio is signalled in an amount such that the balance is once again restored to the return point z.

AN OPTIMAL SOLUTION FOR A SIMPLE SPECIAL CASE

Given that this kind of control policy seems reasonable--and we would argue that it is reasonable not only in dealing with some types of cash management problems but in many other kinds of settings where there is a substantial cost in managerial intervention to restore a "wandering" system to some desired state--the task of the researcher then becomes that of applying mathematical or numerical methods to determine the *optimal* values of the limits. By optimal we mean values that provide the most advantageous trade-off between interest loss on idle cash and the costs involved in transfers of cash to and from the portfolio. As it turns out, there happen to be some simple, but important special cases in which these optimal values can be derived in relatively straightforward fashion and where the results can be expressed in the form of a simple, compact formula. In particular, we have been able to obtain such a formula for the optimal values of the limits for cases which meet the following conditions: (1) Where it is meaningful to talk about both the cash balance and the portfolio as if they were each single homogeneous assets.[1] (2) Where transfers between cash and the portfolio may take place at any time but only at a given "fixed" cost, i.e., a cost that is the same regardless of the amount transferred, the direction of the transfer or of the time since the previous transfer.[2] (3) Where such transfers may be regarded as taking place instantaneously, that is, where the "lead time" involved in portfolio transfers is short enough to be ignored. (4) Where the lower limit on the cash balance is determined outside the model, presumably as the result of negotiations between the bank and the firm as to what the firm's required minimum balance is to be; and (5) Where the fluctuations in the cash balance are entirely random. There may perhaps be a trend or "drift" as it is called in this kind of analysis; but

---

[1] We have also recently been able to develop approximately optimal solutions for certain special kinds of "three-asset" models, i.e., models in which there are two kinds of securities (e.g., a line of credit and commercial paper) in addition to cash.

[2] Simple solutions also have been developed for the case in which the cost is not fixed but proportional to the amount transferred. More complicated, mixed cases involving both a fixed and a proportional component have been analyzed by our colleagues G. Eppen and E. Fama who have developed a very flexible method of obtaining numerical values for the limits under a wide variety of circumstances.

aside from this kind of simple systematic component, the day-to-day changes in the cash balance are completely unpredictable.

As for the specific formula that constitutes the solution under these assumptions, there is little point in discussing it any length here. The complete derivations and other details can be found in a recently-published article.[3] It might, perhaps, just be worth noting here that the solution defines the limits in terms of the fixed transfer cost, the daily rate of interest on the portfolio and the variability of daily changes in the cash balance (exclusive of changes related to the portfolio). As would be expected, the higher the transfer cost and greater the variability the wider the spread between the upper and the lower limits; and the higher the rate of interest, the lower the spread. There are, however, some surprises. In particular, for the "no-drift" case, it turns out that despite the fact that the cash balance is equally likely to go up or down, and it's equally costly to buy or to sell securities, the optimal return point--z--the point at which the average long-run costs of operating the system are lowest--does not lie midway between the upper and lower limits. Instead, it lies substantially below the midpoint. To be precise, it lies at one-third of the way between the lower and upper bounds and it stays at the one-third point regardless of the numerical values that are assigned to the transfer costs or to the daily rate of interest that can be earned on the portfolio. As these values are changed, the whole system expands or contracts, but the relation between the parts remains the same.

A TEST APPLICATION OF THE SIMPLE MODEL

Your initial reaction is likely to be that this model and the assumptions on which it was based are much too special and restrictive to have any important applicability to real-world problems. In management science, however, as in science generally, it is rash to pass judgment on the range of applicability of a model solely on the basis of the assumptions that underlie it. Mathematical models often turn out to be surprisingly "robust" and insensitive to errors in the assumptions. The only safe way to determine how well or how poorly a model works is to try it out and see.

In obtaining the basis for this kind of test of the model we were extremely fortunate in having the active collaboration of Mr. D.B. Romans, Assistant Treasurer of the Union Tank Car Company.[4] Mr. Romans had seen an earlier version of our original paper and was struck by the similarity between the model and his own policies in putting his firm's idle cash to work. The systematic investment of idle cash in short term, money market securities was a relatively new program for his company--one that he had instituted only about a year previously. The interest earnings for that year were quite large, not only in relation to the costs involved but to the total budget of the treasurer's department. Now that the year's experience had been accumulated, he wanted to go back over the record, to study it in detail and to see whether any changes in practice might be suggested that would make the operation even more profitable. He felt, and we agreed, that the model might be extremely helpful in this kind of evaluation. If the model did seem to behave sensibly when applied to the company's past cash flow then it might be used to provide an objective standard or "bogey" against which past performance

---

[3] "Model of the Demand for Money by Firms," by M. H. Miller and D. Orr, *Quarterly Journal of Economics* (Aug. 1966), pp. 413-435.

[4] We have also benefited greatly from discussions of cash management problems and practices with several officers of the Harris Trust and Savings Bank of Chicago. We hope that they will benefit too from this chance to see how the problem looks from the other side of the account.

could be measured.

Since mathematical modeling of business decisions is still quite new, and since few people outside the production area have had much direct connection with it, it is perhaps worth emphasizing that at no time was it intended or contemplated that a model should be developed to do the actual on-line decision-making. The purpose of the study was to be *evaluation* by the treasurer of his own operation. This is a valuable but unglamorous use of models that tends to be overlooked amidst all the hoopla of the Sunday supplement variety surrounding the subject of automated management. An important point that must be kept in mind about mathematical models is that they are not intended to *replace* management--though like any other technological improvement they sometimes have that effect--but that they provide managers with new tools or techniques to be used *in connection with* other managerial techniques (including good judgment) for improving over-all performance.

THE SETTING OF THE OPERATION

Since our objective was to compare the model's decisions over some trial period with those of the Assistant Treasurer, the first step was to examine carefully the setting in which he actually operated and to see how closely or how poorly the circumstances matched the assumptions of the model. As would be expected, the results were mixed. On the one hand, there were some respects in which the assumptions fit quite well. The Assistant Treasurer did behave, for example, as if he were in fact controlling only a single-central cash balance. Note the phrase "as if," because as a matter of fact the firm does have many separate balances in many banks. For purposes of cash management, however, the Assistant Treasurer works with one single balance representing the free funds that he can marshal throughout the system without regard to the particular banks they happen to be in at the monent (or where the funds derived from a portfolio liquidation must ultimately be routed).

It was also clear that there were substantial "order costs" involved in making portfolio transfers. In the case of a portfolio purchase, for example, some of the main cost components include: (a) making two or more long-distance phone calls plus fifteen minutes to a half-hour of the Assistant Treasurer's time, (b) typing up and carefully checking an authorization letter with four copies, (c) carrying the original of the letter to be signed by the Treasurer, and (d) carrying the copies to the controller's office where special accounts are opened, the entries are posted and further checks of the arithmetic made. It is hard to establish a precise dollar figure for these costs, but at least the approximate order of magnitude for a complete round trip is probably somewhere between \$20 and \$50. That this is not a trivial amount of money in the present context becomes clear when you remember that interest earnings at the then prevailing level of interest rates were running at about \$10 per day per hundred thousand dollars in the portfolio and that his average size of portfolio purchase during the test period was about \$400,000.

Not surprisingly, we also found that there was a considerable amount of randomness or unpredictability in the daily cash flow. In fact, the Assistant Treasurer did not even attempt to forecast or project flows more than a day or two ahead except for certain large recurring outflows such as tax payments, dividend payments, sinking fund deposits, transfers to subsidiaries and the like; and even here the forecasts were made more with a view to deciding the appropriate maturities to hold in the portfolio than as part of the cash balance control *per se*. As for the "drift" or trend, analysis of the cash flow over the 9-month test period showed no evidence of any significant drift in either direction.

As opposed to these similarities between the assumptions of the model and the reality of the firm's operation there were very definitely a number of respects in which the fit was much less comfortable. The model assumes, for example, that when the lower bound on cash is hit or breached, there will be an immediate sale of securities out of the portfolio to make up the cash deficiency. The Assistant Treasurer, however, followed a policy of buying only non-marketable securities and holding them to maturity primarily because he wanted to try his new cash management program without requiring any change in the company's standard accounting procedures. Hence, if a large net cash drain occurred unexpectedly on a day on which he had no maturing security he simply let his cash balance drop below his normal minimum which he and his banks regarded as an "average minimum" rather than as the strict minimum contemplated by the model.

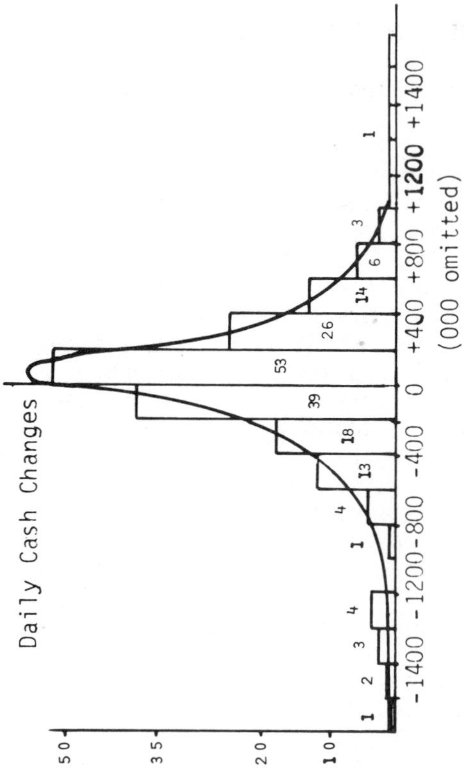

Figure II

A discrepancy between the model and reality that was more disturbing appeared when we constructed the frequency distribution of daily cash changes by size of change over the 9-month sample period of 189 working days. The distribution of these daily changes is shown in graphic form in Figure II. The logic of the model requires that this distribution be at least approximately of a form that statisticians refer to as "normal" or "Gaussian." A hasty glance at the figure might lead one to conclude that this requirement is met. Closer study reveals, however, that not only is the distribution not normal, but it almost seems to be a member of a particularly ill-behaved class of "fat-tailed" distributions that have come to be called "Paretian distributions."[5] In these distributions--which may be familiar to those of you who have been following the debate about random walks in the stock market[6]--large changes occur much more frequently than in the case of the normal distribution. In fact, the frequency of large changes is so much greater that we were quite uncertain as to whether the model would behave in even roughly sensible fashion or whether it would simply find itself being whip-sawed to death by the violent swings through the control range. As indicated earlier, however, there is only one way to tell; and that's by trying it out and seeing what happens.

---

[5] We say "almost seems to be" because despite the conspicuously fat tails, the distributions as computed cumulatively month by month remain roughly similar with no tendency for the tails to get fatter and fatter over time as in a true Paretian process. The Paretian like tails are mainly the reflection of such large, but relatively controllable and definitely size-limited items as dividends, taxes, transfers to and from subsidiaries and the like.

[6] *Random Walks in Stock-Market Prices*, Selected Papers No. 16, Graduate School of Business, University of Chicago.

THE TEST OF THE MODEL AGAINST THE DATA

To get a close basis for comparison with the Assistant Treasurer's actual decisions it was decided to run the model under various alternative assumptions about the true value of the transfer cost. That is, we would start with a conservatively high value of say $90 per transfer; compute the optimal upper limit h and return point z; run the model against the actual data and tabulate its portfolio purchases and sales. If, as expected, the model made fewer transfers than the Assistant Treasurer, then we would go back; use a lower value for the costs; recompute the new optimal limits and so on until we had finally forced the model to make approximately the same number of transfers over the sample interval as the Assistant Treasurer himself. Then, assuming the model was behaving sensibly, we could compare and contrast their patterns of portfolio decisions over the interval as well as get at least some rough idea of what figure for the cost of a transfer the Assistant Treasurer was implicitly using in his own operation.

The only difficulty encountered in implementing this straightforward kind of test was in the matter of deciding precisely how many transfers the Assistant Treasurer should be regarded as having made. Because of his policy of holding only non-marketable issues, his portfolio tended to be of quite short average duration. Hence there were inevitably days on which he had a maturity that proved to be too early. If he had merely rolled these issues over there would have been no problem; we would simply have washed that transaction out and not counted either the maturity or the reinvestment as a transfer. But it is clearly not always efficient just to roll over the maturing issue. Given that a purchase must be made anyway on that day, it would be wise to pick up any additional cash that also happened to be lying around, even if the amount involved would not have been large enough by itself to have justified incurring a transfer cost. Accordingly, we decided not to count any transfers on roll-over days unless the Assistant Treasurer indicated that the balance was so large even without the maturing issue that he would almost certainly have bought anyway (in which case he would be charged with the purchase, but not the sale). Similarly with the case of net sale days. If there was a larger maturity on a given day than was actually needed to meet the cash drain and if some small part of the excess proceeds were rolled over, then he was charged with a sale, but not a purchase. By this criterion we were able to agree on a figure of 112 total transactions by the Assistant Treasurer during the 189 test days of which 58 were purchases and 54 were sales (maturities).

THE RESULTS OF THE TEST

When we commenced the trial-and-error process of matching the total number of transactions by the model with those of the Assistant Treasurer our hope was that the model might be able to achieve an average daily cash balance no more than say 20 to 30 percent above the Assistant Treasurer's average. We felt that if we could get that close and if the model did behave sensibly, then there was a very real prospect of being able to use the model as a bogey against which to measure and evaluate actual performance. As it turned out, however, we found that at 112 transactions, the model not only came close but actually did better--producing an average daily cash balance about 40 percent *lower* than that of the Assistant Treasurer ($160,000 for the model as compared with about $275,000). Or, looking at it from the other side, if we matched the average daily cash holdings at $275,000, the model was able to reach this level with only about 80 transactions or about one-third less than the 112 actually required.

It can be argued, of course, that this sort of comparison is unfairly loaded in favor of the model, not only because it was applied on a hindsight basis, but because the transfer costs would actually have been higher for the model than the simple matching of total numbers of transfers would seem to suggest. The Assistant Treasurer, it will be recalled, never really sold a security; he merely let it run off. Hence the model would have had to incur additional costs on at least those sales that did not occur on the easily forecastable, large-out-flow days. Check of the numbers involved showed, however, that the model would still have dominated in terms of net interest minus transfer costs over the sample period even if these extra costs of liquidation were included on every sale. And, of course, that is much too extreme an adjustment. Many of the actual sale days of the model coincided with the large out-flow days and appropriately maturing securities could have been purchased to hit these dates. In fact, the post-mortem showed that about half the model's sales took place on days then the Assitant Treasurer also "sold" and nearly 80 percent occurred either on the same day or within one day either way of a day on which he scheduled a maturity.

Furthermore, the model too is operating under some handicaps in the comparison. At no time, for example, did the model ever violate the minimum cash balance marked on the Assitant Treasurer's work-sheets, whereas no less than 10 percent of his total dollar days invested were represented by the cash deficiencies on the days in which he let his balance dip temporarily below the minimum. In addition, the model did not receive instructions to change its policies before weekends and holidays. The Assistant Treasurer, on the other hand, always knew when it was Friday and was thus able to sock away additional amounts on which he could get two extra days interest.

All in all then the comparison would seem to be basically a fair one; and it is a tribute to the Assitant Treasurer's personal and professional character that he never became ego-involved in the comparison or wasted time alibiing. He was concerned about one thing and one thing only: How to do an even better job.

THE COMPARISON OF OPERATING POLICIES

With this question in mind, we then went on to make a detailed comparison of the actual decisions with those called for by the model. The complete record of these comparisons is, of course, too long and too specialized to be spelled out at length here, but there are at least a few simple contrasts that can be presented to illustrate the sorts of things that turned up.

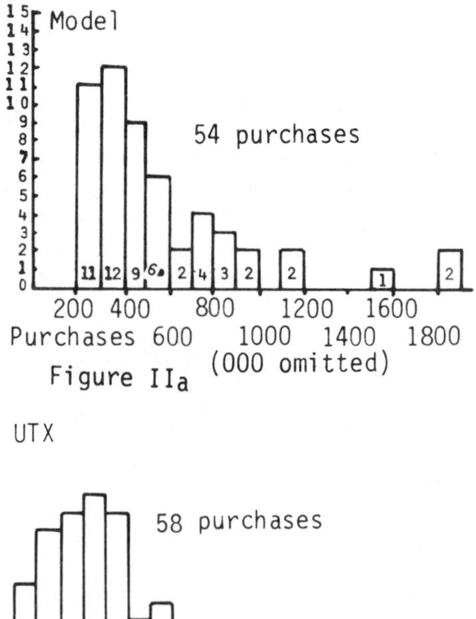

Figure IIa

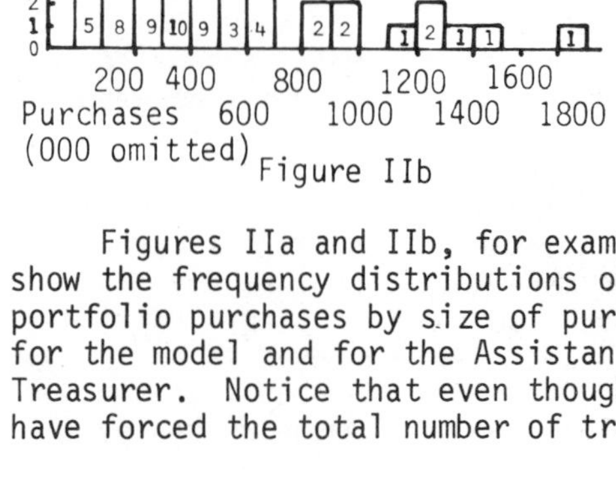

Figure IIb

Figures IIa and IIb, for example, show the frequency distributions of portfolio purchases by size of purchase for the model and for the Assistant Treasurer. Notice that even though we have forced the total number of transfers to match, the model makes somewhat fewer purchases (54 as against 58) and does so in considerably larger average size (about $600,000 as compared with only $440,000). The difference in operating policy is particularly striking at the lower end of the size scale because of the rigid rule built into the model that keeps it from ever buying in units smaller than h-z, which was about $250,000 when the model was set to produce 112 transfers. The Assistant Treasurer, by contrast, made about 13 purchases (or nearly 25 percent of his total purchases) in amounts smaller than that size including 5 in amounts of $100,000 or less. Even allowing for the fact that some of these small transactions were for weekends, the total impression conveyed is one of an excessive amount of small-lot purchasing activity. This impression was further reinforced both by the very low implicit transfer cost that was necessary to force the model to make 112 transfers as well as by the fact that more than 90 percent of the total interest earnings achieved by the model with 112 transfers could have been attained with only about 50 total transfers. Of these 50, moreover, only some 20 were purchases and all were of fairly large size.

Even more revealing are Figures IIIa and IIIb which show the distribution of the closing cash balance by size on days when no portfolio action was taken in either direction. Notice again that because of its rigid upper limit the model never lets the cash balance go above h which in this case is about $400,000. The Assistant Treasurer, however, seems to be much less consistent in this respect, having foregone no less than 23 buying opportunities of this amount or larger including 3 of over a million dollars. When and why so many opportunities were missed is still not entirely clear. Part of the trouble undoubtedly stems from the fact that the Assistant Treasurer has many other responsibilities and cannot always count on being at his desk at the time of day when the decision has to be made. And without actually interrupting to construct his worksheet, there is no way for him to determine whether an interruption of his other work would really be profitable. Hopefully, however, by making his limits more explicit (in the spirit of the model) and by delegating to others much of the purely mechanical task of monitoring these limits, he will be able to achieve in the future a significant reduction in the size and frequency of these lost opportunities.

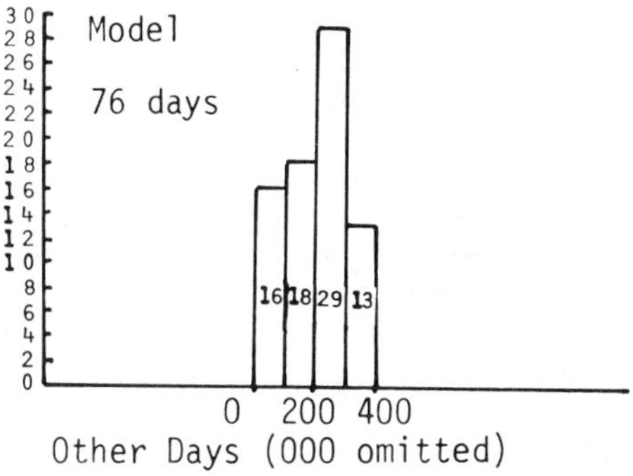

Figure IIIa

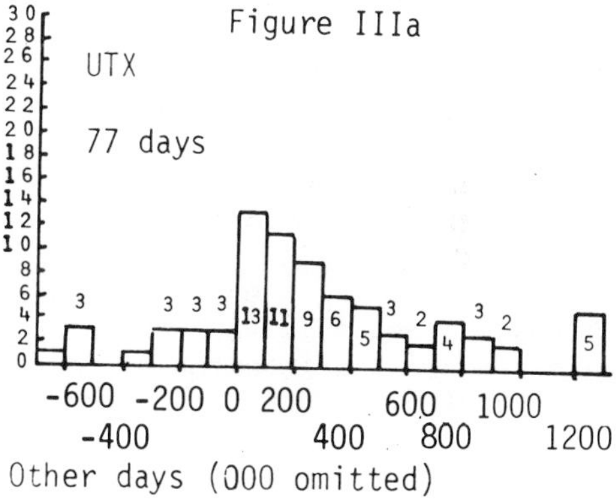

Figure IIIb

CONCLUSION

We have tried here to present a concrete example of how mathematical methods can be and are being applied to management problems in the field of finance. The example happens to be a particularly simple one. But it does at least serve to illustrate very neatly a number of points about this kind of research that senior financial managers would do well to keep in mind.

First, it is important for financial managers to disabuse themselves of the notion that there is something special or unique about financial problems. In particular, we have seen that what is commonly regarded as a peculiarly financial problem--to wit, managing the cash balance and a portfolio of liquid securities--turns out to be nothing more than an inventory problem.

Second, mathematical models of decision or control problems should not be thought of as something fundamentally different from ordinary management principles or techniques. They are merely more disciplined and systematic ways of exploiting these principles. In particular, control-limit models of the kind we have seen here--and remember that many additional variations are possible--are essentially extensions of the fundamental notion of "management by exception."

Third, be careful not to prejudge mathematical models solely on the basis of the lack of literal realism in the assumptions underlying them. To develop a workable model, simplifications--sometimes, extreme simplifications--must be made. But, if it has been properly conceived, a simple model may still perform extremely well. It is not a matter of getting something for nothing; rather that the gains made by doing a good job on the really essential parts of the problem are often more than large enough to offset the errors introduced by the simplifications (errors, incidentally, that often cancel out).

Finally, remember that there is a trade-off between improving decision-procedures and improving the information and forecasts used in arriving at the decisions. In the present instance, for example, we saw a case in which a model that assumed the cash flow to be completely random was still able to do a very successful job of decision-making. Nor is this result unique or exceptional. The slogan everywhere today is "more, better and faster information for management." We suspect, however, that thanks to the computer, many firms may already be in the position of having more, better and faster information than they can use effectively with present management techniques. There is likely to be as much or more real pay-off in the years ahead in rationalizing and improving decision procedures than there is in simple trying to get an even bigger bang from the information explosion.

READING 13

The Use of Forecasts and Smoothing in Control-Limit Models for Cash Management

Bernell K. Stone
Georgia Institute of Technology

In the literature of finance there are two classes of inventory approaches to the cash management problem—one initiated by Baumol [1] postulates complete certainty; the other, presented by Miller and Orr [2], postulates complete uncertainty. Although these two models represent the two extremes between certainty and uncertainty in cash management, both have in common a desire to specify the appropriate timing and size of marketable security transactions in the framework of two assets—cash and a single interest-bearing security with no maturity structure. Both view the problem as a trade-off between incurring transaction costs and holding idle cash balances.

Baumol assumes: (1) a constant continuous net cash flow that is known with certainty; (2) a constant fixed transaction cost; (3) an opportunity cost for idle cash. Baumol finds the economic order quantity that minimizes the cost of cash management (defined as the sum of the transaction cost and the opportunity cost of holding money). Both the existence of a maturity schedule and the problem of reinvesting maturing short-term assets are ignored.

The Miller-Orr cash management model postulates a control-limit inventory policy and assumes: (1) cash flows are completely random in nature (stochastic); (2) the cash flows have no "net drift," i.e., there is neither a net inflow (positive drift) nor a net outflow (negative drift), but an average *net* flow of zero; (3) the day-to-day cash flows are independent and identically distributed; (4) transaction costs are fixed and are the same for sales and purchases; (5) maturing securities are automatically reinvested and are not regarded as a part of the cash flow; (6) cash balances may not fall below a fixed minimum level; (7) the sizes of security purchases and sales are continuous—there are no unit order quantities. Miller and Orr find the control limits and return point that will minimize the sum of transaction costs and the opportunity cost of idle cash.

Reprinted from FINANCIAL MANAGEMENT (Spring 1972), pp. 72-84, by permission of the publisher and author.

ASPECTS OF REAL-WORLD CASH MANAGEMENT

Real-world cash flows are neither completely certain, uniform, and continuous nor are they completely unpredictable. The day-to-day flows are generally not independent. Most firms can and do forecast their cash flows, but there is an element of uncertainty in the forecast. Thus a firm's net daily cash flow is lumpy, discontinuous, and partially known (forecastable) and partially unknown (stochastic). It may be positive one day, negative the next; it may have a net drift.

Within this environment of partially forecastable cash flows, corporate cash managers generally attempt to:

1. "Look ahead" when buying and selling securities—they consider not only their present cash position but also incorporate data from their cash forecasts.
2. Smooth cash flows by coordinating security maturities with forecasted cash needs.
3. Buy the highest yielding securities subject to portfolio and liquidity constraints unless transaction savings are achievable by cash flow smoothing.
4. Maintain cash balances sufficient to meet the average net collected balance requirements arising from banking arrangements.

For most large firms, net collected balances required by banking arrangements are much larger than average daily cash flows. Since most banking arrangements only call for the maintenance of *average* balances, a firm can tolerate fairly large fluctuations in its cash balances as long as net collected balances are not negative. It can also adjust its target level of cash balances to make up for the fact that past balances have been above or below the target within the time period over which the average is calculated.

In addition to activities that relate directly to cash position management, corporate financial managers also make portfolio switches, sell before maturity, and employ other devices to improve the return on their portfolio. In this article, however, we shall focus only on the management of aggregate cash position and not include portfolio management.

In the following sections, we shall formulate a control-limit inventory model of cash management that incorporates imperfect forecasts of future cash flows and employs heuristics (i.e., simple decision rules) to take advantage of the information contained in the cash forecasts. These heuristics will attempt to: (1) look ahead a short period to take account of the forthcoming forecasted cash flows and thereby avoid unnecessary transactions and (2) match security maturities with cash needs to smooth cash flows and reduce transactions.

A MODEL OF CASH FLOWS

Representation of Cash Flows. We seek to represent cash flows when there is: (1) a cash forecast for daily flows over a time horizon of N days—in a variable period model, for instance, one could have a daily forecast for a period and then a weekly forecast, (2) an estimate of the uncertainty associated with the forecast, and (3) a schedule of maturities for current holdings of marketable securities.

Let ε_t be the error in the forecasted cash flow for any given day, t. The expected value or forecasted arithmetic mean of the positive and negative error terms over a relatively large number of days is zero. Mathematically speaking, when the expectations operator, E, is applied to the error term, we get $E(\varepsilon_t) = 0$. Then the actual net cash flow that occurs on day t, C_t, can be represented as the sum of the forecasted cash flow, $E(C_t)$, and of ε_t. That is:

$$C_t = E(C_t) + \varepsilon_t \, .$$

We can break the expected net cash

flow on day t, $E(C_t)$, into the sum of the expected flow from operations on day t, $E(F_t)$, and the flow from maturing marketable securities, M_t (assumed known with certainty). Thus, C_t can be expressed as:

$$C_t = M_t + E(F_t) + \varepsilon_t \, .$$

When we assume M_t is known with certainty, then the error in the forecast is due to inability to forecast the flow from operations.

The Miller-Orr and Baumol Models as Special Cases. To obtain the Miller-Orr model from our general cash flow representation, we ignore the cash flow from maturing marketable securities, M_t, set the expected flow from operations, $E(F_t)$, equal to zero for all t days, and assume that the unknown error terms (which are the only remaining component of the cash flow) are independently and identically distributed random variables [mathematically, these assumptions mean that: (1) for all t, $E(C_t) = E(\varepsilon_t) = 0$; (2) covariance $(\varepsilon_t, \varepsilon_{t'}) = 0$ unless $t = t'$].

To obtain the Baumol model from our general cash flow representation, we set the error term, ε_t, equal to zero for all t days, again ignore M_t, and assume that the expected cash flow from operations (which will now be the actual cash flow) is the *same* constant amount every day.

From this reformulation of the Miller-Orr and Baumol models in the context of our general cash flow representation, we see the sense in which these models represent extremes of certainty and uncertainty. In Miller-Orr, $E(C_t) = 0$ and ε_t is the only component of the cash flows; in Baumol, $\varepsilon_t = 0$ and $E(F_t)$, and therefore C_t, is a constant.

PROBLEM FORMULATION

Basic Assumptions. In addition to the use of a control-limit inventory model, we assume:

1. There are two assets—cash and an interest-bearing security.
2. There is a series of maturities for this security with a schedule of yields for different length maturities. (No special assumptions are required about the shape of the yield curve.)
3. Maturing securities are not automatically reinvested, but are part of the firm's cash flow—for example, securities maturing on day t of dollar amount M_t are part of the forecasted cash flow for day t.
4. There exists a forecast of future net cash flows over a time horizon of N days. The cash forecasts are updated whenever new information becomes available; the schedule of maturity dates and dollar values is updated whenever the firm makes purchases or sales of securities. There is a rolling time horizon; $t = 0$ is the current day and $t = N$ is the final day.
5. A firm attempts to maintain a specified level of cash ledger balances such that it can meet the average net collected balance requirement consistent with its planned credit and banking needs.

A firm with many banks will be concerned with the allocation of balances among its banks and, of course, with the prevention of overdrafts. The problem of distributing cash over a firm's banks (which can be called the "cash allocation problem") is not of concern in this article.

Specification of the Objective Function. Past inventory models of the cash management problem have been concerned with the trade-off between the carrying cost of idle balances and transaction costs; they have ignored the maturity structure problem.

The basis for the concern with carrying costs has been the assumption that idle balances have an opportunity cost related to the rate that can be earned on short-term funds. Consideration of the constraints imposed on the firm by the bank implies that the problem is more complex.

For loans, lines of credit, and even tangible services, banks require a firm to maintain specified levels of average new collected balances. All cash in demand deposits counts toward these requirements; hence, unless the firm maintains cash in excess of its net collected balance requirements, the opportunity cost of cash is really zero because these balances must be met (if it is assumed these services can only be provided by the company's bank—a not unreasonable assumption). Moreover, if at any time the firm maintains excessive balances, it can generally apply these balances to another time period. Hence, all cash can be regarded as counting toward the compensating balance requirement. On the average, a firm that acts optimally should never have excess balances. Thus, the carrying cost is not an important component of the objective function for aggregate cash position management. There is a wide range of bank practice with respect to how compensating balance requirements must be met. The most common arrangement is to require a monthly average. Many banks allow a yearly average, while some expect balances to be met on a moving-average basis (e.g., the ten-day average balances shall not fall below the target). A more limited number of banks specify a minimum (other than zero) level below which net collected balances may not fall. Terms between a firm and its bank are a subject for negotiation, but almost all major banks will allow a firm to meet balance requirements in terms of a monthly or yearly average. In any case, all that is required to justify the ability of the firm to tolerate fluctuations in its aggregate balance is for at least one of a firm's major banks to allow meeting requirements on an average basis. It is not necessary that every bank treat balances on an average basis or that no bank specify a minimum acceptable level of net collected balances.

The ability to buy securities of different maturities provides an opportunity to reduce transaction costs by smoothing cash flows and thereby reducing the number and dollar value of security transactions. When investing excess cash, cash flow smoothing consists of buying securities that will mature at times of large forecasted outflow; when providing cash by selling securities, cash flow smoothing consists of selling securities that would mature (if not sold) at or near times when excessive cash inflows are forecasted. The cost trade-off in smoothing is between reduced transaction costs and possible loss of return on a portfolio of short-term securities. An objective function that reflects this trade-off is formulated in a later section.

An important cost of aggregate cash position management is the cost of running the system. A model that structures the problem, handles information, and performs calculations quickly and cheaply will probably have as its major benefit, not the increased return on the portfolio of marketable securities, but rather cost savings from saved executive time and reduced accounting cost.

OPERATION OF THE CONTROL-LIMIT MODEL

This section formulates the decisions of timing and amount in the context of a control-limit inventory model. The succeeding one treats the maturity structure problem.

When cash forecasts are available, an automatic and immediate return to a target level of balances after disturbance is generally not optimal. For example, consider a firm with a target balance of 4.0 (in millions of dollars) and control limits of 5.0 and 3.5. If current balances were 5.2, an automatic return model would require the purchase of 1.2 in marketable securities to restore balances to 4.0. If the cash manager expected additional inflows of .3 and .2 over the next two days, he might want to purchase 1.7 (instead of 1.2) so that he would be back on target in two days rather than immediately.

On the other hand, if the cash manager expected outflows of 1.0 and .2 over the next two days, then he might prefer to make no purchase (depending on the rate for overnight money), since he will probably have to sell to restore the balance to 4.0 on the next day.

Assume we know the current level of cash balances, CB_o and can make a forecast of the net cash flow $E(C_t)$—positive or negative—that will occur on each day, t, over the next k days. Then the expected level of cash balances k days from now is the sum of the current level of cash balances and the algebraic sum of k daily net cash flows. Mathematically, the expected balance in k days can be represented as:

$$E(CB_k) = CB_o + \sum_{t=1}^{k} E(C_t) .$$

If the net cash flows over the next k days are lumped into a single net cash flow figure for the k-day period, SC_k, the expected level of cash balances in k days is the sum of the present cash balance and the expected value of SC_k, i.e.:

$$E(CB_k) = CB_o + E(SC_k) .$$

Exhibit 1 depicts the two-level control-limit structure to be presented. The target level of cash balances is denoted by TB. There are two sets of control limits. One is defined by h_1 and h_o, the upper and lower control limits for initiating consideration of a transaction; the other set is defined by $h_1 - \delta_1$ and $h_o + \delta_o$, the upper and lower limits that determine whether a transaction will actually be made.

In the operation of the model, no action is taken unless the current cash balance CB_o is outside of the control limits defined by h_1 and h_o. If these limits are exceeded, then (rather than returning automatically to the target level of balances TB) the information contained in the forecast over the next k days is used to decide whether a marketable security transaction should be made. A transaction will be made only if expected cash balances in k days, $E(CB_k)$, will exceed the control limits defined by $h_1 - \delta_1$ and $h_o + \delta_o$. If a transaction is made, the amount is such that expected balances in k days will be at the target level of cash balances. Thus, when a transaction is made, the model returns the expected level of balances in k days to the target level rather than immediately returning the current balance to the target.

EXHIBIT 1. Structure of Control-Limit Model With Two Sets of Limits

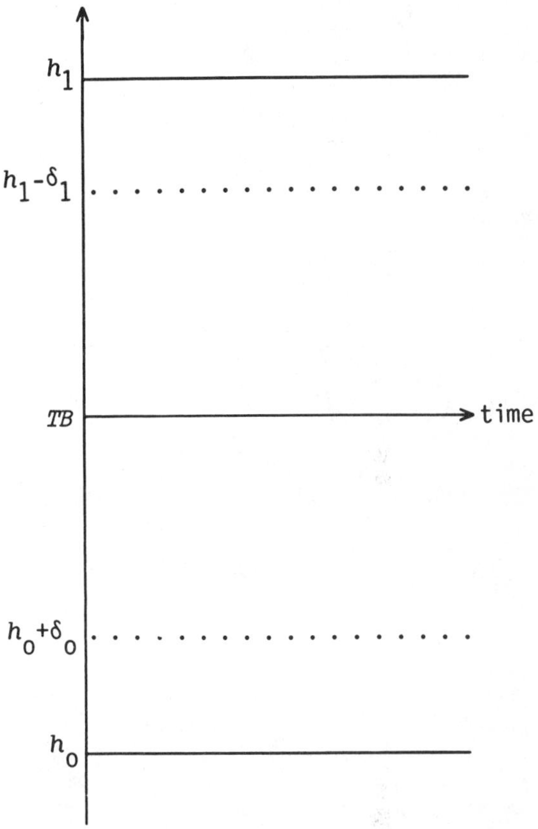

Both the number of days, k, in the look-ahead horizon and the values of the control limits are model parameters that must be assigned. (There

is further discussion of the specification of model parameters in a later section.) Typical values of k are on the order of 3 to 12 days; this period is less than the number of days for which most large firms have fairly accurate forecasts.

The look-ahead technique has the effect of smoothing out day-to-day cash flows so that a firm makes decisions on the *net* flows over k days rather than responding to day-to-day fluctuations. Two of the major benefits of the k-day, look-ahead technique (combined with a recognition of the ability of a firm to tolerate fluctuations in its balances) are that the number of transactions should be reduced and the average maturity of the portfolio can (if profitable) be increased. A major benefit of maturity lengthening is shifting from overnight and 1-day maturities to greater-than-k-day maturities. (Although this model requires no assumptions about the shape of the money market yield curve, the sharpest rise *on average* is at the start of the curve, say from 1 to 15 days.)

With this model, the expected cash balance in k-days will be the target balance; the actual balance will be the target plus the net cumulative forecast error. Thus, if the cumulative forecast error is between levels of errors ranging from e_1 to e_o, then CB_k will be between $TB + e_1$ and $TB - e_o$. For instance, if $e_1 = h_1 - TB$ and $e_o = TB - h_o$, then we know that cash balances on day k will be between h_1 and h_o. Although forecast errors are not likely to be substantial over a short horizon, it is necessary to monitor for errors for k days after a transaction has occurred, since cash policy is fixed over a horizon of k-days *unless* specified error tolerances have been exceeded.

Exhibit 2 is a logic diagram of the buy-sell decision process. "Update" is simple a program module that adds in current cash flows, keeps track of errors, adjusts for the passage of time, and performs various housekeeping functions. The major steps in the operation of the model are as follows:

1. If any transactions have taken place within the last k days, go to 2; otherwise to to 3.
2. If prespecified error tolerances have not been exceeded, make no transaction and go to 7; otherwise go to 3.
3. Compute the expected value of the net cash flow for the k-day period, $E(SC_k)$, by algebraically summing each day's positive or negative expected cash flow.
4. If the current cash balance falls between the outer control limits h_o and h_1, make no transaction and go to 7; otherwise, go to 5 if CB_o exceeds (or equals) h_1 or go to 6 if CB_o is less than (or equal to) h_o.
5. Since the present cash balance, CB_o, exceeds the upper outer control limit, h_1, *buy* an amount of securities equal to CB_o plus the expected value of k-day net cash flow, $E(SC_k)$, less the target balance, TB, *if* $CB_o + E(SC_k)$ exceeds the upper inner control limit, $h_1 - \delta_1$; otherwise make no transaction and go to 7.
6. Since the present cash balance, CB_o, is less than the lower outer control limit, h_o, *sell* an amount of securities equal to the target balance, TB, less both CB_o and the expected value of k-day net cash flow, $E(SC_k)$, *if* $CB_o + E(SC_k)$ is less than the lower inner control limit, $h_o + \delta_o$; otherwise make no transaction and go to 7.
7. Update and begin again at Start in one day.

Example of Operation of the k-Day Look-Ahead. Exhibit 3 gives a hypothetical set of forecasted net cash flows and the actual net cash flows that occurred, the forecast error, a summary of security transactions, and actual cash position on each day *after* security transactions for both a three-day and a no-day look-ahead. Exhibits 4 and 5 plot cash balances as a function of time for each case; the dashed lines

EXHIBIT 2. Buy-Sell Decision Algorithm with a k-Day Look-Ahead

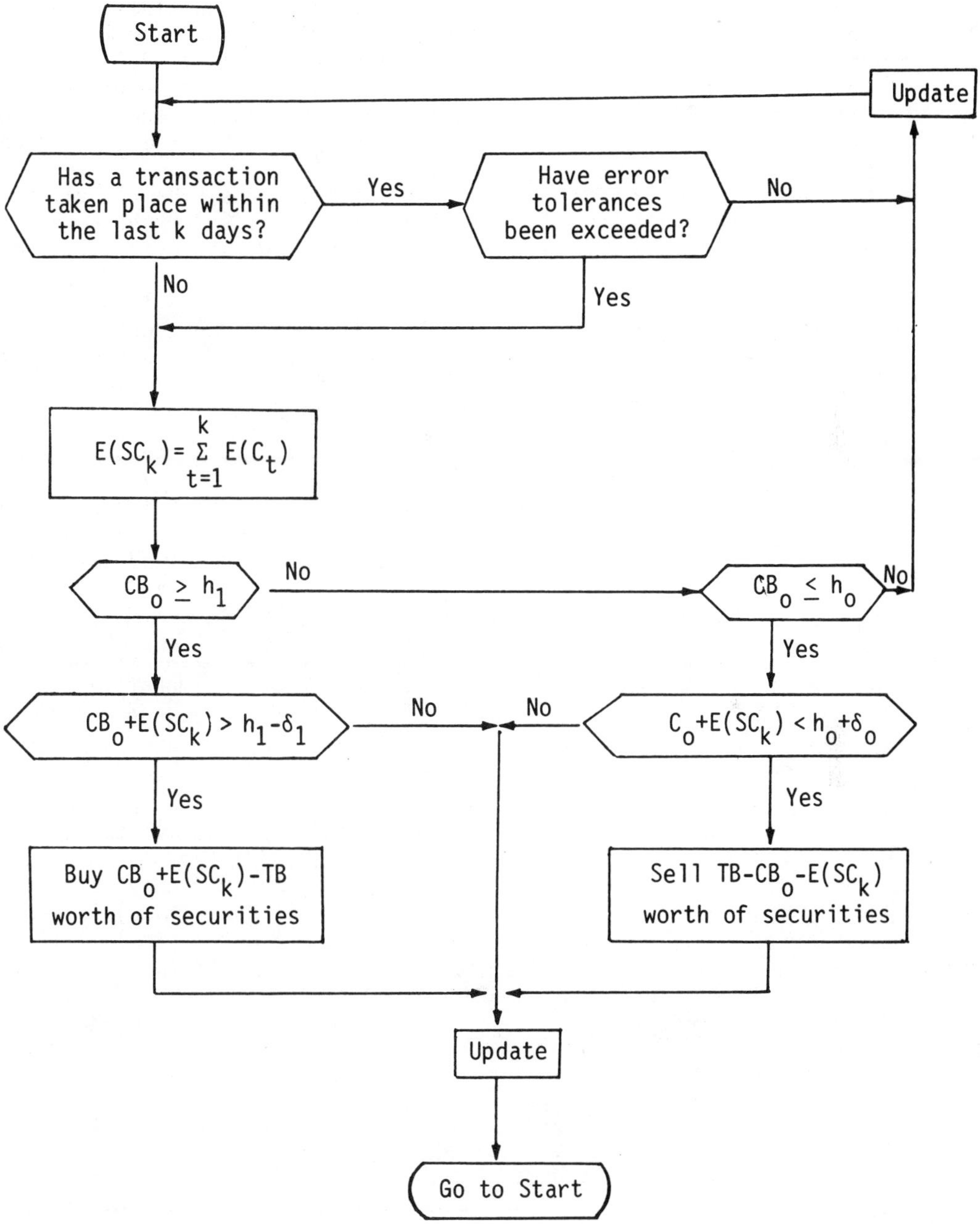

EXHIBIT 3. Cash Flow, Security Transactions, and Cash Position Data

Cash Forecast and Cash Flow Data				Three-Day Look-Ahead		No Look-Ahead	
Day Number	Cash Flow Forecast	Actual Cash Flow	Forecast Error	Transaction Cash Flow	Final Cash Position	Transaction Cash Flows	Final Cash Position
1	1	1	0	--	21	--	21
2	2	1	1	--	22	--	22
3	3	6	-3	--	28	-8	20
4	-1	-1	0	--	27	--	19
5	-2	-3	1	--	24	--	16
6	-3	-3	0	--	21	+7	20
7	-8	-9	1	--	12	+9	20
8	5	6	-1	--	18	--	26
9	6	4	2	--	22	-10	20
10	4	6	-2	-17	11	--	26
11	5	3	2	--	14	-9	20
12	4	4	0	--	18	--	24
13	0	1	-1	--	19	--	25
14	2	-1	3	--	18	--	24
15	-3	-2	-1	--	16	--	22
16	1	2	-1	--	18	--	24

EXHIBIT 4. Cash Position With Three-Day Look-Ahead

(In millions of dollars)

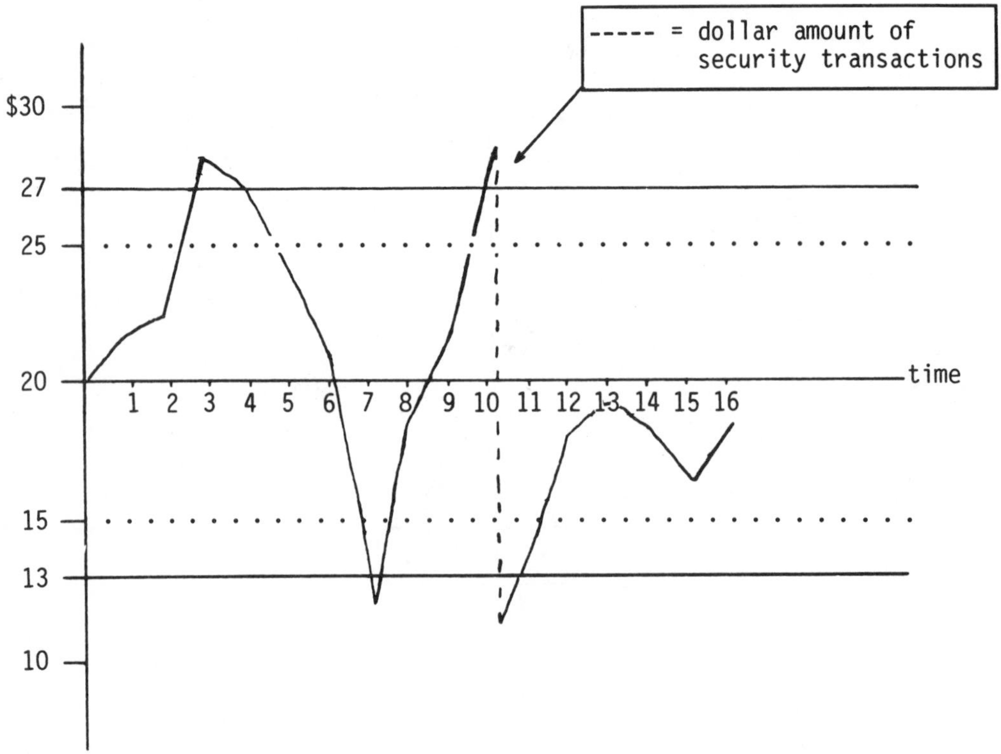

EXHIBIT 5. Cash Position with No Look-Ahead
(In millions of dollars)

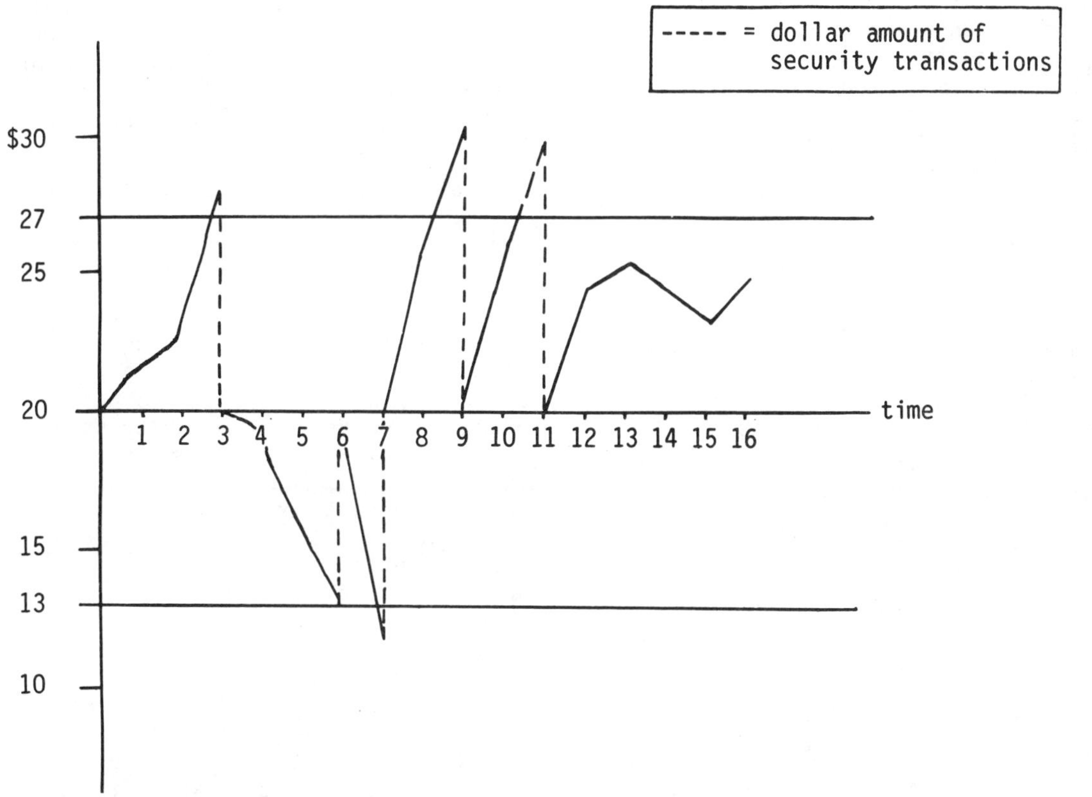

represent changes in level due to security transactions. In this example, $TB = 20$, $h_1 = 27$, and $h_o = 13$; $\delta_1 = \delta_o = 2$ (in millions of dollars). It is clear by inspection that the cash position shows greater variability with no look-ahead than with the three-day look-ahead. There are also more transactions—5 versus 1; there is a greater dollar volume of transactions—$43 million versus $17 million. However, the average size of a transaction is lower with no look-ahead.

THE SECURITY MATURITY DECISION

The look-ahead procedure determines whether or not a transaction is necessary when the cash level exceeds the control points and, when it is necessary, specifies the size of the recommended transaction. Once it is decided to transact a given amount, it is necessary to specify the maturity structure of the transaction.

To formulate this decision, let q_t be the quantity transacted in a marketable security of maturity t. For a purchase transaction, q_t will be the cash invested in securities of maturity t; for a sale, q_t will be the amount of maturity t that is sold.

The maturity structure decision involves a trade-off between obtaining the best possible return and the opportunity to smooth cash flows and thereby reduce transactions. To get an expression for the savings from reducing cash flows, let B_o and S_o be an estimate of the number of purchases and sales respectively over the next N days *before* the transaction; let B_a and S_a be the estimate *after* the transaction. Then the change in B, $\Delta B = B_o - B_a$, and the change in S, $\Delta S = S_o - S_a$, will be the estimated improvement (i.e., reduction) in the number of purchase and sale transactions respectively.

Let the costs per transaction be A_B for each purchase and A_S for each sale. Then the estimated savings from reduced transactions due to cash flow smoothing is the sum of the products of the costs per transaction times the respective estimated reductions in the number of transactions: $A_B \cdot \Delta_B + A_S \cdot \Delta_S$. Let r_t be the average daily yield for a security of maturity t. For the case of a purchase, the problem can be formulated as maximizing the return on invested funds adjusted for transaction savings—that is, maximizing the sum of the dollar returns on the amount of securities purchased, $r_t q_t$, from the day following the look-ahead period, $k+1$, to the end of the time horizon, N, added to the average daily estimated savings from reduced transactions due to cash flow savings. Mathematically,

$$\max OBJ = \sum_{t=k+1}^{N} r_t q_t + \frac{1}{N}(A_B \cdot \Delta_B + A_S \cdot \Delta_S)$$

such that all funds are invested[1] and portfolio constraints are satisfied.

For the case of a sale, the problem can be formulated as minimizing the return that could have been earned on securities sold adjusted for transaction cost savings. Now instead of adding the average daily cost savings to the sum of the dollar returns and maximizing, the cost savings are deducted from the sum of the dollar returns and the resulting quantity is minimized. Mathematically,

$$\min OBJ = \sum_{t=k+1}^{N} r_t q_t - \frac{1}{N}(A_B \cdot \Delta_B + A_S \cdot \Delta_S)$$

such that required funds are provided and portfolio constraints are satisfied.

Although these expressions are using a constant transaction cost for concreteness, the procedure to be presented for determining maturity structure will allow a variable cost component. In fact a nonlinear schedule of transaction costs could be used.

This formulation views the problem as a sequential decision process. At the time of each transaction, the goal is to attain the best possible return adjusted for the potential savings from reduced transaction costs. The factor $1/N$ is present in the objective function to reduce total savings over the time horizon to average daily savings to make it comparable with the portfolio return which is measured in units of average dollar return per day since r_t is the average daily yield.

Let $\underline{q} = (q_{k+1}, \ldots, q_N)$ represent the amount of each maturity that is transacted. To solve the problem it is necessary to specify a procedure for estimating transaction costs and a rule for determining $\underline{q}$. The transaction cost will depend on both the pattern of expected cash flows and the value of $\underline{q}$. This nonlinear dependence of transaction costs on $\underline{q}$ complicates the objective function.

Since the objective function is nonlinear in $\underline{q}$, we shall use a simple decision procedure (heuristic) to specify maturity structure. The essence of the heuristic is first to select maturities solely on the basis of yield (and portfolio constraints)

---

[1] For a purchase, all funds will be invested if

$$\sum_{i=k+1}^{N} q_i = CB_o + E(SC_k) - TB.$$

For a sale, all funds will be invested if

$$\sum_{i=k+1}^{N} q_i = TB - CB_o - E(SC_k).$$

The requirement that all funds be invested can be relaxed to require that all funds be invested to within the nearest unit order quantity.

and then to shift maturities to smooth cash flows if the foregone yield is exceeded by savings from cash flow smoothing. In the remainder of this section, we first present an algorithm for estimating purchases and sales and then present and discuss the smoothing heuristic.

A Buy-Sell Forecasting Algorithm

We can estimate the time and amount of purchase and sale transactions by assuming that the actual cash flows are the forecasted cash flows and successively applying the k-day look-ahead procedure from day $k+1$ to day N.

Exhibit 6 provides a detailed logic diagram of the buy-sell forecasting procedure. The major steps in the logic of the algorithm are:

1. Compute the current level of cash balances and the level in k days.
2. If current cash balances are within the control limits, no transaction is necessary, go to 6; otherwise go to 3.
3. If the current cash balance, CB_t, is equal to or greater than h_1, go to 4; otherwise go to 5.
4. Since $CB_t \geq h_1$, see if the cash balance k days later, C_{t+k}, is greater than the upper inner control limit, $h_1 - \delta_1$; if it is, make a purchase to restore balances to the target, count the purchase, record the amount and the date in a list, adjust future cash flows, and move ahead k days where we know that the cash balance will be TB; otherwise go to 6.
5. Since $CB_t \leq h_o$, see if the cash balance k days later, C_{t+k}, is less than the lower inner control limit $h_o + \delta_o$; if it is, make a sale to restore balances to the target level in k days, count it, record the amount and the date in a list, adjust future cash flows, and move ahead k days to where we know that the cash balance will be TB; otherwise, go to 6.
6. If we are now at the end of the forecast horizon, stop; otherwise, update and go to 1.

The input to the buy-sell forecasting algorithm is a cash flow forecast and specified values of the decision variables $\underline{q}$. The output is a count of the estimated number of purchases and sales expected over the time horizon and a list of the time and the amount of expected transactions. By running the algorithm for two different values of $\underline{q}$, we can compute the expected change in transactions and transaction costs.

The Smoothing Heuristic

When buying securities, the logical maturity dates for smoothing cash flows are those dates on which a sale is forecast. Similarly, when selling securities, the candidate maturity dates for smoothing cash flows are those which are on or near a forecasted purchase day. These facts suggest a heuristic procedure for specifying $\underline{q}$—first ignore smoothing and choose $\underline{q}$ to maximize return per day (subject to portfolio constraints); then sequentially reassign maturities to take advantage of smoothing opportunities. The reassignment should continue as long as the objective function improves and there remain opportunities for smoothing.

Exhibit 7 is a logic diagram for this heuristic in the case of a purchase. The following is a verbal statement of the major steps in this heuristic:

1. Ignore smoothing at the outset and choose $\underline{q}$ to produce the largest possible yield subject to portfolio constraints.
2. Rank the dates of the nonzero q_t by their corresponding values of r_t from smallest to largest r_t so that the least desirable maturity times occur first.
3. Rank the forecasted sell dates according to the perceived value of eliminating a given sell so that the sell which should be executed first is ranked first.

EXHIBIT 6. A Buy-Sell Forecasting Algorithm

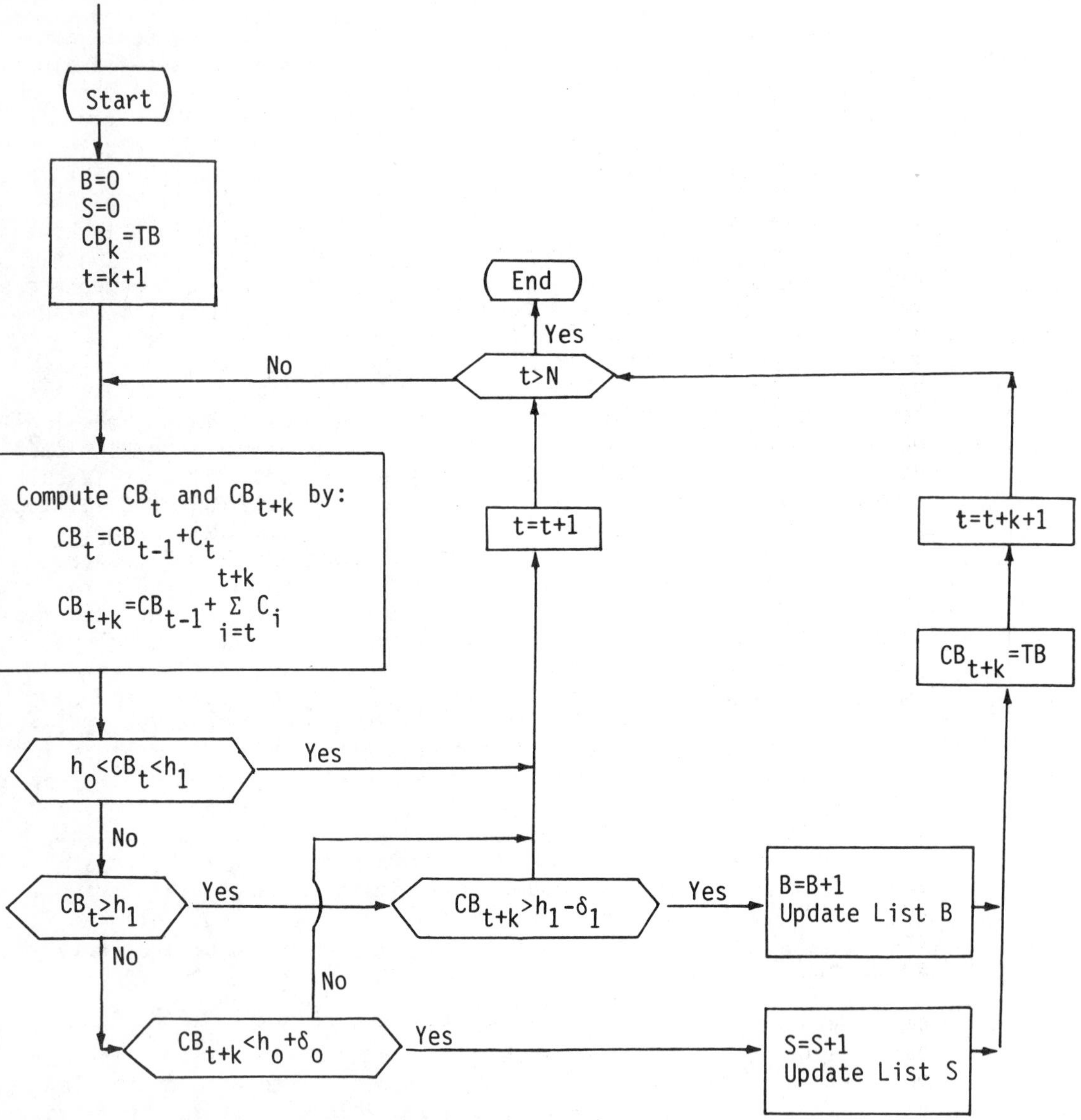

List B is a list of purchase dates and amounts.
List S is a list of sale dates and amounts.

4. Assign dollars from the currently highest ranked maturity date (determined in Step 2) to the currently highest ranked sell date (determined in Step 3). (The amount assigned is the minimum of the dollars remaining to be assigned in the currently top-ranked maturity time and the amount of the forecasted sale to the nearest unit order quantity.)

5. Produce a new count of estimated purchases and sales that reflects the effect of portfolio transactions.

6. If the objective function was improved, go to 7; otherwise stop.

7. If either all forecasted sell

EXHIBIT 7. Logic Diagram of the Smoothing Heuristic for a Purchase Decision

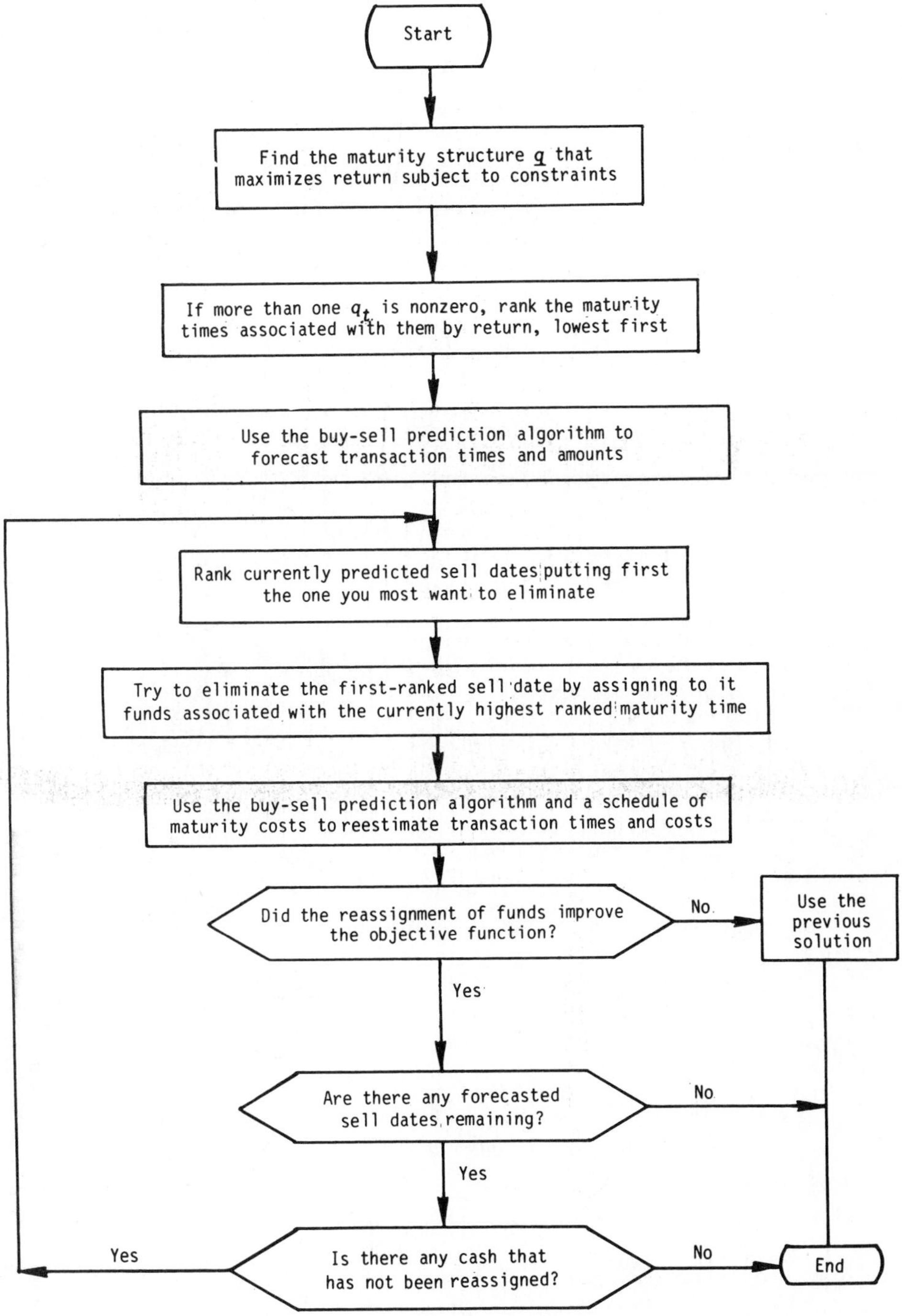

dates have been eliminated or all cash has been reassigned, stop; otherwise, update and go to 3.

The case of a sale is analogous except that it is necessary to match forecasted purchase dates with maturities. The only forecasted purchases that can be eliminated by selling are those near to dates at which securities in the portfolio are maturing (and which are possibly caused by the large cash inflow due to a maturing security).

Ranking the Attractiveness of Transactions

The key to a good heuristic is to have a good ranking rule for deciding which opportunities for smoothing are most attractive and thus which should be the first selected for elimination. Factors which affect attractiveness are: (1) the size of the transaction cost to be eliminated; (2) the amount of the opportunity cost to be eliminated; (3) the probability that the transaction will actually be eliminated. In general, we prefer to eliminate a nearer rather than a more distant transaction because we are more certain to be successful and will have fewer opportunities to eliminate it by smoothing in the future. An approach to ranking can be to compare the benefits (saved transaction costs) with the costs (foregone return) adjusted for our preference for near returns.

A suggested ranking criterion is savings less costs. That is, from the dollar transaction cost that is saved by avoiding a sale are deducted two quantities: (1) the dollar return of the alternate maturity foregone and (2) a preference (quantified in dollar terms) for early or late transactions. Let Δr_t be the foregone yield per day in switching to maturity t from the best yield available, s_t be the dollar amount of a sale that is forecasted to occur on day t (that is obtained from list S of the buy-sell counting algorithm), t be the number of days, and f be a constant factor that can reflect preference for early or late transactions. If $f > 0$, the ranking will tend to force an early transaction; if $f = 0$, there is no preference; if $f < 0$, the ranking will tend to force a late transaction.

When $f = 0$, the ranking criterion is simply transaction costs saved net of return foregone. With a ranking criterion of this type, a failure of the model to make the best choice for elimination will occur when one is near the indifference point between return and transaction cost savings. Hence, with this criterion, the model should be fairly insensitive to errors in ranking. One further point: it is not required that A_S be a constant—it can be replaced by an expression for the transaction cost as a function of the size of the transaction.

SPECIFICATION OF MODEL PARAMETERS

The values of the control limits and the length of the look-ahead period k should not be treated as fixed parameters, but rather should be adjusted as necessary. In particular:

1. The parameter TB should not be the target level of balances that a firm has to hit over a time period, but should be the "adjusted target" to reflect past history. If balances were 10% too low the first third of a month, the firm should attempt to have them 5% too high the next two thirds of the month. In effect, the adjusted target should reflect past history and even possibly forecast data (such as knowledge of a monthly cycle or a period of net drift in cash flows).

2. The length of the look-ahead period k can vary. It can be longer at the start of the period or when there is "more information" (greater certainty) associated with the forecasts.

3. The levels of the control limits do not have to be (and in the author's opinion should *not* be) fixed.

They can be wider at the start of the period when greater fluctuations can be tolerated and can then be narrowed at the end of the period to force one to hit the target level of balances.

One of the merits of the *k*-day look-ahead is its adaptiveness and robustness. By specifying the target balance, control limits, and look-ahead as a function of time, a cash manager can specify the time path about which his balances fluctuate and the size of fluctuations he will tolerate as a function of time.

The best approach to parameterization is a combination of a cash manager's judgment and simulation. The author suggests testing over historical cash flow and cash forecast data. If the model is programmed for use on a time-shared computer with a flexible command structure for changing parameters, an experienced cash manager with an hour or two of interaction with the *k*-day, look-ahead model can test dozens of parameter levels and strategies, and he will arrive very quickly at the best values for the parameters. Moreover, this type of parameterization has the side benefit of getting the cash manager involved in the model and gives him confidence in its ability to assist him.

Although it has been argued that carrying costs should not be a significant component of the firm's objective function, acceptance of this argument is not necessary for the use of the short-period, look-ahead heuristic. It will only affect how one parameterizes the model. In conducting Monte Carlo tests of the short-period look-ahead, it produced fairly substantial savings when compared to an automatic return model.

One does not have to use the matching heuristic for security maturity decisions to effectively use the *k*-day look-ahead for specifying the timing and amount of transactions. It is possible to use the *k*-day look-ahead and make maturity structure decisions on a judgmental basis. This may be particularly appropriate for those cash managers who try to incorporate forecasted shifts in yield curves in their maturity structure decisions. However, even if the maturity structure decision is made judgmentally, the output of the buy-sell forecasting algorithm can be an important aid to the decision maker by giving him a schedule of forecasted transaction times and showing him the effect of maturity structure decisions on forecasted transaction requirements. With this approach, the *k*-day look-ahead and buy-sell forecasting represent aids to the cash manager who makes the more complex maturity structure decisions on a judgmental basis.

It is the author's opinion that the greatest saving will come from the look-ahead technique rather than the matching procedure, especially for firms that currently hit their target balance on a daily basis and purchase a lot of over-night and very short-term commercial paper.

However, the potential savings in people time and operational cost (assuming a well-designed information system) will probably greatly exceed the savings from reduced transactions and opportunity cost. For firms that use marketable securities primarily as a buffer for fluctuations in their cash position (and depend on credit lines for contingency liquidity), another potentially large saving is represented by the ability to reduce the size of the portfolio of marketable securities. This reduction means shifting from assets earning money-market rates to cost-of-capital rates. This reduction in marketable securities is made possible by letting the cash maintained as compensating balances serve the function of the buffer.

CONCLUSION

This model (when embellished) is fairly complete and realistic in that it includes the important aspects of cash management. It is highly flexible, adaptive, and robust (insensitive to errors). Although it has many parameters and a fairly complex structure, it does not require advanced mathematics or sophisticated optimization techniques, and hence can be understood and controlled by a cash manager. Since the model is a formalization of activities of the current practice of many cash managers, and since the information requirements are low (assuming that a firm is already making forecasts), the interface of the model to the cash manager and the organization should not be difficult. Finally, model implementation costs are very low relative to the potential savings.

REFERENCES

1. William J. Baumol, "The Transactions Demand for Cash: An Inventory Theoretic Approach," *The Quarterly Journal of Economics* (November 1952), pp. 543-546.
2. M.H. Miller and Daniel Orr, "A Model of the Demand for Money by Firms," *The Quarterly Journal of Economics* (August 1966), pp. 413-435.

READING 14

Are Cash Management Optimization Models Worthwhile?

Hans G. Daellenbach
University of Canterbury, Christchurch, New Zealand

The objective of this paper is to determine upper bounds of the potential savings that can be realized by the application of cash management optimization models. These upper bounds are found by simulation as the difference between the performance of a deterministic optimization model -- which finds the optimal policy in hindsight -- and the simulated performance of a hypothetical treasurer who uses simple heuristic cash management rules as informally practiced by many treasurers, based on prediction of random cash flows. The results of this analysis leave serious doubts as to profitability of cash management optimization models.

I. INTRODUCTION

In recent years a large number of cash management models have been published: Baumol's [2] and Tobin's [20] deterministic models; the linear programming (*LP*) formulation by Robichek et al. [19], Calman [4], and Orgler [17]; and finally the control-limit models by Miller and Orr [13,15], Eppen and Fama [8,9, and 10], Girgis [11], Neave [16], Daellenbach and Archer [6], and Daellenbach [7]-- the last seven models using dynamic programming (*DP*). These models have taken us a long way from the common-sense study by Pflomm [18]. If Baumol [2] and Tobin [20] and, to a minor degree, Miller and Orr [13] (but not [14]) viewed their models as descriptive for the demand for money by firms, the emphasis of the other models was on actual cash management. Miller and Orr [14] were the only authors to compare the performance of their model with the actual decisions made by a company treasurer, although no estimates of benefits were provided.

This paper attempts to develop upper bounds of the potential savings that can be obtained from such models. Section II briefly contrasts cost factors and other aspects considered by these models with those deemed important by a group of 20 company treasurers. Section III develops a

Reprinted from the JOURNAL OF FINANCIAL AND QUANTITATIVE ANALYSIS (September 1974), pp. 607-626, by permission of the publisher.

dynamic programming model for cash management under certainty which is used in Section IV to find the optimal cash management policy with perfect hindsight, i.e., what it should have been with perfect knowledge of the cash flows experienced. Any model dealing with uncertain future cash flows will incur higher costs. The costs of the *DP* model under certainty are then compared with simulated costs incurred by a hypothetical treasurer who uses simple decision rules as practiced informally by many treasurers. The latter bases his decisions on imperfect predictions of random cash flows. The difference between the two represents an upper bound on potential savings that can be provided by the use of optimizing models. In Section V the prospects of realizing these potential savings are discussed for some of the optimizing models proposed in the literature.

II. CASH MANAGEMENT COMPONENTS THEORY VERSUS PRACTICE

Personal interviews with top financial officers of 20 medium and large size companies were conducted on the west coast of the United States.[1] On the investment side, the types of marketable securities *(M/S)* considered for short-term use of idle cash and listed in their order of preference were: (1) treasury bills; (2) prime commercial papers; (3) repurchase agreements; and (4) certificates of deposits.

The investment criteria listed in their order of importance as stressed by the financial officers were: (1) security; (2) ease of purchase and liquidity (including maturity); and (3) yield. This explains why treasury bills rate so high. All financial officers stated that *M/S* are as a rule always held to maturity. Only *LP* models can handle this feature. Due to dimensionality, this is not possible for *DP* models.

On the borrowing side, the instruments used to cover short-term cash deficiencies, again in their order of preference, were: (1) short-term bank credit; (2) issue of commercial papers; (3) extension of accounts payable; and (4) use of bank "float." As was to be expected, none of the companies considered stocks or bonds for short-term investment of idle cash.

To adjust their cash balances, all companies engaged actively in *M/S* as well as short-term borrowing transactions. Thus in general, at least three state variables describe a firm's short-term cash position, namely its cash balance, its *M/S* holdings, and the amount of short-term loans outstanding. In contrast, more than half of all cash management models discussed consider only one state variable, namely the cash balance. This implies that *M/S* holdings will never be depleted or that lending and borrowing rates are identical. Eppen and Fama [10], Miller and Orr [15], Daellenbach and Archer [6], Daellenbach [7] and all LP models [4, 17, and 19] consider more than one state variable.

Ideally, cash flow predictions should be broken down on a daily basis for the immediate future, say the coming months, and on a weekly basis thereafter for another three to four months. Although all companies reviewed their cash balances daily, only eight made short-term cash flow predictions broken down on a weekly or daily basis. Nineteen of the 20

[1] Most of this survey was done in early 1970 by M. F. Collins as part of an M.B.A. research paper at the University of Washington. Composition of firms interviewed by size and line of activity was as follows:

1969 Gross Sales Revenue (in millions of dollars)	Number of Companies
1 - 5	3
5 - 10	4
10 - 50	4
50 - 100	4
100 - 300	3
over 300	2

Activity	Number of Companies
Manufacturing	10
Retailing	4
Insurance	2
Utilities	3
Services	1

companies reported that their cash outflows were highly predictable. This is not an unexpected result since a large portion of the cash outflows is given by payments for wages and salaries and other contractual periodic obligations. On a very short-term basis, however, even cash outflows generated by accounts payable can be predicted within narrow limits. Five companies considered their cash inflows predictable within a 5 to 10 percent margin. It was also apparent from these interviews that daily cash flows for most firms can be decomposed into several components, such as highly predictable weekly, biweekly, and monthly cycles plus residual components, resulting in a fairly strong degree of autocorrelation. Assumptions of stationary daily cash flow distributions as made by most authors of cash management models seem thus not to be warranted.[2] This conclusion seems to be true even for public utilities.

Most models reported in the literature consider the following cost and return factors as relevant:

1. Fixed transaction costs of buying or selling *M/S* and increasing or decreasing the amount of borrowings. These costs are assumed to be independent of the transaction size, i.e. they cover the costs associated with selecting the appropriate instruments -- clerical cost as well as any fixed bank and dealer charges.
2. Variable transaction costs of buying or selling *M/S* and increasing or decreasing the amount of borrowings. These costs are assumed to be proportional to the size of the transactions. They are supposed to cover commission and reduction in yield due to the spread between selling and buying prices.
3. Cost of foregoing return on idle cash. This is an opportunity cost included either as a penalty for idle cash balances or as a charge on borrowing balances or return on *M/S* holdings.

The *LP* formulations by necessity ignore fixed transaction costs, and so do the models by Eppen and Fama [8] and Daellenbach [6 and 7], whereas Baumol [2] and Miller and Orr [13] ignore variable transaction costs.

In order to assess the fixed transaction costs, the financial officers were asked to estimate the amount of time spent by senior people in the daily review of cash balances and, in particular, the time spent in preparing and executing cash balance adjustments. The most frequent response was one of embarrassment, since in most cases the actual time spent daily on reviewing the size of the cash balance amounted to less than five minutes. This can be considered as part of the fixed costs of operating the system. The actual time spent by the financial officer and his assistants in preparing and executing a cash balance transaction consisted generally of the time needed for a telephone call to one of the firm's banks or a dealer, and the signing of the documents for the transaction. Most financial officers also agreed that there were small clerical costs associated with the transaction. Full cost estimates ranged from $10 to $50 per transaction, with more than half being $20 or less.[3] At interest rates of about 5 percent, two to three days' interest on $100,000 -- often the minimum transaction size even considered by most firms -- covers fixed

[2] Miller and Orr [14 and 15] mention predictable heavy cash outflows and tailoring of maturities of marketable security holdings to match these requirements in time, but ignore this fact in their models.

[3] In [14] Miller and Orr state that for large firms a fixed cost of "*$20 to $50 dwindles into insignificance,*" but that for medium-size firms the fixed cost element will be significant. In the Miller-Orr model [13] the two control limits are proportional to the cubic root of the fixed transaction cost for the no-drift case and could thus be zero if the fixed cost is neglected.

transaction costs of that size.[4] The question is, however, should one use full costing? In inventory control where a firm might deal with thousands of different items, even a small change in the number of replenishments placed per item may have an impact on the total clerical load. Hence, the marginal cost change probably coincides with the full cost change (exclusive of overhead). However, in cash management we are dealing with a single item, and with at most one setup per day. Hence the marginal change in the total cost of cash management is probably negligible, as far as the time of senior people is concerned as well as in terms of clerical costs. It is therefore not surprising that all 20 financial officers interviewed categorically stated that these costs never entered into their decisions.

Most financial officers felt that there were no variable transaction costs associated with *M/S*. Additional probing into this aspect revealed that *M/S* are usually held to maturity; hence the firms do not incur the cost given by the spread between selling and buying price which constitutes the dealers' profit margin. The same conclusion was true for short-term borrowing transactions, except commercial papers sold through a dealer, in which case the dealer would charge a small commission. This could, however, be avoided by placing the papers directly.

One cost, ignored by all financial officers but those of the three largest firms, was the opportunity cost on funds tied up in transactions. When *M/S* are liquidated or commercial papers are placed, there is at least a one-day delay before it is possible to draw on the proceeds if the transaction goes through a dealer or bank. The firm thus either foregoes one day's interest in the first instance, or incurs an additional day's interest in the second instance, since such transactions have to be planned one day ahead of actual cash needs. This cost is proportional to the size of the transaction and can be considered a variable transaction cost. It can be avoided by not going through a clearing house but by transferring the funds directly via a Federal Funds transfer between banks. In this case, however, the firm also has to maintain a bank account at the location where the payee executes his obligation. It seems that many financial officers are not aware that they incur these variable costs.

III. A TWO-SOURCE OPTIMIZING MODEL UNDER CERTAINTY

An optimizing model that assumes perfectly predictable cash flows -- which essentially corresponds to an after-the-fact analysis of what the optimal policy should have been given the actual cash flow experienced -- will consistently do at least as well as any model which by necessity must use imperfect forecasts of future cash flows. Hence, any cost estimates obtained on this basis will provide optimistic lower bounds of the actual costs incurred by the use of cash management models that have to work with imperfect forecasts.

The model assumes that controllable cash balance adjustments can be made either through purchases and sales of *M/S* or through increasing or decreasing the amount of borrowings. Successive cash balance review periods can be of different length.

Let B_n be the ending cash balance in period n;

R_n be the sum of uncontrollable cash transactions in period n;

Z_n be the ending balance of loans in period n;

[4] Although there may be institutional reasons why most firms tend to have a minimum transaction size of $50,000 or $100,000 and why many keep their transactions to multiples of these minima, it is clear that this may not be optimal.

S_n be the ending balance of M/S holdings in period n;

X_n be the amount of borrowing transactions in period n; and

U_n be the amount of M/S transactions in period n.

X_n and U_n, $n = 1,2,\ldots,N$, constitute the decision variables and are positive for increases and negative for decreases in the cash balance. The following material balance equations link period n-1 to period n:

(1) $B_n = B_{n-1} + R_n + X_n + U_n$,

(2) $Z_n = Z_{n-1} + X_n$, $Z_n \geq 0$,

(3) $S_n = S_{n-1} - U_n$, $S_n \geq 0$.

At the end of each period n, the state of the cash balance situation can be described in terms of the balances (B_n,S_n,Z_n). In view of the relations (1) to (3), this state description can be reduced to (Z_n,S_n), since the three variables are not independent.[5] Then, for any combination of values (Z_n,S_n), the total cost in period n is given by the sum of (a) fixed and variable transaction costs for borrowing transactions, (b) fixed and variable transaction costs for M/S transactions, (c) interest cost on borrowings, (d) return on M/S holdings (shown as a negative cost), and (e) a penalty cost for cash shortages $(B_n < 0)$ as follows:

(4) $T_n(X_n, U_n, Z_n, S_n) =$

$$\begin{Bmatrix} a_1^+ + b_1^+ X_n & \text{for } X_n > 0 \\ 0 & \text{for } X_n = 0 \\ a_1^- - b_1^- X_n & \text{for } X_n < 0 \end{Bmatrix} + \begin{Bmatrix} a_2^+ + b_2^+ U_n & \text{for } U_n > 0 \\ 0 & \text{for } U_n = 0 \\ a_2^- - b_2^- U_n & \text{for } U_n < 0 \end{Bmatrix}$$

$$+ \{c_{1n} Z_n - c_{2n} S_n\} + \begin{Bmatrix} -c_{3n} B_n & \text{for } B_n > 0 \\ 0 & \text{for } B_n \geq 0 \end{Bmatrix}$$

where

$a_1^+, a_1^-, b_1^+, b_1^-$ are fixed and variable borrowing transaction costs for cash increases (+) and cash decreases (-);

$a_2^+, a_2^-, b_2^+, b_2^-$ are fixed and variable M/S transaction costs for cash increases (+) and cash decreases (-);

c_{1n} is the interest cost on ending loan balances in period n;

c_{2n} is the return on ending M/S holdings in period n;

c_{3n} is the penalty on negative ending cash balances in period n.

All cost coefficients are nonnegative. The total cost over the entire planning horizon of N periods is given by summing (4) over all periods subject to (1) to (3), where B_0, Z_0, and S_0 are given. The problem consists of finding a sequence of decision variables (X_n,U_n) which minimizes the total cost. Let $F_n(Z_n,S_n)$ be the minimum cost from period 1 to n given an ending position of (Z_n,S_n) in period n. By the principle of optimality of dynamic programming, we can form the following recursive relations:

(5) $F_1(Z_1, {}_1) =$

$$\underset{X_1,U_1}{\text{MIN}} \; T_1(X_1,U_1,Z_1,S_1), \text{ and}$$

---

[5] Let $Q_n = B_n + S_n - Z_n$, all $n \geq 0$, where n=0 denotes the beginning balances. By (1), $Q_n = B_{n-1} + R_n + X_n + U_n + (S_{n-1} - U_n) - (Z_{n-1} + X_n) = B_{n-1} + P_n + S_{n-1} - Z_{n-1}$. But Q_n can also be obtained recursively as $Q_n = Q_{n-1} + R_n$ for all $n \geq 1$, and is a known constant in each period. B_n can thus be determined through Q_n.

$$(6)\quad F_n(Z_n,S_n) = \underset{X_n, U_n}{\text{MIN}} \left[T_n(X_n,U_n,Z_n,S_n) + F_{n-1}(Z_n - X_n, S_n + U_n)\right]$$

for $n > 1$ subject to (1) to (3).[6]

IV. UPPER BOUNDS TO ESTIMATED ANNUAL SAVINGS OF CASH MANAGEMENT OPTIMIZATION MODELS

By simulation the performance of the *DP* model under certainty described in Section III is now compared with the performance of a hypothetical treasurer. The simulated cash flows are generated by random normal deviates superimposed onto different expected cash flow patterns.[7] These patterns exhibit weekly and monthly cycles of net cash inflows, as commonly encountered in practice. Each week is divided into four one-day periods from Monday to Thursday, followed by a three-day period covering Friday to Sunday.

All cash flow patterns used assume the no-drift case, i.e., the long-run expected net cash flow is zero. Three sets of basic cash flow patterns differing with respect to the degree of uncertainty and the strength of autocorrelation present in the data were used. Patterns 1 and 2 are based on the same recurrent one-month sequence of expected daily cash flows, as shown in Table 1. The behavioral assumptions underlying the sequence of expected cash flows reflect cycle payments of accounts payable on Wednesday, wage disbursements on Thursday, and salary disbursements and other monthly contractual payment (such as utility bills, rentals) at the beginning of every fourth week. Cash receipts from cycle billing occur throughout the week but are more heavily concentrated towards the end of each week. The fluctuations in receipts are also assumed larger towards the end of each week as shown by the doubling of the standard deviations.

Pattern 1 has standard deviations of $50,000 and $100,000 about the expected daily cash flows. As a result, it exhibits a very strong autocorrelation in the cash flows generated and corresponds to the situation in which cash flows are relatively predictable. The sample autocorrelation coefficient for a five-period lag for the actual cash flows generated for pattern 1 amounts to .75. The standard deviations about the expected daily cash flows are doubled for pattern 2, lowering the degree of autocorrelation. The sample autocorrelation coefficient for a five-period lag for the actual cash flows generated for pattern 2 amounts to .5.

Pattern 3 has the highest degree of uncertainty with no autocorrelation and simulates a stationary daily cash flow distribution with an expected daily cash flow of 0 for all periods and a population standard deviation of $140,000. Pattern 3 is the exception rather than the rule in practice. However, it is the situation assumed by a majority of cash management models that explicitly deal with uncertain cash flows [8, 9, 10, 11, 13, 14, 15, and 16].

---

[6] Given that the transaction cost coefficients are the same for all periods and $c_{1n} \geq c_{2n}$, all n, by the usual relationship between lending and borrowing rates, the solution method can be simplified since: (1) an optimal policy will never contain sales of marketable securities and repayments of borrowings, or purchases of marketable securities and new borrowings in the same period, and (2) if $B_{n-1}+R_n \geq 0$, it will never be optimal to obtain additional cash (i.e., to have $X_n>0$ or $U_n>0$), and if $R_n<0$, it will never be optimal to withdraw any cash (i.e., to have $X_n<0$ or $U_n<0$). Both propositions follow from the fact that to postpone or advance such transactions, whichever case applies, by one period results in a cost reduction without causing additional costs, except maybe for the first or last period of the planning horizon in response to beginning or ending conditions imposed on the balances.

[7] See Appendix.

TABLE 1

RECURRENT SEQUENCE OF CASH FLOW DISTRIBUTIONS USED TO GENERATE SIMULATED CASH FLOWS FOR PATTERNS 1 AND 2 (in $1000)

Period:	1	2	3	4	5	6	7	8	9	10
Expected Cash Flow	110	110	-290	-90	210	110	110	-290	-90	210
Standard Deviation:										
Pattern 1	50	50	50	100	100	50	50	50	100	100
Pattern 2	100	100	100	200	200	100	100	100	200	200
Period:	**11**	**12**	**13**	**14**	**15**	**16**	**17**	**18**	**19**	**20**
Expected Cash Flow	110	110	-290	-90	210	-190	110	-290	-110	210
Standard Deviation:										
Pattern 1	50	50	50	100	100	50	50	50	100	100
Pattern 2	100	100	100	200	200	100	100	100	200	200

The *DP* model finds the after-the-fact optimal policy for the cash flows so generated. The hypothetical treasurer, on the other hand, makes his decisions on the basis of expected daily cash flows and associated cash flow standard deviations, similar to Archer [1]. The policy, which for simulation purposes is expressed as highly formalized rules, attempts to capture the essential aspects of the informal decision process used by many treasurers.

Let:

$$(7)\quad K_j = \Sigma_{i=1}^{j} E(R_i) - k\sqrt{\Sigma_{i=1}^{j} \mathrm{VAR}(R_i)}$$

be the k-adjusted cash flow over j days, where R_i is the cash flow on day i. $E(R_i)$ is adjusted for any *M/S* maturing on day i, and k is chosen by the decision maker and reflects his attitude towards risk. His rules are:

1. At the beginning of each day the treasurer determines the minimum k-adjusted cash flow for the coming n days, denoted by K^*, where

$$K^* = \underset{1 \leq j \leq n}{\mathrm{MIN}}\ K_j.$$

If $B + K^* > A$, where A is minimum transaction size, $B + K^*$ is applied to reduce loans and/or purchase *M/S*, in this order of preference. If $0 < B + K^* < A$, no action is taken. and if $B + K^*$ is negative, rule 3 applies.

$B + K^*$ positive can be interpreted as a conservative estimate of the amount of cash that will remain idle over all n days. It seems reasonable to select both n and A as increasing functions of the fixed transaction cost. A value of k=1 was used in all simulation runs to find K^* for rule 1.

2. All *M/S* purchased are held to maturity. Maturities are tailored to coincide with days when the expected cumulative cash position during a 14-day interval becomes negative for the first time or else at the end of this interval.

3. If $B + K^* < 0$ and the current day's k-adjusted ending cash position $B + K_1 < 0$, an amount $-\mathrm{MIN}(B + K_1, -A)$ is borrowed. If $B + K_1 \geq 0$, no action is taken.

Some experimentation showed that for the shortage costs used, k=0 gave better results than $k > 0$ to find K_1 in rule 3. Note the asymmetry in rules 1 and 3.

In order to assess the sensitivity of the results to fixed transaction costs, separate simulation runs using the same sequence of cash flows were made for fixed transaction costs of $0.00, $10.00, $20.00, $40.00, and $80.00. Other cost factors used were: variable transaction costs on sales of *M/S* of $25 per $100,000, variable transaction costs on loan repayments of $15 per $100,000, interest earned on *M/S* of 3.6 percent per year, interest paid on loans of 5.4 percent per year, and a penalty cost on negative cash balances of 7.2 percent per year. Ten runs were made for each fixed cost level. Corresponding optimization and simulation runs started out with the same initial values for the state variables B_0, S_0, and Z_0. Table 2 summarizes the estimated average upper bounds to the potential savings.[8]

As expected, the hypothetical treasurer performs less well the larger the fixed transaction costs and the larger the degree of uncertainty present in the cash flows. However, even for the stationary pattern 3, where the rules of the hypothetical treasurer are not really suitable, the upper bounds on the potential savings seem to be surprisingly small.[9]

V. CLASSIFICATION AND EVALUATION OF CASH MANAGEMENT MODELS

The models reported in the literature can be grouped into two basic types:

Type A: Deterministic models, in which future cash flows are assumed known with certainty or point estimates are substituted for uncertain cash flows. This group includes the models by Baumol [2] and Tobin [20], which are positive models describing the demand for cash by firms rather than normative, and the linear programming formulations for a finite planning horizon by Calman [4] and Robicheck et al. [19], which are both normative models.

Type B: Stochastic models in which uncertain future cash flows are described in terms of probability distributions. They all take the form of control-limit models: for instance, if the cash balance in period n is below a lower control limit L_n, it is increased to $L_n + l_n$; if the cash balance is above an upper control limit U_n, it is decreased to $U_n - u_n$; and if it is in the range of L_n and U_n, no change is made. If fixed transaction costs are assumed to be zero, both l_n and u_n are zero. This group can be subdivided further into stationary

[8] The results reported in Table 2 are based on ten runs of two months each, extrapolated to annual figures. Both these numbers are small, due to the amount of computer time taken to run the *DP* model. However, the small standard errors obtained, which for most fixed transaction cost levels amount to less than 5 percent, indicate that the results would only be marginally different for a larger number of longer runs and would thus not alter the conclusions. See Appendix for estimation model.

[9] Note the results in Table 2 can within limits be extrapolated to cash flows that differ in their relative size. For instance, for cash flows similar to pattern 3 but with a standard deviation of only one-half of $140,000, or $70,000, the cost difference for fixed transaction costs of one-half of $80, or $40, and a minimum transaction size of one-half of $200,000, or $100,000, and n=5 is equal to one-half of $8,860, or $4,430 --where $8,860 is the table entry for pattern 3 and fixed costs of $80. Similarly, since both models are linear in the cost factors, these results can also be extrapolated for proportional shifts in all costs (with no changes in the cash flow sizes). Such changes will not affect the optimal policy of the *DP* model and will only change the total costs by the same factor for both models. For instance, for a doubling of borrowing and lending rates and all variable transaction costs, the entries in Table 2 are equal to half the annual difference for fixed costs levels twice the ones shown in column 1 (for all positive fixed cost levels).

TABLE 2

ESTIMATED AVERAGE ANNUAL COST DIFFERENCES BETWEEN THE POLICIES OF THE DP MODEL AND THE HYPOTHETICAL TREASURER

Cash Flow Pattern			1		2		3	
Range of daily cash flows generated			-400,000 to +450,000		-550,000 to +700,000		-400,000 to +400,000	
Sample standard deviation of cash flows generated around long-run daily population mean (rounded)			180,000		220,000		140,000	
Sample standard deviation of cash flows generated around daily expected cash flow pattern (rounded)			70,000		140,000		140,000	
Sample autocorrelation coefficient for five-period lag			.75		.5		not significant	
			Annual Cost Difference		Annual Cost Difference		Annual Cost Difference	
Fixed Transaction Cost Level	n	Minimum Transaction Size For Hypothetical Treasurer	Estimate	Standard Error	Estimate	Standard Error	Estimate	Standard Error
$ 0	2	$ 50,000	880	60	3,340	130	4,590	110
$10	3	$100,000	3,130	80	5,300	150	5,530	120
$20	3	$150,000	3,840	80	6,350	190	6,170	170
$40	4	$150,000	5,440	90	8,370	240	7,330	190
$80	5	$200,000	8,040	140	10,330	220	8,860	210

and non-stationary models. Stationary models assume that the cash flow distributions remain constant over an unbounded planning horizon. This covers the Eppen-Fama models [8, 9, and 10], the models by Girgis [11] and Neave [16], all of which are dynamic programming formulations, and the Miller-Orr models [13 and 15]. Taking advantage of the fact that Markovian decision models (a special case of *DP*) can be reformulated as linear programs, Eppen and Fama solve their models by linear programming. Nonstationary models allow the cash flow distributions to be different from period to period over a finite planning horizon. This covers the models by Archer [1], Daellenbach and Archer [6], and Daellenbach [7], the latter two being DP formulations.

How much of the upper bounds of the potential savings are these models likely to realize? The answer to this will to a large extent depend on the frequency with which these models are run. Deterministic *LP* models of type A will require frequent reruns, say weekly, on possibly several different sets of point estimates for the predicted cash flows. Only decisions for the first few periods in the planning horizon can usually be implemented as the unfolding of events renders the decisions for the remaining periods obsolete. These models will only perform reasonably well if the unexplained variation about the predicted cash flow pattern is relatively small, such as for pattern 1. Furthermore, *LP* models cannot cope with fixed transaction costs and perform worse the larger these costs. In the light of these two points, the upper bounds of the potential savings relevant for deterministic *LP* models are those of pattern 1 for small fixed cost levels. But these are rather small and may not even cover annual computer running costs. According to Orgler [17, p.101] such models require between 300 and 500 constraints in 2000 to 4000 variables, which have run times of several minutes even on large computers.

Stationarity of the daily cash flow distribution is in most instances just a convenient simplifying approximation made to allow the use of a given mathematical tool, such as Markovian decision processes. In real life, true stationarity over any extended length of time is rare. Hence, stochastic models based on stationary cash flow distributions will have to be rerun periodically in response to observed or predicted changes in the cash flow distribution. Even so, these models will not be able to cope properly with predictable large cash outflows, such as outlays for capital equipment, periodic large tax payments, or other periodic financial obligations. Whether such events are incorporated into the stationary cash flow distributions, resulting in large variances that do not reflect the actual degree of variation present during most of the periods, or are excluded, the models are unlikely to perform properly and may only capture a small portion of the potential savings.

To check this point, the Miller-Orr model [13] and the Eppen-Fama model [9] were tested on the same set of cash flows as that used to derive the results in Table 2. Comparisons with the Miller-Orr model are somewhat difficult since this model does not include any variable transaction costs nor any shortage costs and assumes that borrowing and lending rates are equal. The simulations produced the lowest costs for using the *M/S* returns and provide no protection against possible cash shortages. The simulation results show that, if both fixed and variable transaction costs are charged, the average annual costs of the Miller-Orr model are about twice those of the hypothetical treasurer for patterns 1 and 2 and are larger by at least 10 percent for all fixed cost levels for the stationary pattern 3. If variable transaction costs are excluded from both models, the Miller-Orr model can just better the hypothetical treasurer's performance for pattern 3. The results for patterns 1 and 2 are not unexpected. However, the results for pattern 3 are disappointing.

The Eppen-Fama model in [9] performs somewhat better. It is on the average just able to match the hypothetical treasurer for pattern 2, but not for 1. For pattern 3, Table 3 shows that this model realizes approximately 30 percent of the upper bounds on potential savings for all fixed cost levels.

TABLE 3

PERFORMANCE OF THE EPPEN-FAMA MODEL IN [9] FOR PATTERN 3

Fixed Cost Level	$10	$20	$40	$80
Ave. Savings Achieved:				
%	29.6	31.1	34.3	25.6
Amount	$1,640	$1,920	$2,510	$2,270
Standard Error	$120	$150	$190	$340

We can thus conclude that the Eppen-Fama models may offer some moderate improvement over the hypothetical treasurer for highly uncertain cash flows with little or no recurrent cycles, such as the stationary pattern 3, provided these cash flow distributions only change slowly over time so as to reduce the number of updating runs needed.[10]

Stochastic models based on nonstationary cash flow distributions by necessity cover only a limited planning horizon of several weeks or months, and only the optimal policy for the first few periods can be implemented. As time advances, events past the planning horizon will have an increasingly significant effect on the optimal current decision, and the model has to be rerun using a rolling planning horizon. Experience with dynamic models in water reservoir management, which have many features in common with cash management, shows that such models may have to be run at least once a week, if not daily. Stochastic models based on one state variable will have fairly short run times, but they also risk realizing only a small portion of the potential savings. On the other hand, models with two or three state variables evaluated on a fairly coarse grid will even with a fast computer, such as an IBM 360/67, easily take ten minutes or more. Annual operating costs are thus likely to be large. These models will do fairly well for cash flows with a low degree of uncertainty, such as pattern 1, but will hardly do better than the Eppen-Fama models for highly uncertain cash flows, such as pattern 3. For pattern 1, the upper bounds to the potential savings are only sizable for very large fixed transaction costs. However, none of the 20 financial officers interviewed estimated that these costs exceeded $50. The prospects for these models are thus not promising.

If the cash flows exhibit a stable recurrent pattern, such as weekly or monthly, few updating runs may be needed. However, most of the remarks for models assuming stationary cash flow distribution apply to this case as well.

---

[10] Assume that two state variables are represented by discrete values of $20,000. For pattern 3 one would need a range of about $2 million for the cash balance and $5 million for *M/S* holdings or loans. Such a problem formulated as a Markovian decision process as for the Eppen-Fama model [10] would yield an *LP* with well over 70,000 constraints. Using a coarser grid with increments of $100,000, this number would be reduced to about 3,000. For one-state variables only (cash balance), such as [8] and [9], the number of constraints using a grid unit of $20,000 would amount to about 300--still a fair-size linear program.

Let us add a few words about development costs for the various models. Development costs not only cover problem analysis and model formulation but also the cost of developing computer programs, including data input, such as the coefficient matrices for *LP* or Markov processes, and including programs to present the output in a form readily usable to the decision maker who generally will have little or no background in sophisticated operations research techniques, as well as testing and implementation costs. The data basis for all models is essentially the same, so that data acquisition costs can be ignored in any comparisons. Processing of raw data will be somewhat cheaper for models working with summary measures of location and dispersion only, such as the deterministic *LP* models, the Miller-Orr models, and the hypothetical treasurer. Development costs are likely to be similar for most optimization models. Experience with setting up large-scale operational *LP* and *DP* problems as well as experience from inventory control suggests that this will involve at least two to four man-months of a highly qualified analyst and programmer. The Miller-Orr model [13] and the hypothetical treasurer are again exceptions, since in both cases all computations can easily be performed on a desk calculator.

Finally, it is instructive to compare the results in Tables 2 and 3 with the minimum annual savings, exclusive of operating costs, needed to guarantee various rates of return for each $1,000 of initial investment in development costs. The numbers in Table 4 are based on productive lives of five and ten years which seem to be a reasonable range for investments of that sort. For instance, for an initial investment of $5,000 and a desired rate of return of 10 percent, the annual savings have to lie between $815 and $1,320. Comparing these numbers with the estimated savings of the Eppen-Fama model in Table 3, this leaves little room for operating costs.

TABLE 4

SAVINGS NEEDED (EXCLUSIVE OF OPERATING COSTS) PER $1,000 OF INITIAL DEVELOPMENT COSTS BEFORE TAXES

Savings Needed For A Rate Of Return Of	Productive Life	
	5 Years	10 Years
5%	230	130
10%	264	163
20%	334	239
50%	576	509

V. CONCLUSIONS

When the hypothetical treasurer was simulated, little experimentation was performed with respect to the various decision parameters, such as the length of the immediate planning horizon n, the minimum transaction size A, and the values of k. The simulation followed a strict and rigid pattern. It goes without saying that an experienced treasurer should be able to do considerably better, particularly by proper choice of short-term instruments used and close tailoring of *M/S* maturities to predicted heavy cash outflows. In this respect the results of Table 2 are thus even more optimistic. It is also recognized that the benefits to be gained from operations research projects are in most cases highly uncertain. Therefore, management tends to insist on fairly high expected rates of return --25 percent to 50 percent being not uncommon.

With these points in mind, the analysis provides sufficient evidence that, for nonstationary cash flows, cash management optimization models cannot offer any improvements over simple decision rules commonly practiced by treasurers as long as fixed transaction costs are below \$50. Extrapolation of the results in Table 1 shows that his conclusion is unlikely to be different even for cash flows with a considerably wider range than those used to derive the results in Table 2. Only if fixed transaction costs are well above the range of \$10 to \$40 do these models become attractive for very large firms. However, none of the 20 financial officers interviewed estimated that these costs exceeded \$50. In limited tests with stationary distribution models applied to nonstationary cash flows, some of these models were just able to marginally better the hypothetical treasurer's performance for cash flows with a low degree of autocorrelation.

Only in the case where a firm faces a stationary or close to stationary distribution -- which according to survey results is the exception rather than the rule -- are the results of this analysis not definitely negative. Provided the initial investment into such projects as well as annual operating costs can be kept low, these models can offer a moderate but uncertain rate of return for firms with cash flows of daily standard deviations well in the hundred-thousands. The size of the savings achieved is, however, disappointingly small.

The present high interest rates do not change these conclusions in substance, but only render some of the models marginally more attractive for large firms.

This analysis points to the disconcerting conclusion that a very large amount of research -- albeit academically interesting research -- was directed into a problem that offers no economic returns for small and medium size firms and very limited returns for large firms.

It has been recognized in the literature that inventory control offers in most cases small savings per product. What makes inventory control profitable is the fact that one project may cover thousands of individual products, pooling individually small savings. For cash management there is only one item to be controlled. Even if this single item may under favorable circumstances generate net annual savings of a few hundred or thousand dollars, this may be insufficient for the risk associated with such an investment.

APPENDIX

Let μ_t denote the expected cash flow in period t,
σ_t denote the standard deviation of the cash flow in period t,
z_t be a random normal deviate with mean 0 and variance 1 generated by a random number generator.

Then the cash flow experienced in period t is

$$x_t = \mu_t + z_t\sigma_t .$$

Let r_i be the minimum cost of the DP policy over T days for simulation run i, and
s_i be the cost of the policy followed by the hypothetical treasurer over T days for simulation run i.

Then $d_i = s_i - r_i$ is the cost difference (≥ 0) over T days for run i;

$$\bar{d} = \frac{1}{n} \sum_i d_i$$

is the sample mean of the cost difference over n simulation runs, and

$$s^2 = \frac{1}{n-1} \sum_i (d_i - \bar{d})^2$$

is the sample variance of the cost difference over n simulation runs. The point estimate for the annual average cost difference is

$$\hat{\mu} = \frac{\bar{d}}{T} 365$$

and the estimated standard error of this estimate is

$$\hat{\sigma} = \frac{s}{\sqrt{n}} \sqrt{\frac{365}{T}}$$

REFERENCES

1. Archer, S.H. "A Model for the Determination of Firm Cash Balances." *The Journal of Financial and Quantitative Analysis*, Vol. 1 (March 1966).
2. Baumol, William J. "The Transactions Demand for Cash: An Inventory Theoretic Approach." *Quarterly Journal of Economics*, Vol. 66 (November 1952).
3. Bierman, H., and A. K. McAdams. *Management Decisions for Cash and Marketable Securities.* Ithaca, N.Y.: Cornell University, 1962.
4. Calman, R.F. *Linear Programming and Cash Management: CASH ALPHA.* Cambridge, Mass.: The MIT Press, 1968.
5. Congress, 86th, 2nd Session, Joint Economic Committee, *A Study of the Dealer Market for Federal Government Securities.* Washington, D.C., 1960.
6. Daellenbach, Hans G., and S.H. Archer. "The Optimal Bank Liquidity: A Multi-Period Stochastic Model." *Journal of Financial and Quantitative Analysis*, Vol. 4 (September 1969).
7. Daellenbach, Hans G. "A Stochastic Cash Balance Model with Two Sources of Short-Term Funds." *International Economic Review*, Vol. 12 (June 1971).
8. Eppen, Gary D., and Eugene F. Fama. "Cash Balance and Simple Dynamic Portfolio Problems with Proportional Costs." *International Economic Review*, Vol. 10 (June 1969).
9. Eppen, Gary D., and Eugene F. Fama. "Solutions for Cash Balance and Simple Dynamic Portfolio Problems." *Journal of Business*, Vol. 41 (January 1968).
10. Eppen, Gary D., and Eugene F. Fama. "Three Asset Cash Balance and Dynamic Portfolio Problems." *Management Science*, Vol. 17 (January 1971).
11. Girgis, Nadio Makary. "Optimal Cash Balance Levels." *Management Science*, Vol. 15 (November 1968).
12. Maldonado, R.M., and L.S. Ritter. "Optimal Municipal Cash Management: A Case Study." *The Review of Economics and Statistics*, Vol. 53 (November 1971).
13. Miller, Merton H., and Daniel Orr. "A Model of the Demand for Money by Firms." *Quarterly Journal of Economics*, Vol. 80 (August 1966).
14. Miller, Merton H., and Daniel Orr. "An Application of Control-Limit Models to the Management of Corporate Cash Balances." In *Financial Research and Management Decisions*, edited by A.A. Robichek. New York: Wiley, 1967.
15. Miller, Merton H., and Daniel Orr. "The Demand for Money by Firms: Extensions of Analytic Results." *The Journal of Finance*, Vol. 23 (December 1968).
16. Neave, Edwin H. "The Stochastic Cash Balance Problem with Fixed Costs for Increases and Decreases." *Management Science*, Vol. 16 (March 1970).
17. Orgler, A.E. *Cash Management.* Belmont, Calif.: Wadsworth Publishing Company, Inc., 1970.
18. Pflomm, Norman E. *Managing Company Cash.* New York: National Industrial Conference Board Inc., Business Policy Study No. 99.
19. Robichek, Alexander A.; D. Teichroew; and J. M. Jones. "Optimal Short-Term Financing Decision." *Management Science*, Vol. 12 (September 1965).
20. Tobin, James. "The Interest-Elasticity of Transactions Demand for Cash." *Review of Economics and Statistics*, Vol. 38 (August 1956).

READING 15

Riding the Yield Curve — A Useful Technique for Short-Term Investment of Idle Funds in Treasury Bills?

Jerome S. Osteryoung
Florida State University

Gordon S. Roberts
Dalhousie University

Daniel E. McCarty
University of Louisville

Over the last decade, rising interest rates have contributed to heightened concern over the management of cash. Cash managers have focused attention on accelerating collections of accounts receivables, slowing cash disbursements and minimizing cash balances. Rather than hold idle cash balances, firms and non-profit organizations invest in risk-free, highly-liquid, and interest-earning marketable securities when their actual cash balances exceed their minimum cash balances. U.S. Treasury Bills have long held a favorable position as an investment instrument with a frequent strategy being to purchase bills of maturities longer than a planned holding period and to sell them prior to maturity.

This strategy, referred to as riding the yield curve, enjoys support from academicians and financial executives [4, 14, 15] yet seems to have escaped close scrutiny. The objective of this paper is to measure the potentially higher returns and risk (from interest-rate variation) resulting from riding the yield curve using Treasury Bills. The paper first discusses the mechanics of riding the yield curve; second, the results of the empirical tests are presented; and finally, conclusions are drawn.

THE MECHANICS OF RIDING THE YIELD CURVE

If an investor has funds idle for recurring periods of 28 days (holding period) and if Treasury Bills are the desired investment instrument, there are three alternatives available. An investor may purchase T-Bills with a maturity less than the holding period, invest in a Bill with a maturity equal to the holding period or purchase a Bill maturing after the end of the holding period. For example, an investor can invest in Bills maturing in 14 days (or any maturity under 14 days) with the intention of rolling over the investment into another Bill maturing in 28 days. As a second alternative, the investor might match the maturity with the planned 28-day holding period. Finally, the investor may choose to ride the yield curve—purchase a 56-day

This paper has not been previously published. Reprinted by permission of the authors.

or an 84-day Bill (or some other maturity longer than 28 days) with the intention of selling it at the end of the 28-day holding period. For the purpose of this paper, only the 14-day rolling, 28-day matching, 56-day riding and 84-day riding strategies are considered assuming a 28-day period of funds availability.

In order to evaluate these strategies, the investor must obtain bid (*B*) and ask (*A*) yields, convert them to selling (*SP*) and purchase (*PP*) prices, and use the selling and purchase prices to compute the annualized 28-day holding period yields for each strategy before a decision on the "right" strategy can be made. To illustrate and to review the mechanics of riding the yield curve, Exhibit 1 contains bid and ask yields for the four maturities (*M*).

EXHIBIT 1

ILLUSTRATIVE BID AND ASK YIELDS AND PRICES

	Yield		Price	
Maturity	(*B*) Bid	(*A*) Ask	(*SP*)* Selling	(*PP*)** Purchase
14	8.55%	8.40%	$99.6675	$99.6733
28	8.80%	8.50%	$99.3156	$99.3389
56	9.16%	8.66%	$98.5751	$98.6529
84	9.54%	8.94%	$97.7740	$97.9140

$*SP = \$100 - \frac{B \cdot M}{360}$ $\quad **PP = \$100 - \frac{A \cdot M}{360}$

m = maturity in days.

The equations in the exhibit were used to calculate prices: e.g., the purchase price to the investor on a 56-day maturity is \$100 - (8.66)(56)/360 or \$98.6529 per \$100 of the face amount of the T-Bill, and the selling price the investor receives is \$100 - (9.16)(56)/360 or \$98.5751. Note that the yields were used in the calculations as a percentage, i.e., they were not converted to a decimal, and the year contains 360 days. Both practices are conventional among Treasury Bill market participants [15].

Exhibit 2 reports the annualized (365-day) holding-period yields for the four strategies, calculated by using the prices from Exhibit 1 and the equation in Exhibit 2. For example, the investor pays \$98.6529 for a 56-day Bill and sells it for \$99.3156 at the end of the 28-day holding period (*H*), for a holding period yield of

$$\frac{\$99.3156 - \$98.6529}{\$98.6529} \text{ or .6716 percent.}$$

EXHIBIT 2

HOLDING PERIOD YIELDS FROM ALTERNATIVE STRATEGIES

Strategy	Yield*
14-Day Rollover	8.545%
28-Day Maturity-Matching	8.675%
56-Day Riding	8.757%
84-Day Riding	8.802%

$*Y = [\frac{SP - PP}{PP}] \cdot [\frac{365}{H}]$.

H = holding period in days.

This holding-period yield is annualized by multiplying it by the number of holding periods in a 365-day year, producing a yield of (.006716)(365/28) or 8.757 percent. An investor using a single decision-making criterion of maximizing return would opt for the 84-day riding strategy since it produces the highest holding-period yield.

However, this analysis explicitly assumes an ascending and, implicitly, a stationary yield curve. That is, yields increase progressively as time to maturity increases and the structure of yields remains the same throughout the year. If, however, interest rates rise during the holding-period, the yields on the 56 and 84-day riding strategies will be reduced. Consequently, an investor electing to follow a riding strategy must have confidence in a superior ability to forecast either a lower future structure of Bill rates or a stable yield curve.

Conversely, if the investor elects the maturity-matching strategy, it is riskless by construction and the yield is immunized and certain.[1] A 14-day rolling strategy affords the investor an opportunity to obtain a higher return on the second purchase if Bill rates rise during the first 14-day period; however, if Bill rates fall, a lower yield is received during the second half of the 28-day holding period. The purchase of a T-Bill with a maturity longer than the holding period subjects the investor to uncertainty as to the sale price at the close of the holding period. Further, given an equal random fluctuation in Treasury-Bill rates across maturities, possible losses would be greater the longer the maturity of the Bills employed in riding the yield curve. This follows from Malkiel [11] and is proven for T-Bills in the Appendix.

The remainder of the paper examines the above arguments with empirical data and with the maturity matching strategy serving as the basis for comparing and evaluating the risks and yields of the rolling and riding strategies.

EMPIRICAL TESTING

Actual quotes on T-Bills were obtained from a Louisville, Kentucky, bank for the period of January 4, 1973, through December 30, 1976.[2] The prices, both bid and asked, were ascertained for T-Bills with maturities of 14, 28, 56 and 84 days. This data was collected for each two-week period during the four-year testing period. All transaction costs were imbedded in the quoted prices assuming a round-lot transaction of $100,000 and all T-Bills were bought at the asked price and sold at the bid price. The data reflect investment possibilities open to investors outside large financial centers. To the extent that transaction costs (bid-asked spreads) are higher than obtainable in New York, a bias is introduced in favor of the buy-and-hold alternative, conservatively underestimating the benefits of riding the yield curve.

The returns are computed from the four different strategies in two ways. First, yields are compared and risks using all observations. Additionally, another set of tests was performed except that time periods in which the yield curve was descending were excluded (six observations were eliminated). Decision makers who follow the discussion above would not consider riding a descending yield curve.

Shown below in Exhibit 3 are the respective means, standard deviations, and correlation coefficients between each specific strategy and the 28-day buy-and-hold alternative.

In order to test whether there is a significant difference between the strategies, the data is restated to examine only the risk-premium measured in basis points between the 28-day buy-and-hold and the other strategies. Since the 28-day is a riskless (immunized) strategy, all other strategies must be measured as differences away from this strategy. Shown below in Exhibit 4 are the results of an analysis of the incremental differences between the respective strategies at the 28-day holding period measured in basis points.

Exhibits 3 and 4 present four comparisons among strategies, both raw data (Exhibit 3) and risk premiums (Exhibit 4); including all observations (left-hand panel) and excluding descending yield curves (right-hand panel). In the interest of realism and of simplifying our discussion, only

[1] Immunization is defined in terms of duration but since duration and maturity are identical for pure-discount instruments (i.e., without coupons), we may use the term here. See Grove [8].

[2] A very small number of observations were missing. For these, we substituted for the missing data from alternative sources.

EXHIBIT 3

ANNUAL YIELDS FOR ALTERNATIVE T-BILL STRATEGIES
1973-1976, MEASURED OVER 28-DAY HOLDING PERIODS

	52 Observations			46 "Non-Descending" Observations		
Strategy	Mean	Standard Deviation	Correlation Coefficient With Locked -In Yield	Mean	Standard Deviation	Correlation Coefficient With Locked -In Yield
28-day locked-in	5.997	1.377	1.000	5.8774	1.317	1.000
14-day roll-over	5.883	1.358	.968	5.8187	1.344	.983
56-day bills held for 28 days	5.769	1.549	.856	5.5993	1.399	.849
84-day bills held for 28 days	6.975	1.915	.756	5.9076	1.736	.728

EXHIBIT 4

ANNUAL RISK PREMIUMS IN BASIC POINTS

	52 Observations, Full Sample		46 "Non-Descending" Observations	
Strategy	Mean Excess Return	Standard Deviation of Excess Return	Mean Excess Return	Standard Deviation of Excess Return
28-day	0.000	0.000	0.000	0.000
14-day	-11.350	34.592	-5.870	24.400
56-day	-22.800	80.260	-27.800	75.000
84-day	+7.808	125.441	3.020	119.100

the 46 "non-descending" observations stated in risk premiums—the right-hand panel of Exhibit 4—are analyzed. The results reported carry over to the other three comparisons, however.

The following statistical tests seek to measure and evaluate the excess returns from the rolling or riding strategy. Normality is assumed because of the reasonable sample sizes and the use of a one-tailed Z test to detect differences *above* the "maturity-matching yield." Exhibit 5 displays the results of the statistical analysis.

This test failed to reject the null hypothesis at the .05 level for all risky strategies. The findings suggest that these returns are not significantly higher than can be obtained

EXHIBIT 5

Z-TEST FOR SIGNIFICANT RISK PREMIUMS TO RISKY STRATEGIES—46 "NON-DESCENDING" OBSERVATIONS

Strategy	Mean Excess Return (Basis Points)	Standard Deviation	Z-Value	One-Tailed Significance Level
14-day	-5.87	24.40	-.24	1.64
54-day	-27.80	75.00	-.37	1.64
84-day	3.02	119.10	.0025	1.64

by matching the maturity of the T-Bill with the time period of excess funds availability.[3]

A key element in the data is the rising standard deviation of the risk premiums. That is, the excess returns are not significantly different from zero, yet the standard deviation increases from 0 (the maturity-matching yield) to 119.10 basis points for the 46 non-descending observations of the 84-day strategy.

The effects of the rising risk level can be put into perspective by examining the coefficient of variation of excess returns as shown below in Exhibit 6.

The rising coefficient of variation along with the rising standard deviation suggest that risk is

EXHIBIT 6

COEFFICIENT OF VARIATION (CVAR) OF EXCESS RETURNS

	52 Observations	46 "Non-Descending" Observations
CVAR of excess returns from 14-day strategy	-3.07	-4.15
CVAR of excess returns from 54-day strategy	-3.63	-2.70
CVAR of excess returns from 84-day strategy	16.06	39.43

increasing with the lengthening of the maturity of the T-Bill purchased. An F-test was performed to ascertain at the 5% confidence level whether the variance of returns of the alternative strategies is significantly different from the variance of the 28-day holding period strategy. This is equivalent to testing the hypothesis that the distributions of the excess returns had variances equal to zero. (A decision maker who immunizes his purchase of T-Bill has zero interest rate risk.) The results of both of these tests with both data sets rejected the null hypothesis of no significant difference. Consequently the statistical

[3] We are maintaining our treatment of the 28-day, locked-in strategy as riskless and our focus on excess returns. This approach has deep roots in tests for excess returns in equity markets.

Following this argument, we calculate each excess return in Exhibits 4 and 5 by simply subtracting the return on a 28-day bill for the corresponding holding-period. This buy-and-hold yield is the only one known to the investor *ex ante*. In Exhibit 3 the standard deviation of all strategies but the first reflects risks. The standard deviation of the 28-day strategy reflects the fluctuation of short-term rates over time. Since each rate is known *ex ante*, it does not reflect risk, to an investor who plans to liquidate his holdings after 28 days.

tests support the notion that risk increases as alternative strategies are employed.

CONCLUSIONS

This research project has attempted to ascertain if riding the yield curve could produce higher returns than the naive buy-and-hold strategy. The results indicate that riding the yield curve does not produce higher returns than the naive strategy for our data set. Additionally, risk was significantly increased by all of the alternative strategies.

Riding the yield curve involves higher transaction costs. Whether these costs or the structure of liquidity premiums for Treasury Bills is the primary factor in our results remains a question for future research. Put another way, riding the yield curve is advanced as a vehicle for achieving higher returns (positive risk premiums) for taking on greater risk consistent with market efficiency. We now believe that this advice is questionable in light of our finding that returns are not significantly higher.

APPENDIX: PROOF THAT TREASURY BILL PRICES OBEY MALKIEL'S BOND THEOREMS

We limit our discussion to Theorems 1 and 2 [10]:

Theorem 1: $\frac{\partial P}{\partial y} < 0$, Bill prices move inversely to yields;

Theorem 2: $\frac{\partial[\partial P/\partial y]}{\partial N} > 0$, for a given change in yields, changes in Bill prices are greater, the longer is the term to maturity.

We define:

P = price;
y = *daily* yield for a 360-day year;
N = *days* to maturity;
D = discount.

Translating from the arithmetic method discussed in the text and used by Bills dealers to an exact formula for daily compounding gives:

$$(1)\quad P = 100 - D \times \frac{N}{360} = \frac{100}{(1+y)^N}.$$

For Theorem 1, N is constant, so

$$(2)\quad \frac{\partial P}{\partial y} = -\frac{\partial D}{\partial y} \times \frac{N}{360}.$$

To find $\partial D/\partial y$, we solve Equation (1) for D.

$$(3)\quad D = \left(100 - \frac{100}{(1+y)^N}\right) \times \frac{360}{N}.$$

Differentiating $\partial D/\partial y$ gives:

$$\frac{\partial D}{\partial y} = -\frac{100 \times 360}{N} \cdot \frac{\partial\left[\frac{1}{(1+y)^N}\right]}{\partial y}$$

$$= -\frac{100 \times 360}{N} \cdot \frac{[(1+y)^N \cdot \frac{\partial 1}{\partial y} - 1 \cdot \frac{\partial (1+y)^N}{\partial y}]}{(1+y)^{2N}}$$

$$= -\frac{100 \times 360}{N} \; \frac{[0 - N \cdot (1+y)^{N-1} \cdot 1]}{(1+y)^{2N}}.$$

Combining minus signs,

$$= \frac{100 \times 360 \cdot N(1+y)^{N-1}}{N \cdot (1+y)^{2N}}.$$

Canceling N, and powers of $(1+y)$:

$$(4)\quad \frac{\partial D}{\partial y} = 100 \times 360 \cdot \frac{1}{(1+y)^{N+1}} > 0.$$

We return to Equation (2) and substitute for $\partial D/\partial y$ from Equation (4):

$$(5)\quad \frac{\partial P}{\partial y} = -100 \times 360 \cdot \frac{1}{(1+y)^{N+1}} \times \frac{N}{360}$$

$$= -100N \cdot \frac{1}{(1+y)^{N+1}} < 0,$$ and this is the desired result for Theorem 1.

Turning to Theorem 2, we differentiate Equation (5) with respect to N.

$$(6)\quad \frac{\partial[\partial P/\partial y]}{\partial N} = -100N \cdot \frac{\partial}{\partial N}\left[\frac{1}{(1+y)^{N+1}}\right] + \frac{1}{(1+y)^{N+1}} \cdot \frac{\partial}{\partial N}\left(-\frac{100}{N}\right)$$

$$= -\frac{100}{N} \cdot [-(N+1) \cdot (1+y)^{N} \div (1+y)^{2N+2}] + \frac{1}{(1+y)^{N+1}} \cdot [-- \frac{100}{N^2}] .$$

Simplifying Equation (6)

$$(7)\quad = -\frac{100}{N} \cdot \left[\frac{-(N+1)}{(1+y)^{N+2}}\right] + \frac{1}{(1+y)^{N+1}} \cdot \frac{100}{N^2} > 0 .$$

This completes the proof of Theorem 2.

REFERENCES

1. G.O. Bierwag and M.A. Grove, "Model of the Term Structure of Interest Rates," *Review of Economics and Statistics* (Jan. 1967), pp. 50-62.
2. Peter W. Bacon and Richard Williams, "Interest Rate Futures Trading: New Tool for the Financial Manager," *Financial Management* (Spring 1976), pp. 32-38.
3. George J. Benston, "Interest Rates are a Random-Walk Too," *Fortune* (Aug. 1976), pp. 107-13.
4. Nicholas J. De Leonardis, "Opportunities for Increasing Earnings on Short Term Investments," *Financial Executive* (July 1966), pp. 48-53.
5. J. Walter Elliott and Michael E. Echols, "Expected Near-Term Yield Curve Movements and Rational Term Structure Expectations for U.S. Government Securities," Working Paper, University of Wisconsin - Milwaukee, (mimeo) (May 1975).
6. J. Walter Elliott and Michael E. Echols, "Expected Yield Curve Movements and Rational Term Structure Expectations: An Empirical Note," *Journal of Money, Credit and Banking* (Feb. 1977, Part 1), pp. 90-96.
7. Peter C. Fishburn, "Mean-Risk Analysis With Risk Associated With Below-Target Returns," *American Economic Review* (March 1977), pp. 116-126.
8. Myron J. Grove, "On Duration and Optimal Maturity Structure of the Balance Sheet," *Bell Journal of Economics and Management Science* (Autumn 1974), pp. 696-709.
9. Edward J. Kane, "The Term Structure of Interest Rates: An Attempt to Reconcile Teaching With Practice," *Journal of Finance* (May 1970), pp. 361-374.
10. Burton G. Malkiel, "How Yield Curve Analysis Can Help Bond Portfolio Managers," *The Institutional Investor* (May 1967), pp. 17, 32-33, 41-44.
11. Burton G. Malkiel, *The Term Structure of Interest Rates: Theory, Empirical Evidence, and Application*, McCaleb-Seiler (1970).
12. James E. Pesando, "Determinants of Term Premiums in the Market for United States Treasury Bills," *Journal of Finance* (Dec. 1975), pp. 1317-1328.
13. Richard Roll, "Investment Diversification and Bond Maturity," *Journal of Finance* (March 1971), pp. 51-66.
14. James C. Van Horne, *Financial Management and Policy*, 3rd edition (Englewood Cliffs, New Jersey: Prentice-Hall, 1974), p. 444.
15. Ben Weberman, "Playing the Yield Curve," *Forbes* (Aug. 15, 1976), p. 86.
16. Jess B. Yawitz, George H. Hempel and William J. Marshall, "A Risk Return Approach to the Selection of Optimal Government Bond Portfolios," *Financial Management* (Autumn 1976), pp. 36-47.

READING 16

Is Aggressive Cash Management a Myth?

Julie Connelly
Institutional Investor

Much is heard these days about how skilled corporate financial men have become at squeezing more yield out of their companies' ballooning cash balances. The impression is left that companies have found a lush new profit source to bolster their overall earnings. In fact, just the opposite is true: The increased sophistication of corporate cash managers is basically a defensive development, to keep the mushrooming cash holdings from dragging down overall earnings. For there are very definite limits to how much added income a cash manager can generate and on how aggressively he can pursue it.

The cash buildup at American corporations has been enormous, although cash and marketable securities have retreated somewhat from their 1976 high-water mark of more than $70 billion to around $60 billion. At Avon Products, for example, cash assets now amount to 37 percent of total assets. At General Electric, the cash pile is now larger than the assets of any operating division of the company. And IBM is literally awash with cash assets—$5.2 billion, or almost one-third of total assets.

Deliberate hoarding by nervous managements has accounted for much of the buildup. Top executives remember the money squeeze of a few years ago and are uncertain about the future. So they are content to let the cash pile up. Adding to the accumulation is the steady improvement of corporate profits during the past two years and the prefunding of long-term borrowing requirements. Standard Oil of Indiana's $400 million debt issue last summer, at a time when it had more than $1 billion of cash on hand and no immediate spending plans, is a somewhat exaggerated example of what's been happening throughout the economy.

Many companies, to be sure, have the feeling that they've accumulated too much cash—far more than they need. But for now, their concern about the excessive buildup goes only to a point. "Managements are more aware that a larger percent of assets has been

Reprinted from the INSTITUTIONAL INVESTOR (May 1978), pp. 45-50, by permission of the publisher.

residing in cash over the past two years," says Richard O'Sullivan, the treasurer of Monsanto. But to date their attention has been focused primarily on making the cash yield more, not on reducing its size. "Even top management is no longer happy with the guy who will just roll over the 90-day Treasury bill," says one cash manager.

The trouble is that cash management is a losing battle as balances grow. Cash simply cannot earn what any reasonably healthy company's operating assets can earn. Skilled as he may be, the corporate cash manager is hard-pressed to generate a yield much higher than 6-1/2 to 7-1/4 percent right now. And when the ravages of inflation are factored in, many cash managers are probably operating in the red. Moreover, as a company's cash pile grows larger and larger, it can actually pull down its overall rate of return. "It doesn't do our balance sheet any good to carry cash for cash's sake," concedes Equitable Life vice president John Dudley, who currently runs a short-term portfolio of $400 million. "This is not the optimal use of our money."

At General Electric, for example, cash and securities, which amounted to $2.2 billion at year-end, produced only $88 million in income. That's a return of only 4.5 percent on GE's average cash and securities holdings for the year as against a pretax return of 13 percent on the rest of GE's $13.7 billion of assets. AT&T, always a heavy capital spender, keeps its cash account much leaner. At the end of 1977, it held $1.4 billion of cash and securities out of total assets of $94.9 billion. The company earned more than $50 million on that cash last year, but profits for the entire company were $4 billion, or 80 times the amount made on the cash. So it's not surprising to hear David Feldman, Ma Bell's director of banking relations, say, "We're not interested in piling up cash; it can earn more invested in telephone plant."

It is not likely, however, that any great amount of the cash held by U.S. companies will find its way into fresh plant investment during 1978. McGraw-Hill's economics department forecasts a 14 percent increase in capital spending this year, which is hardly what anyone would call a capital spending boom—especially in view of the cash available. The fact is that corporate spending policy continues to be tight-fisted in the face of economic uncertainty, high construction costs and expensive environmental regulations. Companies, while mindful of the hazards of excessive cash holdings, seem content to sit on them for now. "Cash is always a drag," says the treasurer of a major airline, "but it's also an insurance policy."

The idea of accumulating cash as a form of corporate insurance—which is the case at many companies—means that it also tends to be managed conservatively, even at the risk of seriously underperforming other corporate assets. Even today, with the increased sophistication of cash managers, the traditional short-term investing trade-off between safety and yield continues to favor safety. "I am not encouraged to make the yield on the portfolio resemble the profit of an operating division," says one treasurer stiffly. Indeed, says Roger Hill, director of investments at National Distillers, "There was a lot more pressure on you to maximize yield back in the mid-1960's." A typical view nowadays is that of Kenneth Siger, who manages Alcoa's $65 million short-term portfolio. "We're not trying to get the highest rates possible," says Siger. "We're not trying to make every additional dime on the portfolio. We are trying to have the money there when Alcoa needs it."

REACHING FOR SAFETY

But if the emphasis is still on safety, and not on reaching aggressively for maximum yield, the fact is that the horizons of cash managers have been broadened. As a result, they can do things now that once might have seemed overly aggressive with a fair degree of safety. Part of this stems from the activity of the dealers in short-term securities—both brokers and banks—in alerting cash managers to a greater variety of instruments. In bidding for corporate business, brokers may have a slight edge over the banks because they offer a wider array of short-term securities. The banks confine themselves to their own liability instruments—CDs, repurchase agreements, acceptances—and short-term tax-exempt securities. Even so, the banks "have been banging on the door," says assistant treasurer Carol Mickelsen of Hershey Foods. "Those that used to call only on Philadelphia and Pittsburgh companies now venture out into the hinterlands."

So determined have been the marketing efforts of the dealers that several corporate treasurers interviewed for this article refused to be quoted on the grounds that they "don't need any *more* dealers pounding on the door." But the determined door-pounding has paid off. "Investors are now willing to look at alternatives," says Garret Thunen, who runs the liability management department at Bankers Trust. "If a CD can't be tailored to their specific maturity requirements, they'll look at an acceptance."

Thanks to dealers' efforts, for example, Eurodollar CDs, which normally yield a 25-basis-point premium over U.S. domestic CDs, have attracted enough U.S. corporate funds to balloon from $16 billion in 1977 to more than $20 billion by early 1978. There is sovereign risk in holding Eurodollar CDs of American branch banks in London: Exchange controls could be clamped on this London-based market, making it impossible to repatriate the funds after maturity, for the U.S. parents are not obligated to pay off the debts of the branches. But as one cash manager puts it, "If there were foreign exchange controls put on London, we'd all be in a lot more serious trouble than worrying about our CDs."

In short, Eurodollar CDs are a new vehicle for cash managers, but not one that involves undue risk. They are fully negotiable, and the trading turnover has grown from 25 percent of the total CDs outstanding to 81 percent in the past five years. Moreover, the participation of U.S. investors, according to figures from Citibank, has risen from 15 percent of the market five years ago to 70 to 80 percent today.

From Eurodollar CDs, cash managers have broadened into Eurodollar time deposits with the American bank branches in London, Nassau and Grand Cayman Island. These, too, are subject to sovereign risk, and, unlike CDs, they are not negotiable. But their maturities can be tailored to any length, from overnight to five years. Mobil Oil, for one, has a good part of its $1 billion cash portfolio in time deposits with large multinational banks, with the maturities tied to the large payments the company must make twice a month for its oil. "The rate is 25 to 50 basis points higher over time than the domestic CD rate," reports Charles Clune, the manager for corporate investments, "and there have been times when it has been as much as 75 to 100 basis points for a fifteen- to 45-day deposit." Again, the vehicle is new and somewhat exotic but is basically conservative as well.

Another new wrinkle: Bank dealers and independent money managers are now starting to offer separate cash management services to individual corporate accounts of $100 million or less. This is a natural outgrowth of their commingled short-term money management funds. "We get calls several times a month from money managers in this business or who are looking to get into it," says one treasurer with a sizable pile of cash. One large leisure time company has hired Scudder Stevens & Clark, Morgan Guaranty, Harris Trust and Dreyfus Corp. to manage about 75 percent of its $135 million cash flow, at a fee under one-half of 1 percent for each manager. An assistant treasurer handles the remainder in-house. "We could just as well have only one of them managing the cash, but we wanted a diversity of opinion to help us run our funds in-house," he says.

DOING WHAT THEY KNOW

The broadening process is not solely the work of the dealers, however. As corporations have marketed their products globally and become better acquainted with foreign financial markets, they've also become more willing to invest their short-term funds abroad. "People will gravitate to something they know," says Richard Shanahan, the president of First International Money Markets. "Corporate treasurers are willing to parlay a business knowledge of foreign banks and trading companies into buying their securities."

Weyerhaeuser, for instance, has invested a portion of its $220 million short-term portfolio in variable-rate Japanese Eurodollar CDs. "We became comfortable with the variable-rate note because we do so much business in Japan with the companies associated with the banks issuing the CDs," explains assistant treasurer David Edwards. The notes have four- and five-year maturities, but the interest rate changes every six months, and there's an active trading market for them. Best of all, the spreads run to 50 basis points above the U.S. 90-day CD rate. Dealers admit, however, that most companies are still leary about floating-rate CDs—because they still consider them fairly esoteric and because the maturities run longer than the eighteen months to two years favored by most cash managers. But Edwards says they fit nicely into Weyerhaeuser's objective of seeking "safety and liquidity."

Floating-rate Asian dollar CDs are starting to make their appearance in short-term portfolios as well. Morgan Guaranty and Bank of America have each issued them, as have five other banks, and they trade on the Singapore market at about a ten-basis-point premium over the Eurodollar variety.

There are, of course, some companies that play the cash management game far more aggressively than the majority. NCR, whose largest foreign division is in Japan, has about five percent of its $300 million portfolio tucked away in fully hedged yen debentures of Japanese banks. "They happened to be desirable from a rate standpoint on the day we were looking to put out funds," says treasurer Robert James. "Our preference would be to buy something totally ordinary, but the spread plus hedging was wide enough to attract us." Unhappily for NCR, the spreads on yen debentures evidently attracted a lot of other investors. The Japanese Ministry of Finance has now decreed that they can no longer be sold to foreigners, for fear of pushing the value of the yen still higher against the dollar.

Fully hedged Canadian short-term securities are about as exotic as many cash managers are inclined to get in seeking safety as well as attractive yield. Treasurer Harold Hoss emphasizes that Union Camp's corporate policy for cash management is conservative. "Safety is primary, then liquidity, then return," he says. And he feels that investing a portion of Union Camp's $70 million portfolio in fully hedged Canadian commercial paper issued by Canadian subsidiaries of U.S. companies and guaranteed by the parents falls within those guidelines. "We get an effective return of 25 basis points over domestic paper," Hoss says. Canadian Treasury bills with a spread of 150 basis points over U.S. bills are also attracting short-term corporate money, even though 100 basis points of that spread must be given up in hedging costs.

Treasurers, too, are jettisoning some of their old favorites from their portfolios. Tax exempts, for example, are no longer so attractive on a rate basis since they currently yield little better than a Treasury bill. Preferred stocks, once a favorite among cash managers because of the 85 percent dividend exclusion from taxes that appeared to offset their relative illiquidity, have fallen victim to a greater short-term orientation among cash managers.

WELL-TAILORED MATURITIES

Indeed, the maturities on short-term portfolios are contracting dramatically. "Last April, our average maturity was 210 days, and we shrank that down to 90 days in two weeks," recalls one cash manager. "Now, we're putting new money out at about 60 days, and the portfolio as a whole averages just under 60 days." In general, the maturities of corporate portfolios now fall into the 60- to 70-day range. And while shorter maturities do suggest a fear of being caught by rising interest rates, they also tend to confirm the underlying conservatism of today's cash managers. Their horizons are still limited to buying securities with maturities tailored only to specific cash requirements such as tax payments or dividend payouts, just as always. Says one treasurer, "The one thing I can't do is say, 'Well, the credit markets are a little shaky today; can you wait until next week?' Why, I'd be out on my ear." Because the cash must be there when called for, safety of principal remains the overriding concern in cash management.

Once the safety criterion has been met, however, cash managers can and do look for the best yield within a given maturity range. It can be a tricky game, says Robert Westoby, who manages Monsanto's approximately $100 million of short-term securities. In March, Westoby bought some Eurodollar CDs on a delayed delivery basis that expired on April 18. The yield was 6.97 percent. The CD maturing five days earlier, on April 13, yielded 6.75 percent because there was considerable demand for paper with a maturity date falling just before April 15 tax payments were due. Had Westoby been investing only to keep his money busy until tax time, he'd have sacrificed 22 basis points of yield. "And you can be sure that the April 20 Treasury bill will be sold at ten basis points higher in yield than the April 14 bill because after April 15 a number of companies won't have the cash to invest," he says.

In line with their fairly conservative bent, today's cash managers don't do much trading. Once a piece of short-term paper finds its way into the portfolio, it generally stays there until it matures. Rarely is an attempt made to swap or trade for a few more basis points of yield. "There are a lot of cash managers who never look at the portfolio again after 10:30 in the morning when they've put out their cash," says a dealer.

Even as sophisticated a short-term investor as NCR's James prefers to play his cards close to the vest. "There are two choices," he says. "You can take somewhat less marketable securities like regional bank CDs and lock in return. Or you can buy more marketable securities and bet that you can guess interest rates and trade at the right time. We'd rather lock it in." The reluctance to trade stems basically from the fear of taking a loss on a portfolio that is supposed to provide for corporate contingencies. "But there are opportunity costs in holding to maturity," says Thomas Gardner of Morgan Guaranty Trust. "Companies take market risks in their basic businesses all the time. They introduce new products or they buy materials based on the price of copper in six months. But most don't do it in the portfolio; they don't ride the yield curve."

Yet riding the yield curve can have a place in even the most conservatively run portfolio. CDs and commercial paper are the backbone of AT&T's $1.4 billion short-term portfolio. "Maturity dates are plugged into our cash needs so we're not forced to sell," says David Feldman. But when it comes to the Treasury bill portion of the portfolio, which he says is much smaller, the approach is very different. "We don't hold bills to maturity," he says. "We swap them for a rate advantage and to match our perceived needs." The result is a "layered" portfolio consisting of a base layer of CDs and commercial paper invested in maturities out to 100 days for new money and tied into specific needs for cash. The top layer consists of the actively managed Treasury bills kept very short to meet emergencies. The average maturity of the whole AT&T portfolio is around 50 days.

Despite the reluctance of most cash managers to trade, more of them are following the layered concept as rising interest rates encourage more active management. After all, layering is a way to buy and hold while taking advantage of higher yields. Union Camp, for instance, has up to one-third of its portfolio invested very safely in the tax-exempt securities of AAA-rated states and MBIA-insured cities with maturities going out to eighteen months. "This is the base layer," says treasurer Hoss, "and then there's a rolling short-term portion for liquidity" consisting of domestic CDs, Treasury issues and some commercial paper. But unlike AT&T, Hoss says Union Camp is not a very active short-term trader.

It is true, then, that cash managers have grown more sophisticated and willing to try new approaches. But their basic emphasis is still on safety and liquidity rather than on yield. And this means that most will generate good but fairly modest returns on their companies' cash assets. "We get 7 percent on the portfolio," says one assistant treasurer proudly. "We're not doing too badly."

But could he and other corporate financial men do better? Probably not—at least not as long as their companies continue to accumulate huge sums of cash. They can stretch a little here and stretch a little there for a few extra basis points. But about the best they can do, even so, is try to conserve the cash and keep it from being too large a drag on overall profitability. Down inside, of course, many finance men know that their companies are piling up too much cash. But they know, too, that they can only play a defensive game until management decides to invest it in assets with greater profit potential. As one treasurer puts it rather solemnly, "I have to remember that I'm the tail, not the dog."

SECTION IV
Accounts Receivable Management

The use of credit in our economy has increased dramatically over the last few decades. While cash sales continue to predominate in certain industries, situations where customers purchase goods and services in exchange for a promise to pay later are increasing. While credit terms are relatively fixed in some industries, there still is a wide range of credit terms whereby goods and services are sold to both individual and corporate consumers. Determining credit terms, selecting credit customers, and monitoring the level of accounts receivable thus become important areas for managerial decision making. This section of the book contains eight readings related to the management of accounts receivable.

Credit scoring techniques have proven to be a useful means of balancing the advantages and costs of good and bad credit risks. A readable discussion of credit scoring as used in screening new credit customers is presented by Boggess (Reading 17). He explains how a profile of demographic and other variables for a potential credit customer can be suitably weighted, using multiple discriminant analysis, to obtain a numerical index of the customer's credit worthiness. Boggess also shows how a credit scoring system provides an information system from which managers can vary the credit policy of the firm in response to changing business conditions. A brief case study is used to illustrate the development of a credit scoring system, and how the relative weightings assigned to variables in the profile may vary over time.

An interesting paper by Buckley (Reading 18) integrates concepts from marketing, statistics, and accounting in determining appropriate cutoff criteria for granting credit to different credit risk groups. A marketing model utilizes credit scoring to calculate a numerical score for each potential credit customer. A statistical model is used to classify each customer into one of several credit risk groups and to determine the sales potential for each group. An accounting model identifies the fixed and variable costs associated with each credit risk group. Focusing on the contribution margin of each credit risk group, the cutoff point between groups that maximize profit to the firm is seen to vary with the extent of its operating leverage.

Hill and Riener (Reading 19) attempt to determine the optimal cash discount for the firm as part of its overall credit policy. The result of their analysis is a usable decision guideline. The authors show that the maximum discount which should be offered depends on the proportion of accepted credit customers who choose to pay earlier and avail themselves of the cash discount, the expected reduction in payment schedules as a result of the discount, the growth in sales that may result, the firms variable cost percentage, and the firm's opportunity cost. The authors provide several numerical examples which illustrate the sensitivity of the discount rate to these several parameters.

Lock-box collection systems are used by many firms to reduce the length of time before payments from their credit customers are available for use. Levy (Reading 20) explains how lock-boxes are utilized and how to evaluate the savings from reduced collection times. He also explains a heuristic programming method for determining the optimal set of lock-box locations. The method involves a comparison of the savings available from each system of lock-boxes with the variable and fixed costs of managing the system.

Lewellen and Johnson (21) explain why many of the traditional measures for monitoring the accounts receivable of a firm may lead to incorrect signals. The difficulty is that the traditional measures may reflect both a changing sales pattern for the firm and a changing payment pattern by its customers. The authors suggest that a preferable tool is to keep track of the percentages of a given month's sales that are outstanding in subsequent months. A schedule of receivables outstanding over time provides timely signals on changes in customer payment patterns, as well as provides the basis for forecasting future collections of credit payment.

Similar arguments are pursued by Stone (Reading 22). Using equations and examples, he explains the interrelationships among various measures of accounts receivable. He points out the difficulties in trying to make a single measure summarize the entire payment pattern of credit customers. The author shows how moving averages and weighted averages of past payment patterns can be used to forecast future cash flows and future levels of receivables. Stone also presents the results of his survey of how 148 large firms plan and control accounts receivable. He finds that many firms are dissatisfied with their use of the traditional measures.

Mehta (Reading 23) argues that a sequential decision process offers improvement over the more traditional approaches to credit management that appear in the financial literature. He proposes a multi-state process for deciding (accept, inquire further, or reject) on potential credit customers. A key aspect of the decision process is not to purchase additional information on the potential customer unless the expected benefit from that information exceeds its cost. Using an example firm, the author shows how a sequential process leads to a series of linear decision rules that can be used in granting credit. Mehta also shows how the decision rules may vary over time with changes in costs and other variables, and how aggregate indices reflecting the status of accounts receivable and bad debt experience can be developed for managerial control purposes.

Copeland and Khoury (Reading 24) analyze conceptually the problem of granting credit in a world of uncertainty. They view credit extension as a certain investment by the firm at the beginning of a period, but with an uncertain result to the firm at the end of the period. The authors develop a one-period model which shows that credit should be extended to the point where the expected rate of return on the firm's investment just equals the market-determined rate of return for projects of that risk. Using the capital asset pricing model, Copeland and Khoury show that the relevant risk measure is based on how the cash flows of the customer firm are correlated with the return on the market portfolio.

READING 17

Screen-Test Your Credit Risks

William P. Boggess
Booz, Allen & Hamilton, Inc.

Consumer credit has become a major factor in the United States, with the "buy now, pay later" philosophy increasingly achieving permanence in the American family's way of living. But because of its rapid growth in the last two decades, consumer credit, as an established business practice, has not yet reached that stage in its development where the lender can feel confident in extending the maximum amount of credit at the lowest possible risk. In other words, consumer credit has not yet the attraction for the lender that it has for many buyers.

Business managers tend to approach consumer credit from one of two extremes. Some businesses use credit vigorously as a sales tool with initial success; but then, after experiencing serious bad debt losses, they resort to dramatic cutbacks in credit sales. Others, fearing losses, have been cautious in promoting the use of credit to expand sales. These companies have used extensive and costly procedures to evaluate applicants and have been very restrictive in granting credit. So, though they do minimize bad debt losses, they also lose sales and potential profits. Neither approach is the most profitable way to achieve success with consumer credit.

A new system for managing consumer credit has been developed, and in one large company with which I am familiar this system has meant a substantial profit improvement. (I shall discuss its experience in detail later.) Specifically, the system provides management with a basis for measuring and controlling profits from credit sales because it balances the probabilities of both good and bad credit risks and enhances the user's ability to vary credit policy with changing market conditions.[1]

In the system, customer characteristics are rated by a series of point scores to determine the likelihood of the prospective buyer's repaying. This is known as a credit scoring system.

[1] For an approach to analyzing business credit risks, see Robert M. Kaplan, "Credit Risks & Opportunities," HBR March-April 1967, p. 83.

Reprinted from HARVARD BUSINESS REVIEW, Vol. 45, No. 6 (November-December 1967), pp. 113-122, by permission of the publisher.

It should be noted that such systems are not new. David Durand first used discriminant analysis in measuring credit risks more than a quarter century ago, although the idea had to wait until the advent of the computer to be put to work.[2] Credit procedures using some kind of scoring of applications--both those based on scientific techniques and those based on the personal experience of the credit manager--have been used by many lenders, such as mail-order houses and finance companies.

The system described in this article, however, has an added dimension, it provides management with an ability to refine its policy continuously to produce optimum profits. But before describing this new system and demonstrating its application in a specific case, let us review briefly the significance of consumer credit in our economy today and the traditional way in which credit is extended.[3]

STATUS OF CREDIT CONTROL

In the last 20 years credit has become one of the principal ingredients in the expansion of retail and other consumer sales. More than 50% of the nearly 8.5 million automobiles sold annually are purchased on some kind of installment basis, and about a third of the used car sales are on a credit basis. A similar proportion of such other durables as refrigerators, washing machines, and air conditioners are sold on credit. Mail order houses have had an enormous success in selling a wide range of consumer products "on time." And in recent years the banking industry has aggressively sought the consumer dollar with its rapidly expanding credit card and installment credit operations.

Businesses have moved into the credit field to stay competitive, to promote sales growth, particularly with higher priced new products developed from our expanding technology, and to reap added income from the service or interest charges. Many businesses have averaged an additional 15% return on the price of the item through service charges. To a $20 million credit sales operation--of which there are many--this means another $2 million in profit even at a conservative 10% interest charge.

So it seems safe to assume that the extension of credit to the consumer, either directly by the retailer or by a third party such as a bank, will continue to be a fact of our business life. It follows, then, that a business must extend credit to the maximum possible number of buyers to increase sales and profits, while withholding credit from those consumers whose purchases would result in a net loss to the company.

The traditional procedures used to decide whether to grant or refuse credit can be time-consuming, costly, and inaccurate. Typically, a credit sale application asks for fairly extensive information about the applicant--employment status, business, credit and personal references, address, home ownership situation, and, in some cases, his annual income. While routinely reviewing applications, credit managers look for characteristics which indicate the possibility of poor risk. They usually have some rules of thumb, based on their own and industry experience, that help them identify the riskier applicants. For example, certain areas of the country or a city are generally low in average personal income and ability to pay. Job description and home ownership are other clues to financial reliability and the subtler, unknown intent to pay.

Those who have been identified in preliminary credit review as poorer risks generally get a more thorough check via credit bureaus and, in many cases, investigations in depth. Combining the information on an application

[2] See David Durand, *Risk Elements in Consumer Instalment Financing* (New York, National Bureau of Economic Research, Inc., 1941; now out of print, but obtainable from University Microfilms, Ann Arbor, Michigan).

[3] For an extensive survey of credit practices, see Merle T. Welshans, "Using Credit for Profit Making," HBR January-February 1967, p. 141.

and the results from an investigation with his own judgment, the credit manager then makes a decision to accept or reject the application.

There is one fundamental difficulty with this procedure that even the most experienced credit executive acknowledges. It is the simple fact that some risks appear to be good but turn out to be bad and, similarly, some that appear to be bad actually are good risks. If the truly "bad" application is accepted, the company will lose money and, conversely, if the truly "good" one is turned down, a potential profit is lost.

A BETTER APPROACH

Any credit control system must consider all of the many factors involved in selecting the most profitable applications. Specifically, the system must take into account that:

√ Investigation of suspected poor risks can be expensive. Clerical and outside credit bureau costs can range from $1 to $10 for each credit check made, and extensive investigations can be even more expensive. So it is important to make an investigation only where the probable loss will exceed the cost of the investigation.

√ The stream of incoming applications is dynamic, and the proportion of good to bad business varies with time, product, geographic area, and many other factors. Therefore general guides, like percentage of rejections, can be misleading.

√ Some traditional factors, such as marital status, may be of little significance in certain segments of a market, though a fairly good predictor in other segments. Furthermore, the ultimate outcome of a credit sale cannot be predicted with certainty by a single or even several characteristics.

√ Granting of credit, at best an uncertain business, is made critical by the fundamental bearing that credit policy has on a company's ultimate profit or loss. Without a systematic way of reducing this uncertainty, the cost of being wrong and the cost of the entire credit operation cannot be weighed together, and the creditor company must rely solely on judgment and experience to optimize its profit.

The credit control system that will be examined here correlates these key elements. It has four significant advantages over traditional credit systems:

1. Management has assurance that the level of credit business being accepted will improve expected total profits.

2. The level of business accepted can be varied in a precise manner as business conditions change.

3. The credit manager has up-to-date information on the performance of credit business.

4. Credit policy can be intelligently altered to meet changing competitive, economic, or new product situations.

With this system, credit management can be more effective by using the credit policy it chooses, rather than being obliged to use a time-honored procedure. Why? Because the system provides for:

√ A screen that measures the degree of risk of each applicant. It is translated into a score that forms the basis for accepting or rejecting the applicant.

√ A management information system. Customer profiles are retained for credit experience research to establish new or improved screens.

√ More adequate data on a routine basis to update credit criteria and the screen to reflect changes in markets and business conditions.

There are many independent and interdependent calculations involved in the system, as well as storage and report requirements. Therefore the use of a computer, while not mandatory, is desirable. There are two essential elements of the system: (1) the credit screen and its point-scoring system, and

(2) the management information system.

Setting up the Credit Screen

Exhibit I shows a simplified flow chart of the decision sequence for a credit screen. New credit applications are first scored with a point system that weights applicants' characteristics according to their usefulness as criteria to determine risk. Those applications with scores above the cutoff score are accepted; those below, rejected. Fundamental to the system, of course, is the method of scoring the applications.

To establish the point scores or weights and the best credit rating cutoff level, a representative sample of good (profitable) and bad (unprofitable) risk accounts is selected from recent company credit experience. A statistical analysis of profiles of customer characteristics determines the relative weights of each characteristic for predicting good and bad risks. The numerical weights and data on average cash profits and losses on good and bad accounts are applied to another sample of accounts. A profit curve can then be drawn indicating profits versus point-score cutoff levels for the sample.

Applicants' characteristics: To understand how point scores are established, let us look more closely at customer or new application profiles. Exhibit II gives a typical picture of the profiles of some known good and bad risks. Note that 90.5% of the good risks were married, and 86.2% of the bad risks were married. But in most of the other seven personal characteristics, the disparity between the two groups is more than 10 percentage points. There is nothing startling about these figures, since credit managers have learned

Exhibit II.
PROFILES OF GOOD AND BAD RISKS

Characteristics possessed	Percentages of two groups having these characteristics: Good risks	Bad risks
Is married	90.5%	86.2%
Owns his home	80.4	42.3
Owns his auto	80.7	68.0
Age is 35 or over	97.0	89.5
Has lived at least 3 years at present address	91.8	70.3
Has a bank reference	93.6	71.0
Has a telephone	75.4	70.3
Has fewer than 3 children	65.8	49.3

Exhibit I

THE CREDIT SCREENING PROCESS

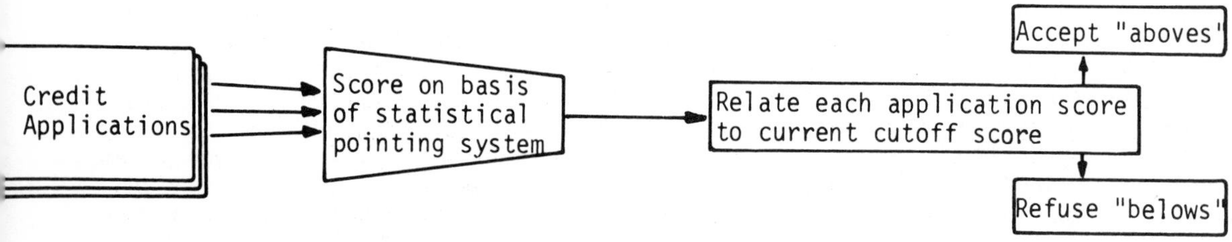

about risk characteristics, at least qualitatively, from experience. In fact, home ownership has become a criterion for quickly identifying good and bad risks. Let us look more closely at using this single characteristic in a simple credit screen.

Assume that a credit manager reexamines a number of old applications that had a mix of characteristics according to Exhibit II. If he had rejected all the applicants who did not own their homes, he would have lost the profit from 19.6% of the applicants who turned out to be good risks, because only 80.4% of them were homeowners. On the other hand, if he had applied this rule of thumb alone to those who had been accepted and then turned out to be bad risks, his company would have suffered losses on credit extended to 42.3% of them, since that percentage of them were homeowners.

It is obvious that using two, three, or more characteristics in some combination to identify potentially good and bad risks is substantially more efficient than using a single characteristic. With a multiple-characteristic approach fewer profitable risks are turned down and fewer unprofitable applications are accepted. To make the most efficient use of the multiple-characteristic approach, the most significant characteristics among the dozens available must be selected and mixed in the right proportions at the time an application is screened.

One method to examine these characteristics and to determine their effectiveness is discriminant analysis, a statistical technique described in many texts.[4] Through this technique many characteristics can be evaluated to determine relative weights or "scores" for each, and the most efficient ones identified for use. The sum of the scores of the most significant characteristics determines the credit score, and the higher the score, the better the probable risk.

Once the weights of the selected characteristics are determined from the statistical analysis, they are converted to a scale usually having a point total of 100. These points can now be used to score each new credit application. Exhibit III shows how points can be assigned to characteristics in rating an application. They are typical questions but nowhere near all-inclusive. Usually, however, fewer than 20 characteristics are adequate for a scoring system.

Exhibit III WEIGHTING OF CHARACTERISTICS OF CREDIT APPLICANTS

Characteristics possessed	Points if answer is "yes"
Is the applicant married?	10
Does the applicant own his home?	15
Does the applicant own an auto?	7
Is the applicant's age 35 or over?	9
Has the applicant lived at least 3 years at his present address?	14
Does the applicant have a bank reference?	18
Does the applicant have a telephone?	8
Does the applicant have fewer than 3 children?	19
	100

<u>Best cutoff score</u>: The next step in developing a credit screen is establishing the appropriate cutoff score to achieve maximum profits. In order to do this, the weights established by statistical analysis are used on another random sample of credit applications that have already proved by performance to be good (profitable) or bad (unprofitable). Each application is scored using the appropriate weights for its various characteristics, and

[4] Two of them are T.W. Anderson, *An Introduction to Multivariate Statistical Analysis* (New York, John Wiley & Sons, Inc., 1958); and M.G. Kendall, *The Advanced Theory of Statistics* (London, Charles Griffin & Company, Ltd., Third Edition, 1951).

then all applications are ranked by values of credit score, in ascending order from 0 to 100 points. The curves for profits and losses are plotted, assuming a cutoff or rejection of all accounts below each point 0, 1, 2, 3, ··· and so on, through 100 points. Exhibit IV illustrates the approach to establishing the cutoff score level, using a relatively small base of applications to make my point clear. (For an actual situation with many thousands of applications, see Exhibit V.)

Exhibit IV.
ESTABLISHING THE CUTOFF SCORE

Credit score	Number of applications below score "Good"	"Bad"	Profits added (lost) by rejecting all below cutoff*
0	1	10	$ 400
5	5	300	14,500
10	25	600	27,500
15	75	900	37,500
20	125	1,100	42,500
25	200	1,200	40,000
30	400	1,300	25,000
35	800	1,400	(10,000)
40	1,300	1,450	(57,500)

*For purposes of this example, each good account lost below a cutoff level represents $100 in lost direct profit and each bad account lost below a cutoff level represents $50 direct profit improvement.

The added dollars of profit at each cutoff score shown in Exhibit IV can be easily computed. At the 5-point cutoff level, note that the *cumulative* number of good applications with 5 points or fewer equals 5. Similarly, the cumulative number of bad applications with 5 points or fewer equals 300. If the cutoff score is set at 5 points, this would mean that all applications at or below that total are rejected. The profits on 5 good accounts, or $500 at $100 each, would be lost, but losses on 300 bad accounts or $15,000 at $50 each, would not be incurred either. The net profit improvement shown is $14,500. Continuing on the scale, the profits added by accepting some risks increase substantially over the profits lost by rejecting others, until an optimum level is reached (in the exhibit this level is underlined). From there the losses increase as more and more good risks are rejected and their profits lost.

Other considerations: In this discussion I have not complicated the example by considering the effect of additional credit investigation on accounts rejected by the screen, i.e., those with scores at or below 20 points in these examples. A major effect of the additional credit investigation is reducing losses of good accounts that might normally be rejected. An additional benefit is use of the investigation to verify suspected bad accounts.

There are other elements in establishing the screening procedure which I have not gone into in presenting its broad outlines. One I might mention is refining the screen to account for recovery in case of default. The cost versus the probability of recovery can be factored into the economics used in establishing the screen. This may be worth doing when the unit of sale is large enough, such as an auto, to make the recovery exceed the cost of collection.

Another source of information that can improve prediction of good and bad risks is the Bureau of the Census. A company can compare the information in a credit application with the Bureau's socioeconomic profile of the country in which the customer lives.

Management Information System

The other major element of this approach to consumer credit control is a comprehensive management information system.

The customer data necessary to establish an effective screen are usually not included in more traditional management information and accounting systems. First, information on home ownership, car ownership, telephone, business references, number of children, bank references, and so forth, while used by credit grantors, is not programmed into the data processing system because it is not needed for routine accounting and collection activities.

A second important missing factor is data on the mix or ratio of good and bad business that was accepted during any given period. In traditional systems, as new applications are approved, they are put into the system for accounting and collection purposes along with previously approved business. The most recent stream of business is mixed with business still on the books from previous periods. In a typical company the number of open credit contracts represents an average of 24 months' worth of business. This average, however, contains accounts with 7 months to 5 years of life remaining, and the "paid in full" accounts have been purged from the file. So at any point in time the accounts receivable file can tell management only what is still on the books; it does not contain a representative mix of current good and bad business.

To establish a screen, a precise measure of the mix of current good and bad business is essential, since the ratio affects the screen's cutoff score. As I showed in Exhibit IV, the number of good and bad risks varies with the cutoff level. If this ratio is inaccurately estimated or measured, the conclusion as to the best cutoff score is in error. Factors influencing credit--for instance, seasonality, new products, and business cycles--also make precise and representative information on the mix of credit business imperative.

A complete management information system tailored for credit control goes beyond the normal accounting system, since it:

1. *Includes all pertinent customer profile data.* Information from every credit application is retained in the records. Any special investigative action taken prior to approval or rejection is also recorded in detail. Since it records what was sold to whom, the system can provide an additional check on reliability of "old" customers. For instance, a customer who did not default on a refrigerator may not be quite as good a risk on that stereo he wants to buy "on time," since consumers tend to pay more faithfully for necessities than they do for luxuries.

2. *Retains all accounts for mix purposes.* No accounts are purged from the special credit information file. It is possible at any time to ascertain the original mix of good and bad applications during a span of time by referring to the file for applications received in that period.

3. *Provides a detailed accounting of performance.* A history month by month, or for shorter intervals--depending on the company's situation--is maintained on the accounts in the credit information file. In time the data become useful for measuring credit screen effectiveness and revising screens in response to changing conditions factored into the scoring system.

4. *Provides a base for testing, analysis, and forecasting.* The more detailed data on collection performance, mix of business, and characteristics become a valuable source for market research. Collection methods and strategies can be evaluated on a sample basis. Knowledge of how well brands and varieties have sold on credit can also be used as a tool for evaluating in advance the market for new products. The data can further be used to select customers for direct mail solicitation.

5. *Gives a user the information and controls for other purposes.* With important financial data already on the computer, a company can improve supervision of the flow of funds and analysis of cash requirements. The technique can be used even in hiring procedures; for instance, salesmen's personal characteristics can be collected and weighed to provide an extra reference point in considering applicants for the

Exhibit V. STEPS IN ESTABLISHMENT OF THE CREDIT CONTROL SCREEN

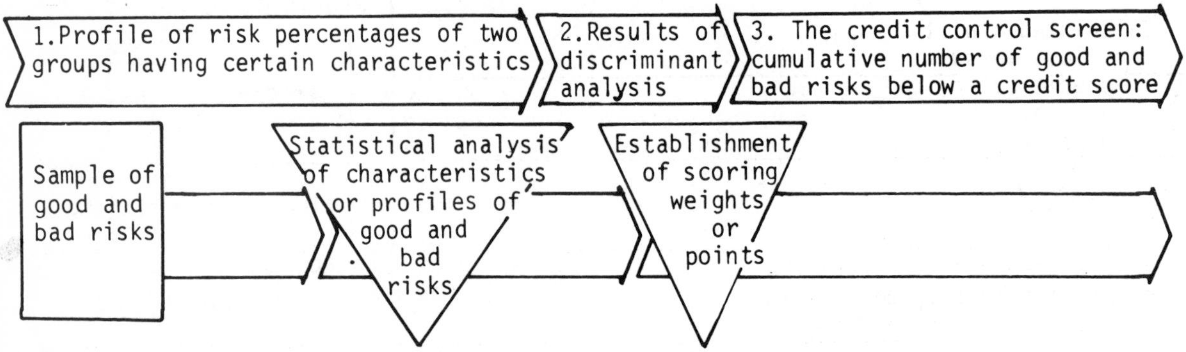

Characteristics possessed	Percentage having these characteristics		Points if answer is "yes"
	Good risks	Bad risks	
Married	90.5	86.2	10
Owns home	80.4	42.3	15
Owns auto	80.7	68.0	7
Age 35 or over	90.0	88.5	11
3 yrs. or more at address	91.8	70.3	14
Has bank reference	96.6	71.0	18
Has telephone	75.4	70.3	6
Fewer than 3 children	65.8	49.3	19
		Total	100

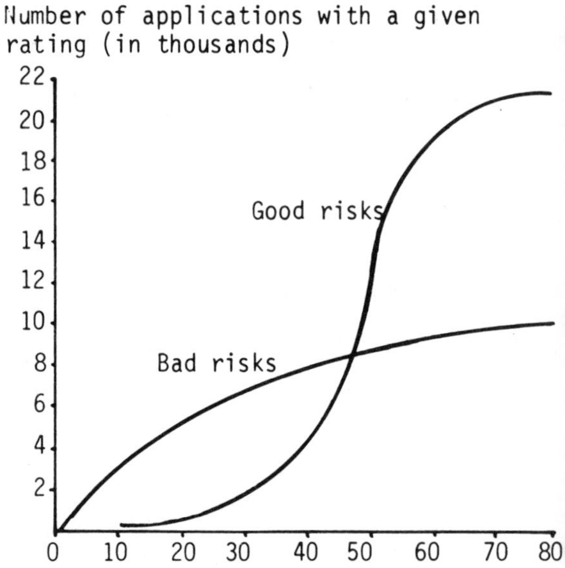

sales force.

CASE OF COMPANY X

On the surface, Company X, my case study, was not in trouble. Annual sales had been growing at a rate of more than 15% and exceeded $100 million. It had a vigorous marketing program and was successful in introducing new products as well as in improving its basic line.

But almost 90% of sales were on an installment basis, though the average single sale was only $50. Accounts receivable totaled about $200 million, due over a 36-month period. Bad debt write-offs had reached $5 million a year and were still climbing. Losses were also occurring in market areas of high penetration and in larger contract sales. In addition, new product sales made up a major percentage of the increasing bad debt volume, as these products reached new markets and new types of credit risk.

Some of the company's executives wanted to curtail these rising bad debt losses by a wholesale cutback in extension of credit. Sales management naturally resisted, citing the company's momentum and its plans for growth and more new products. It was finally decided to have the credit manager, a marketing executive, and a financial executive examine the company's credit

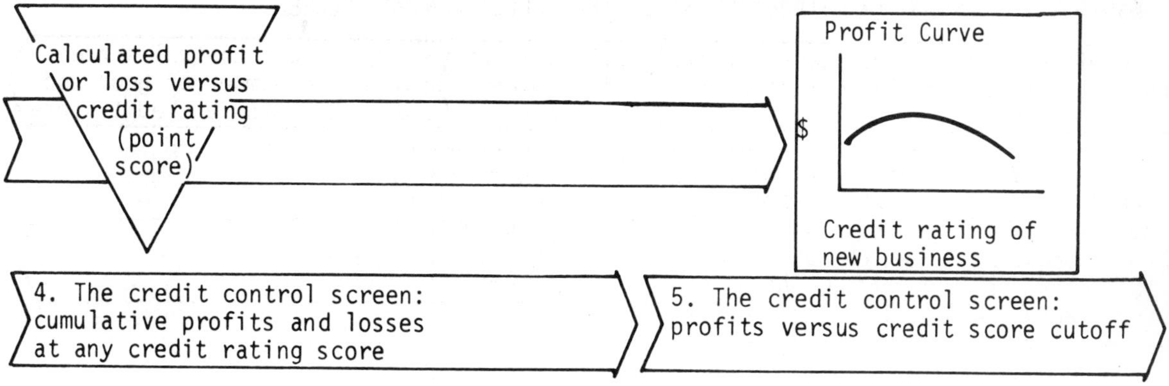

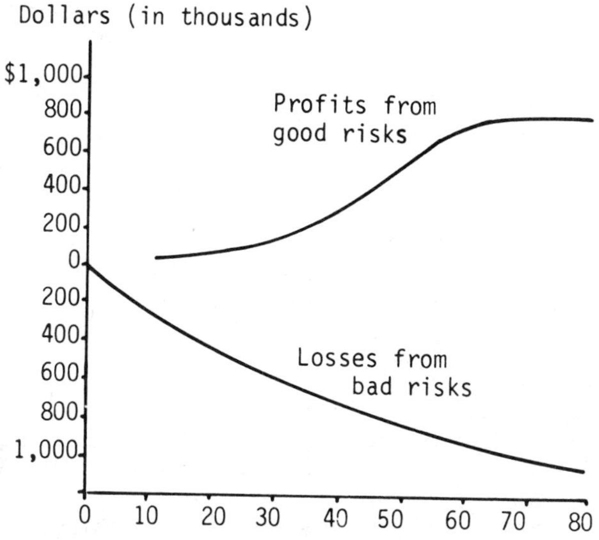

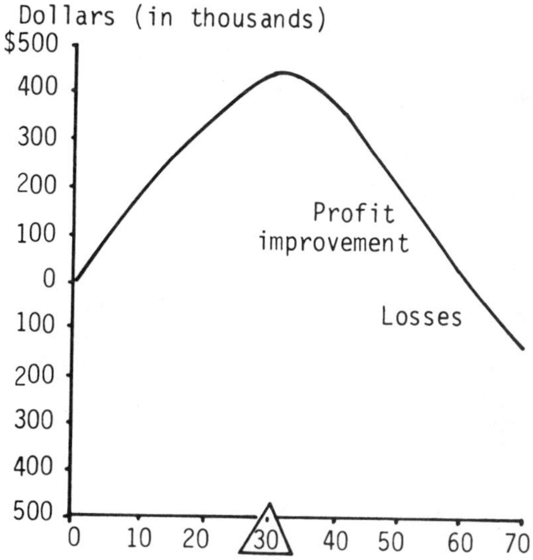

granting and collection operation. The team was supported by operations research and computer personnel.

The three men first drew up a list of basic questions which the study should investigate:

1. Can credit risks be measured and related to profit and bad debt losses from qualitative data on customer applications?

2. Can scoring techniques that measure risk be developed and used to accept and reject new business, thus realizing better profits?

3. Can a system be developed enabling management to tighten or loosen credit extension policy in light of changing conditions?

4. What information is needed to pinpoint when and how to change credit policies?

5. Can collection methods be scientifically analyzed and improved at low cost?

6. What is the makeup or "profile" of our good customers, and what other marketing opportunities exist among our customer groups?

Next, the team made an extensive investigation of the existing credit-granting and collection practices and policies. This study quickly revealed that the company's internal procedures, particularly the accounting system, did not provide the information the group needed to answer its basic questions.

Building the System

It was obvious that a new information system had to be created. The one that was eventually designed and installed, in six months' time, had these features:

✓ Individual customer data, market history statistics, and sales force characteristics were collected and stored.

✓ Accounts opened and sales made in the same time period were grouped together and kept together so that the company could measure changes over time.

✓ The history and performance of each collection action were recorded and compared to measure the effectiveness of alternative collection procedures.

To collect, prepare, and store this much data--about 1,000 characters of information per account on all the company's customers--would have been a prohibitively costly, if not impossible task. So the team, using a computer with a proven random number generating technique, designed a procedure that sampled about 4% of the company's accounts and new applications for the credit information system--a statistically significant number of account for analytical purposes. Now Company X had an accurate and economical system that yielded hitherto unavailable, current information.

The team then developed a credit screening system to cut the bad debt losses. Before analysis could begin, however, it was necessary to let the accounts in the information system age sufficiently to identify the obviously bad or unprofitable business (with new business, of course, there is less time for the customer to default). A study of payment patterns indicated that only nine months's time, rather than a long period, was necessary before the good and bad accounts could be predicted with acceptable accuracy.

(Company X's application rejection rate before introduction of the screen was less than ½ of 1% of the total, so it had a quite unbiased sample. A company whose rejection rate is higher must take into account that the historical data on which its sample is based may be biased, since they include little information on rejected applications. A company with a 25% rejection rate, say, may have to run two or three screens simultaneously, accepting some known bad business for experience purposes, in order to offset the old system's "prescreening.")

The analytical work and calculations in establishing a credit screen out of several thousand accounts made the use of a computer essential. The steps in the analysis are pictured in Exhibit V. The final step in making the new system operational was installing the credit-scoring method in the company's procedures and providing for automatic scoring and processing of new applications on the computer.

As the system now operates, applications completed by the customer are encoded by key punch operators on receipt. They are then audited by the computer for technical acceptance. If the terms of the sale (amount of down payment, payment amounts, contract length, and so on) are within policy limits, the application is automatically scored by the computer and the results are forwarded to the credit department for acceptance or rejection. The full cycle is 24 hours, compared to a week under the old system. The increase in staff necessary to implement the new procedure was less than 2%.

Managing the Screen

An extremely important aspect of Company X's system is its ability to look beyond day-to-day needs. The team was able to give management a tool to loosen or tighten credit policy in meeting changing conditions. The company was able for the first time to identify shifts in the underlying factors that affected its business.

Such factors as changes in customers' income levels, effects of new product introductions, business cycles, and the cost of borrowing money could be accurately weighed in the credit screen. These factors caused shifts in the significance of the key customer characteristics.

Exhibit VI shows these shifts in characteristics in Company X's screen after it was installed in 1964. Note that "has a bank reference" and "owns his home" decreased in point value. Although the exact reasons for this shift are not known, discriminant analysis of these characteristics from the company's credit control information system indicated that, in fact, there was a change in their relative importance or weight. As we have seen in the explanation of the credit screen, such a change in characteristics will generally result in a change in the "best" cutoff score.

Continual updating of the screen by this method is the fundamental advantage of having current and representative customer data from a special credit information system. Every six months Company X extracts from its sample file all accounts that are from 9 to 15 months old. After classifying them as either good or bad, based on projected profitability, the company establishes a new screen.

By controlling the cutoff score for maximum profits, management can really *manage* credit policy. The company cut bad debt losses enough to realize a $1.5 million profit improvement on more than $100 million in sales in the first full year of the system's operation (comparing the results from the initial sample file with the results, using the same sample group, that would have been obtained under the previous credit extension system). In the collection procedure, another $300,000 was "saved." Moreover, the new system gave the company a wealth of customer and market information which was heretofore unavailable.

Exhibit VI CHANGES IN COMPANY X'S CREDIT SCREEN 1964-1967

Characteristics of applicant	Credit rating points allowed			
	1964	1965	1966	1967
Is married	7	8	8	10
Owns his home	20	16	15	15
Owns his auto	7	4	9	7
Age is 35 or over	9	9	8	11
Has lived at least 3 years at present address	13	18	15	14
Has a bank reference	26	20	21	18
Has a telephone	6	9	6	6
Has fewer than 3 children	12	16	18	19
	100	100	100	100

CONCLUSION

This duscussion and case example illustrate the method and potential benefits of an organized approach to managing extension of consumer credit that goes beyond traditional accounting systems. As the case of Company X shows, it is feasible to institute a management information and control system that improves identification of bad risks, avoids rejection of potentially good risks, and increases profits and collection efficiency.

The potential for this system is enormous. Bad debt losses in consumer credit are estimated to total several hundred million dollars annually, and no one knows the amount of business lost because good risks are refused credit. There is no reason for these losses to continue when management has the techniques and the equipment available to establish credit policy scientifically, control it, and vary it with changing business conditions.

READING 18
A Systematic Credit Model

John W. Buckley
University of California, Los Angeles

INTRODUCTION

A critical facet of information systems design and management is the interrelationship of models. While we often tend to think of models in discrete terms, the empirical fact is that most models interact with other models. C. West Churchman has described this interdependency quite vividly in his recent book *The Systems Approach*.[1]

While there are ample descriptive statements of the systemic relationship among models, there are few practical examples. This paper is an attempt to provide such an example. The credit problem is the case in point. The appropriate solution to this problem requires simultaneous consideration of three interactive models: (1) a marketing model, (2) a statistical model, and (3) an accounting model.

While credit-scoring and similar issues are raised, the intent of the paper is not to address those topics *per se*. The literature has attended to those problems in some detail.[2]

THE MARKETING MODEL[3]

The function of the marketing model is to differentiate credit risks in quantitative terms. Immediately we face the problem of measuring subjective matters such as "character"

[1] C. West Churchman, The Systems Approach, (New York: Dell Publishing Co., Inc., 1968).

[2] See, for example, James H. Myers and Edward W. Forgy, "The Development of Numerical Credit Evaluation Systems," Journal of the American Statistical Association (September 1963), pp. 799-806, which is also contained in Kalman J. Cohen and Frederick S. Hammer, (Ed.), Analytical Methods in Banking, (Homewood, Ill: Irwin 1966), pp. 118-134. Also, Carl C. Greer, "Measuring the Value of Information in Consumer Credit Screening," Management Services (May-June 1967), pp. 44-54, and Robert A. Morris, "Credit Analysis: An Or Approach," Management Services (March-April 1966), p. 52.

[3] This paper is based on a marketing model for individuals but a similar process would be used for firms.

Proceedings of the International Symposium on Model and Computer Based Corporate Planning, March 1972, pp. 1-24, by permission of the author.

and "capacity."[4] We turn to measurement theory for an answer. We find that complex principles such as character and capacity cannot be measured directly. Instead surrogates or representative measures are used for this purpose.[5] Most complex principals call for several surrogates, and each one should be capable of objective measurement.

Our search for surrogates is guided by information and decision theories. Our inquiry is inductive.[6] By studying information flows which have led to good (or bad) credit decisions in a sufficient number of cases, we begin to generalize as to an optimum decision structure.

Assume for example, that the following surrogates are cited for character and capacity:

Exhibit I. ILLUSTRATIVE SURROGATES FOR CHARACTER AND CAPACITY

	Character[7]	Capacity
	Occupation	Earnings
	Specific credit record[8]	Dependents
	General credit record	Debt load
Stability	Age	Savings
Stability	Personal references	Equity(wealth)
Stability	Length of residence	
Stability	Length of employment	
Stability	Marital status	

Next, these surrogates must be ranked in order of their importance, as they are unlikely to be of equal value. For example, *earnings* may be a much more significant surrogate for capacity than is *savings*. Again, these weights are derived inductively.

Weighting makes it apparent that we need not exhaust the universe of surrogates. Once we have accounted for a high percentage of our measure, additional data adds little to the decision structure. For example, we can reduce the number of character surrogates to four without losing much statistical significance (Exhibit III). The same could be done for capacity.

Exhibit II. WEIGHTED SURROGATES

	Character	%
	Occupation	40
	Specific credit record	20
	General credit record	10
Stability	Age	10
Stability	Personal references	5
Stability	Length of residence	5
Stability	Length of employment	5
Stability	Marital status	5
		100

Capacity	%
Earnings	50
Dependents	15
Debt load	15
Savings	10
Equity (wealth)	10
	100

[4] "Character" (the intent to pay promptly) and "capacity" (the ability to pay promptly) should be viewed somewhat independently, as one quality does not presume the other. Some persons with great capacity are poor credit risks because they lack the will to pay, while other persons of best intentions are poor credit risks because they lack the means to pay. Data assembled by the National Credit Bureaus, Inc., (see Appendix A) suggest a strong relationship between occupation and character. Data analysis of this type leads to the selection of better surrogates.

[5] For a more extensive treatment of principals and surrogates see Yuji Ijiri, The Foundations of Accounting Measurement, (Englewood Cliffs, N.J.: Prentice-Hall, Inc., 1967), pp. 3-31, and S.I. Hayakawa, Language in Thought and Action (New York: Harcourt, Brace & World, Inc., Second Ed. 1964).

[6] Inductive inquiry begins with systematic observations in the real world. Patterns of consistency in these observations lead to the development of theories. Deductive inquiry, on the other hand, begins with theories which may or may not be supportable. These theories are then tested in the real world to determine their validity.

[7] Race, creed, etc., although they may bear on credit character, must be omitted for legal reasons.

[8] A specific credit record is distinguished from a general credit record in that most persons have their own debt-paying priorities. Some will pay a mortgage or utility bill before a department store account. Others may reverse this order. It is important then to look to the person's credit performance in those areas most closely related to the creditor's line of business.

Exhibit III. SIGNIFICANT CHARACTER SURROGATES

Original Weights %		Revised Weights %
40	Occupation	50
20	Specific credit record	25
10	General credit record	12½
10	Age	12½
20	Others	--
100		100

We shall see presently that some firms need more credit information than others. The ability to expand or contract the number of surrogates enables us to have a more or less *sensitive* model as the situation requires.

The marketing model is used to accept or reject a credit risk, and to minimize accepted risks. The latter objective is met in part by assigning persons to *credit risk groups* in which the credit limit per person decreases in relation to increased risk.

Credit risk groups can be identified by a factor which expresses the ratio of incremental costs to sales. Hence the designation "10% credit risk group" means that the cost of extending credit equals 10% of the sales to that group.

The credit risk factor is a composite of three types of cost, or:

$$F = \Sigma r, n, e$$

where F = credit risk factor
r = cost of capital
n = normal credit costs
e = extraordinary credit costs

Let us examine the nature of these costs in more detail.

1. *Cost of Capital.* This is the cost of carrying receivables. The firm's internal rate of return or some opportunity cost of capital can be used as an index. The cost of capital increases in relation to added risk in that capital is outstanding for longer periods in the event of tardy payments. Thus, while the cost of capital index is itself a constant, the total cost of capital will vary among credit risk groups in relation to collection periods.

2. *Normal Credit Costs.* These are the normal costs of supporting a credit function, such as credit department costs. These costs will increase slightly in relation to risk, e.g., several reminders are required with lower credit groups.

3. *Extraordinary Credit Costs.* This category includes legal, collection agency and other expenses of settling overdue accounts, as well as uncollectible amounts ("bad debts"). Extraordinary credit costs rise sharply in relation to increased risk.

As stated, the credit risk factor is a complex index comprising three subordinate factors, as illustrated in Exhibit IV.

Exhibit IV. COMPOSITION OF THE CREDIT RISK FACTOR

Cost of Capital %	+	Normal Credit Costs %	+	Extra-ordinary Credit Costs %	=	Credit Risk Factor %
5		2		3		10
6		3		6		15
7		4		9		20
8		5		12		25

The credit risk factor can be depicted graphically as a cost function which increases as a percentage of credit sales in relation to increased risk (Exhibit V).

Exhibit V. THE MARKETING MODEL

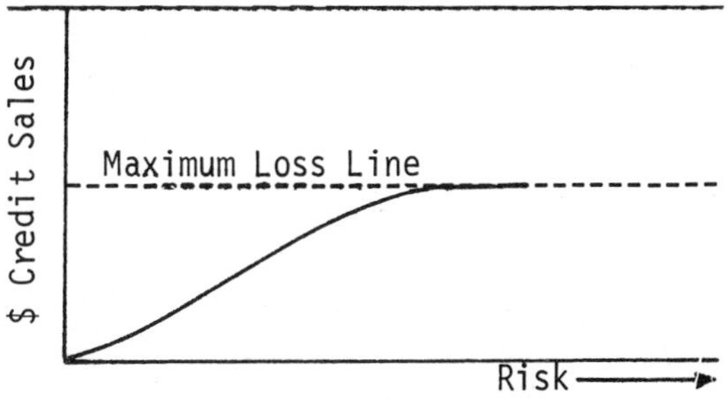

Exhibit VI. APPLICATION FORM & SCORING PROCEDURE

Application Form	Scoring Procedure			
	Verify*	Compute Score	Score Sub-total	Score Total
1. State your occupation: college professor	1	Multiply the percentage in Appendix A by 40 in each case. The college professor rates. 87% x 40		35
2. List the department store credit cards you have at present: Sears	1	0 for none, 5 to 10 for one depending on record, 10 to . 20 for two or more depending on record. (Maximum of 20 points)		10
3. Do you have the following accounts? With whom? checking ✓ Wells Fargo savings ✓ Home S & L loan	 1 1 1	*Checking Account* 0 to 10 based on average balance & number of overdrafts. *Savings account* 5 to 20 based on average balance & withdrawal record *Loan account* -10 to 0 based on amount, duration, and purpose (such as refinancing) (Maximum of 20 points)	10 5 0	15
4. Age: Over 65 61-65 36-60 ✓ 25-35 Under 25	3	4 8 10 6 2		10
5. Personal references: John Flash Rudy Might	2	Lists two = 5 Lists one = 3 Leaves blank = 2 States "none" = 0		5
6. Length in residence: pres. form. Less than 1 yr 1 - 2 years Over 2 years ✓ ✓	2 present 3 former	Present / Former Less than 1 year 1 / 1 1 - 2 years 3 / 2 Over 2 years 5 / 4 (Maximum of 5 points)	9	5
7. Length of employment: pres. form. Less than 1 yr 1 - 5 years Over 5 years ✓ ✓	1 present 2 former	Present / Former Less than 1 year 1 / 0 1 - 5 years 3 / 2 Over 5 years 5 / 4 (Maximum of 5 points)	9	5
8. Marital status: Married ✓ Single or widowed Divorced or separated	3	5 3 1		5
9. Gross earnings per annum of head of household: $ 17,000	1	Over $20,000 50 $15,000 to $19,999 40 $10,000 to $14,999 30 $ 7,200 to $ 9,999 20 Under $7,200 10		40
10. Number of dependents, excluding self 1 2 3 ✓ 4 5 Over 5	3	15 12 9 6 3 0		9
11. Debt load: House payment/rent is $ 200 per month Total monthly installment debt is $ 300	2 3	Total debt load as a percentage of gross income Under 25% = 15 26 to 50% = 10 51 to 75% = 0 Over 75% = -10 Minus 10 points if house payment/rent exceed 25% of earnings		10
12. Equity: Do you own ✓ rent your own home	3	10 0		10
		Total		159

Numbers obtained from credit application forms can now be used to classify risks into credit groups. Let us examine this process. Our surrogates in Exhibit II are the bases for developing the application form and scoring procedure shown in Exhibit VI.[9] The maximum score in our example is 200 points. Assume that the application is for a major department store credit card. Our applicant--a hypothetical college professor--scores 159.

The scoring process utilizes decision theory. In most cases *decision rules* (referred to as "scoring procedures" in our example) are explicit. But as illustrated by items #2 and #3, subjective judgment is desirable to some extent. While it is possible to specify decision rules for items #2 and #3, it is important from a behavioral point of view to leave room for the exercise of judgment to prevent making the process entirely mechanical and hence void of human interest.

By means of our marketing model we recognize the need for credit risk groups and are able to quantify the attributes of credit risk in terms of numerical scores. However, to close the link between scores and credit risk groups we need a statistical model.

THE STATISTICAL MODEL

The statistical model furnishes us with knowledge (or assumptions) as to the attributes of a population. We need this information to extend our credit model. Actually we should refer to statistical models as many are available.[10] Only three of these are pertinent to our credit model--the *uniform*,[11] *Gaussian*, and *Poisson* distributions.

The uniform model should be used with large populations whose attributes are known. The Gaussian model should be used with large populations whose attributes are not known but where they are presumed to conform to a normal distribution. The Poisson model should be used to screen relatively small groups of low credit risk. We proceed in terms of large populations whose attributes are known. Because we are seeking to classify our population into groups, the *uniform* distribution expressed as a histogram is appropriate. We assume that the population consists of 11 credit risk groups, identified A thru K, (Exhibit VII). "A" customers can be defined as *cash* customers, in which event there are no credit costs. "K" customers are deemed to have credit risk factors of 100%. The other credit risk groups, B thru J, range between these values as shown in Exhibit VIII.

Exhibit VIII prescribes the information which is needed to complete the statistical model. We need to know how many potential customers are in each credit risk group, as well as their purchasing or credit power. From this data we derive total potential sales. The score column relates application data to credit risk groups. In our example we assign scores to the full range of credit risk. In practice,

[9] Appendix B contains a credit scoring form used by a national general purpose credit card company. Appendix C illustrates a proposed scoring form for business, as opposed to personal, credit.
Note that we are using bank and savings and loan references for general credit record purposes. Item 3 on the application form combines the character general credit record factor having a maximum of 10 points, with the capacity savings factor also with a maximum of 10 points, making a 20 point total for item #3. This demonstrates that it is possible to combine a character and capacity factor through the use of one source of information.

[10] Statistical distribution models can be classified into three groups: (1) distributions of a discrete variable: Uniform, binomial, multinomial, hypergeometric, Poisson and geometric; (2) distributions of a continuous variable: uniform, normal, beta, gamma, exponential, log-normal and Weibull; and (3) distributions which express relationships among other distributions: Chi-square, F, and t distributions.

[11] The uniform distribution derives from an analysis of population attributes. Its properties are not known mathematically. Where population attributes are not known the Gaussian model should be used.

Exhibit VII. HISTOGRAM OF A UNIFORM DISTRIBUTION OF CREDIT RISKS

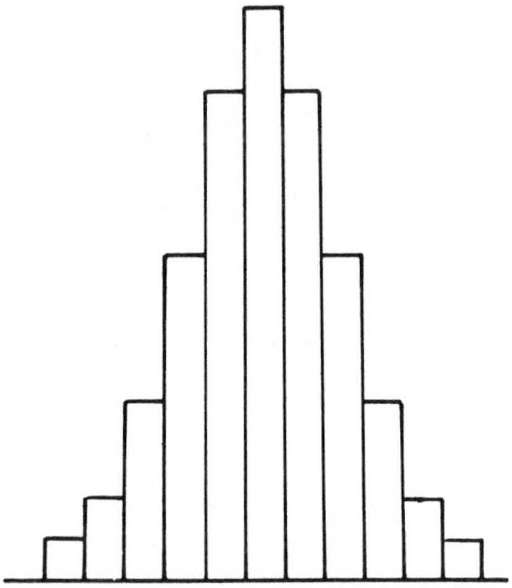

of course, it is not necessary to differentiate risks below a *cutoff* point. For example, if we declined all risks under group E, we would not need to relate scores to credit risk groups below that level, (Exhibit IX).

Our college professor, with a score of 159, falls into group D. But as he is at the upper limit of D, some secondary verification as mentioned in footnote 9 and/or review of the subjective analysis in items #2 and #3 of the application can be employed to see if he should be placed in group C. This action is only of consequence to the professor in the event that he wishes to have his credit limit raised from $700 to $800. However, a change in category is more important to the firm as it affects the accept-reject decision as well as sales forecasts and credit controls.

Exhibit VIII. PROPERTIES OF OUR ASSUMED CREDIT RISK GROUPS

Score	Credit Risk Factor	Credit Risk Group	Potential Number of Persons	Average Sales[12] Per Person (Limit)	Total Potential Sales
None	0%	A	1,000	$100	$ 100,000
180-200	10	B	2,000	900	1,800,000
160-179	20	C	3,000	800	2,400,000
140-159	30	D	4,000	700	2,800,000
120-139	40	E	5,000	600	3,000,000
100-119	50	F	6,000	500	3,000,000
80- 99	60	G	5,000	400	2,000,000
60- 79	70	H	4,000	300	1,200,000
40- 59	80	I	3,000	200	600,000
20- 39	90	J	2,000	100	200,000
0- 19	100	K	1,000	0	0

Exhibit IX. CUTOFF OF CREDIT RISKS

	Score	Credit Risk Factor	Credit Risk Group
Accept	None	0%	A
	180-200	10	B
	160-179	20	C
	140-159	30	D
	120-139	40	E
Reject	Below 120		

[12] (a) In practical terms the limit may be different from average sales, but we are assuming these expressions to be equal in our example.
(b) A point to be stressed is that credit risk factors assume a distribution of risk, e.g., if all of the sales in group B are to a very few persons the 10% factor would no longer be applicable. Geographical dispersion and enforcing credit limits are two ways in which to assure a distribution of risk.
(c) The limit of $100 in the case of group A is a purchasing power rather than a credit limit.

The statistical model enables us to segment a population into credit risk groups. It also furnishes us with sales forecast data and allows us to disperse risk through the medium of the credit limit. While our systemic credit model is greatly refined through the application of statistics, it is still incomplete. The remaining question relates to *cutoff*. But this is an important question for it deals with (1) which risks to accept or reject, and (2) the extent to which we need credit information. For these answers we turn to an accounting model.

The statistical model can also be represented graphically, as in Exhibit X. It shows that on a cumulative basis the more risk a company is willing to accept the higher its cumulative sales potential will be. The sales slope will peak out partly, (because as Exhibit VIII shows), the higher risk groups have progressively less purchasing power, and partly because there is a limit where the granting of credit ceases to be a sales inducement.

Exhibit X. THE STATISTICAL MODEL

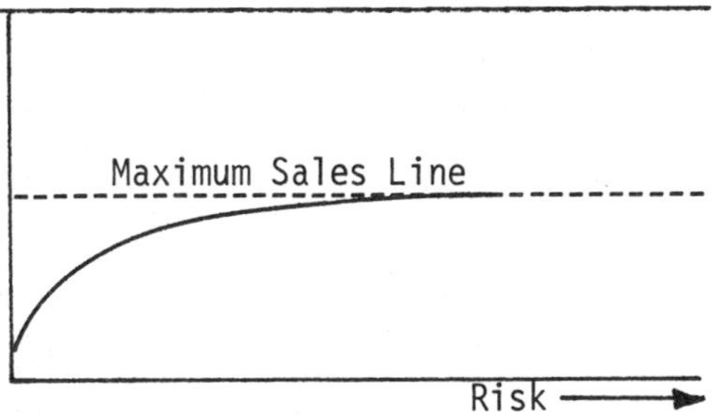

THE ACCOUNTING MODEL

The *cost-volume-profit* (CVP) model in accounting is applicable to this problem. Underlying the CVP model is the observed fact that some costs, such as rents and salaries, relate to time periods and are *fixed* in terms of volume. That is, fixed costs do not vary in relation to changes in activity level. For example, rents and property taxes do not vary as a function of sales. Other costs do vary in relation to volume, such as production costs, the cost of acquiring goods and services, or sales commissions. These *variable* costs are responsive to changes in activity level. For example, a sales commission of 5% is paid out of every sales dollar, hence this cost item will always be 5% of sales, whereas a fixed salary will not change in relation to sales volume. We will not dwell on this elemental concept of cost behavior as it is present in every standard textbook in management and/or cost accounting.

The CVP model is readily depicted by conventional break-even graphs, (Exhibit XI).

Exhibit XI. BREAK-EVEN GRAPHS ILLUSTRATE COST-VOLUME-PROFIT RELATIONSHIPS

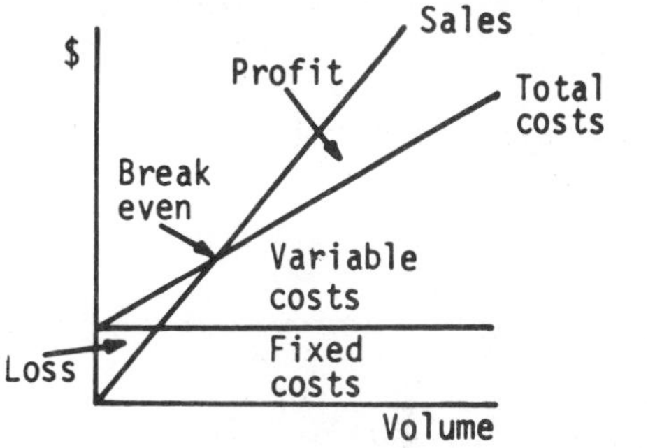

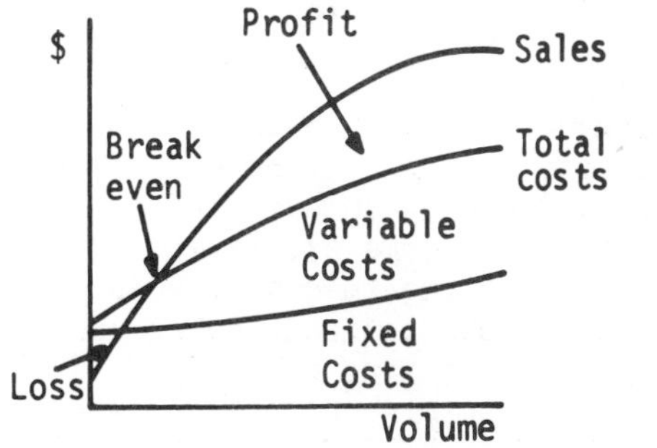

We will limit our discussion to linear CVP functions in which case fixed costs do not vary *at all* in relation to volume, and variable costs change in *direct proportion* to changes in volume. By reversing the position of fixed and variable costs we have what is called a *marginal income* break-even graph, (Exhibit XII).

Exhibit XII. MARGINAL INCOME BREAK-EVEN GRAPH OF LINEAR FUNCTIONS

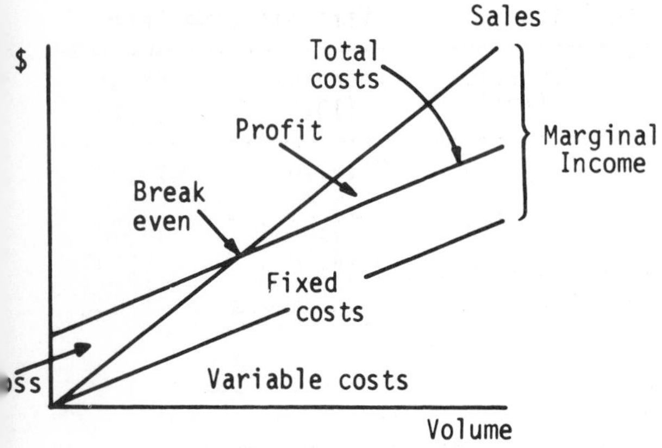

This graph is of interest to us in that it readily shows that marginal income + variable costs = sales, and that marginal income = fixed costs + profit (or - loss). This leads to the *marginal income statement* which has this structure:

Exhibit XIII. MARGINAL INCOME STATEMENT

Sales
- Variable costs
= Marginal Income
- Fixed costs
= Profit

The distinction between *marginal income* and *profit* is crucial. In a linear CVP model, both variable costs and marginal income are fixed percentages of sales regardless of volume, given a fixed relationship between two factors: (1) selling price, and (2) variable cost rate. A change in these factors leads to the following consequences where volume is held constant (Exhibit XIV).

This feature of the CVP model means that once fixed costs are covered, additions to marginal income are a direct increase to profit, (Exhibit XV).

Because marginal income is a constant ratio of sales, (while profit is not), and because of the difficulties in attempting to apportion fixed costs, it is useful to analyze projects in terms of their "contribution to margin" rather than their contribution to profit. Conditions being equal, the project with a higher marginal income ratio would be selected.

Let us return to the credit model. Credit risk factors are variable costs. These variable costs must be added to the basic variable costs, as previously defined, to reach total variable costs. The basic CVP behavior of the firm can be viewed best in terms of a cash structure in which there are no variable credit costs. Suppose that the basic cash structure is:

		%
Sales	$10,000	100
Variable Costs	6,000	60
Marginal Income	$ 4,000	40
Fixed Costs	3,000	30
Profit	$ 1,000	10

The basic variable costs in our example are 60% of sales. Using the credit risk factors in Exhibit VIII, the total variable costs for each credit risk group would be as in Exhibit XVI.

The cutoff problem is now clarified. If we decide on a minimum contribution to margin of 10%, credit would only be extended to groups A through D. Given our basic structure, suppose that potential sales to each credit group is $10,000. Pro forma income statements would appear as in Exhibit XVII.

It is clear that the contribution to margin decreases with lower credit groups. The determinant of cutoff is not the greatest contribution to margin ratio (as this would restrict us to cash customers only), but rather to some minimum rate such as 10%. Given the fact that group A recovers the fixed cost of $3,000, the marginal income of each of the other groups contributes directly to increases in profit. Extending credit to group E would be a break-even proposition, while the inclusion of groups F through K would result in increasing reductions to profit.

Exhibit XIV. EFFECT OF CHANGES IN SELLING PRICE OR VARIABLE COST RATE

		Change in Selling Price		Change in Variable Cost Rate	
	Basic	Increase (10%)	Decrease (10%)	Increase (10%)	Decrease (10%)
Sales	$ 10,000	$ 11,000	$ 9,000	$ 10,000	$ 10,000
Variable Costs	6,000	6,000	6,000	6,600	5,400
Marginal Income	$ 4,000	$ 5,000	$ 3,000	$ 3,400	$ 4,600
Fixed Costs	3,000	3,000	3,000	3,000	3,000
Profit	$ 1,000	$ 2,000	$ 0	$ 400	$ 1,600

Exhibit XV. INCREASES IN MARGINAL INCOME, AFTER RECOVERY OF FIXED COSTS RESULTS IN DIRECT INCREASES TO PROFIT (Volume Increases 20%)

	Old Volume $	Old Volume %	Increase $	Increase %	New Volume $	New Volume %
Sales	10,000	100	2,000	100	12,000	100
Variable Costs	6,000	60	1,200	60	7,200	60
Marginal Income	4,000	40	800	40	4,800	40
Fixed Costs	3,000	30	---		3,000	25
Profit	1,000	10	800	40	1,800	15

Exhibit XVI. TOTAL VARIABLE COSTS OF CREDIT RISK GROUPS

Group	Basic Variable Rate %	Credit Risk Factor %	Total Variable Rate %
A	60		60
B	60	10	70
C	60	20	80
D	60	30	90
E	60	40	100
F	60	50	110
G	60	60	120
H	60	70	130
I	60	80	140
J	60	90	150
K	60	100	160

Exhibit XVII. PRO FORMA INCOME STATEMENTS ON A MARGINAL BASIS

	Group A	Group B	Group C	Group D	Total
Sales	$10,000	$10,000	$10,000	$10,000	$40,000
Variable Costs	6,000(60%)	7,000(70%)	8,000(80%)	9,000(90%)	30,000
Marginal Income	4,000	3,000	2,000	1,000	10,000
Fixed Costs	--	--	--	--	3,000
Profit	--	--	--	--	$ 7,000

PRO FORMA INCOME STATEMENTS ON A CUMULATIVE BASIS

Sales	$10,000	$20,000	$30,000	$40,000
Variable Costs	6,000	13,000	21,000	30,000
Marginal Income	$ 4,000	$ 7,000	$ 9,000	$10,000
Fixed Costs	--	--	--	3,000
Profit	--	--	--	$ 7,000

Exhibit XVIII. DIFFERENT CVP STRUCTURES

	Structure X (High Variable Costs)		Structure Y (High Fixed Costs)	
Sales	$10,000	100%	$10,000	100%
Variable Costs	8,000	80	1,000	10
Marginal Income	2,000	20	9,000	90
Fixed Costs	1,000	10	8,000	80
Profit	1,000	10	1,000	10

Exhibit XIX. DIFFERENCE IN CUTOFF BASED ON CVP STRUCTURES

Credit Groups	Total Variable Cost Ratios Structure X	Structure Y
A	80	10
B	90 —cutoff	20
C	100	30
D	110	40
E	120	50
F	130	60
G	140	70
H	150	80
I	160	90 —cutoff
J	170	100
K	180	110

The CVP model provides the key to cutoff, as mentioned before. We can dramatize this point by using two extreme "basic" structures, (Exhibit XVIII).

While the basic profit ratio is the same, X and Y are radically different organizations insofar as credit management is concerned. Given a minimum 10% contribution to margin in both cases, note the difference in cutoff, (Exhibit XIX).

The nature of the credit problem can be viewed as a continuum with respect to CVP structures, (Exhibit XX).

Exhibit XX. THE CVP-CREDIT CONTINUUM

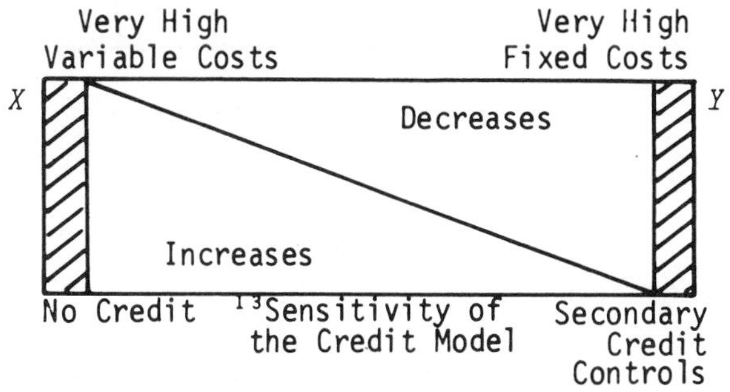

No credit problem exists at the extreme of X. In industries such as retail food, margins are so low that the credit function is essentially ruled out. Below the extreme, very sensitive models are needed, as we are screening for a rather small number of low credit risks from a very large population. National, general-purpose credit card companies tend toward high-X. As we move down the continuum, less sensitive credit models are required. At the extreme of Y we need no credit screening mechanism. Our CVP structure is such that we assume the distribution of credit risks inherent in the population as a whole.[14]

Instead of screening we rely on secondary controls such as terminating service if payments are not made on time. Most utilities follow this approach.

In general terms, capital intensive industries tend toward Y, while personal service and retail organizations tend toward X. Given the enormous investment in plant and equipment, for example, what does it cost a utility or telephone company to service one additional customer? Magazine publication is another example which tends toward extreme Y. If the circulation of the TV Guide in the United States is 8,500,000 annually, (1970 figure), what is the risk of extending credit to the TV population as a whole, given that mailing of the Guide can cease after one or two issues in the event of non-payment?

Financing automobiles, building homes, or repairing automobiles, are examples which tend toward high-X. The variable costs of providing these services is a high percentage of sales. Firms engaged in these activities require sensitive credit models.

The accounting model completes the loop. It provides the elements which are needed to complete our systemic credit model, i.e., (1) where to make the cutoff, and (2) how sensitive a credit model is required.

The basic CVP model in accounting, with credit costs added, appears as follows, (Exhibit XXI).

SUMMARY

We have taken a complex problem, (credit management), and illustrated why a systems approach is necessary to its solution. In this case marketing, statistical and accounting models were integrated to achieve what we have called a *systemic model*, as depicted graphically

[13] We mentioned earlier that a model could be made more or less sensitive by changing the number of surrogates, i.e., by requiring more or less information.

[14] The distribution of credit risks in the total population of the United States, within the definition of legal age, is probably Gaussian in nature. This means that there are just as few poor risks as there are very good risks.

Exhibit XXI. THE ACCOUNTING MODEL WITH CREDIT COSTS ADDED

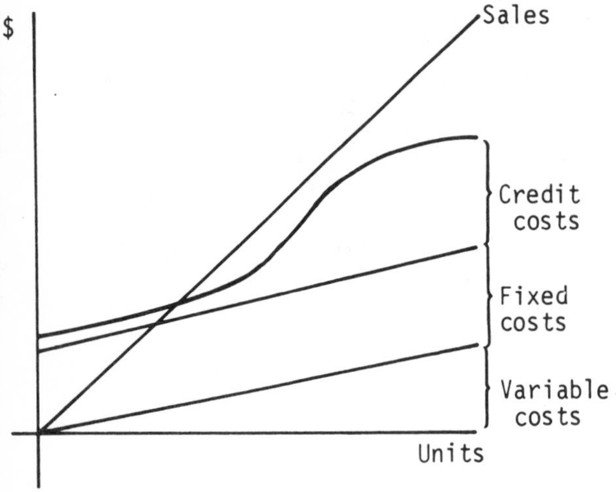

of credit risk. The statistical model deals with population attributes, and yields estimates as to the number of persons in each credit group and an estimation of their purchasing power. Statistics also leads us to distribute risk through the use of credit limits and geographic dispersion. The accounting model (CVP) scrutinizes the basic financial structure of the firm and indicates where cutoff should occur, and how sensitive a credit model is required given the nature of the business. The CVP-credit continuum in Exhibit XX illustrates that no credit is possible at high-X, that the sensitivity of the credit model decreases as we move toward Y, and that secondary controls are preferable to credit applications and screening at high-Y.

While we have shown the progress of the systemic model as moving from marketing to accounting, (Exhibit XXIII), the nature of these complex problems is such that these variables must be considered simultaneously in Exhibit XXII.

The marketing model converts subjective information into quantitative data which is used to identify classes

Exhibit XXII. THE SYSTEMIC CREDIT MODEL
Composite of the Marketing, Statistical and Accounting Models

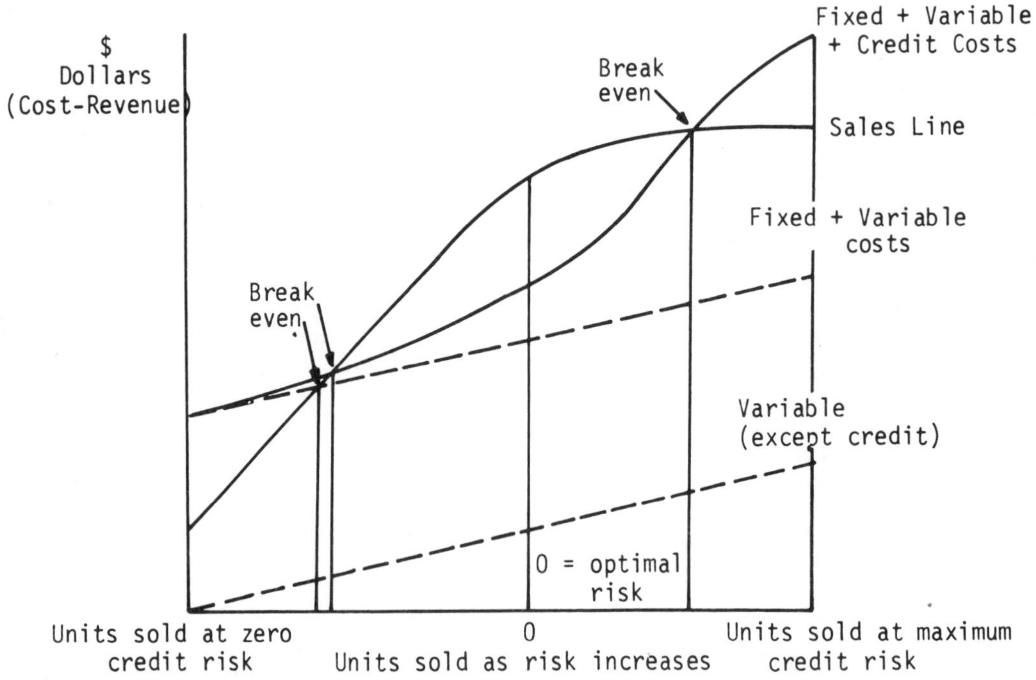

Exhibit XXIII.

Marketing → Statistics → Accounting → Systemic Credit Model

Exhibit XXIIIA

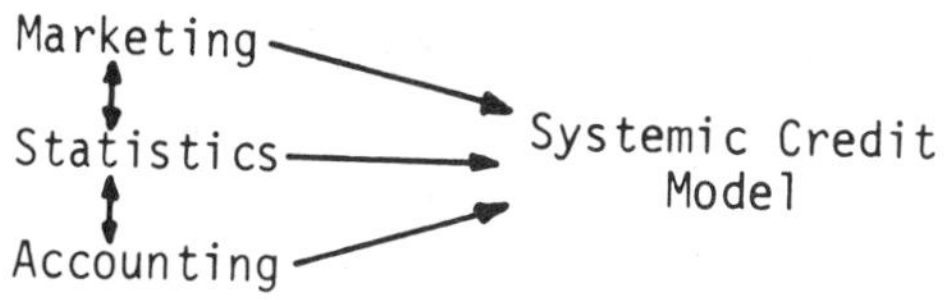

rather than in sequence, (Exhibit XXIIIA).

This exercise points to the need for close cooperation between various specialists in solving complex problems. In addition, the systemic credit model which is developed in this paper should have practical value to those who face the problem of designing or managing credit functions.

APPENDIX A

National statistics on paying habits of various occupations.

	% of Prompt Payment		% of Prompt Payment
1. Business executives	91	19. Lawyers & judges	78
2. Accountants & auditors	90	20. Traveling salesmen	77
3. Store managers	89	21. Plumbers	76
4. Physicians & dentists	89	22. Policemen & firemen	76
5. Engineers	89	23. Carpenters	74
6. Farmers & ranchers (owners)	88	24. Farmers & ranchers (tenants)	73
7. Commissioned officers	87	25. Truck & bus drivers	71
8. Office workers	87	26. Enlisted personnel	71
9. College professors	87	27. Janitors	70
10. Railroad clerks	86	28. Plasterers	69
11. Post office employees	85	29. Barbers	68
12. Hotel & cafe managers	84	30. Bartenders	63
13. School teachers	83	31. Musicians	63
14. Preachers	82	32. Painters	61
15. Nurses	82	33. Laborers	60
16. Public officials	82	34. Cooks	60
17. Sales people	81	35. Waitresses	59
18. Printers	80	36. Laundry workers	58

	% of Prompt Payment
37. Housekeepers	58
38. Models	58
39. Actors	54
40. Singers	53
41. Loggers	52

Source: Committee on Education & Research, U.S. Credit Bureau, Inc., 1970.

APPENDIX B

Credit Scoring Forms for a National, General-Purpose Credit Card Company

Marital Status	Score
Married	0
Single or Widowed	-1
Divorced or Separated	-2
Age	
36 to 60	1
25 to 35	0
61 to 65	0
Under 25 or over 65	-3
Residence	
Own	2
Rent	0
Time at Residence	
6 years or longer	2
2 to 5 years	0
Under 2 years	-1
Time Previous Residence (if presently under 2 years)	
4 years or longer	1
2 and 3 years	0
1 year or less	-2
Occupation (Note #1)	
Professional and Executive	5
Managerial	3
Technical	1
Owners, Partners & Other	0
Questionable	-1
Length of Employment	
Under 2 years	-1
2 to 5 years	0
6 years or longer	2

Company Rating	Score
D + and above	1
F thru D	0
Not listed	0
G and under	-5
Annual Income	
Over $20,000	2
$10,000 to 19,999	1
$7,200 to $9,999	0
Under $7,200	-1
No. of Dependents (if income under $10,000)	
2 or less	0
3 to 5	-2
6 or more	-3
Bank	
Checking account	0
Checking and Loan	1
Other All-Purpose Cards	
Yes	1
No	0
Credit References	
Left blank	0
States "none"	-1
Loan Company Reference	
No	0
Yes	-2

Scores may range from +1 to -3

#1 "Professional" includes physicians, surgeons, dentists, CPA's, architects, etc.

APPENDIX C. PROPOSED CREDIT SCORING GUIDE FOR COMMERCIAL LOANS

Age of business	Under 1 year 1	1-3 years 7	4-7 years 19	8-12 years 36	13-21 years 49	Over 21 years 67
Years of present management	Under 1 year 1	1-3 years 6	4-7 years 17	8-12 years 32	13-21 years 45	Over 21 years 50
Successive years of increased profit	Loss -10	2-3 years 5	4-5 years 12	6-8 years 30	9-12 years 47	Over 12 years 62
Number of days inventory	Over 210 1	150-209 4	90-149 10	60-89 22	30-59 53	Under 30 72
Number of days receivables	Over 210 1	150-209 4	90-149 11	60-89 28	30-59 57	Under 30 70
Debt to net worth	Over 10:1 1	9:1 to 5:1 4	4:1 to 2:1 20	1:1 35	1:2 52	1:3 or better 70
Trade reports	Suits & judgments 1	All slow 2	Mixed slow & satisfactory 5	All satisfactory 20	Pays prompt & takes all discounts 40	--
Industry groups*	I 1	II 5	III 10	IV 15	V 19	VI 24
Audit	Own audit 1	Qualified Audit 20	Unqualified audit by unknown CPA firm 40	Unqualified audit by known CPA firm 60	--	--

*Banks could set up industrial groupings to reflect their preferences in the granting of credit. If, for example, a bank has had very poor experience with a particular industry, the industry could be categorized as "Group 1" and given a correspondingly low score. Conversely, industries with good past records would be categorized by a group receiving a high score.

Source: W.T. Maloan, "What Bankers are Now Looking for In Financial Statements," The Practical Accountant, January--February, 1970, pp. 40-46.

REFERENCES

Ackoff, Russell L., A Concept of Corporate Planning, (New York: John Wiley & Sons, Inc.), 1970.

Amstuz, A.E., Computer Simulation of Competitive Marketing Response, (Cambridge, Mass.:MIT Press), 1967.

Britt, S.H. and H.W. Boyd, Jr., Marketing Management and Administrative Action, (New York: McGraw-Hill Book Co., Inc.), 1963.

Churchman, C. West, The Systems Approach, (New York: Dell Pub. Co., Inc.), 1968.

Clark, W.A. and D.E. Saxton, Jr., Marketing and Management Science: A Synergism, (Homewood, Ill.: Irwin, Inc.), 1970.

Cohen, Kalman J. and Frederick S. Hammer (Eds.), Analytical Methods in Banking, (Homewood, Ill.: Irwin, Inc.), 1966.

Cooley, William W. and Paul R. Lohnes, Multivariate Procedures for the Behavioral Sciences, (New York: John Wiley & Sons, Inc.), 1962.

Donelly, J.H., Jr., and J.M. Ivancevich, Analysis for Marketing Decision, (Homewood, Ill.: Irwin, Inc.), 1970.

Durand, David, Risk Elements in Consumer Installment Financing, Study No. 8, (New York: National Bureau of Economic Research, 1941).

Greer, Carl C., "Measuring the Value of Information in Consumer Credit Screening," Management Services, (May-June, 1967), pp. 44-45.

Ijiri, Yuji, The Foundations of Accounting Measurement, (Englewood Cliffs, N.J.: Prentice-Hall, Inc.), 1967.

Horngren, Charles T., Cost Accounting: A Managerial Approach, (Englewood Cliffs, N.J.: Prentice-Hall, Inc.), 1967 edition.

McGrath, James J., "Improving Credit Evaluation with a Weighted Application Blank," Journal of Applied Psychology, (Vol. 44, 1960), pp. 325-328.

Montgomery, D.B. and G.L. Urban, IEds.) Applications of Management Science in Accounting, (Englewood Cliffs, N.J.: Prentice-Hall, Inc.), 1970.

Neuwirth, Sidney I. and Michael Shegda, "Discriminant Analysis," Management Services, (April, 1964), pp. 28 ff.

Myers, James H. and Warren Cordner, "Increase Credit Operations Profit," Credit World, (February, 1957), pp. 12-13.

Myers, James H. and Edward W. Forgy, "The Development of Numerical Evaluation Systems," Journal of the American Statistical Association, (September, 1963), pp. 799-806.

Smith, Paul F., "Measuring Risk on Installment Credit," Management Science, (November, 1964), pp. 327-340.

Williams, E.J., Regression Analysis, (New York: John Wiley & Sons, Inc.), 1959.

Determining the Cash Discount in the Firm's Credit Policy

Ned C. Hill
Indiana University

Kenneth D. Riener
Texas A & M University

INTRODUCTION

A key decision in the firm's credit policy is whether or not to offer a cash discount for the early payment of invoices; and, if a discount is offered, how much it should be. Credit terms involving cash discounts are common in many industries. A typical credit term is "2/10, net 30;" the customer may take a 2% cash discount from the stated invoice price if payment is made by the tenth day from the date of invoice. If the customer neglects (or chooses not) to pay by that date, the full invoice price is due on the thirtieth day.

Although there is at least one report that suggests discounts substantially affect profitability [2], the role cash discounts play in credit policy has received little attention in the finance literature. The purpose of this study is to structure the cash discount decision in terms of the tradeoff between costs and benefits. There are costs involved in giving up some percentage of the full invoice amount, but there are three possible benefits. First, cash is received sooner, reducing the need to borrow or allowing more cash for investment. Second, sales volume may increase, since a discount is, in effect, a price reduction. Third, if customers can be induced to pay early, it may be possible to reduce bad debt losses.

Assume the firm now has some credit policy that results in a particular pattern of cash flows over time. We then examine how the pattern might change with the introduction of a cash discount. The decision criterion is the present values of the two cash flows. Our approach is similar to the discounted cash flow analysis of the accounts receivable problem described by Atkins and Kim [1], which we prefer to other techniques that do not explicitly consider the timing of the cash flows (see [3], for example). We find a break-even policy by computing the maximum discount the firm can offer given a set of assumptions about timing, change in sales volume, fraction

---

Reprinted from FINANCIAL MANAGEMENT (Spring 1979), pp. 68-73, by permission of the publisher and authors.

of credit sales expected to be paid with a discount, and any change in the bad debt loss rate. The firm would not want to offer a larger discount because the present value of cash flows with the discount policy would be less than the current policy. We also demonstrate how the decision model can be extended to the computation of an optimal discount rate, given relationships between the discount rate and 1) the fraction of customers taking the discount, and 2) the change in sales volume. The model is then applied to a variety of credit problems.

COMPUTING THE MAXIMUM DISCOUNT

CASE 1: CASH DISCOUNT ACCOMPANIED BY A CHANGE IN TIMING

We assume the firm's current credit policy offers no discount on a particular product line, resulting in cash payments, on average, on day N. "On average" refers to a simple arithmetic average. Appendix A shows that a time weighted average is more exact but that the arithmetic average is entirely sufficient for normal interest rates and periods under one year. Exhibit 1 illustrates the cash flows under the current credit policy. Initially, we assume the firm has no bad debt losses. This assumption is relaxed in Appendix B. The present value factor is $(1+i)^{-N}$, where i is the opportunity cost per day of the firm's funds. The appropriate determination of i is beyond the scope of this paper. The net present value of cash flows under the current policy is

$$(1) \quad NPV_0 = S(1+i)^{-N},$$

where S represents total sales.

We now consider a proposed credit policy offering a cash discount of δ for early payment of invoices. We assume some fraction p of net sales will be paid on average on day M, while the remainder $(1-p)$ will be paid on average on day N'. Exhibit 2 represents

EXHIBIT 1. Cash Flow Patterns Under Current Credit Policy

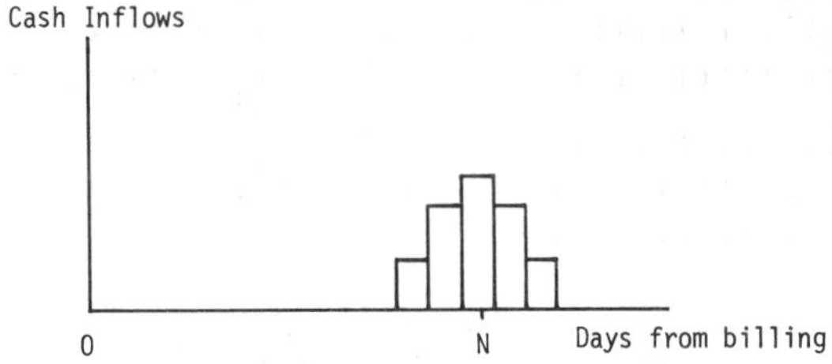

EXHIBIT 2. Cash Flow Patterns Under Proposed Credit Policy

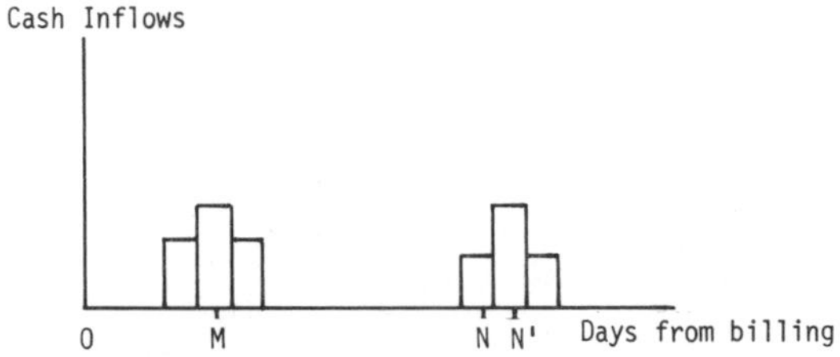

the cash flow pattern under the proposed policy. Note that N' need not equal N—for example, if the percentage of customers taking the discount were higher among early payers than among late payers. The present value of cash flows under the proposed policy is the sum of the amount paid with a discount on day M plus the remainder paid in full on day N':

$$(2) \quad NPV_1 = p(1-\delta)S(1+i)^{-M} + (1-p)S(1+i)^{-N'}.$$

In deciding on the discount rate, the firm should insure that the present value of cash flows under the proposed policy is at least as great as that under the current policy or,

$$(3) \quad NPV_1 \geq NPV_0 .$$

Substitution Equations (1) and (2) into Equation (3), and solving for δ, gives

(4) $\delta \leq 1-(1+i)^{M-N'}[1-\frac{1}{p}+\frac{(1+i)^{N'-N}}{p}]$.

Equation (4) specifies a range of possible discounts that would make this condition hold. We define δ_{max} to be the maximum justifiable discount rate to offer or that discount rate which equates NPV_1 and NPV_0,

(5) $\delta_{max} = 1-(1+i)^{M-N'}[1-\frac{1}{p}+\frac{(1+i)^{N'-N}}{p}]$.

Equation (5) specifies the maximum cash discount the firm should consider. A higher rate cannot be justified on a present value basis because the costs of reduced revenues would exceed the benefits of receiving cash sooner.

We note that δ_{max} depends on p, the fraction of sales being paid with a discount. This value could be estimated using a variety of techniques such as past experience with individual accounts, market surveys, or observations of similar terms for other product lines.

If the average payment date before the credit policy change equals the average payment date after ($N = N'$), we can simplify δ_{max} to

(6) $\delta_{max} = 1 - (1+i)^{M-N}$.

Now the maximum feasible discount is independent of p. N would equal N' if 1) all customers were taking the same amount of time to pay under the old credit terms, or 2) the same dollar fraction of early and late paying accounts were moved forward.

NUMERICAL EXAMPLE

Under the firm's current credit terms, 50% of credit sales are collected on day 60 and 50% on day 120. The average collection day is therefore 90. The firm wants to know what discount it can offer for payment by day 10. It is assumed that all the customers now paying on day 60 will take the discount while the late customers will not. Financing costs are 10%. In terms of Equation (5), $N = 90$, $N' = 120$, $M = 10$, $p = .50$, and $i = .10/365 = .00027$. The maximum feasible discount rate is

$$\delta_{max} = 1 - (1.00027)^{10-120} \cdot [1 - \frac{1 - (1.0027)^{120-90}}{.5}]$$

$$= .0137 = 1.37\% .$$

This means the firm could not benefit from offering a discount of greater than 1.37%.

While this example uses a very simple payment pattern, the model can easily handle complex ones.

CASE 2: CASH DISCOUNT ACCOMPANIED BY CHANGES IN TIMING OF PAYMENTS AND SALES VOLUME

Changing the cash discount could result in a change in sales volume. When sales volume changes we must also consider the change in cash outflow reflecting the change in variable costs. Let g represent the fractional change in sales volume. If v represents the variable costs per sales dollar, then a change of sales volume gS will result in the change of cash outflow vgS. The present value of this cash outflow depends on the firm's pattern of cash payments for variable costs. Let Q be the average payment date of variable costs. The present value of cash flows under this credit policy, assuming fraction p of credit sales will be paid on day M, will be

(7) $NPV_2 = p(1-\delta)S(1+g)(1+i)^{-M} + (1-p)S(1+g)(1+i)^{-N'} - vgS(1+i)^{-Q}$.

Setting $NPV_0 = NPV_2$ and solving for δ gives

(8) $\delta_{max} = 1 - (1+i)^{M-N'}[1 - \frac{1}{p} + \frac{(1+i)^{N'-N} + vg(1+i)^{N'-Q}}{p(1+g)}]$.

NUMERICAL EXAMPLE

A gas station currently accepts only cash. The owner is considering the possibility of honoring a national bank card. Experience of other stations shows this would likely result in a 10% increase in sales. Payments from the bank card company are discounted 5%. The owner expects 50% of his customers will take advantage of the bank card. If variable costs are 80% payable on average on day zero, would the gas station owner be better off accepting the bank card or sticking to a cash only basis? Assume cost of funds to be 10% or .027% per day.

In this case, $N = N' = 0$, $M = 0$, $Q = 0$, $p = .5$, $g = .1$ and $v = .8$. Using Equation (8),

$$\delta_{max} = 1 - [1 - \frac{1}{.5} + \frac{1+.8(.1)(1.0)}{.5(1.10)}]$$

$$= .0364 = 3.64\% .$$

The maximum justifiable discount rate in this case is 3.64% compared to the bank card 5% discount. Hence, the firm should not accept the bank card.

It is easy to see how sensitivity analysis could be employed in this problem to examine the impact of various changes in sales, or in different fractions of customers taking the discount. For example, we could use Equation (8) to determine the minimum volume increase that would be necessary to justify acceptance of the bank card. Setting $\delta_{max} = .05$ and solving for g, we find g must equal 14.3% before the station would break even.

DETERMINATION OF THE OPTIMAL DISCOUNT RATE

We now consider the obvious interdependence of the discount rate with both the fraction of sales to be paid with a discount and the change in sales volume. The higher the discount, for example, the higher the number of customers taking the discount. If these dependencies can be specified, an optimal discount can be computed instead of simply the maximum feasible discount.

Assume that p, the fraction of credit sales paid with a discount, depends on the size of the cash discount offered, or $p = f(\delta)$. We define the optimal discount to be that discount which maximizes the present value of the cash flows, NPV_1. This will occur when $dNPV_1/d\delta = 0$. Using Equation (2), and letting $f'(\delta)$ represent the first derivative with respect to δ,

$$(9) \quad \frac{dNPV_1}{d\delta} = -f(\delta)S(1+i)^{-M} + (1-\delta)S(1+i)^{-M}f'(\delta) - S(1+i)^{-N'}f'(\delta) = 0 .$$

Cancelling the redundant S we obtain

$$(10) \quad -f(\delta)(1+i)^{-M} + [(1-\delta)(1+i)^{-M} - (1+i)^{-N'}]f'(\delta) = 0.$$

The solution to Equation (10) depends on the specific relationship between p and δ. The relationship should be such that $p = 0$ when no discount is offered, and $p = 1$ when the discount approaches 100%. An example of a very simple function satisfying this relationship is $p = \delta$. By substituting $f(\delta) = \delta$ and $f'(\delta) = 1$ into Equation (10), we obtain

$$(11) \quad \delta^* = \frac{[1 - (1 + i)^{M-N'}]}{2} .$$

OPTIMAL DISCOUNT EXAMPLE

Under the firm's current credit terms, payments are collected on average on day 90, with no discount offered. The firm discounts cash flows at 10%. It is assumed that, if some customers take a discount, the average payment date for the remaining customers will not differ much from 90 (or $N' = N$). Assume that the relationship between δ and p is approximated by $p = 20\delta$ (or with a 2.5% discount 50% of the customers would pay early). What is the optimal discount rate, if any, the firm should offer?

Using Equation (11), the optimal discount rate is computed:

$$\delta^* = \frac{[1 - (1 + \frac{.10}{365})^{10-90}]}{2} =$$

$$.0108 = 1.08\% .$$

Hence, the firm can afford to offer a discount of 1.08% (or in more realistic terms, 1%).

OPTIMAL DISCOUNT WHEN SALES VOLUME CHANGES

To determine an optimal discount rate in the case of both timing and sales volume changes, it is necessary to specify how both p and g depend on δ. Let $p = f(\delta)$ and $g = h(\delta)$. NPV_2 from Equation (7) then becomes

$$(12) \quad NPV_2 = f(\delta)(1-\delta)S[1+h(\delta)](1+i)^{-M} + [1-f(\delta)]S[1+h(\delta)]^{-N'} - vh(\delta)S(1+i)^{-Q}.$$

For almost any realistic functions for $f(\delta)$ and $h(\delta)$, determining δ^* from the derivative of Equation (12) is most efficiently handled using computer approximation methods rather than finding an explicit solution.

SUMMARY AND CONCLUSIONS

This paper shows how the cash discount decision in a firm's credit policy can be structured in terms of timing of payments, change in sales, variable costs, the firm's cost of funds, the proportion of sales expected to be paid with a discount, and the bad debt loss rate. The model focuses on the maximum feasible discount rate for a given set of circumstances. The firm cannot afford to offer a discount above this specified rate. Second, by taking into account the dependencies between the size of the discount and both the fraction of sales paid with a discount and the change in sales volume, a model can be developed to specify the optimal discount rate.

With the discount problem structured in this manner, we can make several observations pertinent to credit policy decisions.

1. Products with different variable costs should have different credit terms. In general, the lower the variable costs, the higher the feasible discount.

2. Since the cash discount offered depends on the firm's own cost of funds, managers should consider changing credit policy as the firm's opportunity costs change.

3. The timing of cash flows is critical to the discount decision model. The manager must consider not only how the discount shifts some payments forward but also how it affects the timing of cash flows from non-discount taking customers.

4. Since the cash discount depends on how sensitive demand is to price changes, knowledge of price elasticity is important.

5. As demonstrated in Appendix B, bad debt losses affect the maximum justifiable discount. Firms with higher bad debt loss rates can afford to offer higher cash discounts, provided the discount helps reduce the loss.

APPENDIX A

When using present value methods, care must be taken to define the average time of two or more cash flows occurring at different times. For example, assume a cash flow of A dollars on day N_1 and B dollars on day N_2. The present value of these cash flows is

$$PV_1 = A(1+i)^{-N_1} + B(1+i)^{-N_2}.$$

We wish to compute an average time, N^*, such that the present value of $A+B$ discounted at rate i for N^* periods will have the same present value as PV_1. In symbols:

$$(A+B)(1+i)^{-N^*} = A(1+i)^{-N_1} + B(1+i)^{-N_2}$$

$$(1+i)^{-N^*} = \frac{A}{A+B}(1+i)^{-N_1} + \frac{B}{A+B}(1+i)^{-N_2}$$

$$(1+i)^{-N^*} = f_A(1+i)^{-N_1} + f_B(1+i)^{-N_2},$$

where $f_A = A/(A+B)$ and $f_B = B/(A+B)$. By taking logs and solving for N^*, we get

$$N^* = \frac{-ln[f_A(1+i)^{-N_1} + f_B(1+i)^{-N_2}]}{ln(1+i)}.$$

The same procedure works for any number of cash flows (M), so we may write:

$$N^* = \frac{ln[f_1(1+i)^{-N_1} + f_2(1+i)^{-N_2} + \ldots + f_M(1+i)^{-N_M}]}{ln(1+i)}.$$

To see how much N^* differs from a simple arithmetic average, we will recompute the average for the numerical example of Case 1:

There $f_1 = .50$, $f_2 = .50$, $N_1 = 60$, $N_2 = 120$, so

$$N^* = \frac{-ln[.50(1+\frac{.10}{365})^{-60} + .50(1+\frac{.10}{365})^{-120}]}{ln(1+\frac{.10}{365})}$$

$$= 89.8.$$

The arithmetic average is given by $.5(60) + .5(120) = 90$. A difference of 0.2 days is hardly worth the effort required to use the more exact formulation.

APPENDIX B. CASH DISCOUNT ACCOMPANIED BY CHANGES IN TIMING, SALES VOLUME, AND BAD DEBT LOSS RATE

When a discount is offered, it is possible that in some cases the bad debt loss rate is reduced. This might happen, for example, when a firm goes from a policy of accepting checks to accepting a credit card. It would also be the case where "cash only" is instituted as the alternative policy.

We define net sales to be $(1-b)$, where b is the fraction of sales never collected, or the bad debt loss rate. The present value of cash flows under the current policy is

(B-1) $NPV_0' = (1-b)S(1+i)^{-N}$.

We assume that under the alternative credit policy some customers responsible for the bad debt loss will take advantage of the discount, thereby reducing the overall loss. We define the fraction of total sales thus restored by k. Net sales under the current policy would then be $S(1-b+k)$. If we let p represent the fraction of net sales (including restored sales) paid with a discount on day M, the present value of cash flows becomes:

(B-2) $NPV_1' = p(1-\delta)S(1-b+k)(1+i)^{-M} + (1-p)S(1-b+k)(1+i)^{-N'}$.

Setting $NPV_0' = NPV_1'$ and solving for δ gives

(B-3) $\delta_{max} = 1 - (1+i)^{M-N'}[1 - \frac{1}{p} + \frac{(1-b)(1+i)^{N'-N}}{p(1-b+k)}]$.

From this equation we see that as k increases, other things being equal, δ_{max} increases. Hence, if a firm has reason to believe that offering a discount would reduce bad debt losses, it can offer a higher discount than that justified by simple timing effects. The relationship between discounts and bad debt loss reduction is not well understood and deserves empirical investigation.

An equation analogous to Equation (8) can be developed to include bad debt losses as well. If we let NPV_2' be the present value of cash flows under the proposed policy:

$$\text{(B-4)} \quad NPV_2' = p(1-\delta)S(1-b+k)(1+g)(1+i)^{-M} + (1-p)S(1-b+k)(1+g)(1+i)^{-N'} - vgS(1+i)^{-Q}.$$

Setting $NPV_2' = NPV_0'$ and solving for δ gives

$$\text{(B-5)} \quad \delta_{max} = 1 - (1+i)^{M-N'}\left[1 - \frac{1}{p} + \frac{(1-b)(1+i)^{N'-N} + vg(1+i)^{N'-Q}}{p(1+g)(1-b+k)}\right].$$

Equation (B-5) is the most general equation for computing δ_{max} with previous expressions being special cases.

EXAMPLE

The firm currently accepts cash only and is considering meeting its competition by offering terms of net 30. It is expected that some payments will be stretched beyond 30 days with the average cash flow on day 45. Extending credit will increase bad debt losses to an estimated 1%, but sales should increase 3% with no price change. Cost of funds is .05% per day, and variable costs are 80% of sales paid on average on day 0. It is likely that all customers will take advantage of the more liberal policy. Should the firm extend credit for 30 days?

In terms of Equation (B-5), $i = .0005$, $p = 1.0$, $b = 0$, $k = -.01$, $g = .03$, $m = 45$, $N' = N = 0$, $v = .80$, and $Q = 0$. Solving for δ_{max} gives -2.7%. The negative "discount" implies the firm should not accept the proposed change since it would have to raise prices by 2.7% just to break even. This example shows how well the model can handle a common type of credit policy problem in which timing, bad debt loss, and sales volume change simultaneously.

REFERENCES

1. Joseph C. Atkins and Yong H. Kim, "Comment and Correction: Opportunity Cost in the Evaluation of Investments in Accounts Receivable," *Financial Management* (Winter 1977), pp. 71-74.
2. E.F. Frantz and J.A. Viscione, "What Should You Do About Cash Discounts?" *Credit and Financial Management* (May 1976), pp. 30-36.
3. John S. Oh, "Opportunity Cost in the Evaluation of Investment in Accounts Receivable," *Financial Management* (Summer 1976), pp. 32-36.
4. G. Schiller, "How to Sharpen Your Credit and Collection Efforts," *Credit and Financial Management* (September 1975), pp. 14-15.

READING 20

An Application of Heuristic Problem Solving to Accounts Receivable Management†

Ferdinand K. Levy
Georgia Institute of Technology

INTRODUCTION

The growth of quantitative techniques as an aid to business decision making in recent years has been phenomenal. Under the headings of "management science" and "operations research," these techniques have found a myriad of applications to business, particularly in its production and distribution areas. The terms, mathematical programming, critical path method, exponential smoothing, computer simulation, etc., have now become integral parts of the average executive's vocabulary. These techniques have been used both at day to day operating and in executive level planning decisions in the production and distribution areas of firms[1] and have also recently been applied in finance areas. For example, there is now a great deal of literature in management science concerned with such financial problems as financial planning, transfer pricing, and capital budgeting.[2] This paper describes another very apparent application of a simple method of management science to the routine operations of the financial sector of a business, namely in locating "lock-boxes." These are post office boxes selected in a company's distribution area in order to minimize the time necessary for the company to collect and have available the funds remitted to it by its customers in payment of their obligations.

Reprinted from MANAGEMENT SCIENCE (February 1966), Vol. 12, No. 6, by permission of the publisher.

† The research and writing of this paper was supported by the Research Sponsors' Fund at Rice University. The author is solely responsible for the ideas, opinions, and conclusions expressed in the paper.

[1] At the day to day operations (or micro level) in production and marketing are found management science methods useful in assembly line balancing, advertising media selection, production scheduling, etc. The executive level uses are seen in modern forecasting methods, aggregate inventory and workforce planning, and in allocation of the manufacture of different products to specific plants.

[2] For a good example of this literature, see [6].

To see the usefulness of lock-boxes, we first note that one of the principal duties of the financial manager is to make sure that his firm always has the maximum amount of funds available to it to carry on its daily operations. The main source of these funds is of course the collection of obligations due the firm from its customers. Any method that the financial manager can use to speed the collection of these funds, or to put it another way, to reduce the firm's "accounts receivable float" will result in cost savings to the firm. Lock-boxes present a convenient method to facilitate this.

To illustrate the use of lock-boxes, consider a company located in New York and having customers throughout the United States. Suppose the company does business with only one bank which is in New York and suppose further that the company's terms of sales are ten days net. Now for example, the company sells a thousand dollar order to a firm in San Francisco. On the tenth day following the rendering of the invoice for its order, this firm in San Francisco remits a check most probably drawn on a San Francisco bank to our firm in New York. The average mail time to New York from San Francisco is three days, so the firm waits not ten days but thirteen days for collection of its invoice. However, it still doesn't have use of the funds, as it must then deposit the check in its New York bank and wait until the New York bank clears the check back to the San Francisco bank on which it was drawn. This clearing time, given by standard availability tables published by the Federal Reserve System, is two days from New York to San Francisco. So if the firm in New York is fortunate enough to deposit the check on the same day as it receives it, there will be a minimum of fifteen days before our firm can possibly have the use of the money.

Now assume the firm tells its New York bank it wants to locate a lock-box in San Francisco. This is a post office box to which the customer in San Francisco will remit rather than sending the check to New York. The New York bank will designate a bank in San Francisco which in turn will pick up checks a few times a day from the post office box and deposit them for our New York firm's account in San Francisco. In this case, our firm will have its funds available to draw upon in twelve days. There will only be one day for the mailing and one day for the bank clearing time. This represents a saving of three days availability time on the $1000. Thus if the firm could extend this saving to all of its accounts receivable, the savings would become quite significant. For example, the savings on $100 million available in twelve rather than fifteen days at an interest rate of 5% would be $41,667.[3]

The savings illustrated above are gross in that the cost of the lock-box is not included. This consists usually of a fixed charge in the form of a minimum balance which the firm must keep in the banks that collect its checks at the post office and a variable charge per check collected and deposited by the banks. Thus the lock-box location problem is to select a number of lock-boxes so that the cost saving attributed to the shortened fund availability time less the cost of the lock-boxes themselves is maximized.

This paper begins with a discussion of the problem of measuring the goodness of one set of lock-box locations relative to another. After proposing a solution to this problem, we shall formulate a heuristic program designed to select lock-boxes for a particular company from a set of possible locations. The paper closes with an application of the heuristic program to an actual problem.

---

[3] 5%/year for three days is .05 x 3/360. Thus the savings would be given by:

$$\text{Savings} = (\$100\text{ million})[.05 \times 3/360] = \$41,667.$$

Before proceeding to describe methods to locate lock-boxes, we should note the symmetry between this problem and the warehouse location problem. Here the problem is to determine the location of warehouses so that distribution costs of goods are minimized. As in the lock-box problem, there are cost savings associated with being geographically close to customers which are offset to some degree by the fixed and variable costs of maintaining warehouses. Thus for the most part the procedures described below are also useful in locating warehouses. However, some of the cost savings in warehouse location problems and their concomitant effects on overall profit are subjective since a firm's being closer to potential customers and being able to service them faster might bring added sales. This part of the warehouse problem is not in the lock-box problem.[4]

THE PROBLEM OF MEASUREMENT

The cost of collection of a set of checks consists of the variable charge per check and the interest lost on the face values of the checks while they are in the process of collection. Thus it costs more to have the funds available on ten one thousand dollar checks than on one ten thousand check because of the variable check charge even though the opportunity cost of the funds for both sets are identical.

To show this equivalence between a group of checks having the same total face value as another single check, we assume that $1000 not available for 10 days is equivalent to $10,000 not available for one day. Thus we can speak of lost availability days per thousand dollars. For example, in both of the above, we have ten availability days lost; that is, the firm is losing the equivalent of $1000 for ten days. Another implicit assumption in this definition, of course, is that the interest rate does not change during the ten days, or in general, that the collection time is short enough so that we can assume a constant interest rate.

It is easy to translate availability days lost into costs. At an interest rate of r, the interest lost on $1000 for one day is $r/360 \times \$1000$. Thus the interest lost when a firm has Y availability days lost is just $Y(r/360 \times \$1000)$. If r is 6%, then for Y availability days lost, the cost to the firm is $\$.167Y$. For example, the firm's interest cost on 7 availability days lost ($Y = 7$) is $1.17. Thus the cost of one set of lock-box locations vis-a-vis another includes the interest cost as measured above in addition to the sum of the fixed charges associated with maintaining each lock-box. A selected group of lock-boxes is optimal, then, if its charges computed in this manner are minimum when compared to the costs of each of all other possible sets of locations.

A HEURISTIC PROGRAMMING METHOD FOR LOCATING LOCK-BOXES

Obviously the lock-box location problem is a huge exercise in combinatorial analysis, If there are n possible locations, then there exist $2^n - 1$ possible sets of locations. In the face of similar problems, management scientists have turned to so-called heuristic problem solving methods to facilitate their solutions.[5] As defined by Simon [4] a heuristic problem solving procedure is a collection of rules of thumbs that assist in reaching a satisfactory solution to a problem. As in any heuristic, there is no guarantee that the lock-box location procedure described in the following paragraphs will reach the optimum solution that a mathematical programming approach would achieve.

---

[4] For a description of an excellent heuristic program for locating warehouses, see [3].

[5] For some examples of heuristic problem solving procedures applied to practical business problems, see [3] and [5].

TABLE 1

Check Number	Potential Lock-Box Locations 1	2	...	j	...	n-1	n
1	Y_{11}	Y_{12}	...	Y_{1j}	...	$Y_{1(n-1)}$	Y_{1n}
2	Y_{21}	Y_{22}	...	Y_{2j}	...	$Y_{2(n-2)}$	Y_{2n}
⋮	⋮	⋮	...	⋮	...	...	...
i	Y_{i1}	Y_{i2}	...	Y_{ij}	...	$Y_{i(n-1)}$	Y_{in}
⋮	⋮	⋮	...	⋮	...	...	...
m-1	$Y_{(m-1)1}$	$Y_{(m-2)2}$	...	$Y_{(m-1)j}$	...	$Y_{(m-1)(n-1)}$	$Y_{(m-1)n}$
m	Y_{m1}	Y_{m2}	...	Y_{mj}	...	$Y_{m(n-1)}$	Y_{mn}
Fixed Charge: F_j	F_1	F_2	...	F_j	...	F_{n-1}	F_n
Total Charges: $L_j = \Sigma_i Y_{ij} + F_j$	L_1	L_2	...	L_j	...	L_{n-1}	L_n

Yet the locations obtained for a given firm will exhibit cost savings over present locations[6] and can easily be adjusted to reflect changes in the firm's distribution of accounts receivable.

To begin our discussion, we assume that the firm has picked a sample of size m from its incoming checks on a stratified basis so that the sample is correct on both a geographical and amount distribution of the checks. Next we assume that the firm has selected n possible sites for its lock-boxes and has calculated the mail availability and bank availability days for each of the sampled checks.[7]

[6] That is, unless the firm's selection of these locations happens by chance to correspond to the ones chosen by the program.

[7] Rather than rely on post-office mail day tables, the firm should take the elapsed time between the postmark on the check's envelope and the date of receipt. The reason for this is simple: most businesses try to take advantage of their suppliers' accounts receivable float and therefore have a tendency to mail payments over a weekend. This causes the mail time to be understated.

We adopt the following notation:

(1) A_i = the face amount of check i, $i = 1,2,\ldots,m$

(2) M_{ij} = the number of mail days of check i to lock-box j, $j = 1,2,\ldots,n$

(3) B_{ij} = the number of days that the bank (lock-box) holds the check before the funds are available for use, $i = 1,2,\ldots,m$; $j = 1,2,\ldots,n$

(4) C_j = the variable charge per check collected in lock-box j, $j = 1,2,\ldots,n$

(5) F_j = the fixed charge associated with maintaining lock-box j, $j = 1,2,\ldots,n$

(6) r = the interest rate to the firm

We now calculate

$$Y_{ij} = [r(A_{ij})(M_{ij} + B_{ij}) + C_j]$$

for each check i and possible lock-box location j and arrange the Y's as in Table 1.

The L_j's in the bottom row of Table 1 represent the cost of maintaining only one lock-box. This is L_1 is the cost assuming all checks are assigned to lock-box 2, etc. We select lock-boxes sequentially. The first lock-box to be selected is that where L_j is minimum, i.e.,

(1) $L_j^* = \min_j L_j$
$j = 1,2,3,\ldots,n.$

Let's assume that lock-box 2 was selected. (1) asserts that if only one lock-box is to be selected, lock-box 2 represents the minimum cost one.

Next all checks whose collection are minimum for the selected box are assigned to it. That is, assign those Y_{ij} to selected lock-box L_j such that those chosen Y_{ij}^* are in accordance with

(2) $Y_{ij}^* = \min_j Y_{ij}$
$i = 1,2,\ldots,m;\ j = 1,2,\ldots,n$

As these checks are allocated to the selected lock-box, their corresponding costs should be subtracted from the remaining column totals; that is, their rows should be eliminated from the table. However, the selected lock-box's column remains in the table, as there are still some checks in it that haven't been assigned. The fixed charge is subtracted from its new total, though, as this has already been absorbed.

The second lock-box is selected from the remaining ones and checks allocated to it on the same basis as the first. Now the remaining checks are *tentatively* allocated to the two selected ones. The criterion is, of course, that they are allocated on the basis of the minimum cost between the two selected lock-boxes. The total cost of this allocation call it L_J assuming J lock-boxes have been tentatively selected (here, 2) is compared to the cost of selecting L_{J-1} (here, 1) lock-boxes. That is, is the cost more or less to select one $(J-1)$ or two (J) lock-boxes? If it is more, only the first is selected. If it is less, the second is also selected and the checks that were not minimum for either the first or the second, i.e., those tentatively allocated, are put back in the table.

The third lock-box or in general, the Jth lock box is selected from the remaining ones as described above. The same calculations are repeated and if the total cost for J boxes is less than for J-1, a $(J+1)^{st}$ one is selected. If not, only the first $(J-1)$ are used and checks are allocated on the basis of minimum cost to those lock-boxes already selected.

The output of this procedure is a set of lock-boxes to be used and a list of geographical regions, based on where the checks in the sample originated, which should use each of the regions. That is, the check identification number should contain its geographical region. The Appendix gives a flow diagram for a computer program for this procedure. In the following section, we show how the simple example in the preceding section is solved by this method and give a few details on an actual problem solved by a computer program written in FORTRAN IV.

SOME EXAMPLES OF THE HEURISTIC METHOD

Suppose we have two checks and two possible lock-box sites and the above calculations have been made and arranged in Table 2. The program then begins by selecting lock-box 1, because it has the total minimum cost and check 1 is assigned to it. The cost thus far is \$5 or (\$3 + 2). This gives Table 3. The program then tentatively selects lock-box 2 and allocates check 2 to it. This yields a total cost of \$12 = 7 + 5. But \$12 > \$10, the cost of using only lock-box 1. Thus lock-box 2 is removed and all checks are allocated to the first lock-box.[8]

To test this procedure written as a FORTRAN IV computer program, we obtained accounts receivable data from a large industrial manufacturer, whose annual sales are in excess of $1 billion. Data for three months amounting to 52,000 checks representing approximately $400 million were used. The stratified sample selected contained 7,620 checks whose aggregate amount was slightly over $161 million. Data entered for each of the checks included their bank and geographical region identification, their amounts and the number of mail days. The computer was programmed to calculate the bank availabilities and the corresponding Y_{ij}'s for each of the selected checks. Eighteen locations were used as possible lock-box sites.[9] The program selected seven of these after 2.5 minutes run time on a 7040 computer.[10]

The firm had previously used only one bank and the selection of the seven lock-boxes enabled it to reduce its accounts receivable float by 64%, and to achieve a once and for all saving of $180,000 in interest costs.

Even for smaller size firms, the use of lock-boxes can represent significant cost savings in the handling of accounts receivables. The program outlined here is a simple easily accessible method of locating these lock-boxes and hopefully can be of immediate benefit to a wide range of businesses.

TABLE 2

Check Identification	Possible Lock-box Locations	
	1	2
1	$3	4
2	5	3
F_j	2	4
L_j	10	11

TABLE 3

Check Identification	Possible Lock-box Locations	
	1	2
1	$--	--
2	5	3
F_j	--	4
L_j	5	7

[8] An obvious alternative to the above heuristic is a fixed charge integer programming formulation. Yet, even in the simple example described above, the programming formulation would need ten constraints. In general for m checks and n possible lock-boxes, there would be $m+2mn$ constraints. Thus for any large collection of checks, this approach becomes quite unwieldy.

[9] The potential lock-box sites are given in Appendix 2.

[10] Sample output and the data for this firm is available by request from the author.

APPENDIX 1

Flow Chart for Heuristic Program

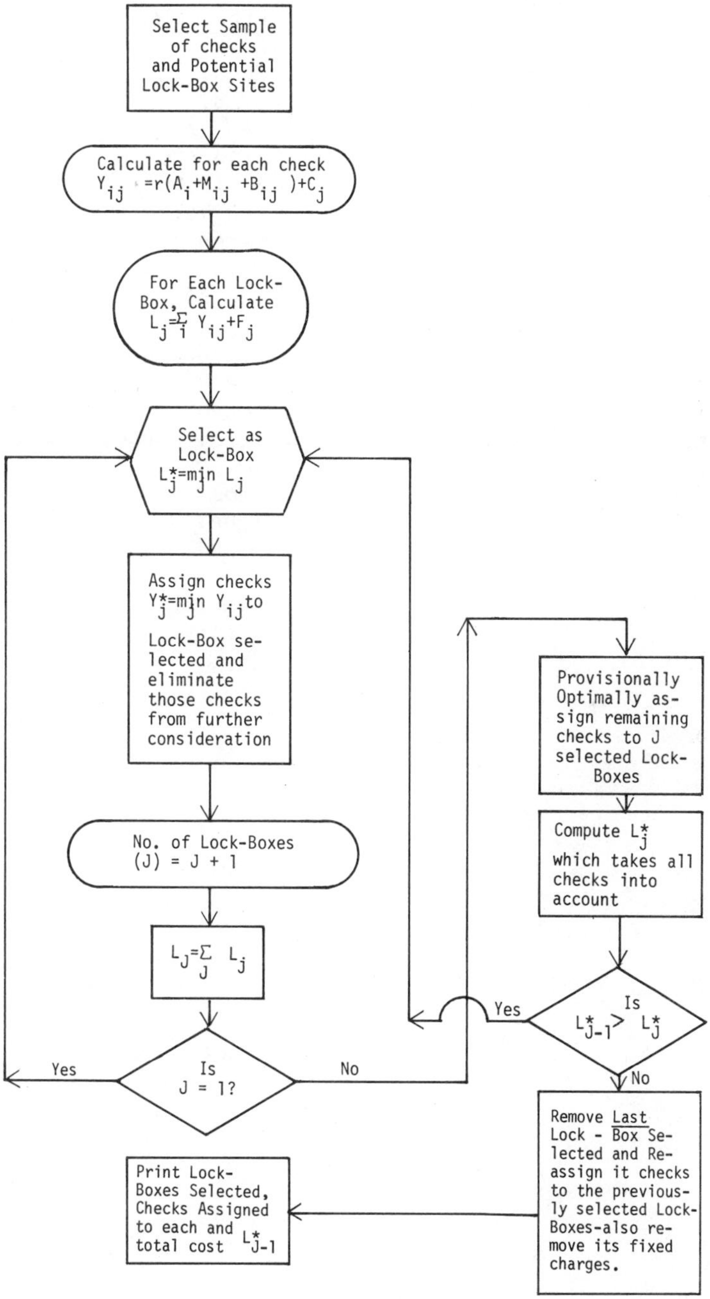

APPENDIX 2

Potential Lock-Box Locations Used in Sample Problem

1. Atlanta
2. Boston
3. Chicago
4. Cincinnati
5. Cleveland
6. Dallas
7. Denver
8. Detroit
9. Houston
10. Kansas City
11. Los Angeles
12. Minneapolis
13. New Orleans
14. New York
15. Philadelphia
16. Pittsburgh
17. San Francisco
18. St. Louis

REFERENCES

1. A. Charnes and W. W. Cooper, *Management Models and Industrial Applications of Linear Programming*, 2 Vols., New York: John Wiley and Sons, Inc., 1961.
2. G. B. Dantzig, *Linear Programming and Extensions*, Princeton: Princeton University Press. 1963.
3. A. Kuehn and M. Hamburger, "A Heuristic Program for Locating Warehouses", *Management Science*, Vol. 9, No. 4, July, 1963, pp. 643-666.
4. H. A. Simon, "Modeling Human Mental Processes", *Proceedings of the 1961 Western Joint Computer Conference*.
5. F. M. Tonge, *A Heuristic Program for an Assembly Line Balancing Problem*, Englewood Cliffs: Prentice-Hall, Inc., 1961.
6. H. M. Weingartner, *Mathematical Programming and the Analysis of Capital Budgeting Problems*, Englewood Cliffs: Prentice Hall, Inc., 1963.

READING 21

Better Way to Monitor Accounts Receivable

Wilbur G. Lewellen
Purdue University

Robert W. Johnson
Purdue University

When a warning signal flashes on the instrument panel of his aircraft, the skilled pilot immediately questions whether the signal mechanism is faulty or whether the airplane is indeed in trouble. The financial executive charged with overseeing the management of accounts receivable for his company faces a similar problem. When the reporting device he uses to monitor collection experience flashes a warning, he confronts a dilemma: Is the monitoring device defective, or are accounts receivable in fact moving out of control? Just as the pilot may endanger his passengers if he responds to a false signal light, so may the financial executive compromise the profitability of his company by his reactions to an erroneous credit indicator. Equally dangerous, of course, is the warning signal that fails to operate when it should.

It is our contention that most of the procedures now widely used for monitoring the management of accounts receivable are, by their very nature, misleading and capable of frequent errors - of both omission an commission. We shall show how commonly used control mechanisms may signal improvement or deterioration in the status of accounts receivable when there actually has been no change in the rate of customer payments. We will also show that the same faulty control mechanism which permits such false signals can fail to flash a warning when one *is* needed. We shall then go on to suggest an alternative analytical framework that does provide meaningful and reliable information for managers.

COLLECTION EXPERIENCE

As a starting point, it is necessary to specify exactly what is meant by the term "collection experience" as it applies to an enterprise that sells to customers on credit. It seems to us logical to define that notion simply as the rate at which remittances for credit sales are received over time; that is, the chronological pattern according to which the receivables created during

Reprinted from the HARVARD BUSINESS REVIEW (May-June 1972), pp. 101-109, by permission of the publisher.

a given interval are converted into cash. If we take a month to be our standard unit of account, the issue is the liquidation rate for each month's new credit sales. A *constant* collection experience -- receivables "in control"-- denotes a situation wherein the fractions of credit sales still uncollected as time passes follow a stable and predictable pattern from month to month. To illustrate:

Suppose a company finds that, say, 90% of the credit sales made during a month always remain outstanding at the end of that month, 60% always remain outstanding at the end of the following month, and 20% always are still uncollected at the end of an additional month, but all are liquidated within the succeeding 30 days. If, for instance, we assume that the company in question has $100,000 of credit sales in January of a particular year, the receivables--and collections--generated by those sales would be as shown in Exhibit I.

Likewise, another $100,000 of credit sales in February would give rise to a set of collections and receivables running from February to May; March's sales would affect events until June; and so on throughout the year. The total of collections and receivables attributable to the various individual months would combine to produce, at any stage, aggregates for the company as a whole.

EXHIBIT I. Collection experience of hypothetical company for January sales (In thousands of dollars)

Month	Collections during month	Receivables outstanding at end of month
January	$10	$90
February	30	60
March	40	20
April	20	0

REASONS FOR FAILURE

The concept of collection experience, therefore, refers to nothing more than this standard notion of the rate of account conversion into cash -- and will be used in just that sense here as we consider whether the usual techniques for assessing a company's receivables provide accurate signals about customer payment patterns. We shall examine with some care the two most common criteria -- days' sales outstanding and aging of accounts receivable.

(A critical discussion of other systems may be found in the Appendix to this article, which begins on page 273.)

Days' Sales Outstanding

A widely used index of the efficiency of credit and collections is the collection period, or number of days' sales outstanding in receivables (DSO). It is calculated for any point in time by dividing the recent average dollar sales volume per day into the dollar amount of receivables outstanding at that time. The equivalent reciprocal index, called receivables turnover, is simply DSO divided into 360 days. Thus, if receivables "turn over" six times a year, the collection period is necessarily 60 days. Our comments therefore apply to both measures of credit circumstances.

The manifest unreliability of these measures can be seen by examining the signals flashed to the credit manager of a company whose collection experience is stable, but whose monthly sales vary over time. Consider the hypothetical case earlier described, wherein the percentages of receivables still uncollected for a given month's credit sales consistently follow a 90%-60%-20% sequential end-of-month pattern --in short, a fixed and definite rate of customer payments. Exhibit II indicates the effect on the DSO calculation of three sales profiles under this steady collection experience:

1. Level sales for three months at $60,000 per month.
2. Rising sales for the next three months at $30,000, $60,000, and $90,000, respectively.
3. A declining sales profile of $90,000, $60,000, and $30,000.

Thus, in all three situations, *total* sales for the calendar quarter are identical. Only their distribution differs.

Exhibit II reveals the collection period the credit manager would record at the *end* of each of the three quarters. Clearly, the signals are both misleading and capricious. They are sensitive not only to the sales pattern observed but also to the sales-averaging period selected. Indeed, the choice of averaging period virtually determines the nature of the signals.

If, for example, the most recent 30 days were chosen for computing average daily sales, then it would appear that collection experience had improved for the company during April through June, as compared with January through March, because the collection period had fallen from 51 to 41 days. Similarly, as the sales pattern of July through September unfolded, the DSO figure would climb to 81 days and generate concern that remittances were slowing significantly. Throughout, however, the rate of customer payments is *invariant*, by stipulation. The problem lies entirely with the monitoring device.

Comparable ambiguities prevail for any averaging period. If 90 days were selected instead, the chronological sequence of erroneous signals would simply be reversed. Balances at the end of the second quarter would indicate 62 days' sales outstanding and imply a deterioration in collection, but, by the end of the third quarter, an apparent improvement to 41 days would be reported.

Thus, no single averaging period will consistently yield a correct appraisal where there are fluctuations in sales. In fact, within any given sales interval, even the *direction* of the signal depends on the averaging period chosen.

It should be emphasized that these observations do not rely for their validity on sales variations as sharp as those depicted in Exhibit II. Milder increases and decreases in volume would merely moderate -- not eliminate -- the discrepancies identified. Moreover, 60 days cannot be recommended as a kind of "happy medium" averaging period that can be counted on to minimize the extent of potential errors. This interval looks relatively good here only by accident. Consider, for example, the DSO figures based on the most recent 60 days' sales that would emerge if the sales for April and May, or July and August, were reversed.

Insuperable difficulties: Despite a vague awareness of the existence of problems of this sort, it has been argued in the literature that valid comparisons of DSO figures may be made if the calculations pertain to the same point in a company's seasonal sales cycle from year to year, or that comparisons among companies are legitimate so long as the same date is utilized in the computations for each.[1] We cannot agree. Intertemporal or intercorporate reliability of such an index can be counted on only if the credit sales patterns involved for the months preceding the analysis point are *literally* identical. This condition is, of course, unlikely.

An added difficulty is the fact that a mechanism which transmits false signals about nonexistent changes in collection experience may also fail

[1] See, for example, Pearson Hunt, Charles Williams, and Gordon Donaldson, *Basic Business Finance*, 4th Edition (Homewood, Illinois, Richard D. Irwin, 1971), p. 62.

EXHIBIT II. Days' sales outstanding (DSO) with varying sales patterns and varying averaging periods
(Dollar figures in thousands)

		Receivables outstanding at end of quarter		Sales per day if averaging period is most recent:			Reported end-of-quarter collection period, if averaging period is:		
Month	Sales	Percent of sales	Dollar Amount	30 days	60 days	90 days	30 days	60 days	90 days
January	$60	20%	$ 12						
February	60	60	36						
March	60	90	54						
			$102	$2	$2.0	$2	51 days	51 days	51 days
April	$30	20%	6						
May	60	60	36						
June	90	90	81						
			$123	$3	$2.5	$2	41 days	49 days	62 days
July	$90	20%	$ 18						
August	60	60	36						
September	30	90	27						
			$ 81	$1	$1.5	$2	81 days	54 days	41 days

to send the *true* warning when needed. To illustrate:

Suppose that during the April to June period in Exhibit II, customer payments slow down in such a way that the pattern of successive end-of-month uncollected balances becomes 60%-80%-95% instead of 20%-60%-90%. Receivables at the end of June would then amount to $152,000. A 30-day sales averaging period for the DSO calculation would suggest 51 days' sales outstanding--matching the value for the end of March, and concealing the underlying deterioration in payment patterns. The financial executive would be lulled into believing that credits and collections are in control when actually they are not.

Aging of Receivables

Another common device for monitoring receivables is the "aging" criterion. Again, however, we must ask how dependable this monitoring method is when sales can vary from month to month.

The aging schedules in Exhibit III--derived as of the end of each calendar quarter from the data in Exhibit II--show that rising sales (Quarter 2) create an impression of improved customer payment patterns, whereas falling sales (Quarter 3) produce a schedule that suggests a deterioration in collections. This is understandable when one recognizes that the most recent month's sales always dominate the calculations. Thus, the proportion of total receivables in accounts less than 30 days old will naturally be relatively high in a period of rising sales, and low in a period of falling sales--even when, as is the case here, the payment profile is completely stable.

This will result in a continual series of spurious warning signals being flashed to the credit manager simply in response to normal sales fluctuations. Only during the unusual intervals when sales are level from month to month will the indicator be of any potential use.

Even at that, the aging schedule suffers from an inherent deficiency. It is difficult to interpret meaningfully any figures that are contributed from differing sources but are constrained to add up to 100%. The fact that, say, 30% of a company's receivables outstanding at a point in time are under 30 days old, and 70% are 30-60 days old, may not mean that there is an extraordinarily large number of overdue accounts and that receivables are out of control. It could merely be that an unusually--and desirably--high percentage of rapid payments were made on the most recent month's sales, leaving very few of them outstanding and raising the apparent weight of old accounts.

EXHIBIT III. Reported receivables aging schedules
(Dollar figures in thousands)

Age of account	Receivables outstanding at end of qtr.*	Percent of total
End of Qtr. 1 (March 31):		
60-90 days	$ 12	12%
30-60 days	36	35
0-30 days	54	53
	$102	100%
End of Qtr. 2 (June 30):		
60-90 days	$ 6	5%
60-30 days	36	29
0-30 days	81	66
	$123	100%
End of Qtr. 3 (September 30):		
60-90 days	$ 18	22%
30-60 days	36	45
0-30 days	27	33
	$ 81	100%

*Figures from Exhibit II.

The latter, however, may be no greater than normal in relation to the original sales that created them.

From the aging proportions per se there is no way of detecting this phenomenon, and erroneous conclusions could easily be drawn by management. Any criterion according to which the role of one element is automatically affected by changes in the others embodies this defect.

Adjusting for the Biases

One response to the foregoing observations might be that it would be possible to live with the distortions inherent in the various procedures described, so long as the credit manager is aware of the general nature and direction of the relevant biases. Again, we would demur.

In the illustrations cited, we have employed rather basic patterns of progressive increases and decreases in sales. While one might conceivably develop some rule-of-thumb adjustment allowances to handle the effects of such simple changes in volume, it would be much more difficult -- if not impossible -- to compensate correctly for all the peculiar, nonsystematic variations in sales confronted in actual practice. Even if the *direction* of the distortion were known, the *extent* would still be an issue -- and would still be obscured. For example:

Suppose that in a period of rising sales it turns out that the collection period has lengthened from 40 days to 50 days. The financial executive would have to know whether that is more or less than the "normal" result for the specific monthly sales growth rate being experienced.

AN EFFECTIVE TOOL

The central difficulty with the two most commonly used monitoring devices (as well as those discussed in the Appendix) is that, in one form or another, the view taken of collection experience is conceptually inappropriate. Either collections or balances are *aggregated* in the calculations, making it impossible to detect changes in remittance rates for particular components of credit sales.

If aggregation is the problem, *dis*aggregation is the key to its solution. The remittance rates for each individual component of sales should be identified and separated out if the data are not to be confounded by external influences, such as sales variations.

Can this be done? Fortunately, there is an analytical technique that meets the need. It involves nothing more than casting up the periodic receivables status report in the same form as the basic definition of "collection experience" with which we began our discussion, i.e., balances outstanding as a percentage of the respective *original* sales that gave rise to those balances. In this fashion, customer payment rates are automatically traced to their source, and the appraisal of collection success is rendered independent of sales patterns and of the impact of changes in relative account composition. A typical report-- prepared as of the end of each calendar quarter for our illustrative situation -- is offered in Exhibit IV.

Not surprisingly, this record of the ratio of receivables balances to original sales indicates that the collection rate on accounts has been perfectly stable throughout the period in question. Exactly 90% of the most recent month's, 60% of the next most recent month's, and 20% of the third more recent month's credit sales show up as outstanding at each point in time examined. (These figures do not -- and will not, except by accident -- sum up to 100%, since they do not purport to describe the makeup of a fixed total. Each is calculated according to a *different* sales base.)

The same answer would emerge at the end of every one of the nine months tabulated, and will persist under any conceivable sales pattern we might stipulate, so long as customer payment rates are in fact stable. Conversely, any deviation in those rates for any of the relevant sales intervals would be immediately detected and would not be concealed by aggregation or changes in other collections.

EXHIBIT IV. Uncollected balances as percentages of original sales
(Dollar figures in thousands)

Month of origin	Sales during that month	Receivables outstanding at end of quarter	% outstanding (receivables/sales
January	$60	$ 12	20%
February	60	36	60
March	60	54	90
		$102	
April	$30	$ 6	20%
May	60	36	60
June	90	81	90
		$123	
July	$90	$ 18	20%
August	60	36	60
September	30	27	90
		$ 81	

Accurate Analysis

To illustrate the improvement from a management standpoint, consider a simple example:

Suppose the group of customers to whom merchandise was sold during February happen to be slow payers and remit for only 15% of their purchases during the month following the month of sale, rather than the 30% figure which has been normal. In that case, balances at the end of March would be as shown in Exhibit V, instead of as portrayed in Exhibit IV. Since only the figure for February would show up as out of line with past experience in the status report, the problem could be tracked to its source without difficulty.

EXHIBIT V. Effect on percentages outstanding of slow payment on February sales
(Dollar figures in thousands)

Month	Sales during month	Receivables outstanding at end of quarter	% outstanding (receivables/sales)
January	$60	$ 12	20%
February	60	45	75
March	60	54	90
		$111	

Of equal importance, an acceleration of the payments on other months' sales would not obscure the analysis by exerting offsetting effects. Assume, for instance, that collections on credit sales originally made during January are simultaneously higher than normal, amounting to fully 55% of original balances during March rather than the usual 40%. Those extra receipts would neutralize the concurrent decline attributable to the customers from February, and put total receivables back at $102,000 as of the end of March (Exhibit VI).

EXHIBIT VI. The combined effect of fast payment on January sales and slow payment on February sales
(Dollar figures in thousands)

Month	Sales during month	Receivables outstanding at end of quarter	% outstanding (receivables/sales)
January	$60	$ 3	5%
February	60	45	75
March	60	54	90
		$102	

Nonetheless, the credit executive could see from the report that changes *have* occurred even though the totals are "normal." He would not be lulled into thinking that payment patterns have remained stable--as would be indicated by, say, a

DSO calculation--and could institute policy changes before it is too late to prevent some unpleasant surprises. In particular, if the shift in collection rates persists, then, as sales begin to rise, the increase in the funds committment necessary to support receivables could be anticipated.

Value in Forecasting

The virtues of the framework we propose are, in fact, as notable in the context of forecasting funds requirements as in the contemplation of changes in policy. It may often be that the financial executive cannot do much about a slowdown in customer payment patterns without adversely affecting profitability. Competitive conditions--or the simple undercapitalization of many customers--may render it impossible to tighten terms and raise standards of acceptability without a substantial loss of revenue. Whatever the constraints, the need to project receivables balances for budgeting purposes is always present, and it is clear that the usual techniques leave a great deal to be desired. To illustrate:

Consider the forecasts that would be made by the credit manager of a company whose sales and collection experience has for some time been steady, as in the January-March period in Exhibit II. Assume that total sales in the upcoming calendar quarter are predicted to be $180,000 again, but that they follow the monthly pattern of April through June.

If the executive were monitoring receivables in terms of DSO--with a 90-day sales averaging period--he would see 51 days' sales outstanding consistently, and would therefore use that standard to forecast balances. Because total sales anticipated for the next 90 days just match those experienced during the most recent 90, the DSO prediction would simply be for $102,000 in receivables outstanding as of the end of June. Given the 90%-60%-20% uncollected balance sequence that actually prevails, however, receivables would turn out to be $123,000 instead--an error that could be uncomfortable.

If sales of $180,000 were then forecasted for the third quarter, $102,000 in outstanding accounts would once more be the DSO-based estimate for the end of September, but $81,000 would turn out to be the actual figure. Comparable mistakes would -- or could, depending on the circumstances -- occur from use of the other techniques described earlier and in the Appendix, since none really gets at the rate of customer payments in a meaningful way.

Only by ascertaining that the normal uncollected balance profile *is* 90%-60%-20% (that is, collections are 10%-30%-40%-20%) can one disentangle the independent effects of remittance rates and sales patterns and thereby achieve an accurate forecast. Accuracy, of course, is important not only to the credit executive but also to the company's banker, who may be confronted with a working-capital loan request based in large part on receivables predictions.

Tracking Flows Over Time

The parameters of the model, for forecasting purposes, are easily obtained from past data. Ordinarily, a simple record of historical end-of-month balances (like that shown in Exhibit IV), broken down into percentages of original monthly sales for, say, the most recent two years, will suffice. This number of observations should provide a reasonably good indication of the trend, or lack thereof, of payment patterns.

The analysis might resemble the one presented in Exhibit VII, where it appears that the fraction of sales made in a given month which are uncollected at the end of that same month has varied from 86% to 97% during the year considered; the fraction still on

EXHIBIT VII. Status report on receivables outstanding as a percent of original sales

	Month											
	J	F	M	A	M	J	J	A	S	O	N	D
Percentages outstanding for 1970 from sales of:												
Same month	90%	89%	91%	95%	97%	93%	86%	92%	91%	90%	91%	90%
One month before	60	62	59	68	73	69	59	54	62	63	61	60
Two months before	20	19	18	35	37	33	23	20	17	21	22	20
Percentages outstanding for 1971 from sales of:												
Same month	90%	91%	90%	93%	96%	96%	89%	91%	90%	88%	89%	90%
One month before	60	61	59	70	72	68	57	62	59	61	61	60
Two months before	20	22	21	33	39	33	19	18	21	20	19	20

Note: To ascertain the payment flows for one month's original sales, see the numbers in a descending left-to-right diagonal pattern. Thus the sequence 89%-62%-21%, singled out for July-August-September of 1971, refers to balances originating in July's sales as they remain outstanding as of the end of three successive months.

the books 30 days later has ranged from 54% to 73%; and the proportion after another 30 days has been between 17% and 39%. (Balances for four, five, or more months might also be shown if customers took longer to pay.)

Whether tabulated in this manner or plotted on a graph, the indicated percentages summarize very quickly and conveniently for management the company's ongoing collection experience. A continual updating of the record will then keep the appraisal current.

It would appear, in the situation shown in Exhibit VII, that remittance rates *are* fairly stable; no secular trend is evident in the 24 months examined. On the other hand, it seems characteristic for payments to slow down during April, May, and June of each year before returning to the "normal" pattern of roughly 90%-60%-20%. Additional data for earlier years might be collected to confirm this interpretation. Various standard statistical techniques, including regression analysis, could be applied to test rigorously whether a trend is present, as judged by whether the more recent percentages tabulated differ significantly --in the statistical sense --from those of earlier periods.

Alternatively, and less formally, a simple moving average of perhaps the last six months' percentages at each of the three levels could be maintained and compared with the corresponding averages for the same intervals one and two years earlier. Or, if no seasonal variations were apparent, a comparison of *any* successive six-month intervals would do. Note that seasonality in *sales* is not the issue. That effect has been factored out by the percentage calculations. Indeed, as is obvious, the volume of sales need not be recorded in the receivables status report. Only payment patterns are of concern.

The average collection experience suggested by these calculations would then be used in forecasting receivables balances, given monthly sales estimates from the company's marketing department. Thus, the average end-of-month outstanding balance percentages listed in Exhibit VII for July through December of 1970 and 1971 are 90%, 60%, and 20%; and for April through June of both years, 95%, 70%, and 35%. Projections of balances for 1972 would logically be based on these relationships.

Whatever the evidence for the particular company involved, and whatever the preferred averaging technique, the percentages displayed provide the financial executive with an effective tool *both* for detecting changes in remittance rates and for forecasting.

Control Limits

As far as policy is concerned, the signal to management that something has happened with customer payments would be either an affirmative statistical significance test, of the kind just described, or a deviation of the moving average greater than a specified tolerance limit. To illustrate:

The credit manager might establish a rule that a 5% change in the most recent six-month outstanding balance averages in comparison with the averages for the preceding six months, or for the corresponding period a year earlier, would be reason to consider a revision in credit policy. Thus, if the July-December 1971 end-of-month receivables averages come out to a 95%-65%-25% profile, whereas 1970's July-December figures were 90%-60%-20%, that might well be grounds for reexamining sales terms and credit standards. In fact, a 5% increase or decrease even in *one* of the three percentages in the profile could suggest the need for action. Alternatively, an observation of three consecutive monthly percentage deviations (other than seasonal) of 5% above or below the average at that position in the profile over the preceding 6 or 12 months might trigger the manager's attention.

A potential increase in bad debts in particular might be foreshadowed by a rise in the percentages at the tail end of the receivables schedule, or the appearance of balances for an additional end-of-month interval. For instance, the profile might begin to change to 90%-60%-20%-3%; the last figure could represent not merely slow payers, but prospective default cases.

It should be emphasized that a below-average outstanding balance tendency can be as important to management as an upward shift. A general acceleration in remittance rates may indicate that credit guidelines or collection practices are becoming *too* stringent, and that many legitimate customers are in fact being excluded.

CONCLUDING NOTE

No single measure of deviation will fit every company's circumstances and tastes for "fine tuning" credit policy. Purely random fluctuations in the relevant percentages may be much larger for one company than for another. The important thing is to organize the detection and control of collection experience around an analytical framework that provides input information useful to the decision process.

We believe the scheme outlined in this article meets that requirement far better than any other currently available. It does not mix together receivables originating in different sales periods; and it is the only procedure which is not distorted by changes in sales patterns.

APPENDIX: DEFICIENCIES OF OTHER SYSTEMS

In this article we have described the shortcomings of the best-known approaches used by management to monitor accounts receivable. Here we describe some variations of these approaches that are familiar to many businessmen, and point out their deficiencies.

Average Age of Receivables

Some companies employ a receivables-monitoring device which summarizes, in a single number, the information contained in the aging schedule. This number or index is the so-called "average age of receivables." It is typically calculated with the assumption that the average duration of outstanding accounts that are less than 30 days old is exactly 15 days, that the average for those 30 to 60 days old is 45 days, and so on, for as many categories as are relevant. The product of these figures times the proportions of each age segment in the total, when summed, yields a global average age measure of overall balances. By this criterion, the schedules depicted in Exhibit III would imply that an average account was 32.8 days old as of the end of Quarter 1. The computation would be:

	.12 x 75 days =	9.0 days
+	.35 x 45 days =	15.8 days
+	.53 x 15 days =	8.0 days
	Total =	32.8 days

Similarly, an average account would be 26.8 and 41.8 days old, respectively, as of the close of Quarters 2 and 3.

The signals given by "average age" must, of course, coincide with those given by the complete aging schedule-- and can only incorporate the same shortcomings.

TABLE A. Distribution of collections by age of account (Dollar figures in thousands)

Age of account (in days)	March		June		September	
	Collections	Percent of total	Collections	Percent of total	Collections	Percent of total
0-30	$ 6	10.0%	$ 9	17.7%	$ 3	4.0%
30-60	18	30.0	18	35.3	18	24.0
60-90	24	40.0	12	23.5	36	48.0
90-120	12	20.0	12	23.5	18	24.0
	$60	100.0%	$51	100.0%	$75	100.0%

Relative Changes

Another technique often followed compares the periodic changes in the level of receivables to the concurrent changes in the level of sales. The misleading signals that result are in the same direction as those generated by collection period methods, and they occur for the same reason: rising (falling) sales necessarily produce quarter-end receivables that are large (small) relative to the sales for the entire quarter, despite a constant collection experience for each individual monthly bloc of credit sales.

Percentage Collections

It has also been argued that the collection/balance ratio should be used by management. For example:

"A further means of checking upon the quality of a firm's credit and collections policies is the preparation of periodic reports to show what percentage of customers' balances on the books at the beginning of each period is collected during that period."*

The reliability of this scheme can be tested by comparing the results it would show for the nine-month sales pattern of our standard illustration. If we assume that the company's sales for the last several months of the preceding fiscal year were steady at $60,000 per month, the ratio of monthly collections to beginning-of-month receivables for January through September would vary from 54% to 68%. Since these indexes can fluctuate so widely even under conditions of no change in customer payment rates, their usefulness as inputs to credit policy decisions is in serious question.

Aging of Collections

Finally, the distribution of monthly collections by age of account involved has been suggested as a possible monitoring device.† Table A presents such a breakdown for March, June, and September of our example. Examination of the data would lead the credit manager to believe that collections were speeding up in the vicinity of June, since a larger percentage of collections are in the 0-30 day and 30-60 day age groups than was true three months earlier. Similarly, he would become concerned that collections were slowing in September because the percentage distribution of receipts shifted back toward the 60-90 day and 90-120 day categories.

* R.P. Kent, *Corporate Financial Management*, 3rd Edition (Homewood, Illinois, Richard D. Irwin, 1969), p. 194.

† "Managerial Controls of Accounts Receivable: A Deterministic Approach," *Journal of Accounting Research*, Spring 1965, p. 114.

This distortion, of course, is nothing more than the normal result of rising and falling monthly sales volumes. Payment rates being stable, the higher the proportion of more recent sales, the heavier will be the weight of collections on recent accounts compared to total collections --and vice versa for a declining sales pattern. The financial executive might, in consequence, be led to undertake "remedial" action that could be detrimental to profitability, when in fact no revisions are warranted.

READING 22

The Payments-Pattern Approach to the Forecasting and Control of Accounts Receivable

Bernell K. Stone
Georgia Institute of Technology

INTRODUCTION AND OVERVIEW

Under the simplifying assumption that payment behavior is stable from month to month, this paper develops and illustrates forecast and control procedures based on the time distribution of cash flows that arise from credit sales at a point in time. Next, a variety of forecast and control procedures now used in practice are reviewed and evaluated and it is argued that most of the popular procedures are technically deficient. Alternative procedures are then considered for measuring the payment distribution. Here the assumption of stable month-to-month payment behavior is relaxed and seasonals and other factors that can impact payment behavior, such as the level of interest rates and the quality of accounts, are considered. Finally, it is shown how an ability to explain payment behavior makes possible meaningful evaluation of collection performance and how it can assist in making credit policy decisions.

CHARACTERIZING PAYMENT BEHAVIOR: PAYMENT AND BALANCE PATTERNS

A *payment pattern* refers to the time distribution of cash flows that arise from credit sales at a point in time. A *monthly payment pattern* can be characterized by the proportion of credit sales in a given month that become cash flows in that month and a series of subsequent months. Such a pattern can be summarized by a histogram as illustrated in Exhibit 1, where the horizontal axis is time *after* the month in which the sales were made with time measured in months. Month zero denotes the month of sale. In this histogram, 10% of the cash flows are received in the month of sale, 40% in the first month after the sale, 30% in the second month, and 20% in the third month.

Once the payment pattern is known, a value of credit sales in a given month can be converted into a

Reprinted from FINANCIAL MANAGEMENT (Autumn 1976), pp. 65-82, by permission of the publisher and author.

schedule of the associated monthly cash flows and the end-of-month receivable balances associated with those credit sales.

Example

January credit sales on a certain product line with credit terms of net 30 were $2,000,000 and were expected to conform to the payment pattern given in Exhibit 1. By applying the payment proportions in the histogram, the following schedules of monthy cash flows and end-of-month receivables associated with January sales are obtained.

	January	February	March	April
Cash Flow	200	800	600	400
Receivables	1800	1000	400	0

This example shows that knowing the schedule of cash flows that arise from a given month's credit sales is equivalent to knowing the schedule of receivables that arise from the same month's credit sales. In effect, there is a receivable balance pattern associated with any payment pattern. The monthly *receivable balance pattern* can be characterized by the fraction of credit sales in a month that remain outstanding at the end of each subsequent month. Exhibit 2 shows the receivable balance pattern associated with the payment pattern of Exhibit 1.

These cash flows and receivables are not the monthly totals. Rather, they are only the values associated with credit sales in January. To obtain the total monthly cash flow and end-of-month receivables for March also requires knowledge of the level of credit sales in February and March as well.

Exhibits 3 and 4 present projection matrices that illustrate how knowledge of the payment pattern enables one to convert a schedule of monthly credit sales into the corresponding schedules of total monthly cash flows and total end-of-month receivable balances. The schedule of credit sales is given in the far left-hand column of each exhibit. The procedure for generating the matrix and the monthly totals is straightforward. First, each month's credit sales are converted into a schedule of associated cash flows and receivables. These values are given in the rows of the matrix. Second, monthly totals are obtained by summing down the columns. The values used in Exhibits 3 and 4 are based on the simple payment pattern of Exhibit 1.

For expositional purposes, several simplifications were used in the development of Exhibits 3 and 4. First, receipt of all payments within 3 months constitutes a fairly short payment period; second, the same payment behavior has been assumed to occur in every month with no month-to-month variation; and finally, there has been no explicit consideration of bad debts. Extending the method to allow for longer payment periods is easily accomplished by using more nonzero entries in the matrix.

In subsequent sections, payment behavior is allowed to change from month-to-month due to seasonality in payment patterns and dependence of payment behavior on factors such as the state of the economy, the level of interest rates, and the quality of accounts. Further consideration of month-to-month variation in payment behavior is deferred until that point.

A simple way to treat bad debts is to view the credit sales projection as the net value after allowance for bad debts. A more complex but more complete approach is to include a pro forma bad debt recognition pattern. Since it is straightforward to extend the equations given here to reflect bad debts, for the sake of expositional simplicity, the credit sales variable will continue to be viewed as net credit sales. Bad debts will be treated explicitly when measurement issues are considered.

The term *payment horizon*

EXHIBIT 1. A Histogram Illustrating a Monthly Payment Pattern

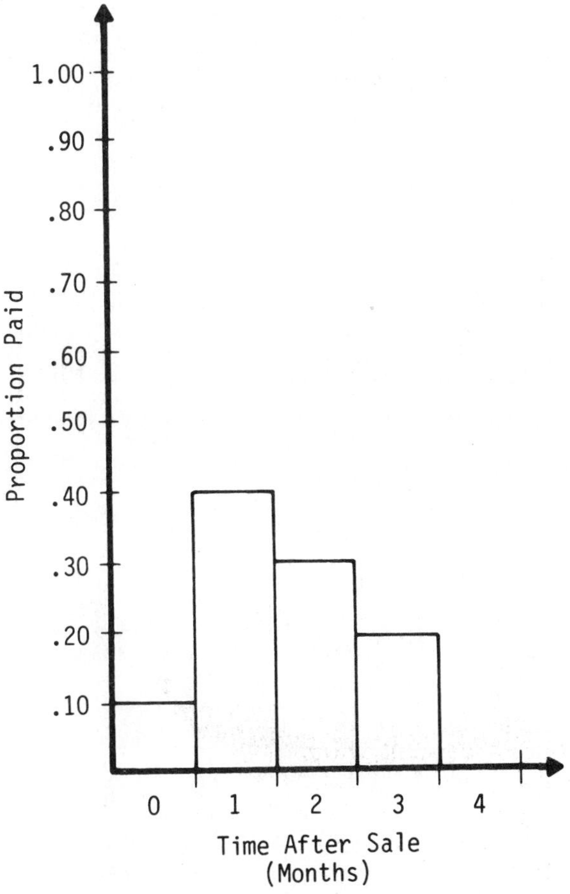

EXHIBIT 2. The Receivable Balance Pattern Corresponding to the Payment Pattern of Exhibit 1

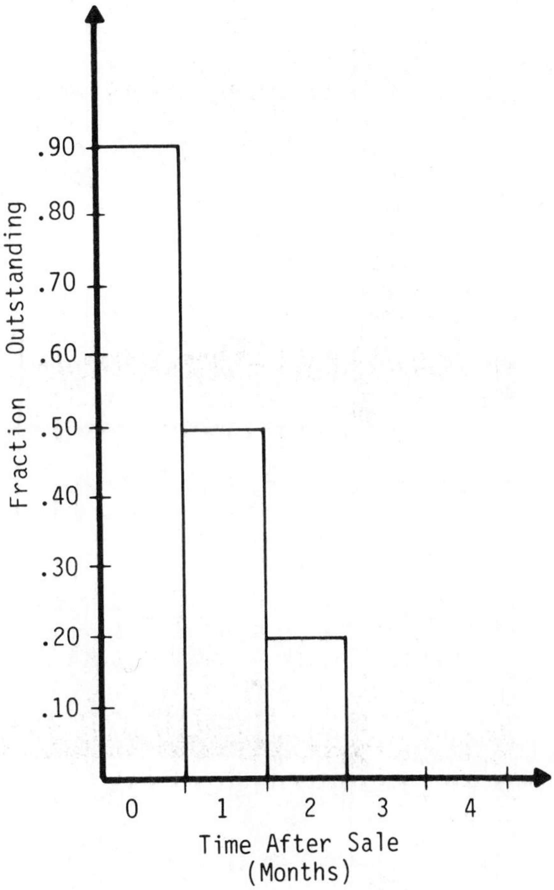

refers to the number of months required for a given month's credit sales to be completely collected. Thus, receivables associated with a given month's credit sales are zero at the end of the payment horizon. The payment horizon is denoted by H, which, for the payment pattern of Exhibit 1, is 3.

P_i denotes the proportion of credit sales paid i months after the month of sale. For the payment pattern of Exhibit 1, $P_0 = .10$, $P_1 = .40$, $P_2 = .30$, and $P_3 = .20$. The P_i's are referred to as *payment proportions;* and the set of such proportions, $(P_0, \ldots, P_H)$, are a complete numerical summary of the payment pattern.

If TCF_t denotes total cash flow forecast for month t and if CS_{t-j} denotes the credit sales received in month t-i, then total cash flow is the sum of the cash flows from credit sales in month t, month t-1, and so on back to

EXHIBIT 3. The Cash Flow Matrix: An Illustration of the Conversion of a Credit-Sale Forecast into a Conditional Forecast of Monthly Cash Flows

Month	Credit Sales	Monthly cash flows (All figures in thousands)											
		Jan.	Feb.	Mar.	Apr.	May	June	July	Aug.	Sept.	Oct.	Nov.	Dec.
Oct.	4000*	800											
Nov.	3000*	900	600										
Dec.	2000*	800	600	400									
Jan.	2000	200	800	600	400								
Feb.	3000		300	1200	900	600							
Mar.	4000			400	1600	1200	800						
Apr.	5000				500	2000	1500	1000					
May	6000					600	2400	1800	1200				
June	7000						700	2800	2100	1400			
July	8000							800	3200	2400	1600		
Aug.	7000								700	2800	2100	1400	
Sept.	6000									600	2400	1800	1000
Oct.	5000										500	2000	1500
Nov.	4000											400	1600
Dec.	3000												300
	Total	2700	2300	2600	3400	4400	5400	6400	7200	7200	6600	5600	4400

*Figures for October, November, and December contain only the cash flows for January on projected as if there were perfect conformity to the pro forma pattern.

EXHIBIT 4. The Receivable Matrix: An Illustration of the Conversion of a Credit-Sale Forecast into a Conditional Forecast of End-of-Month Receivables

Month	Credit Sales	End-of-month accounts receivable balances (All figures in thousands)											
		Jan.	Feb.	Mar.	Apr.	May	June	July	Aug.	Sept.	Oct.	Nov.	Dec.
Oct.	4000*												
Nov.	3000*	600											
Dec.	2000*	1000	400										
Jan.	2000	1800	1000	400									
Feb.	3000		2700	1500	600								
Mar.	4000			3600	2000	800							
Apr.	5000				4500	2500	1000						
May	6000					5400	3000	1200					
June	7000						6300	3500	1400				
July	8000							7200	4000	1600			
Aug.	7000								6300	3500	1400		
Sept.	6000									5400	3000	1200	
Oct.	5000										4500	2500	1000
Nov.	4000											3600	2000
Dec.	3000												2700
	Total	3400	4100	5500	7100	8700	10300	11900	11700	10500	8900	7300	5700

*Figures for October, November, and December contain only the values for January on projected as if there were perfect conformity to the pro forma pattern.

month H, i.e.,

$$(1)\quad TCF_t = P_0 CS_t + P_1 CS_{t-1} + \ldots + P_H CS_{t-H} = \sum_{i=0}^{H} P_i CS_{t-i}$$

The terms in this summation are clearly the nonzero terms in the t-th column of the cash flow matrix. The formula is a symbolic statement of the procedure of adding down the columns to obtain the forecast of the total monthly cash flow.

Letting F_i denote the fraction of credit sales outstanding i months after the month of sale, the receivable pattern of Exhibit 2 is $F_0 = .90$, $F_1 = .50$, and $F_2 = .20$. (Of course, since the payment horizon is 3 months, $F_3 = 0$). The F_i's are defined as *balance fractions*; and the set of such fractions, $(F_0,\ldots,F_{H-1})$, is a numerical summary of the receivable balance pattern.

The total values of receivables at the end of month t is the sum of the receivables arising from credit sales in month t, in month $t-H$, and so on back to those from credit sales H-1 months earlier. If TAR_t denotes total accounts receivable at the end of month t, then

$$(2)\quad TAR_t = F_0 CS_t + F_1 CS_{t-1} + \ldots + F_{H-1} CS_{t-H+1} = \sum_{i=0}^{H-1} F_i CS_{t-i}\ .$$

The terms in this summation are clearly the nonzero terms in the t-th column of the receivable matrix. The formula is a symbolic statement of the procedure of adding down the columns of the receivable matrix to obtain the total receivable balance.

Payment Patterns and Control

Control concerns the detection of deviations from expected or intended behavior and the initiation of corrective action where appropriate. For accounts receivable, two levels of control exist. Account-level control concerns the conformity of individual accounts to credit terms. Management control concerns the aggregate behavior of receivables, ideally at the product-line, credit-term level, and thus focuses on the net effect of the company's credit granting and collection effort.

Since payment proportions and balance fractions are measures of payment behavior that are independent of the sales pattern, they are the logical focus of control. Conceptually, using payment patterns for control consists of comparing a pro forma payment distribution with the one that actually occurred and asking if the differences are significant in the sense of exceeding normal month-to-month fluctuations in the payment pattern. For example, assume that a company's historical payment proportions and balance fractions were those summarized in Exhibits 1 and 2. In early March, assume that the report on actual payments for January and February credit sales showed a current balance fraction for January sales of $F_1 = .60$ versus the pro forma value of .50 and a realized value for February sales of $F_0 = .94$ versus the pro forma value of .90. Because the deviations are adverse and larger than usual and because there are two consecutive months of adverse behavior, this report would indicate possible problems and the need for further action.

THE STATE OF CURRENT PRACTICE

The payment-pattern approach to receivable forecasting and control seems simple and straightforward.

The reader not familiar with corporate practice might even be asking: "If that is all there is to receivable forecasting and control, why is it perceived to be so hard and why the great concern?"

The fact is that few corporations use payment-pattern measures for forecasting and controlling receivables. The alternatives used in practice and advocated in much of the finance-accounting literature contain serious defects. This section of this article surveys the current state of corporate practice, relates alternative forecasting and control procedures to payment patterns, and indicates why the popular forecast and control procedures typically fail.

Conventional Measures of Receivable Status

The two standard measures used to characterize the status of receivables are average days outstanding and the aging schedule. These measures are presented in most basic finance texts, many accounting texts, and almost any work on financial analysis that deals with receivables, e.g. [1, 3]. They have been the common basis for recommendations on receivable management and control [2, 11]. Of the works known to this author, the only ones using measures of receivable status based on payment-pattern concepts of Lewellen and Edmister [8] and Lewellen and Johnson [9], both of which introduce balance fractions and criticize average days outstanding and the aging schedule.

An Overview of Corporate Practice

There is a dearth of published information on current corporate practice with respect to receivable forecasting and control. This author has surveyed financial officers of nearly 150 companies participating in executive development seminars. The annual sales of these companies ranged from $10 million to $8 billion with 80% having annual sales in the range of $25 million to $250 million. The average sales were just over $100 million. While neither the sample selection nor survey procedure allow meaningful statistical inference to the general population of companies, the results are at least roughly indicative of corporate practice.

Exhibit 5 summarizes the reported use of alternative projection approaches. Over 80% of these companies reported using some systematic procedures to project receivables. Of those using formal methods, the great majority (86%) used either a pro forma projection of average days outstanding or some other ratio of receivables to a measure of sales. Another 10% based projections on the assumption that a certain percentage of receivables are paid in each period. Only 5% (six companies) projected receivables as a linear function of past sales, the projection mode implied by the payment-pattern approach.

In contrast to the diversity of forecasting behavior, Exhibit 5 shows considerably more uniformity in control practice. The great majority of the firms using formal control procedures report that aging schedules are their primary control measure. Almost all these companies also used one or more secondary control measures such as average days outstanding, percent of overdue accounts, percent of doubtful accounts, and bad debt loss rates, but generally regarded them as subordinate information that complements the aging schedule. Of the remaining companies using formal control procedures, approximately 10%, which tended to be smaller companies, used average days outstanding. Only two companies, one of which regarded bad debt loss rates as an equally important control measure, used balance fractions, the measure implied by payment patterns.

Alternative forecast and control procedures used by companies are now elaborated upon and are related to payment patterns. Further comment is also made upon corporate practice.

The Aging Schedule

The aging schedule is the proportion of accounts receivable that are in different age classes. While some companies use weeks, the usual practice seems to be months, which will be used here.

The aging schedule is closely related to the payment pattern. In fact, the projected aging schedule for each month can be obtained directly from the column data of projection matrices such as Exhibit 4. For each column, one simply divides each nonzero value of receivables by the total at the bottom to obtain the proportion in each age class, where the most recent receivables are the bottom of the nonzero column entries.

To illustrate, let A_0, A_1, and A_2 denote the proportion of receivables in each age class. These quantities are labeled *aging fractions*. For the receivables in Exhibit 4, the aging fractions for March and October are:

	A_2	A_1	A_0
March	$\frac{4}{55} = .07$	$\frac{15}{55} = .27$	$\frac{36}{55} = .66$
October	$\frac{14}{89} = .16$	$\frac{30}{89} = .34$	$\frac{45}{89} = .50$

Despite the fact that the payment proportions used to develop Exhibit 4 were the same in every month, these aging schedules are quite different because the latter depends on both payment behavior and the pattern of sales. When there is no change in payment behavior, rising sales produce a more current aging schedule and falling sales a less current one. As is shown in Appendix A, sufficient conditions for the aging fractions to be independent of sales are extremely restrictive; namely *uniform sales* defined as sales growing at a constant month-to-month rate, a special case being constant month-to-month sales. Uniform sales preclude any kind of annual sales cycle as well as random month-to-month variation.

Throughout this paper, the term *uniform* credit sales means credit sales that grow at a constant month-to-month rate. Uniform credit sales are a slightly more general restriction for the acceptability of aging and average days outstanding than the restriction of constant month-to-month sales stated by Lewellen and Edmister (8), which is a special case of constant growth in which the growth rate is zero.

The dependency of the aging schedule on sales is recognized by most practitioners. For this reason, many of the companies using the aging schedule for control reported that they used a seasonal schedule for comparison purposes. For instance, October's aging schedule would be compared with the one for last October or even an average over several past Octobers. Several companies also reported attempts to correct judgementally for variations in sales. Most companies described themselves as "extremely dissatisfied" or "dissatisfied" with the aging schedule as a control measure with only a few characterizing themselves as "satisfied" or "extremely satisfied". Interestingly, larger companies characterized themselves as extremely dissatisfied much more frequently than small companies. Post-questionnaire discussion indicated a concensus view that sales variation was much larger than shifts in payment behavior, so that aging schedules tended to reflect sales changes more than the payment shifts that receivable control is intended to detect.

Most of the larger multiproduct companies reported in questionnaire follow-up that they applied their control measures at subunits such as subsidiaries or product lines. Many expressed frustration at trying to implement exception reports using aging schedules. One problem with

EXHIBIT 5. Survey Summary of Primary Methods Used to Forecast and Control Accounts Receivable

Primary forecast method	% Responses	% Formal model
1. ADO-based projection (see note 2)	26	32
2. Ratio Projection other than ADO (see note 3)	44	54
3. Percentage balance (see note 4)	8	10
4. Linear function of past sales (see notes 3 and 5)	4	5
5. Pro forma aging schedule (see note 6)	0	0
6. No formal systematic procedure (judgement)	15	n.a.
7. No knowledge	2	n.a.
8. Incomplete response	2	n.a.
	101	101

Primary control measure	% Responses	% Formal model
1. Aging schedule (see note 2)	76.0	80.0
2. ADO-based (see note 3)	9.0	9.5
3. Percentage overdue	4.5	4.8
4. Bad debt loss rate	2.5	2.6
5. Balance fraction (see note 4)	1.5	1.6
6. Other (see note 1)	1.5	1.6
7. No formal system (see note 5)	6.0	n.a.
8. Incomplete response	1.0	n.a.
	102.0	100.1

Notes on Forecasting

1. A number of respondents listed "other" as their primary method. However, their explanation of the method and/or post questionnaire follow-up enabled almost all of these responses to be placed in one of the listed categories

2. A few respondents listed "average age" as their method. Questionnaire follow-up indicated that most were using this term synonomously with average days outstanding. A few also listed "pro forma turnover rate" as their primary method. Questionnaire follow-up showed most of these were also variants of the conventional ADO forecast as discussed in the paper, however, a few were closer to the percentage balance method and were grouped under this procedure.

Notes on Control

1. "Other" was listed frequently. Generally, the explanation and/or post questionnaire follow-up enabled most of these to be placed in one of the listed categories. Exceptions are percent over credit limit (.5%), change in quality class composition (.5%), and percent not taking discounts (.5%). Each of these respondents also listed the aging schedule as their primary method.

2. "Aging Schedule" also includes responses, the essence of which was "distribution of overdue accounts" since this is readily derived from the aging schedule by excluding current accounts.

3. ADO includes "turnover measures" and "average age" methods since these are all closely related concepts.

3. Six respondents (4%) reported a "moving ratio" using a weighted average of recent sales. This does involve a linear function of past sales but not a simple linear function. If these responses were reclassified, methods 3 and 5 would change from 44% and 4% to 40% and 8% respectively. However, none of those using a moving ratio assessed weights within a payment-pattern framework.

4. Early versions of the questionnaire did not have "percentage balance" listed as a method; it was added as an explicit choice after being listed under "other" with some frequency. While this omission could bias the early responses against this approach, the questionnaires after its inclusion had a lower selection rate than before.

5. Three of these responses (2%) indicated that the weights were determined via a least-squares regression of accounts receivable on a lagged function of sales.

6. "Pro Forma Aging Schedule" was a possible method. Those few companies indicating this method were reclassified on the basis of questionnaire follow-up, generally as linear function of past sales.

4. Both firms using balance fractions do so implicitly via an adjusted forecast in a lagged regression model rather than directly, i.e., they would use realized sales in their receivable forecast equation and then compare differences in theoretical and actual receivables. One of these firms thought that bad debt loss rate was an equally important control measure.

5. Most firms without a formal system and many using ADO measures were either smaller companies or companies for whom receivables were not a significant problem (e.g., because of ability to enforce credit terms by stopping delivery or credit devices such as liberal discounts).

6. Questionnaire follow-up revealed that most firms that were serious about control used seasonalized measures, regardless of their particular control measure. Most larger companies applied their control measures to subunits such as subsidiaries or product lines; most wanted more subunit detail than they were getting.

Comments on Survey Size and Procedures

1. Forecast data is based on a 148 company sample. Control data is based on a 102 company subsample.

2. To assess forecast techniques, respondents were first asked to indicate all methods used to forecast receivables for budgeting, planning, and cash management as opposed to control and then to indicate the primary (most important) method.

3. To assess control techniques, respondents were first asked to indicate all methods used for management control of receivables and then to indicate the primary (most important) method. Because of confusion on early questionnaires (not included in sample), care was taken to differentiate management control (defined as the identification of payment problems and/or detection of changes in overall payment behavior) from account-level control.

4. Fractional weights were assigned when: 1) more than one primary method was indicated; 2) multiple respondents from the same company indicated different primary methods and questionnaire follow-up could not reconcile differences; 3) more than one method was used and no primary method was indicated on either the questionnaire or post questionnaire follow-up.

5. Totals differ from 100% because of rounding.

implementation was defining a summary measure. Some tried using a sum of either current or overdue aging fractions, e.g., a company might sum the aging fractions in the first two or three age classes. In fact, a few questionnaire responses even listed such summary measures as either the primary control measure or one that is as important as the aging schedule itself.

In questionnaire follow-up, some companies described a very interested attempt to correct for sales variation. The essence of the procedure was to assume a "pro forma aging schedule" and use realized sales to impute pro forma receivables that would be compared with actual receivables to see if there were deviations from the pro forma behavior. Such companies were very close to discovering balance fractions. In terms of the projection matrices, their problem lay in an attempt to apply aging fractions (which arise from column data) to sales rather than applying the correct procedure of using balance fractions (which apply to row data). The basic problem faced by these companies was that of specifying a pro forma aging schedule when they knew their actual schedules were seasonal.

When use of payment proportions and balance fractions was presented to such companies as sales-independent summaries of payment behavior, the general reaction was favorable in recognizing sales independence as a key criterion for control. The most common questions concerned how to measure payment proportions and/or balance fractions and the extent to which they were stable.

Payment Patterns Versus the Aging Schedule

It is claimed in this paper that payment proportions and balance fractions are superior to aging fractions for control. Their obvious advantage over aging fractions is their independence of the level of credit sales. There is no substantive difference in terms of simplicity. The aging schedule is no easier to compute than balance fractions or payment proportions once the receivable data base is properly organized along the lines of the projections matrices illustrated in Exhibits 3 and 4. For stable payment behavior, the number of ratios involved in the aging schedule is the same number of balance fractions. In fact, when one uses seasonal aging schedules to reflect seasonal sales, considerably more data is required to use aging fractions. Finally, in the case of time-dependent payment behavior, it is shown subsequently that control is logically organized by the concept of an underlying *basic payment pattern* (defined in the measurement section) that corrects for the effect of seasonals in payment behavior and other factors such as changing interest rates. In contrast, there is no obvious measure of a "basic aging fraction" that corrects for shifts in payment behavior.

Control Based on Average Days Outstanding

There are several closely related one-parameter summary measures of receivable status--average age, average days outstanding, and turnover. Average age is usually defined as the receivable-weighted average of the median number of days in each age class. As a one-parameter summary of the aging schedule, it contains all the defects of the aging schedule plus loss of information due to averaging. In addition, the receivable weighting in computing the average tends to magnify sensitivity to sales.

Average days outstanding (hereafter *ADO*) is usually measured as the ratio of receivables to a measure of daily sales. With the conventional practice of using annual sales per day as the measure of daily sales, the formula for average days outstanding at the end of month t is

(3) $ADO_t = 365[TAR_t/(\text{annual credit sales})]$.

The usual turnover measure is the ratio of annual sales to receivables, and thus is the reciprocal of the term in brackets. For this reason, average days outstanding and turnover are viewed as essentially equivalent measures.

Computing average sales over a shorter time period than a year can eliminate some of the sales cycle from the *ADO* measure, but it still leaves the *ADO* measure quite sensitive to the pattern of sales. To illustrate, the *ADO* measures for annual, quarterly, and monthly measures of daily sales and average age for the March and October receivables of Exhibit 4 are:

	March	October
ADO (annual)	34	54
ADO (quarterly)	55	45
ADO (monthly)	41	53
Average Age	28	35

Even though the payment proportions used to develop Exhibit 4 were the same in every month, the March and October values of the alternative *ADO* measures and the average age are quite different. These differences arise solely because of month-to-month sales variation. Except for the unusual special case of uniform sales, both average age and average days outstanding vary with sales even when there is no change in payment behavior.

Almost all companies using *ADO*-based control measures recognize its dependence on sales and the fact that sales variations can and do mask changes in underlying payment behavior. Most companies using such measures used a seasonal value as their comparison standard but generally felt *ADO*-based measures were poor control tools. The usual reason for using *ADO*-based measures seemed to be simplicity and a perceived lack of any meaningful alternative.

Projection Based on Average Days Outstanding

The essence of forecast procedures based on average days outstanding is to solve the usual defining equation for average days outstanding for total receivables and then to use a pro forma value for average days outstanding to project receivables. For instance, solving equation (3) for total receivables gives

(4) $TAR_t = ADO_t(\text{annual credit sales})/365$

Given a forecast of annual credit sales and a pro forma value of average days outstanding, an associated value is obtained for accounts receivable.

As this formula makes clear, when the relation between receivables and average days outstanding is expressed in terms of average daily credit sales, the value of average days outstanding must generally be a function of time, especially if sales are cyclical. For this reason, most companies use a time dependent value of average days outstanding, usually one based on past history. For instance, the measure of average days outstanding in month t could be based on the average value in the same month in prior years. Then the forecast equation is

$$TAR_t = (\text{average past } ADO \text{ for month}) \times (\text{annual credit sales})/365.$$

An obvious problem here is that annual credit sales may be unrepresentative of the recent rate of average daily credit sales, especially when sales are highly cyclical. Thus, another way that companies try to improve *ADO*-based forecast procedures is to use a sales measure for a time period shorter than a year. Quarterly sales seem to be a common substitute, especially for companies doing quarterly financial statement projection. With quarterly sales, the projection equation can be stated as

$TAR_t = (ADO_t)$[(credit sales in previous three months)/Q],

where Q is the number of days in the previous 3 months.

Finally, some companies used both a time varying ratio and shorter periods for measuring average receivables. For instance, a synthesis of the two previous equations gives

TAR_t = (average past ADO for month) x (credit sales in the previous 3 months)/Q.

Both the use of more recent measures of average daily sales and of a time dependent ratio are attempts to improve the basic forecast. However, except for such restrictive special cases as uniform sales, these refinements fail to reflect properly the effect of varying sales levels even when payment behavior is stable. Even the use of time varying values for average days outstanding requires joint stability in payment behavior and sales patterns, so that deviations from past sales patterns cannot generally be treated properly.

The underlying problem with ADO-based projections is an attempt to use a single number, and generally a single representative value of sales, to summarize the relationship between receivables and credit sales at a point in time. Trying to make one number summarize the entire payment pattern is an oversimplification that generally omits important information. Knowledge of payment patterns shows that a complete summary of monthly payment behavior generally requires H numbers, where H is the payment horizon.

The average-days-outstanding method must be viewed as a simple but incomplete forecast framework. Its degree of adequacy depends either on essentially uniform sales or, in the case of cyclical sales, on the joint stability of year-to-year sales and payment patterns.

Follow-up discussions with companies using ADO-based projection indicate that the main reasons for using it are simplicity and the fact that average days outstanding is a universally accepted way of summarizing receivable collections. Almost all companies using ADO-based projection report general dissatisfaction with its accuracy and their ability to reflect what they know about receivable behavior within the ADO framework. The reasons for elaborations on the basic ADO framework such as time varying values are attempts to use more information and cure deficiencies in the basic method.

Ratio-Based Projection

Ratio-based projection refers to any forecast procedure that assumes that receivables at a point in time are proportional to some measures of sales. There appear to be many variations to the ratio projections with varying degrees of sophistication. In fact, the various ADO forecasts can be viewed as a particular type of ratio projection. Thus, ratio-based projection other than ADO-based approaches is now considered.

In its simplest form, ratio projection makes receivables at the end of time period t proportional to sales during that time period. If r denotes the proportionality factor, this relation can be expressed as

(5) $TAR_t = rCS_t$.

A simple variant of this equation involves replacing current sales by sales in the previous month (or quarter).

The use of a single constant is incapable of treating the fact that the ratio of sales to accounts receivable typically changes over time. This form of the expression is so simple that it is rarely used. An extension of the simple constant is the use of a "moving ratio" to treat seasonality in the relation of receivables to sales. With monthly projection, this approach assumes that the ratio of receivables to sales in a given month will be the same as the past ratio in that same month. A projection equation for the moving ratio is

$$(6) \quad TAR_t = \left(\frac{TAR_{t-12}}{CS_{t-12}}\right) CS_t \ .$$

In addition to moving ratio, terms used to describe the projection method included seasonal ratio, sales scaling, and sales shifting. (Another closely related term is "growth scaling". When sales grow at a constant rate g so that $CS_t = CS_{t-12}(1+g)$, then the moving ratio means receivables show the same growth pattern, i.e. $TAR_t = TAR_{t-12}(1+g)$.) The central idea of this approach is that shifts in accounts receivable are proportional to shifts in sales. It implicitly assumes that historical relations between sales and receivables persist in the future and that a single value of sales is representative of the entire series of recent sales.

Equation (6) scales sales by the actual ratio of receivables to sales 12 months earlier. A variant of this method is to use the average value on the ratio for a given month over some number of previous years. For instance, if one weighted a given month's values for the past 3 years with weights of .2, .3, and .5 respectively, the formula for the proportionality factor at time t would be

$$r_t = .2\left(\frac{TAR_{t-36}}{CS_{t-36}}\right) + .3\left(\frac{TAR_{t-24}}{CS_{t-24}}\right) + .5\left(\frac{TAR_{t-12}}{CS_{t-12}}\right).$$

Ratio-based projection is another attempt to summarize the relation between receivables and sales by a single number or at least a single number at a point in time. Even with stable payment behavior, the constant ratio requires uniform credit sales to be correct, while the moving ratio requires joint stability of seasonal sales and payment patterns to be an acceptable projection method. When such joint stability exists, then it can be a reasonable way to convert credit sales forecasts into receivable projections.

Ratio projection is often used within the framework of a computer-based financial statement generator. One of the main reasons for using ratios is simply that many of these statement generators require that the user specify relations between financial statement variables in terms of user-specified ratios.

Interestingly, many companies using moving ratios report reasonable to high satisfaction with the accuracy of the receivable forecast for planning purposes but not for control purposes. There are several explanations for this. One is that control generally requires greater accuracy than forecasts for planning (budgeting) and cash management. A second involves the way companies plan. For one-year and two-year cash plans, the most common method of projecting sales is a seasonalized average growth projection, often obtained by scaling some smoothed measure of past sales. Hence, the pro forma sales projections have built into them the required stability, even though the sales ultimately realized may deviate from the historical pattern. This explanation is consistent with the fact that the forecast is adequate for projection purposes but not for control, which requires an ability to deal with what receivables should be for realized sales. Third, for companies making quarterly rather than monthly projections, moving ratios have a built-in smoothing feature that tends to average out month-to-month sales fluctuations. In questionnaire follow-up, 3 companies reported being unpleasantly surprised when they shifted from quarterly to monthly projection and found that the quality of their forecasts had deteriorated. This deterioration reflects a major defect of moving ratios, namely, excessive sensitivity to the extent to which a given value of sales is representative of the immediately preceding series of sales.

One attempt to cope with this sensitivity has been to replace the single value of sales at a point in time with a moving average of recent sales. If MAS_t and MAS_{t-12} reflect the moving average of recent sales computed at time t and a year earlier, this refinement of the moving ratio can be expressed as

$$(7)\quad TAR_t = (TAR_{t-12})(MAS_t/MAS_{t-12}).$$

Appendix B relates this projection technique to payment patterns. It shows that, with properly chosen weights, the use of a moving average of past sales in a ratio projection can be viewed as a special case of a payment-pattern projection. However, Appendix B also shows that this technique is generally an inefficient way to use payment-pattern information.

Five of the six companies using a weighted average of past sales within the framework of a moving ratio were among the larger companies surveyed. All used the approach as part of a computer-based projection system, and all but one of the six reported reasonable to high satisfaction with its use for forecasting purposes. The consensus was that it did a good job of reflecting seasonality in receivables and an acceptable job of reflecting the effect of past sales. The most common complaint was an inability to reflect changing business conditions and the fact that the previous year would generally differ from the projected one, so that the ratio interjected a scaling error, a problem noted in Appendix B.

In questionnaire follow-up, all six of these companies indicated that weights were specified judgmentally without any formal statistical measurement designed to find a best set of weights. Several indicated that knowledge of the aging schedule was the primary input to specifying weights and had even described their forecast procedure as aging-schedule-based projection on their questionnaire. None indicated an awareness of balance fractions as the logical basis for specifying weights.

When asked why they did not use a simple lagged function of sales rather than the moving ratio, two basic explanations emerged. Three of these companies had introduced the moving average of sales when they changed from quarterly to monthly projection and found the simple moving ratio no longer satisfactory. Thus, this approach was viewed primarily as a refinement of the simple moving ratio rather than as a representation of receivables as a lagged function of sales. The essence of the other reason was that the use of the ratio tended to correct for misspecification of weights to the extent that past and projected sales patterns were stable.

Percent of Balance

The *percent-of-balance method* of forecasting receivables assumes that payments received in a given month are some constant proportion of the start-of-month receivables. In addition to percent of balance and percentage balance, other practitioners have used the terms "percentage payment" and "percent of payment." Still others described it as "monthly turnover." Thus, there seems to be a lack of well-defined terminology for this projection technique. This author is unaware of any reference to it in the finance-accounting literature, although the Cyert-Davidson-Thompson [4] model of bad debt forecasts via a Markov process is conceptually similar.

Accounts receivable at the end of month t is equal to accounts receivable at the end of month $t-1$ less payments made of these receivables in month t plus new credit sales in month t less any bad debts recognized in month t. In the absence of bad debts, this accounting identity can be expressed in the notation of this paper as

$$(8) \quad TAR_t = TAR_{t-1} - TCF_t + CS_t.$$

There seem to be two variants to the percentage balance approach. In one, it is assumed that the total cash flow from receivables in a month is proportional to the starting balance. If q denotes the proportionality factor, then this assumption means that the identity in equation (8) can be rewritten as

$$(9) \quad TAR_t = (1-q)TAR_{t-1} + CS_t.$$

In the other variant, the proportionality factor between receivables and cash flow is defined in terms of only the cash flow on outstanding receivables. If q^* denotes the fraction of receivables outstanding at the start of a month that are paid off during that month, the $(1-q^*)TAR_{t-1}$ is the change in receivables initially outstanding and $(1-P_0)CS_t$ is the net addition from credit sales during the month. In this case, the identity in equation (8) can be written as

$$(10) \quad TAR_t = (1-q^*)TAR_{t-1} + (1-P_0)CS_t.$$

Comparisons of equations (8) and (9) shows that the two scaling factors must be related by the expression $q = q^* + P_0(CS_t/TAR_{t-1})$. Equation (9) appears to be more commonly used than equation (10), although the latter is more complete and more congruent with the verbal statements of what practitioners say they are doing. However, in the common situation in which there are practically no payments made on credit sales within 30 days, P_0 is essentially zero, q and q^* are practically equal, and there is no substantive difference in the two equations.

We have focused attention upon the accounts receivable projection implied by the percent-of-balance method. However, discussions with users of the method indicate that it is employed more often simply to obtain a cash flow projection rather than a receivable projection *per se*. Often the time horizon of the projection is short, e.g., a 3-month rolling cash flow projection.

Whether used to project receivables or cash flow, the use of either q or q^* as the basis for projection is a questionable procedure. Like *ADO* and simple ratio projection, this approach is another attempt to use a single number to summarize payment behavior. Like the other one-number forecasts, these ratios are complete summaries only in the special case of uniform sales.

Like ratio projection, the percent balance technique can be extended to treat seasonality, although few companies reported trying such extensions. Most users reported general dissatisfaction with the approach.

Linear Functions of Past Sales and Lagged Regression

The payment-pattern approach to forecasting cash flows and receivables expresses the quantities as a linear function of past credit sales. In the survey summarized in Exhibit 5, a number of companies reported using some linear function of past sales. The approach was generally described as a "moving average," "weighted average," or "lagged average," although the weights were generally not normalized in the usual sense of an average. Except for companies using the lagged regression described in the subsequent measurement section, these companies indicated in questionnaire follow-up that the relative importance of each month's credit sales was determined judgmentally rather than by any formal empirical procedure. Some indicated that the basis of judgment was knowledge of the company's aging schedule. Some even described their approach as an aging-schedule-based forecast on the questionnaire.

Most companies applied their model to aggregate sales rather than at the product-line, credit-term level. Nevertheless, a majority of these companies generally described themselves as being "satisfied" to "highly satisfied" with the approach, especially those using a lagged regression to measure the balance fractions.

A Summary of Current Practice

The popular control measures depend on the sales pattern. Thus, the greater the variation in sales, the more likely they are to prove unsatisfactory. Using seasonal measures can help cope with seasonal sales patterns but only to the extent that past patterns repeat exactly. The high general level of dissatisfaction with these measures reflects an inability to separate the effect of sales variation from payment shifts and the fact that normal sales variation is generally much greater than shifts in payment behavior.

The one-parameter forecast techniques (*ADO*, ratio, and percent of balance) attempt to summarize payment behavior by a single number. Even the attempts to improve these techniques by using seasonal parameters still use a single number at a point in time rather than a set of numbers. Except for companies with an unusual amount of stability in their sales, such one-parameter forecast measures generally produce poor accuracy. Much of the current dissatisfaction with forecasting accounts receivable and the associated cash flows must be imputed to the forecast procedures in widespread use and the fact that they are conceptually incomplete approaches.

In most forecasting situations, there is a trade-off-between simplicity and completeness. Except for the unusually stable company, basing forecasts on any of the one-number summaries of the payment behavior must be viewed as erring on the side of oversimplification, especially given the ease with which a set of given payment proportions enables one to fill in forecast matrices such as those illustrated in Exhibits 3 and 4. For computer-based projection with preprogrammed measurement of payment patterns, there is no substantive difference in actual difficulty.

THE MEASUREMENT OF PAYMENT PATTERNS

Alternative ways to use past data to measure payment proportions and balance fractions are now considered. Stable payment behavior is first treated and then measurement when payment behavior shifts over time is considered.

Simple Average

The most straightforward way to estimate payment proportions is to compute the average value realized from past data, i.e.,

$$(11)\quad P_i = AVE(CF_{ti}/CS_t) = \frac{1}{N}\sum_{t=1}^{N}\frac{CF_{ti}}{CS_t},\quad i = 0,\ldots,H$$

where CF_{ti} is cash flow in month $t+i$

from credit sales in month t and N is the number of months of past history used to compute the average. The caret denotes the fact that the value is an empirical estimate.

The analogous expression for balance fractions is

$$(12)\quad \hat{F}_i = AVE(AR_{ti}/CS_t) = \frac{1}{N}\sum_{t=1}^{N}\frac{AR_{ti}}{CS_t}, \quad i = 0,\ldots,H-1$$

where AR_{ti} is the receivable balance at the end of month $t+i$ due to credit sales in month t.

Lagged Regression

As was indicated in the review of forecasting practice, several companies using a payment-pattern approach to forecasting did so within the framework of a lagged regression in which past receivable balances were regressed on a lagged function of past sales. The regression equation can be expressed as

$$(13)\quad TAR_t = f_0 CS_t + f_1 CS_{t-1} + \cdots + f_{H-1} CS_{t-H+1} + u_t$$

where $f_0, f_1,\ldots,f_{H-1}$ are the regression coefficients and u_t is the usual error term. Their values represent historical estimates of the relative importance of sales in the previous months in determining the values of outstanding receivables.

Comparison of this regression equation and expression (2) for total receivables shows the two equations have the same structure. Estimating the regression coefficients is a method for imputing balance fractions from past data. The main issue is whether such a regression of receivables on lagged sales is the best way to measure balance fractions. It is argued shortly that it generally is not.

An alternative lagged regression approach can be based on explaining total cash flows rather than receivable balances. The analogous equation for directly estimating the payment proportions is

$$(14)\quad TCF_t = p_0 CS_t + p_1 CS_{t-1} + \cdots + p_H CS_{t-H} + u_t .$$

Again, $p_0,\ldots,p_H$ are regression coefficients and u_t is the usual error term. The regression coefficients are estimates of the payment proportions with the property that they minimize the variance of month-to-month "errors" in their prediction of total cash flow from receivables over the sample of past data. These regression coefficients do not necessarily sum to one; they can be made to do so by simply scaling the estimates. With scaling, the actual estimate of the payment proportion is obtained from the regression coefficients in accord with the expression

$$\hat{P}_i = p_i / (\sum_{j=0}^{H} p_j), \quad i = 0,\ldots,H.$$

A more complex but more technically correct approach is to use constrained regression in which the least squares estimate is developed subject to the constraint that

$$\sum_{i=0}^{H} p_i = 1 .$$

Measurement is one area where explicit note of bad debt considerations is pertinent. When estimation is based on gross credit sales, then the normalization condition should be revised to say that the sum of payment proportions should equal one less the fraction of credit sales written off as bad debts. In fact, payment proportions and bad debt loss rates should be estimated simultaneously as shown below.

Measurement Focus: Payment Proportions Versus Balance Fractions

Payment proportions and balance fractions are logically equivalent ways to characterize payment behavior in the sense that knowledge of one implies knowledge of the other. From this equivalence, it would seem that empirical measurement could focus on either payment proportions or balance fractions. The fact that most of the forecast equations for receivables in this article are expressed in terms of balance fractions even suggests that they are the logical focus for measurement. They were in fact the implicit focus of all companies using a lagged regression of receivables on sales. Lewellen and Edmister [8] and Lewellen and Johnson [9] concentrated solely on balance fractions and did not even consider payment proportions.

Contrary to the apparently natural tendency to focus on balance fractions, this author believes that payment proportions are the proper focus for empirical measurement. The primary reason for this preference is that there is no obvious way to impose a normalization restriction of balance fractions, especially in the context of constrained regression.

Note that the normalized balance fractions imply a tautological identity when expressed in terms of the balance fractions, i.e.,

$$1 = \sum_{i=0}^{H} P_i = (1 - F_0) + (F_0 - F_1) + \ldots$$

$$+ (F_{H-2} - F_{H-1}) + F_{H-1}.$$

It is possible to estimate balance fractions, solve for the implied payment proportions, and then recursively adjust the balance fractions until consistent estimates are obtained. However, such a circuitous procedure is unnecessarily complex when the payment proportions can be estimated directly.

A second reason involves treatment of bad debts. By focusing measurement on payment patterns, one obtains a comparatively simple problem structuring for simultaneous estimation of bad debt and payment behavior. For instance, if GCS_t denotes gross credit sales at time t, BD_t denotes total bad debts realized in month t and primes denote values expressed in terms of gross credit sales, then the joint estimation of payment patterns and bad debt loss rates can be expressed in the lagged regression framework as

$$BD_t = \sum_{t=0}^{H} B_i' \, GCS_{t-1}$$

$$TCF_t = \sum_{t=0}^{H} P_i' \, GCS_{t-1}$$

subject to the joint contraint that

$$\sum_{i=0}^{H} P_i' + \sum_{i=0}^{H} B_i' = 1.$$

The associated balance fraction is given by

$$F_t' = 1 - \sum_{i=0}^{t} P_i' - \sum_{i=0}^{t} B_i'.$$

The reason for the "nice" structuring is that payment proportions and bad debt loss rates characterize flows that occur in a single month, while balance fractions represent the net effect of flows over the preceding months.

Constant Versus Time Varying Payment Behavior

The estimation of payment patterns via either the simple average method or the lagged regression implicitly assumes that the payment proportions are the same from month-to-month aside from random disturbances. In most companies, payment behavior shifts in response to a variety of factors. Some product lines may have a seasonal variation in their payment pattern. Also, payment behavior typically shifts in response to economic variables such as the level interest rates and the state of the economy. Moreover, changes in the quality of receivables and shifts in the company collection effort can also alter payment behavior.

The way to allow for variation in payment behavior over time is to have a different set of payment proportions and balance fractions in each month. As before, total cash flows and receivables are projected by first developing the row of the projection matrix and then summing down columns. Control is still based on comparing pro forma and realized values. The only increase in complexity is the nominal requirement for more data.

Measurement in the Presence of Shifting Payment Behavior

Allowing for time varying payment proportions and balance fractions provides the conceptual generality necessary to develop forecasts in the presence of shifting payment behavior. However, without additional structuring, it provides neither for meaningful empirical measurement of payment behavior nor for a coherent framework for either control or performance evaluation. Variation in payment behavior can be meaningfully structured by assuming that there is a stable underlying payment pattern characterized by a constant set of payment proportions and associated balance fractions. Actual payment behavior can be shifted from these underlying values by other factors such as seasonality, interest-rate levels, and company collection effort.

Some illustrative estimation equations are now developed to show how the postulate of a basic underlying payment pattern leads to a meaningful conceptual framework for empirical measurement.

Seasonality

Seasonality of payment behavior refers to systematic changes in payment proportions over the course of a quarter or year. It is important to distinguish it from the seasonal receivables and cash flows that arise from seasonal sales.

To illustrate the measurement of a yearly seasonal, let S_{mi} denote the seasonal shift in the payment proportion P_i for month m of the year (where the months are indexed from 1 to 12 with January being 1). The regression equation for jointly estimating the basic payment proportions and the seasonal shift is

$$\frac{CF_{ti}}{CS_t} = P_i + \sum_{m=1}^{12} S_{mi} D_{mt} + u_{ti}, \qquad (15)$$

where D_{mt} is a dummy variable that is one if time t occurs in month m of the year, and zero otherwise; and u_{ti} is the usual residual error.

Credit managers, who are accustomed to correcting the standard receivable measures for seasonality, tend to worry about seasonal payment behavior. In this author's experience, payment proportions for highly seasonal sales are often not significantly seasonal, especially when estimated at the product-line, credit-term level.

Readers are warned to beware of measurement induced seasonals. These can be caused by measuring a payment pattern for overall sales when sales subunits each have a different but stable (non-seasonal) payment pattern and the mix of sales subunits has a stable relative seasonal. Of course, instability in the sales mix itself means a degradation in the ability to impute an overall payment pattern to characterize total sales.

Accounting practice can be another source of spurious seasonals.

For instance, in a company that recognized bad debts on a quarterly basis, the every-third-month adjustment to receivables gave the appearance of a small quarterly cycle in payment behavior. It vanished when bad debts were recognized monthly.

Interest-Rate Effects

To illustrate the inclusion of interest-rate effects along with seasonal effects, let I_t be a measure of the level of interest rates in month t and $\bar{I}$ be a measure of "normal" interest rates. A regression equation for jointly estimating the basic payment pattern, any yearly seasonal, and interest rate shifts is

$$(16) \quad \frac{CF_{ti}}{CS_t} = P_i + \sum_{m=1}^{12} S_{mi} D_{tm} + a_i (I_t - \bar{I}) + u_{ti}$$

where the coefficient a_i measures the sensitivity of payments i months after the sale to deviations in interest rates from the so-called normal level.

Synthesis of Measurement

Equations (15) and (16) illustrate how past data can be used to estimate both basic payment proportions and the way that payment behavior shifts in response to a yearly seasonal and interest rates. Other appropriate factors can be added to the estimation equation in an analogous fashion and their explanatory importance assessed.

It is noted that equations (15) and (16) are extensions of the simple average approach to estimation and not lagged regression. Analogous relationships can be put in the lagged regression framework by, for example, extending the lagged regression to reflect a seasonal variation in payment behavior by adding a seasonal constant to equation (14), i.e.,

$$(17) \quad TCF_t = \sum_{m=1}^{12} C_m \Delta_{mt} + \sum_{i=0}^{H} p_i CS_{t-i} + u_t$$

where Δ_{mt} is the seasonal dummy that is one when time period t is month m and zero otherwise. However, including shifts in the payment pattern from effects such as interest rates requires modification of the sales coefficients and usually leads to nonlinear estimation problems requiring recursive techniques.

Dealing with time dependent payment behavior complicates considerably the estimation problem compared to the estimation of simple averages in a stable environment. Dealing with these econometric issues is beyond the scope of this paper. The reader is referred to econometric texts such as Johnston [7] and Theil [14] and related literature such as references [5, 6, 10, 12, 13]. The objective here is not to specify completely all pertinent factors that can influence payment behavior or to deal extensively with the many statistical issues that arise in this type of measurement problem. Rather, the intent is to structure the problem sufficiently to make clear the basic conceptual approach implied by the postulate of the existence of an underlying stable payment pattern.

Measurement Focus and the Need for Disaggregation

In the course of this article, it has been mentioned several times that the logical focus for receivable forecasting and control is the product-line, credit-term level. A more precise criterion for the logical measurement focus is that payment proportions should be assessed for sales units that can logically be expected to have the same payment behavior. Credit terms are often more important than product lines.

When payment proportions are measured for sales mixtures with different underlying payment patterns, then the imputed payment pattern is an average of those for the particular sales mix in the sample. The use of such averages for forecasting and control involves an implicit assumption that the same sales mix will prevail in the future. Hence, the basic benefit of payment-pattern measures, independence of sales, is lost. Moreover, to the extent that the sales mix shifts over the sample period, measurement precision is unnecessarily sacrificed and the company foregoes control quality and forecast confidence.

The criterion of focusing measurement on sales units expected to have stable payment behavior can even go beyond the product-line, credit-term level. For instance, in a company that classified accounts into 5 credit quality classes, this author has found that measurement of payment patterns for different quality classes is an easy but particularly beneficial refinement. Deciding how far to go in refining measurement involves two basic issues. One is theoretically attainable accuracy. The other is trading off the greater measurement cost and accuracy with the benefits of tighter control and possibly improved decision making and performance measurement.

Performance Evaluation and Decision Making

Meaningful measures of the performance of a company's collection effort must be based on measures of behavior that do not depend on factors beyond the control of those responsible for collections, e.g. the sales pattern, the level of interest rates, and the quality of the accounts, the latter being determined by the company's credit granting decisions. Underlying basic payment proportions and balance fractions represent such measures.

An Example

A Fortune 100 company instituted a major program to speed up collections in 1973 because of apparently dedetiorating collections. As sales declined and interest rates rose throughout the first 9 months of 1974, both the aging schedule and unadjusted balance fractions indicated further deterioration in receivables despite even greater collection effort. There was talk of replacing the credit manager and reorganizing the collection function. Then, as interest rates declined in late 1974 and 1975 and sales stopped falling and then increased, there was apparently dramatic improvement in collection behavior as measured by both the aging schedule and an indication of some improvement even on the basis of unadjusted balance fractions. However, when basic payment patterns were measured with correction for seasonals, interest-rate-effects, and receivable quality, the picture was dramatically different. It indicated a large favorable shift in the basic payment patterns for almost every product line within a month of the initiation of the new collection program in 1973 that was followed by further month-to-month improvements that continued into mid-1974 when the impact of the new collection effort fell to near zero. Interestingly, when both the aging schedule and the unadjusted balance fraction indicated significant improvement, the basic balance fraction had stabilized in that it showed no statistically significant change.
The explanation for the difference in the unadjusted balance fraction and the basic balance fraction was primarily

the effect of interest rates, especially in product lines with discounts that were foregone by almost all customers when interest rates were high. This interest-rate-effect was reinforced by a normal seasonal in some product lines and lower quality of accounts arising from the extension of credit to poorer risks as sales declined.

Credit Policy Decisions

Making intelligent credit policy decisions (such as relaxing or tightening credit granting, changing discount terms, introducing or eliminating discounts) requires knowledge of how the decisions will impact payment behavior. The "explanation" of payment behavior inherent in the measurement of basic payment patterns is useful input to such decisions. In the company of the example above, measuring payment patterns at the product-line, credit-term level for different credit quality classes led to the relaxation of credit granting in some product lines and the tightening of others and the revision of discount terms in several product lines.

SUMMARY AND CONCLUSIONS

Payment proportions and balance fractions are two closely related sets of ratios that completely summarize the conversion of credit sales into cash flows and receivable balances. These ratios are independent of the pattern of credit sales, a key property for a meaningful summary of company payment experience first recognized in the pioneering works of Lewellen and Edmister [8] and Lewellen and Johnson [9].

Implications for Forecasting

Popular forecast techniques (average days outstanding, ratios, and percentage balance) are based on one-number summaries of the relation of credit sales to receivables. Except for the special case of uniform sales (or of jointly stable seasonal sales and payment behavior for seasonal forecast parameters), these one-number summaries do not properly reflect the dependence of receivables on sales. Hence, their use introduced structural forecast error into both receivable and cash flow projections.

For the typical company, the payment-pattern approach to receivable forecasting promises greater forecast accuracy within a logically consistent framework that places no restrictions on sales patterns. For the company that cannot measure payment patterns with any meaningful statistical accuracy, the approach indicates the inherent uncertainty in receivable levels and cash flows.

Given the apparently widespread dissatisfaction with current forecast procedures, there seems to be a clear need for the use of improved method.

Implications for Control

Rather than the usual aging schedule, control should focus on monitoring payment proportions, bad debt loss rates, and balance fractions. Meaningful control should focus on the patterns at the product-line, credit-term level. Realized values should be compared to pro forma values implied by past data with adjustment made for factors that shift payment behavior such as seasonals and interest rates. In effect, the control focus should be the basic payment pattern. By eliminating measurement noise arising from sales variation, seasonal payment behavior and other factors, more precise control is attainable at any given level of administrative effort.

Implications for Performance Evaluation

The proper focus for the evaluation of company collection effort is impact on basic payment patterns. Either realized payment patterns or sales dependent measures such as the aging schedule can give spurious indications of company performance.

Implications for Information System Design

A basic principle of modern information systems theory is the idea of working backward from the decision to be made to the required data to the implied data gathering and data organization. The two projection matrices illustrated in Exhibits 3 and 4 are the basic data-structure units for a receivable information system. The various forecast equations define key data manipulation. The measurement section specified the types of data that must be captured. Thus, the decision foundations and much of the data identification and organization necessary to develop a decision-centered receivable information system are provided.

APPENDIX A. THE FUNCTIONAL DEPENDENCY OF THE PARAMETERS OF VARIOUS FORECAST AND CONTROL PROCEDURES ON BALANCE FRACTIONS AND THE SCHEDULE OF CREDIT SALES

This appendix develops formulas expressing the parameters of popular techniques as functions of balance fractions and the schedule of credit sales. It considers sufficient conditions for these parameters to be complete summaries when payment behavior is stable.

Aging Fractions

Let A_{jt} denote the fraction of receivables in age class j at time t. The convention is adopted that the most current receivables are indexed by $j = 0$. The formula that relates the aging fraction to the balance fractions and the schedule of credit sales is

$$A_{jt} = F_j CS_{t-j} / \sum_{i=0}^{H-1} F_j CS_{t-j}$$

$$j = 0,1,\ldots,H-1.$$

A time subscript is used here because the aging schedule generally changes from month-to-month even when the balance fractions are constant.

In the special case of uniform sales that grow at a constant month-to-month rate of g, the expression for the balance fraction simplifies to

$$A_{jt} = F_j(1+g)^{-j} / \sum_{i=0}^{H-1} F_i(1+g)^{-i}$$

$$j = 0,1,\ldots,H-1.$$

Here, the aging schedule is the same in every month.

For constant month-to-month credit sales, the growth rate g is zero and the expression above simplifies to

$$A_{jt} = F_j / \left(\sum_{i=0}^{H-1} F_i\right), \quad j = 0,1,\ldots,H-1.$$

In the special case of constant sales, the aging schedule is simply a normalized schedule of balance fractions.

Average Days Outstanding and Average Age

If the conventional *ADO* measure is used based on the ratio of total receivables to a measure of average daily sales, then with a Q-day quarter as the time period, it is found that

$$ADO_t = \frac{TAR_t}{\text{average daily sales}}$$

$$= \frac{Q \sum_{i=0}^{H-1} F_i CS_{t-i}}{\sum_{i=0}^{2} CS_{t-i}}$$

With the conventional approximation that the average of the receivables arising from sales i months prior to time t is $30_i + 15$, the overall average age of receivables is

$$\text{average age} = \sum_{i=0}^{H-1} F_i CS_{t-i}(30_i + 15) / \sum_{i=0}^{H-1} F_i CS_{t-i} .$$

When payment behavior is stable, both average days outstanding and average age depend on sales. They will be constant only for restrictive assumptions about sales such as uniform sales.

Ratio Forecasts

The following expression relates the receivable-to-sales ratio to balance fractions and sales levels:

$$r_t = TAR_t / CS_t = \sum_{i=0}^{H-1} F_i CS_{t-i} / CS_t$$

$$= F_0 + F_i\left(\frac{CS_{t-1}}{CS_t}\right) + F_2\left(\frac{CS_{t-2}}{CS_t}\right) + \ldots + F_{H-1}\left(\frac{CS_{t-H+1}}{CS_t}\right).$$

The moving ratio approach of equation (6) requires the consistency of the following expression in each month:

$$\frac{\sum_{i=0}^{H-1} F_i CS_{t-i}}{CS_t} = \frac{\sum_{i=0}^{H-1} F_i CS_{t-i-12}}{CS_{t-12}} .$$

For the constant ratio to be independent of the sales pattern requires restrictive conditions such as uniform sales. In contrast, the moving ratio allows for seasonal sales variation but requires year-to-year stability of seasonal patterns to within a scale factor.

Percent of Balance Parameters

The two variations of the percent of balance method were characterized by the parameters q and q^*. By definition, q is the ratio of total cash flow to total receivables in the previous periods, i.e.,

$$q \equiv \frac{TCF_t}{TAR_{t-1}} = \frac{\sum_{i=0}^{H} P_i CS_{t-i}}{TAR_{t-1}}$$

$$= \frac{(1 - F_0)CS_t + \sum_{i=1}^{H} (F_i - F_{i+1})CS_{t-i}}{\sum_{i=0}^{H} F_i CS_{t-i-1}}$$

By definition, q^* is the ratio of cash flow from receivables outstanding at the end of the previous period to those receivables, i.e.,

$$q \equiv \frac{TCF_t - P_0 CS_t}{TAR_{t-1}} = \frac{\sum_{i=1}^{H} (F_i - F_{i+1})CS_{t-i}}{\sum_{i=0}^{H} F_i CS_{t-i-1}}$$

APPENDIX B. THE RELATION BETWEEN FORECASTS BASED ON A MOVING RATIO USING WEIGHTED AVERAGES OF PAST SALES AND PAYMENT-PATTERN PARAMETERS

The ratio between total receivables at time t and 12 months earlier can be expressed as

$$\frac{TAR_t}{TAR_{t-12}} = \frac{\sum_{i=0}^{H-1} F_i CS_{t-i}}{\sum_{i=0}^{H-1} F_i CS_{t-12-i}} .$$

Let $W_i = F_i / (\sum_{i=1}^{H-1} F_i)$ denote a normalized balance fraction. By multiplying both the numerator and denominator of the right-hand-side of this expression by $1/(\sum_{i=1}^{H-1} F_i)$,

$$\frac{TAR_t}{TAR_{t-12}} = \frac{\sum_{i=0}^{H-1} W_i CS_{t-i}}{\sum_{i=0}^{H-1} W_j CS_{t-12-i}}$$

is obtained. This last expression is clearly a moving ratio involving a weighted average of credit sales. It has the structure of equation (7). This result shows that the moving-ratio forecast based on a weighted average of past sales is equivalent to a payment-pattern projection when the weights are based on normalized balance fractions. It also shows that any other choice of weights in equation (7) must be an incomplete characterization of the dependency of receivables on the sales pattern. The aging schedule is appropriate only when sales are constant and payment behavior is stable.

This expression shows that the standard moving-ratio projection with a single value of sales is an extreme case of assigning the entire weight to the current value of sales. This overweighting of the current value is the reason for the unnecessary sensitivity of the receivable forecast to the value of sales used and the reason that companies have moved to the intuitively more acceptable approach of weighting several values.

While a moving ratio in the form of equation (7) is a logically correct way to project receivables when weights are based on normalized balance fractions, it is unnecessarily redundant. Once the balance fractions are known, equation (2) is all that is necessary. Moreover, once it is recognized that payment behavior can shift over time, using a ratio based on balance-fraction weighted sales rather than the simple use of balance fractions introduces an element of statistical noise that can improperly scale the correct forecast.

REFERENCES

1. W. H. Beaver, "Financial Statement Analysis," Chapter 5 in *Handbook of Modern Accounting*, Sidney Davidson, Editor, New York, McGraw-Hill Book Co., 1970.
2. H. Benishay, "Managerial Control of Accounts Receivable: A Deterministic Approach," *Journal of Accounting Research* (Spring 1965), pp. 114-132.
3. L.A. Bernstein, *Financial Statement Analysis*, Homewood, Illinois, Richard D. Irwin, Inc., 1974.
4. R. M. Cyert, H. J. Davidson, and G. L. Thompson, "Estimation of the Allowance for Doubtful Accounts by Markov Chains," *Management Science* (April 1962), pp. 287-301.
5. Z. Griliches, "A Note on the Serial Correlation Bias in Estimates of Distributed Lags," *Econometrica* (January 1961), pp. 65-73.
6. A. W. Jastram, "A Treatment of Distributed Lags in the Theory of Advertising Expenditures," *Journal of Marketing* (July 1955), pp. 36-46.
7. J. Johnston, *Econometric Methods*, second edition, New York, McGraw-Hill Book Co., 1972.
8. W. G. Lewellen and R. O. Edmister, "A General Model for Accounts Receivable and Control," *Journal of Financial and Quantitative Analysis* (March 1973), pp. 195-206.
9. W. G. Lewellen and R. W. Johnson, "Better Way to Monitor Accounts Receivable," *Harvard Business Review* (May-June 1972), pp. 101-109.

10. N. Liviatan, "Consistent Estimation of Distributed Lags," *International Economic Review* (January 1963), pp. 44-52.
11. G. L. Marrah, "Managing Receivables," *Financial Executive* (July 1970), pp. 40-44.
12. T. W. McGuire, J. U. Farley, R. E. Lucas, Jr., and W. L. Ring, "Estimation and Inference for Linear Models in which Subsets of the Dependent Variables are Constrained," *Journal of the American Statistical Association* (June 1972), pp. 348-368.
13. T. W. McGuire and D. L. Weiss, "Logically Consistent Market Share Models II," *Journal of Marketing Research* (August 1976), pp. 296-302.
14. H. Theil, *Principles of Economics*, New York, John Wiley, 1971.

READING 23

The Formulation of Credit Policy Models

Dileep Mehta
Georgia State University

This study examines two problems: first, formulation of credit extension policy for a specific request or account; and second, evaluation of the effectiveness of such a policy. In literature, the relevant area of credit management is covered by three categories: credit management textbooks,[1] empirical surveys of credit management practices,[2] and finance textbooks[3] dealing with credit as a part of financial management. On a very general level, the structure of analysis in all these categories is quite uniform: the objectives of the credit department are (a) to maximize sales, (b) to minimize bad-debt losses, and (c) to minimize the cost of investment in accounts receivable. The methodological approaches differ considerably among different categories, even though the treatment of the subject within each category is fairly uniform. Credit management textbooks are comprehensive compilations of credit *procedures*, while the surveys and the finance textbooks tend to explore the conceptual aspects of credit management. Irrespective of these categories, however, the existing literature suffers from two major limitations:

(a) Credit extension decision is accepted as a pivotal point in credit management. It is also conceded, explicitly or implicitly, that it is amenable to routine decision procedures. However, very rarely have attempts been made to show methods through which these procedures can be devised in a systematic way. Even when such attempts are made, they are only partial in that they ignore the *economic worth* of sources of information used in arriving at a decision. Thus, though Beranek's Linear Discriminant Function[4] is superior to the conventional measures in that it enables one to employ past experience in a meaningful way, it may

[1] One of the most comprehensive works in this category is by Beckman [1].

[2] A trenchant analysis is provided in a relatively obscure work by Thompson and Langer [6].

[3] The textbooks that have treated the subject of credit management in some depth and distinguishable ways are by Weston [7], Lindsay and Sametz [4], and Beranek [2].

[4] See Beranek [2, pp. 327-333].

Reprinted from MANAGEMENT SCIENCE (October 1968), Vol. 15, No. 2, pp. B-30 - B-50, by permission of the publisher.

not be economically worthwhile in *all* cases.

(b) Similarly, for control purposes, conventional ratio measures or aggregates are suggested. There is nothing wrong with ratios; the objection is against the standards to which they are compared. These standards, derived from the historical experience of the firm (or the industry to which the firm belongs), assume that historical performance has been optimal, and that the efficiency path is a linear function of change. Both assumptions are of questionable validity for internal control purposes, even though they may be considerably useful to creditors and investors who do not have access to more detailed information.

Even when attempts are made to derive systematically indices or aggregates,[5] they are not derived from or interrelated with the routine decision-rule framework; hence, this reduces the operational usefulness of these measures to a great extent.

In this study, attention is first focused upon the credit-extension phase of credit policy, since management primarily exercises its discretion during this phase, and since subsequent phases of credit policy are closely related to this particular phase. Thus, operating decision rules for credit-extension are derived from examination of past experience concerning bad-debt levels, credit period length, collection acitivities, and lost sales levels. The situation is then reversed; indices in terms of bad-debt levels, receivable levels, etc., are computed to measure the impact of credit extension procedures on the subsequent phases of credit policy.

The strength of the suggested approach lies in the logical relationship between operating rules concerned with routine decisions and the control indices. This consistent relationship is extremely helpful to management in formulating the optimal credit policy.

DECISION RULES FOR CREDIT EXTENSION

The method proposed here for handling individual credit requests is known as the "Sequential Decision Process."[6] It rests on two premises: first, since all relevant information cannot be secured in time or without cost, all relevant information is not worthwhile in making a decision. Second, past experience can be effectively employed in dealing with uncertainty as to the future.

The underlying process is simple. Once we acquire a piece of information relevant to the credit extension decision, we attempt in the light of past experience to estimate costs associated with the three alternatives; namely, credit grant, rejection of request, and postponement of the decision until a piece of further information is secured. We select that alternative which has the minimum expected cost.

Associated with credit grant are the costs of average investment in receivables and of collection efforts made before the final payment. Moreover, in bad-debt cases, there will be the added cost of the product shipped to the customer.

Rejection of a credit request entails loss of the contribution margin composed of profit margin and indirect and overhead cost. When the volume of sales and production fluctuates widely, the indirect and overhead cost may be replaced by the "unabsorbed overhead (and indirect) burden." Unabsorbed overhead burden is the difference between the burden rate at the "normal" or capacity volume and the standard burden at the actual (or anticipated) volume. As the actual volume approaches the "normal" volume, this difference decreases. Consequently the rejection cost will be smaller, and credit standards more stringent, as the actual volume approaches capacity.

The cost of postponing a decision comprises two elements: (a) the cost

---

[5] See Beranek [2, pp. 275-320].

[6] For a lucid exposition of this process, see Schlaifer [5].

of securing and processing a piece of further information, and (b) the *expected* cost of each subsequent move made by chance. This latter element is difficult to explain in the abstract, and yet it is of crucial importance in the sequential decision process. The difficulty arises because of the use of inductive logic.

The sequential decision process will be explained here with the help of an example based upon a real situation. In this example, the credit policy of the firm is first briefly described. Second, cost information relevant to our example is considered. Third, the investigation process and the criteria for classification of accounts are described in detail, since they are pivotal points for credit management. Finally, the mechanism of the sequential process is explained with the help of a simplified example, and then the actual process is carried out to derive the decision rule set. The figures have been generally modified for simplicity in exposition. Even though the study stresses illustrative value rather than a claim for empirical significance, the detailed description of the methodology of the field study is given so as to enhance its usefulness.

Description of the Credit System

The firm under investigation sells one product with annual sales in the vicinity of $3 million. Sales are almost uniform throughout the year, and mostly on credit terms of 2%-10 days; net-30 days. Very few customers, however, take advantage of the cash discount.

Orders for the product range from 1 unit to 100 or 150 units, but have never exceeded 200 units. Many orders are repeat, but about 10% of the orders are from customers with whom the firm has had no previous experience.

Cost Information. Each unit of the product is sold for $10. The cost breakdown of the product unit is given below:

Variable cost (materials plus direct & indirect labor)	$6.00
Indirect and overhead cost	2.50
Profit margin	1.50
Contribution margin	4.00

Investigation Process. The investigation procedure can be broken down into five stages:

1. No investigation,
2. Past experience,
3. Risk classification by an outside credit rating agengy,
4. References of other creditors and banks,
5. Financial statements analysis.

It should be noted that there is nothing sacrosanct about the *number* or *order* of the stages. In some companies, outside agency ratings may not be relied upon; in others it may be necessary to conduct a personal interview of the potential customer before making any final decision. Similarly, in some cases the order of creditor references and the financial statements analysis may be reversed.

The *number* of stages is limited here to *five* for three reasons: (a) a customer account in the firm under observation rarely exceeds $1,500 so an added stage, say of a personal visit, entails expenses that immediately rule out such investigation (in fact, it is never undertaken); (b) in many cases, as we shall see later, there is no need of undertaking investigation even of earlier stages; and (c) our primary purpose is an illustrative analysis where a slight gain in refinement is far outweighed by the cost of obscuring the basic principles in a maze of figures.

The rationale for the *order* of stages in this illustration is two-fold: (a) the process cost of investigation is lower for earlier stages; and (b) delay or inaccessibility of data increases at later stages. From a slightly different viewpoint, each successive stage may be regarded as a stronger but more expensive filter of requests.

Criteria for Determination of Categories. Each *stage* is divided into the following categories:

Stage 1. *No investigation* (no categories).

Stage 2. *Past Experience* (four categories).

a. *Good* -when payments have been consistently made within the prescribed period of one month.

b. *Fair* -when the formal credit period has been frequently exceeded, but there has been no need for stronger than formal payment reminders; or the customer has given a satisfactory explanation for delinquency.

c. *Poor* - when stronger and personal reminders have been necessary in the past, and credit has been at times exceeded beyond a three-month period without reasonable or satisfactory explanations.

d. *New* -when there is a credit request from a customer with whom the firm has no previous dealings.

Stage 3. *Agency Ratings*. In our firm, Dun and Bradstreet ratings are used. They are reclassified into three groups for convenience.

a. *A ratings*: *Aa* to *E* -High, Good, and Fair; *F* to *H* -High and Good; *J* to *L* -High.

b. *B ratings*; *Aa* to *E* -Limited; *F* to *H* -Fair and Limited; *J* to *L* -Good and Fair.

c. *No rating*: when there is a blank rating, or no ratings are available.

Stage 4. *References*.[7] Creditors' references, three to five for each customer, fall into the following classifications.

a. *Strong*-when all references are highly favorable, and are made by banks or reputable firms.

b. *Fair*-when a majority of references are favorable, but one or two (particularly from banks) are cautious, or when a majority of references are not from well-known creditor firms.

c. *Evasive*-when most of the creditors are either outright unfavorable or very reluctant to commit themselves; or, when references are exclusive of banks and include only obscure firms.

Stage 5. *Financial Statement Analysis*.[8] When a firm, in extending credit heavily emphasizes the liquidity of the customer's assets, primary reliance is placed upon working capital. Hence, the current ratio may be computed. When emphasis is on both liquidity and financial viability, the Linear Discriminant Function suggested by Beranek may be computed: it is an index based upon the current ratio and the leverage measure.[9] This index falls into three categories dictated by past experience.

a. *Strong*-an index value not less than 2.5 indicates definite probability of payment, and payment within the period of one month.

b. *Weak*-an index value lower than 1.0 identifies submarginal customers with whom the firm had collection difficulties.

c. *Fair*-an index value larger than 1.0 and smaller than 2.5 indicates payment not always within the prescribed period of one month; however, this delinquency tendency rarely results in bad debts.

---

[7] The area of credit reference is not particularly amenable to classification criteria. This is largely because it is a matter of interpretation. One way to circumvent this difficulty is to send with the inquiry a form letter, requesting referees to complete and return only this form letter.

[8] This stage has been included here for illustrative purposes, even though it is almost non-existent in the firm in the example.

[9] See Beranek [2, pp. 327-334].

Classification criteria for the above categories were supplied by management. The length of the *actual* credit period, for instance, was the major criterion stressed by the treasurer in describing the "past experience" category.

Data Sources and Processing. Information on a customer was available from mainly two sources:

(a) *Ledger Card*-showing date and amount of shipment, and date of payment. It goes as far back as five years.

(b) *File*-containing a variety of materials such as special D&B reports on the customer, creditors' references, and collection correspondence, if any. From the ledger cards, the aging statement of accounts is prepared every month in this firm.

Aging statements for two consecutive months were available. From the first, customers with initials "A" to "M" were selected, and from the second those with "N" to "Z" were taken. The following information was sought on each group and then was averaged so as to derive the probabilities and average credit period of Table I.[10]

[10] For a detailed description of the method by which information was collected and processed, see Appendix.

Table I

	Prob.of Pmt.	Prob.of Bad Debt	Av.Credit Period	Av.Coll. Cost	Acceptance Cost	Rejection Cost
1. *No Investigation*	.95	.05	2	1.00	$1 + .40x$*	$3.8x$
2. *Past Experience*						
a. Good	1.00	.00	1	0.25	$0.25 + .05x$	$4x$
b. Fair	.95	.05	2	1.00	$1.00 + .40x$	$3.8x$
c. Poor	.70	.30	4	4.00	$4.00 + 2.0x$	$2.8x$
d. None**	--	--	-	--	---	
3. *Agency Rating*						
a. *A*	1.00	.00	1	0.50	$0.50 + .05x$	$4x$
b. *B*	.94	.06	2	1.50	$1.50 + .46x$	$3.7x$
c. No Rating	.75	.25	3	3.00	$3.00 + 1.65x$	$3x$
4. *Creditor Reference*						
a. Strong	1.00	.00	1.5	0.50	$0.50 + .08x$	$4x$
b. Fair	.95	.05	2	1.25	$0.25 + .40x$	$3.8x$
c. Evasive	.50	.50	6	8.00	$8.00 + 3.3x$	$2x$
5. *Financial Statement Analysis*						
a. Index $\geq$ 2.5	1.00	.00	1	0.25	$0.25 + .05x$	$4x$
b. 2.5 > Index $\geq$ 1.0	.95	.05	2	1.00	$1.00 + .40x$	$3.8x$
c. 1.0 > Index	.30	.70	6	8.00	$8.00 + 4.50x$	$1.2x$

* x is the integral number of units on order *plus* the number of units delivered but unpaid.

**It is difficult to distinguish between this category and the first stage, since there is no way to knowing whether, in the case of new requests, credit was granted without any investigation or a search was made to ascertain past experience. Hence, all requests (a) that were granted credit without any evidence of agency check and subsequent investigations and (b) that had no cards showing past experience were assumed to be granted credit "without investigation."

Customers on whom no files were maintained were assumed to be extended credit without any investigation.[11] New customers were those whose ledger cards were new, and had no previous transactions record. Some of these customers, however, were listed in Dun & Bradstreet "regular" report books. Ratings were assumed to have been checked on these customers.

Customers receiving monthly statements were assumed to have been granted credit on the basis of past experience.

Customers whose files contained "special" D&B reports but had no creditor references were assumed to have been extended credit on the basis of D&B ratings.

Customers whose files did contain creditors' references were assumed to have been extended credit on the basis of these references.

Only in one case were financial statements available. As indicated above, this stage was added purely for illustrative purposes. Hence, values in Table I are fictitious.

There had been no refusal of requests during the two months under observation.

Once the stage at which credit was extended was determined, the average length of the credit period was ascertained from the ledger cards. Also, the files were checked to determine the frequency and nature of collection correspondence.

Formally, a bad debt was recognized three months after a one-month credit period (or four months after shipment). *Actually*, accounts were written off six months after shipment. Hence, the bad-debt period was recognized as six months. Upon this basis, probabilities of payment and non-payment were computed.

Computation of Acceptance and Rejection Costs. Collection cost was based upon the frequency of collection letters, use of stationery and stamps, telegrams (if any), and relevant clerical and supervisory time.

Investment cost was computed on the basis of a 6% interest rate.[12] It is at this rate that the company raised money on the collateral of accounts receivable.

Cost of credit grant and cost of request refusal were computed in the following way:

Acceptance Cost = (Probability of Non-payment) (variable product cost) + average investment cost + average collection cost.

Rejection Cost = (Probability of Payment) (contribution margin).

It should be noted here that as far as the bad debt cost is concerned, only the variable cost is relevant because of its incremental nature (fixed cost is a sunk cost). So far as the investment cost is concerned, the relevant unit cost will be \$10 (and not \$6), since it represents the opportunity cost, where the alternative of discounting or factoring is based upon \$10 value per unit.

The above information is recorded in Table I. Its interpretation is simple. For instance, when a credit request comes in and is granted credit without any kind of investigation, the probability that it will be paid is 0.95, with an average of two months to pay the amount.

Based upon this experience, the acceptance cost will be:

$$\$[(.05)\ (6x) + (.06)\ (2/12)\ (10x) + 1.00] = [1.00 + .40x]$$

where x is the integral number of units

[11] This and subsequent assumptions were necessary since no information was available as to the stage at which each account was granted credit, and the treasurer, who is also credit manager, was reluctant to go over 500 accounts.

[12] Logically, the cost of capital--as suggested in the finance literature--should be used as investment cost. Even though the interest rate has some justification here, it is used solely for the purpose of arithmetic convenience.

on order, *plus* the number of units delivered but unpaid.

Rejection cost, similarly, will be:

$$\$[(.95)\ (4x_1)] = \$(3.8x_1)$$

where x_1 is the integral number of units on order.[13]

Since the rejection cost is larger than the acceptance cost for all $x \geq 1$, the request should *not* be *immediately* rejected.

Mechanism of the Sequential Decision Process. Once we know the category to which a request belongs, we can decide logically whether to extend credit. However, we still do not know whether to seek further information before ultimately accepting or rejecting the request. The following simplified example is used to explain the method for handling this situation.

Suppose the company relies only on past experience, and does not seek agency ratings, other creditors' references, financial statement analysis, etc., as defined above. The company will have two alternatives: (a) to make the decision without taking into account past experience; and (b) to have past experience guide the decision of extending or refusing credit. Assume that investigating past experience costs, on the average, 50 cents worth of clerical time. Now the situation is as shown below.

Immediate refusal is ruled out, since it is more expensive than immediate extension. Now the question is whether to investigate further. Investigation cost is 50 cents--which is, by itself, less than immediate extension cost. Consequently, immediate investigation is not ruled out.

However, this is only one component of investigation costs. We have to make the decision at the second level; and this entails costs that should be reflected in the present investigation.

If previous experience belongs to the *good*, *fair*, or *none* category, the request will be accepted, since rejection cost is obviously too high. If previous experience is poor, we would extend credit only when extension costs

[13] The reason for defining x to include the unpaid account will become obvious when we derive the decision-rule set below. If x includes only the current order, all that a customer has to do is to order one unit at a time--thus avoiding any investigation. This will naturally defeat the purpose of the analysis. On the other hand, when we are considering rejection cost, it will be only to the extent of contribution margin on the request *times* the probability of payment, and not on the unpaid order already executed; hence x_1 includes only the current credit request under consideration. In the subsequent analysis, the assumption of $x = x_1$ will be made for convenience; this assumption implies that there are no unpaid orders already executed, when a credit request is made.

[14] These values do not appear in Table 1. They are assumed here only for this illustration.

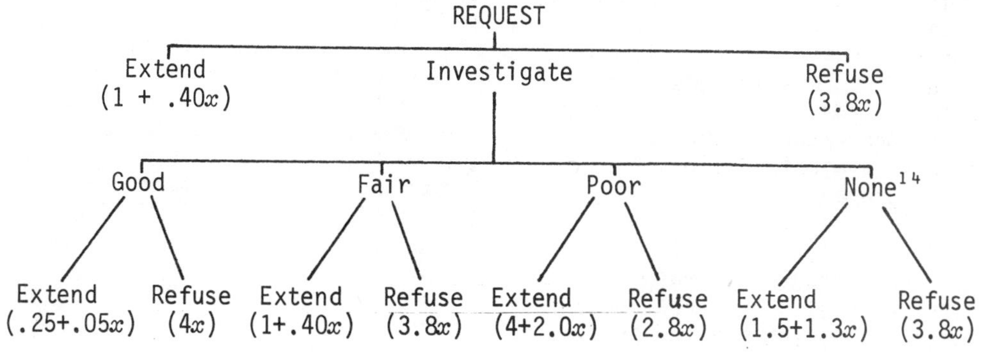

are less than rejection costs, i.e., $4.00 + 2.0x < 2.8x$. This condition would be clearly satisfied for $x > 5$, and thus the request for more than 5 units should be accepted. Similarly, the request for less than 5 units should be rejected. Since $x = 5$ turns inequality into equality, we would be indifferent towards requests for 5 units. Hence, if the request is for more than 5 units, credit will be granted no matter to what category it belongs.

But the question is what will be the cost of accepting at a second level. Here again, past experience is helpful. Assume that our past experience indicates that whenever we have investigated previous dealings, *50%* of the time it has belonged to the category *good*, *30%* of the time to the category *fair*, *10%* of the time to the category *poor*, with new requests composing the remaining 10%.

This implies that if we investigate, our *expected* cost of investigation will be:

$0.50 process cost
$+(.50)\$(.25+.50x)+(.30)\$(1.00+.40x)$
$+(.10)\$(1.50+1.3x)+(.10)\$(4.00+2.0x)$
$=\$(1.48+.475x)$, for $x > 5$;

and $0.50 process cost
$+(.50)\$(.25+.50x)+(.30)\$(1.00+.40x)$
$+(.10)\$(1.50+1.30x)+(.10)\$(2.8x)$
$=\$(1.08+.555x)$, for $x \leq 5$.

Since in either case the investigation cost is higher than the cost of immediately extending credit, i.e., $\$(1 + .40x)$, the request should be granted.

Now we can return to our example with the five-stage investigation process. All we need to know is the process cost of investigation at each stage, and the frequency distribution that Chance determines for each dategory at every stage. This frequency distribution can be determined by finding the proportion of the *number* of requests in each category. In our example, instead, the proportion of the *amount* is the determinant of the frequency distribution. Thus, if there were four requests worth $100, and the amount of requests belonging to the category *good* was $40, *fair* was $30, *poor* was $10, and *new* was $20, the frequency distribution would not be .25 for each category, but would be .40, .30, .10, and .20 respectively. This does distort the picture slightly, since collection cost was computed per request, and not per dollar of request. However, the immense ease of computation at the aggregate level, as will be seen in the next section, seems to compensate for distortion of the present.

To determine the cost of seeking further information at each stage, we have to go to the last stage--financial statement analysis--and progress toward earlier stages. We can demonstrate the proposition in the following way.

Figures I-IV provide the needed information in a decision-tree form. Figure I starts with an incoming request and traces the investigation cost related to the "poor" past experience category. Similarly, Figures II, III, and IV trace costs related to "good," "fair," and "no" (new) past experience categories respectively. Since we are interested in development of investigation cost, let us trace in detail the decision-tree branch belonging to "good" past experience in Figure II.

At the place marked (1) in Figure II, the cost of seeking further information is the sum of the process cost[15] of $1.00 *and* the expected cost of making a rational decision after Chance has made the move. If the index computed is not smaller than 2.5, the rational decision would be to grant the request. Since the likelihood is 1.0 that the index will not be smaller than 2.5, when investigation is carried out at place (1), the expected investigation cost at place (1) will be $\$(1.00 + 0.25 + .05x)$ or

$$\$(1.25 + .05x).$$

---

[15] Process cost is $0.25, $0.30, and $0.50 for processing past experience, agency rating, and creditor references, respectively. Processing cost was assumed to be $1.00 for the fictitious last stage.

Figure I

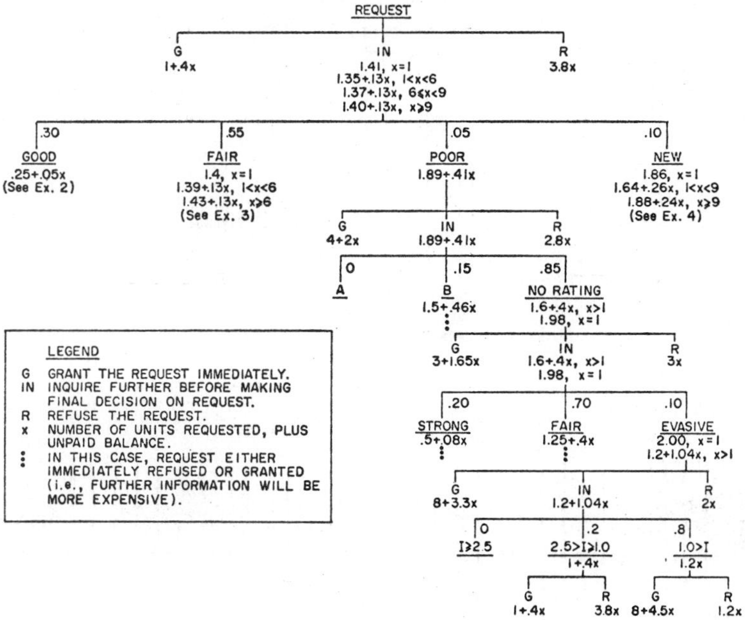

Figure II

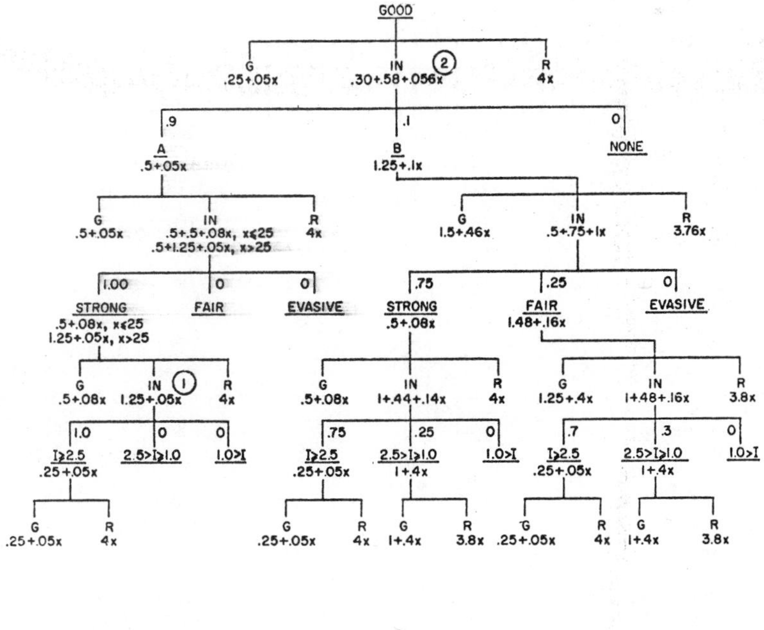

Figure III

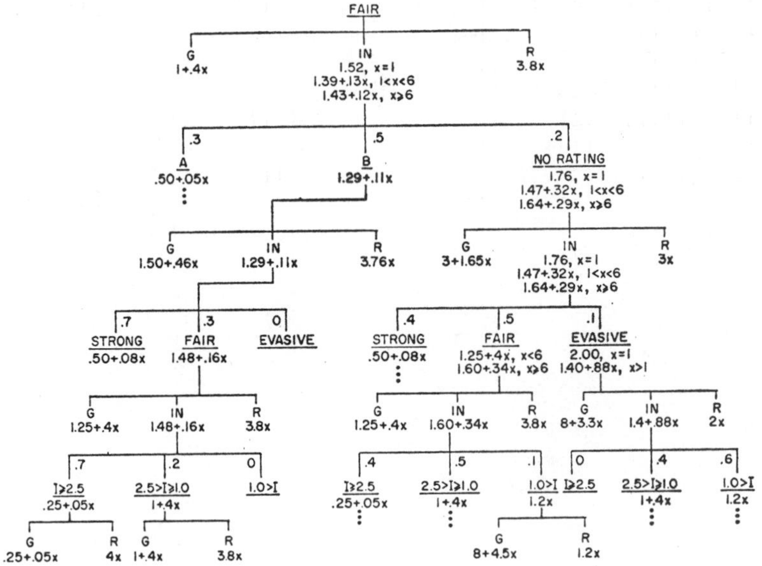

Figure IV

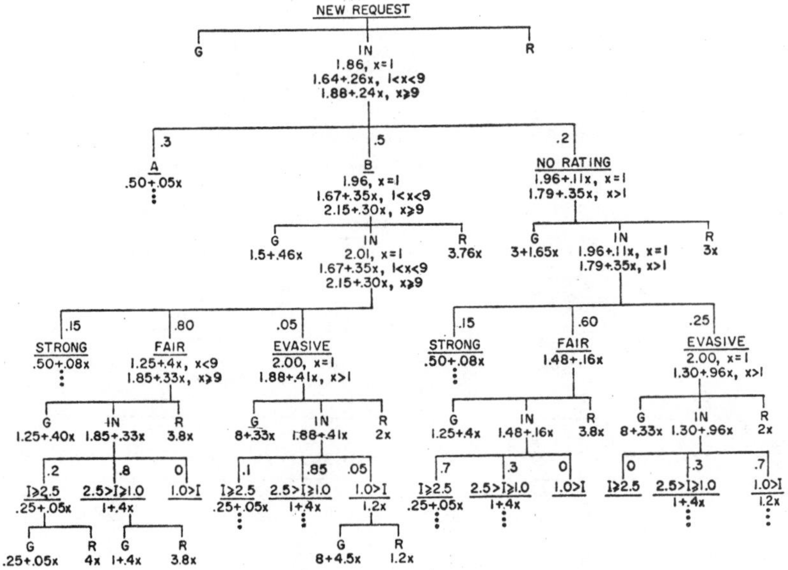

Thus, when the past experience is "good," credit rating is an "A", and references are favorably strong, the expected cost of granting the request is $\$(0.50 + .08x)$ and the cost of carrying further investigation is $\$(1.25 + .05x)$. This implies that further information is worthwhile, if and only if the number of units ordered *and* unpaid exceeds 25.

Now let us explore whether it is worthwhile to investigate further when the past experience is "good," *and* credit rating is an "A". The cost of correspondence for references is $0.50. And in this case, past references were invariably found to be favorably strong. Hence, the expected cost of seeking references is $\$(.50 + .50 + .08x)$, for $x \leq 25$, and $\$(.50 + 1.25 + .05x)$ for $x \geqq 25$. Since the cost of immediately granting credit upon finding "good" past experience and an "A" rating is $\$(0.50 + .05x)$ and thus, less than the expected cost of carrying out further investigation, such investigation is not worthwhile.

We find that a customer with whom the firm had "good" past experience but who has a "B" rating needs to be investigated on the grounds of similar reasoning. The expected cost of investigation and ultimately granting or rejecting the request to such a customer is $\$(1.25 + .10x)$.

Since the customers with whom the firm had "good" past experience have been rated in categories "A" and "B" by the outside agency, there is no need to find the expected cost of the ultimate decision in the case of customers who had "no rating."

Now, going one stage still farther up, we find that at the place marked (2), the cost of getting the agency rating is $0.30. When such investigation was undertaken in the past, it was found that nine times out of ten the "good" customer had an "A" rating, and one time he had a "B" rating. Hence, the expected cost of further investigation at place (2) is:

$$\$(0.30) + .90\ \$(.05x + 0.50) + .10\ \$(1.25 + .10x)$$

or

$$\$(0.88 + .055x).$$

Again, this cost is more than the cost of immediately granting the request, when the past experience is found "good," i.e., $\$(0.88 + .055x) > \$(0.25 + .05x)$. Hence, in this case, it is not worthwhile to investigate further.

Similarly are found costs under categories of "fair," "poor," and "no" experience, as shown in Figures I, III, and IV.

The weighed cost estimate of past experience added to the cost of 25 cents for processing the customer's past record gives us the expected cost of investigation for an incoming request, i.e., $1.41 for $x = 1$, $\$(1.35 + .13x)$ for $1 < x < 6$, and so on. Since this cost is less than the cost of immediately granting a request for credit on orders exceeding on unit, i.e., $\$(1 + .4x) < \$1.41$ for $x = 1$, but $\$(1 + .4x) > \$(1.35 + .13x)$ for $1 < x < 6$ and so on, requests for credit on orders exceeding one unit should be investigated.

Decision Rules

The following set of decision rules for individual credit requests emerges from the above analysis of the sequential decision process.

A. If the order is for exactly one unit, grant the request without further investigation.

B. If the order exceeds one unit, investigate the past experience.

1. When past experience with the customer is *good*, credit should be immediately granted.
2. If past experience belongs to the *fair* category, agency ratings of the customer should be checked. If it belongs to category *A*, no further investigation is needed, and credit should be granted. Otherwise, further in-

vestigation if the form of credit references should be undertaken.

If credit references are *strong*, grant credit. If the rating is *B*, references other than strong require investigation of financial statements. Only if the Linear Discriminate Function (LDF) is *greater than one* should credit be extended.

If there are *no* agency ratings available, *fair* references permit the firm to grant credit up to *five* units. When an order is larger than that or when the references are *evasive*, financial analysis should be undertaken. As above, credit should be granted only if the LDF is *greater than one*.

3. When the past experience is *poor*, an agency rating of *B* permits credit extension; if there is *no* agency rating, an order with *strong* or *fair* references should be granted credit. If references are *evasive*, it is necessary to undertake financial statement analysis. Credit should be granted in that case only if the LDF is *greater than one*.

4. When the firm has had *no* experience with a customer, it should investigate its agency rating. An *A* agency rating allows credit extension without further investigation. Otherwise, credit references are desirable.

Strong references allow immediate credit extension, irrespective of whether there is a *B* or *no* agency rating.

If references are *evasive*, irrespective of whether there is a *B* or *no* agency rating, *or* if references are only *fair*, when there is *no* agency rating available, financial statement analysis should be undertaken.

When financial statement analysis is desirable, credit should be granted only if the LDF is *greater than one*.

One apparent paradox in the decision rules should be noted: credit should be immediately granted when the experience with a customer is *poor*, but the outside agency rating is "B." However, if past experience is *fair* and the outside agency rating is "B," a customer's references should be checked.

This paradox can be resolved by the following reasoning: filtering subsequent to outside agency ratings does not add much pertinent information in the case of *poor* experience. For the category of *fair* experience, when there is a "B" rating, the cost of subsequent filters is less than the expected costs of bad debt and collection upon immediate credit extension.

Stability of the System

Initially, when the system is established, it will not be a final solution. Revisions of estimates, particularly of frequency distributions at various investigation stages, will be necessary. In our example, the frequency distribution of past experience may change, for instance, so as to increase a "fair" category to 5% and decrease a "good" category by 5%.

Such revisions need not be--and usually will not be--violent, since filters do exist at various investigation stages prior to installation of the system, even though they may not be explicit and rational.

Once the system has gone through the initial "learning process," it will achieve equilibrium. This equilibrium will be reflected in the stability of the frequency contributions of various categories at each stage, if the company's cost estimates and the customer's payment behavior are accurate.

If sales are seasonal or cyclical, ti may be desirable to devise rules appropriate for the time period of the year or for the amount of sales. For instance, customers may extend the formal credit period, without bad intentions, during times when sales have hit the bottom and are expected to go up. Hence, credit sales at that level should be expected to be paid in, say, 45 days instead of 30 days. Thus collection letters may be sent from 45th day onward, and the bad debt period may be recognized after, say, 7 months.

Since these modifications are valid only for a limited time or range of sales, we may construct a different set of decision rules that may be preferable to revision of the set applicable at a higher amount or at another phase of the cycle.

In general, our model is based on the assumption of the linear behavior of cost. This assumption is generally reasonable within a certain range. Beyond that range, the assumption, the approximation to linearity, is either not valid or unreasonable. In such cases, a different set of decision rules, based on the different nature of cost estimates, should be relied upon.

Periodical review of the system may be necessary to check its stability and, hence, its effectiveness. Thus we may select a small number of requests according to a pre-determined plan and undertake their detailed investigation. It should be noted that for this purpose, investigation should be carried out for all stages, no matter what may be the category to which the sample requests belong. Thus, a few requests in the sample may belong to past experience with the "good" category. Our decision rule dictates that credit should be extended immediately. In this case, agency ratings, creditors' references, and financial statement analyses should be carried out, since it is necessary to check estimates of costs and frequency distributions of later stages upon which the present decision rule is based.

Since this cost of periodical review will not depend upon the volume of receivables, it may be treated as a fixed cost.

AGGREGATE MEASURES FOR MANAGEMENT CONTROL

The set of decision rules derived in the previous section need not remain constant. Changes in the relevant conditions, initiated by management or otherwise, decrease the effectiveness of rules valid under previous conditions.

An obvious solution is to derive a new set of decision rules. The ability to derive a new set of decision rules, however, presupposes actual knowledge of changed conditions which need not be the case. Hence, there is a need for developing indices--aggregate measures--that flag the attention of management.

Even when changes in conditions are deliberately introduced by management, these indices are useful in that they indicate some of the implications of such intended changes.

Our concern here centers around the financial implications of the cecision rules: the impact on fund flows of volume of receivables, bad-debt experience, and lost sales.

The task of defining fund flows implications of receivables management involves the following phases:

1. Identifying variables whose variations set into motion forces which necessitate changes in the decision rules.
2. Developing aggregate measures that indicate changes in the above-mentioned variables; and
3. Testing the sensitivity of such standards to changes in the variables so as to determine critical variables.

Variables Affecting the System

At the outset, we assume an absence of conscious infringement of rules by lower management that may result in changes in the variables affecting the system. Not that such conduct is insignificant, but such problems are beyond the scope of this work.

The following are the variables whose behavior will affect the decision-rule set:

(a) uncontrollable[16] cost estimates--

[16] The magnitude of control that can be exercised by management depends on the time element. In the long run, investment in fixed assets is controllable. Over a short period of time, such as a day, even wages may be uncontrollable.

interest rate and product cost;

(b) controllable and semi-controllable cost estimates--process costs of investigation and collection;

(c) length of credit period;

(d) bad debt experience;

(e) frequency distributions of various *categories* at different *stages* of the investigation process.

Uncontrollable cost estimates are not a direct concern of credit management.

Processing costs of investigation and collection activities are of significance to credit management. Changes in processing may be at the initiative of credit management. The credit manager may decide to send personal, elaborate, but non-committal replies to requests rejected, instead of impersonal form letters. This may increase the cost of processing.

Changes in processing often are not at the initiative of higher management; nor are they meant to be a conscious infringement of the directions of higher management. Fortunately, processing costs are engineering estimates, and deviations are easily revealed by periodic check-up or are reflected in, for example, increased overtime during a given period.

It is the last three cateferies of variables that are of critical importance to credit management. Credit management is generally evaluated in terms of the average length of credit period (turnover ratio) and the bad-debt experience (bad-debt ratio).

Changes in the average credit period and bad-debt experience often affect the frequency distribution of various *categories* at different *stages* of the investigation process. Frequency distributions, in turn, magnify or diminish the impact of such changes on decision rules and fund flows. For instance, various categories of "past experience" are defined in terms of average credit period. A change in this average period will be reflected in a change in the frequency distribution of the various categories. On the other hand, bad-debt experience in the "poor experience" category may increase from 30% to 40%, and it may decrease from 5% to 3% for the "fair experience" category. In this case, since 55% of the results belong to the "fair" category, and only 5% to the "poor" category, the average bad-debt experience may decrease despite a phenomenal increase in bad-debt experience for the "poor" category.

Aggregate Indices

As mentioned earlier, credit policies affect fund flows through the volume of receivables (or the average credit period, given sales), bad-debt experience, and lost sales. Stringent policies of investigation and collection reduce the volume of receivables and bad debts, but only through increased lost sales. Indiscriminate extension and lax collection procedures result in decreased lost sales but an increased receivables volume and bad-debt level.

Adherence to decision rules, in our example, should result in credit extension for not more than three months. The theoretical aging of accounts which results from such adherence can be found by dtermining the stage at which credit should have been extended.

Let the volume of requests be X dollars, for a given month.[17] No request is assumed to be for one unit only. Perusal of the decision rules in the previous section will indicate at which stage various types of requests should be granted credit. Perusal of the sequential decision charts indicates the proportion of requests at various stages. When these proportions are combined with the appropriate average credit periods given in Table I, we derive the theoretical aging of accounts. Similarly, we can also derive the proportion of refused requests resulting in lost sales. When the proportions, mentioned above, are combined with bad-debt probabilities, instead of

[17] See footnote 13, above.

average credit periods, we are able to determine the bad-debt estimate.

We derive below the three indices in the form of (1) aging of accounts, (2) lost sales, and (3) bad-debt level for the firm in illustration.

1. Aging of Accounts

a. Receivables which will be paid in one month:

(i)	Good = (.30)	.300000X
(ii)	Fair → A = (.55)(.30)	.165000X
	New → A = (.10)(.30)	.030000X
(iii)	Fair → B → Fair → $I \geq 2.5$ = (.55)(.50)(.30)(.70)	.057750X
	Fair → No → Fair → $I \geq 2.5$ = (.55)(.20)(.50)(.40)	.022000X
	New → B → Fair → $I \geq 2.5$ = (.10)(.50)(.80)(.20)	.008000X
	New → No → Fair → $I \geq 2.5$ = (.10)(.20)(.60)(.70)	.009400X
	New → B → Evasive → $I \geq 2.5$ = (.10)(.50)(.05)(.10)	.000250X
	Amount of receivables paid in one month	.591400X

Line 1 in (ii) may be paraphrased as follows: the probability that a request will belong to "fair" category of the past experience *and* to "A" agency rating is (.55)(.30). Once it has an "A" rating, there is no need to investigate this request any further. Thus x times the probability of a request belonging to "Fair" past experience "A" rating will give us the expected amount of payment in one month under one category.

b. Receivables paid in 1.5 months. Whenever references are required and a decision to grant credit has been made upon the basis of strong references, such credit extensions have taken on the average of 1.5 months to pay. Hence:

Fair → B → Strong = (.55)(.50)(.70)	.192500X
Fair → No → Strong = (.55)(.20)(.40)	.044000X
Poor → No → Strong = (.05)(.85)(.20)	. 00850X
New → B → Strong = (.10)(.50)(.15)	.007500X
New → No → Strong = (.10)(.20)(.15)	.003000X
Amount of credit paid in 1.5 months	.255500X

c. Receivables paid in two months. When a decision to extend credit has been made on the basis of fair references or on that of a financial index between the values 1.0 and 2.5, credit has been paid in two months.

Poor → B	= (.05)(.15)	.007500X
Fair → B → Fair → $I \geq 1.0$	= (.55)(.50)(.30)(.30)	.029750X
Fair → No → Fair → $I \geq 1.0$	= (.55)(.20)(.50)(.50)	.027500X
Fair → No → Evasive → $I \geq 1.0$	= (.55)(.20)(.10)(.40)	.004400X
Poor → No → Evasive → $I \geq 1.0$	= (.05)(.85)(.10)(.20)	.000850X
New → B → Fair → $I \geq 1.0$	= (.10)(.50)(.05)(.80)	.032000X
New → B → Evasive → $I \geq 1.0$	= (.10)(.50)(.05)(.85)	.002125X
New → No → Fair → $I \geq 1.0$	= (.10)(.20)(.60)(.30)	.003600X
New → No → Evasive → $I \geq 1.0$	= (.10)(.20)(.25)(.30)	.001500X
	Amount paid in two months	.133975X

2. Receivables Outstanding for Six Months (Request Refused). A financial index less than 1.0 involves a six-month investment. Note that in this case the request will be refused.

Fair → No → Fair → $I < 1.0$	= (.55)(.20)(.50)(.10)	.005500X
Fair → No → Evasive → $I < 1.0$	= (.55)(.20)(.10)(.60)	.006600X
Poor → No → Evasive → $I < 1.0$	= (.05)(.85)(.10)(.80)	.003400X
New → No → Evasive → $I < 1.0$	= (.10)(.20)(.25)(.70)	.003500X
New → B → Evasive → $I < 1.0$	= (.10)(.50)(.05)(.05)	.000215X
	Amount of credit requests refused	.019125X

Thus, according to the above interpretation, if there are requests worth $1 million, requests worth $19,125 will be *refused*.

Out of the other requests granted --for about $981,000--$591,400 will be paid in about a month, and the remaining should be paid by the end of the next month.

3. Bad-Debt Experience. Table I indicates that the probability of default is *0* when credit has been extended upon (i) "good" experience, (ii) agency rating "A," (iii) "strong" references, or (iv) financial index at least as large as 2.5. Note that this enumeration exhausts all the sequences listed above under receivables which will be paid in 1 and 1.5 months.

The probability of default is .06 when credit is extended on the basis of "B" agency rating, and it is .05 when based upon a financial index at least as large as 1.0 but smaller than 2.5. This includes all sequences possible for receivables that will be paid in 2 months.

The aging of accounts shows that .007500X dollars worth of credit will be extended to customers immediately upon discovering an agency rating of "B" following the "poor" experience and .126475X dollars worth of credit will be extended upon finding a financial index at least as large as 1.0, but smaller than 2.5. Hence, bad-debt experience can be estimated as

$$(.0075\ )(.06) + (.126475)(.05)X$$
$$= .006774X$$

since all other sequences of credit granting lead to no defaults or rejection.

In other words, when requests amount to $1 million, bad-debt experience should average $6,774.

In brief, whenever the actual aging of accounts, bad-debt level, and amount of refused requests are different from their estimates (derived in the above fashion), credit management should be concerned.

Of course, the actual values realized for the aging of accounts, bad-debt level, and amount of refused requests will rarely correspond to the estimates derived by the above procedures. Naturally, it is the extent of deviation that is important. This leads us to the third part of our analysis: testing sensitivity of the three indices to changes in the variables, and distinguishing between random and non-random deviations.

Sensitivity Analysis

Only an outline of sensitivity analysis will be sketched, since the procedure underlying such an analysis are similar to those already shown.

Three sets of elements whose estimates will affect the decision-rule set, and through it the indices are:

(a) average credit period;

(b) probability of default;

(c) frequency distribution.

Their estimates are used for each category at different stages.

First, upper and lower limits whould be established for each element with the help of past experience or managerial judgment.

Second, varying only one subset of elements at a time to their extreme limits (provided by the first step), while keeping all other elements constant should enable us to derive a decision-rule set in the manner indicated in the previous section. If this new set is identical with the decision-rule set in practice, another subset of variables should be varied for examination or the third step should be undertaken, if all subsets are exhausted. If the new set is not identical, managerial judgment should be called upon to determine whether changes in the decision rules are significant; if they are significant, these elements should be first observed when the system is suspected to be out of order. The tolerance limits of these "critical" elements may be established by decreasing their extreme limits initially undertaken to the extent of providing the decision-rule set identical to the present set. This process will provide us with the tolerance limits of the particular subset under observation.

Third, the aggregate indices should be computed for tolerance limits of each subset of elements. This will give us the range of permissible values for the indices. Beyond these ranges, management should regard changes as non-random, demanding correction.

Fourth, combinations of various subsets should be made. Their impact on decision-rules and indices should be computed. This enables us to determine critical elements and susceptibility of the system to the changes in such variables. Also, one subset of elements, when combined with another, may have much less impact; in other words, the loss on the one side may be compensated by the gain on the other. Even though this appears formidable, it need not be: first, computers can undertake such calculations in a fraction of time; second, certain combinations are intuitively more important than others. For instance, in our illustration, "good" and "fair" past experience comprises 85% of requests; combinations of both of them with higher agency ratings may be more significant than, say, "poor" experience with "no" agency rating.

In brief, the simulation process can distinguish "critical" elements through their impact on the decision-rule set. At the same time, management can derive the permissible range of receivable volume, bad-debt level, and the amount of requests refused through this process. Periodically, then, actual experience can be compared to these indices so as to determine non-random fluctuations. If fluctuations are non-random, reasons for these deviations should be investigated with particular attention to the subsets of critical elements.

NEED FOR FURTHER RESEARCH

In this paper, an attempt was made to apply the sequential decision theory to routine credit investigation problems. The focus was on the following question: In view of the past experience of a company, what information should be sought before an eventual decision of credit extension or refusal is made. Since management primarily exercises its discretion during the credit-extension phase, and since subsequent phases of credit policy are closely related to this particular phase, attention is naturally focused on credit-extension. The following variables affect the investigation process: bad-debt level, length of the credit period, amount of collection expenditure, and level of lost sales resulting from refusal of requests and rigorous collection measures.

The *overall* impact of credit extension policy on the subsequent phases of credit policy is measured through reversal of the above process. Thus the operating decision rules and indices for control are logically derived.

The proposed approach effectively employs past experience, and provides unambiguous operating procedures. It does so without jeopardizing the managerial prerogative of policy formulation and changes in it. However, by itself, it does not provide the optimal framework. In the first place, improvement stems from past experience, and only in the long run will the approach be optimal. Second, some significant aspects of credit policy are ignored--the most relevant being discount policy.[18] More important, the behavioral aspect of implementing changes and policy formulation in the broader framework of investment scheme and control are ignored. In this sense also the suggested approach does not provide an answer. It can only be an initial step toward an integrated framework of financial policy formulation.

APPENDIX

The investigation process devised to derive Table I was carried on as follows:

1. Monthly aging statements for two consecutive months (ending on March 31 and April 30 of 1964) were available. From the first, accounts with initials A to M (inclusive) and from the second, accounts with initials N to Z (inclusive) were selected; the totals of the accounts were 305 and 209 respectively. Upon inspection, it was found that three General Electric plants and nine Sears, Roebuck stores were treated as separate, independent accounts for convenience. Since the purpose of the present study is risk determination of an account, General Electric plants were grouped together, as were Sears stores. For convenience in computation, two accounts (which were the last ones) from the first list were dropped so as to bring the total of accounts in that list to 300.

The file on each account was checked. Criteria given above in the section *Criteria for Determination of Categories* were observed in determining the stage at which credit was extended. For example, when there was no file on an account, credit was assumed to have been extended without any investigation. The following distribution was found:

	First Group	Second Group	Average Percentage
No investigation	45	37	16
Past experience	78	46	25
Ratings	138	72	42
Creditor references	39	45	17

2. Ledger cards were checked so as to determine the date of shipments. Early in November, 1964, ledger cards of all accounts were again checked. Dates of payment on transactions under observation, and hence, the credit period, were ascertained. Customers who were sent monthly statements or who placed an order before paying the prior

[18] Rationalizations may be offered for rigid adherence to the industry practice of discounting: quick competitive reprisal, low profit margins, inability to maintain an informal nature (as in the case of length of credit period) of discount policy, insignificant number of customers taking advantage of discount. A combination of these factors may make a flexible discount policy unpalatable to management.

one were assumed to be paying in the same order. Sometimes a payment was made which covered fully some orders but only partially the others; in such cases the following procedure was adopted. Assume that goods worth \$100 were shipped to a customer on March 1, 1964 and goods worth \$200 shipped on April 1, 1964. The customer made the first payment of \$200 on May 1, 1964 and \$100 on June 1, 1964. In this case, the length of the credit period was:

(a) 1st order
2 months (March 1-May 1)

(b) 2nd order
½ 1 month (April 1-May 1),
½ 2 months (April 1-June 1)
Average: 1.5 months

(c) Average credit period
½(1.5 + 2) = 1.75 months

3. An account was written off after six months (or, as is the practice now, handed over to the credit insurance company, even though the contract terms require handing it over upon expiration of a credit period of four months). The following table was prepared, with the numerator the number of accounts written off and the denominator the total number of accounts in that category.

Collection activities are comprised of:

(i) A form-letter requesting payment after one month of credit period;
(ii) one or two other similar form-letters every month subsequently;
(iii) personal letters (or letter) if prior experience is poor, or in case of a new account with poor rating or not strong references, or both;
(iv) telegrams, telephone calls (if in vicinity) if previous steps are not effective.

Cost of the form letters was based upon two elements: clerical time and use of stationery. Clerical time spent in typing the address and mailing the correspondence was 5 minutes at the rate of \$2.00 per hour and the cost of the form letter, envelope, and stamp was \$0.07. For convenience, the total cost was estimated as \$0.25.

Cost of personal letters involved supervisory time in dictation. The average time for this was 5 minutes at the rate of \$5.00 per hour. Clerical time increased to 8 minutes. Stationery cost dropped to \$0.55. The total cost was slightly less than \$0.75 but was estimated, for convenience at \$0.75.

ACCOUNTS NOT PAID WITHIN THE CREDIT PERIOD OF 6 MONTHS

	First Group	Second Group	Total
1. *No Investigation*	2/45	2/37	4/82
2. *Past Experience*			
a. Good	0/31	0/15	0/46
b. Fair	2/40	1/19	3/59
c. Poor	1/7	4/12	5/19
d. New	-	-	-
3. *Agency Rating*			
a. A	0/22	0/12	0/34
b. B	6/80	2/45	8/125
c. No	8/36	5/15	13/51
4. *Creditor References*			
a. Strong	0/11	0/15	0/26
b. Fair	0/20	2/20	2/40
c. Evasive	4/8	6/10	10/19

Cost of telegrams and telephone calls was difficult to ascertain, since only partial records were available. Managerial judgment was thus relied upon for average estimates for each category at various stages.

The following table was derived:

COLLECTION EXPENSES

	Form Letter	Personal Letters	Telegrams and Telephone Calls
1. *No Investigation*	$0.25	$0.75	$--
2. *Past Experience*			
a. Good	0.25	--	--
b. Fair	0.25	0.75	--
c. Poor	0.25	1.50	2.25
d. New	--	--	--
3. *Agency Rating*			
a. A	0.50	--	--
b. B	0.25	0.75	0.50
c. No	0.25	1.50	1.25
4. *Creditor References*			
a. Strong	0.50	--	--
b. Fair	0.50	0.75	--
c. Evasive	0.25	1.50	6.25

REFERENCES

1. Beckman, Theodore, *Credit and Collections: Management and Theory*, McGraw-Hill, New York, 1962.
2. Beranek, W., *Analysis for Financial Decision*, Irwin, Homewood, Ill., 1963.
3. Cyert, R.M., Davidson, H.J. and Thompson, G.L., "Estimation of the Allowance for Doubtful Accounts by Markov Chains," *Managerial Science*, Vol. 8, No. 3 (April 1962).
4. Lindsay, R., and Sametz, A., *Financial Management: An Analytical Approach* (rev. ed.), Irwin, Homewood, Ill., 1967
5. Schlaifer, Robert, *Probability and Statistics for Business Decisions*, McGraw-Hill, New York, 1959.
6. Thompson, L., and Langer, L.C.R., *A Study on Measurement of Credit Department Effectiveness*, Credit Research Foundation, New York, 1954.
7. Weston, J.F., and Brigham, E.F., *Managerial Finance* (2nd ed.), Holt, Rinehart and Winston, New York, 1966.

READING 24

Analysis of Credit Extensions in a World with Uncertainty

Thomas E. Copeland
University of California, Los Angeles

Nabil T. Khoury
Laval University

The problem of deciding the size of a credit line to be extended to a new customer involves not only the difference between expected gains and losses but also the effect of the credit extension on the riskiness of the lending firm. A line of credit should be extended only if the expected return is sufficiently large to compensate shareholders for the additional risk they are taking. Therefore, receivables policy is analogous to asset expansion decisions.

Part I is a brief review of the literature on receivables policy. Part II identifies the marginal costs associated with credit extension. Part III develops a one-period model which yields the required rate of return on a new credit line. The required rate of return determines the maximum line of credit which can be extended so that the value of the firm does not decrease. If the acceptable line of credit is greater than or equal to that requested by the customer, then the credit request should be granted. Otherwise, it should be rejected. Part IV summarizes the argument and draws conclusions.

I. A BRIEF REVIEW OF THE LITERATURE ON RECEIVABLES POLICY

Parallelling the rapid increase in credit sales, various models related to the management of receivables have been developed in the last two decades. From a theoretical viewpoint, these models could be roughly divided into two groups depending on whether they deal with the *techniques* of credit extension or with the *theory* of credit expansion. The first group of models is addressed mainly to operational questions such as the screening of credit applicants, monitoring the collection of receivables and providing for bad debts. The second group emphasizes the risk-return characteristics of credit expansion as viewed in a capital budgeting framework.

On the techniques of credit extension, Beranek [1] has investigated the optimal discount rate that would maximize profits and has

This paper has not been published previously. Reprinted by permission of the authors.

used discriminant analysis to classify customers into risk classes mainly on the basis of their past liquidity and debt ratios. In the same vein, Boggess [3] has also used discriminant analysis to develop an index of creditworthiness for applicants mainly on the basis of their personal characteristics. Using partial equilibrium analysis, Wrightsman [9] has attempted to analyze credit terms. He studied the impact of a) the interest rate to be charged to credit customers, and b) the period of credit on expected sales, expected receivables, and expected profits. The purpose of his analysis is to find the optimal interest rate and credit period that would maximize net profits (i.e., after deducting the cost of carrying receivables and credit charge income). Regarding the problem of monitoring receivables, Lewellen and Edmister [7] have suggested a scheme based on detecting changes in customers' payment patterns. Their scheme boils down to a matrix notation of the percentage of receivables still unpaid at any given date relative to the time when they originated. This technique focuses on the rapidity of conversion of credit sales into cash. Finally, to provide for bad debts, Cyert, Davidson, and Thompson [4] have suggested the use of Markov chains to estimate at a certain date the percentage of credit that will still be outstanding one period hence. The provision for bad debts can then be calculated as a proportion of the estimated unpaid credit.

There are, of course, many other models in the literature dealing with the techniques of credit extension. The above-mentioned examples, however, provide an adequate overview of the approaches which have been adopted in this respect. For the purposes of this paper, such an overview is sufficient.

Fewer models deal explicitly with the theory of credit expansion, and until now none of these have adopted a capital asset pricing model framework. This is somewhat surprising because credit decisions are basically short-run and therefore fit well into the one period assumptions under which the capital asset pricing model is derived. Friedland [5] has argued that risk should be considered along with return (or net gain) when a credit sale is analyzed. He used the standard deviation as a measure of risk without justifying this choice on theoretical grounds. Furthermore, he did not address himself to the question of how to explicitly combine risk and return to reach an efficient investment decision. Bierman [2] has presented a dynamic analysis of credit expansion based on risk-return characteristics, but again his work has not been framed on the modern theory of capital asset pricing.

II. MARGINAL COSTS OF CREDIT EXTENSION

The marginal costs of credit extension are interpreted here to be those undertaken when extending credit to a new account. Examples of such costs are extra credit department expenses created by the need for special credit checks, extra sales commissions paid to salesmen who bring in the new account, and delinquency expenses which may be incurred.

Bad debt expenses, a priori, cannot be attached to specific accounts. Instead, as will be demonstrated in Part III, they are reflected in the mean and variance of the firm's end-of-year receipts. Hence, it is appropriate to charge a risk premium to customers of greater risk. The specification of this risk premium will be seen to arise from usage of the market price of risk as determined by the capital asset pricing model.

The timing of credit expenses is important. Extra credit department expenses such as clerical and secretarial time are usually incurred shortly before the credit line is extended. Sales commissions are paid at the same time as the credit extension. However, delinquency expenses such as the cost of phone calls, reminders, and personal visits occur after the credit line has been outstanding for some time. They can therefore be considered proportional to the fraction of credit sales which become delinquent.

III. DETERMINATION OF THE APPROPRIATE CREDIT POLICY

To simplify matters, assume a one-period world with no taxes. At the beginning of the period, the firm produces a certain quantity of output, Q_1 (which it sells at price P), and incurs fixed and variable production costs (F and b respectively). The firm also pays sales commissions and extra credit costs, a, which are expressed as a percent of nominal sales, PQ_1. At the end of the period, the firm has uncertain collections, $P\tilde{Q}_2$ on the amount of goods sold, and pays delinquency expenses, $\tilde{e}$, which are a proportion of $P(Q_1 - \tilde{Q}_2)$, the delinquent amount.[1] Note that Q_1, must, by definition, be greater than or equal to $\tilde{Q}_2$.[2]

Figure 1 shows the timing of the cash flows in a one-period model. In order to simplify the notation, let M be the markup on sales

$$(1) \quad M = \frac{PQ_1 - bQ_1 - F}{PQ_1} = \frac{(P-b)Q_1 - F}{PQ_1}$$

Because of anti-trust laws and other institutional constraints, we assume that M does not vary with the creditworthiness of the customer under consideration. Therefore, M is not a decision variable. Let C_j be the dollars of credit extended to customer j. The maximum line of credit can be found by equating the present value of the outlays with the present value of the profits

$$\underbrace{C_j(1-M) + aPQ_{j1}}_{\text{Time 0}} = \underbrace{\frac{P\tilde{Q}_{j2} - eP(Q_{j1} - \tilde{Q}_{j2})}{1+\tilde{R}_j}}_{\text{Time 1}}$$

$\tilde{R}_j$ is the rate of return on the jth line of credit which is C_j dollars with expected revenues of $P\bar{Q}_{j2}$ dollars. Note that the rate of return is a random variable because $\tilde{Q}_{j2}$ is random.

FIGURE 1. The Timing of Cash Flows

Beginning of period = 1	End of period = 2

F = fixed costs
bQ_1 = variable costs
aPQ_1 = marginal credit expenses and sales commissions
$P\tilde{Q}_2$ = uncertain revenues
$eP(Q_1 - \tilde{Q}_2)$ = uncertain delinquency expenses

[1] It is possible that delinquency expenses will affect the amount collected, $\tilde{Q}_2$. For the sake of simplicity, we have assumed that $e(Q_1-\tilde{Q}_2)$ is independent of the expected value of $\tilde{Q}_2$. Two other interpretations of delinquency expenses are (1) that delinquent receivables are factored at a constant fraction of their value or (2) that all of the uncollected amount is written off, in which case $e \geq 1$.

[2] The implicit assumption is that there are no receivables left outstanding from the previous period.

The analysis proceeds by solving for the maximum line of credit, C_j, which satisfies a required rate of return, $\tilde{R}_j^*$. If the amount of the purchase, PQ_1, is less than the maximum line of credit, C_j, the credit request should be granted, otherwise not. Hence we are dealing with a [0, 1] decision variable. Note that the return on investment is simply the expected cash inflow at the end of the period divided by the cash outlay at the onset. The outlay is really the cost of goods sold plus administrative costs. The smaller this outlay is relative to the dollars of sales it is expected to generate, the larger the line of credit can be.

Of course, the decision of whether or not to grant credit to a customer will depend on the relationship between the maximum line of credit and the dollar amount of the purchase requested. At the margin the maximum line of credit will just equal the amount requested. In these cases the marginal *expected* rate of return on investment, $E(\tilde{R}_j)$, will equal the market determined *required* rate of return, R_j^*, for projects of the same risk class. The credit should be extended if the expected rate of return, $E(\tilde{R}_j)$, is greater than or equal to the required rate, R_j^*.

$$(2) \quad E(R_j) = \frac{P\bar{Q}_{j2} - eP(Q_{j1} - \bar{Q}_{j2})}{C_j(1 - M) + aPQ_{j1}} - 1 \geq R_j^*$$

The maximum line of credit then is

$$(3) \quad C_j \leq \frac{P\bar{Q}_{j2} - eP(Q_{j1} - \bar{Q}_{j2}) - (1+R_j^*)aPQ_{j1}}{(1+R_j^*)(1-M)}$$

$$= \frac{P\bar{Q}_{j2}(1+e) - PQ_{j1}[e+a(1+R_j^*)]}{(1+R_j^*)(1-M)} .$$

Customers who seek to purchase more than the maximum should have their request refused.

For the sake of exposition, assume a company that sells all its products on credit. A customer wishes to purchase 10,000 units (Q_{j1}) at \$100 a unit. The end-of-period distribution for $\tilde{Q}_{j2}$, the number of units to be sold, has a mean of 10,000 units and a standard deviation of 814 units.[3] Delinquency expenses (e) are estimated at 4%, fixed costs of production (F_j) at \$200,000, variable costs (b) at \$60 per unit, and initial credit costs (a) are 3%.

If the required rate of return is 25%, the maximum line of credit will be \$962,500. At \$100 per unit this is 9625 units, hence the maximum credit extension is less than what the customer requests (10,000 units), and therefore the credit request should be refused.

Up to this point there has been no mention of how to adjust the required rate of return so that it is appropriate given the riskness of the customer. Therefore, the analysis proceeds by using the market information about the price of risk provided by the capital asset pricing model.

Assume, for the sake of simplicity, an all equity firm. The return on equity, before considering the new customer, is

$$(4) \quad \tilde{R}_e = \frac{P\tilde{Q}_2 - bQ_1 - F}{S}$$

where S is the market value of the equity. Should the firm allow a line of credit, the return on equity becomes

---

[3] Because the distribution of $\tilde{Q}_2$ has a finite upper bound of Q_1 and a finite lower bound of zero, the distribution of $\tilde{Q}_2$ is only approximately normal. However, a firm with many receivables decisions, all of different size, might rely on central limit effects resulting from the sums of non-normal distributions to view the class of receivables decisions as being normally distributed.

$$(5)\quad \tilde{R}'_e = \frac{P(\tilde{Q}_2 + \tilde{Q}_{j2}) - bQ_1 - F - eP(Q_{j1} - \tilde{Q}_{j2}) - C_j(1-M) - aPQ_{j1}}{S}.$$

Therefore the change in the expected return on equity can be found by taking the expectations of (4) and (5) and subtracting.

$$(6)\quad E(R'_e) - E(R_e) = \frac{P\bar{Q}_{j2} - eP(Q_{j1} - \bar{Q}_{j2}) - C_j(1-M) - aPQ_{j1}}{S}.$$

It is necessary to equate the change in the *expected* rate of return on equity with the change in the *required* rate of return for projects of the same risk in order to determine the line of credit. The capital asset pricing model (CAPM) can be used to determine the required rate of return.[4] It is usually expressed as

$$(7)\quad E(\tilde{R}_j) = R_f + [E(\tilde{R}_M) - R_f]\,\frac{\mathrm{Cov}(\tilde{R}_j, \tilde{R}_M)}{\sigma^2(\tilde{R}_M)}$$

where

$E(\tilde{R}_j)$ = the expected rate of return on the jth risky asset (in our case the equity of the jth firm)

$E(\tilde{R}_M)$ = the expected rate of return on a value-weighted portfolio of all risky assets

R_f = the one-period rate of return on a riskless asset

$\mathrm{Cov}(\tilde{R}_j, \tilde{R}_M)$ = the covariance between the return on the jth asset and the return on the market

$\sigma^2(\tilde{R}_M)$ = the variance of return on the market.

The required rate of return, $\tilde{R}^*$, *before* the new line of credit is considered is (an asterisk is used to designate required rates of return):

$$E(\tilde{R}^*) = R_f + \frac{E(\tilde{R}_M) - R_f}{\sigma^2(\tilde{R}_M)}\,\mathrm{Cov}(\tilde{R}^*, \tilde{R}_M)$$

and since the covariance is

$$\mathrm{Cov}(\tilde{R}^*, \tilde{R}_M) = E\left[\left(\frac{P\tilde{Q}_2}{S} - \frac{P\bar{Q}_2}{S}\right)(\tilde{R}_M - \bar{R}_M)\right]$$

$$\downarrow \qquad = \frac{P}{S}\,\mathrm{Cov}(\tilde{Q}_2, \tilde{R}_M),$$

the required rate of return can be rewritten as

$$E(\tilde{R}^*) = R_f + \frac{E(\tilde{R}_M) - R_f}{\sigma^2(\tilde{R}_M)}\,\frac{P}{S}\,\mathrm{Cov}(\tilde{Q}_2, \tilde{R}_M).$$

The required rate of return *after* the new line of credit is $\tilde{R}^{*\prime}$.

$$(8)\quad E(\tilde{R}^{*\prime}) = R_f + \frac{E(\tilde{R}_M) - R_f}{\sigma^2(\tilde{R}_M)}\,\mathrm{Cov}(\tilde{R}^{*\prime}, \tilde{R}_M)$$

and since the covariance is

$$\mathrm{Cov}(\tilde{R}^{*\prime}, \tilde{R}_M) = E\left[\left(\frac{P\tilde{Q}_2 + P\tilde{Q}_{j2} + eP\tilde{Q}_{j2} - ePQ_{j1} - C_j(1-M) - aPQ_{j1}}{S} - \frac{P\bar{Q}_2 + P\bar{Q}_{j2} + eP\bar{Q}_{j2} - ePQ_{j1} - C_j(1-M) - aPQ_{j1}}{S}\right)(\tilde{R}_M - \bar{R}_M)\right]$$

$$= E\left[\frac{P}{S}[(\tilde{Q}_2 + (1+e)\tilde{Q}_{j2}) - (\bar{Q}_2 + (1+e)\bar{Q}_{j2})](\tilde{R}_M - \bar{R}_M)\right]$$

$$= \frac{P}{S}\,\mathrm{Cov}(\tilde{Q}_2, \tilde{R}_M) + \frac{P}{S}(1+e)\,\mathrm{Cov}(\tilde{Q}_{j2}, \tilde{R}_M),$$

the required rate of return can be rewritten as

$$(9)\quad E(\tilde{R}^{*\prime}) = R_f + \frac{E(\tilde{R}_M) - R_f}{\sigma^2(\tilde{R}_M)}\,\frac{P}{S}[\mathrm{Cov}(\tilde{Q}_2, \tilde{R}_M) + (1+e)\,\mathrm{Cov}(\tilde{Q}_{j2}, \tilde{R}_M)].$$

Subtracting (8) from (9) yields the change in the required rate of return.

[4] The CAPM assumes frictionless capital markets with homogeneous investor expectations, zero bankruptcy costs, and riskless borrowing and lending. In addition, we have assumed an all equity firm. The reader who is interested in extending the results into a world where corporations are levered with risky debt is referred to Rubinstein [8], or Hamada [6].

$$(10)\quad E(\tilde{R}^{*\prime}) - E(\tilde{R}^{*}) = \frac{E(\tilde{R}_M) - R_f}{\sigma^2(\tilde{R}_M)} \frac{P}{S} (1+e) \operatorname{Cov}(\tilde{Q}_{j2}, \tilde{R}_M).$$

The change in the *expected* rate of return on equity must equal the change in the *required* rate of return for projects of equal risk. Therefore, equating (6) and (10) gives a solution for the line of credit, C_j.

$$\frac{P\bar{Q}_{j2} - eP(Q_{j1} - \bar{Q}_{j2}) - C_j(1-M) - aPQ_{j1}}{S} = \frac{E(\tilde{R}_M) - R_f}{\sigma^2(\tilde{R}_M)} \frac{P}{S} (1+e) \operatorname{Cov}(\tilde{Q}_{j2}, \tilde{R}_M).$$

$$(11)\quad C_j = \frac{P\bar{Q}_{j2} - eP(Q_{j1} - \bar{Q}_{j2}) - aPQ_{j1} - \lambda P(1+e)\rho(\tilde{Q}_{j2}, R_M)\sigma(\tilde{Q}_{j2})}{1-M}$$

where

$$\lambda = \frac{E(\tilde{R}_M) - R_f}{\sigma(\tilde{R}_M)}$$

$$\operatorname{Cov}(\tilde{Q}_{j2}, \tilde{R}_M) = \rho(\tilde{Q}_{j2}, \tilde{R}_M)\sigma(\tilde{Q}_{j2})\sigma(\tilde{R}_M)$$

$\rho(\tilde{Q}_{j2}, \tilde{R}_M)$ = correlation between collections and market return.

Equation (11) may be rewritten as

$$(12)\quad C_j = \frac{P\bar{Q}_{j2} - eP(Q_{j1} - \bar{Q}_{j2}) - aPQ_{j1} - [E(R_M) - R_f]P(1+e)\beta_{j2}}{1-M}$$

where

$$\beta_{j2} = \frac{\operatorname{Cov}(\tilde{Q}_{j2}, \tilde{R}_M)}{\sigma^2(R_M)}.$$

An analysis of (11) and (12) reveals that the maximum line of credit increases with the profit margin, M, and the expected collections $\bar{Q}_{j2}$. It decreases with increasing costs of extension, a, and collection, e; and as the covariance of collections with the state of the economy increases.

The example which was started earlier can be used to show that firms with lower covariance with the economy (lower systematic risk) are more likely to receive credit. Suppose that the customer in question has a business with cash flows correlated .783% with the economy. The expected rate of return on the market is 14% with a standard deviation of 2.5% and the risk-free rate is 6%. Given these facts, as well as those mentioned earlier, the maximum line of credit is approximately 9625 units, and the credit would be refused. However, if the firm had a correlation coefficient of only .4 [of course this means that his systematic risk is also lower since

$$\beta \equiv \frac{\rho(\tilde{Q}_{j2}, \tilde{R}_M)\sigma(\tilde{Q}_{j2})}{\sigma(\tilde{R}_M)}],$$

the maximum line of credit would increase to 10,875 units and the credit request would be accepted.[5] Therefore, customers who have lower covariance with the economy are more likely to receive credit.

Expression (11) could serve as a guideline for the credit policy of the firm whenever it deals with a new credit request. The firm should take on additional credit risk so long as the expected increase in total profit minus the increase in the associated expected credit expenses is greater than the relevant risk premium. That risk premium is determined by the added magnitude of the dispersion of collections that would result from the acceptance of the additional credit account and by the correlation of collections with the economy. These parameters are both included in the covariance of $\tilde{Q}_{j2}$ with the economy. In a sense then, expression (11) could be viewed as the firm's demand function for additional credit customers belonging to lower risk classes.

It should be noted that credit expenses are usually fixed for a wide range of variations in credit sales. The profit margin on goods sold is also usually fixed over the relevant range of production. To decide on an additional credit sale, the firm must estimate the impact of the new credit extension on the dispersion and correlation of total collections. The greater these parameters are, the higher will be the required rate of return, and hence the lower will be the line of credit that should be extended.

In order to operationalize the decision rule implied by equations (11) and (12), it is necessary to measure $\mathrm{Cov}(\tilde{Q}_{j2},\tilde{R}_M)$. This is the covariance between the uncertain payment and the return on the market portfolio. Because trade credit is an unsecured debt obligation which in bankruptcy has lower priority than (among other things) taxes due and payments to holders of secured debt, a good proxy for the covariance in question would be the covariance between the cash flows after interest and taxes for the creditor firm and the return on the market portfolio. Note also that the relevant stream is for the firm as a whole rather than a particular line of business. This is true because the unsecured trade credit is a claim on the assets of the firm as a whole, hence in the event of overdue payments, cash flows other lines of business in the firm may be used to fund trade credit in the jth line of business.

SUMMARY AND CONCLUSIONS

The premise of this discussion has been that receivables should be considered as an investment rather than the passive consequence of sales. From this viewpoint, the extension of credit and its recuperation is an operation which should be planned and controlled with great care in order to avoid its becoming a source of financial weakness to the firm.

Before investing in receivables, the enterprise should evaluate the impact of such an action upon its overall financial position. Credit should be extended up to the point where the expected rate of return just equals the market-determined required rate of return for the firm with its new risk. This risk is seen to arise out of the product of the firm's correlation with the market and the new standard deviation of revenues resulting from taking on questionable accounts.

---

[5] Alternatively, one can operationalize the credit acceptance decision by using (2) and (6) to rewrite (11) as a required rate of return

$$(11')\quad R_j^* \geq \frac{S\left[\frac{E(\tilde{R}_m)-R_f}{\sigma^2(\tilde{R}_m)}\,\frac{P}{S}(1+e)\,Cov(\tilde{Q}_{j2},\tilde{R}_m)\right]}{C_j(1-M)+aPQ_{j1}}$$

If the expected rate of return on the right-hand side of (11') is less than the required rate of return, the project should be rejected.

REFERENCES

1. W. Beranek, *Analysis for Financial Decisions*. Homewood, Illinois: Richard D. Irwin, Inc., 1963, Ch. 10.
2. H. Bierman, Jr., *Financial Policy Decisions*. New York: The MacMillan Co., 1970, Ch. 3.
3. W. P. Boggess, "Screen-Test Your Credit Risks." *Harvard Business Review*, Vol. 45, No. 6 (November-December 1967).
4. R. M. Cyert, H. J. Davidson, and G. L. Thompson, "Estimation of the Allowance for Doubtful Accounts by Markov Chains." *Management Science*, Vol. 8 (April 1962), pp. 287-303.
5. S. Friedland, *The Economics of Corporate Finance*. Englewood Cliffs, N.J.: Prentice-Hall, Inc., 1966, Ch. 4.
6. Robert S. Hamada, "Portfolio Analysis, Market Equilibrium and Corporation Finance." *The Journal of Finance* (March 1969).
7. W. G. Lewellan and R. O. Edmister, "A General Model for Accounts Receivable Analysis and Control." *Journal of Financial and Quantitative Analysis*, Vol. 8, No. 2 (March 1973).
8. M. Rubinstein, "A Mean-Variance Synthesis of Corporate Financial Theory." *Journal of Finance* (March 1973), pp. 167-181.
9. D. Wrightsman, "Optimal Credit Terms for Accounts Receivable." *Quarterly Review of Economics and Business*, Vol. 9, No. 2 (Summer 1969). Reprinted in K. V. Smith (ed.), *Management of Working Capital*. St. Paul, Minn.: West Publishing Co., 1974, pp. 101-108.

SECTION V
Inventory Management

Though it is the least liquid of the firm's current assets, inventory represents an essential component of working capital for most business firms. The problem of its management is complicated by the varying nature and use of inventory within the firm, and the many different cost components and other variables which must be considered. In contrast to the management of either cash or accounts receivable, all functional areas of the typical business, directly or indirectly, are affected by inventory decision making. It is not surprising, therefore, that far more has been written on inventory management than on the management of other current assets. This section on inventory management contains six readings.

The first three readings are concerned with appropriate policies for acquiring and holding inventory. Snyder (Reading 25) sets forth clearly the cost tradeoffs that are inherent in deciding how to replenish the firm's inventory. Specifically, he focuses on the economic order quantity relationships that have received considerable attention in the literature. After pointing out that for many firms a small number of inventory items account for a large percentage of total inventory values, the author goes on to discuss the ordering, holding, and shortage costs associated with inventory. Snyder argues that the optimal order quantity, which minimizes the sum of such costs, may be on a relatively flat segment of the total cost curve. Solution to the inventory problem thus is effectively a range instead of a single point, and the order quantity can be selected within that range to facilitate the production scheduling activity of the firm.

In 1956, Magee published a series of three important papers on inventory management. The second paper in that series is included here (Reading 26). It expands on the usual cost balancing formulation that is based on rather restrictive assumptions about demand and delivery times. Magee also shows how safety stocks can be used to greatly reduce the variability in production schedules, and thereby enhance the firm's overall profitability. The author shows by example and case study the complexity of production scheduling and inventory control, and how greater improvements can be made as the scope of the analysis is broadened.

Austin (Reading 27) reports on an economic order quantity approach to military procurement. In particular, he shows how a team of graduate students, faculty, and military personnel were able to develop guidelines for soliciting price discounts from suppliers that resulted in potential savings of millions of dollars. An interesting part of the project was in working around the considerable constraints that exist in military procurement. Austin argues that the actual implementation of an improved system is an important part of the total project.

The next two readings of this section are important by virtue of how they capture interrelationships between inventory and other working capital accounts. Schiff (Reading 28) uses aggregate statistics for manufacturing companies to suggest that control of inventory has been better than control of accounts receivable. He believes that this may be due to better models for inventory control, to different responsibilities within the firm, to credit managers not considering all relevant costs associated with receivables policy, and particularly to the fact that inventory and receivables are not considered together. He illustrates briefly how carrying costs for both inventory and receivables should be included in an economic comparison of alternative marketing plans.

Beranek (Reading 29) also recognizes the potential problem of suboptimization within the firm. His focus is on how financing considerations inherent in holding inventory may distort the use of the traditional economic order quantity models. Beranek argues that the loan repayment schedule should be explicitly considered in conjunction with the cash inflows both from purchasing materials and in selling inventory. This means that collections from customers and disbursements to suppliers become additional variables in the inventory problem. This paper thus identifies interfaces between inventory and receivables as part of current assets, and accounts payable and short-term bank borrowing as part of current liabilities.

The paper by Shapiro (Reading 30) also considers both inventory and receivables, but it adds the important dimension of foreign exchange. Specifically, it considers the financial implications to firms whose business activities include international divisions or subsidiaries. The author uses linear and dynamic programming methods to develop the conditions whereby firms should purchase raw materials or grant credit in the face of continuing inflation, or under the threat of current devaluation.

READING 25

Principles of Inventory Management

Arthur Synder
Behr-Manning Company

INTRODUCTION

"Why are we always out of stock?" Behind this question lies one of the most perplexing problems facing businessmen today. They are confronted with the dilemma of attempting simultaneously (1) to meet ever-increasing demands for improved customer service, (2) to maintain stable production operations, and (3) to keep the investment in inventory at a reasonable level. As a result, during the past decade we have seen a great deal of interest and attention devoted to the subject of inventory management. Unfortunately, considerable doubt and confusion still exist as to what the basic tools of inventory control are, where they come from, and how they should be used.

It is the purpose of this study to analyze the development and application of the principles of inventory control. In discussing these techniques, it is often necessary to use concepts and terminologies which might be foreign to many businessmen. It is impossible, however, to acquire a sound knowledge of these principles without becoming familiar with the fundamental tools upon which they are based.

Hundreds of articles have been written on this subject. Unfortunately, very few provide the reader with anything but generalizations. The contents of this study, therefore, should not be looked upon as either an academic exercise in mathematics or a review of clever clerical devices which can help shortcut the labyrinth of confusion. Properly understood, these concepts will help the businessman make better policy decisions, which in turn will generate more useful and satisfying procedures. As such, these techniques are worth some time and thought, commensurate with the importance of inventory policy in your business operation.

Included is a new theory on economic ordering quantity (EOQ) which shows how the EOQ can be interpreted as a quantity range rather than a fixed quantity. It is current practice rigidly to adhere to the specific quantity obtained by using the EOQ formula.

Reprinted from FINANCIAL EXECUTIVE, Vol. 32, No. 4 (April 1964), pp. 13-21, by permission of the publisher.

Deviations are made only under the assumed penalty of increased inventory costs. This myth will be exposed, and it will be shown that the EOQ can be interpreted as a quantity range imparting flexibility to the production and inventory control system.

THEORIES OF INVENTORY CONTROL

Particular attention must be given to acquiring a thorough knowledge of the three fundamental concepts which form the foundation of any sound inventory control system:

1. Classification: What to control.
2. Order point: When to make or buy.
3. Economic lot size: How much to make or buy

Let us briefly examine each of these concepts to see how it is derived and adapted to practice.

CLASSIFICATION: WHAT TO CONTROL

The purpose of classification techniques is to provide a means whereby inventory control efforts can be directed toward those areas in which they can be most effective. On items of small value, it is seldom justifiable to use the same close and detailed control that is applied to high-valued or critical items. If you do, you may be spending more to keep these low-valued items within a prescribed limit than a slight excess in inventory might cost, or you are stealing time from controlling those items that require close policing.

Studies have shown that the average manufacturing company has an inventory which is distributed as to number of items and dollar value as shown in Table I.

Table I

Group	No. of Items	Inventory Value
A	15%	70%
B	30	20
C	55	10
	100%	100%

As shown, group A contains only 15 percent of the physical number of items, but represents 70 percent of the total inventory value. It is logical to assume that the more valuable items merit greater attention. This can be accomplished by giving them an A rating and reviewing these items more often. This system is often referred to as the "ABC analysis of inventory."

Other factors, which are just as important as dollar value, to consider when developing a classification plan include the frequency and quantity of demand for an item, its rate of obsolescence, and whether it is a critical item, the lack of which would create a serious inconvenience to the company or a customer. In short, the development of a sound method of classification and record keeping is the first step toward improved inventory control.

ORDER POINT (OP)

The order point (OP) equation is a tool for evaluating the factors affecting the question: "When should I make or buy?" The purpose of the order point is to signal when the inventory level of a particular item has reached the point where, based on forecasted usage, it will be completely exhausted during the time required to manufacture or produce a replenishment stock. The equation is:

$$\text{Order Point (OP)} = S(P - L) + F\sqrt{SQ(P - L)}$$

S = Sales or usage
L = Lead time
Q = Units per demand
F = Stockout acceptance factor
P = Production or procurement cycle

The definitions of the variables used in the order point equation are included in the Appendix.[1] These schedules should be studied carefully, as it is important that the individuals responsible for the development of an inventory control program thoroughly understand the tools they are about to use.

It is the function of the order point to optimize the two opposing conditions of minimizing the inventory investment while satisfying demand and reducing the possibility of stockouts to an acceptable level. While, in theory, it is desirable never to have a stockout, for all practical business applications a certain level of stockouts must be planned for and tolerated. Stockouts are the result of fluctuations in usage from the forecasted level. These fluctuations are intensified for those items which have large variations in their usage (Q) or in the average number of units per demand (S).

In order to allow for these fluctuations in the demand pattern, the order point equation provides for the addition of safety stock. The determination of how much safety stock is required to establish an acceptable stockout level is based on the application of a formula known as the "square root approximation of the Poisson distribution." Statistical studies have shown that there is an acceptable correlation between the fluctuations in an average industrial demand pattern and the Poisson distribution. If the fluctuations for a given industry or product line are abnormal, the formula will break down under testing, and modifications to the value of the stockout acceptance factor (F), as it relates to the percentage of stockouts, will be required. These situations can occasionally be anticipated by testing the order point with historical data.

Almost every business requires some safety stock; the amount is largely determined by competitive practices and demands of the trade. Weighing the cost of additional inventory against the loss of a sale and customer goodwill is an important inventory policy decision. It is possible to develop a formula which equates (1) the loss resulting from a stockout in terms of either a lost sale and/or customer goodwill to (2) the cost to carry the additional inventory necessary to prevent the stockout. Such a formula, however, has proven to be quite theoretical and impractical. The problems to resolve are: What portion of the safety stock is responsible for the stockout; what percentage of the stockouts result in an actual lost sale; what is the value of customer goodwill, etc.? The general practice is, or should be, to establish an OP using tentatively agreed-upon safety stock limits and adjust the latter based on experience and desired objectives.

A common mistake made in the administration of the OP is the practice of releasing a stock replenishment order (when the OP is reached) for a lot size as determined by the EOQ without giving consideration as to whether or not the remaining stock balance is significantly below the OP. For example, an item has a current OP of 100 units and an EOQ of 50 units. The present stock balance of 140 units is reduced to 80 units by orders for 60 units. Many inventory systems would trigger off a stock replenishment order of 50 units (instead of 70 units), ignoring that 20 units are needed to restore the stock balance to the OP.

The result is usually frequent stockouts. To correct this situation, the OP's are raised, which in turn increases the inventory levels. These factors naturally generate dissatisfaction with the system. The practice of rigidly adhering to the EOQ is based on the assumption that the EOQ is a specific quantity and any deviation will result in increased inventory costs. As will be shown later on, the EOQ under

[1] An analysis of the derivation of the equation, as well as other material, is available in booklet form from the Behr-Manning Company, Troy, N.Y.

most conditions can be interpreted as a rather broad quantity range, thereby imparting flexibility to the inventory control system.

Another implied condition, but worthy of emphasis, is that the administration of the OP should carefully distinguish between items "in stock" and items "in process." Using the previous example, after release of a 70-unit stock replenishment order, the 150 units of stock would be distributed as follows: 80 units in stock and 70 units in process. An order for 50 units would reduce the stock balance to the OP and require the release of another stock replenishment order. The number of units in stock, however, has been reduced to a dangerously low level of 30 units; and the system should automatically "flag" this condition to permit, if deemed necessary, one of the previous stock orders to be expedited through production to avoid the possibility of a stockout condition. If possible, all in-process orders should show the date released, or the expected date of completion.

ECONOMIC ORDERING QUANTITY (EOQ)

The determination of order quantities is primarily a matter of economics. By increasing the size of an order, we reduce the unit cost because we spread the one-time production and/or procurement costs over a larger number of units. On the other hand, there are factors which argue for limiting the lot size, such as the increased inventory investment, higher inventory carrying charges, and a greater risk of obsolescence and spoiled work.

The economic ordering quantity equation (or EOQ, as it is more frequently called) provides a means whereby the several factors affecting the cost of a unit can be evaluated simultaneously to determine which lot size will generate the lowest unit cost for a given set of conditions. This familiar equation takes the following form:

$$\text{EOQ} = \sqrt{\frac{2SO}{RU} + \frac{PSO}{U} - \frac{O}{U}} \cong \sqrt{\frac{2SO}{RU}}$$

S = Sales or usage
O = Ordering costs
U = Unit costs
R = Investment factor
P = Production or procurement cycle

The simplified version of the EOQ formula is sufficiently accurate for most business applications, as the last two functions do not significantly contribute to the final value of the EOQ.

As previously emphasized, the development of a sound inventory control program requires that the responsible individuals be thoroughly familiar with the basic theories involved. By itself, the EOQ formula is meaningless unless we understand the function of the factors it is based upon and what assumptions are used in its derivation.

EOQ RANGE THEORY

There are two misconceptions concerning the use of the EOQ formula for determining economic ordering quantities: (1) that the EOQ is a specific quantity and (2) that a small deviation from this specific quantity substantially increases the total cost per unit. The implied inflexibility of the EOQ has always been a source of concern to those individuals charged with the responsibility of managing the inventory control system. In actual practice, it is often necessary to release a lot size which is greater or less than the EOQ. These deviations from the EOQ are usually reluctantly approved because it is believed there will be a significant increase in the total unit cost. We shall show that for all practical purposes the EOQ can be interpreted as a quantity range within which can be realized the minimum total unit cost.

ADVANTAGES OF EOQ RANGE

The ability to interpret the EOQ as a range of quantities, rather than a specific quantity, has many advantages. In general, it imparts flexibility to the inventory and production control system, permitting desired adjustments to the ordering quantity without the fear of increased cost. Deviations from the EOQ might be prompted by one of the following reasons:

√ Less than EOQ. The use of ordering quantities less than the EOQ is often prompted by conditions such as the desire to reduce work-in-process inventory, fear of product obsolescence when the EOQ exceeds more than 6-12 months' supply, conservative adjustment to an optimistic sales forecast, or the desire to smooth out the production load by staggering the release of several small lot sizes.

√ More than EOQ. Those situations which pressure for the release of ordering quantities larger than the EOQ are (1) to permit an adjustment of the production load by providing work during a temporary slack period; (2) to build inventory in lieu of anticipated loss of normal capacity due to material shortages, strike, or heavy vacation periods; or (3) to make up for shortages between the stock balance and the OP.

Other types of adjustments include the desire to modify the EOQ to utilize the full capacity of a machine or to facilitate handling. Whatever the reason may be, there is general agreement that a system which is flexible within controlled limits is preferred over an inflexible system. The latter often creates more problems than it solves.

EOQ FORMULA

The assumption that the EOQ is a specific quantity and any deviation from this quantity increases the total cost per unit stems primarily from the popular concept that cost per unit, plotted as a function of the ordering quantity, results in a curve with a distinct minimum point, as shown in Figure I. The implied unity of the EOQ point is further supported by the EOQ formula, which provides only one answer for any given set of data.

Figure I

TOTAL COST CURVE*

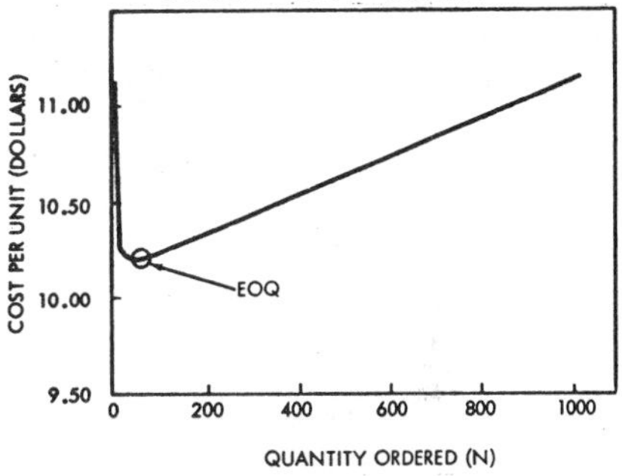

*Data based on Case Problem--Widgets.

Let us direct our attention to Figure II, which represents an enlargement of the area new the EOQ point in Figure I. Figure II shows that what appeared to be a distinct minimum point in Figure I is really a flat portion of the curve which extends on either side of the specific EOQ point. It

Figure II

ENLARGED SECTION OF TOTAL COST CURVE*

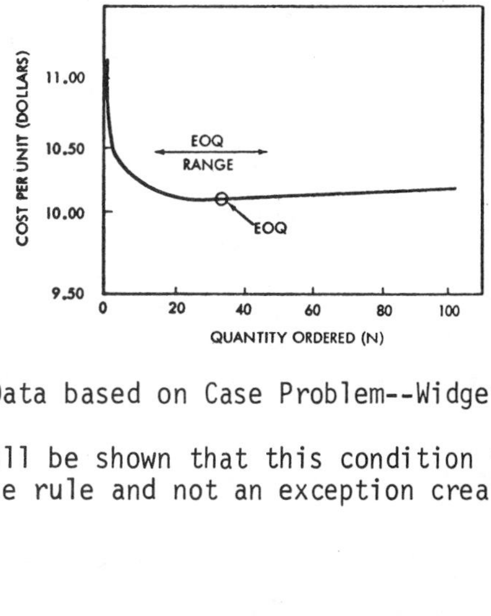

*Data based on Case Problem--Widgets.

will be shown that this condition is the rule and not an exception created by the data chosen for the illustration.

Based on the above example and an understanding of the mathematical derivation of the EOQ formula, two observations can be made: (1) The EOQ is a precisely determined point on the total cost curve, and (2) this curve has an extremely long and flat portion at the theoretical minimum cost (or EOQ) point. What we intend to prove, therefore, is that the EOQ is not a specific point, but a section of the total cost curve. This section represents the economic order quantity range which will provide the same minimum total cost per unit as the specific EOQ.

CASE PROBLEM

To illustrate this point clearly, let us use a case problem choosing fairly representative data for the variables involved. Suppose the XYZ Company manufactures Widgets and the necessary production and inventory control data for this product are as shown in Table II.

Table II

Symbol	Definition	Value
S	Sales volume	100 per month
P	Production cycle	1 month
O	Ordering costs	$1
U	Unit cost	$10 each
R	Investment factor	24% per year
L	Lead time	½ month
Q	Units per demand	5
F	Stockout acceptance	10% (1.29)

Based on the given data and respective formulas, the inventory control procedure for this product would be to establish an order point (OP) of 70 units and a lot size (EOQ) of 32 units.

$$\text{OP} = S(P - L) + F\sqrt{SQ(P - L)} = 70 \text{ units}$$

$$\text{EOQ} = \sqrt{\frac{2SO}{RU}} = 31.6 \text{ units}$$

We are satisfied with the determination of an order point (OP) of 70 units. As explained, the OP is primarily a function of our sales forecast and the production cycle. To the minimum OP of 50 units, we have added a buffer stock of nine units to reduce the probability of stockout to 10 percent and 11 units to adjust the OP for the fact that we average five units per order. We recognize that the latter may have to be adjusted based on actual experience.

The lot size of 32 is interpreted as the most economic manufacturing quantity based on the given values of S , O, R, and U. It is implied that a deviation from this quantity will result in a significant increase in the total cost per unit. Rather than accepting this statement, let us actually examine the effect on the total unit cost (TUC) as the ordering quantity is increased or decreased from the EOQ of 32 units. The equation for calculating the TUC for a given quantity (N) is as follows:

$$\text{TUC} = \left[\frac{O}{N} + U\right]\left[1 + \frac{RP}{2} + \frac{RN}{2S} - \frac{R}{2S}\right]$$

Substituting the given data for Widgets, the total cost per unit as a function of the ordering quantity (N) simplifies to:

$$\text{TUC} = \$10.10 + \frac{\$1.01}{N} + \$0.001\,N$$

Using the above expression, the total cost per unit for lot sizes from one to 1,000 is shown in Table III. These data were also used for plotting the graphs shown in Figures I and II.

EOQ VERSUS COST

The function of the EOQ formula is to provide an answer to the question: "What ordering quantity will generate the minimum total cost per unit?" Using the data chosen for our case problem, the EOQ is calculated as 31.6 units, which results in a minimum total

Table III

Order Quantity(N)	Total Cost per Unit Exact	Total Cost per Unit Nearest Cent
1	$11.1101	$11.11
5	10.3061	10.31
10	10.2101	10.21
15	10.1814	10.18
20	10.1696	10.17
25	10.1645	10.16
EOQ = 31.6	10.1627	10.16
40	10.1644	10.16
45	10.1665	10.17
55	10.1725	10.17
60	10.1759	10.18
75	10.1876	10.19
100	10.2092	10.21
200	10.3042	10.30
300	10.4025	10.40
500	10.6011	10.60
1,000	11.1011	11.10

cost of $10.16 per unit. If we look at Table III, however, we find that this is the minimum cost only if we extend the value to four positions after the decimal, or $10.1627. Any lot size between the quantity range of 25-40 has a total variable cost of $10.16 when rounded off to the nearest cent.

This quantity range is not clearly evident if we inspect Figure I, which represents the universal impression of what the total cost curve looks like. Due to the large quantity range used for the X axis, the curve appears to have a distinct minimum point or EOQ. As previously discussed, if we enlarge the section of the curve near the EOQ as shown in Figure II, we readily see what the unit cost figures tell us: The curve near the EOQ point is almost flat. The EOQ is merely the precisely calculated low point of this flat section. Hence, for most conditions the EOQ can be considered a range of quantities rather than a specific quantity.

Let us carry these observations to a further conclusion using our case problems for illustration. The management of the XYZ Company desires to impart flexibility to the ordering quantities of its new product, Widgets. It is agreed that 32 units is the theoretical quantity that will produce the minimum total cost per unit, but it is recognized that the values of the variables chosen for calculating the EOQ are not necessarily exact. Management is willing, therefore, to work within an EOQ range that does not exceed one half of 1 percent of the theoretical minimum total cost per unit. An increase of one half of 1 percent over the minimum cost of $10.16 would extend the acceptable cost range to $10.21. On this basis, instead of an EOQ of 32 units, sales and production management could gear their operations to the release of lot sizes which vary from 10 to 100 units.

EOQ VERSUS COST RATIO

The EOQ formula can be thought of as a function of sales volume (S), investment factor (R), and cost (O, U). The equation, when separated in this manner, appears as follows:

$$\text{EOQ} = \sqrt{\frac{2SO}{RU}} = \sqrt{S \times \frac{2}{R} \times \frac{O}{U}}$$

When viewed in this manner, it becomes evident that it is the ratio of ordering to unit costs (O/U), rather than their absolute values, which determines the EOQ. For example, in the case problem we chose a value of $1 for ordering costs and $10 for unit costs, giving a ratio of 1:10. For the same values of S and R, any combinations of absolute values for O and U which maintain the same 1:10 ratio will result in the same EOQ, as shown in Table IV.

It is often difficult to establish accurate and acceptable ordering and unit costs. The interpretation of these costs as a ratio, rather than as individual absolute amounts, can serve as a very useful approach to handling the cost aspect of the EOQ formula. The use of a cost ratio (O/U) establishes the proper relationship between the two costs. For instance, if the unit cost

Table IV

Variable	Examples #1	#2	#3
S(month)	100	100	100
R(year)	24%	24%	24%
O	\$ 1.00	\$ 5.00	\$ 2.20
U	\$10.00	\$50.00	\$22.00
$K = O/U$	0.1	0.1	0.1
EOQ	32	32	32

for an item is \$22, there is no need to fret over whether the ordering cost is \$2.00 or \$2.20. The effect on the cost ratio, and hence on the EOQ, is insignificant. Further, it often simplifies the problem of how much variable overhead cost should be added to each cost. If overhead is a percentage addition to each cost, then it can be ignored, as it will not change the ratio. Another advantage to the cost ratio approach is that it permits products with similar cost ratios to be grouped and handled with the same inventory control charts and procedures.

EOQ VERSUS SALES VOLUME

Under most conditions, once the cost ratio (O/U) and investment factor (R) have been determined and agreed upon for a given product, they can be considered constant unless involved in a major cost change. This therefore reduces the EOQ formula to the function of one true variable--sales volume.

In the case problem, we chose a sales volume (S) of 100 units per month and arrived at an EOQ of 32 units and an EOQ range of 10-100 units for the control limit on one half of 1 percent increase in minimum total variable cost. Table V shows the effect on the EOQ and EOQ range for changes in the sales volume (S) from one to 250 units per month. The EOQ was calculated using the standard EOQ formula, and the EOQ range was determined by substituting the value T = 0.005 for the control limit of one half of 1 percent. If a control limit of one tenth of 1 percent were desired, a value of T = 0.001 would be used.

Table V

Sales Volume (S)	EOQ	EOQ Range (+ ½%)
1	3	2-5
5	7	4-13
10	10	4-20
20	14	6-32
30	17	7-42
50	22	8-61
75	28	9-86
100	32	10-105
250	50	12-214

Table V shows that for the given data of the case problem, the EOQ range is significant for all levels of sales volume. When the forecasted sales volume drops to five per month, a quantity range of four to 13 units provides the same minimum cost as the EOQ of seven. At a forecasted sales volume of 250 units per month, the EOQ is 50 units, but the same minimum cost will be realized for any lot size within the limits of 12 to 214 units. Working within the EOQ range, the production control manager could stagger the release of lot sizes to fit a daily, weekly, or monthly schedule if such is desired.

APPLICATION OF EOQ RANGE THEORY

At this point a criticism could be made by the practitioners of production and inventory control that the availability of an EOQ range complicates the problem, as it introduces a decision as to what lot size to use, whereas previously the choice was limited to a specific EOQ. If this is a problem, then the solution lies in a well-defined management policy describing the procedure to follow in determining the proper lot size. To explore some of the ways the EOQ range can be adapted to practice, let us return to our case problem of Widgets.

Figure III

CASE PROBLEM: EOQ RANGE CURVE

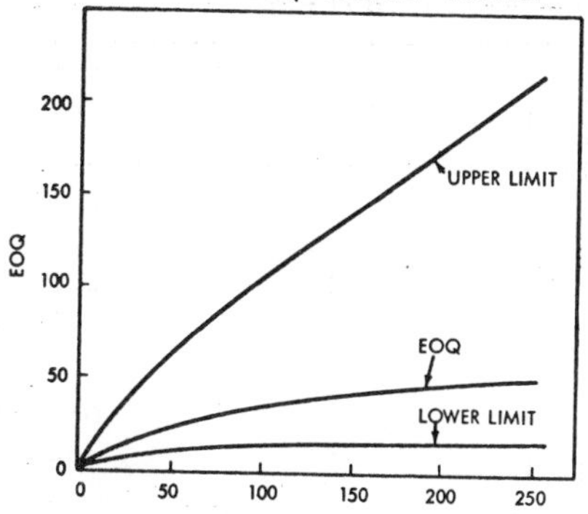

Figure III shows one way in which the EOQ range, as a function of sales volume, can be represented graphically for easy reference. In a similar manner, Figure IV shows a graph of the order point as a function of sales volume. The order point is shown with and without the addition of safety stock, the latter being based on a 10 percent stockout acceptance level. Using these graphs, which could be combined, variations in management policy concerning the inventory control of Widgets could be introduced.

Figure IV

CASE PROBLEM: ORDER POINT CURVE

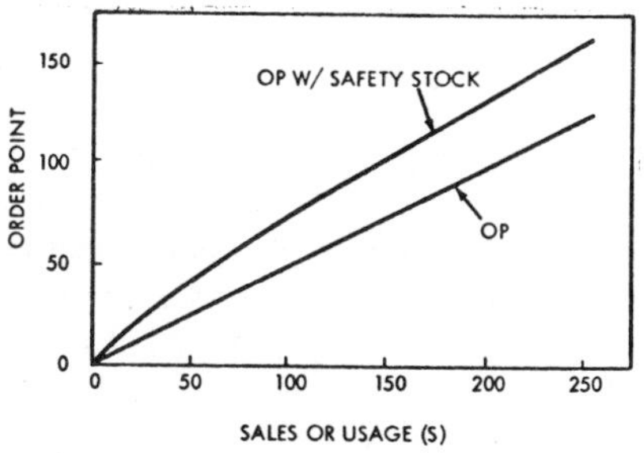

1. During the initial stages of introducing the product to the market, the EOQ lot size will be standardized at 20 units. The release of small lot sizes is desired by the factory to minimize spoilage usually associated with a new product and reduce the possibility of building excess inventory in case sales do not reach forecasted volumes. An OP of 50 units will be established, which represents the order point for sales (*S*) of 100 units per month without the addition of safety stock.

2. After the production "bugs" have been worked out, the EOQ will be increased to 50 units and the OP to 70 units, provided the forecasted sales volume and buying pattern materialize.

3. Since this is a seasonal item with peak demand during the fourth quarter, additional inventory will be built in the third quarter by increasing the lot size to the maximum level (105 units for forecasted sales of 100 units per month).

4. As the product matures or obsolescence is feared, the OP could be reduced by eliminating the safety stock and reducing the lot size to 20 units.

The important conclusion to draw from the above discussion is that management, by reference to charts or graphs of this type, could establish some simple rules which would effectively control the production of this product.

CONCLUSION

Interpretation of the EOQ as a quantity range rather than a specific quantity is an important concept to understand in the formulation of your inventory control program. It will provide the line organization responsible for the day-to-day management of your inventories with the flexibility they must have to meet the demands placed on the system by daily production and sales problems.

PURCHASE QUANTITY

Occasionally, you will hear a purchasing agent or distributor ask the question: "The EOQ formula is fine for advising the manufacturer how much to make, but can we use it to determine how much to buy?" The answer to this question is a very definitely yes.

$$EOQ = \sqrt{\frac{2SO}{RU}}$$

S = Sales or usage
R = Investment factor
O = Ordering costs
U = Unit costs

The EOQ formula shown above is applicable to both manufacturing and purchasing situations. The Appendix provides a thorough analysis of how each variable used in the EOQ equation is evaluated, depending upon whether the item is manufactured or purchased.

QUANTITY DISCOUNT

A common practice in industry today is the quantity discount, which is used to encourage buyers to place larger orders. Many suppliers offer a discount schedule wherein the discount increases with the number of units ordered. The result is a variable unit cost for the item which is dependent on the quantity ordered. This problem does not exist for the manufacturer, as his unit cost (U), as defined and used in the EOQ formula, can usually be considered constant. This brings us to the question: "How are the quantity discount and the resulting variable unit cost recognized in determining the EOQ for purchased items?"

The procedure for handling a quantity discount in the EOQ formula is not difficult, particularly if we analyze the problem and break it down into its logical components. The effect of a quantity discount is to produce several unit costs for the same item. These unit costs are dependent on the order quantity, which determines the applicable discount. For each unit cost, we can calculate an economic order quantity using the EOQ formula. The optimum order quantity will be the largest EOQ, provided it falls within the quantity range upon which the unit cost and respective discount are based. Let us use an example to illustrate this.

A company has a monthly usage of 100 units of item A which can be purchased according to the discount schedule shown in Table VI. Assume the company has an established procedure for determining purchase order quantities based on the use of the EOQ formula and the following data are applicable to item A:

Investment factor (R) = 24% per year
Ordering costs (O) = \$1.20 per order
Unit costs (U) = Net purchase price per unit *plus 20%* for inventory-carrying costs, taxes, handling, insurance, inspection, etc.

Table VI

Purchase Quantity	Discount	Net Purchase Price per unit
a) 1-9	--	\$10.00
b) 10-49	10%	9.00
c) 50-99	25	7.50
d) Over 100	40	6.00

Using the above data and sales (S) of 100 units per month, we can calculate the respective EOQ's for the four unit costs provided by the discounts schedule (see Table VII).

As shown in Table VII, the four EOQ's vary from 32 to 41. The optimum EOQ is 34, as it is the largest EOQ which falls within its respective purchase quantity range (10-49). Theoretically, the EOQ of 36 cannot be used, as it is based on a unit cost of \$9.00, which can be realized only if the order quantity is for 50-99 units. For the same reason, the EOQ of 41 cannot be used, as its unit cost of \$7.20 requires an order quantity of 100 or more units.

Table VII

	(a)	(b)	(c)	(d)
Monthly sales (*S*)	100	100	100	100
Investment factor (*R*)	24%	24%	24%	24%
Ordering costs (*O*)	\$ 1.20	\$ 1.20	\$1.20	\$1.20
Unit costs (*U*)	\$12.00	\$10.80	\$9.00	\$7.20
EOQ	32	34	36	41
Purchase quantity*	1-9	10-49	50-99	Over 100

* Purchase quantity required to obtain net purchase price per unit upon which unit cost (*U*) is based.

CONCLUSION

The above procedure is shown for those who wish to apply an exact and rigorous method to the determination of an EOQ for purchased items, the net price for which is determined by a quantity discount schedule. Although the above example is based on a single set of conditions, it supports the conclusion that very little is gained by this detailed probing of the problem. All four of the EOQ's which range from 32 to 41, are within the discount bracket established by a purchase quantity of 10 to 49 units. Based on an expanded series of similar examples, it can be shown that the typical quantity discount schedule has no significant effect on the EOQ. At best, recognition of a purchase quantity discount will increase the order quantity only to the next discount bracket.

An easy solution to this problem is to base the purchase order quantity on an evaluation of the EOQ range for the item and the respective discount schedule.

Here, then, is another valuable use for the EOQ range formula. By interpreting the order quantity as a range rather than a specific amount, judgment can be used in selecting and optimizing an available purchase quantity discount schedule.

SUMMARY

The universal question we all seek to answer is: "What is an optimum inventory level?" The problem of answering this question is compounded by the fact that within a management group there are usually several conflicting opinions. The sales manager will not tolerate stockouts. The factory manager desires long manufacturing runs and stable employment. The treasurer feels that a minimum of working capital should be tied up in inventories.

Many companies blame their inventory problems on a large volume of small orders for diversified products. "We inventory 100,000 items." "Our sales forecasts are too general." "We're really a job shop." Each company feels that its problems in this respect are unusual. Refuge, however, cannot (and should not) be taken behind this smoke screen. These problems are shared by most manufacturers today. If it is not apparent in some companies, perhaps the answer lies in the fact that their managements have been able to minimize the problem.

The key to good inventory control primarily rests in sufficient knowledge of the fundamental techniques to develop enough self-confidence to permit their practical adaptation to the specific needs of the company. Many programs are defeated before they start by imposing upon the group responsible for the execution of the program a "bag of tools" in the guise of mysterious mathematical equations and unique concepts. Seldom is any attempt made first to educate the group on how to use these new tools. The result is distrust of the techniques, poor application, and eventual confusion when things get worse rather than better.

In establishing or improving upon inventory control procedures, it is important to remember that the following fundamentals largely determine the degree of your success:

1. The order point (OP) is singularly the most significant factor affecting your inventory control procedure, as it establishes your inventory levels. Hence, it determines your investment in inventories and your ability to provide satisfactory customer service. Careful attention must be given to the development of your order point procedure. Despite the several factors involved in the formula, remember it is primarily dependent on the accuracy of your sales or usage forecast.

2. The EOQ is usually given far too much emphasis; and often a disproportionate amount of time is spent worrying about unit costs, setup costs, and the investment factor. Keep in mind that these factors are not involved in determining your order point. The only factor common to both the OP and the EOQ is the sales or usage variable. As already shown, the EOQ under most conditions can be interpreted as a broad quantity range.

It is perhaps appropriate to close this article with a reminder that regardless of how sophisticated your inventory control techniques, the results will be no better than the day-to-day data fed into the system. Before embarking on any elaborate inventory control program, be sure your accounting and record-keeping procedures can provide the system with current and reliable data. The bottleneck in most inventory control procedures is data input and utilization. It is in this area that we have seen many successful applications of data-processing equipment.

A modern inventory control program affects all phases of your business; therefore, it must be an integral part of your business operation. The degree of success of an inventory program depends largely on how well management conceives the problem, formulates its policy, and executes the program.

APPENDIX

This schedule contains a discussion of the eight basic variables used in the ordering point (OP) and economic ordering quantity (EOQ) equations. In relating specific data to these variables it is most important to recognize the dimension of these variables as discussed in the last section of this schedule.

S = Sales or Usage

This represents the forecast of future sales or usage. How far into the future the forecast is made is dependent primarily on the production or procurement cycle and the characteristics of the sales pattern. The usual practice is to make a forecast of from three to six months, normally through the projection of historical data. Sales forecasting is at best an inexact science, but every effort should be made to develop the very best possible projections.

P = Production or Procurement Cycle

This is the total elapsed time normally required to procure or manufacture the unit. In determining this time cycle, it should start when the decision is made that additional units are required and end with their delivery to the stock room of customer. If there are significant fluctuations in the time cycle, the effect on the order point should be tested for the probable extreme ranges of the cycle.

O = Ordering Costs

These are the variable costs associated with the manufacture or procurement of the lot size which are independent of the quantity. A typical list of these costs includes variable labor and expenses for purchasing, receiving, accounting, planning and manufacturing setup.

U = Unit Costs

This includes the variable costs related to the production or procurement of each unit, such as the manufacturing cost or net purchase price per unit. To this must be added inventory carrying costs per unit for space, taxes, handling, insurance, inspection, etc.

K = Cost Ratio

K is the ratio of ordering costs (*O*) to unit costs (*U*) or $K = (O)/(U)$.

K = Investment Factor

The function of the investment factor is to provide a rate of return on the inventory investment (before taxes) which is commensurate with the risks and costs associated with the business, such as obsolescence, cost of working capital, and spoiled work. In actual application, different interest rates can be used depending on the degree of risk involved. Factors which should be considered in evaluating the degree of risk are type of product, reliability of the sales or usage forecast, working capital requirements, etc.

L = Lead Time

Lead time can be devined as the average time span between the acceptance of an order and the promised delivery date. For repair parts and critical stock items, the lead time is often zero, whereas for a large machine tool the lead time may vary from three to nine months. Lead time is primarily a function of the nature of the product and competitive practices.

Q = Units Per Demand

Units per demand refers to the average number of units per order. For instance, an automotive distributor will usually receive orders for spark plugs or valves in six or eight units per demand.

F = Stockout Acceptance Factor

The significance of the stockout acceptance factor (*F*) is discussed in the report under the section "Order Point." The value of *F* in the order point equation for a given percent stockout level, assuming a Poisson distribution in the demand pattern, can be read from the graph shown in Figure VII.

T = EOQ Control Limit

An equation has been developed for the calculation of the EOQ range. This function is based on an acceptable percentage increase in the minimum total variable cuit cost. The percentage increase is termed the EOQ control limit and designated by the letter (*T*).

Dimension of the Variables

In the use of the order point (*OP*), economic order quantity (EOQ), and EOQ range equations, it is critical that all data be in the same time or units dimension, for example:

Variable	Value of Raw Data	Formula Value	
		Per Month	Per Week
S	200 per month	200	46.2
P	6 weeks	1.39	6
L	1 month	1	4.33
R	24% per year	.02	.0046
O	50 cents per lot	.50	.50
U	$3.00 per unit	3.00	3.00
Q	5 per demand	5	5
F	2.06	2.06	2.06
T	½ of 1%	.005	.005

Figure VII

STOCKOUT ACCEPTANCE FACTOR

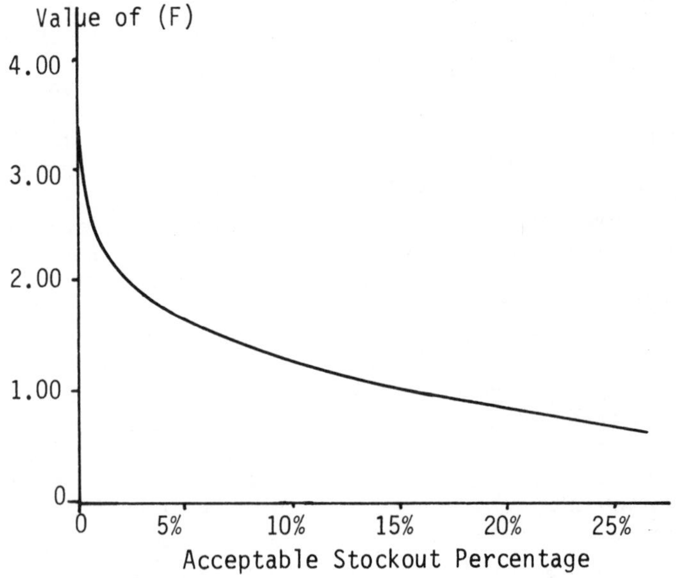

READING 26

Guides to Inventory Policy: Problems of Uncertainty

John F. Magee
Arthur D. Little, Inc.

Marketing and production executives alike have an immediate, vital interest in safety stocks. In these days of strong but often unpredictable sales, safety stocks afford, for the factory as well as for the sales office, a method of buying short-term protection against the uncertainties of customer demand. They are the additional inventory on hand which can be drawn upon in case of emergency during the period between placement of an order by the customer and receipt of the material to fill the order. However, in practice their potentials are often needlessly lost.

One reason for the failure is a very practical one. Because safety stocks are designed to cope with the uncertainties of sales, they must be controlled by flexible rules so that conditions can be met as they develop. But sometimes the need for flexibility is used as an excuse for indefiniteness: "We can't count on a thing; we have to play the situation by ear." And, in any sizable organization, when people at the factory level start "playing it by ear," one can be almost sure that management policy will not be regularly translated into practice.

Our studies have shown that the methods used by existing systems in industry often violate sound control concepts. The economy of the company is maintained, in the face of instability and inefficiency in the inventory control system, only because of constant attention, exercise of overriding common sense, and use of expediting and other emergency measures outside the routine of the system.

Actually, it is possible to have inventory controls which are not only flexible but also carefully designed and explicit. But the task needs special analytical tools; in a complicated business it defies common-sense judgment and simple arithmetic. Methods must be employed to take direct account of uncertainty and to measure the response characteristics

---

Reprinted from the HARVARD BUSINESS REVIEW (March-April 1956), pp. 103-116, by permission of the publisher.

of the system and relate them to costs. Such methods are the distinctive mark of a really modern, progressive inventory control system.

Here are some of the points which I shall discuss in this article:

√Basically, there are two different types of inventory replenishment systems designed to handle uncertainty about sales—*fixed order*, commonly used in stockrooms and factories, as in bins of parts or other materials; and *periodic reordering*, frequently used in warehouses for inventories involving a large number of items under clerical control. While the two are basically similar in concept, they have somewhat different effects on safety stocks, and choice of one or the other, or some related variety, requires careful consideration. Certain factors which should be taken into account in the choice between them will be outlined.

√The fundamental problem of setting safety stocks under either system is balancing a series of types of costs which are not found in the ordinary accounting records of the company—costs of customer service failure, of varying production rates (including hiring and training expenses), of spare capacity, and others. Often specialists can find the optimum balance with relatively simple techniques once the cost data are made explicit. However, part of the needed data can come *only from top management*. For example, the tolerable risk of service failure is generally a policy decision.

√The specific problem of inventory control, including production scheduling, varies widely from company to company. Where finished items can be stocked, the important cost factors to weigh may be storage, clerical procedures, setup, supervision, etc. But where finished items cannot be stocked, the problem is one of setting capacity levels large enough to handle fluctuating loads without undue delay, which involves the cost of unused labor and machines. Despite the great variety of situations that are possible, specific mathematical approaches and theories are available for use in solving almost any type of company problem.

√Both to illustrate the various techniques and by way of summary, a hypothetical case will be set forth where a company moved through a series of stages of inventory control. Significantly, the final step brought a large reduction in stocks needed for efficient service and also a great reduction in production fluctuations. Out of the range of this company's experience, other managements should be able to get some guidance as to what is appropriate for their own situations.

BASIC SYSTEMS

Like transit stocks and lot-size stocks (discussed specifically in the previous article in this series[1]) and also anticipation stocks (to be taken up in the subsequent article), safety stocks "decouple" one stage in production and distribution from the next, reducing the amount of over-all organization and control needed.

But the economies of safety inventories are not fairly certain and immediate. The objective is to arrive at a reasonable balance between the costs of the stock and the protection obtained against inventory exhaustion. Since exhaustion becomes less likely as the safety inventory increases, each additional amount of safety inventory characteristically buys relatively less protection. The return from increasing inventory balances therefore diminishes rapidly. So the question is: How much additional inventory as safety stock can be economically justified?

---

[1] John F. Magee, "Guides to Inventory Policy: I. Functions and Lot Sizes," HBR January-February 1956, p. 49.

To answer this question we need to look at the two basic systems of inventory replenishment to handle uncertainty about sales and see how they produce different results.

Fixed Order

Under any fixed order system—the old-fashioned "two-bin" system or one of its modern varieties—the same *quantity* of material is always ordered (a binful in the primitive system), but the *time* an order is placed is allowed to vary with fluctuations in usage (when the bottom of one bin is reached). The objective is to place an order whenever the amount on hand is just sufficient to meet a "reasonable" maximum demand over the course of the lead time which must be allowed between placement of the replenishment order and receipt of the material.

Where the replenishment lead time is long (e.g., three months) compared with the amount purchased at each order (e.g., a one-month supply), there are presumably some purchase orders outstanding all the time which, on being filled, will help replenish the existing inventory on hand. In such cases, of course, the safety stocks and reorder points should be based upon both amount on hand and on order. Where, on the other hand, the lead time is short compared with the quantity ordered, as in most factory two-bin systems, the amount on hand and the total on hand and on order are in fact equivalent at the time of reordering.

The key to setting the safety stock is the "reasonable" maximum usage during the lead time. What is "reasonable" depends partly, of course, on the nature of short-term fluctuations in the rate of sale. It also depends—and here is where the top executive comes foremost into the picture—on the risk that management is prepared to face in running out of stock. What is the level of sales or usage beyond which management is prepared to face the shortages? For example:

EXHIBIT I. Brown and Brown's Safety Stock

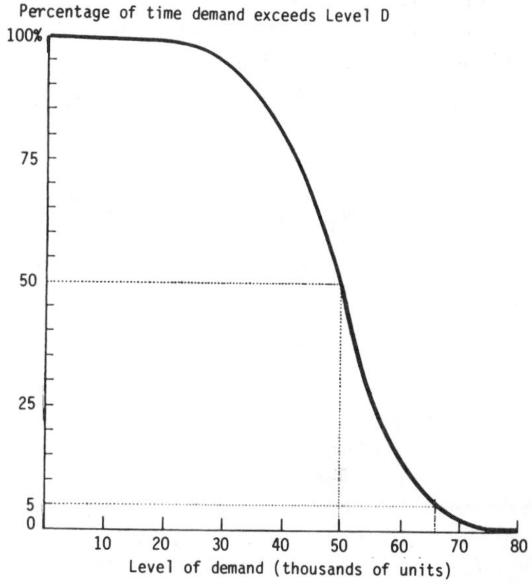

In Exhibit I, continuing the hypothetical case of Brown and Brown, Inc., discussed in the first article in this series,[2] the curve shows the number of weeks in which the demand for casings may be expected to equal or exceed any specified level. (Such a curve could be roughly plotted according to actual experience modified by such expectations or projections as seem warranted; refinement can be added by the use of mathematical analysis when such precision seems desirable.)

Now, if it takes B. and B. a week to replenish its stocks and the management wishes to keep the risk of running out of stock at a point where it will be out of stock only once every 20 weeks, or 5% of the time, then it will have to schedule the stock replenishment when the inventory of casings on hand drops to 66,000 units. Since the expected or average weekly usage is 50,000 units, the safety stock to be maintained is 16,000 (making a total stock of 66,000).

This example, of course, assumes a single, rather arbitrary definition

[2] Ibid., p. 57.

of what is meant by risk or minimum acceptable level of customer service. There are a number of ways of defining the level of service, each appropriate to particular circumstances. One might be the total volume of material or orders delayed; another, the number of customers delayed (perhaps only in the case of customers with orders exceeding a certain size level), still another the length of the delays. All of these definitions are closely related to the "probability distribution" of sales—i.e., to the expected pattern of sales in relation to the average.

Cost of Service Failure. It is easy enough to understand the principle that setting a safety stock implies some kind of a management decision or judgment with respect to the maximum sales level to be allowed for, or the cost of service failure. But here is the rub: service failure cost, though real, is far from explicit. It rarely, if ever, appears on the accounting records of the company except as it is hidden in extra sales or manufacturing costs, and it is characteristically very hard to define. What is new in inventory control is not an accounting technique for measuring service cost but a method of self-examination by management of the intuitive assumptions it is making. The progressive company looks at what it is in fact assuming as a service-failure cost in order to determine whether the assumed figure is anywhere near realistic.

For example, characteristically one hears the policy flatly stated: "Back orders are intolerable." What needs to be done is to convert this absolute, qualitative statement into a quantitative one of the type shown in Exhibit II. Here we see the facts which might be displayed for the management of a hypothetical company to help it decide on a customer service policy:

√To get a 90% level of customer service (i.e., to fill 90% of the orders immediately), a little over three weeks' stock must be carried—

EXHIBIT II. Relation Between Safety Stocks and Order Delay

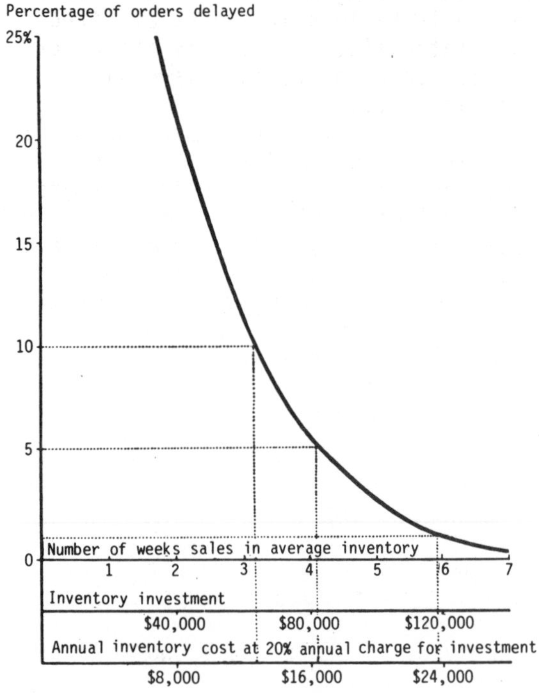

an investment of $64,000 with an annual carrying cost of $12,800.

√Filling another 5% of orders immediately, thereby increasing the service level to 95%, would mean about one week's more stock, with an extra annual cost of $3,800.

√Filling another 4% immediately (a 99% service level) would cost an extra $7,400 per year.

At each point the management can decide whether the extra cost is justified by the improved service. Thus, the chart becomes a device for comparing policies on service and inventories for consistency and rationality.

Periodic Reordering

The periodic reordering system of inventory replenishment—the other basic approach to handling uncertainty about demand—is very popular, particularly where some type of book inventory control is employed and where it is convenient to examine inventory stocks on a definite schedule. The idea underlying all varieties of this system is to look at stocks at fixed *time* intervals, and to vary the order *amount* according to the usage since the last review.

The problem is that many seemingly similar ways of handling a cyclical ordering system may have hidden traps. A typical difficulty is instability in reordering habits and inventory levels caused by "overcompensation"; that is, by attempting to outguess the market and assuming that high or low sales at one point, actually due to random causes, indicate an established trend which must be anticipated. For example:

An industrial abrasives manufacturer found himself in a characteristic state of either being out of stock or having too much stock, even though his inventory control procedures were, at least judging by appearances, logically conceived. The procedures worked as follows: Each week the production scheduling clerk examined the ledger card on each item, and each month he placed a replenishment order on the factory based on (a) the existing finished stock on hand in the warehouse, (b) a replenishment lead time of six weeks, and (c) a projection for the coming two-month period of the rate of sales during the past two-month period.

The manufacturer blamed the instability of his market and the perversity of his customers for the difficulties he faced in controlling inventory, when in fact the seemingly logical reorder rule he had developed made his business behave in the same erratic fashion as a highly excitable and nervous driver in busy downtown traffic. The effects of sales fluctuations tended to be multiplied and passed on to the factory. *No use was made of inventories—especially safety stock—to absorb sales fluctuations.*

The most efficient and stable reorder scheme or rule has a very simple form:

A forecast or estimate of the amount to be used in the future is made for a period equal to the delivery lead time plus one reorder cycle. Then an order is placed to bring the totel inventory on hand and on order up to the total of the amount forecast for the delivery lead and cycle times, plus a standard allowance for safety stock. Under such a scheme, the average inventory expected to be on hand will be the safety balance plus one-half the expected usage during a reorder cycle.

Note the contrast between this scheme and that used by the abrasives manufacturer. Here inventories are used to "decouple" production and sales. An upward fluctuation in sales is "absorbed" at the warehouse; it is not passed on to the plant until later (if at all). Many companies subscribe to this plan wholeheartedly in principle but only halfheartedly in practice. A common tendency, for instance, is to make the forecast but then, if sales increase, to revise it upward and transmit the increase back to the plant. The whole value of a safety stock based on a balancing of the costs of running out and the costs of rush orders to production is thus lost.

Readers may recognize the application here of servo theory, the body of concepts (including feedback, lags or reaction times, type of control, and the notion of stability) developed originally by electrical engineers in designing automatic or remotely controlled systems.[3] An inventory system, though not a mechanical device, is a control system and as a consequence is subject to the same kinds of effects as mechanical control systems and can be analyzed using the same basic concepts.

Choice of System

Each system of reordering inventories has its own advantages. Here

---

[3] See H.J. Vassian, "Application of Discrete Variable Servo Theory to Inventory Control," *Journal of the Operations Research Society of America,* August 1955, p. 272.

are the conditions under which the fixed order system is advantageous:

√Where some type of continuous monitoring of the inventory is possible, either because the physical stock is seen and readily checked when an item is used or because a perpetual inventory record of some type is maintained.

√Where the inventory consists of items of low unit value purchased infrequently in large quantities compared with usage rates; or where otherwise there is less need for tight control.

√Where the stock is purchased from an outside supplier and represents a minor part of the supplier's total output, or is otherwise obtained from a source whose schedule is not tightly linked to the particular item or inventory in question; and where irregular orders for the item from the supplier will not cause production difficulties.

For example, the fixed order system is suitable for floor stocks at the factory, where a large supply of inexpensive parts (e.g., nuts and bolts) can be put out for production workers to draw on without requisitions, and where a replenishment is purchased whenever the floor indicates the supply on hand has hit the reorder point.

By contrast, the periodic reordering system is useful under these conditions:

√Where tighter and more frequent control is needed because of the value of the items.

√Where a large number of items are to be ordered jointly, as in the case of a warehouse ordering many items from one factory. (Individual items may be shipped in smaller lots, but the freight advantages on large total shipments can still be obtained.)

√Where items representing an important portion of the supplying plant's output are regularly reordered.

In general, since safety stocks needed vary directly with the length of the period between orders, the periodic system is less well suited where the cost of ordering and the low unit value of the item mean infrequent large orders.

It should be noted that modifications of the simplest fixed order system or intermediates between the fixed order system and the periodic reordering system are also possible and very often useful; they can combine the better control and cost features of each of the "pure" schemes. For example:

One type of scheme often useful—the "base stock" system—is to review inventory stocks on a periodic basis but to replenish these stocks only when stocks on hand and on order have fallen to or below some specified level. When this happens, an order is placed to bring the amount on hand and on order up to a specified maximum level.

The choice of frequency of review and the minimum and maximum inventory points can be determined by analysis similar to that used for the other systems, but precautions must be taken—such as that stocks on order must always be counted when reorder quantities are figured—in order to avoid problems of instability and oscillation which can easily creep into rules that are apparently sound and sensible.

Interaction Among Factors. As mathematical analysis will indicate, the safety stock, reorder quantity, and reorder level are not entirely independent under either the fixed order or the periodic reordering system (or any combination thereof):

Where the order amount is fixed, the safety stock is protection against uncertainty over the replenishment time (measured by the reorder level). But it is the size of the order amount that determines the frequency of exposure to risk. With a given safety level, the bigger the order placed, the less frequently will the inventory be exposed to the possibility of run-out and the higher will be the level of service.

Where inventories are reordered on a periodic time cycle, the uncertainty against which safety stocks protect extends over the *total* of the reorder period and replenishment time. But here it is the length of the reordering cycle that determines the risk. The shorter the period and the closer together the reorders, the less will be the chance of large inventory fluctuations and, as a consequence, the less will be the size of safety stock required in order to maintain a given level of service.

The interaction among the frequency of reorder, the size of reorder, and safety stocks is often ignored as being unimportant, even in setting up fairly sophisticated inventory control schemes (although the same companies readily consider the *lot-size* problem in relation to the other factors). In many cases this may be justifiable for the purpose of simplifying inventory control, particularly methods for adjusting reorder quantities and safety stocks to changing costs and sales. On the other hand, cases do arise from time to time where explicit account must be taken of such interactions so that an efficient system may be developed.

Note, too, that the factors governing the choice of any reorder scheme are always changing. Therefore, management should provide for routine review of the costs of the system being used, once a year or oftener, so that trends can be quickly identified. Also, control chart procedures, like simple quality control methods, should be used to spot "significant" shifts in usage rates and in the characteristics of customer demand (fluctuations, order size, frequency of order, etc.). Schemes for checking such matters each time a reorder point is crossed are easily incorporated in the programs of automatic data-handling systems used for inventory control; they can also be applied to manual systems, but less easily and hence with some temptation to oversimplify them dangerously.

PRODUCTION SCHEDULING

Now let us turn to the important relationships between safety stocks and production. The safety stock affects, and is affected by, production run cycles, production "reaction times," and manufacturing capacity levels.

Setting Cycle Lengths

In production cycling problems, as in periodic reordering, the longer the run on each product, the longer one must wait for a rerun of that product; therefore, a larger safety stock must be maintained as protection. Shorter, more frequent runs give greater flexibility and shorter waiting periods between runs, and thus lower safety inventory requirements. Also, again the interaction between factors must be taken into account. For example:

A chemical company arrived at production run cycles for a set of five products going through the same equipment on the basis of only setup costs and cycle inventories (e.g., lot-size inventories), ignoring the interaction between cycle length and safety stocks. It found that on this basis an over-all product cycle of approximately 20 days, or one production month, appeared optimum, allowing four days per product on the average. However, when the problem was later re-examined, it was discovered that the uncertainty introduced by long lead times was so great that the over-all product cycle could in fact be economically cut back to less than 10 days. Doubling setup costs would be more than offset by savings in inventory and storage costs resulting from a reduction in the needed safety stocks.

Exhibit III illustrates the cost characteristics found to exist. The

EXHIBIT III. Influence of Safety Stocks on Choice of an Optimum Production Cycle

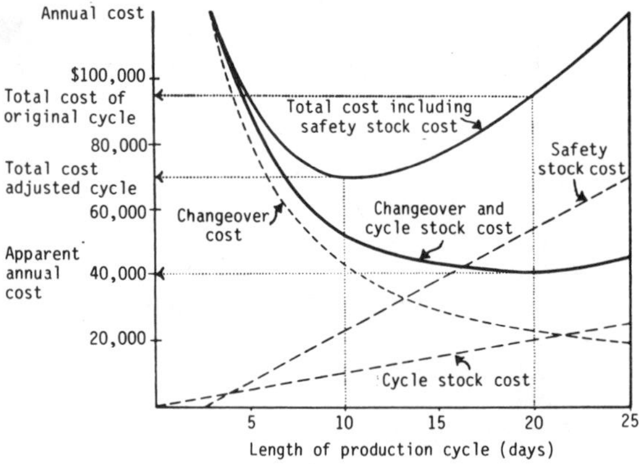

three *dashed* lines show separately the annual costs of changeovers, carrying cycle inventories, and carrying safety stocks, compared with the length of the individual production cycle. Adding together only the first two costs leads to the lower of the *solid* lines. This is at a minimum when the production cycle is 20 days long, indicating an apparent annual cost of $40,000. However, if *all* costs are included (the *solid* line at the top), the total annual cost on a 20-day cycle is $95,000. On this basis total costs are at a minimum when the cycle is 10 days long—only $70,000. This means a saving of $25,000 annually on the products in question.

Setting Production Levels

Safety stocks give only short-term protection against sales uncertainty. If stocks are being replenished from production, the effectiveness of over-all control depends also on the ability to restore them in case of depletion.

If total demand varies, the ability to restore stocks depends, in turn, on the ability of the production facilities to react to chance fluctuations. In order to get low inventories, the process must have fast reactions properly controlled or (equivalently) in some cases large "capacity." If reactions are slow or limited, inventories must be large, and the inventory in effect serves another type of protective function, namely, protection of production rate or capacity from the stresses of demand fluctuation. To illustrate the kind of situation where this may be true:

✓Changes in the throughput rate of chemical processing equipment may be slow and difficult or expensive.

✓The output level of an assembly line operation may depend on the number of shifts working. Some time may be required to change the production rate by changing the number of stations manned at each point along the line.

✓The production output of a job-shop operation may be influenced by the rate at which new workers can be hired and trained, or the cost of making changes in the manning level by bringing in new untrained workers or laying off people.

How fast should production operations respond to sales fluctuations, and to what extent should these fluctuations be absorbed by means of inventory? The costs of warehousing and cash investment in inventory need to be balanced against the costs of changing production rates or building excess capacity into the production system.

The actual cost of making out schedules, which depends on the frequency with which they are made and the degree of precision required, also should be considered, as well as the speed of reaction of production which is physically possible (e.g., the employee training time). When these costs are made explicit, management may find itself having to balance conflicting objectives. To illustrate:

A metal fabricator making a wide line of products to order attempted to provide immediate service to customers. He found that on the average his departments needed a substantial excess of labor over the normal requirements of the jobs flowing through, and this excess was essentially idle time. On the other hand, when he attempted to cut the excess too thin, backlogs began to build up. He had to weigh his desire to get the lead time down against the costs of excess unused labor.

Ordinarily we want to avoid passing back the full period-to-period sales fluctuation by making corresponding changes in the size of orders placed on production because it is uneconomical. What we can do instead is to:

1. Set the production level in each period equal to anticipated needs over the lead time plus the scheduling period not already scheduled, plus or minus *some fraction* of the difference between desired and actual inventory on hand.

2. Alternatively, change the existing production level or rate by *some fraction* of the difference between the existing rate and the rate suggested by the simple reorder rule (i.e., that an order be placed in each period equal to the anticipated requirements over the lead time plus the scheduling period, plus or minus the difference between desired and actual inventory on hand and on order).

Each of these alternatives is useful in certain types of plants, depending on whether the cost of production fluctuations comes primarily from, say, overtime and undertime (work guarantee) costs or from hiring, training, and layoff costs. Each in appropriate circumstances will lead to smoother production, at the expense of extra inventory to maintain the desired level of service.

When the different costs involved are identified and measured, mathematical techniques can be used to show the effect that varying the numbers in the rule (in particular, the size of the *fraction* used) has on inventory and production expense and to arrive at an economical balance between the needs of marketing and manufacturing. These two rules are expressions of servo theory, like that referred to earlier in connection with inventory. Here it may be worthwhile to see in some working detail how the theory can be applied mathematically:

The first rule can be stated as follows:

$$P_i = \sum_{k=0}^{T} F_{i+k} - \sum_{k=1}^{T} P_{i-k} + k(I_0 - I_i)\,;$$

$k \leq I.$

P_i is the amount scheduled for production in period i, F_i is the forecast requirements for period i, I_0 is the desired inventory, I_t is the actual opening inventory on hand in period i, and k is the response number which indicates what fraction of the inventory error or production rate departure is to be accounted for each period.

The fluctuations in inventory resulting from a choice of k in the first rule can be expressed as a function of the fluctuations in sales about the forecast, as follows (if fluctuations from month to month are not correlated):

$$\sigma_I = \sqrt{\frac{T(2k - k^2) + I}{2k - k^2}}\,\sigma_F$$

where σ_I is the standard deviation of inventory levels, and σ_F is the standard deviation of actual sales about forecast sales each period. Similarly, the production rate variations resulting from any choice of k can be expressed as:

$$\sigma_P = \sqrt{\frac{k}{2 - k}}\,\sigma_F$$

The influence of the choice of a response number, k, on the standard deviation of inventories and on the standard deviation of production rates under the first type of rule is shown in Exhibit IV. Frequently the costs of

EXHIBIT IV. Effect of Response Number k on Variations in Inventory and Production Rate

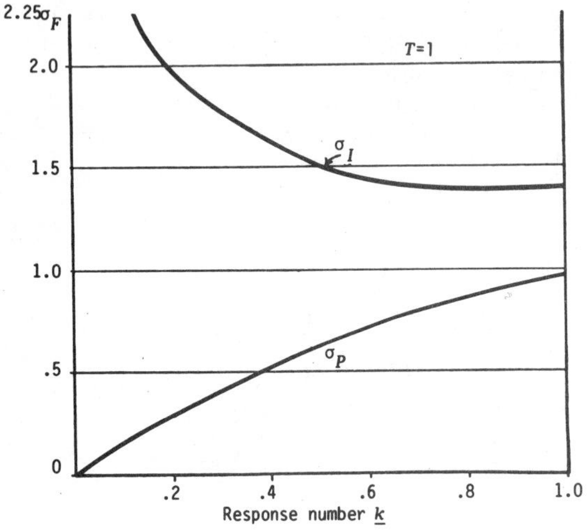

production fluctuations are more or less directly proportional to the standard deviation of fluctuations in the production rate, a measure of the amount of change in production level which can be expected to occur. On the other hand, the normal inventory level, the average level expected, must be set large enough so that even with expected inventory fluctuations, service failures will not occur excessively. This means that the larger the standard deviation in inventory levels, the larger must be the normal level, generally in proportion. Therefore, one can "buy" production flexibility with larger inventories, and vice versa, with the particular costs in the process concerned determining the economical balance.[4]

The second rule can be worked through similarly. Here P^* is the changed amount scheduled for production, and the rule can be stated as follows:

[4] See H.J. Vassian, op. cit. See also Charles C. Holt, Franco Modigliani, and Herbert A. Simon, "A Linear Decision Rule for Production and Employment Scheduling," *Management Science*, October 1955, for another approach to this problem under different cost conditions.

$$P^*_i = P^*_{i-1} + k(P_i - P^*_{i-1}) ;$$

$$k \leq I = (I - k)P^*_{i-1} + kP_i$$

where

$$P_i = \sum_{k=0}^{T} F_{i+k} - \sum_{k=1}^{T} P^*_{i-k} + (I_0 - I_i) .$$

Setting Capacity Levels

In some cases—particularly where output cannot be stocked easily—the problem of controlling the production level is not so much one of adjusting the level to respond to fluctuations in demand, as of setting the capacity of the plant or operation at a high enough level to permit demand fluctuations to be absorbed without excessive delay. If the capacity is set equal only to the desired average rate, fluctuations in demand about this desired rate must either be absorbed by inventories or by orders piling up in a backlog. To illustrate:

√The telephone companies have recognized for many years that telephone exchanges must be built with greater capacity than is required to handle the average load, in order to keep lines of waiting subscribers within reasonable levels.

√Pile-ups often occur around the check-out booths of cafeterias or the ticket windows in railroad stations. Customers are eventually taken care of, but capacity is so close to average requirements, in some cases, that long waiting lines can be built up as a result of customers arriving at random in small bunches.

√The problem of specifying the number of workmen to tend semiautomatic machinery or the capacity of docks to service freighters is complicated by the fact that the units require service more or less at random, so that again there can easily develop an accumulation of units awaiting service if personnel are not immediately available.

A theory of such processes is growing; it is known as waiting-line theory. This is really a branch of probability theory, and is itself a whole body of mathematical techniques and explicit concepts providing a mathematical framework within which waiting-line and similar problems can be studied.[5]

Some examples of applications in production scheduling are: flow of orders through departments in a job shop; flow of items through the stages in an assembly line; clerical processing of orders for manufacture or shipping; filling orders in a warehouse or stockroom; and setting up shipping or berth facilities to handle trucks or other transport units. In each case, fairly well-fixed crews or facilities have to be set up for handling fluctuating orders or items quickly, avoiding delays in service. A balance between the cost of extra personnel or facilities and delays in taking care of demand is needed.

In applying waiting-line theory to such problems, the flow of orders or demand for goods can be considered as a demand for service, analogous to subscriber cost in a telephone exchange. Orders are handled by one or more processing stations, analogous to telephone trunk lines. When the order or unit is produced, the processing station is free to take on the next order in line, as when a call is completed through the exchange. For example:

A wholesale merchandise house planned its order-handling and order-filling activities in advance of peak sales. The company, selling consumer merchandise to a large group of retail dealers, had grown rapidly and in midsummer had looked forward to serious congestion, delayed orders, and lost customers when the Christmas peak hit. An analysis based on waiting-line theory outlined staff and space requirements to meet the forecast load, showed what jobs were the worst potential bottlenecks, and revealed, incidentally, how the normally inefficient practice of assigning two persons to "pick" one order could in this case help avoid tie-ups and save space during the critical sales peak.

STAGES OF CONTROL

The choice and use of appropriate techniques for inventory control is not a simple matter. It takes a good deal of research into sales and product characteristics, plus skill in sensing which of many possible approaches are likely to be fruitful.

To describe these techniques, I shall take a case illustration. This case is drawn from a great deal of business experience, but in order to keep the detail and arithmetic within manageable proportions without distorting the essential points, I have simplified and combined everything into one fictional situation.

Any of the stages of the company's progress toward more efficient inventory management—from the original to the final—might be found to exist in the inventory control practices of a number of sizable companies with reputations for progressive and efficient management. These stages of advancement in the refinement of inventory control should not be used to compare the inventory system of one company or division with that of another, for the reasons just mentioned; but they may prove helpful to management in answering the questions, "Where are we now?" and "What could we do better?"

Briefly, the case situation is as follows:

One division of the Hibernian Bay Company makes and sells a small machine part. Sales run slightly over 5,000 units annually, and the price is $100 apiece. Customers are supplied from

[5] A technical discussion of waiting-line theory and related applications can be found in W. Feller, *An Introduction to Probability Theory and Its Applications* (New York, John Wiley & Sons, Inc., 1950), Chapter 17.

four branch stock points scattered about the country, which in turn are supplied by the factory warehouse. The machining and assembly operations are conducted in a small plant, employing largely semiskilled female help. The level of production can be changed fairly rapidly but at the cost of training or retraining workers, personnel office expenses, and increased inspection and quality problems. The division management has almost complete autonomy over its operations, although its profit records are closely scrutinized at headquarters in Chicago.

Originally the factory and branch warehouse stocking practices were haphazard and unsatisfactory. In total, nearly four months' stock was carried in branches, in the factory warehouse, or in incompleted production orders. A stock clerk in each branch who watched inventories and placed reorders on the factory warehouse was under pressure to be sure that stocks were adequate to fill customer orders. The factory warehouse reorder clerk in turn watched factory stocks and placed production orders. Production runs or batches were each put through the plant as a unit. Fluctuations in production, even with apparently sizable stocks on hand, caused the management deep concern.

Service Improved

The management decided to try to improve inventory practices and appointed a research team to study the problem. The team suggested using "economical order quantities" for branch orders on the factory warehouse and warehouse orders on production, as a basis for better control. The steps followed were:

The research team suggested that the formula for determining the economical order quantity was $x = \sqrt{2As/i}$, where A = fixed cost connected with an order (setup of machines, writing order, checking receipts, etc.), i = annual cost of carrying a unit in inventory, s = annual movement, and x = "economical order quantity."

The team found that each branch sold an average of 25 units a week, or 1,300 per year; that the cost of a branch's placing and receiving an order was \$19 (\$6 in clerical costs at the branch and factory, \$13 in costs of packing and shipping goods, receiving, and stocking); that annual inventory carrying costs in the branches were \$5 per unit, based on a desired 10% return on incremental inventory investment. The reorder quantity for each branch was computed as $\sqrt{2 \cdot \$19 \cdot 1{,}300/\$5} = 100$ unit reorder quantity.

A system was set up where each branch ordered in quantities of 100, on the average, every four weeks. On this basis, without further action, each branch would have had an average inventory of one-half a reorder quantity, or 50 units. (The books would show 75 units, since stock in transit from factory warehouse to branch was also charged to the branch, and with average transit time of one week this would average 25 units.)

The next step was to provide for enough to be on hand when a reorder was placed to last until the order was received. While the average transit time was one week, experience showed that delays at the factory might mean an order would not be received at the branch for two weeks. So sales for two weeks had to be covered.

Statistical analysis showed that sales in any one branch over two weeks could easily fluctuate from 38 units to 62 units and could conceivable go as high as 65-70. The management decided that a 1% chance of a branch running out of stock before getting an order would be adequate.

Calculations then indicated that the maximum reasonable two-week demand to provide for would be 67. (The statistical basis was that sales fluctuate about the average at random; that fluctuations in the various branches are independent of one another; and that the standard deviation is $\sqrt{st}$ where s = sales rate, and t = length of individual time period.)

The branches therefore were instructed to order 100 units whenever the stock on hand and on order was 67 or less. This gave an inventory in each branch made up on the average as follows:

Safety stock	42	(order point, 67, less normal week's usage, 25)
Order cycle stock	50	(one-half 100-unit order)
In transit	25	(one week's sales)
Total	117	or 4.7 weeks' sales

The resulting behavior of the reorder system is shown in Exhibit V—both as it would be presumed in theory and as it actually turned out. Although the actual performance was much less regular than presumed, the two compare fairly well—testimony to the soundness of the procedure.

Application at the Factory

At the factory warehouse end, the "economical order quantity" scheme worked as follows:

√The cost of holding a unit in inventory was \$3.50 per year (at 10% return on investment); the cost of placing an order and setting up equipment for each order was \$13.50; and, of course, a total of 5,200 units was made each year. These indicated that each production order should be for $\sqrt{2 \cdot \$13.50 \cdot 5{,}200/\$3.50} = 200$ units.

√Factory processing time was two weeks; it would take two weeks for each order to reach the warehouse. The warehouse would need to place its replenishment order on the factory when it had enough on hand or on order to fill maximum reasonable demand during the next two weeks.

On the average, the factory warehouse would receive one order a week from the branches (one every four weeks from each of four branches) under the new branch reorder system. In fact, because of the fluctuations in branch sales described before, it

EXHIBIT V. Economical Reorder System of a Branch Warehouse

A. Presumed Operation

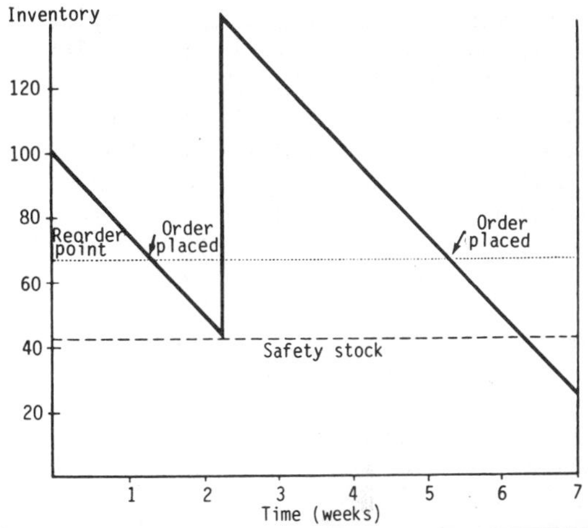

B. Actual Operation

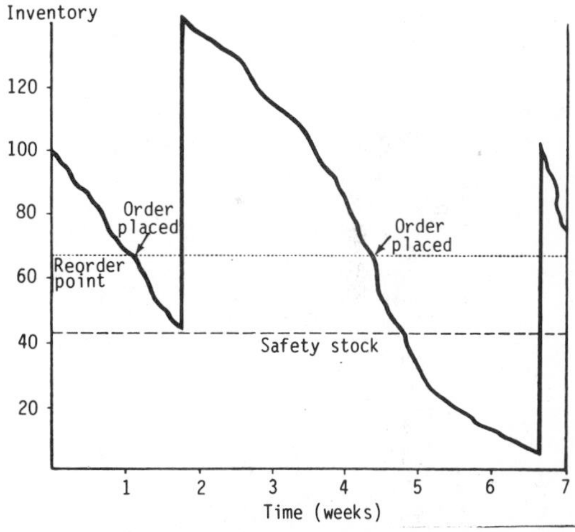

was found that orders on the factory warehouse fluctuated substantially in any two-week period (see Exhibit VI).

It was agreed that to give branches service adequate to maintain their own service, stocks at the factory warehouses would have to be high enough to fill demand 99% of the time, i.e., a replenishment order would have to be placed when 600 units were on hand. This meant a safety stock of 600 units minus 200 (normal usage), or 400 units. Cycle stock averaged half

EXHIBIT VI. Fluctuations of Orders on Factory Warehouse

Number of branch orders	*Number of items ordered*	*Percentage of weeks*
A. Weekly Periods		
0	0	37%
1	100	37
2	200	18
3	300	6
4+	400+	2
B. Biweekly Periods		
0	0	13%
1	100	27
2	200	27
3	300	18
4	400	9
5	500	4
6	600	1
7+	700+	1

a run, or 100 units, and stock in process an additional half run, or 100 units. Total factory stock, then, was:

Cycle stock	100 units
Stock in process	100
Safety stock	400
Total	600 units

Exhibit VII gives a picture of the apparent costs of the "economical order" system. The stock of 1,068 units equaled less than 11 weeks' sales, a fairly substantial reduction, and the management felt that it had a better control, since clerical procedures were set up to adapt readily to

EXHIBIT VII. Costs of Reorder System

	Number	*Cost each*	*Annual cost*
Inventory:			
Factory	600 units	\$3.50/year	\$2,100
4 Branches	468 units	\$5.00/year	2,340
Reorder cost:			
Branch	52/year	\$19.00	990
Factory	26/year	\$13.50	350
Total			\$5,780

any changes in inventory charges (currently 10% per year) or service level requirements the management might choose to make.

Production Stabilized

But the factory still had problems. On the average, the warehouse would place one production order every two weeks, but experience showed that in 60% of the weeks no orders were placed, in 30% one order, and in 10% two, three, or more orders were placed. Exhibit VIII shows orders on the factory and the production level for a representative period of weeks.

EXHIBIT VIII. Factory Orders and Production Level

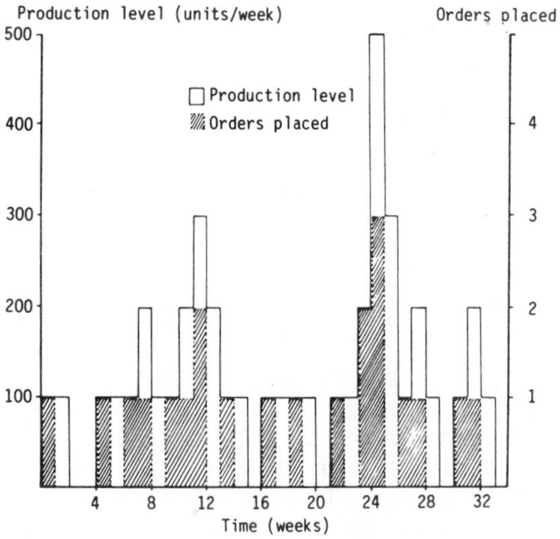

Factory snarls due to these fluctuations occasionally caused the factory to miss deadlines. These in turn led on occasion to warehouse delays in filling branch orders, and forced the branches to hold to the two-week delivery time even though actual transit time was only one week. An analysis revealed the following:

✓Factory fluctuations were very costly. A statistical regression of costs against operating levels and changes showed that annual production

EXHIBIT IX. Summary of Reorder Period Cost Comparisons

	Length of period (weeks)					
	1	2	3	4	5	6
Branch warehouse						
Safety stock	24.0	26.0	27.0	28.0	30.0	31.0
Cycle stock	12.5	25.0	37.5	50.0	62.5	75.0
Transit stock	25.0	25.0	25.0	25.0	25.0	25.0
Total units of stock	61.5	76.0	89.5	103.0	117.5	131.0
Annual inventory cost	$ 310	$ 380	$ 450	$ 515	$ 590	$ 650
Ordering cost	990	495	330	250	195	165
Total cost each branch	$1,300	$ 875	$ 780	$ 765	$ 785	$ 815
Total cost four branches	$5,200	$3,500	$3,120	$3,060	$3,140	$3,260
Factory warehouse						
Safety stock	33	33	41	47	52	58
Cycle stock	50	100	150	200	250	300
Total units of stock	83	133	191	247	302	358
Annual inventory cost	$ 290	$ 465	$ 670	$ 865	$1,060	$1,250
Ordering cost	700	350	235	175	140	120
Total cost factory	$ 990	$ 815	$ 905	$1,040	$1,200	$1,370
Production change costs	$1,600	$2,250	$2,760	$3,180	$3,560	$3,900
Total system costs	$7,790	$6,565	$6,785	$7,280	$7,900	$8,530

costs were affected more by the average *size* of changes in level than by the frequency of change; a few large changes in operative level were much more costly than many small changes.

√Under the "economical reorder quantity" system, production fluctuations were no larger than before, but the average change up or down actually equaled 80% of the average production level. This was estimated to cost $11,500 annually, bringing the total cost of the system, including costs of holding inventories, placing orders, and changing production rates, to $17,280 per year.

This led to the suggestion that the company try a new scheme so that orders on the factory warehouse and the factory would be more regular. A system with a fixed reorder cycle or period was devised, under which branch warehouses would place orders at fixed intervals, the order being for the amount sold in the period just ended. The factory warehouse would ship the replenishment supply, order an equivalent amount from the factory, and receive the order within two weeks or by the beginning of the next review period, whichever was longer.

Under this scheme, each branch warehouse would need to keep its stock on hand or on order sufficient to fill maximum reasonable demand during one review period plus delivery time (tentatively taken as two weeks) on the basis of the reorder rule described previously in this article. The question to be determined was: How long should the review period, that is, the time between reorders, be? Exhibit IX summarizes inventories and costs for reorder intervals ranging from one to six weeks, based on the following facts and figures:

(1) *Branch safety stock* was determined from a study of branch sales fluctuations, to allow for maximum reasonable demand over the reorder interval plus the two-week delivery period.

"Maximum reasonable demand" was defined to allow a 0.25% risk of being out of stock in any one week (equal to the 1% risk on the average four-week interval under the "economical reorder quantity" system described previously).

(2) *Branch cycle stock* would average one-half of an average shipment. Under this system, the average shipment to a branch each period would equal the average sales by the branch in one period (25 units x number of weeks).

(3) *Transit stock* equaled one week's sales.

(4) *Branch inventory carrying cost* was $5 per unit per year.

(5) *Branch ordering costs* equaled $19 per order, with one order per period. A one-week period would mean 52 orders per year; a two-week period, 26 orders per year; etc.

(6) *Factory safety stock* was set to allow a 1% risk that the warehouse would be unable to replenish all branch shipments immediately.

(7) *Factory cycle stock* in process or in the warehouse would be approximately equal to one-half the sales in any one period.

(8) *Factory inventory carrying cost* was $3.50 per unit per year.

(9) *Factory ordering costs* equaled $13.50 per order (see 5 above).

(10) *Production change costs* were proportional to the period-to-period changes in production level, equal under this system to period-to-period changes in branch sales.

The figures show that a two-week reorder interval would be most economical for the company as a whole, and this was chosen. Costs were estimated to be $6,600, compared with $17,300 under the "economical reorder quantity" system. While the new system cut total inventories by nearly 70%; most of the gain came from smoother production operations. Exhibit X shows weekly production for a representative period under the new system.

Further economies became apparent when the system was in operation:

(1) The reduction in production fluctuations made it possible to meet production deadlines regularly, cutting the effective lead time in deliveries to branches and thereby permitting modest reductions in branch safety stocks.

EXHIBIT X. Production Fluctuations Reduced with Fixed Reorder Cycle

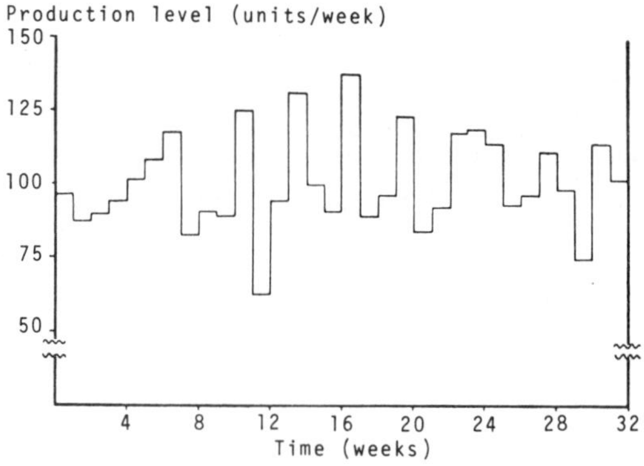

(2) The inventory system was found well suited to "open" production orders. Instead of issuing a new order with each run, the moderate fluctuations made it possible to replace production orders with simplified "adjusting memos" and at the same time to eliminate much of the machine setups.

"Base Stock" System

The success with the periodic reordering system encouraged the company to go further and try the "base stock" system referred to earlier. Under this system, the branch warehouses would *report* sales periodically. The factory would consolidate these and put an equivalent amount into production. Stocks at any branch would be replenished whenever reported sales totaled an economical shipping quantity.

Two possible advantages of this system compared to the fixed period scheme were: (1) Branches might be able to justify weekly sales reports, reducing production fluctuations and safety stock needs still further. (2) It might be possible to make less frequent shipments from factory to

EXHIBIT XI. Optimum Shipping Quantity From Factory to Branch Warehouse Under Base Stock System

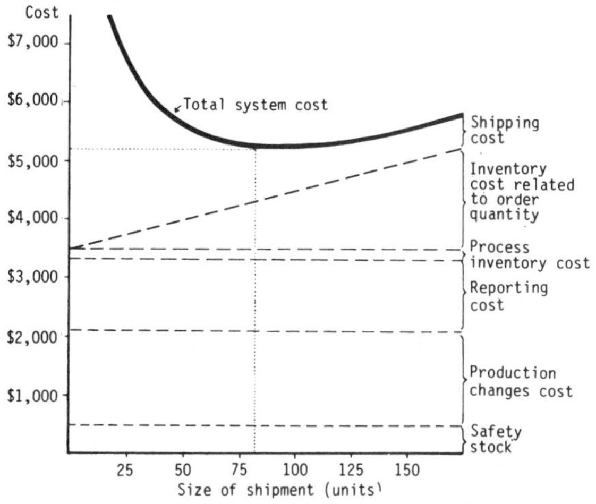

EXHIBIT XII. Cost of Production Changes and Safety Stock Vs. Rate of Response to Sales Fluctuations

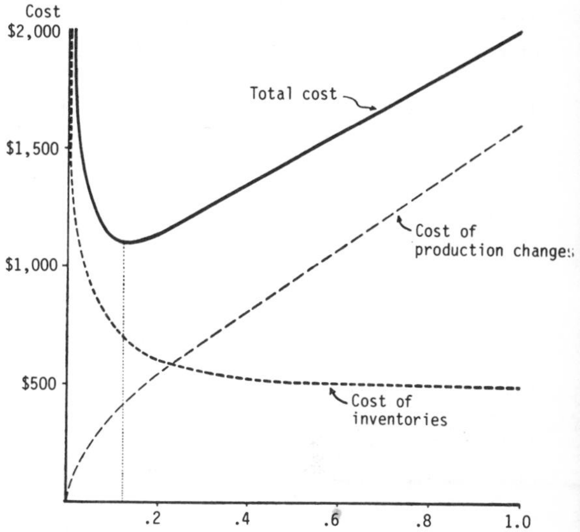

branches and make further savings. The following questions had to be decided:

How frequently should branches report sales? As noted earlier, cost studies showed that of the $19 total cost of ordering and receiving goods $6 represented clerical costs in placing and recording the order. Here is a summary of the costs affected by the choice of reporting interval:

	Reporting Interval			
	One week		Two weeks	
	Number	Cost	Number	Cost
Branch safety stock	100	$ 500	108	$ 540
Production changes		1,600		2,250
Branch clerical costs	4×52	1,250	4×26	625
Total		$3,350		$3,415

Thus, there appeared to be some advantage to reporting sales weekly from branches to the factory.

How big should replenishment shipments be? Exhibit XI summarizes the system costs related to the size of shipment from factory to branch. Each line shows the total of the cost indicated plus those represented by the line below. The total system cost (top line) is lowest at 82; that point is therefore the optimum shipping quantity from factory to branch warehouse. The same answer can be obtained from the formula given before, $\sqrt{2 \cdot \$13 \cdot 1{,}300/\$5} = 82$.

The base stock system therefore was set up with weekly reporting and replenishment shipments of 82 units to branches. The total cost of the base stock system was $5,200 compared with $6,600 under the previous system.

Stabilized Further

The company, cheered by its successes, decided to see if even further improvements might be obtained by cutting down further on production fluctuations. As it was, the production level under the base stock system was being adjusted each week to account for the full excess or deficiency in inventory due to sales fluctuations. It was proposed that production be adjusted to take up only a fraction of the difference between actual and desired stocks, with added inventories used to make up the difference.

The possibilities were analyzed along the lines described previously in the text; the results are summarized in Exhibit XII. The two costs that would be affected are costs of changing production and costs of holding inventories, in particular safety stock. These are affected by the fraction of the inventory departure that is made up each week by adjusting production.

The study showed that the cost would be minimized with the rate of response set equal to 0.125, as seen in the exhibit. (This compared with a response rate of 1.0 under the base stock system.) The additional savings of $970 brought the annual cost of the system down to $4,200.

Summary

The results of all the changes made by the division management were substantial:

(1) *A major reduction in stocks*—They had been cut 35% from what they were even with the "economical reorder quantity" system.

(2) *A substantial reduction in production fluctuations*—Exhibit XIII shows what weekly production levels for a typical period looked like at the end, contrasted with Exhibits VIII and X for the same sales.

The problems of the case are common even among the best-run businesses and can be solved in much the same way with much the same results. Of course, a large part of the effort and expense that were necessary in this step-by-step, evolutionary approach could be saved. Technical methods are available for analyzing and measuring the performance of alternate systems so that management can proceed directly to the ultimate system that is most desirable; management does not have to feel its way. Let me emphasize again, however, that no one kind of system should be considered "the goal." The efficiency of any given inventory control plan depends too much on the demand and cost characteristics of the business.

In the discussion thus far, several large questions remain unanswered. What happens when the business is subject to seasonal sales? What more can be done than to insure that desired levels of service are maintained while cutting inventory and production costs? Where do forecasting and scheduling fit into the picture? I shall discuss these questions in the next and final article in this series.

EXHIBIT XIII. Production Level Under the Base Stock System with a Reaction Rate of 0.125

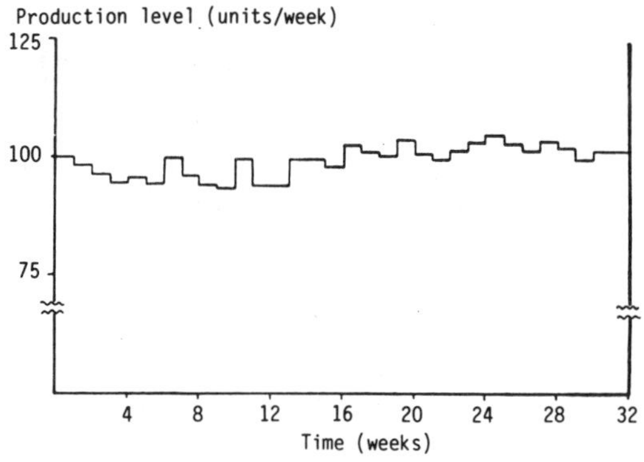

READING 27

"Project EOQ": A Success Story in Implementing Academic Research

Larry M. Austin
Texas Tech University

INTRODUCTION

Inventory theory was one of the earliest, and certainly one of the most successful, operations research techniques to be applied in business, industry and the public sector. As early as 1952, the United States Air Force had developed and implemented a simple economic ordering quantity (EOQ) system for repetitive purchases of expendable (nonreparable) weapon system spares [4], and in 1958 the Department of Defense directed the use of basic EOQ principles by all defense procurement and logistics agencies [5]. Although many changes were made over the years, as late as 1973 Air Force Logistics Command (AFLC) was still using a variation of the basic Wilson model [8] to determine optimal ordering quantities for its 250,000-item active inventory of expendable spares. Annual procurement costs total approximately $350-$400 million, and AFLC managers wanted to explore the possibility of installing a price discount capability in its bid solicitation system.

Since price discount solicitations are common in commercial procurement, and since the mathematical theory involving optimization of total acquisition cost is simple and well known (e.g., [8]), implementation of such a capability by AFLC would appear to have been a trivial undertaking. However, as is so often the case, the complex constraints and requirements of the "real-world" system did not coincide with theoretical models. This paper reports on the frustrating, but highly successful, research and implementation effort which came to be known as "Project EOQ."[1]

ORGANIZATION OF THE RESEARCH EFFORT

At the Air Force Academy, a graduate-level course in logistics management was taken each year by certain academically gifted seniors in their final semester. In the past, the

Reprinted from INTERFACES (August 1977), Vol. 7, No. 4, by permission of the publisher.

[1] Details of the various topics discussed herein may be found in [1].

course had been taught in a seminar format using case studies. Meanwhile, in the spring of 1974, AFLC requested the assistance of the Academy in modernizing its EOQ system to include a price discount solicitation capability, and several faculty members with appropriate academic training and experience had expressed an interest in the proposed research. The Air Force Business Research Management Center had agreed to assist in obtaining the required data and background material, with the Air Force Procurement Research Office acting as on-site project manager. It subsequently occurred to the faculty members involved that this project could provide a unique opportunity for the cadets who would be enrolled in the logistics management course to tackle a "real-world" problem--complete with massive amounts of data and "messy" constraints--rather than a set of neat, well-structured case studies. The nineteen cadets, whose majors were in computer science, economics, management and mathematics, were enthusiastic about the idea. Both the sponsor and the Academy approved the experiment, and "Project EOQ" was initiated in January, 1974.

It became apparent early in the game that opportunities for improvement in AFLC's EOQ system were not limited to installation of a price discount capability. First, the system currently used an eight-quarter moving average to predict demand for each of the 250,000 items in inventory, and it was felt that more sophisticated techniques might significantly improve the accuracy of demand forecasting. Second, AFLC was currently using a holding charge of 32% of average on-hand inventory,[2] which was applied to every item regardless of cost or classification. This factor was thought to be excessively high, as well as inappropriate for application to every item in the inventory. Third, AFLC was currently using a safety stock of one month's demand, undifferentiated as to dollar value or utlization rate, and the team believed that a better fill-rate (the ratio of orders filled from stock to orders received) and lower cost could be attained by developing a more sophisticated approach in this area. Fourth, AFLC was not satisfied with its ordering cost parameters ($142 per order for orders under $2500; $424 per order for larger orders), and research into this facet of the system was indicated.

Finally, many studies had previously been done of AFLC's EOQ system, with very little actual improvement resulting. All parties agreed from the start that "Project EOQ" would not end up as just another theoretical probe resulting in a final report and little else. It was decided, therefore, to build a simulation model using actual data in order to test the effects of recommended changes to the system.

As a result of this preliminary analysis, the research team was subdivided into four operational groups, each composed of four or five students and a faculty member, as follows:

- Group 1: computer model-building;
- Group 2: holding cost analysis;
- Group 3: demand prediction and safety stock analysis;
- Group 4: price discount and ordering cost analysis.

The four teams worked independently during the first phase of the research effort, but the results of their efforts were later integrated into a set of prioritized recommendations. Implementation of these recommendations, in various combinations, was simulated to produce prospective annual cost savings for AFLC. The effect of total implementation of the team's recommendations is given in Table 1.

[2] The 32% charge was composed of: 10% opportunity cost; 1% handling and storage; and 21% obsolescence cost.

TABLE 1. Projected net annual savings

Average Price Discount	Net Annual Savings ($ millions)
3%	21.5
5%	39.6
8%	68.2

PRICE DISCOUNTS

One critical assumption of simple economic ordering quantity models is that the price per unit is constant regardless of order size. In effect, these models attempt to minimize purely *internal* costs (e.g., ordering, holding, backordering, and stockout), while ignoring the supplier's economic *production* quantity (EPQ). Since most expendable weapon system spares have no commercial application, suppliers must incur a setup cost of producing each order obtained. Thus, without an opportunity to quote decreased unit prices for larger order quantities, a match between the buyer's EOQ and the supplier's EPQ is purely a matter of serendipity.

In commercial procurement transactions, solicitation or price discounts is a simple matter: the buyer merely asks for price quotes based upon the supplier's preferred quantities--perhaps within some feasible range. The award is then made to the competing supplier whose bid results in the lowest total annualized cost (all other things being equal), regardless of quantity or price. Either "all-units" or "incremental" discounts may be accepted at the option of the buyer, or offered at the option of the seller.

In defense procurement, however, the situation is much more complex. First, the Armed Services Procurement Regulations (ASPR) prescribe competitive (advertised) procurement in all cases in which such an approach is feasible. Furthermore, competing suppliers must be given the opportunity to bid on the same quantities, which effectively negates the possibility of allowing suppliers to quote prices based upon their individual EPQ's. Since purchase solicitation quantities must therefore be determined by the government in advance, "incremental" discounts are ruled out immediately.[3] The alternative is to solicit "all-units" discounts based upon predetermined solicitation quantities.

Even in the case of "all-units" price discounts, the situation is not straightforward. First, the differential ordering costs mentioned above form a step-function, and are based upon simplified buying procedures which are permitted for small purchases (under $2500),[4] as opposed to more paperwork and higher approval levels for purchases above this amount. This discontinuity in the cost function is tricky to handle, since it is based upon order quantity rather than annual demand. Second, the Department of Defense had directed [6] that no less than a three-month supply, and no more than a three-year supply, of any item be purchased at one time. These artificial constraints on order quantities have several interesting effects: elevating the holding costs on high value, frequently ordered items; and raising the ordering costs on numerous low value, infrequently ordered items. (In fact, the ordering cost for low value items frequently exceeds the cost of the units themselves.) The net effect of these constraints is to complicate the determination of solicitation quantities for price discount purposes.

The most frustrating constraint of all, however, and the one that presented the most serious barrier to

[3] This is true because, when soliciting "incremental" discounts, the order quantity can be any number of units and is determined by the combination of prices quoted for the various increments. Thus, order quantity is determined by the supplier, not the buyer.

[4] This figure has recently been raised to $10,000.

implementation of a price discount capability in AFLC, was the fiscal restriction. Funds to purchase expendable spares are allocated separately by Congress on a year by year basis, and exceeding a given fiscal year allocation--even to save considerable money in the long run--is not permissible under federal law. In addition to legal restrictions, AFLC had further imposed quarterly administrative restrictions on expenditures by its five Air Logistics Centers. The impact of these fiscal contraints was expressed by one senior AFLC manager in the following (seemingly paradoxical) comment following a briefing by the research team: "Your recommendations make sense, and I agree that soliciting price discounts would probably save a lot of money, but we simply can't afford to do it."

The Recommended Price Discount Solicitation System

A thorough study of laws and regulations covering fiscal year obligation authority revealed no feasible way to implement an across-the-board price discount solicitation capability for all of AFLC's 250,000 inventory items. However, since expendable weapon system spares exhibit strong Pareto ("ABC" rule) characteristics, a workable transition scheme was developed by the team. Beginning with the first day of a new fiscal year, it was recommended that all items which would normally be purchased two or more times per year (EOQ $\leq$ half of annual demand) be identified for price discount solicitation, which effectively limited the set of applicable items to those which would have been purchased more than once within current-year obligation authority. While this approach limited application to about 4% of the items, it included almost two-thirds of the dollar value of purchases. Recommended price discount solicitation quantities for the transition year are given in Table 2.

In order to test the actual effect of price discount solicitation, a test, using the approach in Table 2, was initiated at the Ogden Air Logistics Center in April 1974, when actual price discount solicitations were attached to Purchase Requests (PR's). The form was structured in such a way that the lowest quantity solicited was the PR quantity as stated in the usual manner, so that prospective suppliers could ignore the price discount form and still be responsive to the PR. The results of the 2 1/2-month test were better than expected, with 70% of the PR's being returned with price discounts quoted, and with discounts averaging 4 1/2% being offered

TABLE 2. Solicitation quantities for transition year

Normal Line Item Value For the Solicitation	Price Discount Solicitation quantities
Annual Demand (AD)/4[a]	AD/4, AD/2, 3 · AD/4, AD
Between AD/4 & AD/2	EOQ, (EOQ + AD)/2, AD
Between $2500 & AD/2	EOQ, AD, 2 · AD[b]
< $2500	Do not solicit price discounts, use small purchase procedures

[a]Under DOD restrictions, purchase quantity may not be less than three months' supply.

[b]For items in the lower end of the dollar value range, it was decided that one year demand rule could be relaxed without serious risk of overobligation of current-year funds.

by suppliers.[5] On the basis of this successful experience, the test at Ogden ALC was indefinitely extended, and the quarterly internal fiscal constraints were relaxed for this purpose.[6]

The solicitation system for the transition period obviously did not take advantage of all possible savings to be realized through price discounts, since the experiment was artificially limited to large (over $2500) purchases. The "steady state" price discount solicitation system recommended by the research team is outlined in Table 3. Since the computation of these price discount solicitation quantities is obviously complicated, a brief explanation of the logic used to derive Table 3 is in order. Four criteria were used: (1) the DOD constraint on ordering more than a three-year supply of an item must be observed; (2) the effect of the ordering cost step-function between large and small purchases must be taken into account; (3) the order quantities in each case must be sufficiently far apart in magnitude to allow a supplier to differentiate between them as to price discounts; and (4) the DOD constraint on ordering less than a three-month supply of an item must be observed. The effect of criterion (1) is seen in the computation of solicitation quantities in Categories IV and V. Categories II and III are driven by criterion (2), and criterion (4) affects only Category I. Criterion (3) was the most troublesome, and it affects solicitation quantities in Categories I, II, and III, as well as the determination of the cut-off point between Categories IV and V.

The most interesting situation displayed in Table 3 arises as a result of the large purchase/small purchase dichotomy. A legal interpretation of this ASPR provision was obtained from experts in procurement law, and the upshot is that the determination of large vs. small purchase would depend upon the maximum quantity solicited. That is, a particular PR (within a certain range) could be kept within small purchase limits by soliciting bids on a maximum quantity of $2499, or deliberately moved into the large purchase range by soliciting at least one quantity above $2499. Note that the *solicitation, not the final award,* determines the purchase category. For this reason, it was recommended that this option (Category II) be left to the experienced judgment of the buyer. A simple computer program was written to assist buyers in these cases; the program computes the price discount which would have to be obtained in order to cover the additional ordering cost generated by moving to a large-purchase situation.

The Price Discount Simulation Model

Complete information on each of the 250,000 active inventory items was maintained on 26 magnetic tapes. Rather than attempt to simulate the entire inventory (a formidable and very expensive task!), a stratified random sample of 9,767 items was selected. The simulation runs were made on the sample, and the results were then projected to the entire inventory. A description of the sample is given in Table 4. Standard random selection procedures were used to select individual inventory items within each dollar category.

---

[5] Price discounts were calculated on a "cascading" basis in order to derive a conservative estimate. That is, if three prices ($P_1>P_2>P_3$) were quoted on three increasingly larger quantities ($0<Q_1<Q_2<Q_3$), then the price discounts (PD_i) were individually computed as follows: $PD_1=(P_1-P_2)/P_1$; $PD_2=(P_2-P_3)/P_2$. The 4½% average discussed above is the arithmetic mean of all discounts treated separately.

[6] Subsequent to the completion of "Project EOQ," a special revolving fund was set up at Ogden ALC for the purpose of validating savings achieved through price discounts.

TABLE 3. "Steady state" solicitation quantities

Major Category	Subcategories	Price Discount Solicitation Quantities
I AD $\geq$ \$10,000 or EOQ > \$2500	EOQ < 3 · AD/4	EOQ, 2 · EOQ, 3 · EOQ, 4 · EOQ
	3 · AD/4 $\leq$ EOQ < AD	EOQ, 2 · EOQ, 3 · EOQ
	AD $\leq$ EOQ < 3 · AD/2	EOQ, 2 · EOQ
	EOQ $\geq$ 3 · AD/2	EOQ, 3 · AD
II \$2000 $\leq$ AD < \$10,000 and EOQ $\leq$ \$2500	Option of buyer: remain within small purchase limits	EOQ, any quantity up to \$2499
	Option of buyer: exceed small purchase limits	Same quantities as in Major Category I above
III \$833 $\leq$ AD < \$2000	EOQ > \$2000	EOQ, \$2499
	EOQ < \$2000	EOQ, (EOQ + \$2499)/2, \$2499
IV \$300 $\leq$ AD < \$833	-------	EOQ, 3 · AD
V AD < \$300	-------	Do not solicit price discounts

TABLE 4. Composition of stratified random sample

Annual Demand in Dollars	% of Total Items in Sample	Dollar Value in Sample (\$000's)	Number of Items in Sample
< \$25	1%	5	628
\$25-\$500	2%	311	2,305
\$501-\$2500	5%	2,201	2,201
\$2501-\$10,000	10%	6,986	1,613
\$10,000-\$45,000	33%	31,325	1,851
> \$45,000	100%	124,942	1,169
Totals		165,770	9,767

Note that, while the sample contained only about 4% of the inventory items, over 40% of the total dollar value (in terms of annual demand) was represented. The sample records were loaded on a single magnetic tape, which made extensive experimentation and sensitivity analysis possible.

In deciding upon appropriate average price discounts for the simulations, little empirical evidence was available to guide them. A recent test by the General Accounting Office [7] at one Air Logistics Center evoked price discount quotes from suppliers ranging from 1% to 31%, with the average being about 7%. To assure conservative results, simulations were run with all possible combinations of three average discounts (3%, 5%, 8%) and three maximum discounts (10%, 15%, 20%). Due to the conservative nature of the assumed distribution of price discounts,[7] it was found that the maximum allowable discount made almost no difference in the overall results, so subsequent runs were made using a maximum discount of 20%. The results of these simulation runs, with all but price discounts remaining unchanged in the EOQ system, are presented in Table 5.

TABLE 5. Projected net annual savings from price discount solicitation

Average Price Discount	Gross Savings in annual Acquisition Cost ($ Millions)	Net Savings in[a] Total Annual Cost ($ Millions)
3%	19.6	10.3
5%	39.9	25.9
8%	67.2	50.7

[a]Adjusted for net increase in ordering/holding cost caused by higher average inventories.

[7] The Appendix contains an expanded discussion of the simulation model.

An interesting thing occurred while the cadets were making the computer simulation runs. Although they were well aware of the Central Limit Theorem and understood its implications for the simulation model, they nevertheless wanted to be *sure*. Therefore they ran the simulation 25 times on the Academy's B-6700 computer. As could have been predicted, the total annual costs generated varied by only about 1/2 of 1% from maximum to minimum. That they were impressed by this result is a decided understatement! The moral here is clear: it is one thing to establish the validity of a powerful theoretical result by a formal mathematical proof; *it is quite another*--and more convincing--*thing to allow students to demonstrate the result for themselves.*

ADDITIONAL RESEARCH RESULTS

While the research and recommendations with respect to solicitation of price discounts were the most successful part of "Project EOQ", the other areas of investigation also generated potentiall profitable recommendations. These areas are discussed briefly below.

Demand Prediction

The current AFLC demand prediction technique (an eight-quarter moving average) was tested against four more sophisticated techniques[8] for forecasting accuracy. In each case, the most current eight quarters of demand for approximately 6,000 randomly selected items were forecast with predictors constructed from demand in the previous eight quarters. Four criteria were used to compare the results: mean absolute deviation; weighted mean absolute

[8] Single, double and triple exponential smoothing (three different weights for each) and simple linear regression.

TABLE 6. Demand prediction recommendations

Item Category	% of Items in Category	Recommendation
Low Demand Items (less than three quarters of positive demand history in the last eight qtrs.	44%	Item Manager reviews all field demands for appropriateness (management by exception)
Erratic Demand Items (at least three quarters of positive demand history in last eight quarters, but with demand standard deviation greater than average demand)	21%	Use single exponential smoothing with tracking signal to indicate a shift in demand pattern
"Normal" Demand Items	35%	Use single exponential smoothing with $\alpha = 0.1$

deviation; sum of squared deviations; and weighted sum of squared deviations [2]. Single exponential smoothing, with a smoothing constant of $\alpha = 0.1$, was approximately three times as accurate as the next most accurate of the predictors tested,[9] and was twice as accurate as measured by the most conservative criterion (weighted sum of squared deviations). Differential treatment for different categories of demand was also recommended, as outlined in Table 6.

In addition to the overall demand prediction analysis, a special analysis of the 250 highest dollar-demand items was undertaken. Most of these items are aircraft spares, so a multiple linear regression model was constructed using numbers of aircraft, sorties flown, and flying hours for each aircraft type as the independent variables, and demand for each part as the dependent variable in each case [3]. The coefficients of determination (R^2) for the individual spare parts models varied from 0.13 to 0.75, with an average R^2 of 0.47. Introduction of a one quarter time lag between the data for the independent and dependent variables resulted in a slight improvement in the R^2 (average) to 0.52. The team concluded that the results of this investigation were not convincing enough to recommend implementation of this approach, but did suggest further research in this area.

Holding Cost

In June, 1973, AFLC had decreased its holding cost parameter from 39% to 32%, based upon a downward revision of the obsolescense component from 28% to 21%. Partially as a result of evidence generated by "Project EOQ," the obsolescense component was further decreased in April 1974 to 13%, resulting in a holding parameter of 24%. (The 10% opportunity cost and 1%

[9] $D_t = \alpha \cdot d_{t-1} + (1-\alpha) D_{t-1}$, where: D_t = forecast demand for period t; d_t = actual demand for period t; α = smoothing constant.

TABLE 7. Projected net annual savings from use of variable obsolescence

Average Price Discount	Gross Savings in annual Acquisition Cost ($ Millions)	Net Savings in Total Annual Cost ($ Millions)
No Price Discount	7.8[a]	7.8
3%	23.4	17.4
5%	43.0	35.6
8%	69.2	61.8

[a]Note that lower holding costs in certain cases caused price discounts to be economically advantageous that were not so under a constant holding cost situation.

handling and storage cost components, which were established originally by the Department of Defense, were unchanged.) While the research team believed this to be a move in the right direction, there was still concern about the efficacy of the practice of applying an undifferentiated obsolescence to all items in the inventory. In an effort to refine this process, a variable obsolescence approach was investigated. Each item in the inventory is classified in two mutually exclusive and exhaustive ways--by one of 341 System Management Codes (SMC's) which identifies the item with a particular weapon system, and by one of 311 Federal Supply Class Codes (FSCC's) which identifies the item by general type. A computer scan of the inventory tapes revealed that only 634 of the SMC/FSCC pairs contained obsolescent items (while there are technically 106,051 possible SMC/FSCC combinations, most are infeasible). The actual obsolescence percentages ranged, as expected, from 0-100%, with most in the 1-2% category.

The variable obsolescence parameters were input into the simulation model, substituting the actual obsolescence rate for the current parameter, and the rather startling results are exhibited in Table 7 (compare with Table 5).

Safety Stock Analysis

Although a concerted attempt was made, the team was unable to develop a satisfactory method for determining stockout cost for expendable weapon system spares. "Time-weighted mission essentiality" is the criterion preferred by the Department of Defense [6], but no economic surrogate for this operational criterion could be identified. A secondary objective--to minimize total investment in safety stock for a given overall fillrate--was analyzed, but the results were inconclusive. Basically, the optimization of this objective involves high safety stock levels for low cost items, and low (or zero) safety stock levels for high cost items, which totally ignores mission essentiality. Further research was recommended in this area.

Miscellaneous Areas of Investigation

During the course of this research effort, AFLC readjusted its ordering cost parameters to $444 (from $424) per order for large purchases, and to $149 (from $142) per order for small purchases. The combined effect of this change and the previously mentioned downward revision in the holding cost parameter was to decrease the total number of annual purchase actions by approximately 12%. While these changes caused many more dollar actions to be affected by the three-year buy constraint on one hand, they had the salutory effect of moving large dollar actions affected by the three-month buy constraint closer to the true economic order quantities. Even more important, the reduced volume of PR's allowed experienced, highly trained buyers more time to do a better job on the remaining actions, and made implementation of a price discount solicitation capability more manageable.

Finally, AFLC had long employed the practice of using a "standard price" 15% higher than the unit price in its EOQ computations, on the theory that AFLC is acting as a wholesaler. The 15% add-on was viewed as a service charge to its customers. The research team noted that the only real effect of this practice was to cause the EOQ (in units) to be artificially understated by about 7%, and AFLC discontinued this practice prior to the termination of "Project EOQ."

CONCLUSIONS

"Project EOQ" was successful in two distinct ways. First, and most obvious, implementation of key recommendations resulted in savings of $7 million *forecasted** for the first (transition) year--the figure stated in the citation which accompanied the Air Force Business and Procurement Research Award for 1975 to each member of the research team. Full implementation of a price discount capability at all five Air Logistics Centers will soon be a reality, and AFLC subsequently sponsored additional research in all peripheral areas discussed in this paper.

Second, and perhaps even more personally gratifying, was the success achieved in orienting an academic course to the solution of a real problem. As a result, there are nineteen Air Force lieutenants who are convinced of the power and usefulness of management science--not because they heard about it in a classroom, but because they did it themselves.

---

*Note: Savings in excess of $600,000 were confirmed for late FY 1976.

APPENDIX

A one-parameter Beta distibution was used to simulate price discounts (d) randomly as follows:

(1) $f(d;\beta) = ((\beta+1)/M)(1 - d/M)^{\beta}$,
$d \in [0,M], \beta > -1$.

Choosing $M = 0.2$ (maximum allowable discount of 20%), the function becomes:

(2) $f(d;\beta) = 5(\beta+1)(1 - 5d)^{\beta}$,
$d \in [0,\ 0.2]$, with

(3) $E[d] = 0.2/(\beta+2)$;
$\mathrm{VAR}[d] = 0.04(\beta+1)/(\beta+2)^2(\beta+3)$.

Note that, as long as $E[d] < 0.10$, then $\beta > 0$, and f is strictly convex. Since mean discounts of 3%, 5%, and 8% were chosen for the simulations, the probability that a randomly selected discount was less than the mean is greater than 0.5. For example, with an average discount of 5%, than $\beta = 2$, and $\Pr(d_i \leq 0.05) \doteq 0.578$.

Moreover, more than 98% of the simulated discounts in this case are less than 15%. Thus it is seen that (2) represents a conservative approach to simulating price discounts.

(4) The CDF $F(d;\beta) = 1 - (1 - 5d)^{\beta+1}$,
$d \in [0,\ 0.2]$.

Solving (4) for d, we have:

(5) $d = 0.2 - 0.2(1 - F(d;\beta))^{1/(\beta+1)}$.

Since it is well known that F is a uniform random variable on [0,1], the internal random number generator of the B-6700 computer was used to obtain random values for F, which were inserted in (5) to derive randomly generated price discounts.

Solicitation quantities were computed using the logic in Table 3. P_o, the most recent unit price paid, was assumed to be the bid price for Q_o, the normal PR quantity. For additional quantities Q_i, $i = 1 \ldots n$

($n \leq 3$), prices were obtained by generating random discounts d_i and computing the prices $P_i = (1 - d_i)P_{i-1}$. Using the Wilson EOQ formula, total annualized cost was computed for each order quantity, and the optimal quantity and total annual cost was recorded as a "buy."

ACKNOWLEDGEMENTS

A major share of the credit for the success of this project belongs to the nineteen cadets and to Mike Anselmi, Dick Carlburg and Howard Clark, who participated as faculty members. Important contributions were also made by Elsie Akisada, Phil Jorgenson, Sanford Kozlen, John Slinkard, Paul Ste. Marie, Bob Stevens, Dan Strayer and Bill York of AFLC and the AFBRMC.

REFERENCES

1. L. M. Austin, M. S. Anselmi, R. E. Carlburg, and H. A. Clark, Project EOQ: Feasibility of Price Discounts in Procurement of Non-reparable Spares, Technical Report No. 74-18, USAF Academy, Colorado (Sept. 1974).

2. R. G. Brown, *Smoothing, Forecasting, and Prediction of Discrete Time Series*, Prentice Hall, Englewood Cliffs, N.J. (1964).

3. Y. L. Chou, *Statistical Analysis*, Holt, Rinehart, & Winston, New York (1969).

4. J. T. Coile, and D. D. Dickens, History and Evaluation of the Air Force Depot Level EOQ Inventory Model, unpublished Master's thesis, Air Force Institute of Technology, Dayton, Ohio (1974).

5. Department of Defense Instruction No. 4140.31 (June 1958).

6. Department of Defense Instruction No. 4140.39 (July 1970).

7. Private communication, working papers supplied by the Kansas City Regional Office of the General Accounting Office (Mar. 1974).

8. T. Whitin and G. Hadley, *Analysis of Inventory Systems*, Prentice-Hall, Englewood Cliffs, N.J. (1963).

READING 28

Credit and Inventory Management — Separate or Together

Michael Schiff
New York University

The management of working capital has received considerable attention in recent years. Each of the elements of working capital--cash, receivables, and inventory--has been studied separately, and modern quantitative analysis has been applied in the search for better planning and control.

The interface between credit management and inventory management is essential in effecting the trade-off in costs between the two and in achieving more effective planning and control for these elements of working capital.

The need for this interface was underscored by my recent experience in connection with a study of cost control in physical distribution management. After the study was released to some 200 large corporate sponsors, a series of 11 seminars were conducted in New York, Chicago, and San Francisco attended by key marketing, distribution, and financial executives from the sponsoring organizations. Even though the interaction between the management of receivables and inventory was not covered in the study, it was presented as a topic for discussion. At these meetings we learned that not one of the participant companies had recognized the need for the joint management of these functions. And everyone agreed that there is a real need to consider credit and customer service jointly in the marketing decision process.

CURRENT STATUS

How well have financial managers performed in dealing with receivables and inventory? Exhibit I shows index numbers for receivables, sales, profits before income taxes, inventories, and accounts receivable for manufacturing corporations, using 1956 experience as a base. From 1956-1970 sales increased 2.3 times, inventories 2.4 times, while accounts receivable increased 3.3 times. These increases were accompanied by a before-tax profit increase of only 1.6 times. Inventories as a percentage of sales show a range of 17.1 to 18.7 percent over the period studied, while

Reprinted from FINANCIAL EXECUTIVE, Vol. 40, No. 11 (November 1972), pp. 28-33, by permission of the publisher.

Exhibit I INDEX NUMBERS - SALES, PROFITS BEFORE TAX, ACCOUNTS RECEIVABLE, AND INVENTORIES ALL MANUFACTURING CORPORATIONS 1956-1970
1956 = 100

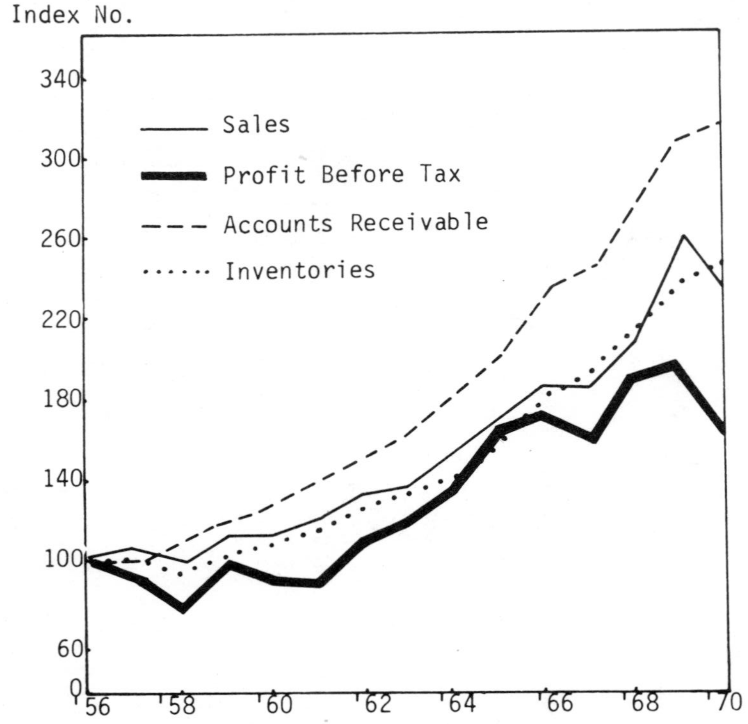

Exhibit II. PROFIT BEFORE TAX, ACCOUNTS RECEIVABLE AND INVENTORIES AS PERCENTAGE OF SALES ALL MANUFACTURING CORPORATIONS
1956-1970

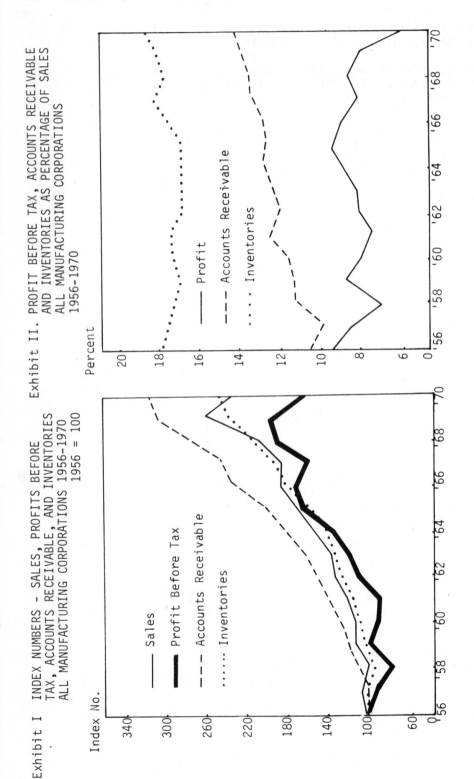

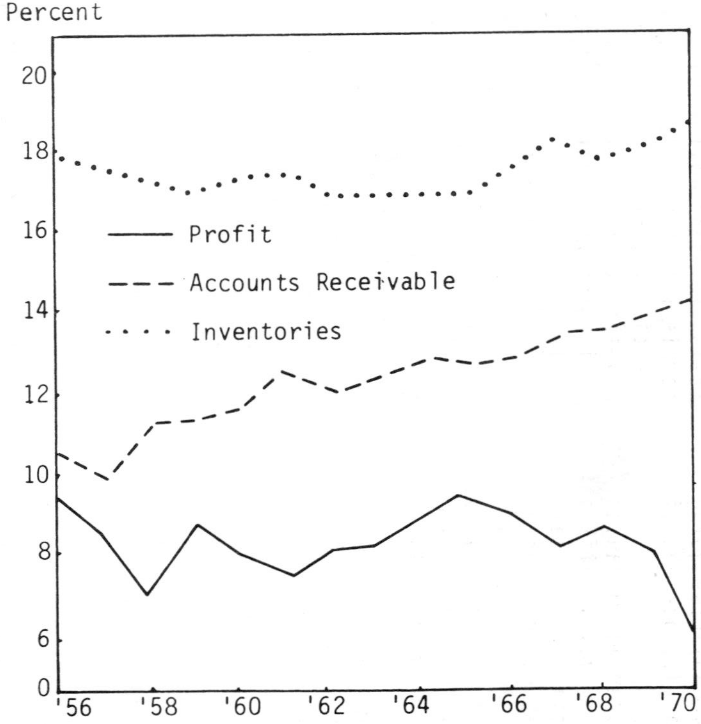

Source: Derived from Quarterly Financial Report for Manufacturing Corporations.
U.S. Federal Trade Commission and SEC

receivables show a steady rise going from 10.1 percent to 14.1 percent of sales. (Exhibit II).

For all manufacturing companies, control of inventories was significantly better than the control of receivables. The fact that the rate of profit growth was slower than sales while receivables increased at a much greater pace than sales suggests a decreasing return on an increased investment in receivables.

One can attribute the trends to external forces such as changes in monetary policy affecting interest rates, varying degrees of uncertainty, changes in customers mix (direct sales vs. sales through wholesalers and distributors), changes in selling price levels and costs, and many other factors. Indeed, business decisions are made under conditions of change and are affected by a host of external factors. The business manager considers these changes as he develops policies and strategies. The strategies must include cost trade-offs. If he fails to recognize available trade-offs, substitutions such as advertising vs. price reduction, packaging vs. advertising, promotion vs. advertising, technical service vs. personal selling, etc., he will not respond in an optimal fashion. Likewise, if he does not consider cost trade-offs in inventory and credit management he will not produce the best possible results.

The data in Exhibits I and II suggest the existence of a problem; what follows is an attempt to identify the causes and possible solutions.

Companies may have been able to maintain better control on inventories as reflected by their close correlation with sales than they have on receivables because executives are more concerned with inventory control and have achieved it by shipping goods on especially attractive terms. The result has been an increased amount of receivables accompanied by a declining rate of turnover.

Why should this be so? Surely, costs are attributable to carrying accounts receivable just as costs are associated with holding inventories. Why should one set of costs appear to be ignored while the other is carefully controlled?

There are three answers to these questions. First, inventory control, with its utilization on inventory models, has received much attention and modern analytical tools generally have been accepted in the field. Not so with accounts receivable. Some attempts have been made to develop mathematical models for studying the effect of changes in credit terms on sales, but no models which integrate receivables and inventories have been reported.

Second, the functions of inventory management and receivables management are separated in the typical business organization. Credit management, which includes granting credit and the collection of accounts receivable, is viewed as a fund management problem and is generally assigned to the treasurer or controller. Inventory management, on the other hand, is viewed as a function of developing and controlling optimum inventory levels by relating production costs, losses due to stock-outs, inventory carrying costs, and customer service costs to seek the optimum inventory levels.

In addition, the position of this function in the organization has undergone some change. Traditionally, it was part of the manufacturing activity, where it remains in many organizations. It was shifted to marketing management in some companies as part of the adoption of the "marketing concept" and, in recent years, some companies have placed it in a separate function called physical distribution. By keeping the two functions of inventory management and receivables management in separate areas of responsibility, limited integration has been achieved.

A third factor accounting for the growth of receivables and inventory is the difference in approach in measuring the effectiveness of each. While inventory management stresses the optimum balance of manufacturing capabilities with marketing needs (a positive approach to profit improvement), credit management still retains bad debt loss minimization (a negative approach). The phrase "bad debt losses" conveys a notion of a cost to be avoided, a form of cost aversion. Realistically, bad debt losses are a cost of marketing goods on credit and should be viewed as part of the marketing mix along with costs such as advertising, promotion, field selling, etc.--costs incurred with a positive purpose to achieve sales and profits. One does not identify advertising or promotion as *bad* advertising or *bad* promotion--costs to be avoided if one is careful. Costs are incurred to achieve benefits ultimately reflected in sales revenue and profits. Credit extension, along with advertising, promotion, customer service, and other elements of the marketing mix, have these attributes and should be viewed constructively.

The failure to integrate receivable and inventory management can, therefore, be attributed to lack of well-developed integrated planning models for receivables and inventory, to the separation of these inventories in the organization, and to differences in the evaluation criteria for judging performance in these functions.

It is interesting to note that during the 1956-1970 period smaller companies ($1-$5 million of assets) displayed a more effective control of receivables. Over the years studied, receivables as a percentage of sales increased at the rate of only 2 percent, while large corporations (assets over $1 billion) showed an increase of 5 percent. Indeed, for smaller companies the relationship of both inventory and receivables to sales has been consistent. The likelihood of companies of this size utilizing sophisticated inventory management techniques is remote. Perhaps their relative success is a result of the closeness of management to decision making and the greater likelihood of the interaction of marketing, production, and credit resulting from better communication and supervision. The larger corporation must rely on more indirect controls.

MARKETING

The importance of the problem can be viewed from another practical operational side. Marketing activities create the demand for accumulating inventories and for credit extension. Since the functions of credit management and inventory management are separate organizational units with minimum communication between them, marketing has two separate sources for bargaining for services which will result in increased sales. It can make its plea for maximum customer service with minimal lag between order placement and shipment and then seek extended terms or more liberalized credit.

The point is frequently made that inventory management and customer service are controlled within the organization, while credit terms are set externally, determined by the marketplace and standardized by industry. One need only examine credit terms in an industry and then calculate actual average credit terms extended as reflected by receivable turnover ratios to observe the variations in extension of credit terms. Similarly, the level of customer service extended by a firm reflects market conditions. In short, the credit extension and customer service policy of a firm reflects its reaction to market demands as much as it reflects reactions to competitive price, advertising, promotion, etc.

Where marketing performance is evaluated on an actual-to-planned-sales measure, the benefits from improved customer service and more liberal credit terms are viewed as free services, and marketing executives increasingly are abusing them. Indeed, it is fair to say that marketing management could be criticized if it does not use free services if the goal is increased sales!

The statistics previously cited suggest that where demands for service are thwarted by well-managed inventory activity, marketing has had greater success in its demand for greater credit extension because credit extension is not profit oriented. The frequent result of this kind of arrangement is increased bonuses for marketing managers and declining profits for the company.

Even where marketing is evaluated and rewarded on contribution to profit, the full cost of extended credit terms is rarely considered in calculating the profit and, as a result, the pressure on credit management for greater extension persists.

The failure to consider the impact of a marketing decision on accounts receivable and inventories can be highlighted in still another way. Consider a proposal to spend $30,000 for a machine or other capital asset in a company today. A capital budget proposal is required with extensive detail on the nature of the expenditure and a projection of cash flows over the life of the project. The proposal, which requires top management approval, is very carefully reviewed relating investment to cash flows.

By contrast, consider a salesman working out of a district office, who after much effort has landed a customer who will purchase on the average $100,000 worth of relatively profitable goods a year. All he needs to do is to get this order through the credit department. One does not usually stop to consider how much additional inventory will have to be kept to service this customer nor does anyone relate to this amount the additional investment in new accounts receivable generated by this sale. If we assume $30,000 as the sum of the average annual investment for both receivables and inventory to sustain the sales volume, then we have made an investment of $30,000 without any evaluation of the return. As a matter of fact, should the customer continue to buy over a long period of time, as expected, the investment in receivables and inventories is far more fixed than was the earlier commitment of $30,000 for the fixed asset.

In the latter situation, the return on investment provided by depreciation is cash flow, which is available for alternative investment from the moment of use (in an asset with a 10-year life the first year would return $6,000--20 percent of $30,000 using double declining balance depreciaiton). The investment in so-called current assets, accounts receivable, and inventory will not be released for alternative investment until the firm stops selling goods to this customer. Small wonder that these assets have increased while profits have declined.

POSITIVE APPROACH

Credit-inventory management is an integrated approach in the management of these functions, an integration which recognizes jointly the costs involved in these functions and measures trade-off in a logical way. Inventory models consider manufacturing costs, annual usage, order handling costs, cost of carrying inventory (physical handling, storage, obsolescence, taxes, insurance, and imputed interest), stockout costs, etc. The costs of credit include credit extension, collection, losses from uncollected accounts, and the imputed interest in carrying accounts receivable. One need not wait for the development of integrated models to achieve the interface between credit and inventory management.

The idea of cost trade-offs has been explored and implemented in inventory management. These relate the costs of physical movement of goods, holding costs, service, production, and sales costs, and are considered on an intrafirm (two or more operations within a firm) and on an interfirm (seller vs. customer) basis. The interfirm trade-offs consider relative costs of seller and customer and aim at that combination of services and service level which is economical to both. Yet these carefully considered trade-offs will be illusory if credit costs are not included. The statistics previously cited suggest that intra-firm trade-offs are deceiving when credit costs are not considered.

An initial step can be taken immetiately by examining inventory and credit policies as they relate to individual customers and channels of distribution. Exhibit III illustrates an income statement wherein inventory and receivables carrying costs are considered. For the assumed carrying costs (inventories 30 percent and receivables 15 percent), it would appear that longer credit terms involving a reduction in inventory (poorer customer service) and its associated costs would be desirable (Alternative B). The more frequently encountered case is Alternative A, where the customer service is not charged and pressure is exerted on the credit department to permit the customer to pay in 60 days. Were this to happen, the company would incur an extra $1,200 in credit carrying costs, thus reducing the contribution income by $1,200.

Inventory carrying costs and receivables carrying costs vary for different firms depending on their physical facilities, financial resources, and investment alternatives. The point should be stressed that the opportunity cost of money identified as interest is common to the tie-up of capital in both inventory and accounts receivable. This interest is automatically incorporated in inventory models and should be included in evaluating alternatives in credit extension. The approach suggested in the illustration will lead to a better matching of the seller's capabilities and costs in customer service and credit extension to the needs and capabilities of the customer. Inventory and credit policies would be

Exhibit III ILLUSTRATION OF CONTRIBUTION INCOME INCLUDING INVENTORY AND RECEIVABLES CARRYING COSTS

	Alternative A	Alternative B
Annual sales 96,000 units @ $1	$96,000	$96,000
Cost of goods sold 96,000 units @ $.75	72,000	72,000
Gross margin	$24,000	$24,000
Direct marketing costs	$ 5,000	$ 5,000
Inventory carrying costs		
8,000 x $.75 x 30%	1,800	--
Receivables carrying costs		
8,000 x 15%	1,200	
16,000 x 15%		2,400
	$ 8,000	$ 7,400
Contribution income	$16,000	$16,600

ASSUMPTIONS

1. Alternative A. Sell 8,000 units per month (one shipment a month), credit terms --30 days net.
2. Alternative B. Sell 16,000 units (one shipment every two months), credit terms 60 days net.
3. Production run: 16,000 units every 2 months shipped directly for Alternative B.
4. Inventory carrying costs equal 30% of factory cost. (Includes 10% for imputed int.)
5. Receivables carrying cost includes credit checking, collection, expected bad debts, and 10% for imputed interest.
6. Customer pays delivery charges.

coordinated to achieve maximum profits.

To assure the administration of this interactive policy, corporate management should review the current corporate structure for inventory and credit management. I suggest combining the credit function and the inventory management function into a new independent organizational unit. This new combined function would be responsible for credit activities, inventory management, and physical distribution. It would be the source for providing marketing management with the inventory and credit costs necessary in developing alternative strategies incorporating the costs of credit and customer service with other elements of the marketing mix--personal selling, promotion, advertising, packaging, etc. The profit plan arrived at with this approach would be comprehensive because it includes the costs of all services available to marketing. It provides for a positive use of credit as an income-generating expense rather than as the negative cost aversion approach typically practiced in credit extension.

Altering traditional organizational structure and responsibilities is not easy. As an alternative, a closer interaction between the two functions recognizing the cost trade-offs between the services of credit and inventory management could achieve desirable results within the current organizational framework.

The statistics cited in Exhibit I and II suggest that control of credit extension is not effective, as is evidenced by the far more rapid increase in investment in receivables as contrasted to the increase in profits. It indicates increasing investment in receivables at decreasing rates of return. This trend can and should be reversed by including costs of credit in the planning process.

CONCLUSION

What is recommended is a coordination of control of inventory and credit management to achieve a maximum return on investment in receivables and inventories. It has been established that inventory control has been achieved in part at the expense of receivables control, the result of dealing with these two interrelated activities as if they were separated and unrelated.

Inventory and receivables policies should and can be developed jointly with a recognition that there are cost trade-offs between them. Combinations of tighter inventory policy and relaxed credit, looser inventory policy, and tighter credit policy in varying mixes can be evaluated together in facing the market to arrive at policies which will generate the maximum return on investment, specifically, the return on the firm's investment in receivables and inventories.

READING 29

Financial Implications of Lot-Size Inventory Models

William Beranek
University of Georgia

The definition of the cost of resources devoted to inventories which is inherent in the economic-lot-size procedure implies financial conditions which may not exist. This would lead to infeasibility and/or to a misstatement of carrying costs. If carrying costs are incorrectly stated, then in these, as well as all standard inventory models which embody the same assumption, the *indicated* optimum inventory is either too high or too low, and needlessly excessive costs are incurred by firms using such models.

These weaknesses can be corrected by reflecting the firm's actual financial arrangements in the model's carrying cost equation and deriving the corresponding optimum lot size. Examples are presented illustrating how this may be done in the face of several different financial circumstances. In each case, the results of our procedure are compared to those that emerge from an application of the standard lot-size model.

Worthwhile savings in inventory cost are indicated, especially if the firm is employing the standard, or classical, model for a number of different products or for a single product which involves a large commitment of resources.

In sum, the model builder must be prepared to develop models which reflect the conditions of his financial environment if he is to choose both an optimal inventory and an optimal means of financing the inventory.

It is not well known that economic lot-size inventory models imply restricted cash-flow and loan-repayment conditions. If funds are not borrowed to finance the inventory, then an equally constraining condition is implied with respect to the availability and the transfer of cash to the firm's next best alternative. The importance of these implications lies in the fact that if these conditions do not correspond to those in a firm's environment, the lot-size-using firm will encounter either (1) *financial infeasibility*, or (2) a *nonoptimal* inventory or (3) both.

Reprinted from MANAGEMENT SCIENCE (April 1967), Vol. 13, No. 8, pp. B-401 - B-408, by permission of the publisher.

It will be shown that the reason lot-size-using firms do not recognize financial infeasibility is because other segments of the firm,are, in effect, subsidizing the lot-size-using suboptimizing departments. Assuming that the model is financially feasible, the added cost of a nonoptimal inventory is often needless, since, as will be shown, models may be developed which eliminate them.

The importance of the problem, however, is broader than might appear at first blush, since these weaknesses are not restricted to lot-size models. They may appear in any inventory model which assumes a carrying cost as in the lot-size, hereafter referred to as the classical, model. There is reason to believe that this includes a host of standard models.[1]

The reason these inventory models contain this difficulty doubtless stems from the high degree of suboptimization practiced by the typical firm. The department seeking an optimum inventory is not the one that must negotiate and provide for the repayment of the firm's loans. This analysis draws attention, therefore, to the need for suboptimization at a higher level within the firm, and hence for inventory models which more accurately reflects the firm's *financing* and *cash-flow* conditions.

The first part of the paper develops the proof of the financial implications of these models; the final section presents some simple illustrations of the computation of carrying costs when these financial conditions do not hold, and, in order to reveal the importance of this analysis, compares the costs of the refined, more accurate models with those of the lot-size models.

THE FINANCIAL IMPLICATIONS

Our focal point of interest centers on the computation of inventory carrying costs. If money is borrowed to finance the acquisition of the inventory, the unit carrying cost, c, is defined to include the interest cost per unit of inventory over the planning horizon T. If demand for units of inventory is uniform over the horizon and if q denotes beginning inventory, the average inventory becomes $q/2$ and it is conventional to define total carrying costs over T as $cq/2$. This assumes that interest cost is proportional to the average inventory $q/2$, a fact which many writers have stated with care.[2] In turn, however, this assumes that within the cycle the average amount of the loan outstanding is proportional to $q/2$. While there are, of course, a host of ways of repaying the loan which involve the same average loan outstanding, each of these methods of repaying the loan involves an associated condition of cash inflow which must hold if the loan is to be repaid in that manner. The implicit assumptions of (1) a loan repayment schedule in combination with (2) a corresponding adequate cash inflow so as to imply an average loan size proportional to $q/2$ have not, to this writer's knowledge, been explicitly treated by authors of inventory models. The classical and numerous other inventory models fail to reflect the fact that a dollar of resources is tied up not only in inventory for a period of time but often also in *accounts receivable* for an *additional* period, a fact which is developed in greater detail in [2].

To illustrate the problem, let us examine some of the loan repayment arrangements which are consistent with the classical carrying cost approach, i.e., the assumption that the amount of interest is proportional to $q/2$. If we let M denote the amount borrowed to finance the purchase cost of the beginning inventory q, then M must be proportional to q. Three possible loan repayment arrangements are depicted in Figure I.

In Part I the loan is repaid continuously while in Part II the loan is repaid in full at time $t/2$. In each

[1] See, for example, [1], [3], [4], [5].

[2] See, for example, [1], [3], [4], [5].

Figure I. LOAN BALANCE AS A FUNCTION OF TIME FOR THREE REPAYMENT ARRANGEMENTS

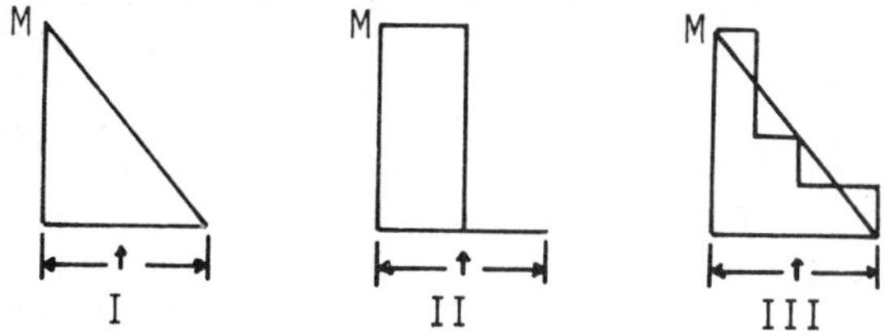

case, however, the average amount of the loan outstanding over the period t is $M/2$. In Part III, the loan is repaid in steps and since the sum of the areas of the two triangles lying above the 45 degree line are equal to the sum of the areas of the small triangles formed on the steps below it, the average amount of the loan outstanding is likewise $M/2$.

While each of these arrangements will yield an average loan proportional to $q/2$, this is not sufficient for *financial feasibility*. For the latter to hold, the cash inflow must be of such a size to make the *loan repayment schedule feasible*. This, of course, need not always be the case. Suppose, for example, that the firm extends credit to its customers under terms which provide that all deliveries during the period (i.e., the inventory cycle) must be paid for at the end of the period. Then cash from sales will not be received in time to make any of these repayment schedules feasible. In such a case, however, the average amount of the loan outstanding over any period will not be $M/2$ but simply M. Moreover, if cash equivalent to the profit for each period is removed from inventory operations (perhaps to pay a dividend or simply transferred to a higher organizational level) the loan size for *each* period will be M. Under these conditions, therefore, the interest cost is actually 100% higher than the amount assumed by the classical model.

Of course, the firm may obtain cash for loan repayment by selling marketable securities or other assets. If so, then this "switching" decision should be implied by the inventory model, i.e., the model should reflect not only inventory costs but also the returns from holding marketable securities and other assets that may be converted into cash. In this way, the optimal decision embodies several acts: the amount to stock, and the amount and date of assets to be sold for the purpose of repaying the proposed loan. The analysis of this paper, however, assumes that cash available for loan repayment is available only from the firm's sales.

The reason why a multiproduct firm can employ the classical model for one or more of its products in the face of financial infeasibility is because some departments of the firm are, in effect, lending cash to the classical-model-using departments. In other words, to this degree these departments are being subsidized, either knowingly or unknowingly, by other segments of the firm.

In summary, it is appropriate to assume that the carrying cost is given by $cq/2$ for borrowing conditions if the following conditions prevail:
(1) the average loan outstanding is proportional to $q/2$;
(2) the cash inflow is actually adequate to make the loan repayment arrangement feasible.

If the firm is employing its own resources for financing the inventory, an analogous set of conditions must prevail. If the firm can earn on its next best alternative a rate of return i on its funds throughout the period, then the cash inflows must be adequate to justify the assumption that the average amount of the firm's resources tied up in inventory is $M/2$, a quantity proportional to $q/2$. Of course, as the cash inflow is used to pay off the internal loan M, so to speak, the firm devotes this cash immediately to its next best alternative which earns the rate of return i.

CARRYING COST WHEN CLASSICAL CONDITIONS DO NOT HOLD

Failure of the classical conditions to correspond to a firm's financial conditions will lead either to infeasibility or to an inaccurate statement of the firm's carrying costs or both. The problem of feasibility can be remedied by an examination of the firm's loan repayment arrangements in combination with its cash inflow conditions. Incorrectly assumed carrying costs, however, are corrected by defining these costs to reflect the firm's actual financial conditions. In this connection, the model builder must be prepared to cope with a variety of financial circumstances and, in particular, to construct a model that corresponds to the financial conditions confronted by his firm.

To show how this may be done, each example that follows is designed to illustrate the computation of financial carrying costs, quantities which may then be inserted into expressions of total inventory costs for the derivation of optimum lot sizes. The suggested procedure consists of first assessing the loan repayment arrangement in order to determine the average amount of the loan outstanding, or the average amount borrowed over the inventory cycle. Interest cost per cycle is then the product of the interest rate and the average amount borrowed. In addition, there may or may not be a fixed commitment fee per borrowing. If there is, the financial cost per cycle is then the interest cost plus the fixed fee. Total carrying costs per cycle are then the sum of nonfinancial carrying costs plus the above financial cost. Since the average amount borrowed is a function of the initial amount stocked (or the initial inventory), total carrying costs may be expressed in terms of the initial amount stocked. The examples below may be helpful in illustrating this procedure.

If we define c to be the unit carrying cost over the horizon T exclusive of interest or opportunity costs, then the quantity $cq/2$ would represent total carrying costs over T exclusive, of course, of either internal or external financing costs. Let i denote either the rate of interest or the firm's opportunity rate over the horizon, whichever may be appropriate, and M, the amount of money borrowed. We shall assume, in each case, that cash profits generated by the system are not available for financing inventory operations.

Example 1. The firm must pay cash upon receipt of its inventory but extends credit to its customers which provides that all purchases during the period (i.e., the inventory cycle) must be paid at the *end* of the period. If the firm borrows money to finance the purchase of q units at the price p per unit at the beginning of each cycle, and if the bank requires a "clean-up" of the loan at the end of each period, then the amount borrowed per period will be $M = pq$ and the interest cost over the horizon will be ipq. The quantity ipq is seen to be twice the amount assumed by the classical model of $ipq/2$.[3] Total carrying cost over the horizon is then $(cq/2) + (ipq)$, a result which may be compared to the

---

[3] We are assuming the absence of a fixed charge or a commitment fee in connection with the borrowing. Such a charge may take the form of a single given fee which applies over the entire horizon or a separate fee for each individual loan. In the former case the financial cost would be $k+ipq$ where k is the commitment fee while in the latter case we would have ipq plus the number of periods (or inventory cycles) multiplied by the fixed borrowing cost per period.

total carrying cost in the classical model of $(cq/2) + (ipq/2)$ by forming the ratio of $(cq/2) + (ipq)$ to $(cq/2) + (ipq/2)$ or $(c+2ip)/(c+ip)$, the ratio of the unit carrying costs. The magnitude of this ratio depends upon the values of ip and c. If, for example, $c = \$1$ and $ip = \$6$ then we have 13/7 or an almost doubling of carrying costs while total interest cost is twice the amount assumed in the classical model. Hence, under these financial conditions the classical model understates unit carrying costs by \$6, or in relative terms by approximately 46%.

The sensitivity of the order-quantity decision to an error of this type can be determined by standard procedures. Assume a fixed reorder cost of \$2, a total demand of 300 units, and a unit carrying cost (computed under classical assumptions) of \$3. Then it is easily verified that the optimal order quantity q_0 becomes

$$q_0 = \sqrt{\frac{2(\$2)(300)}{\$3}} = 20 \text{ units.}$$

Suppose, however, that the correct computation of unit carrying cost leads to a value which, for the sake of simplicity, can be approximated at \$6. Then we have

$$q_0 = \sqrt{\frac{2(\$2)(300)}{\$6}} = 14.14 \text{ units}$$

to the nearest hundredth. Under these conditions, the optimal order quantity is apparently quite sensitive to the firm's financial opportunities.

Observe that if the bank did not require the loan to be repaid until, say, the end of the horizon, the interest cost over the horizon would still be iM. In this case the firm could, if competition so required, find it financially feasible to liberalize the extension of credit to its customers to provide that they may pay at the end of the horizon T for all purchases over the horizon.

Example 2. The firm extends credit to its customers for a period of time equal to the length of the inventory cycle. In other words, each day's deliveries are paid for t days later. Suppose money is borrowed at the beginning of the period and the loan repaid during the next period in the manner corresponding to Part I of Figure I, i.e., as cash is received from accounts it is used to amortize the loan. Thus, while there will not be any cash receipts during the first cycle, there will be cash receipts for t days beyond the end of the horizon T. Therefore, the average loan outstanding will be $M + (M/2)$ or $3M/2$ and hence, the total carrying cost will be $(cq/2) + (ipq3/2)$. The unit carrying cost becomes $c + 3ip$ which compares to the classical result $c + ip$. In this case, the actual interest cost is 200% greater than the amount assumed in the classical model.

A sensitivity analysis of this result as compared to the classical assumption can be made by observing the procedure in Example 1. Note that the expression for the optimal order quantity here has the same form as the corresponding expression in Example 1.

Example 3. The loan is repaid in a lump sum whenever the firm accumulates sufficient cash receipts. Sales to the firm's customers are for cash and the selling price is denoted by p'. The firm must sell q' units to accumulate cash equal to the amount of the loan and hence $p'q' = M$, which implies

$$q' = \frac{M}{p'} = \frac{pq}{p'}.$$

Since sales are made at a uniform rate, the point in time t' at which the accumulated cash will equal $p'q'$ or M must satisfy $q'/q = t'/t$ and hence

$$t' = t\,\frac{q'}{q},$$

or

$$t' = t\,\frac{p}{p'}.$$

The quantity of money M will therefore be borrowed for a period of time t' within each cycle. If we let D denote the total demand over the horizon T, the number of cycles will be D/q and the total time the loan will be outstanding is $(D/q)t'$. In this case the total interest cost will be $iM(D/q)t'/T$, which can be simplified to iMp/p' or iqp^2/p'. Total carrying cost will then be $(cq/2 + (ipq^2/p')$, which, when divided by the classical carrying cost expression $(cq/2) + (ipq/2)$, yields $(c + 2ip^2/p')/c + ip)$. If $p = p'$, then this case reduces to Example 1. However, for $p' > p$ it is seen that the carrying cost for the Example 3 model varies inversely with p' and hence, the ratio of the two carrying costs varies inversely with p'.

To determine how this result affects the classical optimal decision, we note that the carrying cost in this case, $cq/2 + ipq^2/p'$, can be written as $q(c/2 + ip^2/p')$ while the corresponding classical carrying cost can be expressed as $q(c2 + ip/2)$. In order for these two costs to be identical (and hence for the classical decision to be unaffected), it is necessary that the unit carrying costs of each approach be identical or $c/2 + ip^2/p' = c/2 + ip/2$ which, in turn, implies $ip^2/p' = ip/2$ or $2p = p'$. In other words, the unit selling price must be twice the unit cost. When this condition does not hold under the conditions of this example, then the classical decision is affected and, of course, a sensitivity analysis may be conducted to determine the extent. Note that in the above analysis a comparison of the unit carrying cost of each procedure is sufficient since the optimal solution to each model yields the same logical form, i.e., the classic square-root formula.

When a bank offers several loan repayment arrangements, then, from among those that are feasible one would, of course, opt for the one which minimizes total inventory costs (including, of course, carrying costs) over the horizon.

Each of the above examples reflects a financing cost in excess of the corresponding cost in the classical lot-size model. However, Example 4 reveals a case where the lot-size model overstates the carrying cost.

Example 4. The firm purchases its inventory on credit from suppliers on condition that it pay for such purchases at the end of the inventory cycle. It also extends credit to its customers under terms which provide for payment at the end of the cycle for all deliveries during the cycle. Then the period of credit from suppliers will match the period of credit to customers and the firm will not have, on balance, any of its own resources committed to the inventory-accounts receivable cycle. Hence, its financing costs will be zero and total carrying costs will be simply $cq/2$.

It is worth stressing the correspondence of the three periods--the credit period of the firm's suppliers, the credit period of its customers, and the inventory cycle--in the above example. When they do not correspond, the analysis can easily become complicated.

SUMMARY

The carrying cost assumption which is contained in the lot-size inventory model asserts that the amount of resources devoted to inventory is proportional to the average inventory, $q/2$. It was shown that this is valid provided (1) the external (or internal, as the case may be) loan repayment schedule is such that the average amount of the loan outstanding per unit time is $M/2$, and (2) the cash inflow conditions are such as to render the repayment schedule *feasible*. Since these conditions do not often obtain, (1) carrying costs are frequently misstated with the result that the indicated optimal inventory is either too high or too low and/or, (2) cash is implicitly borrowed from other segments of the firm with the result that the lot-size-using department is being subsidized. These difficulties, however are not restricted to the classical model: all inventory models which employ the classical carrying cost assumption may be subject to these weaknesses. Simple examples illustrating the computation of carrying costs under nonclassical conditions were developed and the financial costs compared to those in the lot-size model. Financial offerings, i.e., loans, must be evaluated not only in terms of the interest rate but also in view of the proposed loan repayment arrangement. The firm then may choose the financial offering that minimizes total inventory costs, including carrying costs, over the horizon.

REFERENCES

1. Arrow, K.J., Karlin S. and Scarf, H., *Studies in the Mathematical Theory of Inventory and Production*, Stanford University Press, Stanford, Calif, 1958, p. 6.

2. Beranek, W., *Analysis for Financial Decisions*, Irwin, Homewood, Ill., 1963, p. 303.

3. Fetter, R.B. and Dalleck, W.C., *Decision Models for Inventory Management*, Irwin, Homewood, Ill., 1961, p. 31.

4. Hadley, G. and Whitin, T.M., *Analysis of Inventory Systems*, Prentice-Hall, Englewood Cliffs, N.J., 1963, pp. 13-17.

5. Starr, M.K. and Miller, D.W., *Inventory Control: Theory and Practice*, Prentice-Hall, Englewood Cliffs, N.J., 1962, pp. 10-11.

READING 30

Optimal Inventory and Credit-Granting Strategies Under Inflation and Devaluation

Alan Shapiro
University of Pennsylvania

I. INTRODUCTION

The recent wave of devaluations has again brought to the fore the foreign exchange risks with which most multinational corporations have to live constantly. While these latest parity changes have tended to increase the value of foreign currencies relative to the dollar, most exchange risks arise from pending devaluations.

There are numerous methods used by corporations to hedge, or protect themselves, against devaluations. For example, if a firm believes that the English pound, which is now selling for $2.40, is likely to be devalued within the next six months, it can sell pounds forward for delivery six months hence. At that time, it will receive $2.40 - X per pound, where X is the forward discount. This discount is a risk premium which takes into account the market participants' perceptions regarding the possibility and extent of a devaluation within the next six months. These hedging arrangements are known as forward contracts. The problem of determining an optimal forward contract hedging policy is discussed in [9].

However, in many Latin American and other underdeveloped countries with soft currencies (those likely to be devalued) forward contracts are limited. In these countries, two alternative means of hedging that are popular include the advance purchase of imported materials and credit rationing.

A situation common to all the soft currency countries is a persistent internal currency devaluation otherwise known as inflation. Even if no external devaluation is forecast, expected price rises may lead a firm to increase its investment in inventory and to modify its credit policy.

This paper discusses inventory purchase strategies and credit granting policies in soft currency countries under both inflation and the threat of devaluation. Revaluations can be easily handled with the same basic models.

These problems necessitate sequen-

Reprinted from the JOURNAL OF FINANCIAL AND QUANTITATIVE ANALYSIS (January 1973), Vol. 8, No. 1, by permission of the publisher.

tial decision making. The particular formulation used is the special class of dynamic programming problems known as stopping rule problems (see Breiman [2] for a good treatment of stopping rule problems). A number of published articles have used stopping rule formulations particularly in the areas of evaluating warrants and stock options (See, for example, [5], [8], and [11].)

The following models assume a linear utility function, i.e., there is no risk aversion, at least for the relatively small amounts at stake.[1]

II. INVENTORY PURCHASE STRATEGIES

Suppose a company needs a particular material t periods hence and wants to determine when and at what price to buy. Expected general price rises or an anticipated devaluation may lead a firm to purchase construction materials in advance or to speed up the importation of certain goods. The tradeoff involves tying up money in inventory as well as not being able to take advantage of potentially favorable fluctuations in the specific prices of these materials.

Inventory Purchase Under Inflation

The first model treats the case of inflation. Assume that the price of a unit of inventory in period $j + 1$ can be described by the following random walk:

$$p_{j+1} = p_j + \mu_j + z_j$$

where z has a known density function $f(z)$ with mean zero and $\mu_j \geq 0$, all j. Essentially, μ_j is the expected inflation parameter for period j. Let r_j be the firm's opportunity cost for one unit of local currency in period j.

Suppose that at the beginning of period j the firm has not yet purchased inventory. Its options then are either to buy material at the current price and hold it until period t or to wait until $j + 1$ with the hope of saving enough on the carrying cost to pay for the expected price increase. There are generally additional out-of-pocket holding costs. We summarize these out-of-pocket holding costs from j to t in the parameter $\lambda_{j,t}$. Then one unit of inventory bought in period j at a price p and held until period t will cost $p(1 + \lambda_{j,t})$. This assumes that holding costs are proportional to the number of items purchased.

The problem can then be formulated as the dynamic programming problem (see Figure I), where the return function, $K_{j,t}(p)$ is the minimum expected cost of purchasing a unit of raw materials for period t given that we are in period j and the current price (the state variable) is p.

As shown in [9], there is a critical number c_j in each period j such that, if $p < c_j$, we would purchase the inventory, while if $p \geq c_j$, we would wait till period $j + 1$. In μ_j, c_j is monotonically nondecreasing and in r_j and λ_j it is monotonically nonincreasing. Intuitively this makes sense. The greater the carrying cost, the less we are willing to pay in period j; the larger the expected price increase in period $j + 1$, the more we are willing to pay in j. A necessary condition for buying in period j is that

$$\frac{(1+\lambda_{j+1,t})}{1+r_j}(p + \mu_j) > p\ (1+\lambda_{j,t}).$$

This condition states that we will only buy in period j if the expected cost of buying in period $j + 1$

$$\frac{(1+\lambda_{j+1,t})}{1+r_j}(p + \mu_j)$$

---

[1] For a good treatment of risk aversion in a stopping problem, see Hausman and White [5].

is greater than the price, $p(1 + \lambda_{j,t})$, right now.

The c_j's are monotonic and can also be shown to be increasing in j if

$$\frac{1}{(1+r_j)(1+\lambda_{j+1,t})} \leq \frac{1}{(1+r_{j+1})(1+\lambda_{j+2,t})}$$

and $\mu_j \leq \mu_{j+1}$ for $j = 1, \cdots, t-2$ (see [9]). In other words, we are willing to pay a higher and higher price as time goes on if both inflation and our holding cost discount factor are increasing together. Any computation scheme will assume that p can only take on discrete values. These properties enable us to develop a more efficient dynamic programming algorithm to compute optimal policies by bounding the necessary search space.

In addition, a well-known feature of stopping-rule problems is that they can be converted into linear programming problems if the state variable is discrete (see [2] and [9]). By appending a subroutine utilizing the previously stated properties to the master problem, convergence to the optimal solution should be more rapid.

Inventory Purchase of Imported Raw Materials Under the Threat of a Devaluation

If a devaluation is anticipated and most of a firm's raw materials are imported, then for these imported materials price inflation is not the central problem unless the country exporting these materials is itself facing an inflation. The unit of payment is the foreign currency and the exchange rate is fixed until devaluation. The problem involves determining whether to buy now and tie up capital in inventory or wait until later with the increased chance of having to buy at a post-devaluation price. Even though the price in the foreign currency remains the same, imports become relatively more expensive in terms of the local currency; how much more expensive depends directly on the extent of the devaluation. The discount rate remains r_j in period j. The price in period $j = 1$ can be described as follows:

$$p_{j+1} = p_j + z_j, \text{ if no devaluation occurred in period } j;$$

$$p'_{j+1,k} = \frac{p_j+z_j}{1-d_k}, \text{ if there was a devaluation of size } d_k \text{ in } j$$

where the z_j's are independent, identically distributed random variables with mean zero.

This process assumes that there is no trend in prices and that, even after a devaluation, there is no alteration in the pattern of prices expressed in terms of the foreign currency. However, in terms of the local currency, prices increase in proportion to the extent of the devaluation, i.e., the importing country comprises only a small portion of the total market.

Let $K_{j,t}(p'_{jk})$ (with $\mu_j = 0$) be the optimal inventory purchase plan described in the previous section. $\bar{\pi}_j$ and π'_{jk} are the conditional probabilities, respectively, of no devaluation in period j and a devaluation of size d_k, $k = 1, \cdots, K$, in period j, given that no devaluation occurred

Figure I.

Buy Wait

$$K_{j,t}(p) = \min \{p(1 + \lambda_{j,t}), \frac{1}{1+r_j} E[K_{j+1,t}(p + \mu_j + z_j)]\} \quad j = 1, \cdots, t-1$$

$$= p; \quad j=t$$

Figure II

$$M_{j,t}(p) = \min \{\underbrace{p(1+\lambda_{j,t})}_{\text{Buy}},\ \underbrace{\frac{1}{1+r_j}[\bar{\pi}_j E[M_{j+1,t}(p + z_j)] + \sum_k \pi'_{jk} E[K_{j+1,t}(p'_{j+1k})]]}_{\text{Wait}}\};$$
$$= p;\ j=t$$

previously. Then the new problem becomes to find (see Figure II), where $M_{j,t}(p)$ is the minimum expected cost of purchasing inventory for period t given that we are in period j, that $p_j = p$, and that no devaluation has yet occurred.

Each of the $K_{j,t}$'s would have to be solved separately and then used in determining the $M_{j,t}$'s. This procedure sounds complicated but each of the $K_{j,t}$'s as well as the overall problem can be converted into linear programming problems as proved in [9] and solved using one of the many L.P. packages available. The number of variables and constraints for each K_j and M_j is also discussed in [9].

The necessity of acquiring the key inputs $\bar{\pi}_j$, π'_{jk} looms as a major obstacle to this model. However, some work has been done in this particular area and some information is available. For example, a paper by Ferber [4] utilizes an empirically derived beta distribution for time to devaluation in Brazil. In addition, Shulman [10] quantifies the probabilities of devaluations and revaluations for a number of different currencies. The only claim for this model is that it promises to make better use, than current practice does, of the probabilities, even though they are sketchy and difficult to obtain.

III. CREDIT GRANTING AND THE MANAGEMENT OF ACCOUNTS RECEIVABLE

Bierman and Hausman [1] discuss some of the important considerations that must be made in analyzing any credit policy. They assume that credit is granted for only one period at a time and the gain from a sale is K_1 if collection occurs. However, one aspect of granting credit that poses a constant problem to managers operating in an inflationary environment or in a soft currency country threatened with devaluation is the determination of the length of time for which credit should be granted. The easier credit terms are, the more sales are likely to be made. Against this must be balanced the risk of default and the deterioration of the value of accounts receivable through inflation and/or currency devaluation. Sometimes these additional costs can be partly offset by a firm's being able to raise prices because of the liberalized credit terms. The following models attempt to determine the expected marginal cost, in terms of dollars, of extending one dollar's worth of credit now from t periods to $t + 1$ periods.

Extension of Credit in an Inflationary Environment

Let the firm's discount rate in period j be r_j. Then, in the case of inflation where no means of protection are available, the expected cost of extending credit from period t to period $t + 1$ is:

$$\frac{1}{\prod_1^t (1+r_i)} - \frac{1}{\prod_1^{t+1} (1+r_i)} = \frac{r_{t+1}}{\prod_1^{t+1} (1+r_i)}$$

where r_i, the discount rate in period i, takes into account the anticipated rate of inflation in i.

In general, though, it will be possible to factor (discount) these accounts receivable in advance and convert the local currency into dollars or some other asset which will maintain its real value in terms of present dollars in the face of inflation. Suppose that a firm is now holding one dollar's worth of local currency receivables which are due t periods from now. At the beginning of any period, except the last one, these accounts receivable can be either discounted or held for one more period. A company that discounts one dollar's worth of soft currency receivables (payable at t) in period j will receive $\$(1-\rho_{j,t})$ worth of local currency.

The discount rate $\rho_{j,t}$ incorporates the real interest rate adjusted for the risk of inflation between j and t. In addition, if the receivables are factored without recourse, $\rho_{j,t}$ would also include a default premium.

Let $g(\rho_{j+1,t}|\rho_{j,t} = \rho)$ be the density function for $\rho_{j+1,t}$ given $\rho_{j,t} = \rho$. This assumes that ρ is determined by a Markov process. Markov models of interest rate determination are often used in the literature.[2] The tradeoff for the company then is between paying ρ_j in period j for discounting the accounts receivable and having the money available immediately or waiting until $j + 1$ to see if more favorable discounting terms can be arranged. If the company is willing to wait until period t, full value of the accounts receivable will be collected by the firm. (The problem of defaults can be treated by looking at the expected percentage of collection.)

Then the decision problem can be formulated as

$$R_{j,t}(\rho) = \max \{1-\rho, \frac{1}{1+r_j} E[R_{j+1,t}(\rho_{j+1,t}|\rho_{j,t} = \rho]\}, \quad j = 1, \cdots, t-1$$

$$= 1; \; j=t$$

where $R_{j,t}(\rho)$ is the value of holding one dollar's worth of accounts receivable in period j which are due in period t, and where the present discount cost is ρ.

The expected marginal cost then of extending credit now from period t to $t + 1$ is

$$R_{j=1,t}(\rho_{1,t}) - R_{j+1,t+1}(\rho_{1,t+1})$$

where $R_{j=1,t}(\rho_{1,t})$ is the expected value now of one dollar's worth of accounts receivable due in period t when the present discount rate is $\rho_{1,t}$.

Extension of Credit Under the Threat of a Devaluation

If a devaluation is anticipated, then the marginal cost in dollars, per dollar's worth of local currency credit extension for one more period, is computed in a different manner. Let π_{jk} represent the probability of a devaluation of size d_k occurring in period j. If there are no available means of protection, then for every dollar's worth of local currency due us in period t, we would expect to collect only

$$1 - \sum_{j=1}^{t} \sum_{k=1}^{K} \pi_{jk} d_k$$

dollars. Given that r_j is the firm's opportunity cost of money in j, one dollar's worth of local currency due at the end of t is worth only

$$\frac{1 - \sum_{j=1}^{t} \sum_{k=1}^{K} \pi_{jk} d_k}{\prod_{j=1}^{t} (1 + r_j)}$$

dollars at the beginning of period 1.

---

[2] See Kalymon [6] and Pye [7], for example.

Then the relevant cost of extending one dollar of local credit from t to $t + 1$ is equal to

$$\frac{r_{t+1}[1 - \sum_{j=1}^{t} \sum_{k=1}^{K} \pi_{jk} d_k] + \sum_{k=1}^{K} \pi_{t+1,k} d_k}{\prod_{j=1}^{t+1} (1 + r_j)}$$

If a future market exists, the firm's accounts receivable can be hedged through forward transactions. Let $A(t)$ be the expected minimum cost of protecting one dollar's worth of exposure for the next t periods. Then the expected marginal cost of extending credit for one more period is

$$\frac{1 - A(t)}{\prod_{j=1}^{t} (1 + r_j)} - \frac{1 - A(t + 1)}{\prod_{j=1}^{t+1} (1 + r_j)} = \frac{A(t + 1) - A(t) + r_{t+1} [1 - A(t)]}{\prod_{1}^{t+1} (1 + r_j)}.$$

The values of $A(t)$ and $A(t + 1)$ are found from the models of optimal hedging through forward contracts in [9].

In many underdeveloped countries, however, there are no forward contracts available. It may be possible, though to hedge by discounting accounts receivable in advance and converting the local currency into a dollar account or some other asset that will maintain its fixed dollar value in the face of a devaluation.

A question that immediately comes to mind is whether discounting is possible in a country where no forward market exists for the local currency. According to Business International [3, p. 7]. discounting is "widespread in Latin America; for example discounting is the normal technique of lending in Brazil and Argentina." In addition, while discounting is not very common in India, "local money lenders (or *shroffs*, as they are called) make advances against personal notes called *hundis*. There is a regular market in these notes" ([3, p. 546]).

Let $\rho_{j,t}$ be the discount rate in period j for discounting accounts receivable from period j through period t; i.e., at the beginning of period j, if devaluation has not yet occurred, $(1 - \rho_{j,t})$ dollar's worth of local currency can be received through discounting. At the beginning of any period, except the last one, the accounts receivable can either be discounted or held until the next period. Let $\bar{\pi}_j$ and π'_{jk} be the conditional probabilities, respectively, of no devaluation and a devaluation of extent d_k in period j, given that no devaluation occurred between periods 1 and j.

The optimal policy is then found by solving

$$D_{j,t}(\rho) = \max \{1-\rho, \frac{\bar{\pi}_j}{1 + r_j}$$

$$E[D_{j+1,t}(\rho_{j+1,t} | \rho_{j,t} = \rho)]$$

$$+ \sum_k \pi'_{jk}(1 - d_k)\};$$

$$j = 1, \cdots, t-1$$

$$= 1; \; j=t$$

where $D_{j,t}(\rho)$ is the maximum expected value, in period j, of one dollar's worth of accounts receivable due in period t.

Then the expected marginal cost of extending credit from period t to $t + 1$ is

$$D_{1,t}(\rho_{1,t}) - D_{1,t+1}(\rho_{1,t+1})$$

using our previous notation.

When either forward contracts or the discounting of accounts receivable can be used, the expected marginal cost of extending credit for one more period then becomes

$$\min \left\{ D_{1,t}(\rho_{1,t}) - D_{1,t+1}(\rho_{1,t+1}), \; \frac{A(t+1) - A(t) + r_{t+1}\,[1-A(t)]}{\prod_{1}^{t+1} (1 + r_j)} \right\}$$

However, the expected marginal revenue to be derived by a relaxation of credit terms, both through possibly raising prices as well as by making more sales, must be considered along with the marginal cost of extending credit for one more period.

Let $c(t)$ be the total expected cost of extending credit for t periods. Assume that the firm faces a demand curve $q(p,t)$, $\frac{\partial q}{\partial p} < 0$, $\frac{\partial q}{\partial t} > 0$, where t is the length of time for which credit is extended and q is the quantity demanded at a given dollar price p.

If $f(q)$ is the cost of selling q units (disregarding credit costs), then expected dollar profits will equal

$$pq(p,t)\,[1 - c(t)] - f(q).$$

The optimal pricing and credit decisions have to be determined simultaneously by solving the following two inequalities for p and t:

$$[pq(p,t) + p\,\frac{\partial q}{\partial p}]\;[1 - c(t)] - \frac{df}{dq}\,\frac{\partial q}{\partial p} \leq 0, \text{ and}$$

$$q(p,t)\,[c(t-1) - c(t)] + [q(p,t) - q(p,t-1)]\;[1 - c(t)] \leq 0.$$

Second-order conditions, of course, would have to be checked to ensure that we are at a maximum.

Both of these quantities, the expected marginal revenue as well as the marginal cost of relaxing credit terms, can be used as inputs into a Bierman-Hausman type model which considers only default risk.

REFERENCES

[1] Bierman, Harold, Jr., and Warren H. Hausman. "The Credit Granting Decision." *Management Science*, Vol. 16 (April 1970), pp. B-519-532.

[2] Breiman, Leo. "Stopping Rule Problems." *Applied Combinatorial Mathematics*, ed. by E. Beckenback. New York: John Wiley, Inc., 1964.

[3] Business International Corporation. *FFO: Financing Foreign Operations*. New York, 1966.

[4] Ferber, Robert. "Optimal Hedging Against Devaluation." Paper delivered at T.I.M.S. Sixteenth International Meeting.

[5] Hausman, Warren H., and W.L. White. "Theory of Option Strategy Under Risk Aversion." *Journal of Financial and Quantitative Analysis*, Vol. 3 (Sept. 1968), pp. 343-358.

[6] Kalymon, Basil A. "Stochastic Costs in Multi-Period Decision Models." Ph.D. Dissertation, School of Administrative Science, Yale University, pub. as Technical Report H28, December 1969.

[7] Pye, Gordon. "A Markov Model of the Term Structure." *Quarterly Journal of Economics*, Vol. 80, (February 1966), pp. 60-72.

[8] Samuelson, Paul A. "Rational Theory of Warrant Pricing." *Industrial Management Review*, Vol. 6 (Spring 1965), pp. 13-31.

[9] Shapiro, Alan. "Management Science Models for Multicurrency Cash Management." Ph.D. dissertation, Graduate School of Industrial Administration, Carnegie-Mellon University, April 1971.

[10] Shulman, Robert. "Report on Exchange Rate Developments - September, 1969." Ann Arbor, Mich.: The Robert Shulman Co., Inc.

[11] Taylor, Howard M. "Evaluating a Call Option and Optimal Timing in the Stock Market." *Management Science*, Vol. 14 (September 1967), pp. 111-120.

SECTION VI
Trade Credit Management

Current liabilities represent the sources of short-term financing for business firms. Among the current liabilities, trade credit is an important spontaneous source of short-term financing as firms purchase materials, parts, and products from their suppliers on credit. Despite the dollar importance and potentially low cost of trade credit financing, the financial literature contains much less treatment of accounts payable than it does of accounts receivable. This section of the book contains three readings which deal with the management of trade credit.

Gitman, Forrester, and Forrester (Reading 31) investigate the problem of how the firm should pay its suppliers. They show that by causing payments to be made from geographically dispersed bank accounts, the firm can take advantage of slower check clearing times and thereby increase disbursement float. Their formulation of the cash disbursement problem is shown to be analogous to the cash collection problem in which a lock-box collection system can be used by the firm to decrease collection float (recall Reading 20). The authors illustrate their concept both with a simplified three-bank example, and with a realistic example involving disbursements to 66 different cities.

Maier and Vander Weide (Reading 32) review and compare the problems of cash collections and cash disbursements, and then discuss how both sides of credit management can be considered jointly. In order to solve the joint problem, the levels of net collected balances at each bank must be considered, as well as explicit recognition of how each bank is paid for the cash management services which are rendered to the firm. The joint formulation and solution turns out to be considerably more complicated than when either cash collections or cash disbursements are considered separately.

The paper by Haley and Higgins (Reading 33) demonstrates the interdependency of trade credit financing and patterns of inventory accumulation. They formulate a model in which the optimal order quantity for inventory and optimal payment time for trade credit are determined jointly. The approach is one which minimizes the total costs associated with trade credit deficits (inventory investment greater than trade credit) and trade credit surpluses (trade credit greater than inventory investment). The authors show that optimal conditions depend on the nature of transaction costs, and whether funds are raised externally by borrowing, or internally be decreasing liquid assets.

READING 31

Maximizing Cash Disbursement Float

Lawrence J. Gitman
The University of Tulsa

D. Keith Forrester
The Bank of Oklahoma

John R. Forrester, Jr.
First National Bank of Tulsa

INTRODUCTION

Importance of Cash Management

The management of corporate funds has been a major function of corporate treasurers and bankers for a considerable period of time. Over the past few years increased attention has been devoted to the use of more sophisticated methods of managing corporate cash flows. This increased emphasis can be attributed primarily to the recent high levels of interest rates and also the limited availability of financing alternatives. High interest rates increase the opportunity cost of holding idle cash balances, thereby placing presure on firms to lower their levels of cash balances. Often, the level of a firm's cash balance is considered indicative of the company's success in managing cash. In general, it appears that businesses have made their money work harder for them in recent years, as cash levels have remained relatively constant while sales have doubled [6].

Cash Management Strategy

Each company is unique in its manner both of receiving and disbursing funds from operations, so that each must utilize cash management strategies based upon its own financial condition and objectives. The two basic cash management strategies [4, pp. 169-170] normally applied are: (1) Collect accounts receivables as quickly as possible without losing future sales due to high-pressure collection techniques. (2) Pay accounts payable as late as possible without damaging the firm's credit rating and supplier relationships.

The objective of the *collection system* is to speed up collections by *minimizing* both the amount of mail time for the receipt of payments and the amount of collection float--the latter being the amount of checks in the firm's demand deposit account on which they have not yet received payment from the payor's bank. This

Reprinted from FINANCIAL MANAGEMENT (Summer 1976), pp. 15-24, by permission of the publisher and author.

enables the company to increase interest income by increasing the amount of investable funds or decrease interest expense by reducing the amount of borrowing. In an effort to minimize collection float, firms have employed several useful tools, one of which is the lock-box system. In a lock box system customers send their payments directly to a post office box or drawer located at a major post office [19]. The box or drawer is emptied at least daily by the firm's bank and the contents deposited directly into the firm's account. By strategically locating lock boxes geographically, a firm can reduce mail float--the time it takes for a check mailed by the customer to be deposited in the bank. By reducing both mail float and collection float, such a system should result in savings for the firm if the funds generated are put to more productive uses.

The objective of the *disbursement system* is to slow down payments in order to *maximize* the amount of payment float resulting from all payments (checks) and thereby allow the firm to reduce borrowings or invest excess funds in marketable securities or other productive assets. The goal of the corporate treasurer may be cash conservation, which can be achieved by taking the maximum allowable time to pay bills and by adopting methods of bill paying that result in a need for lower borrowing levels [11]. Methods and procedures for maximizing payment float in order to minimize cash requirements include centralizing payable and disbursement procedures in order to: (1) gain better control over the timing of payments and to streamline banking relationships; (2) insure taking attractive discounts; and (3) employ payment techniques which maximize float by delaying payments until late in the day, by using drafts and by delaying the clearing of checks through the company's bank account [3,5].

Although the concept of maximizing disbursement float is broadly understood by companies in the United States, it is not a broadly adopted technique since some firms do not wish to endanger their supplier relationships. Some companies find the strategy of maximizing disbursement float inconsistent with their overall business conduct. Other companies are known to go to elaborate means in order to maximize their disbursement float. In some cases, firms use the computer to examine the mailing addresses of check recipients and then draw the check from the most remote bank. Further refinements include taking advantage of snowstorms and airline strikes in order to further slow down payments.

Components of Disbursement Float

Three types of float are generated as a result of the payment process. *Mail float* is the amount of time a check remains in the postal system. *Processing float* is the amount of time it takes for the company to receive the check from the post office until it is deposited in the bank. One aspect of *transit float* deals with how long it takes the check to clear the banking system and be charged against the company's account, which must be funded by the paying company at that time. Such transit float applies to disbursing accounts, and is the float most maximizing disbursing systems seek to maximize. Another aspect of transit float is concerned with the fact that the supplier--the one receiving the check--will receive credit on all checks no more than two days after deposit because of an arbitrary guarantee by the Federal Reserve System [2] that all checks will in effect be cleared within two days. If the Fed cannot clear the checks within two days, then the Fed ends up carrying the float. In this type situation the Fed is providing interest-free money to the collecting company. Because of the Fed's guarantee of availability, the paying company can maximize its transit float for as long as one week, while the supplier (the check depositor) is guaranteed availability of funds within two days after deposit. As a result of the Fed's guarantee of availability in instances where the check takes more than two days to clear, the transit float differs for the supplier and customer. This article is concerned with the transit float of the paying company.

Since the amount of time a check remains in the payment process is very important to the financial manager, he funds the company's bank accounts not when the checks are written or released; rather, he does so when the check is expected to be returned to the bank for payment. Although this strategy would be risky for an individual to use in funding a personal checking account, for large firms writing numerous checks--none of which are unusually large--it is relatively simple, through historical studies, to fund the account on the day the check is expected to clear. The larger the number of checks and the smaller the size of checks, the easier it is to determine with a high degree of accuracy the time at which the checks will clear the account. The longer a payment remains in the system, the greater the amount of earnings that will be generated from investable funds. For example, assume that a company averages $1 million daily in payments to suppliers. Each day these payments remain in the system allows the corporation to increase its investable balances by $1 million. This, in turn, means that a company can annually earn (assuming a 10% opportunity rate, which in this paper is assumed to equal the return the firm could earn by investing the money gained through the increased float in marketable securities) $100 thousand in pre-tax earnings for each additional day the $1 million remains in the disbursement system. With special banking arrangements, a company can earn interest for as long as a week of float, thus considerably increasing its cash resources.

State of the Art in Cash Management

Over the last few years a great deal of emphasis has been placed on the collection or cash gathering side of the cash flow system, but relatively little attention has been devoted to the disbursement area of cash management. Only in the last few years have companies begun to exploit new, sophisticated, computer-controlled systems [13] with the main purpose of taking advantage of the inefficiencies in both the check collection procedures of the Federal Reserve System and the postal system.

Many large companies have "played the float" for years. Recently, many corporations have developed effective ways to extend the float a few more days, thereby allowing them, in effect, to use Federal Reserve money interest-free to pay their bills. The company is able to invest its own cash at high interest rates, invest in inventory, or use it to furnish compensating balances to cover the cost of banking services [13]. Levy [11] has developed a heuristic (i.e., a rule of thumb that generates a good--but not necessarily optimal--solution to a problem) applicable to the lock box location problem of managing accounts receivables. Calman [1] has included disbursing activity in his linear programming model that encompasses the entire cash flow system. In this model he includes the cost required by banks to provide services. Pogue, Faucett, and Bussard [14] have expanded Calman's model to more precisely identify costs; they have emphasized minimizing the sum of service fees and the opportunity cost of allocating cash balances to the banks in the system.

The most recent significant development in computerizing

disbursement models was underwritten by 8 banks for Phoenix-Hecht Cash Management Services (PHCMS), a computer software designer, to refine the disbursement computer system [13]. By opening accounts in 100 banks nationwide, PHCMS developed a data base of check clearing times between these banks to use for maximizing disbursement float. Their computer model has the ability to specify the most geographically advantageous disbursing point or drawee bank from which to pay suppliers. Although there have been no published models with respect to this particular cash disbursement problem, several banks along with Phoenix-Hecht have developed similar in-house capabilities.

Objective of this Article

In light of the state of the art, in this article a mathematical model is developed and applied to the cash disbursement problem. The disbursement model presented is believed to be an improvement over previous developments, as it incorporates segments of the previously mentioned studies into a workable, efficient model. The model views the disbursement system as the reverse of a check collection system, since check clearing float is maximized instead of collection float being minimized. The model also computes the marginal cost of each additional bank managers would use to help them evaluate the cost of different banks. By applying the techniques used in the warehouse location problem [8] to the quite similar problem of maximizing disbursement float, a heuristic is described that can efficiently and economically provide for the selection of disbursing banks that maximize disbursement float and provide optimal solutions. The cash disbursement model yields optimum disbursement locations given a specific number of possible drawee banks by maximizing transit or check collection float and minimizing account costs for each disbursing bank or group of disbursing banks deemed necessary.

THE CASH DISBURSEMENT PROBLEM

Importance of Cash Disbursement Management

Most large companies pay their bills--not as received, but rather in batches paid at discrete points in time. Quite often firms pay most of their accounts payable once each month. Of course, when attractive cash discounts are offered, firms pay their bills in order to take advantage of these discounts. Since these firms typically pay their bills with checks, a period of time is likely to elapse between the mailing of the check and the actual withdrawal of funds from its checking account. As a result of this "float" in the check clearing process, a firm is able to reduce borrowings or invest the excess funds in profitable assets. Of course, in order to intelligently do this the firm must arrange for zero-balance accounts with a concentration account at its bank or somehow "scientifically" estimate the amount of checks clearing each day after the checks are issued [19].

Ignoring supplier relations for the moment, in order to efficiently manage its disbursements, the firm should attempt to pay its bills in a fashion that maximizes its disbursement float, thereby delaying the removal of funds from its account and allowing the firm to earn as much on these funds as possible. Of the two aspects of mazimizing payables management, one relates to the actual mailing of the check, independent of the day the check is printed or written, or the date that appears on the check. The most important factor is when the company is going to mail the check to the supplier, which could perhaps be 45 days after receipt of invoice, perhaps on the due date, or perhaps one or two days earlier than the due date so that it is received by the supplier on the due date. (This could also include the additional processing time if the payor mails the check to the office of the supplier rather than the lock box.)

The second aspect of maximizing payables is to attempt to maximize transit float. Only two controllable variables exist which allow the firm to manipulate this float--(1) the location, and (2) the number of banks from which the firm makes its disbursements. If one assumes that in order to avoid late fees, payments must be received by the payment date determined by the payor, then the location and number of disbursing banks are the only variables that can be manipulated in order to maximize payables management. This article operates under this assumption. By selecting disbursing locations (assuming the cost of banking services is the same for all banks) in order to maximize total disbursement float, the result should be a positive contribution toward the firm's profits. Of course, at the same time the firm adds additional disbursing banks, it also must provide added balances or fees as compensation for the bank's services. Therefore, the firm must weigh these costs against the added benefit when choosing the optimal system of disbursement banks.

Problem Configuration

The problem with which the firm is faced can be explained using the data presented in Exhibit 1, which depicts in geographic space the 3 payments to vendors in cities A, B, and C that a firm must make. Exhibit 1 indicates that the firm must make

EXHIBIT 1. Diagram of Payments to Vendors in Cities A, B, and C

A
$100,000

B
$150,000

C
$125,000

the following monthly payments to firms in the associated cities:

City	Amount
A	$100,000
B	$150,000
C	$125,000

If one assumes that the firm can pay these amounts by a check drawn on a bank in any of the above cities, the question becomes from which city(s) the firm should make its disbursement float.

Heuristic Solution

The solution to this disbursement bank selection problem can be obtained heuristically. In order to illustrate the operation of the heuristic procedure, an example is used to show the actual mechanics of the process. To begin with, a table of check clearing times (shown in Exhibit 2) is examined to find the average number of days required for a check to travel from the depository bank (bank where the check is deposited) to the drawee bank (bank on which the check is drawn). Next, the number obtained from the check clearing table is multiplied by the amount of the disbursement to the corresponding city. The resulting product is the total clearing float measured in dollar-days, which are merely the average number of days it takes for a check to clear through the Federal Reserve System or local clearinghouse associations, multiplied by the amount of the payment to a firm in the associated city.

EXHIBIT 2. Check Clearing Times (in days) for Banks A, B, and C

Drawee Banks	Depository Banks A	B	C
A	0.00	4.71	2.87
B	1.80	0.00	4.00
C	4.08	3.20	0.00

The following steps illustrate the mechanical process involved in arriving at the value of the dollar-day float for each combination of disbursement points. In addition, the optimum number of of disbursement or drawee banks will be determined from the available data. In order to keep this sample problem simple, the following analysis is performed on a before-tax basis and only a small dimensional matrix is employed. The firm's opportunity cost of funds is assumed to be 10%, and the monthly cost of each additional bank account is considered to be $150.

The basic operational procedure of the heuristic is simple. Its objective is to maximize the return on float from which the cost of maintaining additional banks can be subtracted to obtain net profit. Using the payment and clearing time data given, the best 1, 2, and 3 bank disbursing systems can be determined. Also, the optimum number of drawee banks can be found. The optimum system is that system that maximizes net profit, which is the difference between the savings gained in the form of investable balances and the cost of maintaining the required bank accounts.

Best 1-Bank Disbursement System. Exhibit 3 presents a matrix of dollar-day float for all possible drawee-depository bank combinations.

By summing each row in the matrix, the amount of dollar-day float for each drawee bank is calculated. The decision criterion for selecting the best disbursement system is to choose that drawee bank which maximizes the dollar-day float. In other words, A would be the best one bank disbursement system, since it represents the highest total of dollar-day float for the 3 possible drawee banks.

To determine the value of the dollar-day float, the following equation is applied:

Value of float = (r)[(Dollar-Day Float) /365 days],

EXHIBIT 3. Dollar-Day Float Matrix for 1-Bank System

Drawee Banks	Depository Banks A	B	C	Total Dollar day float
A	0	706,500	358,750	1,065,250
B	180,000	0	500,000	680,000
C	408,000	480,000	0	888,000

where r = firm's opportunity cost of funds. The firm's opportunity cost of funds, which is stated as an annual rate, is divided by 365 days to arrive at a daily earnings rate which is used to determine the value of total dollar-day float. For example, it was found that drawee bank A provided for the greatest amount of dollar-day float. The value of A's dollar-day float is calculated as follows:

Value of float = (.10)[(1,065,250)/365]

= $291.85.

Therefore, if we assign a fixed cost of $150 per bank account, the net profit for this system would be $141.85 ($291.85 - $150).

Best 2-Bank Disbursement System. Exhibit 4 presents the dollar-day float matrix for each of the 3 possible 2-disbursing-bank systems.

To determine the best 2-bank disbursement system, a comparison is made of each paired combination of drawee banks. Again, the combination that maximizes the total dollar-day float is presumed to be the best disbursing system, which in this case includes banks A and C. Listed below is the total clearing float, value of the float, cost of bank accounts, and the net profit attained from the system:

EXHIBIT 4. Dollar-Day Float Matrix for 2-Bank System

Drawee Banks		Depository Banks A	B	C	Total dollar day float
AB	A	0	706,500	0	1,386,500
	B	180,000	0	500,000	
AC	A	0	706,500	358,750	1,473,250
	C	408,000	0	0	
BC	B	0	0	500,000	1,388,000
	C	408,000	480,000	0	

EXHIBIT 5. Dollar-Day Float Matrix for 3-Bank System

Drawee Banks		Depository Banks A	B	C	Total dollar day float
ABC	A	0	706,500	0	1,614,500
	B	0	0	500,000	
	C	408,000	0	0	

Clearing float. .1,473,250 (dollar-days)
Value of float $403.63
--Cost of Bank accounts (2 x $150). . . . $300.00
Net profit (loss) $103.63

Best 3-Bank Disbursement System. Exhibit 5 presents the dollar-day float matrix for the 3-disbursement-bank system.

The best 3-disbursement-bank system is obviously A, B, and C, since these are the only drawee banks considered. Other drawee banks could have been considered, but for simplicity only the 3 depository banks were consiered. The possibility that the optimal configuration may be one that requires the drawee banks to be in cities other than the depository cities is quite likely since this would be consistent with the objective of float maximization. The pertinent information for the 3-bank system follows:

Clearing float. 1,614,500 (dollar-days)
Value of float $442.33
--Cost of bank accounts (3 x $150) $450.00
Net profit (loss) . . . . ($7.67)

Optimal Disbursement System

The optimal disbursement system is that combination which provides the maximum net profit attainable from all alternatives considered. Therefore, in the example presented, the one drawee bank system, which is bank A, represents the optimal system since its net profit is greater than any of the other combinations examined.

As this exercise illustrates, the more disbursing points considered, the greater the combinatorial analysis. Therefore, a good heuristic should reduce the amount of time needed to perform the iterative processes and provide for an optimum disbursing system.

DEVELOPMENT AND APPLICATION OF THE WAREHOUSE LOCATION PROBLEM TO THE CASH DISBURSEMENT PROBLEM

The Warehouse Problem

The warehouse problem has been developed in the literature as a special class of mixed integer programming [7]. It deals with the minimization of the costs of maintaining warehouses to support demand and the associated handling and transportation costs of supplying customers. Its solution involves the testing of combinations of warehouses that will economically best (optimally) geographically service the given number of customers. The mathematical model parallels that formulated in equation (1) given in the next section. The mechanics to provide the solution have been improved considerably by Khumawala's [7] branch and bound algorithm a number of heuristics [16,18,20].

The Maximization of Dollar-Day Float

The warehouse location problem provides a "best fit" to the cash disbursement problem by merely converting it into a maximization configuration. The location of disbursing points as they relate to a given customer base remains the same in terms of transportation costs and the fixed costs associated with the points of disbursement. However, instead of m potential warehouses, m potential drawee banks are substituted, and n supplier's deposit banks or payment points are substituted for n customers. The problem then becomes one of maximizing clearing time or dollar-days of float that occur as a result of the payment process of checks to n suppliers drawn on m possible banks. The problem then can be formulated in the following manner:

(1) Maximize $$\sum_{i=1}^{m} \sum_{j=1}^{n} D_{ij} X_{ij}$$

Subject to: $$\sum_{i=1}^{m} X_{ij} = 1,$$

for each j, $j=1,2,\ldots,n$

$$X_{ij} = 0,\ 1,$$

for all i, j

where C_{ij} = check clearing time in days from its deposit by the supplier at bank j to its presentation at the drawee bank i; V_j = dollars payable to the supplier banking at bank j; $D_{ij} = C_{ij}\ V_j$ = dollar-day float for payments deposited in bank j and clearing to its presentation at drawee bank i; and V_{ij} = the portion of V_j drawn on bank i.

The reader should recognize that the C_{ij} values in equation (1) would most likely be stochastic. Although the treatment of this variable appears to be deterministic, it would in practice be impossible to know with certainty these clearing times. The specification of the variable could result in problems because the C_{ij} may differ depending upon the drawee bank-depository combination, i, j. Specification of the variances in the model may change the choice of drawee banks and the assignment of payments to these banks. In order not to complicate the model being presented, the C_{ij} variable is, therefore, assumed to be deterministic.

The solution to the maximization of dollar-day float will dictate the number and location of banks that payables will be drawn on. The maximization of float *can* be approached by specifying the number of drawee banks desired. If k represents the number of banks desired, the following constraints (1a) and (1b) must hold:

(1a) for k banks,

$$\sum_{i=1}^{m} X_{ij} > 0, \text{ for each } j,\ j=1,2,\ldots,n$$

(1b) for m-k banks,

$$\sum_{i=1}^{m} X_{ij} = o, \text{ for each } j,\ j=1,2,\ldots,n.$$

The optimal solution of the model could be obtained using a branch and bound algorithm [7]. However, several heuristic algorithms are available that can provide solutions within 2% of optimality, but perform with greater efficiency [16,18,20]. The solution is normally approached in a logical step-wise manner similar to that described in the previous section.

The Optimum Cash Disbursement Model

To further enhance the model maximizing dollar-day float, the fixed costs for additional bank accounts needed to improve disbursement float can be included in the model. Letting a_i equal fixed costs of maintaining drawee bank i, equation set (1) is reformulated to maximize net profit from the cash disbursement system in equation set 2, which assumes that the sample payments are for one month. As a result, the daily opportunity cost of funds would be (r/365), where r is the firm's opportunity cost of funds. The cash disbursement model then becomes:

(2) Maximize

$$\frac{r \sum_{i=1}^{m} \sum_{j=1}^{n} D_{ij} X_{ij}}{365} - \sum_{i=1}^{m} a_i Y_i$$

Subject to:

$$\sum_{i=1}^{m} X_{ij} = 1,$$

for each j, j=1,2,...,n

$$0 \leq \sum_{j=1}^{n} X_{ij} \leq n_i \, Y_i,$$

for each i, i=1,2,...,m

$$Y_i = 0, 1,$$

for each i, i=1,2,...,m

where r/365 = daily opportunity cost of funds assuming monthly dollars disbursed; a_i = fixed costs of having bank account at bank i; n_i = the number of suppliers that can be paid from drawee bank i, which in this case, includes all m of the banks. Therefore, $n_i = m$.

The model then provides the location of the best number of banks, k^*, from which to pay suppliers and also indicates through the X_{ij} values from which of the chosen drawee banks, i, each supplier, j, should be paid in order to maximize the dollar-day float.

COMPUTATIONAL RESULTS

In order to determine the relative effectiveness of the procedure developed in this paper, the monthly disbursements of an actual firm were used to illustrate the practicality of this application. The sample company has monthly payments to be disbursed to 66 different cities from a list of 38 possible drawee banks. The float times represent empirically determined values for the average number of days required for checks placed in each depository bank to clear through each possible drawee bank. Several heuristic rules were applied and each resulted in the same solution; therefore, the resulting solution is believed to be optimal. The data and results of the heuristic solution are summarized in Exhibit 6.

The exhibit indicates what city(s) from which the company should arrange to make its disbursements for each of the depository banks. As is shown in Exhibit 6, the best disbursement system includes 3 banks: El Paso, Helena, and Miami. The total clearing float associated with this sample problem is 64,837,440 dollar-days. By applying the firms' actual opportunity cost of funds of 6% to the total clearing float and dividing by 365 days, the value of the float, which in this case is \$10,658 [i.e., (.06)(64,837,440/365 days)], was determined. The net profit of \$10,208 was calculated by subtracting from the value of the float the monthly fixed cost of \$150 for each of the 3 drawee banks opened [i.e., \$10,658 - (\$150 x 3 banks)].

An important consideration here is that the heuristic procedure usually provides for an optimal solution, which in most cases eliminates the

EXHIBIT 6. Data and Solution of Sample Problem

Depository bank	Amount of payment	Average days of float to drawee chosen bank	Value of float (@6%) associated with drawee banks		
			El Paso	Helena	Miami
Boston	$ 515,000	4.51	$381.81	$	$
New York City	1,937,000	3.96		1,260.91	
Buffalo	11,000	3.83		7.02	
Philadelphia	538,000	4.14		366.13	
Cleveland	881,000	3.32	480.81		
Cincinnati	121,000	3.40	67.63		
Pittsburgh	439,000	3.50		281.34	
Richmond	19,000	4.55	14.21		
Baltimore	6,000	5.10			5.03
Charlotte	34,000	4.08	22.80		
Atlanta	62,000	3.07		31.29	
Birmingham	6,000	6.16		6.08	
Jacksonville	3,000	4.03		1.99	
Nashville	7,000	4.28		4.92	
New Orleans	6,000	5.63		5.55	
Chicago	3,091,000	3.36		1,707.25	
Detroit	295,000	4.05	196.40		
St. Louis	584,000	3.00		288.00	
Little Rock	18,000	4.10		12.13	
Louisville	98,000	3.52	56.71		
Memphis	267,000	3.85		168.98	
Minneapolis	853,000	3.38			473.94
Kansas City	127,000	3.65		76.20	
Denver	18,000	4.16			12.31
Oklahoma City	6,000	3.49			3.44
Omaha	23,000	4.20			15.88
Dallas	229,000	3.64		137.02	
El Paso	2,000	4.97		1.63	
Houston	83,000	3.38		46.12	
San Antonio	1,000	4.21			0.69
San Francisco	149,000	4.18			102.38
Los Angeles	367,000	3.97	239.51		

Portland	22,000	4.29	15.51		
Salt Lake City	9,000	4.98			7.37
Seattle	2,000	4.38	1.44		
Worcester	659,000	5.78		626.14	
Albany	320,000	4.75	249.86		
Rochester	37,000	4.67	28.40		
Allentown	452,000	4.82	358.13		
Akron	610,000	4.31		432.18	
Dayton	37,000	4.31		26.21	
Wheeling	181,000	3.15		93.72	
Columbus	154,000	4.52	114.42		
Raleigh	68,000	4.52		50.52	
Norfolk	12,000	6.03		11.89	
Winston-Salem	179,000	3.98	117.11		
Savannah	124,000	4.42		90.10	
Tampa	173,000	5.05		143.61	
Knoxville	60,000	4.75		46.85	
Baton Rouge	272,000	3.47		155.15	
Miami	45,000	3.18	23.52		
Springfield IL	1,174,000	5.13		990.02	
Lansing	85,000	4.94	69.02		
Springfield MO	140,000	3.97		91.36	
Duluth	161,000	4.16			110.10
Helena	1,000	4.47			0.73
Pueblo	35,000	4.37			25.14
Tulsa	24,000	2.84		11.20	
Lincoln	43,000	4.24	29.97		
Lubbock	45,000	3.92			29.00
Beaumont	2,000	4.04		1.33	
Sacramento	154,000	4.40			111.39
San Diego	146,000	4.37		104.88	
Eugene	5,000	4.36	3.58		
Ogden	11,000	4.76		8.61	
Spokane	5.000	4.48			3.68

Total Dollar-Days = 64,837,440
Value of Float = $10,658
−Cost of Bank Accounts = $ 450
Net Profit = $10,208
CPU Time = 7 seconds

need for more sophisticated techniques such as branch and bound algorithms that normally require more computer CPU time and much more computer core storage.

SUMMARY AND CONCLUSIONS

This presentation has developed a quantitative means by which the accounts payable of a firm can be analyzed to determine the system of disbursement banks that will optimize a firm's check clearing float (ignoring the possibility of manipulating mail times which could be an important factor in maximizing float) and provide benefits through efficient cash management. The maximization of this float increases the amount of time that a firm can invest its available funds and effectively increase its cash reserves or reduce borrowing. The literature does not specifically offer a quantitative solution procedure for the cash disbursement problem. Fortunately, the traditional warehouse location problem can be adapted and applied to select an optimal cash disbursement configuration. The optimum solution can be obtained through the use of a branch and bound algorithm or can be approximated by using one of a number of available heuristics. These solutions can be applied to actual situations to determine if a more profitable disbursement system (drawee bank relationships) is available for minimizing cash requirements and thereby increasing the amount of funds available for investment and/or retirement of debt.

When new disbursement systems are indicated, practical operational considerations exist. In the development of the optimum cash disbursement model, the fixed cost of maintaining a bank account was included for each disbursing bank in the new system. These fixed costs may vary from bank to bank dependent upon the bank's pricing objectives and perhaps its viewpoint of the individual firm's credit standing in the marketplace. However, the following basic consideration is essential to the optimization: the benefits derived by the addition of a new banking relationship for maximizing disbursement float must be offset by the costs associated with the new relationship.

There is a great deal of conjecture that earnings obtained as a result of an optimum cash disbursement system will not be long-lived. Public and private efforts are being made to reduce float as evidenced by the Federal Reserve's attempts to more efficiently perform the check clearing process. They have developed the regional check processing center (RCPC) concept as an effort to reduce float by assisting the check clearing process in high volume areas. Additional efforts to reduce check clearing float have been provided by commerical banks in the form of direct-send programs. These programs depend upon the ability to capture high dollar volume items and physically present them at the drawee bank. They provide a cash management tool that can be used to speed up the collection of checks and pass the benefits on to the bank customer (the supplier) and reduce the disbursement float advantage of the payor (user of the product or service).

Taking advantage of check clearing float may not be a practice that will provide long-term benefits. However, the optimum cash disbursement model will increase earnings for the medium-term. When applied with other disbursing strategies such as paying invoices as late as possible without damaging supplier relationships and credit ratings, the firm's earnings can be further increased. These disbursing strategies should enhance the firm's overall return and allow the firm to better achieve the long-run goal of owner-wealth maximization.

REFERENCES

1. Robert F. Calman, *Linear Programming and Cash Management/Cash ALPHA*, Cambridge, The M.I.T. Press, 1968.

2. *The Federal Reserve System: Purposes and Functions*, Washington, D.C., Board of Governors, September 1974, pp. 20-21.

3. David I. Fisher, *Cash Management*, Ottawa, The Conference Board, Inc., 1973.

4. Lawrence J. Gitman, *Principles of Managerial Finance*, New York, Harper and Row, Inc., 1976.

5. Frederick E. Horn, "Managing Cash," *The Journal of Accountancy* (April 1964), pp. 56-62.

6. "How Business Lives Beyond Its Means," *Business Week* (November 15, 1969), pp. 72, 74, 76.

7. Basheer M. Khumawala, "An Efficient Branch and Bound Algorithm for the Warehouse Location Problem," *Management Science* 18 (August 1972), pp. 718-731.

8. Basheer M. Khumawala, "An Efficient Heuristic Procedure for the Uncapacitated Warehouse Location Problem," *Naval Research Logistics Quarterly* 20 (March 1973), pp. 109-121.

9. Robert L. Kramer, "Analysis of Lock Box Locations," *Bankers Monthly Magazine* (May 15, 1966), pp. 50-53.

10. A. Kuehn and M. Hamburger, "A Heuristic Program for Locating Warehouses," *Management Science* 9 (July 1963), pp. 643-666.

11. Ferdinand K. Levy, "An Application of Heuristic Problem Solving to Accounts Receivable Management," *Management Science* 12 (February 1966), pp. 236-244.

12. James F. Lordan, "Cash Management: The Corporate-Bank Relationship," *The Magazine of Bank Administration* (January 1975), pp. 14-19.

13. "Making Millions by Stretching the Float," *Business Week* (November 23, 1974), pp. 88 and 90.

14. Gerald A. Pogue, Russel B. Faucett, and Ralph N. Bussard, "Cash Management: A Systems Approach," *Industrial Management Review* (Winter 1970), pp. 55-73.

15. Ward L. Reed, Jr., "Cash--The Hidden Asset," *Financial Executive* (November 1970), pp. 54-60.

16. Robert A. Russell, "Heuristic Programming Algorithms for Warehouse Location," in *Scientific and Behavioral Foundations for Decision Sciences*, edited by Laurence J. Moore and Sang M. Lee (1974), pp. 212-213.

17. Frederick W. Searby, "Use Your Hidden Cash Resources," *Harvard Business Review* 46 (March-April 1968), pp. 74-75.

18. R. E. Shannon and J. P. Ignizio, "A Heuristic Proramming Algorithm for Warehouse Location," *AIIE Transactions*, Vol. 2, No. 4 (December 1970), pp. 334-339.

19. William J. Tallent, "Cash Management: A Case Study," *Management Accounting* (July 1974), pp. 20-24.

20. M. B. Teitz and P. Bart, "Heuristic Methods for Estimating the Generalized Vertex Median of a Weighted Graph," *Operations Research*, Vol. 16 (1968), pp. 955-961.

21. James C. Van Horne, *Financial Management and Policy*, third edition, Englewood Cliffs, Prentice-Hall, Inc., 1974.

22. Harry L. Winn, Jr., "A Discussion of Issues Related to Disbursing," *Cash Management Forum of the First National Bank of Atlanta* 1 (Volume 1, Number 2), pp. 2-3, 7.

READING 32

A Unified Location Model for Cash Disbursements and Lock-Box Collections

Steven F. Maier
Duke University

James H. Vander Weide
Duke University

The benefits from an improved corporate cash management system generally stem from three sources. First, the firm can often achieve a considerable reduction in its collection float by locating lock-boxes in strategic customer areas and utilizing devices such as wire transfers to shorten the time between customer mailing and fund availability. Second, the firm can usually increase its disbursement float by choosing wisely the offices and banks from which it disburses. Finally, the firm can reduce the costs of banking services it receives by carefully setting the levels of its bank deposit balances. In this paper, we provide a brief review of the models that are currently available to analyze each of these areas, and then present a unified model which can be used to optimally design an entire cash management system.

THE LOCK-BOX LOCATION PROBLEM

It is well-known that corporate treasurers can sometimes significantly increase the amount of funds available for investment by locating check collection points, commonly called "lock-boxes," in one or more of the firm's major customer areas. The problem of locating those check collection points which minimize the value of uncollected funds can be formulated mathematically as follows:

(1) MINIMIZE
$$W = \Sigma_k \Sigma_m [p(q_{mk} + r_{mk}) + e_{mk}] \cdot Y_{mk} + \Sigma_k f_k^c \cdot Z_k^c$$

(2) s.t. $\Sigma_k Y_{mk} = b_m \qquad \forall m$

(3) $\Sigma_m Y_{mk} \leq (\Sigma_m b_m) Z_k^c \qquad \forall k$

(4) $Y_{mk} \geq 0,\ Z_k^c = 0 \text{ or } 1 \qquad \forall k, m$

Where Y_{mk} = the number of deposit items from customer group m processed by bank k

b_m = the total number of checks to be processed from customer group m

Reprinted from Summer 1976 issue of JOURNAL OF BANK RESEARCH, published by Bank Administration Institute.

q_{mk} = the dollar value of the mail float carried as accounts receivable balances that is generated when one check is mailed by customer group m to bank k

r_{mk} = the dollar value of the collection float that is generated when one check of customer group m is cleared through bank k

e_{mk} = the variable bank costs of processing one check from customer group m through a lock-box operated by bank k (if this cost does not differ for customer groups, then use e_k)

p = the opportunity cost of ledger balances

f_k^c = a fixed charge for using bank k as a collection point

Z_k^c = one if bank k is used as a lock-box site, zero otherwise

The constraint sets (2) and (4) together insure that all the checks will be allocated, while constraint set (3) insures that no checks will be sent to a "closed" lock-box.

In this model, a homogenous customer group is defined as a collection of customers whose combined mailing and clearing time to each potential lock-box site is the same. Although this does not require that customers be geographically contiguous, in practice customers are grouped by the first two or three digits of their ZIP codes.

The lock-box problem is equivalent to the simple warehouse location problem. Both problems have received extensive coverage in the O.R. literature (see, for example, [Drysdale and Sandiford, 1969], [Feldman, et. al., 1966], [Kraus, et. al., 1970], [Kuehn and Hamburger, 1963], [Shanker and Zoltners, 1972], and [Spielberg, 1969].) In fact, both of these formulations are part of a class of models referred to as the fixed charge location allocation problem by Ellwein [1970] and Ellwein and Gray [1971]. The name stems from the fact that the problem may be approached in two stages. First, one selects a subset of the possible bank location sites and second, one allocates the customers among those selected sites in a manner which minimizes the mail and collection float.

The first stage of the problem is combinatorial in nature, since the number of possible subsets of the location sites is $2^k - 1$ where k is the number of banks under consideration. The second stage of the problem can be solved in general as a transportation problem; however, for the lock-box problem this simplifies further because the bank collection activities are uncapacitated. This simplification permits a solution to be obtained for the second stage of the problem by assigning each customer group to the bank location that gives the minimum float. Because of the simple nature of the second stage, the algorithms that have been proposed are primarily concerned with finding an efficient method for searching the feasible subsets of location sites. Both branch and bound and implicit enumeration have been shown to be efficient and capable of finding the optimal solution to a reasonably sized versions of this problem in a matter of seconds. (See, [Bent, 1972], [Bulfin and Unger, 1973], [Ciochetto, et. al., 1972], [Davis and Ray, 1969], [Effroymson and Ray, 1966], [Khumawala, 1971 and 1972] and [Pogue, et. al., 1970].)

In this paper we will not be further concerned with the computational aspects of the lock-box problem. Instead, we will examine whether this model, which focuses only on the collection side of the cash management function, is in fact a useful planning tool. In a previous paper [1974], we focused our attention on the difficulties inherent in implementing this model because of the high cost of obtaining bank service price information. Now we will ask the more fundamental question: Can the cost of operating a lock-box system be considered independently of the other cash management costs? With that as our goal, we proceed to review the models for the disbursement activity.

THE CORPORATE PAYMENT PROBLEM

Corporate cash managers can also often generate significant cash savings from a more efficient use of their disbursement system. This savings is achieved by locating the check disbursement activity at offices and banks with "slow" mail and clearing times, respectively. The problem of locating those disbursement activities which maximize the net benefits from the increased disbursement float was first discussed by Shanker and Zoltner [1972, Spring]. The formulation that follows is an extension of Shanker and Zoltner's work:

$$(5)\quad \text{MAX } W = \Sigma_i \Sigma_j \Sigma_k (p \cdot P_{ijk} - d_{jk}) X_{ijk} - \Sigma_k f_k^D \cdot Z_k^D - \Sigma_i f_i^R \cdot Z_i^R - \Sigma_i \Sigma_k f_{ik}^{DR} \cdot Z_{ik}^{DR}$$

$$(6)\quad \text{s.t. } \Sigma_i \Sigma_k X_{ijk} = a_j \qquad \forall j$$

$$(7)\quad \Sigma_i \Sigma_j X_{ijk} \leq (\Sigma_j a_j) Z_k^D \qquad \forall k$$

$$(8)\quad \Sigma_j \Sigma_k X_{ijk} \leq (\Sigma_j a_j) Z_i^R \qquad \forall i$$

$$(9)\quad \Sigma_j X_{ijk} \leq (\Sigma_j a_j) Z_{ik}^{DR} \qquad \forall i,k$$

$$(10)\quad X_{ijk} \geq 0;\ Z_k^D, Z_i^R, Z_{ik}^{DR} = 0 \text{ or } 1 \qquad \forall i,j,k$$

where X_{ijk} = the number of checks to be issued by regional office i to creditor group j on bank k

a_j = the total number of checks to be issued to creditor group j

P_{ijk} = the dollar value of the float generated by disbursing one check from regional office i to creditor group j on bank k

d_{jk} = the per item bank cost of processing one check for creditor group j through bank k (if this cost does not differ for creditor goups, then use d_k)

p = the opportunity cost of ledger balances

f_k^D = a fixed charge for disbursing at bank k

Z_k^D = one if bank k is used for disbursements, zero otherwise

f_i^R = a fixed cost to the firm for locating and maintaining a disbursement activity at regional office i

Z_i^R = one if a disbursement activity is located at regional office i, zero otherwise

f_{ik}^{DR} = a fixed cost to the firm for maintaining a relationship between regional office i and bank k

Z_{ik}^{DR} = one if a relationship is established between regional office i and bank k, zero otherwise

Here, the constraint set (6) is needed to insure that all of the checks that are owed to creditor group j are processed while the constraint sets (7), (8) and (9) are needed to insure that all activities occur through "open" offices and banks.

On first inspection, it may appear that this model is considerably more difficult to solve than that of the lock-box location problem. This is in fact not the case. The two-stage approach described in the previous section can still be applied to this model with no serious increase in complexity. However, it would generally be true that the number of integer 0-1 variables would be considerably greater here than in the lock-box problem. Again, we must caution against overenthusiastic acceptance of the solution of this model, since it makes the very strong implicit assumption that the cost of operating the disbursement system is independent of other cash management costs.

A SYSTEMS APPROACH TO CASH MANAGEMENT

The two preceding models described in this paper are characterized by their failure to view the collection and disbursement activities in a framework which properly considers the interrelationships between them. Calman[1968] first proposed a comprehensive model of the firm's entire banking system. This model, which was later revised by Pogue et. al, [1970] provides a means of determining the true costs of the various components of the system. A limitation of their model is that it only determines activity levels within the firm's current banking system. As the two previous models indicate, firms often want to consider possible changes in the current banking structure. Therefore, in the next section we present a cash management model which unifies the two previous location models along the lines suggested by Calman and Pogue into a model capable of locating banking activities as well as determining their optimal levels.

A UNIFIED LOCATION MODEL

The key to a unified cash management model is the explicit determination of the optimal level of total bank compensation. In order to appreciate why this is so, one must understand the service pricing policy of commercial banks. Generally, commercial banks offer their services in a package for which they are partially compensated by a minimum balance requirement on a line of credit. When a compensating balance is required, the bank will often allow a service charge credit to be earned on the balance, which may be used to offset charges for other bank services. This policy often permits the firm to obtain double use of such funds. If a firm has already established its lines of credit, it may have a sizable pool of service charge credit that it can use to offset lock-box and disbursement charges. Therefore, unless all of the firm's banking activities are considered simultaneously, it is impossible to establish a basis for a cost analysis. It is this conclusion that makes the cost information required by the first two models impossible to obtain and leads us to the consideration of a unified approach.

In this model we will consider three separate ways of compensating a bank for its services. First, the bank can be paid in the form of cash fees FEE_k. Second, the bank can give a service charge credit C_k^N for each dollar of average net collected balances NCB_k on deposit. (The net collected balance is the true bank balance.) Finally, the bank can give a credit C_k^T for each dollar of tax payments TP_k the firm makes through the bank. (The reason the bank will allow credit is that there is often a substantial delay between the time the firm is required to pay its taxes and the time the U.S. Treasury actually withdraws funds.) We assume that the bank must be compensated for its total cost of processing disbursements TCD_k, its total cost of processing lock-box collections TCC_k and the value of any other tangible or intangible services V_k it performs for the firm. With these assumptions, we can write the bank compensation constraint as:

$$(11) \quad FEE_k + C_k^T \cdot TP_k + C_k^N \cdot NCB_k \geq TCD_k + TCC_k + V_k$$

which must hold for each bank k under consideration in the system. Each of the variables in this equation is subject to additional constraints, which we now explore in some detail.

The tax payments the firm makes thru its bank is constrained by its total tax liability TPP. We express this as:

$$(12) \quad \Sigma_{k=1}^{K} \; TP_k \leq TTP$$

Because of its existing lines of credit, the firm must maintain a minimum level of net collection balances in each bank. Thus,

$$(13) \quad NCB \geq g_k,$$

where g_k is the required minimum balance.

Since an assumption of our model is that all parameters are known with certainty, the firm will generally find it optimal to allocate its cash balances to banks in such a way that equation (13) holds with equality. In practice, firms may desire to keep net collected balances above those required by its credit agreements because of the uncertainties associated with the timing of collections and disbursements and because of the desire to maintain access to bank loans in the event of an unforeseen credit need. These uncertainties can easily be incorporated into the model at this point through the introduction of chance constraints. Since an excellent discussion of these constraints in contained in Pogue, Faucett and Bussard [1970], however, we will proceed under our initial assumption.

In order to evaluate the benefits from a redesigned cash management system, we must find a relationship between the firm's average ledger-cash balance and the net collected balance on which the bank bases its computations. These two figures differ because of delays in the payment of checks written by the firm and the collection of checks received by the firm.

The delay in payments (positive float) is due to two factors: the mail delay between the firm's regional office i that issued the check and the location j of the vendor's receiving address; and the clearing time from the vendor's bank back to the firm's bank k upon which the check was drawn. (In addition to the mail and clearing float, there are generally various small delays such as the time the customer needs to process the check. For the purposes of this model, we assume these delays are independent of the issuing location and the bank on which the check was drawn.) If we let X_{ijk} denote the number of checks to be issued by regional office i to creditor group j on bank k, and let p_{ijk} denote the average dollar value of the float generated by disbursing one check for group j from regional office i through bank k, then $\Sigma_i \Sigma_j p_{ijk} X_{ijk}$ will represent the total amount of positive float associated with bank k.

Similarly, the delay in collections (negative float) has two contributions: The mail time from customer group m's location to a lockbox located at bank k; and the clearing time from bank k back to the customer's bank. The mail time, however, does not affect the relationship between the firm's average ledger cash balance and its net collected balances because both balances are computed after the mail time has elapsed. Using our previous definition of Y_{mk} as the number of deposit items processed from customer group m by bank k, and letting r_{mk} be the average dollar value of the collection float generated when one check of customer group m is cleared through bank k, we can formulate the negative float associated with bank k as $\Sigma_m r_{mk} \cdot Y_{mk}$.

The relationship between NCB_k, the net collected balance, and BAL_k, the ledger balance, can now be expressed as:

(14) $$NCB_k = BAL_k + \Sigma_{i=1}^{I} \Sigma_{j=1}^{J} P_{ijk} \cdot X_{ijk} - \Sigma_{m=1}^{M} r_{mk} \cdot Y_{mk}$$

which holds for all banks k under consideration.

Additional constraints are required to guarantee the assignment of all checks to one of the lock-box or disbursement account locations. These constraints were used in the previous models and are simply rewritten here as:

(6) $\Sigma_{i=1}^{I} \Sigma_{k=1}^{K} X_{ijk} = a_j$ for all creditor groups j.

(2) $\Sigma_{k=1}^{K} Y_{mk} = b_m$ for all customer groups m.

Returning now to the right hand side of the bank compensation constraint (11), we derive a formula that relates the disbursement activity levels X_{ijk} to the bank's total cost for operating the disbursement system TCD_k. We assume that the costs of operating the disbursement system can be divided into fixed and variable portions. If we let d_{jk} be the cost of processing one check from creditor group j through bank k, then the variable portion can be expressed as: $\Sigma_i \Sigma_j d_{jk} \cdot X_{ijk}$. The fixed costs, those costs that do not depend on the level of various activities, can be either attributed to the individual regional offices that use the account or to the bank's maintenance of that account. Therefore, in this model the treatment of the fixed charges f_k^C, f_k^D and F_{ik}^{DR} differs from that of the previous models. We have divided the fixed charges into the portion the bank incurs $\hat{f}_k^C$, $\hat{f}_k^D$, and $\hat{f}_{ik}^{DR}$ and therefore must receive compensation for, and the portion that the firm incurs $\bar{f}_k^C$, $\bar{f}_i^R$. $\bar{f}_{ik}^{DR}$ and must therefore be accounted for, but for which it does not have to compensate its banks.

With these assumptions, we can express TCD_k as:

(15) $$TCD_k = \Sigma_{i=1}^{I} \Sigma_{j=1}^{J} d_{jk} \cdot X_{ijk} + \Sigma_{i=1}^{I} \hat{f}_{ik}^{DR} \cdot Z_{ik}^{DR} + \hat{f}_k^D \cdot Z_k^D$$

which holds for each bank k. The variables Z_{ik}^{DR} and Z_k^D are integer 0-1 variables that indicate the existence of a disbursement account at bank k (Z_k^D) or the existence of regional office-bank relationship (Z_{ik}^{DR}).

The analysis of the total cost of processing lock-box collections is similar. Letting e_{mk} be the cost of processing one customer check from customer group m at the lock-box located at bank k, we have as the variable portion of TCC_k: $\Sigma_m e_{mk} \cdot Y_{mk}$. If we let $\hat{f}_k^C$ be the fixed charge assesed by bank k for servicing the lock-box, then the total cost of collections can be written as:

(16) $$TCC_k = \Sigma_{m=1}^{M} e_{mk} \cdot Y_{mk} + \hat{f}_k^C \cdot Z_k^C \text{ for each bank } k,$$

where Z_k^C is an integer 0-1 variable that indicates the existence of the lock-box at bank k.

A final set of constraints are need to control the values of the integer variables Z_k^D, Z_k^C, Z_i^R and Z_{ik}^{DR}. They are constraints (3), (7), (8) and (9) from the previous models:

(3) $\Sigma_{m=1}^{M} Y_{mk} \leq (\Sigma_{m=1}^{M} b_m) \cdot z_k^C$

for all banks k.

(7) $\Sigma_{i=1}^{I} \Sigma_{k=1}^{K} X_{ijk} \leq (\Sigma_{j=1}^{J} a_j) \cdot z_k^D$

for all banks k.

(8) $\Sigma_{j=1}^{J} \Sigma_{k=1}^{K} X_{ijk} \leq (\Sigma_{j=1}^{J} a_j) \cdot z_i^R$

for all regional offices i.

(9) $\Sigma_{j=1}^{J} X_{ijk} \leq (\Sigma_{j=1}^{J} a_j) \cdot z_{ik}^{DR}$

for all regional office i and bank k combinations.

The last part of the model to be specified is the objective function. We assume that the firm wishes to minimize the cost of its banking system. The cost of the system can be viewed as consisting of two portions. First, there is the direct out of pocket costs. These include the fees paid to the bank and the fixed costs of the various banking relationships:

$$\Sigma_{k=1}^{K} FEE_k + \Sigma_{k=1}^{K} [\bar{f}_k^C \cdot z_k^C + \bar{f}_k^D \cdot z_k^D + \Sigma_{i=1}^{I} \bar{f}_{ik}^{DR} \cdot z_{ik}^{DR}] + \Sigma_{i=1}^{I} \bar{f}_i^R \cdot z_i^R$$

where $\bar{f}_k^C$, $\bar{f}_k^D$, and $\bar{f}_{ik}^{DR}$ represents the fixed cost to the firm respectively of its collection, disbursement and regional office relationships. The cost $\bar{f}_i^R$ represents the fixed cost for locating and maintaining a disbursement activity at regional office i.

The second portion of the objective function evaluates the savings from decreased collection and increased disbursement times in the form of lower cash requirements to operate the banking system. More explicitly, we measure the change in the firm's ledger balance $\Sigma_k BAL_k$ and the reduction in receivables due to reduced mail collection times $\Sigma_m \Sigma_k q_{mk} \cdot Y_{mk}$. We evaluate these savings by using the opportunity cost p of the ledger balances. Combining these savings terms with the previous costs we have as our objective function the following:

(17) $$\text{MINIMIZE } W = p(\Sigma_{k=1}^{K} BAL_k + \Sigma_{m=1}^{M} \Sigma_{k=1}^{K} q_{mk} \cdot Y_{mk}) + \Sigma_{k=1}^{K} FEE_k + \Sigma_{k=1}^{K} [\bar{f}_k^C \cdot z_k^C + \bar{f}_k^D \cdot z_k^D + \Sigma_{i=1}^{I} \bar{f}_{ik}^{DR} \cdot z_{ik}^{DR}] + \Sigma_{i=1}^{I} \bar{f}_i^R \cdot z_i^R.$$

COMPUTATIONAL CONSIDERATIONS

The unified location model fits into the framework of the fixed charge location allocation formulation, and may therefore be solved by the two-stage procedure previously described. Two major considerations in the use of branch and bound or implicit enumeration as a solution technique should be mentioned. First, the second stage of the solution process can no longer be solved by a simple assignment of customers to the nearest bank location and vendors to the furthest bank location; rather one must solve a linear program to find the optimal choice of these assignments. Second, the number of integer 0-1 variables is potentially greater in this model than in either of the previous ones. Because of the sensitivity of integer programs to the number of integer variables involved, the user must be cautious when defining his set of bank and regional office locations. He should be especially cautious about the number of regional office-bank relationships he wishes to consider, since the number of integer variables is given by $I + 2K + IK$ where I is the number of regional offices and K is the number of banks. After careful consideration of reported computational experience, the authors believe that a problem containing 25 potential bank sites and three potential regional offices is within the range of available integer programming codes. (See specifically [Ciochetto, et. al., 1972], [Davis and Ray, 1969], [Ellwein, 1970], [Khumawala, 1971 and 1972] and [Spielberg, 1969].

POST OPTIMAL ANALYSIS

A solution to the dual problem of the proposed unified location model can provide additional information about the sensitivity of the model to changes in some of its parameters. For instance, the shadow price associated with constraint (13) can be used to measure the cost of an increase in a required compensating balance level. In addition, the shadow prices on constraints (2) and (6) can measure the impact of a shift in creditor or customer geographic distrubtion. Unfortunately, the integer nature of the model precludes using simple shadow price information to measure the cost of different office and banking relationships. However, this information could be obtained as a byproduct of the branch and bound or implicit enumeration algorithm chosen as a solution procedure.

CONCLUDING REMARKS

In this paper we were concerned with the question of whether the lockbox and disbursement portions of the cash management problem could be unified in one model. The need for this unification arises from the interrelationship between the costs of these two activities. Following Calman and Pogue, we found that the key to such a unification was the explicit consideration of the total level of bank compensation. The proposed model is designed to locate bank activities as well as to determine the optimal levels of these activities.

APPENDIX A

SUMMARY OF THE MODEL

Objective Function

(18) $$\text{MINIMIZE } W = p\left(\Sigma_{k=1}^{K} BAL_k + \Sigma_{M=1}^{M}\Sigma_{k=1}^{K} q_{mk}\cdot Y_{mk}\right) + \Sigma_{k=1}^{K} FEE_k + \Sigma_{k=1}^{K}\left[\bar{f}_k^{C}\cdot z_k^{C} + \bar{f}_k^{D}\cdot z_k^{C} + \Sigma_{i=1}^{I}\bar{f}_{ik}^{DR}\cdot z_{ik}^{DR}\right] + \Sigma_{i=1}^{I}\bar{f}_i^{R}\cdot z_i^{R}$$

Constraints

All creditor checks must be processed:

(6) $$\Sigma_{i=1}^{I}\Sigma_{k=1}^{K} X_{ijk} = a_j \qquad \forall_j$$

All customer deposits must be processed:

(2) $$\Sigma_{k=1}^{K} Y_{mk} = b_m \qquad \forall_m$$

Definition of net collected balances:

(14) $$NCB_k = BAL_k + \Sigma_{i=1}^{I}\Sigma_{j=1}^{J} P_{ijk}\cdot X_{ijk} - \Sigma_{m=1}^{M} r_{mk}\cdot Y_{mk} \qquad \forall_k$$

Net collected balances can support either compensating balances or supporting balances:

(13) $$NCB_k \geq g_k \qquad \forall_k$$

Definition of TCD_k:

(15) $$TCD_k = \Sigma_{i=1}^{I}\Sigma_{j=1}^{J} d_{jk}\cdot X_{ijk} + \hat{f}_k^{D}\cdot z_k^{D} + \Sigma_{i=1}^{I}\hat{f}_{ik}^{DR}\cdot z_{ik}^{DR} \qquad \forall_k$$

Definition of TCC_k:

(16) $$TCC_k = \Sigma_{m=1}^{M} e_{mk}\cdot Y_{mk} + \hat{f}_k^{C}\cdot z_k^{C} \qquad \forall_k$$

Bank compensation constraint:

(11) $$FEE_k + c_k^{T}\cdot TP_k + c_k^{N}\cdot NCB_k \geq TCD_k + TCC_k + V_k \qquad \forall_k$$

Constraints for integer variables Z_k^C:

(3) $\Sigma_{m=1}^{M} Y_{mk} \leq (\Sigma_{m=1}^{M} b_m) \cdot Z_k^C \qquad \forall_k$

Constraints for integer variable Z_k^D:

(7) $\Sigma_{i=1}^{I} \Sigma_{j=1}^{J} X_{ijk} \leq (\Sigma_{j=1}^{J} a_j) \cdot Z_k^D \qquad \forall_k$

Constraints for integer variable Z_i^R:

(8) $\Sigma_{j=1}^{J} \Sigma_{k=1}^{K} X_{ijk} \leq (\Sigma_{j=1}^{J} a_j) \cdot Z_i^R \qquad \forall_i$

Constraint for integer variable Z_{ik}^{DR}:

(9) $\Sigma_{j=1}^{J} X_{ijk} \leq (\Sigma_{j=1}^{J} a_j) \cdot Z_{ik}^{DR} \qquad \forall_{i,k}$

Constraint on available tax payments:

(12) $\Sigma_{k=1}^{K} TP_k \leq TTP$

We assume the continuous variables, FEE_k, X_{ijk}, Y_{mk}, NCB_k, and TP_k are non-negative and BAL_k is unrestricted in sign. The integer variables Z_k^D, Z_k^C, Z_i^R, and Z_{ik}^{DR} are all restricted to be either 0 or 1.

REFERENCES

1. Egon Balas, "An Additive Algorithm for Solving Linear Programs with Zero-One Variables," Operations Research, Vol. 13, 1965, pp. 517-546.

2. D. H. Bent, "Branch-and-Bound for Facility Location," *Inform*, Vol. 10, No. 1, February, 1972, pp. 1-7.

3. R. L. Bulfin, and V. E. Unger, "Computational Experience with an Algorithm for the Lock Box Problem," *Proceedings of the 28th ACM National Conference*, Atlanta, August, 1973.

4. R. F. Calman, Linear Programming and Cash Management/Cash Alpha, The M.I.T. Press, Cambridge, MA, 1968.

5. F. F. Ciochetto, H. S. Swanson, J. R. Lee, and R. E. D. Woolsey, "The Lock Box Problem and Some Startling But True Computational Results for Large Scale Systems," presented at the 41st National Meeting of ORSA held in New Orleans on April 26-28, 1972.

6. P. S. Davis and T. L. Ray, "A Branch-Bound Algorithm for the Capacitated Facilities Location Problem," *Naval Research Logistics Quarterly*, Vol. 16, No. 3, Sept., 1969, pp. 331-344.

7. J. K. Drysdale and P. J. Sandiford, "Heuristic Warehouse Location--A Case History Using a New Method," *Canadian Operational Research Society Journal*, Vol. 7, No. 1, March, 1969, pp. 45-61.

8. M. A. Effroymson and T. L. Ray, "A Branch-Bound Algorithm for Plant Location," *Operations Research*, Vol. 14, No. 3, May-June, 1966, pp. 361-368.

9. L. B. Ellwein, "Fixed Charge Location--Allocation Problems with Capacity and Configuration Constraints," *Technical Report No. 70-2*, Department of Industrial Engineering, Standford University, August, 1970.

10. L. B. Ellwein and P. Gray, "Solving Fixed Charge Location-Allocation Problems with Capacity and Configuration Constraints," *AIIE Transactions*, Vol. 3, No. 4, December, 1971, pp. 290-298.

11. E. Feldman, F. A. Lehrer, and T. L. Ray, "Warehouse Location Under Continuous Economics of Scale, *Management Science*, Vol. 12, No. 9, May, 1966, pp. 670-684.

12. B. M. Khumawala, "An Efficient Heuristic Algorithm for the Warehouse Location Problem," *Krannert School of Industrial Administration Institute Paper Series*, No. 311, Purdue University, May, 1971.

13. B. M. Khumawala, "An Efficient Branch and Bound Algorithm for the Warehouse Location Problem," *Management Science*, Vol. 18, No. 12, Aug., 1972, pp. 718-31.

14. A. Kraus, C. Janssen, and A. McAdams, "The Lock-Box Location Problem, A Class of Fixed Charge Transportation Problems," Vol. 1, No. 3, *Journal of Bank Research*, Autumn, 1970, pp. 51-58.

15. A. Kuehn, and M. Hamburger, "A Heuristic Program for Locating Warehouses," *Management Science*, Vol. 9, No. 4, July, 1963, pp. 643-666.

16. A. H. Land and A. G. Doig, "An Automatic Method of Solving Discrete Problems," *Econometrica*, Vol. 28, 1960, pp. 497-520.

17. F. K. Levy, "An Application of Heuristic Problem Solving to Accounts Receivable Management," *Management Science*, Vol. 12, No. 6, February, 1966, pp. 236-244.

18. S. F. Maier and J. H. Vander Weide, "The Lock-Box Location Problem: A Practical Reformulation," *Journal of Bank Research*, Vol. 5, No. 2, Summer, 1974, pp. 92-95.

19. G. A. Pogue, R. B. Faucett, and R. N. Bussard, "Cash Management: A Systems Approach," *Industrial Management Review*, Winter, 1970, pp. 55-73.

20. Graciano Sa, "Branch-and-Bound and Approximate Solutions to the Capacitated Plant-Location Problem," *Operations Research*, Vol. 17, No. 6, Nov.-Dec., 1969, pp. 1005-1016.

21. R. P. Shanker and A. A. Zoltners, "An Extension of the Lock-Box Location Problem," *Journal of Bank Research*, Vol. 2, No. 4, Winter, 1972, pp. 62.

22. R. J. Shanker and A. A. Zoltners, "The Corporate Payment Problem," *Journal of Bank Research*, Vol. 2, No. 1, Spring, 1972, pp. 47-53.

23. K. Spielberg, "An Algorithm for the Simple Plant Location Problem with Some Side Conditions," *Operations Research*, Vol. 17, No. 1, Jan.-Feb., 1969, pp. 85-111.

READING 33

Inventory Control Theory and Trade Credit Financing

Charles W. Haley
University of Washington

Robert C. Higgins
University of Washington

The objective of any inventory control system is to minimize the total cost to the firm of maintaining its inventory, where the basic factors which determine this cost are the quantity ordered and the means of financing. These decisions have been treated largely as if they were independent, but it is well known that even in the simple cases the optimal order quantity is a function of the costs of financing. In the case of trade-credit financing, where costs often cannot be stated as a simple interest rate per period, complicated interdependencies can arise.[1]

The purpose of this paper is to determine jointly the optimal order quantity and optimal payment time for the firm when additions to inventory are financed with trade-credit. While the analysis will be confined to a single-product firm where the demand for the firm's product is assumed constant and known with certainty, the implications are much broader than this simple case. Financing costs in many standard inventory models are based on a single interest rate per period similar to the basic certainty model.[2] The optimality of existing solutions to such models depends on conditions which will be developed here.

I. THE PROBLEM

Assume that the firm uses trade credit financing and selects the payment time and inventory order quantity so as to minimize the total cost of its inventory. Abstracting from the non-financial costs of inventory for the moment, the essence of the problem concerns the existence of credit deficits and surpluses. A credit deficit arises when inventory investment exceeds trade credit balances. When payment for purchased inventory is made on receipt of goods, only credit deficits arise.

[1] This point was recognized, but not analyzed by Beranek [4]. In [3] he treats trade credit as a cost-free source of funds and does not account explicitly for the investment of short-term cash balances.

[2] See, for example, [1], [5], [7], [8], and [9].

Reprinted from MANAGEMENT SCIENCE (Dec. 1973, Part I and Part II), Vol. 20, No. 4, pp. 464-471, by permission of the publisher.

In this case trade credit balances are always zero and the firm must finance its investment in inventory at some cost (assumed to be $i\%$ in the initial analysis). The standard treatment of the inventory problem effectively assumes this case.[3]

A credit surplus arises when trade credit balances exceed inventory investment. When payment to suppliers is delayed to some date after the receipt of the goods, trade credit balances take on positive values and may exceed the inventory investment. When this occurs, the difference between trade credit and inventory investment is termed a credit surplus. We argue that the existence of a credit surplus at any point in time implies that the firm has incremental cash balances available for investment equal to the amount of the surplus. We assume that such investment provides a return of $r\%$ per period to the firm. The problem we consider is how to pick the order quantity and repayment time so as to minimize total inventory costs when surpluses and deficits are possible.

Before proceeding, it is worth noting that our treatment of the credit surplus as incremental cash available for investment rests on the proposition that order quantity and payment decisions do not affect the cash inflows of the firm but only a portion of the outflows. Hence only those cash outflows which are affected by the order quantity and payment decisions need be considered in arriving at the incremental impact of those decisions on the firm's cash position. To see why this is true, consider the following.

As in all inventory problems, let us compare the impact of the inventory decisions against a base condition where the firm orders goods continuously and pays for them on receipt. Denoting the net cash flow to the firm for this base condition as K_t, the firm's liquid assets A_t (cash plus securities) at any time m can be represented as

$$A_m = A_0 + \int_0^m K_t dt.$$

Now retaining the assumption of continuous orders, suppose the firm delays payment for all goods received between 0 and m. Letting G_t be the cost of goods received at t, trade credit balances at m will be $\int_0^m G_t dt$ which is also the credit surplus at m given that inventory investment is zero. Then (assuming that stockouts do not occur) cash inflows to the firm are independent of the inventory decision, and the net cash flow to the firm at any point within the interval will now be $K_t + G_t$.[4] This follows from the fact that in the base condition K_t includes a continuous payment stream of G_t by construction. The liquid assets of the firm will be

$$\begin{aligned} A'_m &= A_0 + \int_0^m (K_t + G_t)dt \\ &= A_0 + \int_0^m K_t d_t + \int_0^m G_t dt \\ &= A_m + \int_0^m G_t dt. \end{aligned}$$

The credit surplus $\int_0^m G_t dt$ is therefore the increment to the firm's liquid assets at time m which is what we set out to demonstrate. The proof for the general case when inventory investment is positive is more difficult, but follows similar lines to the above. It will not be provided here since the issue is secondary to the main thrust of this paper.

[3] If trade credit were normally provided at a cost of $i\%$ per period assessed on the outstanding balance, then the standard solutions would be appropriate. It is the fact that such trade credit terms are rare that makes the present analysis interesting.

[4] We also assume that selling prices, credit terms on goods sold, costs of manufacturing, etc., are not affected by inventory and payment decisions. These are reasonable assumptions in a world of certainty where stockouts are not a problem; under conditions of uncertainty the analysis becomes more difficult.

For subsequent reference it will be useful to define the following variables.

s = the number of units sold per period, assumed to be known with certainty and constant over time.
a = the setup or handling cost per order.
u = the cost per item after trade discounts.
h = the holding cost per period of carrying one item in stock excluding financing charges.
q = the order quantity.
n = s/q = the number of orders per period.
p = the number of days per period.
T = pq/s, the time interval between orders,
$d\%/t_1$ net t_2 = trade terms. A discount of $d\%$ in cost of item if paid for on or before t_1 days, due in t_2 days.
$\hat{t}$ = time interval between receipt of goods and payment. If receipt occurs on day 0, $\hat{t}$ equals the payment date.

There are two possible cases that must be considered. In Case I the payment time $\hat{t}$ is greater than or equal to the reorder time T and the firm always has surplus funds. This case leads essentially to the standard solution. In Case II $\hat{t} < T$ and the firm has surplus funds over part of the cycle and must borrow over the remainder. This case leads to a different solution than the standard one when $i \neq r$. Unfortunately, since $\hat{t}$ and T are decision variables, we will not be able to tell in advance which case applies. This point will be clarified later.

Case I: $\hat{t} \geq T$

Suppose we know that the reorder time is less than or equal to the payment time as shown in Figure I. The inventory total cost function in this case is the sum of the setup costs, the holding costs, the surplus funds benefit, and the late payment penalties. Only the latter two are unusual. The surplus

Figure I CREDIT AND INVENTORY BALANCES OVER ONE ORDER CYCLE WHEN $\hat{t} \geq T$.

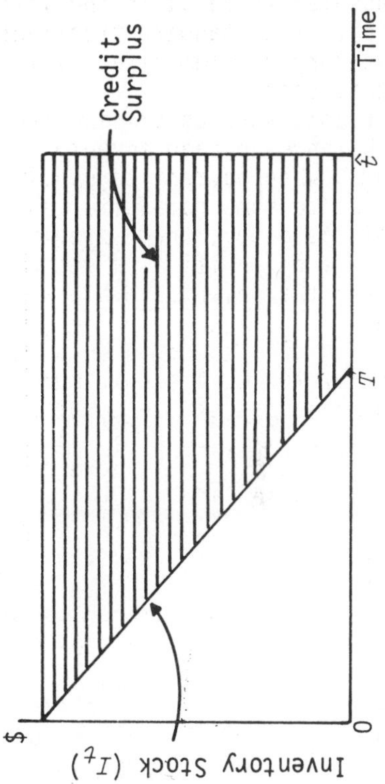

funds benefit arises because the credit surplus in Figure I can be invested to yield a benefit of $r\%$ per period. Integrating over this area and summing over n cycles, this benefit is

$$\frac{rs}{pq} \int_0^T (qu - I_t)dt + \frac{rs}{pq} \int_T^{\hat{t}} qudt.$$
$$= \frac{rsu\hat{t}}{p} - \frac{rqu}{2}.$$

The late payment penalty is $s(u' - u)$ where

$$u' = u \text{ if } \hat{t} \leq t_1$$

$$u' = \frac{u}{1 - d} \text{ if } t_1 < \hat{t} \leq t_2$$

$$u' = \infty \text{ if } \hat{t} > t_2.$$

The possibility of paying beyond the due date is not allowed here.

Treating the surplus funds benefit

as a negative cost and combining it with the usual expressions for setup and holding costs, the total cost function is

(1)

$$TC_I = \frac{as}{q} + (h + ur)q/2 - \frac{rsu\hat{t}}{p} + s(u' - u)$$

Since TC_I contains no cross-product terms in q and $\hat{t}$, the optimal value of q can be found in the usual manner, (setting $\partial TC_I/\partial q = 0$ and solving for q).

(2)

$$q = \left[\frac{2as}{h + ur}\right]^{\frac{1}{2}}$$

The optimal value of $\hat{t}$ will be either t_1 or t_2. There is no benefit from paying prior to t_1, at t_1 a fixed penalty is incurred and payment must be made by t_2. Express the cost of deferring payment from t_1 to t_2 as an interest rate per period i^*

(3)

$$i^* = \frac{p}{t_2 - t_1} \cdot \frac{d}{1 - d}$$

Then if $i^* \geq r$, we should pay at t_1; if $i^* < r$, we should pay at t_2.

In Case I there is one solution for q and two for $\hat{t}$. These solutions generally correspond to those currently appearing in the literature with one exception. We compare i^* with the lending rate (r) whereas the literature on trade credit usually specifies that i^* should be compared with the borrowing rate (i).

Case II: $\hat{t} < T$.

In Case II the firm has surplus funds from 0 to $\hat{t}$ and then must finance its inventory from $\hat{t}$ to T. This is shown in Figure II. If the rate earned on surplus funds, r, is not equal to the financing rate, i, then Equation (1) is inappropriate.

Total cost in this case is the algebraic sum of the following terms:

(a) Average set-up costs: as/q

(b) Average holding costs exclusive of financing: $hq/2$

(c) Late payment penalty: $s(u' - u)$

(d) Average surplus funds benefit (treated as a negative cost):

$$-\frac{rs}{pq}\int_0^{\hat{t}} (qu - I_t)dt$$

where qu is the initial order cost and I_t is the purchase cost of units in stock on day t. $I_t = qu - \frac{su}{p}t$ ∴ the surplus funds benefit is

$$-\frac{rs}{pq}\int_0^{\hat{t}} \frac{su}{p} t dt = -\frac{rus^2\hat{t}^2}{2p^2q}$$

(e) Average cost of borrowing at rate i to finance inventory:

$$\frac{is}{pq}\int_{\hat{t}}^{T} I_t dt$$

Figure II. CREDIT AND INVENTORY BALANCES OVER SEVERAL CYCLES WHEN $\hat{t} < T$.

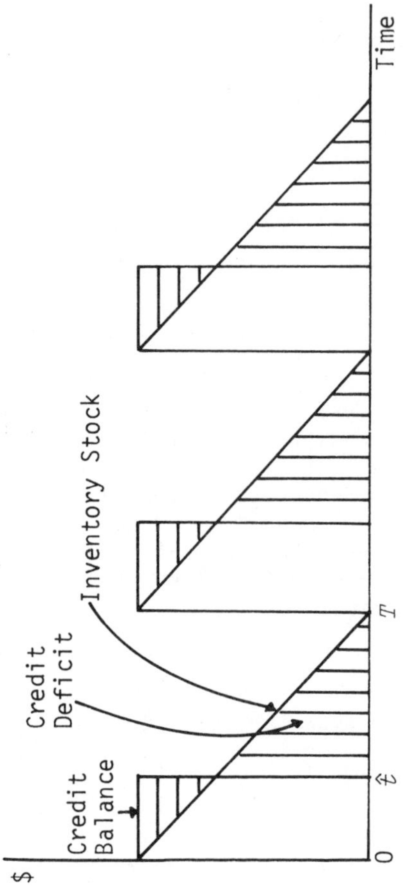

From the definition of I_t above and given that $T = pq/s$, the cost of borrowing is

$$\frac{is}{pq} \int_t^{pq/s} (qu - \frac{su}{p})t\,dt$$

$$= \frac{iqu}{2} - \frac{ius\hat{t}}{p} + \frac{ius^2t^2}{2p^2q}$$

The new total cost function will therefore be

(4)

$$TC_{II} = \frac{as}{q} + (h + ui)q/2 - \frac{ius\hat{t}}{p} + s(u' - u) + \frac{us^2\hat{t}^2}{2p^2q}(i - r)$$

The differences between TC_I and TC_{II} are that i replaces r in the first three terms and another term is added which contains both $\hat{t}$ and q. This cross-product term in t and q forces a simultaneous solution for the values of q and $\hat{t}$ which minimize TC_{II}. Essentially, this cross-product term arises from the fact that unlike Case I, trade credit will be insufficient to cover inventory carrying costs over at least part of the cycle. As it turns out, the relative costs and benefits of the surpluses and deficits depend on $\hat{t}$ and q in the manner shown in the last term.

The nature of the solution can best be understood by referring to Figure III which shows TC_{II} as a function of $\hat{t}$ for typical values of the parameters. As drawn, the minimum cost point with respect to $\hat{t}$ occurs at t_1, however, two other minimum cost solutions are at least theoretically possible; t_2 and what will be called t_m. Except for the discontinuities at t_1 and t_2, TC_{II} is a quadratic function of $\hat{t}$; t_m is the value of $\hat{t}$ corresponding to the minimum point of this quadratic function with respect to $\hat{t}$ and q.

However, differentiating TC_{II} with respect to t, setting the derivative equal to zero, and solving for t_m yields.

$$t_m = T(i/(i - r)).$$

Figure III. TOTAL COST AS A FUNCTION OF PAYMENT TIME WITH MINIMUM COST AT t_1

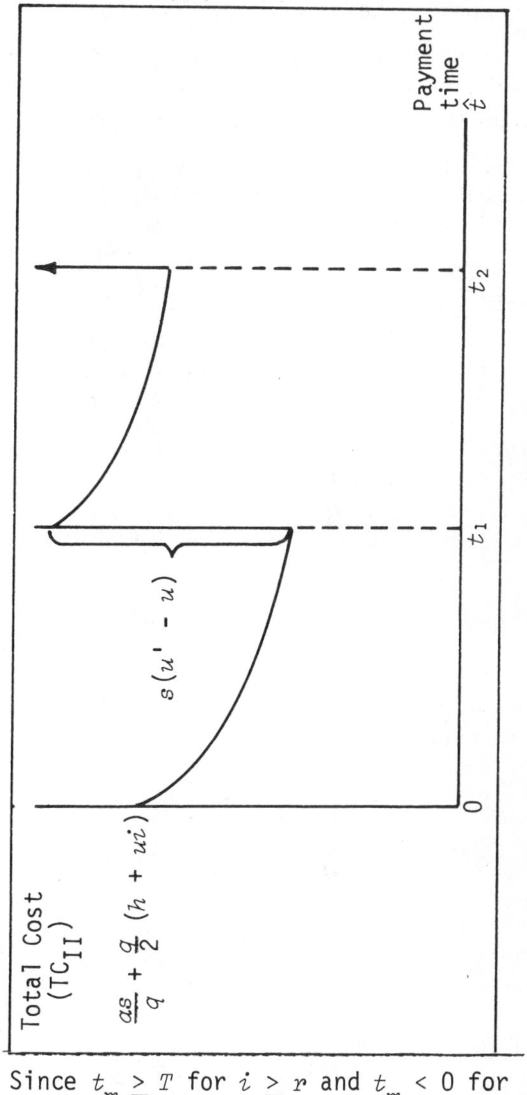

Since $t_m \geq T$ for $i \geq r$ and $t_m < 0$ for $i < r$, t_m is not a feasible solution under the conditions of Case II ($T > t$). Consequently minimum TC_{II} can only obtain at t_1 and/or t_2.

To determine the minimum value for TC_{II}, begin by setting $\partial TC_{II}/\partial q = 0$ and solving for the trough line $q = Q(t)$. Then substituting the two possible values of $\hat{t}$ into this equation yields two sets of values for $\hat{t}$ and q, one of which must correspond to the minimum at

TC_{II}. Thus,

(5)
$$q = \left[\frac{2as}{h+iu} + \frac{s^2u\hat{t}^2(i - r)}{p^2(h + ui)}\right]^{\frac{1}{2}}$$

The substitution of t_1 and t_2 into (5) yields the two possible solutions for Case II. There are, therefore, four feasible solutions in total. Each of the four solutions must be treated as initially feasible for any problem, as we cannot specify in advance whether $\hat{t} \gtrless T$. Although the computational requirements can be reduced somewhat by employing a sequential decision rule, the simplest method is to compute the values of the total cost function for each solution and pick the minimum cost feasible solution.[5]

II. TRANSACTIONS COSTS

The preceding analysis easily generalizes to include transactions costs in utilizing surplus funds and in bank borrowing. While a complete treatment of the subject would be quite laborious, this section will consider one of the more realistic and interesting possibilities. If fixed transactions costs are associated with the investment or liquidation of surplus funds and the take down or repayment of a bank loan, a cash balance problem arises which is in addition to the inventory--trade credit problem already considered. Briefly, with a continuous flow of sales revenue into cash and a fixed cost for purchasing securities, the optimal strategy is to accumulate funds in cash for a time and make a lump-sum purchase of securities. In effect, this is the classic cash balance problem on its head: cash comes in continuously and must be stored, either in cash or securities, in anticipation of a payment at $\hat{t}$.

Analogous reasoning applies to the firm's bank loan. With a continuous cash inflow and a fixed cost for payment or withdrawal, funds should be allowed to accumulate in cash for a time. The problem of interest here is what is the magnitude of the payments, and is this optimal size functionally related to q or $\hat{t}$?

In Case I, the firm does no borrowing and only the investment transactions costs are relevant. Letting C equal the maximum value of cash, and b the cost per transaction, the added costs are the opportunity cost of funds left in cash, $rC/2$, and the transactions costs of going into and out of securities, bus/C.[6] Adding these costs to TC_I, it is apparent that q, $\hat{t}$, and C can all be determined independently. As in the classic cash balance problem, the optimal value of C is $(2bus/r)^{\frac{1}{2}}$.

Case II, is somewhat more involved since both securities investment and borrowing are necessary. Treating first the securities investment part of the problem, the opportunity cost of funds in cash is $rCs\hat{t}/2pq$, and the transactions costs of buying selling securities is $bs^2u\hat{t}/pqC$.[7] Looking next at bank borrowing costs, let L equal the amount repaid per transaction, and let f equal the transaction cost per payment or withdrawal. Then the opportunity cost of funds in cash due to the borrowing transactions costs is $(pq - s\hat{t})iL/2pq$. Similarly, the total transactions costs can be expressed as

[5] It is possible to formulate the problem in a mathematical programming format. Unfortunately the discontinuity in the objective function at t_1 adds an integer condition into the problem. Hence, it becomes a mixed integer, nonlinear programming problem for which algorithms are lacking.

[6] With qu glowing into cash each cycle, and $\$C$ transferred into securities each time, the total number of transfers, including the final liquidation at $\hat{t}$, is qu/C. Over $n = s/q$ cycles at a cost of b per transaction, the total cost is bus/C.

[7] The average cash balance associated with surplus funds is $C/2$ from time 0 to $\hat{t}$ and 0 from $\hat{t}$ to T. Averaging over the cycle, substituting $pq/s = T$, and multiplying by r yields $r\hat{t}Cs/2pq$. For transactions costs, the total revenue flowing into cash from time 0 to $\hat{t}$ is $su\hat{t}/p$. Dividing by C to find the number of transactions and multiplying by $n = s/q$, the total cost at b per transaction is $bs^2u\hat{t}/pCq$.

$(pq - s\hat{t})usf/pqL$.[8] Adding these four expressions to TC_{II} it is clear that in general the decision variables (q, $\hat{t}$, C, L) must be determined simultaneously. In fact, the only instance in which they can be determined independently is when $i = r$ and $b = f$. In this special case, the standard solutions for q, $\hat{t}$ and C are all valid, and in addition, $L = C$.

III. DISCUSSION[9]

From the above analysis it is clear that in the presence of fixed transactions costs for surplus funds and bank borrowing, the standard solutions to the order quantity, repayment time and cash balance problems are generally correct only when $i = r$ and $b = f$. An important issue is, therefore, the specification of the conditions under which these relationships are likely to hold.

There are basically two such conditions.[10] The first is when the firm finances payments to suppliers by reducing liquid assets and, hence, does no bank borrowing. In this case, the cost of funds is just the foregone opportunities on investment in liquid assets, r, and the only relevant transactions cost is b. At the other extreme, the second condition arises when the firm is a continuous borrower and uses its surplus funds to reduce borrowing rather than accumulate liquid assets. Here, the only opportunity cost is i, and the only transactions cost is f.

One should note, however, that these conditions are appropriate only for fixed transactions costs. Thus, for example, suppose the firm does no bank borrowing but faces a transactions cost proportional to the volume transacted whether increasing or decreasing liquid assets. Then, it is easily shown that the net return on surplus funds invested is less than the net opportunity cost of deficits financed out of liquid assets, or in effect $r < i$.[11] Therefore, the standard solutions are not generally correct even though the firm does no borrowing.

Whether or not inventory and trade credit policies can be determined independently in practice is essentially an empirical question. We have shown that the conditions for independence of the two decisions depend upon the particular circumstances of the firm --the nature of its transactions costs and banking arrangements being the more important ones. For many firms it would seem unlikely that these conditions will be met and, therefore, the two decisions, order quantity and payment time, are interdependent.

---

[8] These terms are analogous to those derived in footnote 7. The average cash balance due to the loan is 0 from time 0 to $\hat{t}$, and $L/2$ from $\hat{t}$ to T. Averaging over n cycles, substituting for T and multiplying by i yields the opportunity cost. Since the maximum loan balance is $qu\text{-}su\hat{t}/p$, the total transactions cost is this amount divided by L and multiplied by fs/q.

[9] Our thanks to a referee and the editor for helpful suggestions in this section.

[10] A third obvious situation would be when the firm was operating in a perfect market without transactions costs. In such an idealized market, borrowing and lending rates for the same level of risk must be equal in equilibrium.

[11] Letting g equal the constant of proportionality, the transactions cost of investing in liquid assets over n cycles is

$$\frac{gs}{q}\int_0^{\hat{t}} (qu - I_t)dt.$$

Similarly, the transactions cost of financing the deficit is $\frac{gs}{q}\int_{\hat{t}}^{T} I_t dt$.

We can incorporate these terms into the preceding analysis most easily by defining the net return on surplus funds as $r' = r - pg$ and the net opportunity cost of deficits financed as $i' = r + pg$. Then, replacing r with r' and i with i', the analysis proceeds as before. Clearly, the only condition in which $i' = r'$ is $g = 0$.

We have assumed in the above that the average cash balance will be zero under these conditions. In fact there may be a temporary cash balance just prior to payment. The impact of such balances is to greatly complicate the problem without affecting our basic point.

References

1. Arrow, J.J.; Karlin S.; and Scarf, H. *Studies in the Mathematical Theory of Inventory and Production*, Stanford, Calif.; Stanford University Press, 1958.

2. Baumol, W.J., "The Transactions Demand for Cash: An Inventory Theoretic Approach," *Quarterly Journal of Economics*, LXVI (November 1962), pp. 545-556.

3. Beranek, W., *Working Capital Management*, Belmont, California: Wadsworth, 1966.

4. Beranek, W., "Financial Implications of Lot-Size Inventory Models," *Management Science*, XIII (April, 1967), pp. B401-8.

5. Hadley, G., and Whitin, T.M., *Analysis of Inventory Systems*, Englewood Cliffs, N.J.: Prentice-Hall, Inc., 1963.

6. Magee, J.F., *Production Planning and Inventory Control*, New York: McGraw Hill, 1958.

7. Mao, J.C.T., *Quantitative Analysis of Financial Decisions*, Toronto, Ontario: The Macmillan Company, 1969.

8. Naddor, E., *Inventory Systems*, New York: John Wiley and Sons, Inc., 1966.

9. Starr, M.K., and Miller, D.W., *Inventory Control: Theory and Practice*, Englewood Cliffs, N.J.: Prentice-Hall, Inc., 1962.

SECTION VII
Bank Credit Management

Commercial banks provide firms with short-term financing for their non-spontaneous needs. Commercial banks also provide firms with a range of other services involving the collection of customer payments, the disbursement of payments to employees and suppliers, and the mobilization of liquid funds within the many divisions and facilities of a complex organization. Managing the firm's network of commercial banks, including proper compensation for services received, is an important part of financial management. This section includes five readings that deal with bank credit management.

Conover (Reading 34) pays particular attention to the cost of bank credit, and how the true interest cost to the firm for bank financing may be considerably higher than the simple level of interest rates currently prevailing. The example he uses vividly illustrates that the commitment fee on the unused portion of a line of credit increases out-of-pocket costs to the firm while the compensating balances required by the lending bank decrease the amount of funds actually used by the firm. He also suggests different ways in which a financial manager can attempt to reduce the true interest cost to his firm and thereby lower the firm's average cost of total financing.

The compensating balance continues to be a perplexing institutional phenomenon to many firm managers. Nadler (Reading 35) traces the development of compensating balances from the viewpoint of both the commercial bank and the borrowing firm. He suggests that rising costs of money and more careful analysis of company needs should lead to an incremental pricing of all banks services, rather than a reliance on the traditional method of charging for all bank services using a compensating balance.

The next paper by Diener (Reading 36) is concerned with appraising just how much a firm would be able to borrow for working capital, growth capital, and equity capital. His discussion of working capital financing is particularly useful because it covers both unsecured borrowing and that financing secured by inventory and accounts receivable. A number of rule-of-thumb guidelines used by bankers in determining the amount of bank credit to allow a firm are presented. Diener illustrates the total secured and unsecured financing which a hypothetical firm might be able to raise using such guidelines. In particular, the possibility of secured financing focuses on the linkage between bank credit and some of the current assets of the firm.

Robicheck, Teichroew, and Jones (Reading 37) formulate the overall financing decision of the firm into a linear programming context using the projected cash budget as a starting point. The problem is one of minimizing the total costs associated with various sources of financing subject to a number of constraints that reflect the various terms of bank borrowing. Borrowing terms include lines of credit, term loans, compensating balances, and collateral for secured loans, as well as how accounts payable are handled by the firm. The suggested approach of the authors is illustrated for a number of different cases, and the latitude and power of linear programming becomes quite evident. In addition to obtaining an optimal solution to an important managerial problem, this paper is valuable because of the many linkages between various working capital accounts which are considered explicitly in the formulation.

Folks (Reading 38) explains and illustrates a break-even technique for comparing alternative means of financing the operations of a foreign subsidiary. The break-even point is that foreign exchange rate for which the costs of two alternative financing packages are equal. By specifying a probability distribution for the exchange rate at a future point in time, the financial manager can compare returns and risks for each financing alternative. The author also explains how sensitivity analysis can be used to see how various parameters in the financing arrangements influence the decision which is made.

READING 34

The Case of the Costly Credit Agreement

C. Todd Conover
McKinsey & Company, Inc.

Bill Gordon, vice-president and treasurer of Wellbilt, Inc., had always considered himself something of a whiz at raising money. Wellbilt, a large midwestern manufacturing company (the name, like Gordon's, is fictitious), offered ample scope for his talents. It had always depended heavily on external financing, and two years ago the Board had approved a long-range plan calling for substantial growth over the next five years.

Bill Gordon had risen to the occasion by negotiating a $70 million credit agreement with 18 of the nation's largest and most prestigious commercial banks. That he had obtained such a large agreement at the prime interest rate was a source of much pride to Gordon. It testified, he felt, as much to his own skill as a negotiator as to the credit-worthiness of Wellbilt. In any event, Gordon believed, the company was assured of the financial means to achieve its ambitious growth objectives.

Last month, however, Bill Gordon's complacency received a severe shock. It came as a result of a company-wide profit-improvement program initiated by the president and carried out by several teams under the direction of the corporate controller. One team conducted a detailed study of the company's banking relations and its cash management policies and practices. In the course of the study, they reviewed Gordon's credit agreement and prepared an analysis indicating that, over the previous two years, Gordon had paid almost 29 percent for the funds borrowed under this agreement.

Gordon was flabbergasted, but the analysis was correct. He had concentrated on getting the largest possible agreement at the prime interest rate. In doing so, he overlooked several factors that influence the cost of borrowing. Most critically, the terms of his agreement had specified substantial costs on the unused but still available portion of the agreement. And, since the agreement had not been used to any large extent, the expense was out of all proportion to the funds Wellbilt actually used.

Reprinted from FINANCIAL EXECUTIVE, Vol. 39, No. 9 (September 1971), pp. 40-48, by permission of the publisher.

Like Bill Gordon, many financial executives fail to realize how much they are actually paying for the funds they obtain under borrowing arrangements such as credit agreements or lines of credit. As a result, in their efforts to make sure that funds are available when needed, they may be paying too high a price. The problem here is not high interest rates but the ability to plan bank credit needs more carefully and realistically.

Most financial executives are probably aware of the factors that influence the cost of borrowing, such as compensating balances, commitment fees, and the relationship between the size of an agreement and the amount actually borrowed. What they lack, however, is a good measurement technique that explicitly takes all of these factors into account and thereby provides a safeguard against the trap that Gordon stumbled into.

The purpose of this article is to describe a practical technique for measuring the true cost of borrowing under a credit agreement. This technique may be used by financial executives in planning the amount and terms of their credit agreements and lines of credit. In addition, it can help top management in evaluating the performance of financial executives who have money-raising responsibilities.

Sellers as well as purchasers of credit can make good use of the technique. Since it emphasizes the importance of sound financial planning and careful selection of credit agreement terms, it offers banks another way to strengthen their professional posture vis-a-vis their corporate customers. They can help the customer plan his over-all financial requirements, tailor credit agreements to meet corporate needs by identifying suitable amounts and terms, and determine which other banks might be appropriate participants from the customer's point of view. In short, they can use the technique to enhance both their usefulness to customers and their reputation as professional financial advisers.

CREDIT AGREEMENTS

As every financial man knows, a credit agreement is a written contract between a company and one or more banks. Under its terms the banks agree to lend up to a specified maximum amount during the period of the contract, usually one to three years. In return for this commitment, the company will pay a specified interest rate for the funds it borrows (e.g., one-half to one percent above the prime rate). It will also pay a commitment fee, typically ranging from one-quarter to one-half of 1 percent of the unused portion of the agreement. The company may also have to agree in writing to a number of restrictive covenants, such as the maintenance of a minimum level of working capital or a limitation on the assumption of additional debt. Finally, there is usually the unwritten but well-understood requirement that the company must maintain compensating balances with each of the participating banks.

Rather than enter into a formal credit agreement, of course, companies often establish lines of credit with one or more banks. Unlike credit agreements, these do not involve a written contract, no interest rate is specified, and no commitment fee is charged. However, compensating balances may be maintained to make sure the bank will look favorably on any future loan requests.

The principal reason for credit agreements and lines of credit is to enable a company to borrow funds on short notice with little or no jusitification at the time of borrowing. In effect, these arrangements provide a kind of "liquidity insurance." The borrowed funds are used for a variety of purposes, most commonly to meet seasonal working capital needs, to undertake capital investment projects prior to the arrangement of more permanent financing, or to postpone going to capital markets for debt financing when interest rates are high or are expected to decline.

In addition, financial executives like such arrangements because their performance is often evaluated in terms of their ability to procure funds when needed, rather than by how much they pay for the funds they do procure. In short, credit agreements provide a kind of job insurance for the financial executive--they make his work easier and let him sleep more soundly at night. But unless he knows what kind of premium he is paying for this insurance, his peace of mind can cost his company dearly.

MEASURING TRUE INTEREST COST

What sort of yardstick does a financial executive need for measuring the cost of borrowing under a credit agreement? First, he needs a single measure that can be applied to any credit agreement or line of credit. Second, the measure should, for the sake of convenience, express the cost of borrowing as an interest rate. Third, it should take into account all factors that can influence this cost, namely:

- √ Contract interest rate,
- √ Amount of funds required,
- √ Terms selected and negotiated (e.g., commitment fees and compensating balance arrangements),
- √ Other banking relationships and practices (e.g., normal working balances maintained by the company in each bank) and,
- √ Type of arrangement selected (i.e., credit agreement or line of credit).

By dividing out-of-pocket costs incurred by usable funds, the financial executive can derive a measure that satisfies all three of these criteria. I shall refer to this measure as the "true interest cost of usable funds": TIC for short.

TIC is not difficult to calculate. *Out-of-pocket costs* are equal to the interest on borrowed funds at the contract interest rate plus the commitment fee the company pays on the unused portion of the credit agreement. *Usable funds* are the net amount of a bank loan that the company has available for investment, taking into account (1) the amount borrowed, (2) compensating balance requirements, and (3) the normal working balance, if any, that the company maintains with the bank or banks in order to meet its disbursement obligations.

Exhibit I shows the TIC calculation for the $70 million credit agreement that Bill Gordon obtained for Wellbilt. The company's average borrowings throughout the year totaled $10 million. After taking into account the compensating balance requirements and the company's normal working balance, the amount actually available for use was $4 million. To obtain this amount of usable funds, the company incurred out-of-pocket costs of $1,150,000--the sum of the interest on the average borrowing and the commitment fee on the unused portion of the agreement. Thus, TIC was 28.8 percent.

USING TIC TECHNIQUE

The TIC technique can be put to use in two ways: (1) to plan the amount and terms of an agreement prior to negotiation with banks, and (2) to measure the performance of financial executives in obtaining these agreements.

PLANNING AMOUNTS AND TERMS

If the size of the agreement and the company's normal working balance are held constant, a cost curve can be developed by calculating TIC for different levels of average borrowing. The curve shown in Exhibit II indicates how, for Wellbilt's credit agreement, TIC varies with the level of average borrowing. Of course, the shape of the curve will vary for each different set of terms. In planning his credit agreement, the financial executive should select terms such that his

Exhibit I TRUE INTEREST COST OF USABLE FUNDS
WELLBILT, INC.
($70 Million Credit Agreement)

	Annual Rate	Amount (Thousands)	
Usable Funds			
Average annual borrowing			$10,000
Normal working balance*		$ 2,000	
Less: compensating balances for			
a. Amount borrowed	20%	(2,000)	
b. Unused portion	10%	(6,000)	(6,000)
Average Usable Funds			$ 4,000
Out-of-Pocket Costs			
Interest on average borrowing**	8.5%		$ 850
Commitment fee on unused portion	½ of 1%		300
Total Out-of-Pocket Costs			$ 1,150

True Interest Cost of Usable Funds = $1,150 ÷ $4,000 = 28.8%

*. The amount by which compensating balances exceed the normal working balance represents a burden to the borrower. If compensating balances are less or equal to the normal working balance, usable funds are equal to the amount borrowed.
** At the time this article was written, the prime interest rate was 8.5 percent. At the present rate of about 6 percent, TIC would be 22.5 percent. The difference in prime rates has no effect on the validity of the TIC approach.

Exhibit II. THE TRUE INTEREST COST OF USABLE FUNDS VARIES WITH THE LEVEL OF AVERAGE BORROWING....

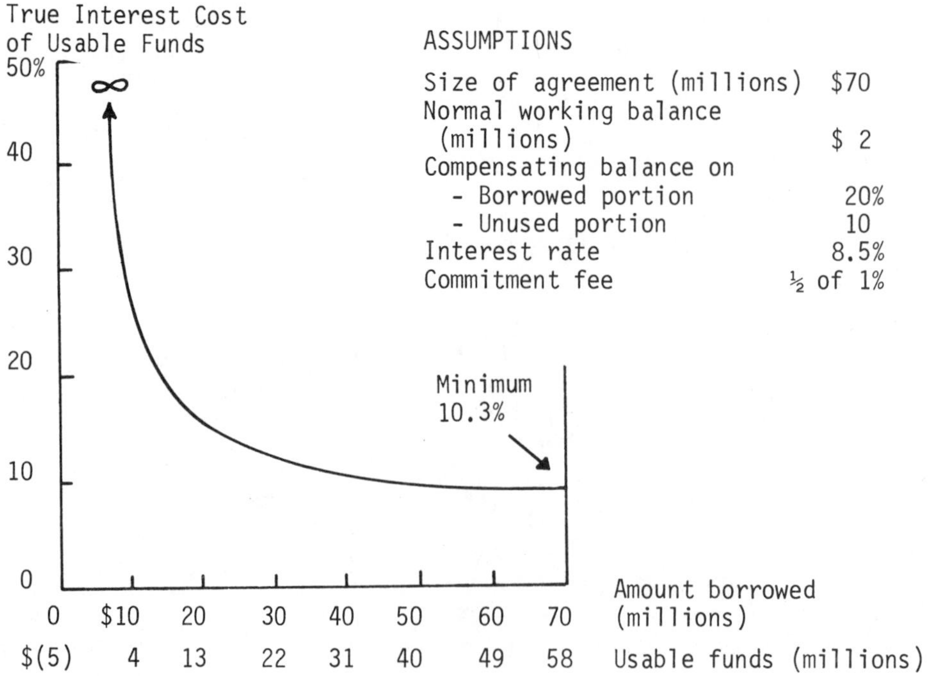

ASSUMPTIONS

Size of agreement (millions)	$70
Normal working balance (millions)	$ 2
Compensating balance on	
- Borrowed portion	20%
- Unused portion	10
Interest rate	8.5%
Commitment fee	½ of 1%

expected level of average borrowing falls on the low-cost portion of the curve.

In the case of Bill Gordon's agreement, as Exhibit II shows, TIC increases sharply if less than $30 million is borrowed. Either Gordon did a less than adequate job of anticipating his short-term borrowing requirements, or he failed to arrange terms that suited his desire to guarantee a large reserve borrowing power. In fact, there are three reasons for the high interest cost he incurred:

1. The small amount actually borrowed in relation to the size of the agreement,
2. The large compensating balances maintained in relation to the company's small level of normal working balances,
3. The commitment fee on the large, unused proportion of the agreement.

Any financial executive who finds himself in Gordon's position can easily calculate the savings obtained by taking one, or any combination, of the following actions open to him:

- ✓ Negotiate a lower interest rate
- ✓ Try to get a lower commitment fee
- ✓ Reduce the size of the agreement
- ✓ Shift the agreement to place a greater proportion of it with banks where normal working balances are concentrated
- ✓ Negotiate a new compensating balance arrangement

The first two actions directly affect out-of-pocket costs and are the most easily recognized and pursued. However, they probably offer the least potential for reducing TIC: an interest-rate reduction would be virtually impossible for a company at or near the prime rate, and a reduction in the commitment fee rate would yield only modest savings. So bypassing these two possibilities, let us consider the impact on TIC of each of the remaining actions.

Exhibit III illustrates the savings in TIC, at $10 million average borrowing, that Gordon could have obtained by:

1. *Reducing the size of the credit agreement.* If Gordon could have improved his financial planning efforts, and thereby improved the predictability of his plans, he could have determined the appropriate size of his agreement more accurately. For example, by reducing its size from $70 million to $50 million, usable funds would increase from $4 million to $6 million, out-of-pocket costs would decline by $100,000 per year, and TIC would decline from 29 percent to 18 percent.

2. *Placing a greater proportion of the agreement with banks where normal working balances are concentrated.* If an additional $3 million of normal working balances were gained by rearranging the credit agreement with banks already carrying such balances, the amount of usable funds would increase by a corresponding amount, and TIC would be reduced to 16 percent.

3. *Negotiating a new compensating balance arrangement.* If Gordon's compensating balance arrangement had been shifted from 20 percent on borrowed funds and 10 percent on the unused portion of the agreement to 30 percent on borrowed funds, the amount of usable funds available at the same out-of-pocket costs would have increased, and TIC would have declined from 29 percent to 13 percent.

4. *Combining all these actions.* If all three of the above actions had been taken together, TIC would have been reduced to 10.5 percent.

MEASURING PERFORMANCE

In addition to planning a low-cost credit agreement, the TIC technique may also be used to evaluate a financial executive's performance. This can be done by developing a cost curve for each credit agreement and calculating TIC for the actual level of average borrowing. In this way, the effectiveness with which the financial executive has planned his financial requirements and determined the size and terms of his agreement may be measured. He can thus

Exhibit III. THE TIC TECHNIQUE MAY BE USED TO DETERMINE THE IMPACT OF DIFFERENT MANAGEMENT ACTIONS.....

	Results of Action at $10 Million Average Borrowing					
	Compensating	Usable	Out-of-Pocket Costs (000)			
Management Action	Balances (000)	Funds (000)	Interest	Commitment Fee	Total	TIC
Maintain the original agreement	$8,000	$4,000	$850	$300	$1,150	28.8%
Alternative Actions						
1. Reduce the size of the agreement from $70 million to $50 million.	$6,000	$6,000	$850	$200	$1,050	17.5%
2. Place a greater proportion of the agreement where normal working balances are concentrated, gain $3 million in normal working balances	8,000	7,000	850	300	1,150	16.4
3. Negotiate a new compensating balance arrangement --30 percent on borrowed funds	3,000	9,000	850	300	1,150	12.8
4. Combine all the alternative actions	3,000	10,000	850	200	1,050	10.5

be evaluated on how much he pays for the money he gets, not just on how good he is at getting it.

AVOIDING COSTLY CREDIT AGREEMENTS

Experience with practical application of TIC suggests these guidelines for financial executives who want to plan low-cost credit agreements and thus ensure good performance.

1. *Select an appropriate time horizon for the company's cash forecast.* The duration of any credit agreement must be related to a practical planning horizon. In other words, unless reasonably accurate cash forecasts can be developed for more than two years ahead, the life of any credit agreement negotiated to help meet capital requirements during that period should not exceed two years.

2. *Carefully determine the amount of anticipated borrowing.* Both the maximum amount required and the expected average borrowing over the appropriate time horizon should be identified. Because TIC varies with the level of average borrowing, the financial executive should try to relate the size of the agreement as closely as possible to the company's probable needs, allowing for a margin of safety but realizing that he will be paying for every bit of that margin.

3. *Identify the company's normal working balance for each bank that might be included in the agreement.* In this way, the financial executive can make sure the company gets the maximum benefit from its normal working balances, which might also serve as compensating balances for the agreement. This step may also help him identify

the proportional share of each bank in the agreement.

4. *Develop a desired set of terms for the credit agreement.* These should reflect both the amount needed and the company's normal working balance. Use the TIC technique to test alternative sets of terms.

5. *Negotiate the desired terms with the appropriate banks.* TIC can be used in the negotiation process to determine the impact of alternative proposals.

Obviously, the task of determining financial requirements and obtaining low-cost credit agreements is more difficult than these guidelines imply. The larger and more diversified the company, and the more international its operations, the more complex its financial planning must be. Moreover, a company's over-all performance and its past banking relationships have an impact on its ability to borrow. Nevertheless, by following the above guidelines and applying the TIC technique, financial executives can see more clearly the costs confronting them and thus avoid an unnecessary and unrecognized drain on company profits.

READING 35

Compensating Balances and the Prime at Twilight

Paul S. Nadler
Rutgers University

Since the outlawing of interest on demand deposits in the early 1930s, the requirement of compensating balances behind loans and the use of the prime rate as the basic lending charge have been integral aspects of commercial banking. Now, however, because of banking's experience in the credit crisis of 1969-1970, and with the greater emphasis on self-analysis that has resulted from the industry's first profit squeeze in more than a decade, bankers are finally reevaluating these concepts.

They are turning instead to incremental costing of lendable funds and tying loan rates to their own cost of money. This development is bound to have major impact on banking in the years ahead and will also influence the operations of those dependent on bank funds.

In this article I shall describe the sequence of events that has brought about this radical redirection of thinking, and also discuss the effect it should have on banks and their customers.

JUSTIFICATION & CRITICISM...

Outsiders as well as the industry's self-appointed soothsayers have spoken out again and again about the drawbacks of these two precepts of loan pricing and have indicated the advantages banks would gain by eliminating them. But most bankers scoffed, and little change took place for decades. How have bankers justified these practices, and what have their critics said?

... of Compensating Balances

In no other industry is the customer sold something and then told he must leave in the store 15% or 20% of what he bought in order to augment the seller's remaining inventory.

In a moment of candor, a banker might justify the balance concept to a customer this way: "If your company is large enough to borrow from a bank,

Reprinted from the HARVARD BUSINESS REVIEW, Vol. 50, No. 1 (Jan.-Feb. 1972), pp. 112-120, by permission of the publisher.

it is also large enough to have a bank account. And if you want to borrow from us, why shouldn't we get that account?"

It is not only a matter of justice and loyalty--the customer being more firmly cemented to his bank--but also a way of gaining more revenue. If a bank requires a borrower to keep on deposit 20% of what he borrows, this raises the effective cost of his loan and thus the yield to the bank.

In addition, bankers have looked on balances as a way of getting a higher yield when usury ceilings and other interest rate limitations prevent getting it directly. Also, a banker may tell a customer that the requirement is a means of getting more raw material to lend to others, and were it not for the balances these others leave, the bank might not be able to grant his loan.

What the critics say: Opponents of the balance requirement consider the bankers' reasoning as specious.

In most cases the borrower already is utilizing all his available liquid funds effectively. So the money he leaves in the bank to back the loan also serves as compensation for the account activity he generates in the normal course of business. When the banker permits the same balances to do such double duty, he is fooling himself if he thinks there is any profit in requiring the balance to enhance the yield he earns on the loan.

As James F. Bodine, Senior Executive Vice President of the First Pennsylvania Banking & Trust Company, has put it:

"The height of illogic is a retailer who prices a shirt at $5 and a necktie at $2.50, but is willing to sell both the shirt and the necktie for $5. The guy is not very smart; I doubt if you'd lend him any of your bank's money.

"Yet this is what banking has done for years--priced deposit service in terms of *X* compensating balances and loan service in terms of *Y* compensating balances, but then accepted in payment for both services only the balances. The borrower who doesn't need deposit service has grounds for complaint on the basis of unfair pricing practice. Ralph Nader would like that one."[1]

When the bank does require the loan-supporting balance to be an idle one, the practice is equally illogical if the customer is sharp in cash management and has no idle funds available. In that case he must borrow enough extra money from the bank to cover the compensating balance requirement. But since this amount comes immediately back to the bank in deposit form, the bank must keep a reserve against it either at the Federal Reserve Bank or, if it is not a member of the Federal Reserve System, at some other bank.

So the practice of requiring balances results both in less money to lend (rather than more, which bankers frequently claim they get in "new business") and in a lower return for the bank than it could earn through a higher loan interest without balances. This can be demonstrated with figures:

✓ A customer who has to raise more than he needs, in order to meet his compensating balance requirement, would be as well off borrowing $100,000 at 7½% without a balance requirement as he would be borrowing $125,000 at 6% and leaving $25,000 in the bank as an idle balance to back the loan. In each case his annual interest cost would be $7,500.

To the bank, however, the alternatives are not equal. It could lend this customer the $100,000 and lend someone else the remaining $25,000--both at 7½%. But if it loaned the entire $125,000 to the first customer and required him to leave $25,000 on deposit, the bank would have to keep idle about one sixth of the deposit as a required reserve and would have only

[1] Address before the annual convention of the American Bankers Association, Honolulu, September 30, 1969.

$20,750 to lend to someone else. Also, if the loan rate is 6% with a balance, the bank would wind up with lower total income than it would have if it had assessed the straight fee of 7½%--even after the $4,150 compensating balance is deposited by the second borrower and reloaned (minus the reserve requirement), and so forth to infinity.

Companies' conduct: Why have corporations objected so infrequently to the balance requirement in years past?

Corporations have often kept more cash in banks than the required minimums. A 1968 study by the Conference Board, for example, showed that more than half of the 291 responding companies maintained larger amounts on deposit than their banks demanded in compensating balances. They typically did this to maintain their own liquidity standards and meet their fluctuating cash requirements.[2]

Because the balance requirement costs them nothing these companies would turn a deaf ear to a bank's suggestion that it be replaced by a higher loan rate.

Even those companies that are short of cash generally have been hesitant to pay with higher loan rates instead of balances, for two reasons:

1. They know that while loan rates remain fixed, they can quietly trim the balances below required levels without much protest from the bank. They can also use the balances on occasion, or even all the time, to back activity in their deposits.

2. Since businesses consider their loan rates to be an indication of their status, few corporate treasurers or presidents care to be labeled "non-prime" borrowers even if their banks are willing to share the added income resulting from elimination of the balance requirement.

...& the prime

Banks set up the prime rate convention in the 1930s to eliminate cutthroat competition and to keep rates from falling below a minimum level. It has been effective in doing that. When it eventually became a status symbol for corporate borrowers, the desire to be a "prime borrower" became an overriding concern for many companies, even at times when maintenance of prime status cost far more in terms of higher balances and other fees than giving it up would have cost.

Academics and other outsiders attack the convention on the ground that it looks like collusion; whenever a leading bank changes it, the vast majority of large banks quickly follow suit. The bankers respond that, on the contrary, competition is so keen that one bank's cut in the prime must be followed by others, lest the initiating bank steal business from them.

Be that as it may, the prime has been adhered to most of the time and has been a far more stable rate than a any other lending charge. Its universality and stability have eliminated some of the disorder in bank lending, even if it has displeased some outsiders.

IMPETUS FOR CHANGE

In the late 1960s as in the early 1930s, compensating balances and the prime rate convention remained as much a part of banking as the clearing of checks and the making of loans. But now things are changing.

Banks are offering loans without balances and with rates tied to their own cost of money, negotiating each loan singly with the customer. And whereas bankers in the past looked solely at balances to determine whether a prime loan was profitable, now they are turning to "profitability analysis"--a means of analyzing the entire relationship with a customer to see if it generates profit, regardless of whether the profit stems from balances, loan interest, or other fees paid.

What has brought about this re-

[2] Commercial Banking Arrangements (New York, 1968), p. 23.

versal? It is a combination of developments, economic and political, which has made the more thoughtful members of the industry realize the limitations of the prime and the balance requirement. Behind these developments is the increased usage of liability management in the middle and late 1960s.

Liability Management

Until recently, banks have traditionally let the level of deposits--as influenced by community growth, public financial habits, and Federal Reserve policy--determine the amount of assets placed on their books.

In the 1960s, however, aggressive banks began to focus on the other side of the balance sheet. They recognized that the money mobilization techniques of acute corporate and municipal treasurers, and the growing financial acumen of individual customers too, were blocking growth of demand deposits.

At first they defensively reverted to solicitation of time and savings deposits to keep from losing their share of the growth in the nation's financial wealth. Then they aggressively stepped up solicitation of these deposits as a means of getting new funds so that asset levels could be controlled rather than accepted as a function of whatever deposit growth occurred.

This meant the development of full-scale liability management. If available loans and investments offered yields attractive enough to merit the purchase of more funds through the time and savings deposit route, the banks would raise their rates and the funds would flow in from the yield-conscious corporate and municipal treasurers and individual savers. If loan and investment outlets became less attractive, so would the rates paid on deposits, with the result that liabilities were managed to meet money needs.

In using liability management--as is the case in most profitable bank transactions--banks borrow short and lend long. Banks that wanted to capitalize on intermediate- and long-term loan and investment opportunities had to rely on short-term certificate of deposit (CD) funds as the wherewithal.

Prime concerns

Bankers believed they could always replace the maturing CDs with new CD money as long as they were willing to pay the rate. But the Federal Reserve opposed this policy--because the smaller banks and nonbanking financial institutions could not compete against the aggressive institutions for the funds in times of tight money--and clamped the Regulation Q ceiling on interest rates that banks could legally pay on CDs.

As interest rates rose in 1966 and the 1969--1970 period, the Regulation Q lid prevented the major banks from gaining renewal of maturing CDs, since investors could obtain higher yields in Treasury bills and other open-market securities than the banks could pay. But the banks had already made loans and investments and had to renew maturing CDs to finance these assets, whatever the cost. So they began to look elsewhere.

One result was the spread of the one-bank holding company. It could sell commercial paper without worrying about the Regulation Q ceiling and thus could provide funds to the subsidiary bank. Another result was the conversion of the Eurodollar market from a dollar-trading vehicle to a market from which dollar claims owned all over the world were channeled to U.S. banks' overseas offices (where Regulation Q did not apply), and then channeled home to replace the maturing CDs.

The competition for Eurodollars drove yields up to as high as 13%. Much of the money was used to underwrite loans that had been made at the prime rate, thus earning the banks 8½% plus any idle balances they could glean. The irony was that the public felt the 8½% rate was extremely high--which prevented the banks from raising it further.

This experience made bankers realize that the uniformity of the prime rate can be a severe handicap, politically as well as economically. They also realized that if they were to maintain aggressive liability management, they must relate their yield on loans more closely to the cost of money. In this way they would not again be caught holding intermediate- and long-term loans offering modest yields while the cost of funds to meet these loan commitments soared.

As a result, industry leaders took three unprecedented steps in an attempt to lessen the significance of the prime rate in the economy:

1. As interest rates fell in 1970, bellwether banks switched to making frequent, small reductions in the prime to keep the rate closer to money-market interest rates. Another goal was to make changes in the prime rate less newsworthy so that the banking industry would not get heat when it came time to raise the prime again.

The prime rate was lowered 11 times between March 1970 and March 1971. The last few cuts received a good deal less attention than the initial ones.

2. Some banks turned to a split prime even before the gradual rate declines began. They kept the basic prime rate on previously determined lines of credit, but when a borrower exceeded his credit limit, he was charged a higher rate tied to the bank's cost of funds.

3. A few banks decided that the only sound approach was to adopt incremental cost pricing completely--at once giving up both the balance requirement and the prime concept and charging a rate tied to their own cost of money under liability management.

For example, one major New York City bank, the Bankers Trust Company, has been arranging loans to some customers with no balances and with the rate set at 2 3/4% over the bank's own CD rate, plus a premium for risk when necessary. The bank can substitute the Eurodollar rate or the next marginal source of funds available (if there is a source cheaper than Eurodollars), just in case the Regulation Q ceiling again makes CD money unavailable and the bank must buy more expensive funds.

<u>More dark clouds</u>: If bankers needed any further evidence that abandonment of the prime makes sense, they got it in 1971. When interest rates turned back up in the spring, the banks found they were criticized sharply for trying to raise the prime rate again--even after 11 declines.

In fact, the major banks were told in no uncertain terms by members of the Administration and the Congress that approval of the $250 million loan guarantees to Lockheed Aircraft Corporation--which the banks needed to protect their credits to the company--would be blocked if the banks raised the prime. As a result of the criticism, the leading banks delayed a prime rate increase for several months after money-market conditions had sanctioned one.

Then, after the wage-price freeze was announced in August, bankers began to fear they could be caught in a new cost-price squeeze.

They realized that raising the prime rate was not politically wise; yet the cost of funds--determined largely by CD rates--would be left to fluctuate according to supply and demand (barring the drastic and unlikely step of governmental capital controls). If interest rates were to climb, the increased cost of CD and Eurodollar sources--coupled with a fixed yield on bank loans--could put the banking industry in a severe profit squeeze which a system tied to the prime rate convention would be powerless to remedy.

The beginning of the end for the convention came in October, when the nation's second largest bank, First National City of New York, announced a shift to a floating base rate to be calculated weekly. Initially, at least, the bank pegged the rate on a spread of ½ of 1% above the effective rate for 90-day commercial paper.

A breakthrough has taken place on the prime. But the breakthrough on balance requirements will take longer.

Out of Balance

The buildup of sentiment to eliminate compensating balances stems from a greater general acceptance of higher interest rates, the new aggressiveness of corporate treasurers in managing cash, profit pressure on banks, and a threat of legal restrictions. I will consider each in turn.

The lid is looser: The United States has always had a low interest rate bias that had made it difficult for lenders to change rates as high as the market would bear. So they have turned to techniques like compensating balances to circumvent limitations such as usury ceilings.

Now, however, after the credit crisis of 1966 and 1969-1970, banks have discovered that the American public is accepting the high cost of money just as it has been accepted in other nations. Despite Washington's reaction, borrowers are much more concerned with the availability of money than with its price. Nor has the deductability of interest cost from net income for tax purposes hurt the growth of this trend.

In addition, states and other public bodies are discovering that usury ceilings and other rate limitations do not bring the potential borrower lower-cost money; rather, they merely lead to the lender's diverting funds to areas where the ceilings do not exist.

Aggressive treasurers: The corporate treasurer is now much more attuned to the opportunity cost of money. He feels that it is foolish to leave money in a bank balance earning the bank 6% net, when he could earn 12% or more on the money for his company elsewhere and compensate the bank with a higher loan fee to replace the balance requirement.

Furthermore, we can look forward to the time when funds are routinely moved electronically from one place to another. Observe what a portentous change in bank policy is reflected in these remarks by the economist of the Cleveland Trust Company:

"An automated payments system will develop because it is clearly advantageous to corporations under conditions of high interest rates to turn idle cash into earning assets as quickly as possible, and because competition within the banking system will drive the banking industry to help them in this endeavor.

"In the future, then, we must think about the day when, instead of making our money by investing and lending our customers' idle balances, we collect a fee for the speed with which we put them to work."[3]

Such an outlook for banking certainly does not correlate with strict maintenance of compensating balance requirments. One can assume that were the Conference Board to survey its members again in 1972, it would not find that over half keep excess bank balances, as they did at the time of the previously mentioned 1968 survey.

One possible counter to this development is the balances that companies maintain to ensure that in periods of credit stringency the banks will take care of them. These customers have always been favored in tight-money periods.

After the Penn Central Company bankruptcy, corporate management became ruefully aware of the value of bank relationships and the impersonality of open-market fund sources which had dried up overnight. So some treasurers "got religion" and built up bank balances to be sure of future credit accommodation. But such religious fervor often fades rapidly.

Profit pressures: Banking historically has been growth-oriented; the typical bank executive can more easily tell someone his "footings" (the figure at the foot of the balance sheet) than he can recall his bank's earnings on assets

[3] Address of Noel A. McBride before the National Automation Conference of the American Bankers Association, New York, May 4, 1971.

or on invested capital.

One reason why banking has been oriented more toward growth than profits is that the profits have come in anyway, so why not concentrate attention on size? But the important sources of profit growth in the 1950s and the 1960s have now largely disappeared. They were:

√ The steady rise in domestic interest rates that brought ever-rising returns on loans and investments held by the banks. (Now interest rates have reached a plateau from which further great advances appear unlikely.)

√ The movement from heavy liquidity and 30% to 40% loan-to-deposit ratios to greater emphasis on loans, resulting in achievement of ratios as high as 70% and 80%. (Now banks have used up their excess liquidity.)

√ The willingness to the saver to remain "sullen but not mutinous" (as a football coach once characterized Yale alumni), earning only 3% to 4% on his savings no matter how high interest rates climbed. (Now he knows what his money is worth.)

So the banks have had to turn inward to build profits, and, as they have done so, they have had to reexamine old policies that brought growth but not profitability.

One multibillion-dollar bank has concluded that it would be better off demanding a balance as the price of a line of credit when the customer is *not* borrowing, instead of charging for this service. But when the customer does borrow, the bank is better off with a higher fee for the entire loan and no balance requirement. Others have come to the conclusion spelled out early in this article--that if the customer is willing to pay a higher loan rate instead of keeping a balance, the bank saves the reserve requirement and actually has more money to lend others and a higher return for itself.

To be sure, there are still many bankers who look at *The American Banker's* lists of the top 10,000 banks (in order of size) and judge their bank's success by its ranking this year compared with last year.

Legal threats: Bankers cannot completely ignore proposals such as that of Senator Edward Brooke of Massachusetts, that the compensating balance requirement be outlawed because it is a tie-in that may violate the antitrust laws.

Bankers recognize how vulnerable they are to lawmakers' attacks. So as they ponder Senator Brooke's proposal and others--like that of Representative Wright Patman of Texas, who suggested that equity kickers and other forms of gaining "a piece of the action" in bank lending should also be made illegal--they have reason to ask themselves if there may be other ways of getting the same income without maintaining the objectionable practices.

PROFITABILITY ANALYSIS

As I mentioned earlier in this article, bankers have been turning to profitability analysis and examination of the entire relationship with customers. This approach eliminates dependence on compensating balance arrangements and on the prime rate as a lending yardstick.

In this procedure, the bank tries to determine whether its dealings with a customer yield a profit from service charges, free balances, and loan interest. If necessary, the bank will assess a fee to make the account earn at least as much as the institution earns on its capital elsewhere.

In considering a customer's loan application, the bank measures its potential profit contribution on the basis of the interest rates charged, cost of money to the bank, risk, idle balances maintained, and services to the borrower.

The depositor is assumed to borrow his own net deposit after deduction of uncollected balances and reserves. The rest of the loan comes from bank capital allocated to loans and from the pool of other bank deposits.

The customer is given credit for

the interest and fees he has paid and is charged for his account activity costs and for the cost of handling his loan. He is also charged at the pool funds rate for the cost of the pool funds he has borrowed. This rate is determined by dividing the total cost of acquiring and maintaining deposits by the amount of the deposit pool.

The bank establishes a profit goal for each borrower based on the desired return on the capital allocated to the loan. The difference between the credits and the charges is the potential profit. The bank compares this amount with the profit goal for this borrower and computes an index number to determine by what percent this transaction would exceed or fall short of the profit goal.

Exhibit I is a reproduction of the "customer profitability analysis" form used by loan officers at the Fidelity Bank of Philadelphia. (To save space, I have greatly condensed the line-by-line instructional footnotes.)

Profitability analysis has not been perfected yet. Bankers debate, for example, whether in a tight-money period the borrower should be charged the marginal cost of funds instead of the average cost, and whether the reserve requirement behind a deposit should be part of the cost of a loan made to the depositor rather than a deduction from deposit profits.

Be that as it may, profitability analysis is a realistic and sound approach. The customer can keep the balances he wants and the bank charges him, on an incremental basis over its costs, for the money he wants above that amount. The approach also encourages the customer to keep funds in the bank rather than put them in Treasury bills or other money-market outlets, since the bank offers him as high a yield.

IMPACT ON CUSTOMERS

Traditions die slowly in banking, and the reader should not conclude that the traditions of compensating balances and the prime rate are being swiftly replaced by profitability analysis and incremental cost pricing.

One reason why the changes are coming slowly is the practice of those corporate treasurers who take advantage of the traditional banks' willingness to sell both the shirt and the necktie for the price of the shirt. These treasurers shop around for rate variations and then whipsaw the innovative banks by threatening to move to the less expensive ones.

Some years ago, forward-looking banks began to price their corporate services to include a profit and give customers realistic earnings credits on their balances. This was a departure from the customary practice of offering services at cost and hoping to gain a profit through low earnings credits. But at first these banks could not make this advance stick because the competition refused to go along.[4]

The same has been true for the more realistic approach to pricing deposit services. But over time, corporate treasurers are becoming aware that dealings with aggressive, profit-conscious banks are better for their companies than deposit relationships with banks that passively accept traditional pricing without periodic examination to account for changes in money-market conditions.

Admittedly, the new approach has disadvantages for the corporate treasurer. His balances will no longer be able to do double duty.

Moreover, companies may no longer be able to immunize themselves from the impact of tight-money conditions by currying favor with banks through leaving generous balances there throughout business cycles. The criterion for getting a loan in tight-money times may be whether these companies can afford the interest rates.

The banks, however, may find that

[4] See James P. Furniss and Paul S. Nadler, "Should Banks Reprice Corporate Services?" HBR (May-June 1966), p. 95.

Exhibit I. PROFITABILITY ANALYSIS FORM USED AT ONE BANK

THE FIDELITY BANK

CUSTOMER PROFITABILITY ANALYSIS — Period ________

Customer ____________________ — SIC No. ________

Loan Quality Rating __________

1) Average Borrowing __________
2) Allocated Capital @ 10% __________
3) Average Collected Balance __________

INCOME

4) Interest Earned __________
5) Earnings Credit on Investible Balance @ ______% __________
6) Service Charges Paid __________
7) Other Income __________
8) Total Income __________

EXPENSE

9) Cost of Funds
   Pool Funds----------Line 1 less Line 2 x ______% ______ __________
   Allocated Capital-- Line 2 x 20% ______ __________
10) Cost of Risk Line 1 x ______% __________
11) Loan Handline Cost Line 1 x ______% __________
12) Activity and Other Charges vs Balances __________
13) Other Service Costs __________
14) Mark-up on Lines 12 and 13 @ 15% __________
15) Total Expense (including Profit Goal) __________
16) Earnings in Excess of Profit Goal (Deficit) __________
17) Line 16 as % of Average Borrowings __________
18) Excess (Deficit) Collected Balances to equal exact Profit Goal __________

#Includes affiliated loans and deposits.

---

19) Confirmed Line of Credit __________
20) Average Free Balances __________ (past 4 quarters)
21) Average Free Balances/ Average Borrowing ______% (past 4 quarters)

Notes:

Line 5. Same rate used for cost of pooled funds under Line 9. The investible balance is the collected balance less applicable reserve requirements

Line 9. Cost of funds pool rate represents average of 89-day CD and federal funds rates over the past four quarters.

Line 10. Designed to recapture average charge-offs; rating of loan determines percentage.

Line 17. Average loan rate during past four quarters should have been higher or lower by the amount of the percentage shown to have achieved the exact profit goal.

Line 20. Amount shown will represent net profit on deposit relationship (Line 5 less Line 12) capitalized at rate used in Line 5.

this development makes their loan demand even more cyclical than it is at present. In the past, when money was easy but expected to get tighter, many businesses borrowed in order to lock up funds at low and relatively inflexible rates. Now, however, as the prime rate is changing more often to correspond with money rates, fewer banks are willing to set fixed rates on term loans and some banks are developing incremental cost pricing. So companies have less incentive to borrow at the slack ends of business cycles.

If banks employ the same flexibility when money is tight but expected to get easier, the action would have the effect of inducing more borrowing. Banks would be the preferred source of funds in tight-money periods, since companies could avoid locking themselves into loans at high, fixed rates.

The result could be a quite different pattern of loan demand at banks over the business cycle, a pattern that would make easy-money conditions easier and tight-money conditions tighter for banks. But the corporate treasurer would be unable to escape some of the impact of rate changes.

On the plus side, companies would know they are getting bank funds at true cost in all phases of the business cycle, and they would not have to worry about how much to maintain in balances to earn their banker's favor in case of need. Frequently these long-idle balances cost the corporation much more than what it would cost in stringent times to get credit accommodation in the open market.

CONCLUDING NOTE

While bankers and their customers have talked for years about discarding the use of compensating balances and the prime rate convention, only now are there signs on the horizon that these traditional banking practices may actually disappear.

The prime rate's drawbacks have become evident through the adverse impact it has had on banking's image and through the pressure that the rate has placed on bank profits when costs of funds rise but the prime remains fixed.

Meanwhile, the shortage of capital has made more bankers and their customers aware that balance requirements frequently only cause borrowers to draw more than they otherwise need in order to meet the requirement. And they realize that both bank and borrower would be better off in many instances with a higher loan charge instead.

The development of more precise loan pricing can help the corporation keep the cost of its bank relationship under better control. The benefits to the bank are even greater. Without the prime convention and balance requirements, bankers improve their chances of getting a fair price for the money they have purchased, particularly in these times when demand and time balances must be paid for dearly with services and interest. In addition, the banks would be rid of a practice that appears to be collusion.

Finally, bank loans are being priced on the basis of the true cost of funds, as determined by supply and demand, rather than on tradition and customer relationships that favor some potential borrowers over others for historical, political, and other noneconomic reasons. Progressive banks are tying their loan charges to the incremental costs of funds and are basing loan decisions on gauges of the profitability of their customers' banking relationships.

Given the tremendous importance of bank loans in the U.S. money and capital market, the movement away from tradition and toward rationality is encouraging to those who feel that a free financial market is worth maintaining and perfecting.

READING 36

Analyzing the Financial Potential of a Business

Royce Diener
American Medical International

Many seekers of business credit--and doubtless all individuals connected with the sources of such credit--will agree that a successful financing program can be achieved only if the applicant has made a prior determination of his exact needs, and if he understands in realistic terms the availability of the type of financing he is seeking. Unfortunately, these understandings are not widely held. In these days of consistently improving technical and marketing proficiencies, it is paradoxical that the means of tapping various capital sources are not generally known. As a result, a businessman whose knowledge of his own industry is far advanced, compared with that of a predecessor a decade ago, may have little more financial know-how than his earlier counterpart. The knowledge gap seems to exist primarily in the realm of recognizing the financing potential of a particular business.

During the past quarter century substantial progressive changes have occurred in the methods of business finance. This evolution, in both domestic and international spheres of trade, derived its basic momentum from the steady growth of our economy. Further impetus came from activation of new government programs, and--surprising for some people to learn--from the development of keen competition among lending institutions to devise new financing applications in an effort to put more of their money to work. The result has been the creation of a broad spectrum of business finance, whose analysis is a prerequisite for every seeker of capital.

Basically, the analysis of the financing potential of a business should be made in a context of the following two criteria: (1) the specific type or types of capital needed for the business, and (2) the eligibility for the types of capital required.

The analytical procedure normally followed to arrive at a determination of financing potential can be simply stated thus: *The measurement of the financial picture of a business against the yardstick of the requirements of each of several specific types of capital.* We must, therefore, initially understand the nature of these types of capital.

In financial circles, capital is usually categorized by referring to its source and to its function. In its simplest form, the categorization stems from two questions: Where is the money to come from? What is it to be used for? We should begin by differentiating between the two generic sources of capital--public and institutional financing.

Public financing is obtained by the issuance of securities to more than a very small group of investors and requires registration with the Securities and Exchange Commission (with the exception of intrastate issues). Public financing almost always involves the services of stock brokerage firms (who refer to this function as investment banking), and it is usually applicable only to experienced businesses that have already traveled the other routes of financing.

Institutional financing encompasses the greatest range of borrowing variations that business firms utilize. These are the types of institutions that may serve as sources: commercial banks, insurance companies, commercial finance companies, pension and welfare funds, Small Business Investment Companies, factors, Small Business Administration, industrial loan banks, and investment bankers (for private placements).

The size of this list presents some idea of the wide variety of institutional funding available. However, we should recognize that all lending institutions stand on one side of a definite boundary line. This line is drawn somewhat short of what we might term "hundred percent financing."

FUNCTIONAL TYPES OF CAPITAL

Some businessmen have the erroneous idea that financial institutions may occasionally provide, on a loan basis, *all* the money required to finance growth or the undertaking of a new operational direction. This is not so, although they may advance as much as 90 percent of the required capital. Of course, reference here is only to the limitations of the lending institutions. Total financing requirements can be obtained on a permanent or semipermanent basis from private sources or public issues. It is this type of financing that leads us into the first functional category of capital--equity.

Equity is usually represented by the original investment in a business plus retained earnings--plus financing later obtained on a permanent investment basis in anticipation of a dividend or capital gain possibility. In the analysis of financing potential, equity is significant because it represents the total value of a business, since all other financing (with the exception of publicly issued equity securities) amounts to some form of borrowing, which must ultimately be repaid. The ratio of these amounts that must be repaid--in other words, the debt--to the net worth, or equity, is a limiting factor on the financing potential of a business. Even then, there are shadings to this definition when it is applied to certain financing arrangements. For example, funds obtained through the issuance of subordinated debentures or notes are usually also considered as equity by lending institutions. This viewpoint can be extremely helpful to any efforts made to pyramid the borrowing abilities of a business.

Equity capital can be more clearly understood if a distinction is made among the following three functionally different types of funding: equity capital; working capital; and growth capital.

Equity capital is not generally obtainable from institutions--at least not during the early stages of the growth of a business. Working and growth capital, on the other hand, can be obtained in a number of ways. Both become necessary when equity capital has been used to the limit of its availability. They extend the effectiveness of equity by providing the leverage on investment present in the financial picture of every successful business.

Working capital needs arise from the generation of activity in a going business. For example, as sales increase, accounts receivable increase and funds are required to carry these. Concurrently, inventories enlarge and payroll costs mount; these, too, require additional money. It is to satisfy such needs that working capital is required. Although borrowed funds may be used for working capital over fairly long periods of time, the amount used fluctuates, depending on the cyclical aspects of a particular business. In fact, it is the varying use of greater or lesser amounts of money over a single year that most quickly identifies the funds used on such a fluctuating basis as working capital. It provides the money to carry a business through its annual period of greatest cash need.

Growth capital, although frequently grouped with working capital by many financiers, is different because it is not directly related to the cyclical aspects of a business. Instead, growth capital is usually involved with a planned program of expansion through purchase of better production or handling facilities, or through increased promotional expenditures. If, based on activating such a program, a projection of greater profits can reasonably be demonstrated, various types of financing can be arranged. Rather than looking toward seasonal liquidity for reducing this type of borrowing, institutions that make growth capital available will rely on the creation of future profits to provide for orderly repayment of such loans over a longer period.

We have reached the point where we can use one-word descriptions in analyzing a need into the three functional types of capital:

1. Fluctuating (working capital)
2. Amortizing (growth capital)
3. Permanent (equity capital)

The differentiation between equity, growth, and working capital which exists in the mind of a lending officer should now be plain. If you are asking for a working capital loan, you will be expected to demonstrate how the loan can be reduced or repaid during your firm's period of greatest liquidity in a cycle of one year. If you are asking for a growth capital loan, you will be expected to demonstrate how the purchase of additional fixed assets, or an increase in funds spent for promotional activities, will yield cash flow enabling you to repay the loan over several years.

If you are not clearly asking for either working or growth capital, an institutional lender will say to you, "We would like to accommodate you, but we cannot *invest* in a business--that is the role of equity capital; we only make loans." Specifically, the lender will explain that the loans he can make are only temporary and that the institution cannot be "locked in" with its money, as would be the case with a stockholder or an investing institution that invests in a private corporation for a dividend return, an advantageous conversion, and/or, a future capital gain.

Actually, working capital loans can be arranged which in practice almost entirely serve equity capital functions and purposes; the differentiation can be very subtle and can depend entirely on the availability of, and the eligibility for, a particular type of institutional financing.

Beginning with an understanding of the three basic types of capital, a business should be analyzed into its financing potential for each of these categories. After a determination of the amount of funding that will be required, we then have a goal for the size and required term of the financing to be sought. Practically every analyst who deals in the broad spectrum of available financing will follow a procedure of sifting the possibilities according to a descending order of desirability. Obviously, each business should analyze its position in an attempt to obtain the best financing available to it on the most attractive terms. Failing that, the other orders of financing are considered, based on the qualifications as revealed by analysis.

ANALYZING FOR EQUITY FINANCING

First in order of desirability is undoubtedly a public equity financing. In modern business, this view is held almost universally by sophisticated financial executives. Particularly since the shake-out of the new issue market in the spring of 1962, a well-conceived public issue has almost always been the most beneficial financing step that any company can undertake. Of course, there have been exceptions; however, these do not usually appear in a well-conceived underwriting sponsored by a responsible investment banking syndicate. In earlier days when analysis was less stringent and criteria less well-defined, there could be debate about the relative merits of a public financing. Within the scope of today's refined practices by responsible financiers if a business qualifies for a public underwriting, this is the route usually most beneficial for it to follow in its financing aspirations. In other words, the requirements of responsible underwriting syndicates today are such that, if these are satisfied, the negative arguments that can be raised against public financing are not valid. Obviously, a public issue should not be entertained prematurely until other forms of financing are used to obtain proper leverage and to build the company to a point where the owners realize their best potential capitalization of earnings by the establishment of a valuation on the business based on an earnings multiplier. Most small businesses, within the federal government's official definition, are not yet ready for a proper public financing. The analyst can quickly make a superficial determination by reviewing the profit-and-loss statement to determine if after-tax earnings are substantial--are growing on a steady curve--and that there are indications from the nature of the business that this growth will be sustained in the future. The role of earnings is preeminent in making this determination, almost to the exclusion of the normal criteria considered in other forms of financing. Regardless of the type of security package ultimately decided upon--common stock, preferred, convertible debentures, or some unitized combination--the present and past earnings (usually for a minimum of five years), plus future increased earnings potential, determine the eligibility for, and the size of, a public issue financing.

Using an oversimplified example, let us assume that a business reflects an after-tax profit of $300,000. It has increased its profits 25 percent each year for the past five years. It is indicated that, with additional capital, the growth rate will not only be sustained but will accelerate. The company operates within an industry, or a marketing field, that has excellent future prospects. Such a firm might easily be evaluated at a worth of $3 million (almost regardless of its book value) on a ten-times earnings-multiplier basis. An investment banking syndicate might underwrite common stock to provide $1.5 million to the company through issuance of 50 percent of its shares to the public.

Obviously, only relatively few firms qualify for public equity financing. Many hundreds of companies can be analyzed for their financing potential before one encounters a firm that is eligible. Therefore the analyst usually moves on to the next order of desirability.

ANALYZING FOR UNSECURED WORKING CAPITAL AND GROWTH CAPITAL LOANS

The simplest means of obtaining working

and growth capital financing is by borrowing on an unsecured basis. The mechanics are the least cumbersome; loan-handling requirements are minimal and therefore the cost is low. For this reason we find that commercial banks--the largest source of this type of financing--prefer to make unsecured loans to operating businesses whenever they can. Analysis for the eligibility of a business to qualify for unsecured financing centers first on the balance sheet of that business. Since unsecured lenders do not enjoy a priority position among creditors, they must place more emphasis on general liquidity, over-all financial strength relative to the size of credit, and present indicated ability to repay. This does not mean that the possibility of obtaining small initial unsecured credit is precluded; it is merely a matter of proposition to the size of credit sought.

A simple approach to the analysis of unsecured borrowing eligibility is found in the net current asset position on the balance sheet. Net current assets are obtained by subtracting the current liabilities from the current assets; the resultant figure is sometimes also called the working capital of a business. Banks normally limit their unsecured lines of credit to 40 percent or 50 percent of working capital, sometimes going a little higher to allow for seasonal peaks. Therefore, a business which shows $200,000 in current assets (cash, inventory, and accounts receivable) and $100,000 in current liabilities (accounts payable, current accrued expenses, and taxes payable) would qualify for approximately $50,000 unsecured credit. This same guideline will apply on much larger amounts; however, consideration must then be given to the current ratio and to the debt-to-worth ratio of the business.

The ratio of current assets to current liabilities is useful primarily as a quick appraisal of the liquidity of a business and its eligibility for unsecured borrowing. Although the ideal current ratios are from two to one and upward, this is not necessarily a minimum requirement for unsecured borrowing. As long as the total amount of unsecured credit is in the neighborhood of 50 percent of the working capital, a current ratio of as low as 1.25 to 1.0 may be tolerated. Obviously, if the current ratio is much lower than that, there will be practically no working capital; thus the possibility of obtaining unsecured loans will disappear on both counts.

As larger unsecured credits are sought for working capital, our analysis will have to take into consideration the debt-to-worth ratio. Here we are referring to total debt, which includes everything but capital and surplus on the liability side of the balance sheet, including all current obligations such as trade accounts payable. There are many mitigating factors in determining the effect of the debt-to-worth ratio as a limitation on unsecured borrowing; however, most companies that qualify for unsecured working capital loans possess debt two to five times the net worth. Since unsecured lenders must look to the general resources of a company for repayment, rather than occupying a secured creditor's prior position, the presence of a higher ratio of debt to worth may preclude unsecured borrowing.

Up to this point, the unsecured borrowing potential we have analyzed has been primarily relative to satisfying working capital requirements. However, we should also analyze for the possibility of unsecured growth capital financing. Here we are talking about a loan which will run for more than one year; in fact the term may vary from two years to more than five years. Many lenders will provide such financing based on the indicated ability to repay--even if the total amount of the financing is in excess of the previously described limitations of unsecured working capital loans in ratio to net current assets. Although there will still be limitations relative to total debt in ratio to worth, here the prime consideration is the annual cash flow.

We will define cash flow as the profits plus noncash expenses such as depreciation. Many businesses that have substantial depreciable physical equipment can obtain unsecured financing in excess of the usual net current asset limitations because the depreciation adds such a material factor to their total cash flow. For example, a company that has $25,000 annual profits and $50,000 depreciation creates $75,000 per year cash flow. If, after deducting all other debt servicing obligations such as mortgage payments and conditional sales contracts for equipment, there is still available $25,000 per year over and above any increased needs for operating capital, such a company might qualify for a three-year unsecured growth capital loan of as much as $75,000. In practice, the determination is not usually set so finely; normally, the "debt coverage" should be at least one and one-half times the annual repayment requirement on the loan.

In more substantial financings, debt coverage can run from three to six or seven times the annual repayment requirement. This is particularly true in the case of private placements of substantial amounts with institutions such as insurance companies, trust funds, and investment companies. These placements--ranging in size from several hundred thousand to millions of dollars--are usually made in the form of debentures or notes. Although some placements are for terms as short as five years, present practice is for terms of twelve to fifteen years with interest-only payments the first several years to help provide the sinking fund.

To qualify for an unsecured debt placement, a company must have a substantial history of earnings for several years--sometimes a minimum of five years or more. Debt coverage--the cash flow available to service the loan--should be from three to six times the required amount. A beginning private placement may be equal to, or greater than, the net worth junior to it, in the case of higher risk placements that include "kickers" of conversion rights or warrants. However, the usual institutional placement rarely exceeds an amount equal to the junior capital and, in fact placements, can be limited to half that.

For example, a company that qualifies on various criteria, including a history of earnings, may have capital and surplus of $1 million. Such a company should qualify for a private placement of at least $0.5 million if the cash flow available to service the placement provides a good cover. Level principal and interest payments on a 6 percent ten-year placement of $0.5 million would be approximately $65,000 per annum; debt coverage should therefore be at least $200,000 out of the available cash flow.

Actually, the financing potential in a funded debt placement of the type described above is not limited to the amounts of the placement itself. This is because such placements are, in one way or another, usually subordinated to current bank borrowings; therefore a leverage is provided. Debentures are normally subordinated on their face. Senior note placements may not be specifically subordinated; however, because they are long term--and current bank borrowings are usually structured on 90-day notes--they are, from a practical viewpoint, subordinated to the bank's position by term. In general, each dollar of subordinated debt that is matched by at least one dollar of equity (capital and surplus) can create one dollar of unsecured bank credit. If, for example, the net worth of a company is 1.5 million and a $1 million placement is obtained, the company should qualify for $1 million in unsecured short-term bank credit. The $1.5 million net worth is therefore leveraged with $2 million in growth and working capital.

To complete the analysis of the unsecured borrowing potential, it should be realized that both working and growth capital financing programs can be combined on a smaller scale with only bank financing. For example, a company with $100,000 net current assets might qualify for a working capital loan of $40,000 that can be repaid during the annual slow season of its operations. At the same time, if its annual cash flow amounted to $40,000, an additional growth capital unsecured loan might be added to the package covering an initial advance of $75,000 to be repaid in equal annual installments of $25,000 over a three-year term. Obviously, at the peak season during the first year, the total financing might amount to nearly $100,000.

These combinations of short-term working capital, plus longer term growth capital on an unsecured basis, will still be subject to the debt-to-worth limitations earlier described. However, here again the financing source will give credit toward the total worth for all subordinated liabilities such as principals' advances to the corporation and other subordinated liabilities from other sources.

ANALYZING FOR SECURED FINANCING

If the use of the various forms of unsecured borrowing heretofore described will not provide sufficient capital, we must then determine the secured borrowing potential. Here we have a drastically different set of criteria because the lender is indeed a preferred creditor on the basis of a statutory lien and he can look to certain assets being allocated strictly to liquidation of his lending exposure. Since he is not on a par with the other creditors of the company, the secured lender does not place as much emphasis on the debt-to-worth ratio. On a secured lending basis, the following assets are analyzed for their financing potential: (1) Fixtures, machinery, and equipment; (2) inventories; and (3) accounts receivable.

Among these three categories of collateral, the simplest form of financing can be obtained by a chattel mortgage on the fixtures or equipment. Loans can be arranged that require merely monthly or quarterly payments over a term, which may run from two to five years. The financing potential will be determined by the liquidation value of the collateral and the indicated ability to repay.

If the collateral is standard equipment, a quick estimate of its liquidation value is that--after about five years' depreciation has been subtracted from the original cost--the net book value is roughly equivalent to the liquidation value. Depending on the rate of depreciation, the net book value will be between 40 percent and 60 percent of the original cost value. At such depreciated book values, we can expect a loan availability of between 100 percent and 125 percent of the liquidation value. This is because the lender feels he knows enough about the present condition of the company to postulate repayment for at least the first year and that thereafter his advance will be below liquidation value. However, the borrower must still demonstrate his ability to repay, based on past or projected cash flow as previously described.

With an understanding of the foregoing information, it is fairly simple to estimate financing potential on furniture, fixtures, and equipment. Let us assume that a manufacturing business has equipment at original cost value of $250,000. The balance sheet indicates that a total of $125,000 depreciation has been taken. Further, from the profit and loss statement we see that the yearly depreciation cost has been $25,000; therefore, the total asset in this category has been depreciated an average of five years. Although an appraisal may be required by the lender, for analysis purposes we can assume that the remaining $125,000 net depreciated asset approximates liquidation value. The collateral consists of punch presses, drills, press brakes, materials handling equipment, and office furniture and machines. (If this total should include some special equipment built by the manufacturer for his own use which would have no ready market and whose liquidation value could not be established, this increment would be ineligible as collateral.) Assuming all collateral to fall into standard equipment categories, however, the manufacturer should be eligible for a secured loan of between $100,000 and $150,000--provided that adequate cash flow was demonstrated. If we assume a maximum loan of $150,000 to be obtained over a three-year term with equal monthly amortizations, the manufacturer would obviously have to demonstrate that he has available yearly cash flow of at least $50,000 after all other debt servicing requirements are met.

Another source of secured financing uses inventory as collateral. In this type of financing, there are several different forms of liens that can be granted to the secured lender; namely, public warehousing, field warehousing, and inventory liens. Each of these arrangements insures a priority creditor position to the lender; however, by their nature they can create differing financing potentials. Public warehousing and field warehousing are known as "ostensible" liens, they are readily apparent to trade creditors and to the general public, and they are more stringently controlled. Therefore, under warehousing arrangements, a higher percentage of loan against collateral may be obtained. The reporting and control of collateral under inventory liens is much simpler and less stringent; therefore, the lender will tend to advance a lower percentage of funds against the cost value of the inventory. The entrepreneur of a business seeking such financing will have to weigh the advantages and disadvantages of these types of lending arrangements in making his choice--a higher loan under more strictly controlled arrangements versus a lower loan under a looser, more flexible arrangement.

The financing potential inherent in an inventory depends on the processing status of the inventory, the commodity nature of the inventory, and the inventory turnover.

The processing status of the inventory is analyzed into three classifications; namely, raw materials, goods in process, and finished goods. If the finished goods are manufactured to fill orders and represent standard marketable products, the percentage of advance over cost can be fairly high, ranging from 65 percent to 85 percent. Advances against raw materials can also be substantial, running from 40 percent to 70 percent. This will depend on the nature of the raw material--whether it consists of basic raw materials for which there is a daily trading market, whether these materials have been specifically produced for special needs of the particular company involved, and whether there is any obsolescence or stale factor in the raw materials. The lowest eligibility for advance will be found in the category of goods in process. Here the raw material has been altered so that it probably can only be sold for scrap value unless money is provided by the lender to complete the productive process. Therefore, goods in process may have a loan potential of only 25 percent of cost value. Retailers or distributors will not be required to make such an analysis because they are almost exclusively handling finished goods for which there is an established wholesale price, which is their basis of cost. Since the wholesaler price is above the cost value of a manufacturer, the percentage of advance against a distributor's inventory of finished goods for resale may be lower than that which can be granted to a manufacturer. If the manufacturer has, for example, $300,000 of inventory broken into three $100,000 increments of raw materials, finished goods, and work in process, an analysis is fairly simple. His advance on $100,000 of finished goods might be 75 percent, or $75,000. His advance on $100,000 of goods in process might be 25 percent, or $25,000. His advance against $100,000 of raw materials might be 60 percent, or $60,000. Therefore, this manufacturer would qualify for a total inventory loan of $160,000 on his total inventory at cost of $300,000.

The commodity rating of an inventory is very significant. We will define a commodity as a material that is very basic, possessing standard qualifications as to size, and quality grading, and immediately saleable on a day-to-day basis. Usual commodities are lumber, metals, grains, cotton, wool, coffee, and so on. There is an active daily market for each of these commodities, according to grade and quantity, and they may be disposed of by a few telephone calls to active dealers or traders in these commodities. Percentage of loan against these commodities can be quite high, varying according to potential price fluctuations. Coffee, for example, can serve as collateral for a loan up to 95 percent of cost. Graded lumber can qualify for 70 percent to 80 percent advance against cost, because price fluctuations over a reasonably short period of time are not very severe.

Except in cases of basic commodities, as described above, the inventory has in the annual turnover its third limitation on financing potential. An inventory that is unusually high in proportion to the sales volume of the company cannot qualify for an otherwise maximum loan. In making this evaluation, the normal inventory turnover for the industry involved is used as a guideline. Whereas some retail and wholesale distribution operations may have an inventory turnover of as high as 10 to 12 times per year, the normal manufacturing company is doing well if it has a turnover of five times per year in its inventory. Let us assume that a company doing $1 million in sales has an inventory cost, including burden, of 75 percent. To create $1 million in sales, $750,000 of inventory would have to be consumed. If a company reported a $150,000 inventory, it would be demonstrating a five times inventory turnover. Depending on the industry, an inventory of up to $250,000 might be acceptable. Anything beyond that figure, however, would probably be disqualified as a basis for additional inventory financing.

The third and certainly one of the most prevalent forms of secured financing is accounts receivable financing. Here the prior lien of the lender is evidenced by the filing of an intention to assign accounts receivable. Accounts receivable, in general, can provide very high percentages of advance because of their liquidity and because of the presence of a third party debtor--the ultimate customer whose receivable is assigned to the lender. The analysis of the financing potential of accounts receivable is dependent upon the credit-worthiness of the debtors (the customers of the borrower), the absence of single debtor concentrations, the prevalence of offsets or claims for faulty materials, and the aging of the total accounts receivable.

The credit-worthiness of the customer of the borrower is certainly an obvious requirement for this type of financing. In fact, unless he follows general credit precaution, the borrower simply will not qualify because the lender will feel that he is not exercising common business prudence for his own protection, as well as for the protection of the lender.

Debtor concentrations provide a different sort of problem. The reason that accounts receivable financing can go as high as a 90 percent loan against collateral is that there are a great number of debtors from whom repayment will come. A distributor or manufacturer selling a volume of $200,000 per month may have 2,000 customers or more, the risk to the lender is therefore spread among 2,000 different business firms as debtors. On the other hand, there are some companies doing $200,000 per month who may have only 20 customers on their books at any one time. Taken on the average, such a company would have accounts receivable of $10,000 from each customer. This situation, in itself, may not be too much of a problem because accounts receivable financing will generally allow concentrations as high as 10 percent of the total outstanding accounts receivable to be owed by one debtor--and, in some cases as high as 20 percent to a single debtor (provided that there are no other debtors who account for this high a percentage of the outstanding receivables). In most cases, heavily concentrated debtors may have AAA-1 credit standings, but it is not their credit-worthiness that creates the problem. Rather, when a large increment of the accounts receivable is concentrated with one debtor, substantial values are at stake if a dispute arises between that single customer and the borrower.

Accounts receivable must also be evaluated with reference to possible offsets and claims for faulty merchandise. Offsets arise normally when a business sells its goods or services to a customer from whom it also purchases. Since the customer can offset his sales against his purchases, the account receivable that has been financed may not be repaid in cash, which will leave the loan made against it unpaid even when the debtor obligation has been satisfied. Therefore, all possible contra accounts (in dealing with which offsets can arise) are considered ineligible for receivables financing. A study is also made of the history of rejections, returns for reworking, and so on. An average is taken to establish a safety factor for the dilution of the accounts receivable arising from this possibility.

The most general yardstick for evaluation of receivables is in the monthly aging. Normally, accounts receivable less than 90 days old are eligible for advance; thereafter, they are ineligible if no special dating arrangements have been made at the outset.

Taking all of the foregoing factors into consideration, we can quickly arrive at the financing potential to be obtained from assignment of accounts receivable. Let us assume that the balance sheet reflects $300,000 as the total accounts receivable outstanding. Normally, after allowing for considerations stated above, an 80 percent advance against *eligible* collateral might be available. As a quick guide, 10 percent of the total accounts receivable can be assumed to be ineligible for one of the reasons stated above. This would bring the total to about $270,000 in the example we are using, and 80 percent of this eligible collateral figure would be $216,000, which is the figure we might assume to be available at a quick determination. Going into the matter a little more in detail, we will assume that there are practically no offsets (which is usually the case), that no single debtor accounts for more than 20 percent of the total receivables, and that no group of the three or four largest debtors accounts for more than 30 percent of the total receivables.

We will assume that the claims for faulty merchandise run only 1 percent or 2 percent of the annual sales. Further, we will assume that the aging reflects that about 75 percent of the total receivables are current or no more than 30 days past due, and that not more than 5 percent to 10 percent of the total receivables are more than 90 days old. Since an 80 percent advance against the total accounts receivable shown on the balance sheet includes a 20 percent reserve for the lender, the example we have used above will probably provide the lender ample protection. In other words, after deducting 10 percent from the total accounts receivable on the balance sheet for the various types of ineligibilities, 80 percent of the remainder can be borrowed on a revolving basis with no requirements for amortization during the time that the accounts receivable financing arrangement is in effect.

SUMMARY

We have seen that, after checking for the possibility of a public financing based on sustained and growing earnings, one should analyze the unsecured and secured borrowing potentials of a business.

If unsecured borrowing can satisfy the financing needs of the business, management should go no further.

If funds greater than those that will be available with unsecured financing are required, then secured financing potential should be analyzed. Here is an example:

Assets		
Cash	$ 25,000	
Accounts Receivable	225,000	
Inventory	300,000	
Total current assets		$550,000
Machinery & equipment	300,000	
Less depreciation	(150,000)	150,000
Real property, net		150,000
Goodwill and prepaid expense		25,000
Total assets		$875,000
Liabilities		
Accounts payable	$200,000	
Current portion, long-term debt	50,000	
Taxes payable	50,000	
Other accruals	50,000	
Total current liabilities		$350,000
R.E. mortgage payable	100,000	
Subordinated notes payable	100,000	
Contracts payable	50,000	
	250,000	
Less current portion	(50,000)	
Total long-term liabilities		200,000
Total liabilities		550,000
Capital & surplus (net worth)		325,000
Total liabilities & capital		$875,000

Earnings are $80,000 plus $30,000 depreciation; therefore, cash flow is $110,000.

Following are the potential financing alternatives:

1. An unsecured working capital loan equal to 50 percent of net current assets of $200,000. Potential:	$100,000
2. An unsecured growth capital loan. The cash flow of $110,000 less $50,000 required for existing debt service results in available debt coverage of $60,000. Maximum growth loan potential for three years:	180,000
3. Secured financing based on the following:	
a. Accounte receivable total of $225,000--less 10 percent for ineligibilities--total eligible is $202,500. Potential at 80 percent advance:	162,000
b. Chattel loan on equipment at 125 percent of liquidation value with $60,000 available cash flow. Potential, 3 or more years term:	187,778
c. Inventory loan at average of 60 percent on cost of $300,000. Potential:	180,000
Total secured financing potential	$529,778

The secured financing can obviously reach a total in excess of the net worth of the company--if this entire amount is needed. In practice, if such a maximum loan is made, provision for additional interest must be equated against the total loan amount in the event that it cannot be immediately postulated that the additional prifits to be developed from the borrowing will absorb the extra cost of money. And here we have the *raison d'etre* for maximum financing; namely that it must create rewards in excess of its cost. Money cost in terms of stated interest is not definitive; for some business situations 5 percent interest may be too high, whereas for others a 10 percent rate can be a bargain. The significant criterion is the total dollar cost versus the additional dollar profits that the money can create by utilizing maximum financing potentials.

READING 37

Optimal Short-Term Financing Decision

A.A. Robickek
Stanford University

D. Teichrow
University of Michigan

J. M. Jones
University of California, Los Angeles

I. STATEMENT OF PROBLEM

The short-term financing decision is a relatively common problem in practice; many companies' financial officers are faced with choosing a source of short-term funds from a set of financing alternatives. If one of the alternatives is clearly superior to all other alternatives the short-term financing problem is easily resolved by accepting that alternative. Sometimes, for example, the company may be able to obtain all the funds it needs under a favorable line of credit. More frequent, however, is the situation where either one alternative is not superior in every respect or where various constraints are placed on the alternatives. In these instances, the financial decision maker must choose from among the alternatives and select a "financing package" as a solution. In practice, approaches to the short-term financing problem vary considerably; consideration is given to such factors as explicit costs, restrictions, expediency, reliability of forecasts, cash "buffers," industry practices, etc.

Consider the problem faced by a firm's financial officer whose staff has prepared the cash budget presented in Table I. The basic objective of the financial officer is to provide the funds needed in the business as shown by the cash budget. He wants to accomplish this objective at a minimum cost to the firm, given the constraints within which he operates.

The Cash Budget

Table I shows, by periods, for twelve periods: total receipts (line 6), total disbursements (line 12), the difference between receipts and disbursements as adjusted by the required change in minimum operating cash balances (line 15) and finally the cumulative cash requirement (line 17). Financial costs of obtaining funds to meet these requirements are not included in the budget. The cash requirements are shown graphically in Figure I.

Only two basic types of cash

Reprinted from MANAGEMENT SCIENCE, (September 1965), Vol. 12, No. 1, pp. 1-36, by permission of the publisher.

Table I - CASH BUDGET (Millions of Dollars)

Receipts	Period 1	2	3	4	5	6	7	8	9	10	11	12
1: Accounts Receivable-Beginning	3.0	3.0	4.5	4.25	4.25	2.0	3.5	4.5	4.5	4.25	3.5	2.5
2: + Sales on Accounts Recv'bl.	2.0	3.0	2.5	2.5	1.75	3.0	3.0	3.0	2.25	2.25	2.0	2.5
3: - Accounts Receivable-End	3.0	4.5	4.25	4.25	2.0	3.5	4.5	4.5	4.25	3.5	2.5	3.5
4: Collections on Accounts Receivable	2.0	1.5	2.75	2.5	4.0	1.5	2.0	3.0	2.5	3.0	3.0	1.5
5: Other Receipts (Cash sales, etc.)	1.5	1.0	1.25	2.0	1.0	4.8	1.0	1.0	1.0	1.6	1.9	1.7
6: Total Receipts	3.5	2.5	4.0	4.5	5.0	6.3	3.0	4.0	3.5	4.6	4.9	3.2
Disbursements												
7: Accounts Payable-Beginning	2.0	2.0	2.5	2.5	2.5	1.0	1.0	2.0	2.5	2.5	1.5	1.0
8: + Purchases (Net)	2.0	2.5	2.5	2.5	1.0	1.0	2.0	2.5	2.5	1.5	1.0	2.0
9: - Accounts Payable-End	2.0	2.5	2.5	2.5	1.0	1.0	2.0	2.5	2.5	1.5	1.0	2.0
10: Payments for Purchases	2.0	2.0	2.5	2.5	2.5	1.0	1.0	2.0	2.5	2.5	1.5	1.0
11: Other Disbursements	2.0	2.0	3.4	1.5	1.9	1.4	2.5	3.5	3.6	1.5	1.5	1.5
12: Total Disbursements	4.0	4.0	5.9	4.0	4.4	2.4	3.5	5.5	6.1	4.0	3.0	2.5
13: Receipts-Disbursements	(0.5)	(1.5)	(1.9)	0.5	0.6	3.9	(0.5)	(1.5)	(2.6)	0.6	1.9	0.7
14: Change in Minimum Operating Cash Balance			(0.1)			0.1			(0.1)		0.1	
15: Cash Requirement for Period Before Interest and Compensating Balance	(0.5)	(1.5)	(2.0)	0.5	0.6	4.0	(0.5)	(1.5)	(2.7)	(0.6)	2.0	0.7
16: Cumulative Requirement Before Interest and Compensating Balance	(0.5)	(2.0)	(4.0)	(3.5)	(2.9)	1.1	0.6	(0.9)	(3.6)	(3.0)	(1.0)	(0.3)
17: Memo-Minimum Operating Cash Balance	0.1	0.1	0.2	0.2	0.2	0.1	0.1	0.1	0.2	0.2	0.1	0.1

Figures in parenthesis denote need to obtain funds and unbracketed figures denote excess cash.

Figure I. CASH REQUIREMENTS BY PERIODS ($1,000)

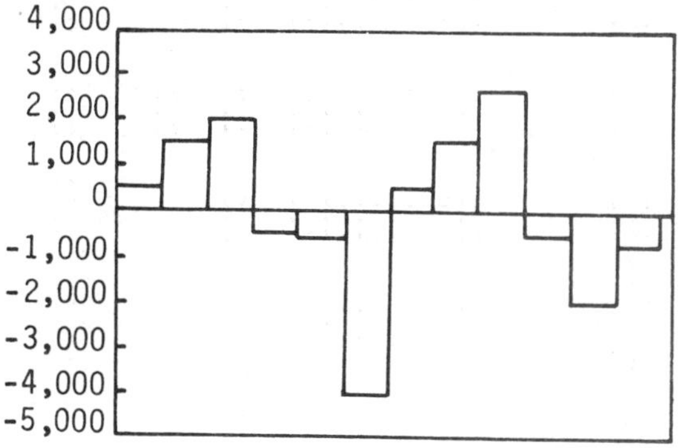

receipts are considered for the particular example in Table I: (1) Collections of accounts receivable; (2) All other receipts, which include sources such as cash sales, proceeds from sale of capital equipment, etc. The detail underlying the determination of the collections of accounts receivable is shown. The financial officer normally does not have any control over the rate of sales, the pattern of collections on accounts receivable, or over "other receipts." However, he is able to use the accounts receivable as security in order to obtain funds.

Similarly, two types of disbursements are shown in The Table: (1) Payments for purchases, and (2) All other disbursements, including payments on outstanding debts. Again, the financial officer normally does not have any control over the rate of purchases or other disbursements. However, he does control the time when payments are actually made on accounts payable.

The change in the minimum operating cash balances (line 14) is obtained by taking the differences from one period to the next in the Minimum Operating Cash Balance (line 17 of Table I). Changes in minimum operating cash balances are also usually not within the control of the financial officer. The cumulative cash requirements before interest and any compensating balance required at the end of any period (line 16) is merely the sum of the adjusted cash requirements for all previous periods.

One of the responsibilities of the financial officer is to provide the cash requirement as shown by the cash budget. Usually a number of sources for short or intermediate term funds exist, including term loans and unsecured lines of credit. Funds can also be acquired by pledging accounts receivable or by delaying payments on accounts payable.

This paper is concerned with the decision of how much and when to acquire money from each of these sources. Other sources of short term funds such as factoring of accounts receivable,[1] etc., and long term sources of funds such as equity capital or bonds will not be considered.

Financial Alternatives

As a first step in formulating the problem, it is necessary to examine the alternatives open to the financial officer, and to determine the costs and the constraints associated with these alternatives. In the description of the alternatives it is convenient to assume that all cash transactions, with one exception, take place at the begin-

[1] Factoring of accounts receivable is not considered because it is usually clearly less desirable than the other alternatives and is not used in practice unless it is the only available alternative.

ning of a period. The exception occurs in the collections on accounts receivable, and is explained in detail below.

1. Unsecured Line of Credit. The company has available an unsecured line of credit with a bank which permits it to borrow up to $1,500,000. The bank requires a compensating cash balance of not less than 20% of the amount actually borrowed under the line of credit; the operating cash balance (line 17, Table I), is available to meet this requirement. The interest rate on this line of credit is 0.9% per period. Money may be borrowed or repaid at the beginning of each period.

2. Pledging of Accounts Receivable. The firm can pledge its accounts receivable as security for a bank loan. The amount outstanding under this alternative is limited to a maximum of $3,750,000. The bank will lend up to 80% of the face value of pledged accounts receivable. A portion of the accounts receivable outstanding at the beginning of the period is repaid in the normal course of the business during the period. It is assumed that these accounts are repaid at a uniform rate throughout the period, and therefore in order to fulfill the requirements at the beginning of a period, it is necessary to borrow at the beginning of the period $1.00 for each 85¢ needed during the period. The cost of borrowing under this alternative is 1.4% per period of the average amount of loan outstanding during the period, which is 85% of the amount outstanding at the beginning of the period. This cost includes not only the interest charged by the lender, but also the out-of-pocket costs associated with the additional work required under this alternative. The amount borrowed under this alternative can be changed at the beginning of each period.[2]

Normally the bank will not allow the company to have an unsecured line of credit and at the same time pledge its accounts receivable on an additional loan, nor does it encourage frequent switches from one to the other.

3. Stretching of Accounts Payable. The financial officer, at his option, may stretch (i.e., delay) payments of accounts payable. In the preparation of the cash budget, it was assumed that the purchases were paid in time to take any discount offered by the vendor. If the payments for purchases are stretched the discount cannot be taken, and this becomes an additional cost to the firm. The discount loss, on the average, amounts to 3½% if the payments are stretched one period. The financial officer may stretch up to 80% of the payments due in the period in which they first become due. Once the accounts payable are stretched, the financial officer may decide to stretch them for one additional period at no loss of discount; the amount which he can stretch one additional period is limited to 75% of the amount already stretched for one period. Although the stretching of payments for one additional period involves no further loss of discounts, it does involve the loss of goodwill on the part of the creditors.

4. Term Loan. The firm has an offer of a term loan from its bank. The term loan must be taken out at the beginning of the initial period under consideration. It is limited in amount to $2,000,000 and it cannot be taken out in an amount of less than $500,000. The principal of the loan must be repaid in ten equal installments; the first installment is due six periods after the loan is initially taken out, with the subsequent installments due at six-period intervals. No speed-up of payments is possible. If the firm takes out a term loan, the bank insists on further constraints on the combined borrowing under the term loan and *either* the line of credit *or* the pledging of accounts receivable. The maxi-

[2] In practice, adjustments under this type of borrowing could take place more often than once per month if, for example, the period is one month.

mum borrowing under the term loan, plus a line of credit is $2,500,000, while the maximum borrowing with a term loan and the pledging of receivables is $4,500,000. The interest rate on the term loan is 0.8% per period. In addition, the bank requires certain restrictions on company operations, such as limitations on officers' salaries, dividend payments, and capital expenditures.

5. Investment of Excess Cash. The financial officer may invest any cash in excess of Minimum Operating Cash Balance in short term securities which yield a rate of return of 0.4% per period. It is assumed that no costs are associated with investing or disinvesting in these short term securities.

Formulating the Objective

The problem that has been considered above is what might be termed a typical short term financing problem of a business subject to seasonal cash flow patterns. The immediate decision that faces the financial officer is whether to take out a term loan and if so, in what amount. Furthermore, at the beginning of each period he must decide how to acquire additional cash if it is needed or what to do with excess cash if any is available. Of those alternatives listed above, the financial officer may use any combination, except that the bank will *not permit* the use of alternative 1, i.e., the line of credit, in combination with alternative 2, i.e., the pledging of accounts receivable, or a switch from one alternative to the other during the periods under consideration.

Using the cash budget as given and the rates as stated, the financial officer can compute the costs of any proposed decision. If possible, he would prefer to use the method which would have minimum interest cost. A few trial calculations are sufficient to show that the optimum decision for this objective is not obvious. The total interest cost will depend on whether or not a term loan is taken. Even without the possibility of a term loan, however, the choice between stretching payables and either the line of credit or pledging of accounts receivable is not obvious. This is partly because the stretching of payables is expensive if done for one period, but much less expensive if done for two periods, and partly because of constraints on the amounts which can be borrowed under the alternatives.

However, as will be shown in the next two sections, it is possible to compute the decision which minimizes the total interest cost. The general technique of mathematical programming, and linear programming in particular, can be used, after some simplifying assumptions are made.

The decision of the financial officer is, however, usually not based solely on the interest cost. He must also consider the qualitative factors. Two of the alternatives have undesirable non-financial "costs." Stretching payables involves a loss of the confidence of creditors and the term loan requires some bothersome restrictions on company operations. A term loan is also a long-range commitment that may prevent the officer from taking advantage of other opportunities if interest rates go down. These qualitative factors may cause a company to use the line of credit in preference to the term loan even though its cost is 0.9% per period compared to 0.8% for the term loan.

Business firms do not usually think of the cost of qualitative factors as being measured in dollars. But, in effect, any decision, assuming rational behavior on the part of the decision maker, imputes a financial cost to a qualitative restriction. In this paper, qualitative factors will be incorporated into the problem through the use of "implicit costs." These are described in detail in section 3 in the discussion of the formulation of the objective.

It should be noted that in this

description of the short-term financing problem a number of assumptions have been made: the term loan is available only at the beginning of the first period; the maximum amount of the line of credit does not change from period to period; all cash transactions, except payment of accounts receivable, occur at the beginning of a period; and all parameters and requirements are known with certainty at the time the initial decisions are made.

These assumptions may be too restrictive for practical applications. There may be random and systematic deviations in the cash requirements from those forecast, and there may be changes in the cost parameters as time goes on. The financial officer, in making his decisions, takes account of the uncertainty by modifying the objective function to include other factors, such as the need for flexibility, safety allowances, etc. In Section 8 some modifications to allow for uncertainty will be considered.

2. PRACTICES AND TECHNIQUES IN SHORT-TERM FINANCING

The literature on the optimization of short-term financing decision is relatively sparse. Two basic topics that are discussed in the literature are: (1) the determination of the size of the cash balance, and (2) the short-term financing decision given the cash balance requirement. These topics are usually discussed with four simplifying assumptions:

1. The minimum cash balance required at all times is specified.

2. The cash inflows and/or outflows are either known with certainty, or else their probability distribution is completely known.

3. The cash flows are partly or wholly discrete. This appears most frequently as the assumption of discrete time periods, within which the time-distribution of flows makes no difference.

4. Costs of all financial alternatives are know.

Determination of Cash Balance

The reasons for holding cash balances are usually considered to be those stated by Keynes [7]: i.e., for transactions, precautionary and speculative motives. The Lutz and Lutz [8] discussion is parallel to Keynes and adopts the same terminology. They discuss the subject in somewhat more detail, but introduce no new concepts.

The specifically financial (as contrasted with economic) literature rarely considers the speculative motive and often concentrates on the transaction motive alone, e.g., see Baumol [1]. This neglect of the precautionary motive implies the assumption that all cash flows other than short-term financing decision flows are given and known with certainty.

Cash inflows and outflows are normally not synchronized, so that a positive cash balance is required to operate the firm. Lutz and Lutz point out that the synchronization of inflows and outflows might be improved, but at a cost. Since excess cash balances can be put to other use, the level of cash at any time is significant.

Baumol's approach to the cash balance problem is exactly parallel to that of the optimum lot size formula used in the management of inventories and production runs. Baumol assumes a simplified model and proceeds to solve for the optimum value of the cash balance. The limitations of Baumol's solution lie in the assumptions of the model itself. Yet, some of the basic conclusions from Baumol's model are in agreement with the empirical findings of Jacobs (1960). For instance, Jacobs finds that large corporations hold proportionately smaller cash balances than small corporations. This outcome would have been predicted from Baumol's model.

Short-Term Financing Decisions Given a Cash Balance Requirement

Discussions of short-term financing usually assume that the interdependence between the short-term financing decision and other decisions can be ignored. The short-term financing "costs" are minimized by taking all other cash flows as given.

Beranek [2] discusses both a certainty model and a risk model of the short-term financing decision. In the certainty model he makes assumptions (1) to (4) given above. In particular, he assumes the existence of a "critical" minimum cash balance. If the firm drops below this minimum penalty costs are incurred. In addition, he assumes that all other inflows and outflows are given and known with certainty, discrete periods, and, as a consequence, discrete cash flows, and that costs of all financial alternatives are known.

Beranek (p. 354) suggests that the treasurer "estimate these (financing) costs in advance and make this information available (to top management) when budgeting decisions are made." No optimizing procedure is provided beyond the statement, "if incremental costs of obtaining cash to accommodate a proposed operating budget are in excess of the incremental operating profit, then, at least, the goal-attaining capability of the budget is suspect."

In his risk model, Beranek changes assumption (3) above. Certain of the inflows are no longer certain, but are characterized by known discrete probability distributions. Beranek illustrates optimization within these assumptions for the one and the two period case. The procedure involves a complete listing of all-possible combinations of events. Extension of Beranek's method to the multi-period problem would necessitate use of dynamic programming algorithms, which may not be feasible in practical situations.

This section can be summarized by stating that, as far as the professional literature is concerned, no generalized optimization techniques have been applied to the multi-period short-term financing problem. Furthermore, a search of the practical literature has not revealed any empirical rules of thumb for making the short-term financing decisions.

The purpose of this paper is to develop the multi-period model for the short-term financing problem with given cash balance requirements and under assumptions (1)--(4) with complete certainty. The model will be solved using linear programming techniques. It may be noted that linear programming has been applied to other problems in financial planning by Charnes et al. [4], Charnes et al. [3], and Ijiri et al. [5].

3. MATHEMATICAL FORMULATION

The following notation will be used to facilitate the discussion of the mathematical formulation of the short-term financing problem described in the previous section.

$x_{i.j}$ = amount borrowed from source i at the beginning of period j.

$y_{i.j}$ = amount voluntarily repaid to source i at the beginning of period j.

$v_{i.j}$ = amount of mandatory repayment to source i at the beginning of period j.

$z_{i.j}$ = net cumulative amount borrowed from source i at the beginning of period j after borrowing and repayment for period j.

$= \sum_{k=1}^{j} (x_{i.k} - y_{i.k} - v_{i.k})$

r_i = interest rate for "borrowing" from source i.

$\alpha_{i.n}$ = nth coefficient used in stating constraints on alternative i.

$\beta_{i.n}$ = nth constraint limit for alternative i.

$s_{i.n}$ = slack variable used to change the nth inequality for alternative i to an equality.

The subscript i denotes the alternatives in the order in which they are discussed in Section 1:

i = 1:unsecured line of credit
2:pledging of accounts receivable
3:stretching of accounts payable
4:term loan
5:investment of excess cash

Through this paper, the x's, y's, v's, z's and s's will be assumed to be non-negative.

The constraints on each of the alternatives are discussed next. This is followed by the cash requirement equation and then the objective function is developed.

Line of Credit

A constraint must be used to ensure that voluntary repayments do not exceed the amount borrowed.

$$\sum_{k=1}^{j} (x_{1.k} - y_{1.k}) \geqq 0$$

or

$$\sum_{k=1}^{j} (x_{1.k} - y_{1.k}) - z_{1.j} = 0;$$

$j = 1, 2, \cdots m$

"The maximum amount of borrowing under the line of credit is limited to $1,500,000."

$$\sum_{k=1}^{j} (x_{1.k} - y_{1.k}) \leqq \beta_1$$

or

$$z_{1.j} + s_{1.j} = \beta_1; \; j = 1, 2, \cdots m$$

where

β_1 = maximum outstanding balance under the line of credit.

"The bank requires a compensating balance of not less than 20% of the amount borrowed."

$$\alpha_{1.1} \sum_{k=1}^{j} (x_{1.k} - y_{1.k}) - s_{1.2.j} \leqq b_j$$

or

$$\alpha_{1.1} z_{1.j} - s_{1.2.j} + s_{1.3.j} = b_j;$$

$j = 1, 2, \cdots m$

where

$\alpha_{1.1}$ = proportion of loan which is required as a compensating cash balance

$s_{1.2.j}$ = additional amount borrowed at the beginning of period j to meet compensating balance requirement

b_j = minimum operating cash balance (line 17, Table I)

Mandatory repayments are not required,

$$v_{1.j} = 0 \qquad j = 1, \cdots m$$

Pledging of Accounts Receivable

A certain proportion of the accounts receivable which are pledged at the beginning of a period would normally be paid by the firm's customers during that period. Once they are paid the "effective" amount borrowed by the firm from the bank is decreased by 80% of the amount of the payment. As stated earlier for the purposes of this model all transactions are assumed to occur at the beginning of the period. If these payments by the customers were treated in the same way, an artificially high amount of borrowing would be required. Therefore it will be assumed that a certain proportion of the receivables outstanding at the beginning of a period are paid by the customers during that period. These payments are treated as mandatory repayments by the firm to the bank at the beginning of the following period or:

$$\alpha_{2.1} \sum_{k=1}^{j-1} (x_{2.k} - y_{2.k} - v_{2.k}) = v_{2.j};$$

$v_{2.1} = 0; \quad j = 2, 3, \cdots m$

or

$$v_{2.j} = \alpha_{2.1} z_{2.j-1}$$

where

$v_{2.j}$ = mandatory repayment of pledged accounts receivable

$\alpha_{2.1}$ = the proportion of accounts receivable that are collected during the period

$\alpha_{2.3} = (1 - \alpha_{2.1}/2)$

At the beginning of period j the amount outstanding is $z_{2.j}$, at the end of the period the amount outstanding is $(1 - \alpha_{2.1})z_{2.j}$. Assuming that the payments from customers are uniform throughout the period, the average amount outstanding is

$$\tfrac{1}{2}(z_{2.j} + (1 - \alpha_{2.1})z_{2.j})$$

$$= (1 - \alpha_{2.1}/2)z_{2.j} = \alpha_{2.3}z_{2.j}$$

This "average" amount is the amount which may be used to satisfy the requirements. (See Fulfillment of Requirements equation.)

Voluntary repayments cannot exceed the amount borrowed

$$\sum_{k=1}^{j} (x_{2.k} - y_{2.k} - v_{2.k}) \geqq 0$$

or

$$\sum_{k=1}^{j} (x_{2.k} - y_{2.k} - v_{2.k}) - z_{2.j} = 0$$

$j = 1, 2, \cdots m$

"The amount outstanding under pledging of accounts receivable is limited to $3,750,000."

$$\sum_{k=1}^{j} (x_{2.k} - y_{2.k} - v_{2.k}) \leqq \beta_2$$

or

$$z_{2.j} + s_{2.1.j} = \beta_2 \quad j = 1, 2, \cdots m$$

where

β_2 = the absolute ceiling on the cumulative amount which can be borrowed by pledging accounts receivable.

"The bank will lend up to 80% of the face value of pledged accounts receivable."

$$\sum_{k=1}^{j} (x_{2.k} - y_{2.k} - v_{2.k}) \leqq \alpha_{2.2}a_j$$

or

$$z_{2.j} + s_{2.2.j} = \alpha_{2.2}a_j$$

$j = 1, 2, \cdots m$

where

$\alpha_{2.2}$ = proportion of maximum loan to a accounts teceivable

a_j = amount of accounts receivable at start of period j (line 1, Table I)

Since the bank will not allow both line of credit and pledging of accounts receivable and will not permit switching from one to the other,

$$x_{1.j} = 0 \quad \text{or} \quad x_{2.j} = 0$$

for $j = 1, 2, \cdots m$

Stretching of Accounts Payable

The firm is able to acquire money to meet requirements by not paying its accounts payable when first due.

An additional subscript here is needed since payables may be stretched for one period and then for another period. Let

$x_{3.j.k}$ = amount of payables, due in period k, which is used to provide funds in period j; $k = j, j - 1$ or $j - 2$

$y_{3.j.k}$ = amount of payables, due in period k, which are actually paid in period j

When an accounts payable payment comes due, it is either paid immediately or stretched.

$$x_{3.j.j} + y_{3.j.j} = p_j, \; j = 1, 2, \cdots m$$

where

p_j = purchases made in period $j - 1$ which are due in period j (line 10, Table I)

"The financial officer may stretch up to 80% of the payments due in the period in which they first become due, i.e., he must pay at least 20%."

$$x_{3.j.j} \leqq \alpha_{3.1}p_j \quad \text{or}$$

$$x_{3.j.j} + s_{3.1.j} = \alpha_{3.1}p_j;$$

$j = 1, 2, \cdots m$

$\alpha_{3.1}$ = proportion of accounts payable which can be stretched in the period in which they first become due.

The p_j's in Table I are computed on the assumption that all discounts are taken by the firm. If an amount $x_{3.j.j}$ is stretched then the discount is not lost and the amount due in period $(j + 1)$ is $(1 + r_3)(x_{3.j.j})$, where

r_3 = discount rate on accounts payable.

As in the first period in which payments are stretched, however, a certain proportion of the outstanding amount must be paid if the payment is stretched to the second period, i.e., only a certain portion can be stretched for another period.

$$x_{3.j.j-1} \leq \alpha_{3.2}(1 + r_3)x_{3.j-1.j-1}$$

$j = 2, 3, \cdots m$

or

$$x_{3.j.j-1} + s_{3.2.j} = \alpha_{3.3}x_{3.j-1.j-1}$$

where

$\alpha_{3.2}$ = proportion of payables stretched first period which can be stretched in second period.

and

$$\alpha_{3.3} = \alpha_{3.2}(1 + r_3).$$

The amount that is not stretched must be paid

$$y_{3.j.j-1} = (1 + r_3)x_{3.j-1.j-1} - x_{3.j.j-1}$$

$j = 2, 3, \cdots m$

This is the amount of "repayment" in period j on payables stretched one period.

Finally, any payables stretched in the second period must be paid in the third period.

$$y_{3.j.j-2} = x_{3.j-1.j-2} \quad j = 3, 4, \cdots m$$

Term Loan

The term loan can only be taken out at the beginning of the first period. The term loan is limited in amount to $2,000,000 and cannot be taken out in an amount of less than $500,000.

$\beta_{4.1} \leq x_{4.1} \leq \beta_{4.2}$ or

$x_{4.1} - s_{4.1} = \beta_{4.1}$ and

$x_{4.1} + s_{4.2} = \beta_{4.2}$

or

$x_{4.1} = 0$

where

$\beta_{4.1}$ = minimum amount of term loan available

$\beta_{4.2}$ = maximum amount of term loan available

"The principal of the loan must be repaid in ten equal installments; the first installment is due at end of six periods (beginiing of seventh period) after the loan is initially taken out with subsequent installments due at six-period intervals. No speed-up of payments is possible."

$$v_{4.j} = \alpha_{4.1}x_{4.1} \quad j = 6k + 1$$

$k = 1, 2, \cdots, 1/\alpha_{4.1}$

$$v_{4.j} = 0 \quad \text{otherwise}$$

and

$$y_{4.j} = 0 \quad j = 1, 2, \cdots m$$

where

$\alpha_{4.1}$ = proportion of the term loan principal repaid at each repayment

$1/\alpha_{4.1}$ = number of installment payments on the term loan

The outstanding balance is given by

$$z_{4.j} = x_{4.1} - \sum_{k=1}^{j} v_{4.k}$$

"The maximum borrowing under the loan plus a line of credit is $2,500,000, while the maximum borrowing with a term loan and the pledging of receivables is $4,500,000."

$$z_{4.j} + \sum_{k=1}^{j} (x_{1.k} - y_{1.k}) \leq \beta_{4.3}$$

or

$$z_{4.j} + z_{1.j} + s_{4.3.j} = \beta_{4.3}$$

$j = 1, 2, \cdots m$

$$z_{4.j} + \sum_{k=1}^{j} (x_{2.k} - y_{2.k}) \leq \beta_{4.4}$$

or

$$z_{4.j} + z_{2.j} + s_{4.4.j} = \beta_{4.4}$$

where

$\beta_{4.3}$ = maximum borrowing with a term loan and a line of credit

$\beta_{4.4}$ = maximum borrowing with a term loan and pledging of receivables

Fulfillment of Requirements

The cash requirements for each period, before interest and compensating balance requirements, are given in line 15 of Table I. These requirements must be adjusted for the interest expense, lost discounts, and any interest earned on investment of excess cash. The requirements inequality for each period states that the adjusted requirements must be satisfied by excess cash, borrowings less repayments, plus any change in compensating balance requirement.

For $j = 3, \cdots, m$ the equation may be written as:

For period 2 the variables with subscript $j - 2$ are deleted. For period 1 the variables with subscripts $j - 2$ and $j - 1$ are deleted and $x_{4.1}$ is added.

The pledged accounts receivable variables are multiplied by $\alpha_{2.3}$ for those pledged accounts receivable which are paid back over the course of the period. This has the effect of using the average amount outstanding for satisfying requirements and for computing interest expense.

Where

R_j = net requirement of period j (line 15, Table I)

$s_{5.1.j-1}$ = excess funds carried over from period $j - 1$

r_5 = interest rate earned on excess funds

r_1 = interest rate on line of credit

r_2 = interest rate on the pledged receivables loan

r_4 = interest rate on the term loan

The discount lost, r_3, does not appear in this inequality since it is already required by the constraints on the repayment variables $y_{3.j.j-1}$ and $y_{3.j.j-2}$.

Using the fact that

$$y_{3.j.j-1} = (1 + r_3)x_{3.j-1.j-1} - x_{3.j.j-1}$$

$j = 2, 3, \cdots m$

and that the repayment $y_{3.j.j-2}$ is the same as $x_{3.j-1.j-2}$ for $j = 3, 4, \cdots m$,

$R_j \leq$	requirements in period j must be less than or equal to new borrowing
$x_{1.j} + \alpha_{2.3}x_{2.j} + x_{3.j.j}$	
$+ (1 + r_5)s_{5.1.j-1}$	+ excess cash from previous period plus interest
$- [y_{1.j} + \alpha_{2.3}(y_{2.j} + v_{2.j}) + y_{3.j.j-1} + y_{3.j.j-2} + v_{4.j}]$	- repayments
$- r_1z_{1.j-1} - r_2\alpha_{2.3}z_{2.j-1} - r_4z_{4.j-1}$	- interest expense in previous periods
$- s_{1.2.j} + s_{1.2.j-1}$	- change in compensating balance requirements

the requirements equation may be written more concisely as

$$R_j = x_{1.j} - y_{1.j} + \alpha_{2.3}(x_{2.j} - y_{2.j} - v_{2.j}) + x_{3.j.j} - (1 + r_3)x_{3.j-1.j-1}$$

$$+ x_{3.j.j-1} - x_{3.j-1.j-2} - v_{4.j} + (1 + r_5)s_{5.1.j-1} - s_{5.1.j}$$

$$- r_1 z_{1.j-1} - r_2 \alpha_{2.3} z_{2.j-1} - r_4 z_{4.j-1} - s_{1.2.j} + s_{1.2.j-1}$$

$$j = 3, 4, \cdots m$$

The slack variable in this equation is $s_{5.1.j}$.

Objective: Cost Equation

For the jth period the explicit costs are interest on loans and discounts lost less the interest earned on excess funds.

$$D_j = r_1 z_{1.j} + r_2 \alpha_{2.3} z_{2.j} + r_3 x_{3.j.j}$$

$$+ r_4 z_{4.j} - r_5 x_{5.1.j}$$

$$j = 1, 2, \cdots m$$

where D_j = total net explicit costs in period j.

As described earlier, the qualitative considerations in the stretching of payables and the term loan will be incorporated by assigning implicit costs. These costs will be assumed to be proportional to the amount of money borrowed and hence can be specified as "rates per period":

$\rho_{3.2}$ = implicit cost of ill will to creditors when payments are stretched more than one period, expressed as a rate per period

$\rho_{4.2}$ = implicit cost of a term loan, expressed as a rate per period

The total implicit cost for the jth period, D^*_j is

$$D^*_j = \rho_{3.2} x_{3.j.j-1} + \rho_{4.2} z_{4.j}$$

$$k = 1, 2, \cdots m$$

In addition an adjustment must be made for terminating the model after m periods. If the cash budget covers a complete seasonal cycle, any difference between the financial conditions at the end of the last budget period and those at the beginning of the initial period must be taken into account in the making of the financial decision. In the formulation developed here it will be assumed that conditions at the end of the last period under consideration need not necessarily be the same as they were at the beginning of the initial period. An "end condition implicit cost or credit" is assigned where the beginning and ending conditions are not the same. This consists of a "one-time" credit for any excess cash available.

However, in the case of the term loan, which can not be paid off, credit is given for having excess cash on hand because of the term loan in the final period. The excess cash available because of the term loan at the end of the mth period is given by

$$z_{4.m} - s_{5.1.m} + s_{5.2} - s_{5.3}$$

where either $s_{5.2}$ or $s_{5.3}$ is zero; $s_{5.2}$ is greater than zero if the excess cash, $s_{5.1.m}$, is greater than the amount outstanding on the term loan.

Let the rate for the implicit end costs be:

$\rho_{1.1}$ for line of credit
$\rho_{2.1}$ for pledged receivables
$\rho_{3.1}$ for stretched accounts payable
$\rho_{4.1}$ for term loan
$\rho_{5.1}$ for excess cash

The end condition implicit cost, F_m, is

$$F_m = \rho_{1.1}z_{1.m} + \rho_{2.1}z_{2.m} + \rho_{3.1}(x_{3.m.m} + x_{3.m.m-1})$$
$$+ (\rho_{4.1} - \rho_{5.1})z_{4.m} + \rho_{5.1}(s_{5.3} - s_{5.2})$$

The total relevant cost, TRC, is the sum of the explicit and implicit costs:

$$TRC = \sum_{j=1}^{m} D_j + \sum_{j=1}^{m} D_j^* + F_m$$

The objective is to minimize TRC, subject to the quantitative restrictions given in this section.

Assumptions

In this mathematical formulation a number of assumptions have been made explicitly or implicitly. At this point it is desirable to restate them and summarize the justification for making them.

The first three are primarily for convenience and can easily be modified if the extra complications are considered worth while.

1. All transactions except collection of accounts receivable occur at the beginning of a period or equivalently the end of the previous period. In practice many of the decisions are in fact made at the beginning of a period, though transactions occur continuously. Increased accuracy can be obtained by dividing the total time into shorter periods.

2. Interest on money borrowed is added to cash requirements at the beginning of the next period. Again greater accuracy can be obtained by using shorter periods.

3. The costs of the various periods are not discounted to the present, because the interest costs are included in the requirements.

The next three assumptions involve more difficult conceptual or computational problems.

4. It has been assumed that the costs of the various alternatives are proportional to the amount borrowed. There is no provision for fixed costs of, say, initiating a "loan." This may not be an unreasonable assumption since the loan initiation cost, under each alternative, is likely to be approximately equal and hence is not a relevant cost.

5. The qualitative factors are incorporated by assigning implicit costs which are proportional to the amount borrowed. Again this is not unreasonable. If only a small amount of payables are stretched, only a small number of creditors may be effected. The conditions on term loans become more restrictive as the amount of the loan increases.

6. The model is terminated after a finite number of periods. In practice the financial officer would seldom consider more than one seasonal cycle in his short term financing decisions. In practice, of course, the short-term financing model should be used in conjunction with a longer-term financing model.

4. LINEAR PROGRAMMING FORMULATION

The Model

With the assumptions made in Section 3 the problem can be formulated as a linear programming problem except for two non-linear restrictions, namely that

$$x_{4.1} = 0 \quad \text{or} \quad \beta_{4.1} \leqq x_{4.1} \leqq \beta_{4.2}$$

and that

$$x_{1.j} = 0 \quad \text{or} \quad x_{2.j} = 0 \quad \text{for}$$

$$j = 1, 2, \cdots m$$

Since there are only four different combinations, each one can be considered a separate linear programming problem. The optimum solution out of these four then is the optimum for the problem.

A summary of the linear programming

Table II. SUMMARY OF LINEAR PROGRAMMING FORMULATION

X_1, Y_1, X_2, Y_2, X_3, Y_3, are m x 1 vectors of decision variables; $X_{3.1}$, $Y_{3.1}$ are m - 1 x 1 vectors of decision variables; $x_{4.1}$ is a decision variable.

Z_i, and $S_{i,j}$ are m x 1 vectors of slack variables except for $S_{3.2}$ which is m - 1 x 1; $s_{4.1}$, $s_{5.2}$ and $s_{5.3}$ are scalar slack variables.

I, T, M, U and W are $m \times m$, or $m - 1 \times m - 1$, matrices defined as follows:
$I_{ij} = 1$ if $i = j$; $= 0$ otherwise $t_{ij} = 1$ if $i \geq j$; $= 0$ otherwise $m_{ij} = 1$ if $j = i - 1$; $= 0$ otherwise $u_{ij} = 1$ if $i = j = m$; $= 0$ otherwise $w_{ij} = 1$ if $i = j = 1$ $= 0$ otherwise

$\mathbf{1}$, θ, and Q are m x 1 vectors defined as follows:
$\mathbf{1}_i = 1$ $i = 1, \cdots m$; $\theta_i = 0$ $i = 1, \cdots m$; $q_i = [(i - 1)/6]$ where $[x]$ is the smallest integer in x;

r_i, $\rho_{i.j}$ and $\beta_{i.j}$ are given parameters, A, B, R and P are m x 1 "input" vectors determined exogenously.

Statement	Equation	Range of j	Matrix Equation
Line of credit			
Non-negativity of balance	$\Sigma_{k=1}^{j}(x_{1.k} - y_{1.k}) - z_{1.j} = 0$	1 to m	$TX_1 - TY_1 - Z_1 = 0$
Maximum balance	$z_{1.j} + s_{1.j} = \beta_1$	1 to m	$IZ_1 + IS_1 = \mathbf{1}\beta_1$
Compensating balance	$\alpha_{1.1}z_{1.j} - s_{1.2.j} + s_{1.3.j} = b_j$	1 to m	$\alpha_{1.1}IZ_1 - IS_{1.2} + IS_{1.3} = B$
Pledging			
Non-negativity of balance	$\Sigma_{k=1}^{j}(x_{2.k} - y_{2.k} - v_{2.k}) - z_{2.j} = 0$	1 to m	$TX_2 - TY_2 - TV_2 - IZ_2 = 0$
	$v_{2.j} = \alpha_{2.1}\,\Sigma_{k=1}^{j-1}(x_{2.k} - y_{2.k} - v_{2.k})$	2 to m	$V_2 = \alpha_{2.1}MZ_2$; $TX_2 - TY_2 - (\alpha_{2.1}TM + I)Z_2 = 0$
Maximum balance	$z_{2.j} + s_{2.1.j} = \beta_2$	1 to m	$IZ_2 + IS_{2.1} = \beta_2\mathbf{1}$
Amount available	$z_{2.j} + s_{2.2.j} = \alpha_{2.2}a_j$	1 to m	$IZ_2 + IS_{2.2} = \alpha_{2.2}A$
Stretching first period			
Amount available	$x_{3.j.j} + s_{3.1.j} = \alpha_{3.1}p_j$	j = 1 to m	$IX_{3.1} + IS_{3.1} = \alpha_{3.1}P$
Stretching second period			
Amount available	$x_{3.j.j-1} + s_{3.2.j} = \alpha_{3.3}x_{3.j-1.j-1}$	2 to m	$IX_{3.1} + IS_{3.2} - \alpha_{3.3}MX_3 = \theta$

Term Loan			
Minimum amount available	$x_{4.1} - s_{4.1} = \beta_{4.1}$	1	$x_{4.1} - s_{4.1} = \beta_{4.1}$
Maximum amount available	$x_{4.1} + s_{4.2} = \beta_{4.2}$	1	$x_{4.1} + s_{4.2} = \beta_{4.2}$
Payments	$v_{4.j} = \alpha_4 x_{4.1}$ if $j = 6k + 1;\; k = 1, 2, \cdots \alpha_4^{-1}$ $= 0$ otherwise	1 to m	
	$z_{4.j} = x_{4.1} - \Sigma_{k=1}^{j} v_{4.k}$	1 to m	$Z_4 = x_{4.1}\mathbf{1} - \alpha_4 x_{4.1} Q;$ $x_{4.1}(\mathbf{1} - \alpha_4 Q) - Z_4 = \theta$
Combined borrowing	$z_{4.j} + z_{1.j} + s_{4.3.j} = \beta_{4.3}$	1 to m	$IZ_4 + IZ_1 + IS_{4.3} = \beta_{4.3}\mathbf{1}$
Combined borrowing	$z_{4.j} + z_{2.j} + s_{4.4.j} = \beta_{4.4}$	1 to m	$IZ_4 + IZ_2 + IS_{4.4} = \beta_{4.4}\mathbf{1}$
Excess Cash	$z_{4.m} - s_{5.1.m} + s_{5.2} - s_{5.3} = 0$	m	$\mathbf{1}'UZ_4 - \mathbf{1}'US_{5.1} + s_{5.2} - s_{5.3} = \theta$
Requirements			
Net borrowing	$x_{1.j} - y_{1.j} + \alpha_{2.3}(x_{2.j} - y_{2.j} - v_{2.j}) - v_{4.j}$		$I(X_1 - Y_1) + \alpha_{2.3} I(X_2 - Y_2 - V_2)$ $+ \mathbf{1}x_{4.1}(W\mathbf{1} - \alpha_{4.1}Q)$
Interest	$+ x_{3.j.j} - (1 + r_3)x_{3.j-1.j-1} + x_{3.j.j-1}$ $- x_{3.j-1.j-2} - r_1 z_{1.j-1} - r_2\alpha_{2.3} z_{2.j-1} - r_4 z_{4.j}$	1 to m	$+ IX_3 - (1 + r_3)MX_3 + IX_{3.1} - MX_{3.1}$ $- r_1 MZ_1 - r_2\alpha_{2.3}MZ_2 - r_4 MZ_4$
Change in compensatory balance	$- s_{1.2.j} + s_{1.2.j-1}$		$- IS_{1.2} + MS_{1.2}$
Change in excess cash	$+ (1 + r_5)s_{5.1.j-1} - s_{5.1.j} = R_j$		$+ (1 + r_5)MS_{5.1} - IS_{5.1} = R$
Objective: Minimize Explicit interest	$\Sigma_{j=1}^{m} (r_1 z_{1.j} + r_2\alpha_{2.3} z_{2.j} + r_3 x_{3.j.j} + r_4 z_{4.j}$ $- r_5 s_{5.1.j})$		$r_1\mathbf{1}'Z_1 + r_2\alpha_{2.3}\mathbf{1}'X_3 + r_4\mathbf{1}'Z_4 - r_5\mathbf{1}'S_{5.1}$
+ Implicit costs	$+ \Sigma_{j=1}^{n} (\rho_{3.2} x_{3.j.j-1} + \rho_{4.2} z_{4.j})$		$+ \rho_{3.2}\mathbf{1}'X_3 + \rho_{4.2}\mathbf{1}Z_4$
+ Implicit end costs	$+ \rho_{1.1} z_{1.m} + \rho_{2.1} z_{2.m} + \rho_{3.1}(x_{3.m.m} +$ $x_{3.m.m-1}) + (\rho_{4.1} - \rho_{5.1})z_{4.m} +$ $\rho_{5.1}(s_{5.3} - s_{5.2})$		$+ \rho_{1.1}\mathbf{1}UZ_1 + \rho_{2.1}\mathbf{1}UZ_2 + \rho_{3.1}\mathbf{1}UX_3 +$ $\rho_{3.1}\mathbf{1}UX_{3.1} + (\rho_{4.1} - \rho_{5.1})\mathbf{1}UZ_4 +$ $\rho_{5.1}(s_{5.3} - s_{5.2})$

formulation is given in Table II. This Table contains the equations in algebraic form, the range of subscripts j for which the equations hold, and the equations in matrix form.

In the matrix expressions the decision variables: X_1, Y_1, X_2, Y_2 and X_3 are m x 1 column vectors; $X_{3.1}$ is an m - 1 x 1 vector and $x_{4.1}$ is a scalar. The subscript denotes the alternative; in the case of the third alternative, stretching of accounts payable, the second subscript represents the stretching of accounts payable which have already been stretched one period, for another period. The slack variables, denoted by Z_i or $S_{i.j}$, are also m x 1 or m - 1 x 1 vectors. The slack variables denoted by x and s are scalars. The first subscript denotes the alternative and the second is a sequential number of the slack variable within the alternative.

The formulation of the problem in terms of matrices is facilitated by the definition of a number of square matrices of size $m \times m$, or $m - 1 \times m - 1$, of particular form. As usual I represents the identity matrix. The T matrix is used to represent cumulative values; it contains ones on and below the main diagonal; i.e.,

$$t_{ij} = 1 \qquad \text{if } i \geq j$$
$$= 0 \qquad \text{otherwise}$$

The jth element in TX gives the sum of x_i for the first j periods.

The matrix M is the "shift" matrix; when a column vector is multiplied the elements are shifted one column, which is equivalent to a shift of one period in time

$$m_{ij} = 1 \qquad \text{if } j = i - 1$$
$$= 0 \qquad \text{otherwise}$$

i.e., the jth element in MX is x_{j-1}.

The matrix W is used for the special initial condition for $x_{4.1}$. It is defined as

$$w_{ij} = 1 \qquad \text{if } i = j = 1$$
$$= 0 \qquad \text{otherwise}$$

The matrix U is used similarly in the special end conditions and has a 1 in the lower right hand position and zeros elsewhere. Its definition is:

$$u_{ij} = 1 \qquad \text{if } i = j = m$$
$$= 0 \qquad \text{otherwise}$$

The vector Q is used to indicate the periods in which payments are made on the term loan. Its definition is:

$$q_i = [(i - 1)/6]$$

where $[x]$ is the smallest integer in x. e.g., [6.1] = 6, [6] = 6.

The LP Tableau is shown in Table III. In this Table each column represents m (or m - 1 for $X_{3.1}$) values of the variables, listed at the head of the column, except in the case of $x_{4.1}$, $s_{4.1}$, $s_{5.2}$ and $s_{5.3}$ where the columns represent one variable. Each line represents m (or m - 1 for stretching of payables for the second period) equations, except the first, the objective, which is a single equation. All mandatory repayments denoted by v in Section 3, have been eliminated by appropriate substitutions.

The model which has been described here was programmed in the linear programming language MATRAN. This linear programming language was developed by Standard Oil Company of California.[3] A brief description of the relevant features of the language is given in Appendix 1. The LP model in MATRAN is given in Appendix 2.

The Parameters

For convenience in the discussion, the parameters appearing in the LP model have been grouped into five categories as shown in Figure II. Three of these

[3] We gratefully acknowledge the cooperation of the Standard Oil Company of California in providing a copy of the MATRAN systems tape.

Figure II. STRUCTURE OF LINEAR PROGRAMMING ANALYSIS SHOWING PARAMETERS GROUPED INTO FIVE MAJOR CATEGORIES

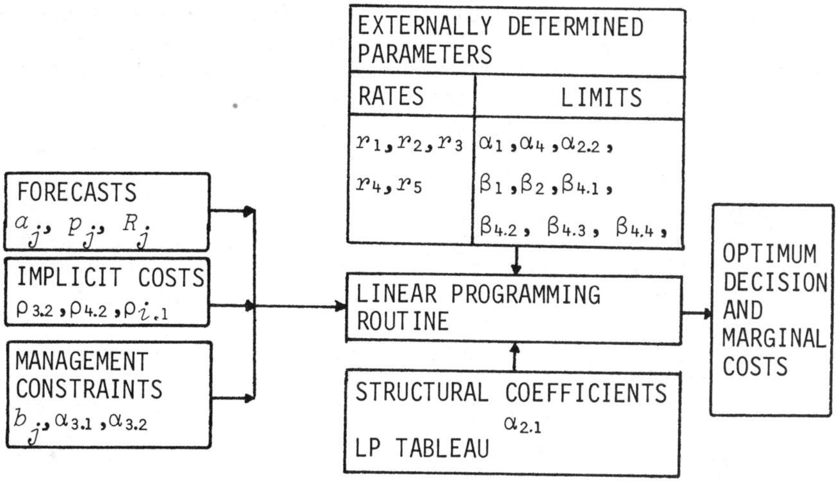

groups are shown in the set of three rectangles at the left; these are the parameters which must be determined by management. First are the forecasts:

a_j : accounts receivable

p_j : purchases on accounts payable

R_j ; cash requirements

The next rectangle shows:

$\rho_{3.2}$, $\rho_{4.2}$: implicit rates set by management

$\rho_{i.1}$: end condition implicit rates

The third rectangle contains the coefficients and limits set by management:

b_j : minimum cash balances

$\alpha_{3.1}$: portion of payables which must be paid immediately

$\alpha_{3.1}$: portion of payables stretched one period which must be paid

The second set of three rectangles shows the linear programming routine in the center and the input of additional information which is ordinarily not under management's control. The top rectangle of the three shows the parameters which are determined externally, usually by the lender:

r_i : interest rates

$\beta^i_{i.n}$: limits on the various alternatives

$\alpha_{1.1}$: proportion of a line of credit required as a compensating balance

$\alpha_{2.2}$: proportion of loan to accounts receivable that the bank allows

α_4 : proportion of the term loan which must be paid each period

The lower rectangle shows the "structural coefficient":

$\alpha_{2.1}$: proportion of the accounts receivable which are ordinarily paid during a period

and the coefficients in the LP tableau.

The result of the LP computation, shown in the rectangle on the right hand side, is a set of values of the decision variables giving the minimum value of TRC, the total relevant cost.

5. SOLUTION TO PARTICULAR CASES

Optimum Solution

In this section the solution to the specific problems presented in Section 1 will be discussed. The parameters a_j, b_j, p_j are given in the cash budget in Table I; the values of the other parameters are given in Table IV.

The minimum values of the objective function, TRC, for a number of cases

TABLE III. LP TABLEAU

	Range of j	X'_1	Y'_1	X'_2	Y'_2	X'_3	X' 3.1	x 4.1	Z' 4	S' 1.1	S' 1.2	S' 1.3	Z' 1	S' 2.1	S' 2.2	Z' 2	S' 3.1	S' 3.2	s 4.1	s 4.2	S' 4.3	S' 4.4	S' 5.1	s 5.2	s 5.3	RHS
Objective: Minimize						$r_3\mathbf{1}$			$r_4\mathbf{1}$				$r_1\mathbf{1}'$			$r_2\alpha_{2.3}\mathbf{1}'$							$-r_5\mathbf{1}$			}
explicit costs	1 }																									
+ implicit costs							$\rho_{3.2}\mathbf{1}$		$\rho_{4.2}\mathbf{1}$																	
+ end implicit costs						$\rho_{3.1}\mathbf{1}U$	$\rho_{3.1}\mathbf{1}U$		γ_1				$\rho_{1.1}\mathbf{1}U$			$\rho_{2.1}\mathbf{1}U$								$-\rho_{5.1}$	$\rho_{5.1}$	
Requirements																										
net borrowing	1 to m }	I	$-I$	γ_5	γ_6	$I-(1+$	$I-M$	γ_2	I		$M-I$					γ_7							γ_3			} R
- interest costs						$r_3)M$			r_4M				r_1M			$r_2\alpha_{2.3}M$										
LC.																										
Definition of Z_1	1 to m	T	$-T$										$-I$													θ
Maximum balance	1 to m									I			I													$\beta_1\mathbf{1}$
Compensating balance	1 to m										$-I$	$+I$	$\alpha_{1.1}I$													B
Pledging																										
Definition of Z_2	1 to m			T	$-T$											$-I+$ $\alpha_{2.1}T_1M$										θ
Maximum balance	1 to m													I		I										$\beta_2\mathbf{1}$
Amount available	1 to m														I	I										$\alpha_{2.3}A$
Stretching 1st period																										
Amount available	1 to m					I											$-I$									$\alpha_{3.1}P$
Stretching 2nd period																										
Amount available	2 to m					$-\alpha_{3.3}M$	I											I								θ
Term Loan																										
Amount available	1							1											-1							$\beta_{4.1}$
Amount available	1							1												1						$\beta_{4.3}$
Payments	1 to m							γ_4	$-I$												I					θ
Combined borrowing	1 to m								I				I													$\beta_{4.3}\mathbf{1}$
Combined borrowing	1 to m								I							I						I				$\beta_{4.4}\mathbf{1}$
Excess cash	1								$\mathbf{1}U$														$\mathbf{1}U$	1	-1	0

$\gamma_1 = (\rho_{4.1} - \rho_{5.1})\mathbf{1}U$ $\quad \gamma_2 = W\mathbf{1} - \alpha_4 Q$ $\quad \gamma_5 = \alpha_{2.3}I$

$\gamma_3 = I - (1 + r_5)M$ $\quad \gamma_6 = \alpha_{2.3}I$

$\gamma_4 = \mathbf{1} - \alpha_4 Q$ $\quad \gamma_7 = \alpha_{2.1}\alpha_{2.3}M$

Table IV. VALUES OF PARAMETERS USED IN THE EXAMPLE

Alternative	Limits($1,000)	Coefficients	Interest Rates	Implicit Rates
Line of Credit	$\beta_1 = 1500$	$\alpha_{1.1} = 0.20$	$r_1 = 0.009$	$\rho_{1.1} = 0.005$
Pledging	$\beta_2 = 3750$	$\alpha_{2.1} = 0.30$	$r_2 = 0.014$	$\rho_{2.1} = 0.006$
		$\alpha_{2.2} = 0.80$		
		$^*\alpha_{2.3} = 1 - (\alpha_{2.1}/2) = 0.85$		
Stretching		$\alpha_{3.1} = 0.80$	$r_2 = 0.035$	$\rho_{2.1} = 0.010$
		$\alpha_{3.2} = 0.75$		$\rho_{3.2} = 0.010$
		$^*\alpha_{3.3} = \alpha_{3.2}(1 + r_3) \cong 0.78$		
Term Loan	$\beta_{4.1} = 500$	$\alpha_4 = 0.10$	$r_4 = 0.008$	$\rho_{4.1} = 0.004$
	$\beta_{4.2} = 2000$			$\rho_{4.2} = 0.003$
	$\beta_{4.3} = 2500$			
	$\beta_{4.4} = 4500$			
Excess Funds			$r_5 = 0.004$	$\rho_{5.1} = 0.003$

*These parameters are combinations of other parameters and are used solely to simplify notation.

Table V. MINIMUM TOTAL RELEVANT COSTS UNDER VARIOUS ALTERNATIVES

Case	Term Loan	Line of Credit	Pledging	Interest Cost	Implicit Costs			Total Relevant Costs Explicit Plus Implicit
					Stretching	Term Loan	End Condition	
1	1,111,111	Yes	No	281,741	23,121	37,997	2,727	345,586
2	1,176,642	No	Yes	270,150	0,204	40,242	2,750	313,346
3	0	Yes	No	366,710	50,033	0	3,503	420,246
4		No	Yes	342,299	13,378	0	4,471	360,148
5	500,000	Yes	No	318,296	33,453	17,100	2,616	371,465
6		No	Yes	301,293	5,773	17,100	2,828	326,995
7	1,000,000	Yes	No	284,886	24,078	34,200	2,637	345,801
8		No	Yes	276,136	0,412	34,200	2,611	313,359
9	2,000,000	Yes	No	288,382	18,459	68,400	3,537	378,778
10		No	Yes	256,914	0	68,400	3,443	328,757

For problem in Section 1 with other parameter values as given in Table IV

TABLE VI. (CASE II). DETAILED STATEMENT OF THE OPTIMUM SOLUTION FOR CASE II, PLEDGING AND OPTIMUM TERM LOAN

Period	1	2	3	4	5	6	7	8	9	10	11	12
Requirement	(500,000)	(1,500,000)	(2,000,000)	500,000	600,000	4,000,000	(500,000)	(1,500,000)	(2,700,000)	600,000	2,000,000	700,000
Interest												
Pledging of Receivables	--	--	(11,621)	(39,548)	(33,328)	(25,812)	--	--	--	(37,919)	(30,168)	(2,709)
Stretched Payables	--	--	--	(919)	--	--	--	--	--	--	--	--
Term Loan	--	(9,413)	(9,413)	(9,413)	(9,413)	(9,413)	(9,413)	(8,472)	(8,472)	(8,472	(8,472)	(8,472)
Less: Income	--	2,707	--	--	--	--	8,484	6,010	--	--	--	--
Total Interest	--	(6,706)	(21,034)	(49,880)	(42,741)	(35,225)	(920)	(2,462)	(8,472)	(46,391)	(38,640)	(11,181)
Adjusted Req't for Period	(500,000)	(1,506,706)	(2,021,034)	450,120	557,250	3,964,775	(500,929)	(1,502,462)	(2,708,472)	553,609	1,961,360	688,819
New Borrowing												
Pledging	--	830,064	2,243,809	403,208	177,295	--	--	--	2,708,472	258,932	--	--
Stretching	--	--	26,244	--	--	--	--	--	--	--	--	--
Term Loan	1,176,642	--	--	--	--	--	--	--	--	--	--	--
Total New Borrowing	1,176,642	830,064	2,270,053	403,208	177,295	--	--	--	2,708,472	258,932	--	--
Repayments												
Pledging	--	--	(249,019)	(847,456)	(714,182)	(1,843,720)	----	--	--	--	(1,961,360)	(193,503)
Stretching	--	--	--	(5,872)	(20,372)	--	--	--	--	--	--	--
Term Loan	--	--	--	--	--	--	(117,664)	--	--	--	--	--
Total Repayment	--	--	(249,019)	(853,382)	(734,554)	(1,843,720)	(117,664)	--	--	(553,609)	(1,961,360)	(193,503)
Net New Borrowing	1,176,642	830,064	2,021,034	(450,120)	(557,259)	(1,843,720)	(117,664)	--	2,708,472	(553,609)	(1,961,360)	(193,503)
Change in Excess Cash	(676,642)	676,642	--	--	--	(2,121,055)	618,593	1,502,462	--	--	--	(495,316)
Req't Financed	500,000	1,506,706	2,021,034	(450,120)	(557,259)	(3,964,775)	500,929	1,502,462	2,708,472	(533,609)	(1,961,360)	(688,819

TABLE VII (CASE I). DETAILED STATEMENT OF THE OPTIMUM SOLUTION FOR CASE I, LINE OF CREDIT AND OPTIMUM TERM LOAN

Period	1	2	3	4	5	6	7	8	9	10	11	12
Requirement	(500,000)	(1,500,000)	(2,000,000)	500,000	600,000	4,000,000	(500,000)	(1,500,000)	(2,700,000)	600,000	2,000,000	700,000
Interest												
Line of Credit	--	--	(8,948)	(12,500)	(11,779)	(12,500)	--	--	(610)	(13,500)	(10,998)	(2,385)
Stretching	--	--	--	(56,072)	--	(21,007)	--	--	--	(48,173)	--	--
Term Loan	--	(8,889)	(8,889)	(8,889)	(8,889)	(8,889)	(8,889)	(8,000)	(8,000)	(8,000)	(8,000)	(8,000)
Less: Interest Earned	--	2,444	--	--	--	--	8,185	5,738	--	--	--	--
Total Net Interest	--	(6,445)	(17,837)	(77,461)	(20,668)	(42,396)	(704)	(2,262)	(8,610)	(69,673)	(18,998)	(10,385)
Adjusted Req't	(500,000)	(1,506,445)	(2,017,837)	422,539	579,332	3,957,604	(500,704)	(1,502,262)	(2,708,610)	530,327	1,981,002	689,615
New Borrowing												
Line of Credit	--	994,167	394,722	--	80,098	--	--	67,771	1,432,229	--	--	--
Stretching	--	--	1,602,059	--	600,188	--	--	--	1,376,381	--	--	--
Term Loan	1,111,111	--	--	--	--	--	--	--	--	--	--	--
Total New Borrowing	1,111,111	994,167	1,996,781	--	680,286	--	--	67,771	2,808,610	--	--	--
Repayments												
Line of Credit	--	--	--	(80,098)	--	(1,388,889)	--	--	--	(277,952)	(956,995)	(265,053)
Stretching	--	--	--	(358,461)	(1,243,598)	(600,188)	--	--	--	(307,952)	(1,068,416)	--
Term Loan	--	--	--	--	--	--	(111,111)	--	--	--	--	--
Total Repayments	--	--	--	(438,559)	(1,243,598)	(1,989,077)	(111,111)	--	--	(585,917	(2,025,411)	(265,053)
Compensating Balance Change	--	(98,833)	21.055	16,020	(16,020)	77,778	--	--	(100,000)	55,590	44,410	--
Net New Borrowing	1,111,111	895,334	2,017,837	(422,539)	(579,332)	(1,911,299)	(111,111)	67,771	2,708,610	(530,327)	(1,981,002)	(265,053)
Remainder	611,111	(611,111)	--	--	--	2,046,306	(611,815)	(1,434,491)	--	--	--	424,562
Excess Cash Balance	611,111	--	--	--	--	2,046,306	1,434,491	--	--	--	--	424,562
Total	500,000	1,506,445	2,017,837	(422,539	(579,332)	(3,957,604)	500,704	1,502,262	2,708,610	(530,327)	(1,981,002)	(689,615)

are shown in Table V. The first four cases are the combination of

optimum term loan ($\beta_{4.1} \leq x_{4.1} \leq \beta_{4.2}$) *or* no term loan ($x_{4.1} = 0$) and *either* the line of credit *or* the pledging of accounts receivable.

In addition, six other cases were computed with given term loans of 0.5, 1, and 2 million dollars with either the line of credit or the pledging. The cost of the optimum solution for each of these cases is given in Table V. Table V shows the explicit interest costs; the implicit costs of stretching of the term loan, and of the end conditions; and the total relevant cost, TRC.

The optimum solution for this particular set of parameters is achieved by a term loan of $1,176,642 and use of pledging of accounts receivable. The optimum solution to the problem would be different if, instead of total interest, only explicit interest is considered. In particular, the explicit interest in the optimum solution with the $2,000,000 term loan with pledging is less than the explicit interest for the optimum (Case II) with the use of pledging; on the other hand, total interest cost is lower for the latter.

A detailed statement of the optimum solution, i.e, Case II, is given in Table VI. The Table shows first the requirements, then the interest paid under the optimum solution less the interest earned. These are added to the requirement to give the adjusted net requirements. Next are shown the borrowing under pledging receivables, stretching payables, and term loan, and the total new borrowing. The repayments under each of the alternatives, and the total net borrowing are shown next. Subtracting the change in the compensating balance and the change in excess cash gives a remainder which is exactly equal to the adjusted requirements. This shows that the cash requirements are satisfied. The implicit interest costs are also shown. From this Table is is easy to verify that the solution shown is feasible; i.e., it satisfies the constraints stated in Section 3.

Similarly Table VII gives a detailed statement of the optimum term loan in combination with the line of credit; i.e., Case I.

6. MARGINAL COSTS AND THEIR USE

In addition to the explicit optimum solutions given in Tables VI and VII, the solution to the LP model can also be used to determine answers to other questions. Management may wish to choose a non-optimal solution because of some factor not included in the model. It may wish to compare the cost of additional short term borrowing, over and above that contemplated in the cash budget (Table I) with the return that it can obtain from the use of these additional borrowed funds. Management may wish to consider changes in the parameters and variables under its control; for example, it may wish to consider delaying capital expenditures included in the cash budget. Management may also wish to request changes in the parameters not under its control, such as maximum limits. For all of these purposes, management can make use of the "marginal costs" of small changes in the optimal decision as an indication of the effect of changes on the objective function. (For the second purpose listed it is also necessary to determine the marginal return on the use of the borrowed funds.) The way these marginal costs are obtained from the LP solution, and their use, will be described in this section.

The linear programming model, summarized in Table III, contains 6 decision variables: X_1, Y_1, X_2, Y_2, X_3, $X_{3.1}$ and $x_{4.1}$. There are a total of $11m + 2$ inequalities: $3m$ for the line of credit, $3m$ for pledging of accounts receivable, $2m - 1$ for stretching of accounts payable, $2m + 2$ for the term

Variable	Basic	Non-basic
Decision variable	Solution gives optimum value of decision variable	Value of decision variable in optimum solution is zero. LP solution gives the marginal cost if the decision variable is set equal to 1000.
Slack variable	Corresponding inequality is satisfied as inequality in optimum solution	Corresponding inequality is satisfied as an equality in optimum solution. The solution gives the marginal cost of changing the right hand side (of the equality) by 1000.

loan, m for the requirements, and 1 for excess cash at the end of the mth period. Each of these inequalities is changed to an equality by the use of a slack variable and therefore $11m + 2$ slack variables are defined in this model.

In the optimum linear programming solution there will be $11m + 2$ basic variables and $6m$ non-basic variables. A decision variable may be either basic or non-basic in the optimum solution and the slack variable may be basic or non-basic. The meaning of the four cases in shown at the top of this page.

The optimum solution gives the value of each basic variable that leads to minimum total relevant cost, TRC. (This value may be zero.) The optimum solution also gives the "marginal cost" for each non-basic variable. The "marginal cost" of a non-basic decision variable is by definition the increase in TRC if this decision variable is set equal to 1000. The marginal cost of a non-basic slack variable is by definition the decrease in TRC if the right hand side of the equality for which the slack variable is defined is increased by 1000.

The optimum values for the basic variables, and the marginal costs for the relevant non-basic variables, are shown in Table VIII for Case II, which is the optimum solution to the cash budget presented in Table I. The fact that this is the solution given in Table VI may be verified by noting that the values of the basic variables appear in Table VI.

To illustrate the use of these marginal costs, suppose that management decides that it should stretch some payables for a second period in period 6. The optimum solution is not to stretch these payables a second time, and the value of $x_{3.1.0}$ is listed in Table VIII as being non-basic with a marginal cost of 0.005725. This means that if the stretching were done, the optimum solution would then have an increased cost of 5.7 dollars per \$1000 stretched. Note that this assumes that the optimum decision is made for all other variables. In general, this optimum solution would be different from the one shown in Table VIII and therefore this new optimum solution usually cannot be obtained from the data available in Table VIII.

As an example of a change in the constraints, suppose that $\beta_{4.3}$, the amount that can be borrowed, were increased. The slack variable associated with this constraint is $S_{4.4}$. From Table VIII it can be seen that $S_{4.4}$ is basic, (i.e., the contraint is not binding) in all periods except period 3. In period 3, $S_{4.4}$ is non-basic with a marginal cost of 0.01624. Therefore if $\beta_{4.3}$ were increased by \$1000, the value of the objective function

TABLE VIII. OPTIMUM VALUES FOR BASIC VARIABLES (B) AND MARGINAL COST COEFFICIENTS FOR NON-BASIC VARIABLES (NB) Case II = $1,176,642 Term Loan, No Line of Credit

	X_2	Y_2	Z_2	$S_{2.1}$	$S_{2.2}$	
1	0.0 B	0.0 NB	0.009807 NB	3750.000 B	2400.000 B	
2	976.546 B	0.0 NB	976.546 B	2773.454 B	1423.454 B	
3	2639.775 B	0.0 NB	3323.358 B	426.642 B	276.642 B	
4	474.362 B	0.0 NB	2800.713 B	949.287 B	599.287 B	
5	208.583 B	0.0 NB	2169.082 B	1580.918 B	1230.918 B	
6	0.0 NB	1518.357 B	0.009085 NB	3750.000 B	1600.000 B	
7	0.0 B	0.0 NB	0.009048 NB	3750.000 B	2800.000 B	
8	0.0 B	0.0 NB	0.000066 NB	3750.000 B	3600.000 B	
9	3186.437 B	0.0 NB	3186.437 B	563.563 B	413.563 B	
10	304.626 B	0.0 NB	2535.132 B	1214.868 B	864.868 B	
11	0.0 NB	1546.943 B	227.650 B	3522.350 B	2572.350 B	
12	0.0 NB	159.355 B	0.01195 NB	3750.000 B	2000.000 B	

	X_3	$X_{3.1}$	$S_{3.1}$	$S_{3.2}$	$S_{4.4}$	
1	0.0 B	---	1600.000 B	0.0 NB	3323.358 B	$x_{4.1}$ =
2	0.0 B	0.04015 NB	1600.000 B	0.04608 NB	2346.811 B	1176.642 B
3	26.244 B	0.006229 NB	1973.765 B	0.03078 NB	0.01624 NB	
4	0.01895 NB	20.372 B	2000.000 B	0.005233 NB	522.645 B	$s_{4.1}$ =
5	0.02253 NB	0.0 B	2000.000 B	0.005023 NB	1154.276 B	823.358 B
6	0.03313 NB	0.005725 NB	800.000 B	0.0 B	3323.358 B	
7	0.02941 NB	0.005742 NB	800.000 B	0.0 B	3441.022 B	$s_{5.2}$ =
8	0.01864 NB	0.0 B	1600.000 B	0.004621 NB	3441.022 B	0.00300 NB
9	0.0 B	0.0 B	2000.000 B	0.004496 NB	254.585 B	
10	0.0 B	0.02372 NB	2000.000 B	0.02801 NB	905.890 B	$s_{5.3}$ =
11	0.02115 NB	0.02353 NB	1200.000 B	0.02762 NB	3213.372 B	563.661 B
12	0.03800 NB	0.01300 NB	800.000 B	0.0 B	3441.022 B	

TABLE IX. OPTIMUM VALUES FOR BASIC VARIABLES (B) AND MARGINAL COST COEFFICIENTS FOR NON-BASIC VARIABLES (NB)
Case I = $1,111,111 Term Loan, No Pledging of Accounts Receivable

	X_1		Y_1		Z_1		S_1		$S_{1.2}$		$S_{1.3}$	
1	0.0	B	0.0	NB	0.005908	NB	1500.000	B	0.004726	NB	100.000	B
2	994.167	B	0.0	NB	994.167	B	505.833	B	98.833	B	0.01315	NB
3	394.722	B	0.0	NB	1388.889	B	111.111	B	77.778	B	0.03758	NB
4	0.0	NB	80.098	B	1308.791	B	191.209	B	61.758	B	0.01258	NB
5	80.098	B	0.0	NB	1388.889	B	111.111	B	77.778	B	0.03782	NB
6	0.0	NB	1388.889	B	0.005381	NB	1500.000	B	0.004305	NB	100.000	B
7	0.0	NB	0.0	B	0.005360	NB	1500.000	B	0.004288	NB	100.000	B
8	67.771	B	0.0	NB	67.771	B	1432.229	B	0.009561	NB	86.446	B
9	1432.229	B	0.0	NB	1500.000	B	0.01648	NB	100.000	B	0.03485	NB
10	0.0	NB	277.952	B	1222.048	B	277.952	B	44.410	B	0.01143	NB
11	0.0	NB	956.995	B	265.053	B	1234.947	B	0.009063	NB	46.989	B
12	0.0	NB	265.053	B	0.007000	NB	1500.000	B	0.007000	NB	100.000	B

	X_3		$X_{3.1}$		$S_{3.1}$		$S_{3.2}$		$S_{4.3}$			
1	0.03419	NB	---		1600.000	B	0.0	NB	1388.889	B	$x_{4.1}$ =	
2	0.006344	NB	0.0	B	1600.000	B	0.003145	NB	394.722	B	1111.111	B
3	1602.059	B	0.0	B	397.941	B	0.02758	NB	0.01988	NB	$s_{4.1}$ =	
4	0.004967	NB	1243.598	B	2000.000	B	0.002518	NB	80.098	B	888.889	B
5	600.188	B	0.0	B	1399.812	B	0.002782	NB	0.02053	NB	$s_{5.2}$ =	
6	0.03336	NB	0.005695	NB	800.000	B	465.896	B	1388.889	B	0.00300	NB
7	0.03323	NB	0.005712	NB	800.000	B	0.0	B	1500.000	B	$s_{5.2}$ =	
8	0.00833	NB	0.000439	NB	1600.000	B	0.0	B	1432.229	B	575.438	B
9	1376.381	B	0.0	B	623.619	B	0.02485	NB	0.002150	NB		
10	0.0	B	1068.416	B	2000.000	B	0.001431	NB	277.952	B		
11	0.02618	NB	0.03202	NB	1200.000	B	0.03109	NB	1234.947	B		
12	0.03800	NB	0.01300	NB	800.000	B	0.0	B	1500.000	B		

Figure III. SEQUENCE OF DECISIONS TO BE MADE

Initial Decision
1. Should a term loan be taken and if so for how much? 2. Should the firm arrange for a line of credit or for pledging of accounts receivable or neither?

↓

Decisions at the beginning of each period
1. Should any money be borrowed? If so, how and how much? By: Borrowing under line of credit, if available, or pledging accounts receivable, if available, or stretching "stretched" accounts payable another period, if available, or stretching accounts payable due this period.
2. Should any borrowing be voluntarily repaid? If so, which and how much? On: Line of credit, or Pledged accounts receivable, or "Stretched" accounts payable.

would be decreased by $16.24.

Similarly, Table IX gives the optimum value for the basic variables and the marginal cost coefficients for the relevant non-basic variables for Case I; the optimum solution for this case was shown in Table VII.

7. ANALYSIS OF THE MODEL

Simplified Decision Rules for Constant Parameter Values

The sequence of decision that must be made by the financial officer is summarized in Figure III. When the model is first used to make the decision in period 1 the amount of the term loan, and either the line of credit or pledging of accounts receivable, is chosen. At the beginning of the first and each succeeding period the financial officer must decide whether he is going to borrow or repay, the order in which he will borrow and repay, and the amounts. It is therefore of interest to investigate whether a simple rule which will give the optimum solution can be developed.

One might expect that a simple decision rule, based on a ranking of the alternatives, would lead to an optimum decision once the amount of the term loan has been decided and the choice between line of credit and pledging of accounts receivable has been made. For Cases I and II, for example, the rule might be as follows:

Case I

Use alternatives in the following order for acquiring funds:
1. Line of credit up to maximum without additional borrowing for compensating balance, then
2. Stretch payable for a second period as much as possible, then
3. Line of credit up to maximum, then
4. Stretch payable for the first period.

Repay when excess funds are available in the following order:
1. Line of credit up to point when no additional funds are required for compensating balance, then
2. Stretched payable for the first period, then
3. Line of credit.

Case II

Use alternatives in order:

1. Stretch payable for second period up to the maximum amount available, then
2. Pledge receivables up to maximum amount available, then
3. Stretch payables for one period.
Repay when excess funds are available in the order:
1. Pledged receivables, then
2. Stretch payables.

This type of rule, of course, will not help in determining the size of term loan required or help in deciding whether the line of credit or pledging of accounts receivable should be used.

Furthermore, such a rule does not always lead to the optimum decision for all possible a_j, b_j, R_j, and p_j even if the parameters do not change. The amount borrowed under an alternative in an optimum solution is not always the maximum allowable under the constraints. For example, the explicit cost of the line of credit may be less than other alternatives up to the point where additional borrowing is required for the compensating balance. The line of credit may therefore be preferable to the other alternatives up to the point where additional borrowing is required for the compensating balance, and less preferable thereafter. A more complex situation occurs in the case of stretching of payables. The discount lost on stretching of payables in the first period may be greater than the cost of the line of credit. However, once the payables are stretched for one period, if excess cash becomes available it may be used to repay the line of credit. This is because stretching payables for one extra period is relatively inexpensive.

A similar situation occurs in the case of the term loan. The optimum amount of the term loan in Case II ($1,176,642) is less than the maximum amount allowable, even though the explicit plus the implicit interest rate on the term loan is less than on the other alternatives. The reason here is that the term loan cannot be repaid voluntarily, hence the interest is incurred whether the money is needed or not. When these excess funds are invested in short term receivables, the earning rate is considerably less than the total borrowing cost.

The above discussion has examined the question of whether it is possible to develop simplified decision rules that lead to optimum decisions if the parameter values are constant. The conclusion is that no such simple decision rules exist.

Decisions as a Function of Parameters

Is it possible to develop a simplified analysis which would indicate the changes in the optimum decision as the parameters change? For example, if the interest rate for alternative (i) is increased, will the amount borrowed under alternative (i) change, in what direction, and by how much?

Here again, the optimum decision will depend on the cash requirements and the parameters of the particular case. For the same reasons as those given in the preceding subsection, a simplified analysis of the direction and magnitude of the changes in the optimum decision as a function of changes in parameters cannot be given. For an explicit optimum solution the LP model must be resolved.

8. THE SHORT-TERM FINANCING DECISION UNDER UNCERTAINTY

The analysis in the previous section has shown that the optimum solution to the model in general, can be obtained only by solving a linear programming problem. There is no simple decision rule which will always give the optimum. This is true even under the simple assumption that all parameters, cash flows, etc. are know with certainty. In practice, this assumption does not hold; the purpose of this section is to examine the changes that would be required to take uncertainty into account.

As was pointed out in the previous

section of this paper, management has to make two types of decisions: those made initially which affect all periods under consideration and those which are made at the beginning of each successive period. At the beginning of each period, certain of the factors which enter into the decision for the coming period are in fact known with certainty. For example, the financial officer knows the commitments, and he also knows the sales that were made in the preceding period which have resulted in receivables this period. He could therefore make immediate decisions which would meet the cash requirements for this period if it were not for the fact that his present decision affects his decisions in the future. Each decision depends on the entire planning horizon and cannot be made only on the basis of known facts at the beginning of the period.

The way in which the management might review periodically the short-term financing decision is shown in Figure IV. This figure shows the review procedure by which management can change those elements of the model that are under its control.

The effect of uncertainty in parameters and forecasts are that management's objective may change from merely minimizing costs to an objective which incorporates protection against dis aster. The LP model under certainty, as developed so far, can be regarded as maximizing expected value for a probabilistic model in which the distribution of parameters and requirements are replaced by their expected values. Furthermore management may wish to provide for flexibility in the alternatives considered so as to take advantage of possible new opportunities as they occur.

A number of changes to the procedure to incorporate the effect of uncertainty could be made. The model may be rerun periodically with existing financial commitments, e.g., amount of term loan, and the current values of the parameters. The model would be expanded to provide optimum solutions for each period given the existing commitments. In addition a number of runs could be made to test the effect of possible divergences from forecasts, e.g., conditions which are ±10% off the forecasts Or, if probability distributions can be estimated for the various elements of the model, available simulation techniques can be used to develop quantitative measures of risk exposure.[4] Quantitative measures of atti-

[4] A simplified simulation model which yields the expected value and the variance of the periodic cash requirements has been developed by one of the authors and will be described in a subsequent paper.

Figure IV. MANAGEMENT REVIEW CYCLE FOR SHORT TERM FINANCING DECISIONS

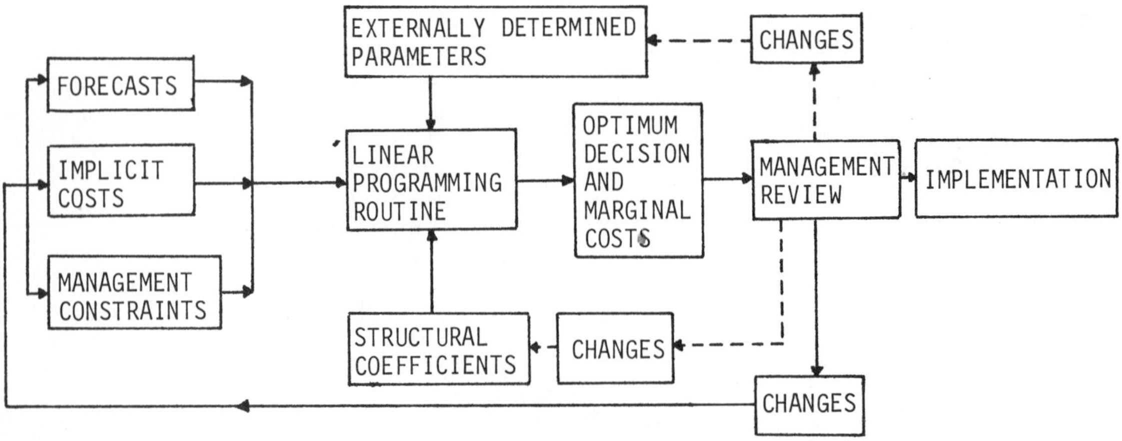

tude to risk would have to be specified before the optimum solution could be computed. The LP solution provides management with the minimum cost alternative. If management, because of uncertainty factors, considers a financial decision which is not optimal, the cost differential can be thought of as the "cost of insurance against uncertainty." The decision maker must then decide whether the added cost is justified.

The discussion of the complications created by uncertainty indicates that the problem requires more detailed analysis. The validity of alternative approaches to the short-term financing problem under uncertainty is left to a future paper.

9. APPLICATIONS

Any firm which has cyclical cash requirements and has the same alternatives and constraints described here can use the model in its present form merely by entering the appropriate parameters. In practice, the set of alternatives and constraints is not likely to be exactly identical to those used here. The model can easily be modified to incorporate other alternatives and/or constraints. The use of the MATRAN language makes it relatively easy to modify the program for such changes. The complete MATRAN program is given in Appendix II. The program is relatively short and its conciseness is another indication of how easy the development or change of an LP has become.

The computer time (7090) required to compile the program is approximately 15 minutes. The solution of a case, for a particular set of parameters and forecasts takes less than 5 minutes.

APPENDIX I

The MATRAN Language

MATRAN is a language in which all MATRAN statements are translated into FORTRAN statements. All FORTRAN conventions and definitions are adhered to. In addition, there are special conventions and statements to facilitate linear programming. These are described briefly in this Appendix.

1. EQUATION Statement. This statement enables the constraint and objective equations to be introduced into the program. All the LP variables are included to the left of the = sign, and all right-hand-side elements to the right of the =. The user must change inequalities to equalities by adding the appropriate slack variable. If the right-hand-side of an LP equation is to be 0.0, MATRAN does not require the = or the right-hand-side (0.0).

2. LP Variables. Each of the LP variables must be preceded by the numeral 1. Otherwise, the same naming rules apply to LP variables as to FORTRAN variables. Coefficients precede the LP variable with an * separating the coefficient and the variable. 1.0 or -1.0 is understood if the LP variable has no coefficient.

3. The SIGMA Function. MATRAN provides for the summation notation

$$\sum_{I=1}^{n} \text{BORR1 (I)}$$

through the Sigma Function.

SIGMAF((I = 1, n) 1BORRI(I))

where the index of summation is enclosed in parentheses within the function argument. Any number of LP variables, with their coefficients, can be included in the SIGMAF argument.

APPENDIX II

The LP Program in MATRAN

The program given on the following pages is the complete LP program for the short-term financing model presented in Section 4. The relation between the names of the variables used in Section 4 and the names used in the program is as follows:

Decision Variables

X_1 : BORR2

Y_1 : PAY2

X_2 : BORR1

Y_2 : PAY1

X_3 : BORR3(I,I)

$X_{3.1}$: BORR3(I, I - 1)

$x_{4.1}$: BORR4 (1)

Slack Variables

$S_{1.1}$: BSLK2

$S_{1.2}$: BALSK

$S_{1.3}$: EXTRA

$S_{1.4}$: SMSLK2 = Z_1

$S_{2.1}$: BCSL1

$S_{2.2}$: BSLK1

$S_{2.3}$: SMSLK1 = Z_2

$S_{3.1}$: PBSLK3

$S_{3.2}$: A4SLK

$s_{4.2}$: TLSLK4

$S_{4.3}$: SLTLC

$S_{4.4}$: SLTP

$S_{5.1}$: EXS

$s_{5.2}$: 07STD1

$s_{5.3}$: OTSTD2

In actual use the MATRAN program would be followed by three statements:

```
WRITE MATRIX
START LP
MINIMIZE OBJECT
```

and a FORTRAN output subroutine.

The first statement computes and stores the LP matrix for the particular values of the parameters that have been read in. The second statement performs the revised simplex method using the objective stated in the third statement. The FORTRAN output subroutine permits the user to print output reports in any form he wishes, using the final values of any LP variables or coefficients in the objective function.

Further, MATRAN statements could also be added to facilitate running a series of related LP problems.

```
C         MULTI-PERIOD, DETERMINISTIC, SHORT-TERM FUNDS MODEL
C                                  READ INPUT PARAMETERS
      READ INPUT TAPE 5, 101, R1, R2, R3, C32, R4, C42, CEIL1, CEIL2,
     1   CEIL4, ALF1, ALF2, ALF3, ALF4, BETA, ALF6, M
  101 FORMAT( 6F4.3, 3F6.1, 6F4.2, I3 )
      READ INPUT TAPE 5, 104, PKTLC, PKTP, ALF7, ALF8, ALF9, ALF10,
     1   ALF11, ALF12, SET
  104 FORMAT( 2F6.1, 6F5.3, F7.2 )
      DO 1000 I = 1, M
      READ INPUT TAPE 5, 102, TQER(1), A(I), PURCH(I), BAL(I)
  102 FORMAT( 5X, 4F10.1 )
 1000 CONTINUE
C
C                                  FACTORING EQUATIONS
      EQUATION   1BORR1(1) - 1PAY1(1) - 1SMSLK1(1)
      DO 10  J = 1, M
      EQUATION   1SMSLK1(J) + 1BSLK1(J) = ALF1*A(J)
      EQUATION   1SMSLK1(J) + 1BCSL1(J) = CEIL1
   10 CONTINUE
      DO 20  J = 2, M
      EQUATION   SIGMAF((K=1,J)  1BORR1(K) - 1PAY1(K)) + SIGMAF((K=2,J)
     1    - ALF2*1SMSLK1(K-1)) - 1SMSLK1(J)
   20 CONTINUE
C
C                                  LINE OF CREDIT
      DO 30  J = 1, M
      EQUATION   SIGMAF((K = 1,J)  1BORR2(K) - 1PAY2(K)) - 1SMSLK2(J)
      EQUATION   SIGMAF((K=1,J)  1BORR2(K) - 1PAY2(K)) + 1BSLK2(J) = CEIL2
      EQUATION   SIGMAF((I=1,J) BETA*1BORR2(I) -BETA*1PAY2(I)) -1BALSK(J)
     1   +  1EXTRA(J) = BAL(J)
   30 CONTINUE
C
C                                  NON-PAYMENT OF A/P
      DO 40  J = 1, M
      EQUATION   1BORR3(J,J) + 1PBSLK3(J) = (1.0-ALF3)*PURCH(J)
   40 CONTINUE
      TERM = (1.0-ALF4)*(1.0+R3)
      DO 50  J = 2, M
      EQUATION   1BORR3(J,J-1) + 1A4SLK(J) - TERM*1BORR3(J-1,J-1)
   50 CONTINUE
C
C                                  TERM LOAN
      EQUATION   1BORR4(1) + 1TLSLK4(1) = CEIL4
      EQUATION   1BORR4(1) - 500.0*1B1 - 2000.0*1B2 - 1TERSLK-1000.0*1B3
     1    - SET*1B4
      EQUATION   1B1+ 1R2+ 1B3+ 1B4 + 1FRCSLK = 1.0
      DO 65  J = 1, 6
      EQUATION        1BORR4(1) + 1SMSLK2(J) + 1SLTLC(J) = PKTLC
      EQUATION        1BORR4(1) + 1SMSLK1(J) + 1SLTP(J) = PKTP
   65 CONTINUE
      DO 67  J = 7, M
      EQUATION   (1.0-ALF6)*1BORR4(1) + 1SMSLK1(J) + 1SLTP(J) = PKTP
      EQUATION   (1.0-ALF6)*1BORR4(1) + 1SMSLK2(J) + 1SLTLC(J) = PKTLC
   67 CONTINUE
```

```
C
C                              REQUIREMENT EQUATIONS
      GAMMA = (R1/2.0)(2.0 - ALF2)
      G = (2.0 - ALF2)/2.0
      H = ALF2*G
      DEL = H + GAMMA
      RA = R4*(1.0-ALF6)
      EQUATION   G*1BORR1(1)-G*1PAY1(1)          + 1BORR2(1) - 1PAY2(1)
     1  + 1BORR3(1,1) + 1BORR4(1) - 1EXS(1) - 1BALSK(1) = TQER(1)
      EQUATION          G*1BORR1(2)-G*1PAY1(2)-H*1SMSLK1(1)+1BORR2(2)
     1  - 1PAY2(2) + 1BORR3(2,2) - (1.0+R3)*1BORR3(1,1) + 1BORR3(2,1)
     2  - 1EXS(2) - 1BALSK(2) - GAMMA*1BORR1(1) + GAMMA*1PAY1(1)
     3                  - R2*1BORR2(1) + R2*1PAY2(1) - R4*1BORR4(1)
     4  + 1BALSK(1) + (1.0+ALF12)*1EXS(1) = TQER(2)
      DO 70  J = 3, 6
      L = J - 1
      EQUATION   G*1BORR1(J) - G*1PAY1(J) + 1BORR2(J) - 1PAY2(J)
     1  + 1BORR3(J,J) - (1.0+R3)*1BORR3(J-1,J-1) + 1BORR3(J,J-1)
     2  - 1BORR3(J-1,J-2) - 1EXS(J) - 1BALSK(J) - DEL*1SMSLK1(J-1)
     3  - R2*1SMSLK2(J-1) - R4*1BORR4(1) + 1BALSK(J-1) + (1.0+ALF12)*1EX
     4S(J-1) = TQER(J)
   70 CONTINUE
      J = 7
      RALF46 = R4 + ALF6
      EQUATION   G*1BORR1(J) - G*1PAY1(J) + 1BORR2(J) - 1PAY2(J)
     1  + 1BORR3(J,J) - (1.0+R3)*1BORR3(J-1,J-1) + 1BORR3(J,J-1)
     2  - 1BORR3(J-1,J-2) - 1EXS(J) - 1BALSK(J) - DEL*1SMSLK2(J-1)
     3  - R2*1SMSLK2(J-1)                  + 1BALSK(J-1) + (1.0+ALF12)*1EX
     4S(J-1) - RALF6*1BORR4(1) = TQER(J)
      DO 72  J = 8, M
      EQUATION   G*1BORR1(J) - G*1PAY1(J) + 1BORR2(J) - 1PAY2(J)
     1  + 1BORR3(J,J) - (1.0+R3)*1BORR3(J-1,J-1) + 1BORR3(J,J-1)
     2  - 1BORR3(J-1,J-2) - 1EXS(J) - 1BALSK(J) - DEL*1SMSLK1(J-1)
     3  - R2*1SMSLK2(J-1) - RA*1BORR4(1) + 1BALSK(J-1) + (1.0+ALF12)*1EX
     4S(J-1) = TQER(J)
   72 CONTINUE
C
C                              OBJECTIVE FUNCTION
      DO 80  J = 1, 6
      EQUATION   GAMMA*1SMSLK1(J) + R2*1SMSLK2(J) + R3*1BORR3(J,J)
     1  + C32*1BORR3(J,J-1) + (R4+C42)*1BORR4(1)
     2  - ALF12*1EXS(J) - 1COST(J)
   80 CONTINUE
      RC = (R4+C42)*(1.0-ALF6)
      DO 82  J = 7, M
      EQUATION   GAMMA*1SMSLK1(J) + R2*1SMSLK2(J) + R3*1BORR3(J,J)
     1  + C32*1BORR3(J,J-1) +          RC*1BORR4(1)
     2  - ALF12*1EXS(J) - 1COST(J)
   82 CONTINUE
      EQUATION   (1.-ALF6)*1BORR4(1) - 1EXS(M) + 1OTSTD1 - 1OTSTD2
      CONS = (ALF10-ALF11)*(1.0-ALF6)
      EQUATION   SIGMA((K=1,M)  1COST(K))
     1             + CONS*1BORR4(1) + ALF11*1OTSTD2 + ALF9*1BORR3(M,M)
     2  + ALF9*1BORR3(M,M-1) + ALF8*1SMSLK2(M) + ALF7*1SMSLK1(M)
     3   - 1OBJECT
```

REFERENCES

1. Baumol, W.J., "The Transactions Demand for Cash: An Inventory Theoretic Approach." *Quarterly Journal of Economics*, November 1952.

2. Beranek, W., *Analysis for Financial Decisions*, Irwin, Homewood, Ill.: 1963.

3. Charnes, A., Cooper, W.W. and Ijiri, Y., "Breakeven Budgeting and Programming to Goals," *Journal of Accounting Research*, I, No. 1 Spring 1963, pp. 16-43.

4. Charnes, A., Cooper, W.W. and Miller, M.H., "Application of Linear Programming to Financial Budgeting and the Costing of Funds," *Journal of Business*, January 1959, reprinted in Ezra Solomon, ed., *The Management of Corporate Capital*; and W. Beranek, *Analysis for Financial Decisions*, Chapter XI.

5. Ijiri, Y., Levy, F.K. and Lyon, R.C., "A Linear Programming Model for Budgeting and Financial Planning," *Journal of Accounting Research*, I, No. 2, Autumn 1963, pp. 198-212.

6. Jacobs, D.P., "The Marketable Security Portfolios of Non-Financial Corporations: Investment Practices and Trends," *Journal of Finance*, September 1960.

7. Keynes, J.M., *The General Theory of Employment, Interest, and Money*, Harcourt, Brace & Co., New York, 1936.

8. Lutz, F.A. and Lutz, V., *Theory of Investment and the Firm*, Princeton University Press, Princeton, N.J., 1951.

The Analysis of Short-Term Cross-Border Financing Decisions

William R. Folks, Jr.
University of South Carolina

INTRODUCTION

Moving needed funds into and out of subsidiaries in countries where exchange regulations and balance of payments weakness are prevalent has always been much more of an art than a science. This paper is not intended to diminish the artistic component of this critical task, which consists in locating and defining the various and sometimes devious methods of inserting and extracting the right amount at the right time. Rather, it is sought to strengthen the skill of the *artiste* in determining which of several possible channels for funds flow should be used.

To provide a framework of practicality for the discussion to follow, suppose the corporate treasurer of XYZ Corporation needs to provide his subsidiary in the country of Parcheesi 10,000,000 Parcheesian rupees (Ru) for a one year period. The local treasurer of the Parcheesian subsidiary proposes that this be funded by a parent company loan of Ru 8,000,000 at 15% per annum and a parent guaranteed loan of $1,000,000 (Ru 1 = US $0.50) from the local branch of a U.S. bank. This funding proposal is referred to as Package 1. Upon checking with another banking connection, the treasurer finds that the possibility exists for the parent to engage in a link financing arrangement. The parent company places $5,000,000 on deposit at 4% per annum with the head office of the bank, whose branch in Parcheesi simultaneously loans the subsidiary Ru 10,000,000 at 21% per annum. This proposal is designated Package 2.

All loans and deposits under both financing packages are for a one year term, with interest payable at the end of the period. Both packages result in the provision of exactly Ru 10,000,000 to the subsidiary. Package 1, however, requires that the parent itself provide only $4,000,000, in contrast to the link financing alternative, which requires $5,000,000. The parent company will find whatever funding is required

---

Reprinted from FINANCIAL MANAGEMENT (Autumn 1976), pp. 19-27, by permission of the publisher and author.

in the Eurodollar market at 9% per annum. Interest income and foreign exchange gains are taxable, and interest income and foreign exchange losses are tax deductible for both the parent and the subsidiary; the marginal tax rate in the United States is assumed to be 50% and in Parcheesi, 10%. For purposes of exposition, the marginal tax rate on foreign source income to XYZ is the same as that on domestic source income, although the approach developed here is extended at a later point in the paper to handle differential tax rates. No market for the forward rupee exists, and thus neither XYZ nor its subsidiary may cover their loan positions by forward operations.

The basic decision problem thus becomes the selection of one of the two competing financing alternatives, and the primary factor complicating the problem is uncertainty about the rate of exchange at the maturity of the loan. Two different approaches may be taken for incorporating this uncertainty into the problem analysis. One analytical technique, suggested by de Faro and Jucker and Shapiro, among others, concentrates on first estimating the expected exchange rate that will prevail at the date of loan repayment, and then calculating the cost of each financing alternative at that exchange rate. The alternate technique suggested here, on the other hand, develops formulae that express the cost of each financing package as a function of the ending exchange rate. These formulae, which are usually linear, are used to calculate a "Breakeven Exchange Rate" (BER) at which the costs of the financing packages are equal. The selection of the appropriate financing package is then made by a comparison of the BER with the spot rate of exchange expected to prevail at the loan maturity date, calculated from the corporate treasurer's subjective probability distribution for that rate.

This BER methodology has been applied to the analysis of several isolated cross-border financing problems. Zenoff and Zwick develop most fully the basic concept of a breakeven rate in their analysis of a specific swap operation. Other analyses of the swap situation by McMillan and Weston and Sorge are based on consideration of the same problem structure but do not clarify the BER methodology as Zenoff and Zwick do. The author has developed a wide variety of breakeven formulae for various types of swap situations, as well as having applied the BER methodology to an analysis of the West German *Bardepot* requirements.

However, the applications of the BER methodology discussed above have been concerned primarily with the analysis of a specific type or class of short-term cross-border financing operations. Development of a general BER methodology applicable to a wide variety of such operations is the objective of this paper. Details of the methodology itself are developed using the example presented above, but the primary purpose of the paper is to acquaint managers with the range of problems BER attacks, and to give them an appreciation of the underlying implications of the method. Further, some precise concepts are developed for sensitivity analysis of decisions reached by BER, an aspect of the methodology not addressed in previous presentations. The concept of Expected Value of Perfect Information (EVPI) as derived from a BER analysis is discussed, and an evaluation of areas where BER should be applied is presented.

THE IMPACT AND MEASUREMENT OF EXCHANGE RATE UNCERTAINTY

One of the major advantages of the BER methodology is that it forces the financial decision-maker to incorporate explicitly into his analysis uncertainty about the spot exchange rate prevailing at the maturity date of the financing packages, a rate designated here by $\tilde{r}$. At the current spot rate of exchange r_0 = $0.50 (the price of 1 Parcheesian rupee), the parent provides in Package 1 the equivalent of $4,000,000 to fund the Ru 8,000,000 loan. A change in the exchange rate to $0.40, for example, alters the dollar equivalent of this loan to $3,200,000, an exchange loss of $800,000 before taxes. The effect of this change must be incorporated in the analysis of the cost of such loans. A recent empirical study by Jilling and Folks indicates that 17.8% of the 90 multinational companies furnishing information on this issue still do not incorporate anticipated exchange rate changes into their calculation of the cost of foreign currency borrowing. The lack of sophistication shown in this regard may perhaps be remedied by the development of a technique of analysis that specifically requires management's best quantification of its uncertainty about the exchange rate.

This quantification takes the form of a subjective probability distribution to be assessed on the future spot rate $\tilde{r}$. In this assessment the financial decision-maker (or his delegated currency forecaster) may utilize macroeconomic variables, such as relative inflation rates and interest rates; political variables, such as expressed exchange rate policies, impending critical elections or other governmental changes; inside information from financial and governmental sources; and a personal feel for the market in the particular currency. Techniques for the assessment of subjective probability distributions are found in Schlaifer, and one example of their application in exchange risk management is given by Wheelwright. The method of performing the assessment of the spot rate depends on the type of exchange rate policy practiced by the country whose rate is being forecast and the interaction of this system with the time horizon of the forecast. Under a par value type system with parity rate changes occurring rather infrequently when compared with the horizon of the forecast, one plausible method would be to assess the probabilities of a devaluation, no change in parity, and revaluation. Conditional probability distributions would be assessed on the actual value of the exchange rate given each of these 3 events. If the option to float the currency were deemed possible by the treasurer, it would be included along with the 3 other alternatives; and a distribution would be assessed on what the rate would be conditional upon floating. In any case, the marginal probabilities of the changes in exchange rate policies would be combined with the conditional probability distributions for $\tilde{r}$ to find the unconditional distribution required for analysis.

On the other hand, if the currency is presently floating and is expected to continue floating, a direct assessment is in order. If there exists a possibility of a return to a fixed rate system, the appropriate method might be to establish marginal probabilities for a continuation of the float and for return to fixed rates, followed by an assessment of conditional distributions for $\tilde{r}$ and their collapsing into an unconditional distribution.

Treatment for countries adopting a crawling peg system depends primarily on the frequency of adjustment and the time horizon of the forecast. Suppose, for example, Parcheesi devaluates its currency *vis-a-vis* the dollar at approximately two month intervals, with randomness present in both the size and timing of the devaluations. A probability distribution for the exchange rate prevailing 3 months into the future would be assessed by first determining a probability distribution on the number of devaluations (0, 1, 2, ...) that will occur over the 3 month period and subsequently assessing conditional distributions on the size of the devaluation. The process of determining an unconditional distribution on the exchange rate would be accomplished by combining these conditional distributions with the marginal distribution on the number of devaluations. The resultant distribution would be rather lumpy and multimodal in nature.

However, were the treasurer called on to assess a probability distribution for the spot rate in 5 years, it would clearly make little sense to adopt a two stage schema of assessment, since one would expect some 30 devaluations if current policies were maintained. To incorporate such a large number of possible devaluations into the analysis would require the assessment of an inordinate number of conditional distributions. Obviously, direct assessment of the distribution is preferable.

In the prototype problem of this paper, the time horizon of one year indicates six expected devaluations of the Parcheesian rupee. In such a borderline case, the treasurer might use either assessment scheme, although a rule of thumb might be to use a direct assessment technique if there are 4 or more devaluations expected over the time horizon of the forecast. In this case problem, the treasurer of XYZ Corporation adopts a direct assessment schema and assesses a smooth unimodal probability distribution on $\tilde{r}$, the spot exchange rate of the Parcheesian rupee one year from the present date.

All calculations involved in the decision-making and sensitivity analysis phase of the BER methodology can be carried out with any assessed subjective probability distribution using numerical approximation techniques. However, substantial reduction in the extent of the calculations involved can be realized if the distribution can be approximated by an analytic distribution. To ease the exposition in the remainder of the paper, therefore, it is assumed that XYZ's treasurer's subjective probability distribution for $\tilde{r}$ can be approximated by a normal probability distribution such that $E(r) = \$0.40$ and $\sigma_r = .03$.

Thus, XYZ's treasurer anticipates a substantial devaluation of the Parcheesian rupee against the dollar, with little or no chance of a maintenance of the existing rate.

EVALUATING THE COSTS OF FINANCING ALTERNATIVES

The next stage of BER analysis requires the development of formulae that express the cost of the competing financial packages as functions of the exchange rate $\tilde{r}$. For almost all financial packages, these functions are linear in $\tilde{r}$, although the methodology can be used in situations where the formulae are nonlinear.

Exhibit 1 presents a detailed schema for the evaluation of financing Package 1. Basically, XYZ's treasurer calculates (on an after tax basis) Interest Cost minus Interest Income plus Exchange Loss for every organizational unit involved in the financing transaction, and then aggregates these amounts for all units involved in the transaction.

All calculations in Exhibit 1 are finally expressed in dollar terms. The subsidiary has a dollar interest charge of \$80,000 on the parent-guaranteed loan and a rupee interest charge of Ru 1,200,000 on the direct loan to the parent. The value of this interest charge in dollars is dependent on $\tilde{r}$, the exchange rate prevailing at the time the payment is to be made. The subsidiary has no interest income, nor has it an exchange gain or loss on the rupee loan provided by the parent. It does have an exchange loss on the dollar portion of its financing, and, because it can deduct this loss for income tax reporting purposes in Parcheesi, the loss is reduced on an after-tax basis.

The parent, on the other hand, has \$360,000 in before-tax interest cost on its funding operations; Ru

EXHIBIT 1. Analysis for Financing Package 1 XYZ Corp.

I. Subsidiary (tax rate = 10%)

A. *Interest Cost*

Borrows Ru 8,000,000 @ 15% = Ru 1,200,000 = \$1,200,000 $\tilde{r}$

Borrows \$1,000,000 @ 8% = \$80,000

After Tax Interest Cost in Dollars = \$72,000 + 1,080,000 $\tilde{r}$

B. *Interest Income*

None

C. *Exchange Loss*

No Loss on Rupee Loan obtained by Subsidiary

Exchange Loss on Dollar Loan by Subsidiary

Borrow \$1,000,000 = Ru 2,000,000

Repay \$1,000,000 = Ru 1,000,000/$\tilde{r}$

Exchange Loss in Rupees = 1,000,000/$\tilde{r}$ - 2,000,000

After Tax Exchange Loss in Rupees = 900,000/$\tilde{r}$ - 1,800,000

After Tax Exchange Loss in Dollars = 900,000 - 1,800,000 $\tilde{r}$

D. *Total Cost to Subsidiary in Dollars*

(A - B + C) = 72,000 + 1,800,000 $\tilde{r}$ + 900,000 - 1,800,000 $\tilde{r}$ = \$972,000 - 720,000 $\tilde{r}$

II. Parent (tax rate = 50%)

A. *Interest Cost*

Borrows \$4,000,000 @ 9% = \$360,000

After Tax Interest Income in Dollars = \$180,000

B. *Interest Income*

Interest on Ru 8,000,000 @ 15% = Ru 1,200,000 = \$1,200,000 $\tilde{r}$

After Tax Interest Income in Dollars = 600,000 $\tilde{r}$

C. *Exchange Loss*

No Loss on Eurodollar Loan

Exchange Loss on Rupee Loan to Subsidiary

Loaned Ru 8,000,000 = \$4,000,000

Repaid Ru 8,000,000 = 8,000,000 $\tilde{r}$

Exchange Loss in Dollars = \$4,000,000 - \$8,000,000 $\tilde{r}$

After Tax Exchange Loss in Dollars = \$2,000,000 - \$4,000,000 $\tilde{r}$

D. *Total Cost to Parent in Dollars Dollars*

(A - B + C) = \$2,180,000 - \$4,600,000 $\tilde{r}$

III. *Total Cost to Corporation in Dollars*

(I, D + II, D) = \$3,152,000 - 5,320,000 $\tilde{r}$

1,200,000 in interest income, the dollar value of which is determined by the value of the rupee at the time of payment; and an exchange loss on the rupee loan it makes to its subsidiary. Interestingly enough, provided Parcheesi allows relatively free repatriation of funds, due to a higher U.S. tax rate XYZ captures a larger tax advantage by denominating the loan in rupees, albeit at the price of leaving more funds in Parcheesi.

The calculations for financing Package 2, as outlined in Exhibit 2, are quite straightforward, as neither XYZ nor its subsidiary suffers an exchange loss on the principal of the loan transaction. In the link financing arrangement, the parent borrows dollars, lends dollars to the bank, receives dollars back and repays dollars. The Parcheesian subsidiary borrows rupees and repays rupees. Yet the total cost to the corporation is *still* uncertain, as the dollar value of the interest payment fixed in the rupee loan is uncertain.

EXHIBIT 2. Analysis for Financing Package 2 XYZ Corp.

I. Subsidiary (tax rate = 10%)

A. *Interest Cost*

Borrow Ru 10,000,000 @ 21% = Ru 2,100,000 = \$2,100,000 $\tilde{r}$

After Tax Interest Cost in Dollars = \$1,890,000 $\tilde{r}$

B. *Interest Income*

None

C. *Exchange Loss*

None

D. *Total Cost to Subsidiary in Dollars*

(A - B + C) = 1,890,000 $\tilde{r}$

II. Parent (tax rate = 50%)

A. *Interest Cost*

Borrow \$5,000,000 @ 9% = \$450,000

After Tax Interest Cost in Dollars = \$225,000

B. *Interest Income*

Lend \$5,000,000 @ 4% = \$200,000

After Tax Interest Income in Dollars = \$100,000

C. *Exchange Loss*

None

D. *Total Cost of Parent in Dollars*

(A - B + C) = \$125,000

III. Total Cost to Corporation in Dollars

(I, D + II, D) = \$125,000 + 1,890,000 $\tilde{r}$

CALCULATING THE BREAKEVEN EXCHANGE RATE (BER)

The results of the previous phase of the BER analysis are linear functions of the period ending exchange rate $\tilde{r}$ for the cost of each alternate financing package. The BER methodology requires the determination of that rate of exchange r_b at which the cost of the two financing packages is the same. The Breakeven Exchange Rate (BER) for the XYZ problem is that rate r_b such that

$$(1) \quad 3{,}152{,}000 - 5{,}320{,}000r_b = 125{,}000 + 1{,}890{,}000r_b.$$

The term on the left of this expression is the cost of the direct parent loan and parent guaranteed bank loan of Package 1, while the term on the right is the cost of the link financing arrangement. The BER is found by solving Expression (1) for r_b; in this situation,

$$(2) \quad r_b = \frac{3{,}152{,}000 - 125{,}000}{1{,}890{,}000 - (-5{,}320{,}000)} = .4198.$$

This breakeven exchange rate deterines for XYZ's treasurer the range of possible future exchange rate levels for which each financing strategy would be superior. If the exchange rate for the Parcheesian rupee stays above .4198, the direct loan plus guarantee arrangement of Package 1 is superior. On the other hand, if the rate falls below .4198, Package 2 proves superior. This determination is made by a comparison of the coefficients of $\tilde{r}$ in the cost formulae for the two packages; the financial package with the larger coefficient for $\tilde{r}$ is assigned the range below r_b.

Here, 1,890,000 is greater than -5,320,000 and thus Package 2 is superior below .4198.

REACHING A DECISION USING BER

The treasurer of XYZ Corporation can now reach a decision in this specific problem situation. He must incorporate into his decision process 3 specific factors: (1) his uncertainty about the exchange rate, already assessed in the form of a probability distribution, (2) the cost of the two alternatives, expressed in the linear formulae developed above, and (3) his philosophy of decision-making under uncertainty. Suppose that XYZ has the philosophy of minimizing the expected cost of its financing. With such an attitude, the treasurer simply compares the expected exchange rate $E(r) = \$0.40$, as calculated from his probability distribution for $\tilde{r}$, with $r_b = \$0.4198$. Since $E(r) < r_b$ $(0.40 < 0.4198)$, the optimal financing package is the link arrangement of Package 2. If $E(r)$ had been greater than r_b, Package 1 would have been preferred. The actual expected cost of the chosen financing package can be found by substituting $r = \$0.40$ into the cost formula as given in Exhibit 2, and is \$881,000.

Of course, an alternate method of analysis would be to evaluate the cost of both strategies at $r = \$0.40$ and determine which package has the lower cost at this expected rate. It is to be noted that such a method requires the performance of all steps in the BER methodology except actual calculation of the BER. Thus, no real savings in effort can be made by its adoption. Furthermore, BER provides a rich structure for sensitivity analysis that is missing in the expected cost comparison approach. After a necessary development of the theory underlying BER, the XYZ problem sensitivity analysis will be discussed further.

THE THEORY OF THE BER METHODOLOGY

The BER methodology requires the development of cost functions for each financial package which are linear in the exchange rate that will prevail at the end of the financing period, the random variable $\tilde{r}$. Theoretically, $\tilde{r}$, the price of one unit of foreign currency in units of the parent's domestic currency, can range upward from 0 without bound, although for all practical purposes reasonable limits to $\tilde{r}$ can be assumed to exist.

α designates the vector of financial variables involved in the decision problem. Components of α in the prototype problem in this paper are the borrowing rate of each loan transaction; the rate of exchange existing at the time the financial decision is to be made; the rate of interest paid in the link financing by the linking bank to the parent; the proportion of Package 1 that is parent direct loan in rupees versus parent guaranteed loan in dollars; tax rates in each jurisdiction; and the total amount borrowed. Some of these components are fixed but mutable market prices; some are subject to managerial decision within limits, such as the rates of the loans and deposits; and some are strictly managerial decisions, such as the rate of interest charged by the parent to the subsidiary. These variables are catalouged and classified in Exhibit 3.

The cost of the first package is designated $\tilde{c}_1(\alpha, \tilde{r})$ and of the second, $\tilde{c}_2(\alpha, \tilde{r})$. We assume that the decision maker prefers a lower financing cost in all instances. The computation of the BER requires the discovery of that non-negative r_b which satisfies the equation $c_1(\alpha, r_b) = c_2(\alpha, r_b)$.

Since $\tilde{c}_1$ and $\tilde{c}_2$ are linear functions of $\tilde{r}$, then

(3) $\tilde{c}_1(\alpha, \tilde{r}) = K_1(\alpha) + k_1(\alpha)\tilde{r}$

EXHIBIT 3. Sensitivity Analysis for Financial Variables

Variable	Variable identification	Variable type	Initial value	Range
i_c	Interest rate on parent loan to subsidiary -- Package 1	Managerial	.15	$i_c \geq .0383$
i_G	Interest rate of parent-guaranteed negotiated bank loan to subsidiary -- Package 1	Negotiated	.08	$i_G \geq -.0789$
θ	Proportion of Package 1 funded by parent loan	Managerial	.80	$\theta \leq 1.285$
i_s	Interest rate on bank loan to subsidiary -- Package 2	Negotiated	.21	$i_s \leq .2497$
i_D	Interest rate on parent deposit at bank -- Package 2	Negotiated	.04	$i_D \geq -.0172$
$i_{\$}$	Interest rate on euro-dollar funding	Market-Environmental	.09	$i_{\$} \leq .3760$
r_o	Spot exchange rate for rupees	Market-Environmental	.50	$r_o \geq .4774$
t_p	Parcheesian tax rate	Government-Environmental	.10	$t_p \geq 1.6875$
t_{us}	U.S. tax rate on domestic source income	Government-Environmental	.50	$t_{us} \leq 1.2150$
t_f	U.S. tax rate on foreign source income	Government-Environmental	.50	$t_f \leq 1.1217$

Cost formula for Package 1:

$$c_1(\alpha,\tilde{r}) = V\{(1-\theta)(1-t_p)(1+i_G)+\theta(1-t_f)(1+i_{\$})+\frac{\tilde{r}}{r_o}(\theta(t_f-t_p)(1+i_c)-(1-t_p))\}$$

Cost Formula for Package 2:

$$c_2(\alpha,\tilde{r}) = V\{i_G(1-t_f)-i_D(1-t_{us})^a\frac{\tilde{r}}{r_o}(1-t_p)i_s\}$$

Breakeven Rate:

$$r_b = r_o\{\frac{(1-\theta)(1-t_p)(1+i_G)+\theta(1-t_f)-(1-\theta)(1-t_f)i_{\$}+i_D(1-t_{us})}{(1-t_p)(1+i_s)-\theta(t_f-t_p)(1+i_c)}\}$$

and

(4) $\tilde{c}_2(\alpha, \tilde{r}) = K_2(\alpha) + k_2(\alpha)\,\tilde{r}$

The functions $K_1(\alpha)$, $K_2(\alpha)$, $k_1(\alpha)$, and $k_2(\alpha)$ are functions of the financial variables of the decision problem whose values can be calculated prior to the calculation of the BER. In the XYZ problem discussed earlier, the values of these functions appear as the constants of the cost functions. Algebraic expressions for these cost functions are useful for sensitivity of the decision problem and are developed in Exhibit 3.

The strategies are numbered for convenience so that $K_1(\alpha) \geq K_2(\alpha)$. For a breakeven rate to exist, it is necessary that $k_1(\alpha) < k_2(\alpha)$. Otherwise, Strategy 2 dominates Strategy 1 for all positive values of r. The breakeven rate is,

(5) $r_b = \dfrac{K_1(\alpha) - K_2(\alpha)}{k_2(\alpha) - k_1(\alpha)}$.

For an Expected Monetary Value decision maker Strategy 1 is optimal if the expected exchange rate $E(r)$ is greater than r_b; if $E(r) < r_b$, Strategy 2 is optimal.

The BER methodology can be of some use in situations where the financial manager is averse to risk and wishes to use expected utility as a guide to action. It is supposed that the decision-maker has assessed a risk averse utility function on his criterion, usually borrowing cost. The variance of each strategy is

(6) $Var[\tilde{c}_1(\alpha, \tilde{r})] = [k_i(\alpha)]^2\, Var\ \tilde{r}$,

for $i = 1, 2$. A comparison of strategy variances can eliminate nonoptimal strategies in two cases as follows, depending on a comparison of the absolute values of $k_1(\alpha)$ and $k_2(\alpha)$.

Case I: $|k_1(\alpha)| < |k_2(\alpha)|$, and $E(r) > r_b$.
Strategy 1 is optimal.

Case II: $|k_1(\alpha)| > |k_2(\alpha)|$, and $E(r) < r_b$.
Strategy 2 is optimal.

These results follow from noting that under these conditions both the expected cost of the optimal strategy and the variance are smaller than the corresponding values of the nonoptimal strategy.

Since in the XYZ Corp. situation, $|k_1(\alpha)| = 5{,}320{,}000 > 1{,}890{,}000 = |k_2(\alpha)|$, the treasurer has found a strategy that is optimal for him provided that XYZ seeks to be either risk averse or risk neutral. Only if XYZ Corp. were risk seeking in the sense that it would be willing to take gambles with negative expected values could the decision to finance using the link financing arrangement be reversed. Thus, XYZ can be confident that its selection of Package 2 is correct without undertaking a direct assessment of its utility function for financing cost. Such an assessment, however, would have been necessary had $E(r) > .4198$ and Package 1 proved optimal on an expected cost basis.

SENSITIVITY ANALYSIS

The sensitivity analysis of a BER problem has two components: (1) an analysis of the sensitivity of the decision reached to the uncertainty in the exchange rate, and (2) an analysis of the sensitivity of the decision to changes in the financial parameters α.

Of the innumerable available ways of looking at the effect of uncertainty in the exchange rate on the financial decision, the author suggests the calculation of 3 values that have an easy interpretation for the financial decision-maker. First, the absolute difference between the expected spot rate $E(r)$ and the breakeven rate r_b, $|E(r) - r_b|$, gives an initial estimation of the sensitivity of the financing decision. In the

XYZ example, the treasurer could be .0198 too high in his estimate and still reach the correct decision according to his criterion. Expressed as a percentage of his estimate, his error in estimation could be 4.95% without affecting the correctness of his choice. Clearly, the higher the allowed percentage error of estimation is, the more confidence the decision-maker can place in his decision.

The allowed error of estimation, however, does not take into account the variability in exchange rate the decision-maker may have assessed. One method of remedying this defect is to determine the probability of correct decision. If the breakeven rate exceeds the expected spot rate, the probability of a correct decision is $P(\tilde{r} \leq r_b)$. If the breakeven rate is smaller than the expected spot rate, $P(\tilde{r} \geq r_b)$ is the appropriate value to compute. Computation of these probabilities requires the use of the entire probability distribution, and not just an estimation of the expectation. Under our supposition that the assessed probability distribution on $\tilde{r}$ is closely approximated by a normal distribution with a standard deviation $\sigma(r) = .03$, $P(\tilde{r} \leq .4198) = .7454$. The higher the probability of a correct decision, the more confidence the decision maker can place in his decision.

Even though the computation of the probability of a correct decision may indicate how sensitive the financial decision-maker's decision is to variability in his exchange rate forecast, it does not take into account the economics of the problem. A concept that does give some idea of the economic consequences of the uncertainty in $\tilde{r}$ is that of Expected Value of Perfect Information, how much the financial decision-maker would be willing to pay in order to ascertain in advance the exact value the exchange rate will assume. Pratt *et al.* [6] give details for computation of this value, either numerically, or by formulae, for specific probability distributions. If $E(r) \leq r_b$,

$$(7) \quad EVPI = [k_2(\alpha) - k_1(\alpha)]L^{(r)}(r_b),$$

and if $E(r) \geq r_b$,

$$(8) \quad EVPI = [k_2(\alpha) - k_1(\alpha)]L^{(l)}(r_b).$$

The functions $L^{(r)}(r_b)$ and $L^{(l)}(r_b)$ are the right and left linear loss functions,

$$(9) \quad L^{(r)}(r_b) = \int_{r_b}^{\infty} (r - r_b)f(r)dr$$

and

$$(10) \quad L^{(l)}(r_b) = \int_{0}^{r_b} (r_b - r)f(r)dr,$$

where $f(r)$ is the probability density function for $\tilde{r}$. If $\tilde{r}$ has a mass function, *EVPI* can be computed directly or a discrete version of $L^{(r)}(r_b)$ and $L^{(l)}(r_b)$ can be computed.

In the example XYZ, computation of *EVPI* is made easier by the assumption that $\tilde{r}$ has a probability distribution that is approximately normal. Then

$$(11) \quad EVPI = [k_2(\alpha) - k_1(\alpha)]\sigma(r)L_{N*}\{\frac{|E\ r - r_b|}{\sigma(r)}\}$$

where $L_{N*}(r)$ is the standardized normal linear loss function. Pratt *et al.* [6] provides tables for this function. Thus, for XYZ

$$(12) \quad EVPI = \{1{,}890{,}000 - (-5{,}320{,}000)\}$$

$$(.03)L_{N*}\{\frac{.0198}{.03}\}$$

$$= (7{,}210{,}000)(.03)(.1528)$$

$$= \$33{,}050.64.$$

Therefore, XYZ Corp. could expect to save $33,050.64 in financing cost if it had an exact forecast of the exchange rate for the Parcheesian rupee available in advance of its selection of a financing package.

The Expected Interest Cost of Uncertainty (EICU) is defined here as the Expected Value of Perfect Information divided by the dollar value of the funds requirement that calls for funding operations, expressed as a percentage. For XYZ, the EICU for the Parcheesian funds requirement of \$5,000,000 is 0.661%. EICU may be considered the ultimate measure of sensitivity of the financial decision to uncertainty about the exchange rate, since it incorporates both the entire spread of values of the probability distribution and the economics of the problem as expressed in the financing costs of the two strategies. The higher the interest cost of the uncertainty in the decision is, the more attention management should pay to further analysis of the decision problem. In fact, *EVPI* provides an upper limit to the amount of funds which should be expended strictly for elimination in uncertainty about $\tilde{r}$.

In addition to this powerful method for analyzing sensitivity to exchange rate uncertainty endemic to cross-border financing operation, the BER technique allows insight into the effect of changes in the other financial factors of the problem on the financing decision itself. Such an analysis first requires the redevelopment of the financing cost formulae for each package in a form where the financial factors appear as variables. A list of variables and the financing cost formulae for the XYZ example are given in Exhibit 3.

Sensitivity to components of the vector of financial variables α is then developed by a ranging operation similar to that used in sensitivity analysis of linear programming. The financial decision-maker seeks to determine a range of values for each component (or groups of components) such that his financing decision remains the same. Let us suppose, for example, that the expected exchange rate $E(r)$ is less than r_b. The financial decision-maker seeks to determine the change in variable i, δ_i such that the calculated breakeven rate remains above $E(r)$. In other words, the values δ_i are found such that

$$(13)\quad E(r) \leq \frac{K_1(\alpha_1,\ldots,\alpha_i+\delta_i,\ldots,\alpha_m)-K_2(\alpha_1,\ldots,\alpha_i+\delta_i,\ldots,\alpha_m)}{k_2(\alpha_1,\ldots,\alpha_i+\delta_i,\ldots,\alpha_m)-k_1(\alpha_1,\ldots,\alpha_i+\delta_i,\ldots,\alpha_m)}$$

If r_b is greater than $E(r)$ the inequality is reversed. Of course, ranging can be done on two or more variables simultaneously.

A complete set of ranges for the XYZ example is also given in Exhibit 3. Financial factors are classified either as (1) environmental, meaning they are determined externally to the company by government or market forces, (2) negotiated, in the sense that the factors are set by negotiation between XYZ and some other entity, or (3) managerial, indicating that they are determined primarily by XYZ management decision. The "Initial Value" column provides the value of the particular variable derived from the XYZ problem. The "Range" column gives the range of values for each variable for which the present financing decision remains optimal. Thus, as long as the interest rate on the parent rupee loan to the subsidiary (i_c) is set at 3.83% or more, XYZ will continue to use the link financing arrangment. No feasible change in the relative composition of Package 1 alone can alter the decision.

The sensitivity analysis can be used to indicate how management can redesign Package 1 to be more competitive. Management has some degree of control over the interest rate it charges its local subsidiary, and the analysis indicates the desirability of lowering this interest rate. Secondly, XYZ's treasurer may be able to substitute parent-supplied funds for the bank guaranteed loan. The sensitivity analysis does indicate that a shift in funding in this direction would be useful. While a reduction in the rate of interest on the parent-guaranteed portion of the package (i_G) would be helpful, an impossibly large reduction would be necessary to achieve optimality for Package 1, and thus, concentration of managerial effort on negotiating this rate downward would not be advisable.

The most sensitive part of the link financing package is the rate charged by the linking bank's subsidiary to XYZ's Parcheesian subsidiary (i_s). Any substantial increase in this rate would change the optimal decision. A negative rate on the parent deposit (i_D) would be required before XYZ would change its decision. Of the environmental variables, substantial changes in the tax structure and Eurodollar funding rate would be necessary before any change in funding pattern would occur, but a decrease in the spot exchange rate (r_o) of more than \$0.0226 before the implementation date would require a re-analysis of the decision. However, any change in r_o should trigger a reassessment of the probability distribution for $\tilde{r}$.

Managerially, XYZ's treasurer should initiate a restructuring of the details of Package 1, seeking to alter the terms as indicated by the sensitivity analysis. The restructured package might then by compared with the existing Package 2 for final decision.

AREAS OF APPLICATION OF BER METHODOLOGY

The BER methodology can be extremely useful for the analysis of cross-border financing. However, its use must be tempered by an appreciation of its limited area of applicability. Basically, BER is the preferred method of analysis when (1) the financing decisions are over a short-term, (2) the amount of funds committed are small compared to the total financial resources of the firm, and (3) the firm is severely restricted in, or precluded from use of, forward exchange markets.

The author believes strongly that the BER methodology should be applied only to financial decisions for a period of no more than one year, and that a more detailed uncertainty analysis be performed for longer term financing decisions. This conclusion is based first on the observation that a financial decision-maker's uncertainty about the exchange rate normally should increase (have greater variance) the farther out in time that uncertainty is assessed. Thus, decisions reached by BER are much more sensitive in the long term than in the short, and corresponding inspire less confidence. Secondly, BER considers two or more alternatives within a given existing pattern of financing. While this backgroup pattern of financing may remain stable over the short-run, and thus allow separate consideration of the two financing strategies, changes in the long-run financing pattern of the firm may introduce side-costs or side-benefits to one or another of the strategies not considered by the BER methodology.

A related recommendation is that BER be used on decisions of rather small scope relative to overall operations of the firm. BER is basically an expected monetary value methodology for decision-making. Managers may wish to use Expected Monetary Value as an approximate guide to action when consequences are small relative to their scope of operations. However, when the financing decision is large enough to affect the overall risk characteristics of the firm, a mean-variance or expected utility method of analysis is preferred.

When the firm has access to a viable market for forward exchange in the foreign currency, it is recommended that short-term financing decisions be based on a calculation of the after-tax covered cost of such borrowing. To borrow without cover is the equivalent of a covered loan and a speculative sale of the currency forward. Any borrowing that is not profitable on a covered basis should not be undertaken, since, in the absence of restrictions on entry into the forward market, a stochastically dominant position can be obtained by engaging in a speculative forward operation. Under these conditions, use of BER is not justified, since a superior analytical guide to action already is available. Nonetheless, adequate forward markets are not available in a number of currencies of importance to direct investors seeking short term funding; in particular, Jilling and Folks [4] report that exchange risk managers generally rate forward markets in the Australian dollar, Brazilian cruzeiro, Mexican peso, and South African rand (all currencies where major rate changes have been experienced in recent years or months) as inadequate. Thus, there exist a number of major direct investment areas where BER may prove useful.

One final word of warning with respect to BER is in order. If financing operations between the country of the parent and that of the subsidiary are relatively free, tax factors relatively equal, and access to local and parent country capital markets generally unrestricted, the relative interest rates on funds of equal maturity in the two countries may be adjusted by market action to reflect prospective currency rate changes in an efficient manner. Under these conditions, great divergence of the breakeven rate r_b from the expected rate $E(r)$ must be justified. One plausible explanation of such a divergence would be that the structure of the corporation provides special financing sources or channels for fund transfer not available to other transactors. Otherwise, the divergence is based on a difference in opinion between the market and the individual corporation's management on the future movement of exchange rates. Corporate financial management would thus be in the position of trying to outguess the market.

However, barriers against access to and free transfer of funds are endemic, and the discovery of more than one alternate financing channel may be a triumph of financial artistry. When such a triumph has been achieved, the BER methodology can be of assistance. The methodology is simple, applicable to a wide range of financing problems, and amenable to illuminating sensitivity analysis. The object of this paper has been to acquaint decision-makers with the requirements, operations, limitations, and possibilities of a decision technique which should be among the capabilities of the financial manager of the multinational corporation.

REFERENCES

1. Clovis de Faro and James Jucker, "The Impact of Inflation and Devaluation on the Selection of an International Borrowing Source," *Journal of International Business Studies* (Fall 1973), pp. 97-104.

2. William R. Folks, Jr., "Break-even Exchange Rates: Some General Results," *Proceedings* of the 1973 Southeast Chapter of the American Institute for Decision Sciences, pp. 349-350.

3. William R. Folks, Jr., "The Theory of Foreign Currency Swaps," *Proceedings of the 1972 Midwest Conference of the American Institute for Decision Sciences*, pp. J-7 through J-8.

4. Michael Jilling and William R. Folks, Jr., "Practices of American Corporations in Foreign Exchange Risk Management: A Statistical Summary," Working Paper 1, Foreign Exchange Risk Management Project, University of South Carolina.

5. Claude McMillan, "The Swap as a Hedge in Foreign Exchange," *California Management Review* (Summer 1962), pp. 57-65.

6. John W. Pratt, Howard Raiffa, and Robert Schlaifer, *Introduction to Statistical Decision Theory*, New York, McGraw-Hill Book Company, 1965.

7. Robert Schlaifer, *Analysis of Decisions under Uncertainty*, New York, McGraw-Hill Book Company, 1969.

8. Alan C. Shapiro, "Evaluating Financing Costs for Multinational Subsidiaries," *Journal of International Business Studies* (Fall 1975), pp. 25-32.

9. J. Fred Weston and Bart W. Sorge, *International Managerial Finance*, Homewood, Illinois, Richard D. Irwin, Inc., 1972.

10. Steven C. Wheelwright, "Applying Decision Theory to Improve Corporate Management of Currency-Exchange Risks," *California Management Review* (Summer 1975), pp. 41-49.

11. David B. Zenoff and Jack Zwick, *International Financial Management*, Englewood Cliffs, New Jersey, Prentice-Hall, Inc., 1969.

SECTION VIII
Planning and Controlling Working Capital

Planning and controlling are key functions in the process of management. With respect to the working capital of the firm, planning is necessary for each of the current assets and current liabilities. Planning should also reflect the interrelationships between the different working capital accounts. Controlling is necessary to ensure that over time the firm consistently moves toward its expressed goals. This final section of the book contains eight papers which in various ways deal with the planning and controlling of working capital.

Welter (Reading 39) suggests a procedure in which management can evaluate alternative ways of reducing total working capital. The procedure is based on a recognition of the several delays that are inherent in the process of producing and distributing goods and services. For an hypothetical manufacturing firm, Welter develops a delay center model consisting of different stages of inventory, stages of manufacturing and assembly, and the final stage of accounts receivable. By specifying the average delay of dollars, together with a measure of value added for each stage, he calculates an overall index of working capital for the firm. This index can be checked systematically to see where in the total process the firm can make effective reductions in its working capital requirements.

A practical approach to short-range financial planning is suggested by Maier and Vander Weide (Reading 40). They develop a linear programming model which determines the optimal portfolio of investments when the firm has excess funds, and the optimal financing mix when there is a shortage of short-term funds. Inputs to the model include cash flow projections, borrowing limitations, descriptions of available marketable securities, and interest rate projections. Because the model can be used on a time-sharing computer system, it is particularly amenable to sensitivity analyses by the financial manager.

Van Horne (Reading 41) proposes a probabilistic forecast of

the cash flows of the firm as a way of making return-risk tradeoffs. He discusses the liquid assets (cash plus equivalents) of the firm, the maturity schedule of the firm's debt structure, and how they are interrelated. By varying the assumptions about sales, collections, purchasing, and so forth, management can determine the relative probabilities of different levels of liquid assets. Since different debt structures cause different costs to the firm, it is possible to make comparisons between the costs of financing and the chances of inadequate liquid assets as a result of that financing.

Smith (Reading 42) shows how parallel projections of monthly borrowing requirements and monthly before-tax profits for the firm provide management with a useful framework for making tradeoffs between liquidity and profitability. The framework also can be used to reflect the uncertainty of future sales, which is the variable that triggers both the cash budget and the projected income statement. In addition, the framework allows sensitivity analyses of working capital policies such as receivables, inventory, and payables.

The next two papers focus on the multiple goals of the firm relative to the management of working capital. Sartoris and Spruill (Reading 43) explain how goal programming allows management to make decisions relative to a set of desired goals. The objective function in a goal programming formulation measures the absolute deviations of each goal from its desired level. The authors illustrate the use of goal programming with an example in which the four goals of the firm include profit for the period, ending cash level, ending current ratio, and ending quick ratio.

Krouse (Reading 44) suggests a different method whereby management can make explicit tradeoffs between the several specified goals of the firm. The method involves hierarchical optimization of a set of firm goals ranked in order of their importance. After the optimal level of the first goal is determined by a mathematical programming approach, a level of satisfaction for that goal is identified, and the second goal is optimized. The process of optimizing one goal subject to the satisfaction of a prior goal continues in a sequential process. While the satisficing levels are determined arbitrarily by managers, it is possible to see the relative tradeoffs at each step in the process. Krouse illustrates the method in an example where profitability and liquidity are two of the three firm goals.

Gentry (Reading 45) discusses a simulation approach in which working capital planning is explicitly integrated into the capital budgeting process of the firm. In each simulation run, values are drawn from the probability distributions for each random variable, the values are interrelated via a set of simultaneous equations, and measures of net present value and rate of return are calculated. By repeating this procedure, distributions for the summary measures of profitability are created. Measures of net present value and rate of return reflect both the benefits and costs of the firms operations, as augmented by the benefits and costs of the working capital that is necessary to sustain those operations. Forecasting errors and inflationary conditions are key factors in how working capital considerations are part of the total investment process.

In contrast to the mathematical programming and simulation approaches to working capital planning, Smith (Reading 46) considers working capital from the standpoint of management control. The idea is to view each change in a working capital account as a corrective action designed to move the firm toward its expressed goals. By examining the benefits and costs associated with each working capital change, a measure of return on investment can be determined. As a result, working capital changes can be viewed as investment projects alongside of other capital budgeting projects. Working capital management thus can be viewed as an integral part of overall financial management, rather than as just a series of independent technologies.

READING 39

How to Calculate Savings Possible Through Reduction of Working Capital

Paul Welter
Olivetti Company
Sistemi Organizzativi S.p.A., Milano, Italy

In many companies, working capital represents an investment superior to investments in fixed assets. (As used here, working capital means the sum of company current assets; i.e., inventiries, current accounts receivables, and liquid assets.) With the increased difficulty of procuring capital for further investments, companies are endeavoring to trim their investments as much as possible and, in order to do so, are asking critical questions regarding the amount of working capital needed and the financial convenience of reducing working capital. It is in answering these questions that the problem of calculation procedure becomes apparent. The purpose of this article is to discuss this calculation procedure.

The starting point is the concept that working capital is the result of a *delay* between the moment an expenditure for the purchase of raw material is made and the moment in which payments are received for the sale of the finished product. Working capital, thus, is the sum of all those expenditures, direct and indirect, which must be made prior to collecting sales revenues.

This being so, working capital originates in "delay centers" located throughout production and marketing functions. In the production function, delay depends mostly on the amount of stock of raw materials, semi-finished and finished goods, and the length of the production cycle. In the marketing function, it depends primarily on the stock of finished products and on payment delays granted to customers.

The delay basic to the formation of working capital may be of two types:

✓ Objective delay: originating from an objective fact, such as the production cycle, which in turn is determined by the production cycles of each single division.

✓ Subjective delay: originating from a decision. This type of delay depends on the quality and quantity of information available on the basis of which the delay is decided; in most cases, it constitutes a security margin

Reprinted from FINANCIAL EXECUTIVE, Vol. 38, No. 10 (October 1970), pp. 50-58, by permission of the publisher.

determined by the manager on his evaluation of inherent risk (for example, the independence of the stock of raw material) and on a commercial necessity (payment terms granted to customers).

Through improving the information on which the decision defining the subjective delay is based, it is possible to reduce risk and consequently to reduce the security margin and the working capital.

A better decision may be the result of two major factors: improved professional ability of the administrative staff, and more rapid and more precise data processing through computers.

These two factors are closely allied. In fact, the computer can give valid information only if the problems it is engaged in solving have been defined with sufficient clarity. The clear definition of a problem and the determination of information fundamental to a correct decision are in direct proportion to the professional quality of the management.

Naturally, more precise data elaboration is not a cost-free matter; it involves expenses both for the availability of data processing equipment and for the availability of prepared management staff (number of staff members, instruction courses, reward system and level).

The following will attempt to outline a way to calculate the savings a company can make from a reduction of its working capital as a consequence of improved information. Should these savings prove greater than the expense required to effect the information improvements, then the expenses constitute a profitable investment.

The first step in organizing the calculation is to determine what are the "delay centers." Then, the amount of added value in each delay center must be indicated (this added value refers to direct and indirect expenses and may be expressed in percentage of list price or sales).

Let us consider a simple production-sales process which includes the following phases:

- ✓ purchase and storage of raw materials
- ✓ manufacture of semi-finished products
- ✓ storage of semi-finished products
- ✓ assembly of semi-finished products
- ✓ storage of finished products
- ✓ sales with granting of payment delays

Each of the above phases is a delay center. We can indicate the average lay-over of stock of raw material, semi-finished products, the length of the production cycle and of the payment delays granted.

In each delay center some value is added, and the sum of these added values gives the sales price of a particular product. Considering each delay center individually, we have:

1. <u>Stock of raw material</u>: The actual cost of the raw materials used to make the invoiced product is added value.

2. <u>Semi-finished products</u>: The direct expenditures made in this phase (e.g., labor) is added value. No consideration should be made of various depreciation and overhead expenses. In fact, if we should pose as an extreme hypothesis the reduction of the production cycle to one day, we would practically eliminate the delay center, which means that for a continuous production cycle no investment in direct expenditure would be necessary in this center. This is not true for investments in capital goods, the cost of which is charged to the various products by means of depreciation (both on the basis of time and quantities produced); the investments in capital goods are not affected by the length of the various delays. This reasoning holds true for overhead expenses as well.

3. <u>Stock of semi-finished products</u>: No value added, as there is no direct expenditure made in this delay center.

4. <u>Assembly</u>: As for the manufac-

Exhibit I

Delay Centers	Costs Borne by Delay Centers	Costs in % of Sales
1. Stock of raw material	Raw material	10%
	Warehouse management	1
2. Manufacture of semi-finished products	Personnel	17
	Depreciation	8
	General production expenses	2
3. Stock of semi-finished products	Warehouse management	2
4. Assembly	Personnel	15
	Depreciation	15
	General assembly expenses	3
5. Stock of finished products	Warehouse management	2
	Total production expenses	75%
6. Accounts receivables	Sales expenses Financial expenses Overhead Profit	25%
	Value of invoice	100%

ture of semi-finished products, the added value is constituted by the direct expenditures only.

5. Stock of finished products: No added value.

6. Accounts receivables (resulting from payment delays): The added value here equals the difference between the final invoice value and the sum of the added values of the other delay centers. In this center, it is actually not a question of avoided or reducing an investment by reducing the delay, but rather of accelerating the collection on sales, which, for the calculation of the economic consequences of reducing delays and reducing working capital, is really the same thing.

EXAMPLE

To illustrate, let us consider the situation regarding Company ABC's actual conditions as put forth in Exhibit I.

The distribution of costs may be made according to various criteria, depending on company organization (standard costs, profit centers, direct costing, etc.). Yet it is consistently true that each center is burdened with the direct expenses which actually arise in it; the different accounting concepts are concerned only with the distribution criteria of the indirect costs.

In order to calculate the working capital of the situation under consideration, we should complete the above information by indicating the *average delays* in each center and giving the value added in the form of *direct expenses* (Exhibit II).

We consider that the addition of the value to the semi-finished products center and to the assembly center occurs uniformly over the entire production cycle, which means that the moment of the addition occurs at mid-cycle. For stocks and accounts, this moment falls at the beginning of the delay period.

With relatively stable sales, the

Exhibit II

Delay Centers	Average Delay	Added Value (in % of sales)
1. Stock of raw material	5 months	10%
2. Manufacture of semi-finished products	1 month	17
3. Stock of semi-finished products	3 months	--
4. Assembly	1 month	15
5. Stock of finished produts	4 months	--
6. Accounts receivables	5 months	58
Total Delay	19 months	100%

Exhibit III

Added Value		Time between moment of charging added value and collection on sales (in months)		Working Capital
10	x	19	=	190.0
17	x	13.5	=	229.5
15	x	9.5	=	142.5
58	x	5	=	290.0
Profit & Overhead				852.0

required working capital can be calculated by multiplying the added value of each center with the time lapse which separates the moment of the addition of this value from the moment of collection on sales. The value added in each center is the amount of direct expense made during the same time unit used for defining the various delays; the exception is made by the delays in payments where added value is considered the difference between the forecasted sales during one time unit and the sum of all the direct expenses already considered (Exhibit III).

The annual sales to be put in relation to the working capital (852) equals the number of times that the time unit used for measuring the delay goes into one year, multiplied by the expected sales during one time unit. In our example, since the month is the time unit and the monthly sales equal 100, the annual sales to consider is:

$$12 \times 100 = 1{,}200.$$

We calculate the following ratio:

$$\frac{\text{Annual sales}}{\text{Working capital}} = \frac{1{,}200}{852} = 1.41$$

On the basis of this ratio, the required working capital for sales of $123 million for Company ABC, which has the delay characteristics indicated in our example, would be:

$$\frac{123{,}000{,}000}{1.41} = 87{,}234{,}000.$$

ALTERNATIVE A

Now let us suppose that, after more precise information has been made available, Company ABC has the possibility of reducing the various delays in the following manner (naturally, the added values for each delay center remain constant) (Exhibit IV).

The working capital resulting from this situation is calculated as follows:

Exhibit IV

Delay Centers	Average Delay (in months)	Added Value (in % of sales)
1. Stock of raw material	4 (rather than 5)	10%
2. Manufacture of semi-finished products	1 month	17
3. Stock of semi-finished products	2 (rather than 3)	--
4. Assembly	1 month	15
5. Finished products stock	3 (rather than 4)	--
6. Accounts receivables	4 (rather than 5)	58
	15 (rather than 19)	100%

Exhibit V

Delay Centers	Average Delay (in months)	Added Value (in % of sales)
1. Stock of raw material	7 (rather than 5)	10%
2. Manufacture of semi-finished products	2 (rather than 1)	17
3. Stock of semi-finished products	4 (rather than 3)	--
4. Assembly	1 month	15
5. Stock of finished products	2 (rather than 4)	--
6. Accounts receivables	3 (rather than 5)	58
	19 months	100%

10 x 15 = 150.0
17 x 10.5 = 178.5
15 x 7.5 = 112.5
58 x 4 = 232.0
673.0

$$\frac{\text{Annual sales}}{\text{Working capital}} = \frac{1,200}{673} = 1.78$$

On the basis of the above ratio resulting from a change in the various delays, the working capital required for Company ABC would be:

$$\frac{123,000,000}{1.78} = 69,100,000.$$

The difference between this result and the working capital determined in the basic situation is:

69,100,100 - 87,234,000 = -18,134,000,

showing a 21 percent reduction of the working capital of the basic situation.

If Company ABC has a cost of capital of 12 percent, the savings--or increase in net profit--resulting from this reduction in working capital is:

18,134,000 x 0.12 = 2,176,000,

that is, *1.77 percent of annual sales.*

ALTERNATIVE B

In this alternative, Company ABC does not manage to reduce the global delay of 19 months with respect to the basic situation, but manages only a redistribution of the global time lapse among the various delay centers, as in Exhibit V.

The calculation of the working capital is made as above:

10 x 19 = 190
17 x 11 = 187
15 x 5.5 = 82.5
58 x 3 = 174
633.5

$$\frac{\text{Annual sales}}{\text{Working capital}} = \frac{1,200}{633.5} = 1.89$$

$$\frac{123{,}000{,}000}{1.89} = 65{,}079{,}000$$
(working capital).

The difference between this result and the working capital of the basic situation is:

65,079,000 - 87,234,000 = -22,155,000,

showing a reduction of 25.4 percent on the working capital of the basic situation.

With a cost of capital of 12 percent, the savings in working capital made through alternative B can be translated in net profit of:

22,155,000 x 0.12 = 2,657,000

that is, *2.16 percent of annual sales*.

CONCLUSIONS

From the above, we can see that, not only is working capital determined by the length of the global delay, but that it is also highly influenced by the distribution of this delay among the single delay centers.

In Alternative A and B, we have assumed a variation in the single delays as a consequence of availability of improved information. As mentioned before, the improvement of information is not gratuitous; its cost is presumably low for reducing too great a delay, but it becomes increasingly expensive with each successive marginal improvement. Attention must naturally be focused on the breakeven point; in other words, the point at which the savings from a reduction of working capital equals the cost (of information processing) which made this savings possible.

READING 40

A Practical Approach to Short-Run Financial Planning

Steven F. Maier
Duke University

James H. Vander Weide
Duke University

INTRODUCTION

Efficient management of the short-run investment/financing portfolio can often generate a significant improvement in a firm's return on investment.[1] Commercial banks, public accounting firms, and cash management consulting firms now offer a variety of computer aids designed to improve short-run financial decision-making, such as information on bank cash balance reports, current interest and foreign exchange rates, lock-box collections, and bank disbursements. The model described here improves the entire planning process by integrating cash forecasting and optimization models with the newly available reporting systems.

The financial manager's short-run portfolio problem was first modeled as a linear program by Robichek, Teichroew, and Jones [6] in 1965. The linear programming model was later expanded by Mao [2], Orgler [4], and Pogue and Bussard [5] to include the possibility of unequal time periods, additional deterministic constraints, and chance constraints. Recently, Srinivasan [7] and Zionts [8] have investigated the use of more efficient solution techniques based on the special structure of one version of the model.

Although linear programming models expand the ability of the cash manager to evaluate alternative short-run financial strategies, they are often extremely cumbersome to use. According to Orgler [3], a linear programming model of the firm's short-run portfolio problem will typically include 300 to 500 constraints and 2,000 to 4,000 variables. Such large models are not only expensive in computer time, but they also require a large amount of data input. Furthermore, the cash manager may often find it difficult to use and interpret models of this complexity. This would appear to make

[1] A good discussion of the potential benefits from agressive portfolio management is contained in "Cash Management" [1].

Reprinted from FINANCIAL MANAGEMENT (Winter 1978), pp. 10-16, by permission of the publisher and authors.

current linear programming models inappropriate for the rapid analysis required fo financial decision-makers.

This paper describes a linear programming model of the short-run financial/investment decision that we feel overcomes these difficulties. Our short-run financial planning model is designed for non-technical users; it is readily available on a world-wide time sharing computer network.[2] The model is designed to provide: rapid input of all necessary user-supplied data, maximum interaction between the user and the model, and output reports that the financial manager can easily interpret. With the aid of this model, the financial officer can plan and execute short-run financial decisions in a matter of minutes.

THE NATURE OF THE PLANNING PROBLEM

The nature of the short-run financial planning problem can be illuminated by the schematic diagram shown in Exhibit 1. The circles in the diagram represent the time period in the firm's planning horizon. Time periods may be measured in days, weeks, months, or any combination of them. It would not be unreasonable, for instance, to have a planning horizon consisting of five daily time periods, three weekly periods, and then five monthly periods.

The arrows at the bottom of the diagram represent the firm's projected cash flows. In this example, the firm expects a net cash inflow of $1,000,000 in Period 1, net outflows of $350,000 in Periods 2 and 3, and net inflows of $200,000 in Periods 4 and 5. Because sources and uses of funds must be equal in every period, the net cash flows indicated by these arrows constrain the firm's short-run financial activities. The firm can invest no more than $1,000,000 in Period 1, must plan to have $350,000 available in cash in Periods 2 and 3, and so on. (Although the diagram has been drawn to depict investment of funds, the model allows both investment and financing opportunities.)

Exhibit 1. THE SHORT-RUN FINANCIAL PLANNING PROBLEM

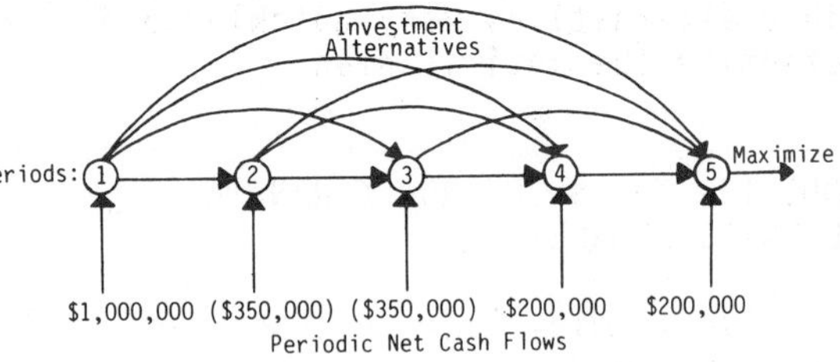

While the arrows at the bottom of the diagram represent externally-generated cash flows, the arrows in the body of the diagram represent all the possible ways the financial manager can choose to invest funds over time. The horizontal arrows, for instance, represent the conservative policy of always investing in a single-period instrument, such as a repurchase agreement. Although this policy assures that the firm will meet its second and third period financial requirement, it very likely will not maximize the rate of return on investment. The uppermost arrow, connecting Periods 1 and 5, represents investment in an instrument with a four-period maturity. If the firm invests $1,000,000 in this instrument at Period 1, it will be forced to borrow to meet the financial requirements of the intervening Periods 2 and 3.

Which investment policy should the firm follow? The answer depends on the magnitude of both current and projected interest rates. Given these rates, the firm could evaluate the total investment return associated with each feasible plan, choosing the one with the highest return. This will be a difficult task in most realistic situations, simply because

[2] The program is available as part of Chemical Bank's CHEMLINK cash management Product System.

there are very many possible plans. A primary virtue of a computerized short-run financial planning model is that it can search the set of possible alternatives very quickly to determine the optimal plan.

MODELING THE SHORT-RUN FINANCIAL PLANNING PROBLEM

Our primary goal is to develop a user-oriented tool for the cash manager. Any model that satisfies this goal should be easily accessible (i.e., no waiting for the computer staff to get to our job), allow rapid input of all necessary data, provide easily interpretable reports, and capture the essence of the short-run financial planning problem described above.

Mathematical Formulation

To meet the stipulation that the input data requirements be modest, it is desirable to use a relatively simple model formulation. One possibility is a network model of the type proposed by Srinivasan [7] and Zionts [8]. Network models, however, are inflexible with respect to the kinds of financial constraints they allow. We therefore elected to use a standard linear programming model along with a sophisticated matrix generator to conserve valuable computer storage. One virtue of a matrix generator is its ability to translate the data input from a very user-oriented form to the equations required by the linear program. A similar report generator handles the translation from the linear programming output to the user reports.

The formulation we chose seeks to maximize the horizon value of the short-term portfolio, subject to a sources equal uses requirement and a limited number of user-specified linear constraints on the dollar amounts invested in various combinations of financial instruments.

In symbols, the formulation is:

Maximize $Z =$

$$\sum_{j=1}^{J}\sum_{i=1}^{T-1} a^j_{iT}\cdot X^j_{iT} - \sum_{k=1}^{K}\sum_{i=1}^{T-1} b^k_{iT}\cdot Y^k_{iT}$$

subject to

$$\sum_{j=1}^{J}\sum_{i=1}^{t-1} a^j_{it}\cdot X^j_{it} - \sum_{j=1}^{J}\sum_{i=t+1}^{T} X^j_{ti} + \sum_{k=1}^{K}\sum_{i=t+1}^{T} Y^k_{ti}$$
$$-\sum_{K=1}^{K}\sum_{i=1}^{t-1} b^k_{it}\cdot Y^k_{it} = e_t \quad t = 1,2,\ldots,T$$

$$\sum_{i=1}^{T}\sum_{t=1}^{T}\left(\sum_{j=1}^{J} c^{jl}_{it}X^j_{it} + \sum_{k=1}^{K} d^{kl}_{it}Y^k_{it}\right)$$
$$= f_l \text{ for } l = 1,\ldots,L.$$

where

X^j_{it} = total dollars invested in security j at decision point i and maturing in period t;

Y^k_{it} = total dollars borrowed from source k at decision point i that must be repaid in period t;

a^j_{it} = principal plus interest received in period t on a dollar invested in security j in period i;

b^k_{it} = principal plus interest due in period t on a dollar borrowed from source k in period i;

e_i = cash requirement in period i. A negative number implies a cash inflow. (Note: this would be net of any compensating balance requirements needed to support lines of credit.);

c^{jl}_{it}, d^{kl}_{it}, f_l = user-specified constants.

Discrete Time Periods

The model user must specify both the length and number of the time periods in his planning horizon. Once these are set, the model assumes that all decisions occur at the beginning of a period. Unfortunately, financial instruments come in a wide variety of maturities, and it is not always possible to choose periods in such a way that all instrument maturity dates coincide with decision points.

To allow for this possibility, we have incorporated two additional assumptions in the model. On the investment side, we assume that any dollars received between decision points from maturing securities are reinvested at the daily repurchase agreement rate, until the next decision is made. On the borrowing side, we require that funds be available on, or before, the due date. Thus, the dollars necessary for repayment of loans are added to the requirement of the preceding decision point and then are invested at a daily rate until they are actually needed. Although the above assumptions are somewhat arbitrary, they are necessary in order to provide flexibility in the length of the time periods and the types of investment instruments.

Finite Horizon

In a world of upward sloping yeild curves, there are only two reasons why the linear programming model will ever select short-term investments. First, the cash manager may predict that interest rates will soon rise, allowing a higher total return to be earned with an initial short-maturity investment and reinvestment at the higher rates. Second, the cash manager may have a net requirement for funds in the near future. Since neither of these factors is relevant for post-horizon time periods, the model will often leave the financial officer with an illiquid portfolio by selecting long maturity investment instruments for decision periods at or near the horizon. If the horizon is relatively distant and the manager intends to implement only the first period recommendation before again solving the model, the "finite horizon" problem can be safely ignored. Where this is not the case, the user can handle the horizon problem by assessing an interest penalty that is proportional to the length of time that a security is held beyond the horizon point. Thus, the interest penalty is most severe for long-term investments, which the model would otherwise have selected.

User Orientation

The short-run financial planning model was especially designed to be user-oriented. The five principal data requirements are 1) number and duration of investment periods, 2) cash flow projection, 3) borrowing limitations, 4) instrument descriptions, and 5) interest rate projection. Since data from previous runs can be stored, the model is especially easy to use once the first case is run, because only data *changes* need be entered on subsequent runs. The optimal short-run plan is reported through a series of financial statements showing the amounts of each instrument bought, sold, and currently held during each period. Because data are easy to enter and solutions are reported rapidly, the user is encouraged to test the implications of various future economic decisions through a series of "what if" questions.

Model Specifications

The short-term financial planning model has the following characteristics: 1) The model accepts up to 25 planning periods. The user can specify the length of each period; 2) The model permits the user to specify a borrowing limitation, which can vary from period to period, on his or her line of credit; 3) The model will accommodate up to 15 investment or financing instruments, each of which can have a unique maturity and yield; 4) The yields on investment instruments can be modified over time via separately specified interest rate projections; and 5) A special feature controls investments that may extend beyond the planning horizon. The user may either entirely disallow such investments, or permit them but extract an interest penalty.

The output from the model gives three sets of information for each time period: maturing securities, new security purchases, and current security holdings. Each of these information sets is given as of the beginning of each investment period. The user has the option to delete any portion of the output not required.

The output also contains a marginal short-term investment rate analysis. This incremental analysis indicates the value of any additional funds the firm can make available for investment in period t, or, when the firm is projecting a net cash outflow in a period, the value of reducing this cash outflow. Such information can help the firm decide whether it should expedite some cash inflows or postpone the payment of specific payable items.

Potential Users

The short-run financial planning model is a potentially useful tool for either the net borrower or the net investor of short-term funds. For a firm that is a net borrower, the model is most useful for analyzing the economic tradeoffs in borrowing long vs. short, as well as the sensitivity of this maturity decision to interest rate fluctuations. For a firm that is a net investor, the model with quantify the added return from investments with greater risk, such as Eurodollar C.D.s, and examine the benefits of longer term investments, such as 180-day C.D.s, compared to a simple policy of rolling over short-term repurchase agreements.

Two conditions determine whether the model will add sufficient additional precision to financial decision-making to justify its cost. The first is rather obvious: the firm must have a large enough short-term investment/borrowing portfolio so that a savings of 5 to 10% will be significant. The second is more subtle: since the model depends on a firm's ability to project its cash flows, a firm that cannot forecast cash flows with reasonable accuracy will not find the model useful. In practice, this consideration depends on both the industry in which the firm operates and the quality of the accounting and information systems available to the treasurer.

The authors have worked with several medium-sized utilities that satisfy both conditions. Over the course of a year, the firms are net short-term borrowers of about \$60 to \$90 million. They rely strongly on the commercial paper market to satisfy their borrowing needs, but they are never sure what maturity paper it is best to float. In this case, the model is used to evaluate the risk-return tradeoff associated with various maturity strategies.

Example

The examples shown in Exhibit 2 demonstrates some of the capabilities of the short-term financial planning model. The example contains two 7-day time periods, followed by two 14-day time periods, and finally three 28-day time periods. At the beginning of each period, the firm is allowed to borrow up to \$2,000,000 from its line of credit or to sell 30-day maturity commercial paper. With its excess cash, the firm can invest in a 30-, 60-, or 90-day C.D. or in an over-night repurchase agreement. During the first two periods the firm expects cash inflows totaling \$3,400,000, with a net cash outflow of \$5,200,000 in the third period. Interest rates over the planning period are anticipated to fall slightly.

We will focus our attention on the decisions made during the first three periods. In the first two periods, the basic problem is to choose the appropriate investment instruments

EXHIBIT 2. Short-Term Financial Planning Model

INPUT DESCRIPTION

1 PERIOD DURATION AND CASH FLOW PROJECTION

PERIOD	DURATION	CASH FLOW
1	7	$ 2,100,000.00
2	7	$ 1,300,000.00
3	14	($ 5,200,000.00)
4	14	$ 2,100,000.00
5	28	$ 2,500,000.00
6	28	($ 3,100,000.00)
7	28	$ 2,100,000.00

2 BORROWING LIMIT ON CREDIT LINE:

PERIOD	LIMIT
1	$ 2,000,000.00
2	$ 2,000,000.00
3	$ 2,000,000.00
4	$ 2,000,000.00
5	$ 2,000,000.00
6	$ 2,000,000.00
7	$ 2,000,000.00

3 INSTRUMENT DESCRIPTION:

# IDENTIFIER	MATURITY	ANNUAL YIELD	INTEREST RATE PROJECTION USED	POST HORIZON INTEREST PENALTY
BORROWING INSTRUMENTS				
1 CREDIT LINE	1	7.25%	1	1.00%
2 CM PAPER 30D	30	6.50%	1	1.00%
INVESTMENT INSTRUMENTS				
3 CERT DEP 30D	30	5.13%	1	1.00%
4 CERT DEP 60D	60	5.35%	1	1.00%
5 CERT DEP 90D	90	5.50%	1	1.00%
6 DAILY REPO	1	4.50%	1	1.00%

4 INTEREST RATE PROJECTION:

PROJECTION NO. 1

PROJECTION DATE	ANNUAL YIELD
1	5.13%
30	5.10%
60	5.08%
90	5.05%
120	5.00%

OUTPUT DESCRIPTION

PERIOD NO. 1
DATE 1

MARGINAL RATE OF RETURN: 4.50%
CAH FLOW FROM EXTERNAL SOURCE: $2,100,000.00

INSTRUMENT ACTION	ACTION DATE	MATURE DATE	AMOUNT	MATURITY VALUE	ANNUAL YIELD
NEW PURCHASES AND SALES:					
DAILY REPO BOUGHT	1	8	$2,100,000.00	$2,101,813.00	4.50%
HOLDINGS AS OF 1					
DAILY REPO BOUGHT	1	8	$2,100,000.00	$2,101,813.00	4.50%

PERIOD NO. 2
DATE 8

MARGINAL RATE OF RETURN: 4.50%
CASH FLOW FROM EXTERNAL SOURCE: $1,300,000.00

INSTRUMENT ACTION	ACTION DATE	MATURE DATE	AMOUNT	MATURITY VALUE	ANNUAL YIELD
MATURING SECURITIES:					
DAILY REPO BOUGHT	1	8	$2,100,000.00	$2,101,813.00	4.50%
NEW PURCHASES AND SALES:					
DAILY REPO BOUGHT	8	15	$3,401.813.00	$3,404,745.96	4.50%
HOLDINGS AS OF 8					
DAILY REPO BOUGHT	8	15	$3,401.813.00	$3,404,745.96	4.50%

PERIOD NO. 3
DATE 15

MARGINAL RATE OF RETURN: 7.25%
CASH FLOW FROM EXTERNAL SOURCE: ($5,200,000.00)

INSTRUMENT ACTION	ACTION DATE	MATURE DATE	AMOUNT	MATURITY VALUE	ANNUAL YIELD
MATURING SECURITIES:					
DAILY REPO BOUGHT	8	15	$3,401,813.00	$3,404,745.96	4.49%

INSTRUMENT	ACTION	ACTION DATE	MATURE DATE	AMOUNT	MATURITY VALUE	ANNUAL YIELD
NEW PURCHASES AND SALES:						
CREDIT LINE	SOLD	15	29	$1,795,254.04	$1,800,244.44	7.24%
HOLDINGS AS OF 15						
CREDIT LINE	SOLD	15	29	$1,795,254.04	$1,800,244.44	7.24%

to maximize profits by minimizing borrowing costs. The case is not clear. On the one hand, interest rates are expected to fall, and longer-term C.D. investments yield more than the repurchase agreement. By buying a C.D., the firm could "lock in" the high current C.D. rate. On the other hand, a large cash outflow is expected in the third period, and the repurchase agreement might allow the firm to minimize the cost of financing this outflow. The computer model has selected the repurchase agreement (see lines 1 and 2 of Output Description).

In the third period, the firm must finance part of its large anticipated cash outflow. Here the tradeoff is between the use of lower cost but less flexible commercial paper and the very flexible but higher cost line of credit. The computer model, taking into account the cash inflows that will occur in periods 4 and 5, chooses to use the higher cost line of credit (see line 3 of Output Description). The logic is simply that it will prove less expensive to borrow for only 14 days on the line of credit than to pay the lower cost commercial paper rate for 30 days.

In examining the data presented in Exhibit 2, the reader should keep in mind that, in practice, a user will probably want to examine the sensitivity of the solution to the interest rate projection and cash flow estimate. It is possible to formulate and test a variety of economic possibilities.

CONCLUSION

The model described in this article provides a tool for corporate financial officers to examine a wide range of possible short-term investment/financing strategies. The power of the model lies in its ability to make such comparisons almost instantaneously, at nominal cost to the user. In a world in which financial decisions must be made quickly, we believe that the computerized short-run financial planning model will prove to be an important new development in the field of cash management.

REFERENCES

1. "Cash Management: The New Art of Wringing More Profit From Corporate Funds," *Business Week*, March 13, 1978, pp. 62-68.

2. J. C. T. Mao, "Application of Linear Programming to the Short-Term Financing Decision," *The Engineering Economist* (July 1968), pp. 221-41.

3. Y. E. Orgler, *Cash Management: Methods and Models*, Belmont, California, The Wadsworth Publishing Company, Inc., 1970.

4. Y. E. Orgler, "An Unequal Period Model for Cash Management Decisions," *Management Science* (October 1969), pp. 77-92.

5. G. A. Pogue and R. N. Bussard, "A Linear Programming Model for Short-Term Financial Planning Under Uncertainty," *Sloan Management Review* (Spring 1972), pp. 69-98.

6. A. A. Robichek, D. Teichroew and J. M. Jones, "Optimal Short-Term Financing Decisions, " *Management Science* (September 1965), pp. 1-36.

7. V. Srinivasan, "A Transshipment Model for Cash Management Decisions," *Management Science* (June 1974), pp. 1350-63.

8. S. Zionts, "A Deterministic Cash Management Problem," *Working Paper #75-2*, European Institute for Advanced Studies in Management (January 1975).

READING 41

A Risk-Return Analysis of a Firm's Working Capital Position

J. C. Van Horne
Stanford University

In this paper, a method is proposed by which management is able to analyze the risk-return tradeoff for various levels of liquid assets for the firm and for different maturity compositions of its debt. Together, these factors determine its working-capital position. Certain probability concepts are employed; and information is provided about the risk of cash insolvency for alternative strategies. In addition, the opportunity costs of these strategies are determined. With the framework proposed, more rational working-capital decisions are possible. The firm is able to achieve a working-capital position that provides the appropriate margin of safety in relation to the cost involved in attaining that position.

The appropriate levels of current assets and current liabilities for a firm, which determine its level of working-capital, are the result of fundamental decisions concerning the firm's liquidity and the maturity composition of its debt. In turn, these decisions are influenced by a tradeoff between profitability and risk. The purpose of this paper is to develop a framework for evaluating decisions affecting the firm's working-capital position, so that optimal decisions can be made more readily. As working-capital management is an area largely lacking in theoretical perspective,[1] it is hoped that the framework presented will place the subject in a clearer conceptual light. In this regard, we examine separately the level of the firm's liquid assets and the maturity composition of its debt in order to illustrate the respective tradeoffs between profitability and risk. We then combine these decision variables in the subsequent development of a framework for analyzing the overall problem. The major input for the method is a cash budget, ex-

[1] Exceptions include Beranek [4], Burton [5], and Walker [8].

Reprinted from THE ENGINEERING ECONOMIST (Winter 1969), Vol. 14, No. 2, pp. 71-88, by permission of the publisher, copyright The American Institute of Industrial Engineers and The American Society for Engineering Education, 25 Technology Park/Atlanta, Norcross, GA 30092.

pressed in probabilistic terms.

DECISION VARIABLES

In a broad sense, the appropriate decision variable to examine on the asset side of the balance sheet is the maturity composition, or liquidity, of the firm's assets--i.e., the turnover of these assets into cash. Decisions that affect the asset liquidity of the firm include: the management of cash and marketable securities; credit policy and procedures; inventory management and control; and the administration of fixed assets. As we wish to reduce the problem to workable proportions, however, we shall hold constant the last three factors. These factors represent separate but important means by which to improve the efficiency of the firm and to change its liquidity.[2] As the purpose of this paper is to provide an underlying theory of working-capital management, however, this theory is developed exclusive of the above factors. The decision variable then becomes the amount of liquid assets held by the firm; these assets are defined as cash and marketable securities. Moreover, our concern is with only the total amount of these two assets and not with the optimal split between them.[3]

Determining the appropriate amount of cash and marketable securities held by the firm (hereafter called liquid assets) involves a tradeoff between risk and profitability. All other things the same, the lower the level of liquid assets, the greater the risk of being unable to meet current obligations. For our purposes, risk is defined as the probability of technical insolvency. Legally, insolvency occurs whenever the assets of a firm are less than its liabilities and the net worth is negative. Technical insolvency, on the other hand, occurs whenever a firm is unable to meet its cash obligations.[4]

The risk of running out of cash can be reduced or even eliminated, of course, by maintaining a high proportion of liquid assets. However, there is a cost involved. This cost is the profit foregone on the investment of these funds in other assets.[5] However cost is measured, it is clear that there exists a tradeoff between risk and profitability.

The maturity structure of the firm's debt also involves a tradeoff between risk and profitability, similar to that affecting its level of liquid assets. A decision here determines the proportion of current assets financed with current liabilities. For purposes of analysis, we assume an established policy with respect to payment for purchases, labor, taxes, and other expenses. These liabilities finance a portion of the assets of the firm and tend to fluctuate with the firm's production schedule, and in the case of taxes, with profits. Our concern is with how assets, not supported by accounts payable and accruals, are financed.[6] We assume also that the firm maintains its existing portion of total debt to equity. Our attention is centered only on the maturity composition of the debt, not on the capital-structure problem.[7]

Depending upon the synchronization of the repayment of debt with the firm's schedule of expected future cash flows, different debt instruments will be more or less risky. The shorter the maturity schedule of the debt

[2] See Van Horne [7], Chapters 2-5, 17, and 18.

[3] For a discussion of the latter issue, see Baumol [2]; and Miller and Orr [6].

[4] See Walter [9].

[5] If the firm does not engage in capital rationing, a case can be made that the appropriate opportunity cost is the cost of capital, particularly if the firm increases its proportion of liquid assets to total assets.

[6] Delaying payment on accounts payable and accruals can be a decision variable for financing. However, there are limits to the extent to which a firm can "stretch" its payables. For simplicity, we assume a definite and consistent policy with respect to payment of current obligations. Consequently, payables and accruals are not active decision variables.

[7] For a review and analysis of this problem, see Van Horne [7], Chapter 7.

in relation to expected future cash flows, the greater the risk of inability to meet principal and interest payments, all other things the same. Generally, the longer the maturity schedule of debt, the less risky the debt financing of the firm. However, the longer the maturity schedule, the more costly is likely to be the financing. For one thing, the explicit cost of long-term financing usually is more than that of short-term financing.[8] In periods of very high interest rates, however, the rate on short-term corporate borrowings actually may exceed that on long-term borrowings. In general, this occurrence is not the case; the firm typically pays more for long-term borrowings, particularly if they are negotiated privately. In addition, if intermediate and long-term financing is used to finance short-term funds requirements, the firm may well pay interest on debt during times when it is not needed. In particular, this situation would hold if there were a seasonal component to the business. Thus, generally, there is an inducement to finance funds requirements, less payables and accruals, on a short-term basis. Offsetting this incentive, of course, is the added risk.

If a firm's future cash flows were known with certainty, it would be able to arrange its maturity schedule of future net cash flows. Because of this synchronization, there would be no need to hold liquid assets. When cash flows are subject to uncertainty, however, the situation is changed. To provide a margin of safety the firm can: (1) increase its level of liquid assets; and/or (2) lengthen the maturity schedule of its debt. To analyze the appropriate margin of safety, management must have information about the expected future cash flows of the firm and possible deviations from these expected outcomes. We turn now to a discussion of how this information can be provided, followed by an evaluation of the use of the information in determining an appropriate margin of safety.

CASH-FORECAST INFORMATION

In order to assess possible adverse deviations in net cash flows, cash forecasts must be prepared for a range of possible outcomes, with a probability attached to each. An initial cash budget should be prepared based upon the expected value of outcomes in each future period. This budget is prepared in the usual manner by: estimating and totaling all cash receipts for each future period; doing the same for cash disbursements; subtracting total disbursements from total receipts to obtain the net cash flow for each period; and calculating the ending cash balance for each period with additional financing. Instead of the cash balance, however, we wish to calculate the liquid-asset balance, the sum of cash and marketable securities. For longer-term forecasts, it is not feasible to prepare detailed cash budgets. Here, estimates of liquid-asset balances based upon major sources and uses of funds probably will be sufficient.

Given an initial cash budget, assumptions with respect to sales, average collection period, production schedule, purchasing, and expenses should be varied by management in keeping with possible deviations from expected conditions. For each change in assumptions, a new set of liquid-asset balances reflecting the change can be generated. Thus, management formulates subjective probabilities of possible future liquid asset balances. These balances are treated as subjective random variables. In determining the effect of a change in assumptions on the liquid-asset balance, simulation techniques can be very helpful in reducing or even eliminating the

---

[8] We ignore consideration of implicit costs that might be associated with short-term financing. These implicit costs in part may be embodied in management's decision, a subject we take up later.

detail work involved.[9]

In summary, changes in assumptions are the bases for alternative outcomes in liquid-asset balances. For each of these outcomes, management attaches the probability of occurrence of the associated change in assumptions. For example, suppose that management felt that there were a .10 probability of a 20-percent drop in sales accompanied by a slowing in the average collection period from thirty to forty days for all periods. Suppose further that production were expected to be cut back only after a month's delay. Given these changes in assumptions, a new set of liquid-asset balances for all periods would be determined, the probability of this outcome being .10. It is not necessary that the decline in sales or the slowing in collections be the same percentage amount for all months. If different changes over time are expected to occur, these changes should be used to determine the new set of liquid-asset balances.

By varying assumptions in this manner, management formulates subjective probability distributions of liquid-asset balances for various future periods; these distributions encompass a range of possible outcomes. To illustrate a probabilistic cash budget, consider the example in Table I. Here, discrete probability distributions of ending liquid-asset balances without additional financing are shown. These balances are reported on a monthly basis for one year, followed by quarterly forecasts for the next two years. We note that the probability of occurrence of a particular liquid-asset balance in one period corresponds to specific liquid-asset balances in all other periods. For simplicity of illustration, absolute changes in liquid-asset balances are made equal over time. While the realism of this example may be questionable, it is meant only to illustrate the framework for analysis.

LEVEL OF LIQUID ASSETS

As discussed earlier, the level of liquid assets and the maturity composition of debt determine the margin of safety of the firm in relation to possible adverse deviations in net cash flows. The level of liquid assets is affected by: (1) the future cash flows of the firm exclusive of new financing; and (2) changes in the total financing of the firm. These factors jointly determine the expected value of liquid assets of the firm. To illustrate, consider in Table I the liquid-asset balance for January, 19X1. The expected value of this balance can be found by

$$\overline{LB_1} = \sum_{i=1}^{11} L_{i1}P_{i1}, \qquad (1)$$

where L_{i1} is the ith possible balance, and P_{i1} is the probability of occurrence of that balance at the end of period 1. Thus, the expected value of liquid-asset balance for period 1 is

$$\begin{aligned}\overline{LB_1} = & -200(.02) - 100(.03) + 0(.05) \\ & +100(.10) + 200(.15) + 300(.20) \\ & +400(.18) + 500(.12) + 600(.07) \\ & +700(.05) + 800(.03) = \$323{,}000. \end{aligned} \qquad (2)$$

If the firm were to increase its total financing by $150,000, the expected value of liquid-asset balance at the end of the period would be $473,000. If we assume a liquid-asset balance of $400,000 at time 0, there would be a $73,000 net increase in the expected value of liquid assets for the period.

A decision to change the total financing of the firm will affect all

[9] We have developed a program for cash budgeting using a time-sharing system. The program allows one to judge the effect of a change in one or more assumptions on cash balances without having to rework the cash budget. See also "Probabilistic Projections," unpublished paper, Amos Tuck School of Business Administration, Dartmouth College, 1967.

Table I

POSSIBLE LIQUID-ASSET BALANCES WITHOUT ADDITIONAL FINANCING (in thousands)

	19X1											
Probability	Jan.	Feb.	Mar.	Apr.	May	June	July	Aug.	Sept.	Oct.	Nov.	Dec.
.02	-$200	-$300	-$400	-$500	-$700	-$900	-$900	-$800	-$700	-$700	-$600	-$500
.03	-100	-200	-300	-400	-600	-800	-800	-700	-600	-600	-500	-400
.05	0	-100	-200	-300	-500	-700	-700	-600	-500	-500	-400	-300
.10	100	0	-100	-200	-400	-600	-600	-500	-400	-400	-300	-200
.15	200	100	0	-100	-300	-500	-500	-400	-300	-300	-200	-100
.20	300	200	100	0	-200	-400	-400	-300	-200	-200	-100	0
.18	400	300	200	100	-100	-300	-300	-200	-100	-100	0	100
.12	500	400	300	200	0	-200	-200	-100	0	0	100	200
.07	600	500	400	300	200	-100	-100	0	100	100	200	300
.05	700	600	500	400	300	0	0	100	200	200	300	400
.03	800	700	600	500	400	100	100	200	300	300	400	500

	19X2				19X3			
Probability	Mar.	June	Sept.	Dec.	Mar.	June	Sept.	Dec.
.02	-$600	-$1000	-$700	-$500	-$700	-$1000	-$700	-$600
.03	-550	-950	-650	-450	-600	-900	-600	-500
.05	-500	-900	-600	-400	-550	-850	-550	-450
.10	-400	-800	-500	-300	-500	-800	-500	-400
.15	-300	-700	-400	-200	-400	-700	-400	-300
.20	-200	-600	-300	-100	-300	-600	-300	-200
.18	-100	-500	-200	0	-200	-500	-200	-100
.12	0	-400	-100	100	-100	-400	-100	0
.07	100	-300	0	200	0	-300	0	100
.05	200	-200	100	300	100	-200	100	200
.03	300	-100	200	400	200	-100	200	300

probability distributions in Table I. For simplicity of illustration, we assume that changes in total financing occur in exactly the same proportions of debt and equity as in the existing capital structure of the firm and that any new debt financing involves perpetual debt. Changes that involve other than perpetual debt are taken into account in the last section of this paper when we consider the total information needed to evaluate alternatives. In our example, then, a decision to increase total financing by \$150,000 at time 0 will increase the liquid-asset balance in Table I by \$150,000 for each probability for each of the periods.[10] As a result, there is obviously a reduced risk of cash insolvency.[11]

For each contemplated change in total financing, we can determine its effect on the probability distributions of possible liquid-asset balances shown in Table I. In order to evaluate the tradeoff between risk and profitability, however, we must have information about the effect of a change in liquid assets on profitability. To determine the cost of a change in liquid assets, we multiply the cost of carrying liquid assets (expressed as a percent) by the change. First, however, we must define a change. While different interpretations are possible, we shall define it as

$$C_j = \sum_{t=1}^{12} (\overline{LB_t} - LB_A)/12 \qquad (3)$$

where C_j = change in liquid-asset balance for alternative j
$\overline{LB_t}$ = expected value of liquid-asset balance in period t for alternative j
LB_A = average liquid-asset balance during previous 12 months

In words, our measured change in the liquid-asset balance represents an average of the expected values of liquid-asset balances for the forthcoming 12 months, less the average of liquid-asset balances for the previous 12 months. If LB_A is not considered typical or appropriate, a more suitable liquid-asset balance may be substituted. The expected value of liquid-asset balance at time t is found with equation (1).

To illustrate the use of equation (3), consider the probability distribution of possible liquid-asset balances for April, 19X1, in Table I. Suppose that the firm increases its total financing by \$200,000. The new probability distribution of possible liquid-asset balances for April is found by adding \$200,000 to each of the eleven liquid-asset balances for that month. The new expected value of liquid-asset balance is

$$\begin{aligned}\overline{LB_4} = & -300{,}000(.02) - 200{,}000(.03) \\ & -100{,}000(.05) + 0(.10) \\ & +100{,}000(.15) + 200{,}000(.20) \\ & +300{,}000(.18) + 400{,}000(.12) \\ & +500{,}000(.07) + 600{,}000(.05) \\ & +700{,}000(.03) = \$214{,}000.\end{aligned} \qquad (4)$$

If LB_A, the average liquid-asset balance of the firm during the previous year, were \$200,000, the change in liquid-asset balance for period t would be \$214,000 - 200,000 = \$14,000. Similarly, we are able to calculate the expected value of change in the liquid-asset balance for the other eleven months of the year. With equation (3), we then average the changes for the twelve months; this average represents our measure of the change in liquid-assets of the firm for a specific change in total financing.

[10] For ease af exposition, we ignore the effect of the payment of interest on new debt and dividends on new stock issued on the cash budget. These factors could be incorporated in the revised cash budget simply by deducting expected new interest and dividend payments in each future period from the \$150,000 increase in liquid assets.

[11] Archer [1] advocates computing the average daily transactions cash balance for a month and the standard deviation about this average. On the basis of this probability distribution, he suggests that the firm should add to its cash balance until the risk of running out of cash is reduced to an acceptable level.

Given our measured change in liquid-asset balance, C_j, this change is multiplied by the opportunity cost of maintaining liquid assets, expressed as a percentage, in order to obtain the total cost of the change. Within a limited range, the opportunity cost of an increase in liquid assets might be approximated by the firm's cost of capital, on a before-tax basis. The product of the above multiplication represents our measure of the impact on profitability of a change in the level of liquid assets of the firm. We defer specific evaluation of the tradeoff between profitability and risk until we have considered the effect of changes in the maturity composition of the firm's debt on profitability and risk.

MATURITY COMPOSITION OF DEBT

Similar to the case for liquid-asset changes, we are able to compute the effect of changes in the maturity composition of the firm's debt on the probability distributions of liquid-asset balances shown in Table I. To illustrate the impact of a change in maturity composition, suppose that the firm had in its existing debt structure a three-year term loan which called for monthly principal payments of $25,000. These payments are assumed to be embodied in the figures in Table I. If the firm renegotiated the term loan into one of 7 1/2 years with equal monthly payments, the principal payment per month would be reduced from $25,000 to $10,000. We can recalculate easily the probability distributions shown in Table I by adding $15,000 to the liquid-asset balance for each probability for each monthly period.[12] Thus, the probability of running out of cash is reduced for three years as a result of this debt lengthening. Of course, for years four through seven and one-half, the firm will be faced with a $10,000 increment in monthly principal payments. For other changes in the maturity composition of existing debt, we likewise can recompute the probability distributions shown in Table I.

A flexible borrowing arrangement for meeting short-term funds requirements is a bank line of credit. A line of credit enables a firm to borrow up to some maximum amount over a period of time, usually one year. With a line of credit, we must recompute the probability distributions in Table I. To illustrate, suppose that the firm increases its total financing by $400,000 of which $200,000 represents a line of credit. Assume further that the firm will borrow upwards to the whole line to maintain a liquid-asset balance of $250,000. For April, the probability distribution of possible liquid-asset balances after financing becomes that shown in Table II. For possibilities 1 through 4, the firm would utilize the full $200,000 under the line. For possibility 5, it would borrow $150,000 under the line; for possibility 6, $50,000. For possibilities 7 through 11, it would borrow nothing under the line; but, of course, there would be $200,000 in regular financing.

With a line of credit, the firm typically is required by a bank to pay off loans for a length of time during the year, perhaps two months. This requirement creates a problem with respect to risk. During the period of expected seasonal slack, the firm must assume the absence of the line so that it is out of debt during the "clean-up" period. For our example in Table I, we see that peak expected liquid-asset balances without additional financing occur in December and January. If the required "clean-up" period were two months, we would not adjust the probability distributions to reflect the availability of the line of credit during this period.

In our cash-flow evaluation, there is an obvious horizon problem. We have estimated cash flows for only three

---

[12] For simplicity of exposition, we ignore again the effect of interest payments on the cash flows.

Table II

Possibility i	Liquid-Asset Balance With New Financing of $400,000	Probability of Occurrence
1	-$100,000	.02
2	0	.03
3	100,000	.05
4	200,000	.10
5	250,000	.15
6	250,000	.20
7	300,000	.18
8	400,000	.12
9	500,000	.07
10	600,000	.05
11	700,000	.03

years hence. Given this horizon, an optimal strategy might call for all debt maturing in three years, one month. Under most circumstances, such a strategy would not be appropriate, for the firm will have funds requirements beyond three years. These requirements no doubt will preclude the paying off of all debt at that time. Consequently, the firm must arrange maturities beyond the cash-budget horizon on the basis of general estimates of future funds requirements and ability to service debt. We might point out, however, that the principles of risk and profitability are the same as those that govern debt maturities falling within the cash-budget horizon.

The opportunity cost of a change in maturity composition of debt must be estimated. If long-term borrowings command an interest rate different from that on short-term borrowings, usually higher, there exists a measureable explicit cost for the operation.[13] Suppose that, in our previous example, the three-year term loan required an interest rate of 6 percent, while the seven and one-half year loan required a rate of 6 1/2 percent. The difference, one-half percent, represents the additional cost of lengthening the debt. If debt were asuumed in perpetuity and the amount of the term loan were $900,000, the opportunity cost of debt lengthening would be $900,000 x 0.5% = $4,500 annually.

The second explicit cost involved with debt lengthening is the payment of interest on debt when it is not needed. Suppose that at January 1 a firm had a short-term loan of $600,000, of which $200,000 matured on August 31, $200,000 on October 31, and $200,000 on December 31. To reduce the risk of running out of cash, the firm might consider changing its borrowing accommodation to a one-year loan, maturing December 31. If the interest rate were 6 percent on both loans, the firm would pay additional interest on $200,000 for four months and on $200,000 for two months. The additional interest cost would be:

.06 x $200,000 x 4/12 =	$4,000
.06 x $200,000 x 2/12 =	2,000
Total	$6,000

The opportunity cost of a line of credit relates principally to the requirement of compensating balances. This requirement, frequently 15 percent of the line, increases the cost of borrowing if balances must be maintained in excess of those ordinarily maintained.

[13] Again, we must recognize the possibility of short-term rates higher than long-term rates when interest rates in general are very high.

One way to measure the cost is to take the interest rate on borrowings times the increase in balances necessary to compensate the bank. This notion assumes that the firm will have to borrow under its line to maintain balances considered compensating.

To summarize, for each feasible change in the composition of the firm's debt, we determine the effect of the change on the probability distributions of expected future liquid-asset balances. In addition, we estimate the incremental explicit cost of the particular alternative. Again, we must point out that we have limited our attention to explicit costs. No consideration has been given to the effect of changes in the maturity composition of debt on the way investors at the margin value the firm's stock. Having taken up the effect of changes in liquid assets and debt composition individually, we now most combine the two factors.

COMBINATION OF FACTORS AND SELECTION

In reducing the risk of running out of cash, the firm can select a combination of changes in liquid assets and in maturity composition of its debt. With a combination, we must estimate the joint effect of the two factors on the probability distributions of expected liquid-asset balances as well as the opportunity cost of the combination. Before proceeding, however, we must digress to relax an assumption made previously. It will be recalled that we assumed that debt issued in connection with an increase in total financing was perpetual. When such is not the case, we must take account of the effect of principal payments on the schedule of expected future cash flows. For example, suppose that the firm obtained a $540,000 three-year term loan payable monthly and that this loan represented new debt. Because the liquid-asset balances previously computed to reflect the change in total financing assumed perpetual debt, we would need to reduce these balances by $15,000 ($540,000/36) for each probability for each monthly period over three years. In addition, we must take account of the effect of the change on explicit costs. Both of these changes should be incorporated into the information provided for evaluating alternatives.

For each feasible alternative for reducing the risk of cash insolvency, a revised schedule of probability distributions of expected future liquid-asset balances should be prepared, accompanied by the estimated opportunity cost of the alternative. Instead of providing the entire probability distribution, it may be suitable to specify only the probability of running out of cash during each future period. The total opportunity cost for each alternative should be denoted on a total annual dollar basis.[14] In this regard, it may be helpful to show not only the total opportunity cost, but also the opportunity cost of each of the changes comprising the alternative. An example of a schedule of possible alternatives is shown in Table III. The probabilities of running out of cash for these alternatives are shown in Table IV.

Given information similar to that found in Tables III and IV, the firm must determine the best alternative by balancing the risk of running out of cash against the cost of providing a solution to avoid the possibility. If the cost of running out of cash were known, the best alternative could be determined easily by comparing the expected cost of a cash stockout with the opportunity cost of a particular solution to avoid that stockout.[15] The expected cost of a cash stockout is the cost associated with a particular stockout times its probability of occurrence. The optimal solution could be found by a comparison of the reduction in the

[14] If there is a change in the average cost of debt financing accompanying a change in total financing, it is necessary to multiply the change in average cost by the total amount of debt financing after the change in total financing.

[15] This assumes that the two costs are comparable.

Table III

SCHEDULE OF ALTERNATIVES FOR REDUCING RISK OF RUNNING OUT OF CASH

Alternative	Description	Opportunity Cost
1	$400,000 increase in total financing	$ 5,100
2	$500,000 increase in total financing	15,100
3	$600,000 increase in total financing	25,100
4	$700,000 increase in total financing	35,100
5	$800,000 increase in total financing	45,100
6	$900,000 increase in total financing	55,100
7	$1,000,000 increase in total financing	65,100
8	Conversion of term loan maturing $200,000 quarterly through 3 years into six-year term loan with $100,000 quarterly payments	9,000
9	Conversion of term loan into ten-year term loan maturing from year 4 through 10	16,000
10	Alternatives 1 and 8	14,100
11	Alternatives 2 and 8	24,100
12	Alternatives 3 and 8	34,100
13	Alternatives 4 and 8	44,100
14	Alternatives 1 and 9	21,100
15	Alternatives 2 and 9	31,100
16	Conversion of term loan from 3 to 6 years and refunding of mortgage maturing May 19X1 into ten-year note maturing quarterly	23,800
17	Alternative 1, and refunding mortgage	19,800
18	Alternative 2, and line of credit of $250,000	17,400
19	Alternative 2, line of credit of $250,000, and extending $1 million in notes from three-year loan to 4 1/2-year loan	26,200
.	. . .	.
.	. . .	.
32	Alternative 1, and refund intermediate-term loan into long-term loan	21,700

expected cost of cash stockout accompanying a particular solution with the opportunity cost of implementing that solution.

The difficulty, of course, is in estimating the cost of a cash stockout. When a firm does not have a sufficient liquidity cushion to cover a cash drain, it may be forced to convert other assets into cash. Frequently, these assets can be converted only at a significant price concession. This concession can be thought to represent the cost of illiquidity; and we would expect it to increase at an increasing rate with the amount of assets to be converted. However, many assets cannot be converted into cash on short notice. The measurement of the cost of illiquidity in this case is very difficult, for it does not involve tangible considerations. The cost will depend upon which obligations cannot be paid--that is, whether they are payments to suppliers, wages to employees, tax payments, bank loans, or other obligations. Because of the obvious difficulties in measuring the cost of a cash stockout and applying it consistently, the method is seldom used.

Table IV. PROBABILITIES OF RUNNING OUT OF CASH FOR VARIOUS ALTERNATIVES

	19X1											
Alternative	Jan.	Feb.	Mar.	Apr.	May	June	July	Aug.	Sept.	Oct.	Nov.	Dec.
1	.00	.00	.02	.05	.20	.55	.55	.35	.20	.20	.10	.05
2	.00	.00	.00	.02	.10	.35	.35	.20	.10	.10	.05	.02
3	.00	.00	.00	.00	.05	.20	.20	.10	.05	.05	.02	.00
4	.00	.00	.00	.00	.02	.10	.10	.05	.02	.02	.00	.00
5	.00	.00	.00	.00	.00	.05	.05	.02	.00	.00	.00	.00
6	.00	.00	.00	.00	.00	.02	.02	.00	.00	.00	.00	.00
7	.00	.00	.00	.00	.00	.00	.00	.00	.00	.00	.00	.00
8	.10	.20	.20	.35	.73	.85	.85	.73	.35	.35	.20	.05
9	.10	.20	.10	.20	.55	.55	.55	.35	.05	.05	.02	.00
10	.00	.00	.00	.02	.10	.20	.20	.10	.02	.02	.00	.00
11	.00	.00	.00	.00	.05	.10	.10	.05	.00	.00	.00	.00
12	.00	.00	.00	.00	.02	.05	.05	.02	.00	.00	.00	.00
13	.00	.00	.00	.00	.00	.02	.02	.00	.00	.00	.00	.00
14	.00	.00	.00	.00	.05	.05	.05	.02	.00	.00	.00	.00
15	.00	.00	.00	.00	.02	.02	.02	.00	.00	.00	.00	.00
16	.00	.00	.02	.05	.10	.15	.15	.13	.12	.08	.06	.04
17	.00	.00	.02	.05	.04	.04	.04	.04	.03	.02	.01	.01
18	.00	.04	.03	.07	.09	.10	.09	.09	.05	.04	.04	.06
19	.00	.04	.04	.05	.06	.07	.06	.06	.04	.03	.04	.03
•												•
•												•
•												•
32	.00	.00	.02	.05	.10	.10	.08	.05	.02	.00	.00	.00

	19X2				19X3			
Alternative	Mar.	June	Sept.	Dec.	Mar.	June	Sept.	Dec.
1	.20	.85	.35	.10	.35	.85	.35	.20
2	.10	.73	.20	.02	.20	.73	.20	.05
3	.02	.55	.10	.00	.05	.55	.05	.02
4	.00	.35	.02	.00	.02	.35	.02	.00
5	.00	.20	.00	.00	.00	.20	.00	.00
6	.00	.10	.00	.00	.00	.05	.00	.00
7	.00	.02	.00	.00	.00	.02	.00	.00
8	.10	.55	.02	.00	.00	.02	.00	.00
9	.00	.00	.00	.00	.00	.00	.00	.00
10	.00	.02	.00	.00	.00	.00	.00	.00
11	.00	.00	.00	.00	.00	.00	.00	.00
12	.00	.00	.00	.00	.00	.00	.00	.00
13	.00	.00	.00	.00	.00	.00	.00	.00
14	.00	.00	.00	.00	.00	.00	.00	.00
15	.00	.00	.00	.00	.00	.00	.00	.00
16	.07	.16	.00	.00	.00	.02	.00	.00
17	.02	.04	.02	.00	.02	.05	.04	.00
18	.06	.10	.08	.07	.06	.12	.09	.08
19	.05	.08	.05	.04	.04	.09	.06	.04
•								•
•								•
•								•
32	.02	.08	.05	.02	.00	.06	.00	.00

A more practical method is for decision-makers to specify a risk tolerance for running out of cash. For example, this risk tolerance might be five percent, meaning that the firm would tolerate upwards to a five percent probability of not being able to pay its bills in a future period. Given an acceptable level of risk, the firm then would seek the least costly solution to reducing the probability of running out of cash to that level. This is done simply by taking those feasible alternatives that provide a probability of cash stockout of approximately five percent or less and picking the least costly. We see in Tables III and IV that this alternative would be number 17. For this alternative, there is a five-percent probability of running out of cash in April, 19X1 and a five-percent probability for June, 19X3. We note that the alternative has a total annual opportunity cost of $19,800.

Another way that decision-makers might select an alternative would be for them to formulate risk tolerances on the basis of the opportunity cost involved in reducing the risk of cash stockout to various tolerance levels. It could well be that the specification of a low risk tolerance would result in a very high cost to provide a solution. If management had information about the cost associated with reducing risk to other levels, it might pick a higher tolerance level that could be implemented at considerably less cost. For example, the least costly alternative in our hypothetical example that will reduce the probability of running out of cash to two percent is number 15, involving a total annual cost of $31,100. This compares with a cost of $19,800 to reduce the probability to five percent. On the basis of this information, management might not feel that the additional $11,300 to reduce the probability of running out of cash from five to two percent was justified. Accordingly, we see that it may be useful to prepare a schedule showing the least costly solution to reducing risk to various levels. In this way, decision-makers can better evaluate the tradeoff between risk and profitability.

Even here, however, there is the problem of not providing enough information. For example, a certain alternative may result in a probability of running out of cash in only one future period, whereas another might result in that probability being reached in several periods. In Table IV, we note that for alternative 17, there is a five-percent probability of running our of cash in two periods, a four-percent probability in six periods, a three-percent probability in one period, a two-percent probability in five periods, and a one-percent probability in two periods. On the other hand, for alternative 14, there is a five-percent probability of running out of cash in three periods, and a two-percent probability in one period. Thus, there are considerably more periods in which the firm may run out of cash with alternative 17 than with alternative 14. As the total cost of alternative 14 is only $21,000, compared with $19,800 for alternative 17, the firm might regard alternative 14 as more favorable.

Therefore, a strong case can be made for providing decision-makers with information about the probability distributions of liquid-asset balances for all future periods for each alternative and the opportunity cost of the alternative. In this way, the firm is able to evaluate the maximum probability of running out of cash and the number of future periods in which there is a chance for a cash stockout. With this additional information, it then can assess more realistically the tradeoff between the risk of running out of cash and the opportunity cost of reducing this risk. On the basis of this assessment, it would select and implement the most appropriate alternative. The actual implementation will determine the liquid-asset level of the firm and the maturity composition of its debt. In turn, these factors will determine the working-capital position of the firm, given the assumptions listed earlier. This position should be the one most appropriate with respect to considerations of risk and profitability.

CONCLUSIONS

In this paper, we have proposed a framework by which management can evaluate the level of liquid assets and the maturity composition of the firm's debt. Employing certain probability concepts, the framework allows a realistic appraisal of the risk of running out of cash for various levels of liquid assets and different debt compositions. Given the opportunity cost of a change in liquid assets and/or maturity composition of the firm's debt, decision-makers are able to evaluate the tradeoff between profitability and risk. The method proposed is designed to provide them with certain necessary information on which to make a decision. However, the decision itself will depend upon management's preferences with respect to risk borne by the firm. The decision itself will determine the current assets and current liabilities of the firm, given the assumptions of the model. The result should be the most desirable working-capital position for the firm.

REFERENCES

1. Archer, Stephen H., "A Model for the Determination of Firm Cash Balances," *Journal of Financial and Quantitative Analysis*, Vol. 1, (March 1966), pp. 1-11.
2. Baumol, William J., "The Transacti tions Demand for Cash: An Inventory Theoretic Approach," *Quarterly Journal of Economics*, Vol. LXVI, (Nov. 1952).
3. Beranek, William, *Analysis for Financial Decisions*, (Homewood, Ill.: Irwin, 1963), Chapter 11.
4. ________________, *Working Capital Management*, (Belmont: Wadsworth Pub. Co., 1966).
5. Burton, John C., "The Management of Corporate Liquid Assets," unpublished doctoral thesis, Columbia University, 1962.
6. Miller, Milton H. and Daniel Orr, "A Model of the Demand for Money by Firms," *Quarterly Journal of Economics*, Vol. LXXX, (Aug. 1966), pp. 413-35.
7. Van Horne, James C., *Financial Management and Policy*, (Englewood Cliffs, N.J.: Prentice-Hall, Inc., 1968).
8. Walker, Ernest W., "Towards a Theory of Working Capital," *The Engineering Economist*, Vol. 9, No. 2, (Jan.-Feb. 1964), pp. 21-35.
9. Walter, James E., "Determination of Technical Insolvency," *Journal of Business*, Vol. XXX, (Jan. 1957), pp. 30-43.

READING 42

Profitability Versus Liquidity Tradeoffs in Working Capital Management

Keith V. Smith
Purdue University

INTRODUCTION

This book contains a series of papers which deal with various aspects of the important problem of working capital management. A recurring theme in many of the readings has been the recognition of linkages between the current assets and current liabilities which comprise the working capital of the business firm. Another theme in considering the management of working capital is the presence of two important goals--profitability and liquidity. It was suggested in the introductory overview to this book (Reading 1) that parallel monthly forecasts of profitability and required borrowing for the firm ought to provide a useful way of connecting those two themes.

The purpose of this final paper is to illustrate the use of such parallel monthly forecasts (1) in making tradeoffs between profitability and liquidity goals of the firm, (2) in estimating the impact of certain working capital policies on those goals, and (3) in reflecting the uncertainty of the future. The methodology employed is not new, but rather it should be viewed as further elaboration and illustration of procedures suggested by several authors whose work is contained in this book. And while the suggested methodology attempts to explain rather than to optimize, it should provide a better basis from which optimizing models can be used to improve working capital policies.

II. SCENARIO[1]

Smith Products is a relatively new firm engaged in the wholesaling of various products to retail outlets in the Northeastern United States. Because of the breadth of their product line and their emphasis on dependable service, the firm has experienced a rapid growth in recent months. It appears that potential exists for continued prosperity during the next few years, provided that their expanding

[1] The illustration used in this paper had its origin in E.W. Walker and Associates, "Case Problems in Financial Management" (Appleton-Century-Crofts 1968), p. 27.

This paper has not previously been published.

business can be handled successfully.

As assistant to the financial manager of Smith Products, suppose that you are asked during the fall of 1974 to prepare a monthly cash budget for 1975 and thereby to determine the firm's financial needs for the year. Your assignment also includes the projecting of monthly income statements for the same period so that profitability and liquidity can be compared. Based on your recent training at a leading business school, you have decided that you also should somehow take into account the considerable uncertainty that exists for future sales. Finally, you are convinced that some of the firm's existing policies for managing working capital might be improved, and you plan to reflect such possibilities in your report, which will be made to the Executive Committee of the firm.

A first step is to accumulate the necessary inputs for preparing your forecasts. In discussion with other managers of Smith Products, you obtain the following information for use in preparing your forecasts.

1. Cash Balances. Based on the current and projected level of sales, it is decided that a beginning cash balance of $20,000 will be appropriate for ensuring the intra-month cash flows.

2. Accounts Receivable. All sales are for credit. The existing collection experience is for 70% of accounts receivable to be collected in the first month following the sale, 20% in the second month, and the remaining 10% in the third month. This experience is expected to continue.

3. Inventory. The existing policy is for the inventory (at cost) at the beginning of any month to be equal to the forecasted sales for the next three months.

4. Purchases. The cost of merchandise purchased for resale averages 75% of sales. On the purchases which are made each month, existing policy is to pay 70% in the first month after the purchase and the remaining 30% during the next month.

5. Selling and Administrative Expenses. At the current level of operations, these amount to $8,500 per month plus 9% of sales. These expenses are currently paid at the rate of 70% in the current month and 30% in the first month following.

6. Interest Expense. It is anticipated that there will be no outstanding borrowing at the beginning of 1975. Also, it is assumed that short-term borrowing can be obtained from some source at an annual interest rate of 8.4%, but with payments being made monthly (at .70% per month). Both borrowing and repayment of outstanding debt take place in increments of $1,000.

7. Capital Expenditures. During March 1975, the company plans to spend $20,000 for production handling equipment. Additional capital expenditures of $30,000 in July and $30,000 in October are also anticipated. Although leasing is a possibility, the existing plan is to pay cash for the capital expenditures at the time of purchase.

8. Depreciation. Existing fixed assets are depreciated at the rate of $1,000 per month. Each capital acquisition will be depreciated on a straight-line basis at the monthly rate of 1%.

9. Taxes. A federal income tax rate of 50% will be used in preparing the forecasts. Smith Products has already paid 1974 taxes, and 1975 taxes will not be due until the end of the year.

10. Forecasted Sales. As a first estimate, the marketing staff of Smith Products provides the following sales forecasts for the remainder of 1974, for the budget year 1975, and for the first three months of 1976. (Figure I) These forecasts reflect a steady growth of sales through the budget year.

Finally, discussions with the treasurer of Smith Products yielded the anticipated balance sheet as of year-end 1974 as shown in Figure II. Values of various assets and liabilities can be shown to be consistent with the information just described. It is noted that total assets are $411,000, most of which is provided by the 10,000 out-

Figure I

FORECASTED SALES

	1974	1975	1976
January		$ 70,000	$130,000
February		80,000	130,000
March		80,000	140,000
April		90,000	
May		100,000	
June		100,000	
July		90,000	
August		100,000	
September		110,000	
October	$40,000	120,000	
November	50,000	120,000	
December	60,000	130,000	

standing shares of common stock. That is, there are no outstanding bank loans or taxes payable at the beginning of 1975.

III. SOLUTION OF BASIC PROBLEM

The next step is to prepare and present profitability and liquidity projections for the budget year 1975 for the "basic problem" just described. Although the preparation of such projections is a relatively straightforward task, you decide to make your presentation in a thorough step-by-step manner so that hopefully there will be no question about the validity of your conclusions. Toward that end, you prepare a detailed worksheet and cash budget covering the first three months of 1975 as shown in Figure III. You note in your accompanying presentation that values in the three columns for the last months of 1974 are needed as input to the calculations for the budget months of 1975. You also note that the worksheet is organized into a series of panels to facilitate a discussion of the budgeting procedures.

Using January 1975 as a typical month, you indicate that forecasted sales are $70,000 as seen in Panel A. Cash receipts in January, which are based on collection of outstanding receivables from the preceding three months, total $56,000 as indicated in Panel B. Panel C reveals that net purchases in January are $72,500 as determined by cost of goods sold plus ending inventory, minus beginning inventory for the month. Cash payments made in January, obtained by applying the appropriate percentages to net purchases in prior months, are $65,750. Selling and administrative expenses, as shown in Panel D, total $14,800 for January, but the associated cash payments are only $14,530. There are no capital expenditures contemplated for January as seen in Panel E.

Panel F contains the actual cash budget for Smith Products. Total cash available of $76,000 when compared to total cash outlays of $80,280 would result in an ending cash deficit of $4,280. In order to cover this deficit and provide an appropriate cash balance of at least $20,000 to begin February, the firm must borrow $25,000 during January. The cash balance after borrowing thus becomes $20,720. This also becomes the beginning cash balance for February 1975, and the same procedure is repeated for each month in the budget year. Notice that in February, interest expense of $175 is obtained by multiplying the $25,000 loan obtained in January by the monthly rate of 0.7%. Although the cash budget in

Figure II

SMITH PRODUCTS

BEGINNING BALANCE SHEET (12/31/74)

Cash		$ 20,000	Accounts Payable	$ 85,250
Accounts Receivable		79,000	Other Accruals	4,170
Inventory		230,000	Loans Payable	0
Fixed Assets	$100,000		Taxes Payable	0
Depreciation	18,000		Common Stock & Surplus	
Net Fixed Assets		82,000	(10,000 shares)	100,000
			Retained Earnings	221,580
Total Assets		$411,000	Total Sources	$411,000

Panel F is not lengthy or complicated, it does depend critically on the information obtained from Panels A-E above. Cumulative required borrowing has grown to $82,000 by the end of March 1975, reflecting the increased level of sales expected by Smith Products.

Once the procedures for preparing a monthly cash budget are understood, the next step is to present the results for the entire year, as in Figure IV, along with projected income statements for each month of 1975. Values in the first three columns (encircled) of the cash budget are identical to Panel F of Figure III just described. The income statement for each month is simply sales minus the sum of cost of goods sold, selling and administrative expenses, interest expense, and depreciation. For January, a before-tax profit of $1,700 is noted.

You indicate to the Executive Committee that the "Cumulative Borrowing" line of the cash budget and the "Net Profit Before Taxes" line of the projected income statement can be used in making tradeoffs between profitability and liquidity for the budget year 1975. You point out that forecasted, monthly, before-tax profits grow steadily during the year from $1,700 in January to a high of $9,002 in December. But such increased profitability can only be achieved if the firm is able to obtain required borrowing in amounts which reach $216,000 also in December. The reason for this, of course, is that expanding sales volume necessitates larger investments, both in accounts receivable and inventory. Projections for Smith Products during 1975 illustrate dramatically the severe financing problem that often accompanies the seeming prosperity of an expanding business.

Figure V includes a projected income statement for the entire year 1975 and also the balance sheet that is projected for year-end 1975. The annual income statement is simply the sum of the monthly income statements in Figure IV, minus the accrued federal taxes at the 50% rate. Although forecasted interest is not particularly large in any single month, it totals $9,184 for the entire year. After-tax profits of $31,658 are anticipated for 1975. This amounts to earnings-per-share of $3.16, and a return on beginning book equity (common stock plus retained earnings) of 9.8%.

The need for additional financing is vividly seen in a comparison of the projected balance sheet for year-end 1975 with the year-end 1974 balance sheet presented as Figure II. Accounts receivable increases from $79,000 to $178,000, while inventory increases from $230,000 to $400,000. Fixed assets also expand by virtue of the three capital expenditures during 1975. Part of the increase in total assets is financed by accounts payable which expand from $85,280 to $137,500 and by other accruals (selling and administrative expenses) which grow from $4,170

Figure III. CASH BUDGETING SOLUTION OF BASIC PROBLEM

	October	November	December	January	February	March
A. Forecasted Sales	$40,000	$ 50,000	$ 60,000	$ 70,000	$ 80,000	$ 80,000
B. Cash Receipts						
Last Month (70%)				42,000	49,000	56,000
Two Months Ago (20%)				10,000	12,000	14,000
Three Months Ago (10%)				4,000	5,000	6,000
Total Cash Receipts				56,000	66,000	76,000
C. Purchase Payments						
Cost of Goods Sold (75%)		37,500	45,000	52,500	60,000	60,000
Ending Inventory (3 mos)		210,000	230,000	250,000	270,000	290,000
Total Needed		247,500	275,000	302,500	330,000	350,000
Beginning Inventory		180,000	210,000	230,000	250,000	270,000
Net Purchases		67,500	65,000	72,500	80,000	80,000
Last Month (70%)				45,500	50,750	56,000
Two Months Ago (30%)				20,750	19,500	21,750
Total Cash Purchases				65,750	70,250	77,750
D. Selling & Administrative						
Fixed Charges ($8,500)			8,500	8,500	8,500	8,500
Variable Charges (9%)			5,400	6,300	7,200	7,200
Total Expenses			13,900	14,800	15,700	15,700
Current Month (70%)				10,360	10,990	10,990
Last Month (30%)				4,170	4,440	4,710
Total Cash Expenses				14,530	15,430	15,700
E. Capital Expenditures				0	0	20,000
F. Cash Budget						
Beginning Cash Balance				20,000	20,720	20,865
Total Cash Receipts				56,000	66,000	76,000
Total Cash Available				76,000	86,720	96,865
Total Cash Purchases				65,750	70,250	77,750
Total Cash Expenses				14,530	15,430	15,700
Capital Expenditure				0	0	20,000
Interest Expense (.007/mo)				0	175	315
Total Cash Outlays				80,280	85,855	113,765
Ending Cash Balance Before Borrowing				(4,280)	865	(16,900)
Cumulative Borrowing				25,000	45,000	82,000
Cash Balance After Borrowing				20,720	20,865	20,100

Figure IV. CASH BUDGET AND PROJECTED INCOME STATEMENT FOR BASIC PROBLEM, 1975

Cash Budget

	Jan.	Feb.	Mar.	Apr.	May	June	July	Aug.	Sept.	Oct.	Nov.	Dec.
Beginning Cash Balance	20000.	20720.	20865.	20100.	20196.	20017.	20053.	20504.	20628.	20719.	20291.	20785.
Total Cash Receipts	56000.	66000.	76000.	79000.	87000.	96000.	99000.	93000.	98000.	106000.	116000.	119000.
Total Cash Available	76000.	86720.	96865.	99100.	107196.	116016.	119053.	113504.	118628.	126719.	136291.	139765.
Total Cash Purchases	65750.	70250.	77750.	80000.	71250.	72750.	82000.	93750.	95750.	100250.	100750.	100000.
Total Cash Expense	14530.	15430.	15700.	16330.	17230.	17500.	16870.	17230.	18130.	19030.	19300.	19930.
Capital Expenditure	0.	0.	20000.	0.	0.	0.	30000.	0.	0.	30000.	0.	0.
Interest Espense	0.	175.	315.	574.	700.	714.	679.	896.	1029.	1148.	1456.	1498.
Total Cash Outlays	80280.	85855.	113765.	96904.	89180.	90964.	129549.	111876.	114909.	150428.	121506.	121428.
Ending Cash Balance	-4280.	865.	-16900.	2196.	18017.	25053.	-10496.	1628.	3719.	-23709.	14785.	18357.
Cumulative Borrowing	25000.	45000.	82000.	100000.	102000.	97000.	128000.	147000.	164000.	208000.	214000.	216000.
Cash Bal After Borrowing	20720.	20865.	20100.	20196.	20017.	20053.	20504.	20628.	20719.	20291.	20785.	20357.

Income Statement	Jan.	Feb.	Mar.	Apr.	May	June	July	Aug.	Sept.	Oct.	Nov.	Dec.
Sales	70000.	80000.	80000.	90000.	100000.	100000.	90000.	100000.	110000.	120000.	120000.	130000.
Cost of Goods Sold	52500.	60000.	60000.	67500.	75000.	75000.	67500.	75000.	82500.	90000.	90000.	97500.
Gross Profit	17500.	20000.	20000.	22500.	25000.	25000.	22500.	25000.	27500.	30000.	30000.	32500.
Selling and Admin. Exp.	14800.	15700.	15700.	16600.	17500.	17500.	16600.	17500.	18400.	19300.	19300.	20200.
Interest Expense	0.	175.	315.	574.	700.	714.	679.	896.	1029.	1148.	1456.	1498.
Depreciation	1000.	1000.	1000.	1200.	1200.	1200.	1200.	1500.	1500.	1500.	1800.	1800.
Net Profit Before Taxes	1700.	3125.	2985.	4126.	5600.	5586.	4021.	5104.	6571.	8052.	7444.	9002.

Figure V

FORECASTED FINANCIAL STATEMENTS FOR 1975

SMITH PRODUCTS

ANNUAL INCOME STATEMENT, 1975

Sales	$1,190,000
Cost of Goods Sold	- 892,500
Gross Profit	$ 297,500
Selling and Administrative Expenses	- 209,100
Interest Expense	- 9,184
Depreciation	- 15,900
Net Profit Before Taxes	$ 63,316
Federal Income Taxes	- 31,658
Net Profit After Taxes	$ 31,658

SMITH PRODUCTS

ENDING BALANCE SHEET (12/31/75)

Cash		$ 20,357	Accounts Payable	$137,500
Accounts Receivable		178,000	Other Accruals	6,060
Inventory		400,000	Loans Payable	216,000
Fixed Assets	$180,000		Taxes Payable	31,658
Depreciation	33,900		Common Stock	100,000
Net Fixed Assets		146,100	Retained Earnings	253,239
Total Assets		$744,457	Total Sources	$744,457

to $6,060. Nevertheless, outstanding loans of $216,000 and taxes payable of $31,658 are included among the sources of financing by year-end 1975. If federal taxes were paid quarterly during the year, the amount of the needed borrowing by the end of the year thus would amount to $216,000 + $31,658 = $247,658.

A natural question at this point is whether or not Smith Products would be able to obtain financing of almost $250,000 during 1975 based on these projections. Banks or other potential lenders would doubtless request additional information on the wholesaling business of Smith Products, its management, its competitors, as well as on overall economic conditions. Another likely factor in the deliberation of potential lenders would be the prognosis for 1976 and subsequent years. For if sales continue to grow during 1976, the amount of needed financing obviously will increase. If monthly sales level off in the $130,000-$140,000 range, then a cursory extrapolation of Figure V suggests that it would take four to five years of after-tax profits to repay the cumulative borrowing needed to sustain growth during 1975. Ironically, the quickest way for this level of borrowing to be repaid is if sales decrease in 1976 and 1977, accompanied by disinvestment in accounts receivable and inventory. Finally, it might be noted that the projections for 1975 suggest that Smith Products may have to consider possible sources of long-term financing, even though the need is primarily from increased levels of working capital. This illustrates vividly the concept of permanent levels of working capital which has been discussed in several leading financial textbooks.

Monthly forecasts of borrowing requirements and profitability in Figure

IV, together with the projected annual financial statements in Figure V, thus represent a useful starting point for both the long-term and short-term financial planning of the firm. Given the main thrust of your report, however, you decide not to pursue further the question of long-term financing at this time. Instead, you turn to consideration of how the information in Figures IV and V can be extended in performing useful sensitivity analyses.

IV. SENSITIVITY TO SALES FORECASTS

Members of the Executive Committee, as well as potential creditors of Smith Products, are likely to inquire--and rightfully so--as to how sensitive the profitability-liquidity comparisons in Figure IV are to the particular sales forecast which triggers the entire budgeting procedure. For that reason, it is well to prepare a series of projections based on alternative sales forecasts for 1975 and 1976. Toward that end, you schedule another series of discussions with the marketing staff of the firm. And while they remain comfortable with their initial forecasts (reflected in prior figures), they do admit that there might be other, less likely outcomes based on a number of possible developments and contingencies in the technology and markets of the industry. The result of your deliberations is four sets of possible sales forecasts as plotted in Figure VI. The original "likely" forecast is assigned a relative probability of 60%, while an "optimistic" forecast is given a 10% probability. On the other side, a low "possible" forecast is believed to have a 25% chance, and an even lower "pessimistic" forecast is given only a 5% chance of materializing. The first three months of each set of forecasts are the same, so that the beginning balance sheet will be identical in each instance. The first eight months are also identical for the likely and possible outcomes. By the end of the year, sales forecasts range from $80,000 per month (pessimistic) to $170,000 per month (optimistic). While this may seem to be an unusually wide range, note that there is an 85% probability that sales will be in the narrower range of $100,000 to $130,000 per month by the end of 1975.

Using each of the four sets of forecasts, parallel monthly projections of cumulative borrowing and before-tax profitability can be prepared. These are included in Figure VII, with the monthly sales forecasts included for comparison. It is seen that the wide range of sales forecasts manifests itself in diverse projections, both of cumulative borrowing which is required, and before-tax monthly profits. As before, the borrowing requirement of the firm is understated by the amount of the federal taxes that would become due at the end of 1975. As seen in Figure VII, maximum borrowing occurs in December under optimistic and likely sales forecasts since further sales growth is anticipated. But under possible and pessimistic sales forecasts with no anticipated growth, maximum borrowing occurs in October 1975. Similar patterns occur for profitability. As a general rule, both cumulative borrowing and before-tax profits decrease as sales forecasts decrease. One exception occurs in the month of August where profitability is greater by a few dollars under the possible sales forecast than under the likely forecast. This occurs only because the cumulative borrowing at the end of July is $7,000 greater under the likely forecast, and thus greater interest expense is incurred.

Comparisons in Figure VII do not reflect the relative probabilities assigned to the four sets of sales forecasts, and thus all available information is not being used. To do that, Figure VIII presents summary measures of expected value and associated standard deviation for selected measures of liquidity and profitability. Expected value is a measure of central tendency for the probability distribution, while standard deviation is a

Figure VI. ALTERNATIVE SALES FORECASTS FOR SMITH PRODUCTS

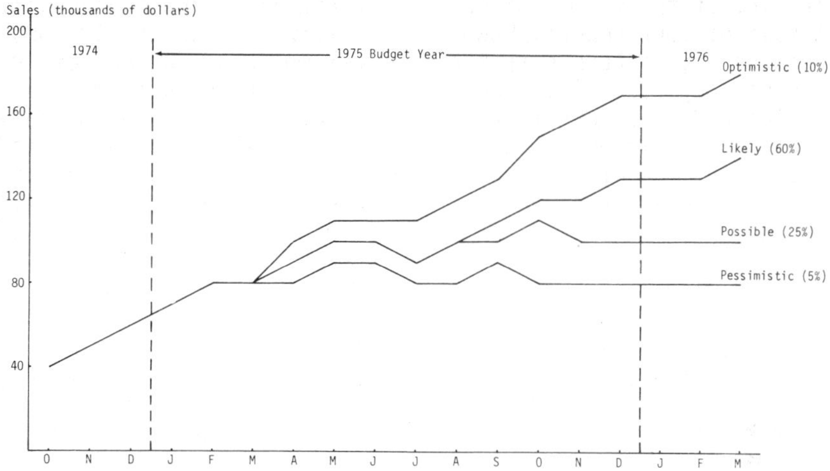

measure of dispersion of the probability distribution. Standard deviation is often used as a measure of risk in conjunction with an expected value since both are in the same units. Moreover, by making assumptions about the underlying probability distribution, one can make probabilistic statements about particular values of the measure being considered.

In Figure VIII, it is seen that after-tax profits and earnings-per-share give similar views of profitability since the former divided by 10,000 outstanding shares gives the latter. For liquidity, maximum cumulative borrowing during 1974 is used as a summary measure. Using values such as in Figure VIII, firm management should be able to make planning decisions with more confidence than if only a single set of forecasts were employed. For example, expected value plus or minus one standard deviation gives a range of $152,600 to $256,400 for cumulative borrowing, and a range of $2.50 to $3.72 for earnings-per-share.

V. SENSITIVITY TO WORKING CAPITAL POLICIES

Members of the Executive Committee and potential lenders also are likely to inquire about possible improvements that might be made by the firm to alleviate the heavy need for borrowing. Again, profitability-liquidity comparisons can be used to see how sensitive the financial status of Smith Products is to changes in some of their management policies. Of interest here are the individual and collective effects of accounts receivable, inventory, accounts payable, and other accruals--four of the central components of working capital.

After further discussions with various managers of Smith Products, you decide that the following changes are feasible with minimal cost to the firm, without any probably effect on forecasted sales for 1975, and without an appreciable increase in risk to the

Figure VII. PROFITABILITY-LIQUIDITY TRADEOFFS FOR ALTERNATIVE SALES FORECASTS (in dollars)

	Jan.	Feb.	Mar.	Apr.	May	June	July	Aug.	Sept.	Oct.	Nov.	Dec.
MONTHLY SALES FORECASTS												
Optimistic	70,000	80,000	80,000	100,000	110,000	110,000	110,000	120,000	130,000	150,000	160,000	170,000
Likely	70,000	80,000	80,000	90,000	100,000	100,000	90,000	100,000	110,000	120,000	120,000	130,000
Possible	70,000	80,000	80,000	90,000	100,000	100,000	90,000	100,000	100,000	110,000	100,000	100,000
Pessimistic	70,000	80,000	80,000	80,000	90,000	90,000	80,000	80,000	90,000	80,000	80,000	80,000
CUMULATIVE BORROWING												
Optimistic	25,000	52,000	99,000	128,000	140,000	144,000	184,000	211,000	243,000	306,000	321,000	323,000*
Likely	25,000	45,000	82,000	100,000	102,000	97,000	128,000	147,000	164,000	208,000	214,000	216,000*
Possible	25,000	45,000	82,000	100,000	102,000	97,000	121,000	130,000	129,000	154,000*	139,000	130,000
Pessimistic	25,000	38,000	65,000	73,000	72,000	61,000	83,000	78,000	74,000	92,000*	85,000	81,000
BEFORE-TAX NET PROFITS												
Optimistic	1,700	3,125	2,936	5,607	7,004	6,920	6,892	7,912	9,323	12,299	13,158	14,653
Likely	1,700	3,125	2,985	4,126	5,600	5,586	4,021	5,104	6,571	8,052	7,444	9,002
Possible	1,700	3,125	2,985	4,126	5,600	5,586	4,021	5,153	5,090	6,697	4,622	4,622
Pessimistic	1,700	3,125	3,034	2,645	4,189	4,196	2,673	2,219	3,854	2,282	1,865	1,905

* Maximum value of cumulative borrowing during 1975.

Figure VIII. SUMMARY MEASURES OF LIQUIDITY AND PROFITABILITY

Outcomes	Probability	Cumulative Borrowing*	Annual After-Tax Profits	Annual Earnings Per Share	Return on Book Equity
Optimistic	.10	$323,000	$45,765	$4.58	14.2%
Likely	.60	216,000	31,658	3.17	9.8
Possible	.25	154,000	26,716	2.67	8.3
Pessimistic	.05	92,000	16,839	1.68	5.2
Expected Value		$205,000	$31,092	$3.11	9.6%
Standard Deviation		52,400	6,060	0.61	2.1

* Maximum value of cumulative borrowing during 1975.

Note: If X_j refers to a particular value of a measure with associated probability P_j, the expected value is given by $EV = \sum X_j P_j$

and standard deviation is given by $SD = \sum P_j (X_j - EV)^2$

where summations are taken over all possible outcomes.

firm.

1. Accounts Receivable. The existing collection pattern of 70% (first month after sale), 20% (second month), 10% (third month) can be tightened to 80% (first month), 15% (second month), and 5% (third month).

2. Inventory. The existing policy of a beginning inventory equal to the next three months of sales can be reduced to 80% of that level.

3. Accounts Payable. Cash payments for purchases can be slowed to 50% in the first month and 50% in the second month following the purchase.

4. Other Accruals. Cash payments for salaries and administrative expenses can be slowed to 50% in the current month and 50% in the following month after the expense is incurred.

Using a similar format from before, Figure IX presents monthly comparisons of cumulative borrowing and before-tax net profits. The "existing" row in each panel refers to the "likely" scenario on which Figures III-V are based. The "receivables" and "inventory" rows refer respectively to the changes in policies for those two current assets. The "payables" row refers to changes in payments both for purchases and selling and administrative expenses. A first observation is that the tightened inventory policy reduces necessary borrowing to a lower level than does faster collection of receivables or slower payments of current liabilities. A second observation is that profitability increases only slightly, a result only of lower interest expenses from lower levels of needed borrowing.

A third observation involving the cumulative effect of the three working capital policies is better seen with the aid of Figure X. Changes in selected measures of liquidity and profitability (the same as used in Figure VIII) relative to those from the "likely" outcome are presented. For the liquidity measure of cumulative borrowing, it is seen that the three individual reductions (from working capital policy changes) just total the aggregate change from implementing all three simultaneously. But in the case of all three profitability measures, the aggregate effect is not exactly equal to the sum of the individual

Figure IX. PROFITABILITY-LIQUIDITY TRADEOFFS FOR ALTERNATIVE WORKING CAPITAL POLICIES (in dollars)

Policy	Jan.	Feb.	Mar.	Apr.	May	June	July	Aug.	Sept.	Oct.	Nov.	Dec.
CUMULATIVE BORROWING												
Existing	25,000	45,000	82,000	100,000	102,000	97,000	128,000	147,000	164,000	208,000	214,000	216,000*
Receivables	23,000	42,000	78,000	95,000	96,000	90,000	120,000	140,000	156,000	199,000	203,000	205,000*
Inventory	20,000	36,000	70,000	84,000	84,000	79,000	108,000	122,000	134,000	175,000	177,000	177,000*
Payables	25,000	43,000	80,000	97,000	102,000	95,000	124,000	140,000	157,000	200,000	206,000	208,000*
All Changes	19,000	31,000	62,000	75,000	76,000	68,000	95,000	108,000	120,000	156,000	158,000*	157,000
BEFORE-TAX NET PROFITS												
Existing	1,700	3,125	2,985	4,126	5,600	5,586	4,021	5,104	6,571	8,052	7,444	9,002
Receivables	1,700	3,139	3,006	4,154	5,635	5,628	4,070	5,160	6,620	8,108	7,507	9,079
Inventory	1,700	3,160	3,048	4,210	5,712	5,712	4,147	5,244	6,746	8,262	7,675	9,261
Payables	1,700	3,125	2,999	4,140	5,621	5,586	4,035	5,132	6,620	8,101	7,500	9,058
All Changes	1,700	3,167	3,083	4,266	5,775	5,768	4,224	5,335	6,844	8,360	7,808	9,394

* Maximum value of cumulative borrowing during 1975.

Figure X. INDIVIDUAL AND COLLECTIVE IMPROVEMENTS IN LIQUIDITY AND PROFITABILITY FROM WORKING CAPITAL POLICIES

Policy	Cumulative Borrowing*	Annual After-Tax Profits	Annual Earnings Per Share	Return on Book Equity
Receivables	-$11,000	+$ 245	+$0.25	+0.3%
Inventory	- 39,000	+ 781	+ 0.78	+1.5
Payables	- 8,000	+ 151	+ 0.15	+0.8
All Changes	-$58,000	+$1,204	+$1.20	+2.9%

* Maximum value of cumulative borrowing during 1975.

changes. This occurs because the beginning balance sheet is not the same for all of the changes being considered.

A more important observation from the results in Figures IX and X is that there is capacity for improvement, particularly with respect to the liquidity goal of the firm. That is, the necessary borrowing during 1975 can be reduced by over 25% if receivables, payables, and inventory policies are tightened in the manner indicated. Such a potential, if realized, seemingly would enhance prospects for obtaining the necessary financing for 1975. However, it probably does not eliminate the need for Smith Products to consider long-term financing at an early date.

This completes the material that you have prepared for the Executive Committee of Smith Products. Hopefully, you can convince members of the Executive Committee of the power and usefulness of the suggested approach wherein profitability and liquidity tradeoffs form the basis for reflecting uncertainty and for examining various working capital policies of the firm.

VI. IMPLICATIONS

This paper has suggested that parallel monthly forecasts of liquidity and profitability can be useful in evaluating tradeoffs between these two management goals, in reflecting the inherent uncertainty of the future, and in estimating the impact of certain working capital policies of the firm. The suggested procedures have been illustrated with a scenario of Smith Products--a wholesaling firm whose anticipated prosperity during the next several months can only be accomplished if considerable financing can be obtained from external sources. It remains in this final section to briefly explore the implications of the suggested procedure.

First, it should be emphasized that parallel forecasts of liquidity and profitability can be no better than the quality or reliability of the input information on which they are based. The well-worn adage of "garbage in-garbage out" is appropos in this context. In fact, inappropriate estimates of future sales, collection experience, operating efficiency, and other parameters could easily result in the firm taking seemingly appropriate actions that in retrospect are detrimental to the best interests of its common stockholders. For that reason, it is incumbent upon those using the suggested procedure to do whatever is necessary to ensure a high quality of input information.

Second, it should be clear by now, that the suggested procedure does not provide an optimal solution to anything. Instead, it offers a forward look at what should occur if the input information proves to be correct. Based on such a forecast of the future, management may decide to take certain actions or to revise certain of its policies. The suggested procedure is not intended as a substitute for "optimizing" models, but rather as a framework within which such models can be exercised. For example, a cost balancing model for determining appropriate levels of inventory for a particular class of products may prove useful to the management of Smith Products. However, parallel forecasts of profitability and liquidity should allow management to trace the full impact of different inventory levels within a total systems context.

Finally, it should be clear that the budgeting and planning of working capital is but part of the total budgeting and planning activity of the firm. Although attention here has focused on the working capital policies of the firm, the suggested procedure is equally useful for examining the impact of capital budgeting, capital structure, leasing, and other management policies.

READING 43

Goal Programming and Working Capital Management

William L. Sartoris
Indiana University

M. L. Spruill
University of Kentucky

INTRODUCTION

In normative financial theory it is usually assumed that the firm has the overall objective of the maximization of the present worth with appropriate consideration of risk. A finer breakdown of this general objective results in more specific and sometimes opposing objectives. Of these spcific objectives, two common ones (but certainly not the only ones of importance) are profitability and liquidity. In most financial decision models that have been developed the dominant objective is profitability with minimal, if any, consideration given to liquidity. Specifically, in working capital models for the determination of the optimal level of a current asset, the liquidity objective is often ignored (see, for example, Soldofsky [12] or Hadley and Whitin [4].

In an article published in the Spring 1972 issue of *Financial Management*, Knight [6] has argued that it is inappropriate to examine the optimal level of the several current assets independently. He also argued that when the investments in these assets are viewed jointly the decision must become one of satisficing rather than optimizing. He suggests a simulation procedure to develop several possible investment alternatives with the manager then choosing the alternative that best satisfies his objectives.

Proposals for the application of mathematical programming techniques in financial decision making are abundant, examples being given in Beranek [1], Mao [9], Quirin [10], and Weingartner [13]. However, most of the applications include only the profitability objective.

Beranek [1] attempted to investigate the liquidity and profitability objectives jointly by using a linear programming (LP) model. The profitability objective is incorporated in the objective function while the liquidity objective is expressed as a constraint on the level of cash and the quick ratio. There are two problems with this approach. First, no effect is given to the implications of investment in working capital

Reprinted from FINANCIAL MANAGEMENT (Spring 1974), pp. 67-64, by permission of the publisher and authors.

for the profitability objective. Secondly, the liquidity objective need not necessarily be a strict constraint. Rather, management may have a desired level of working capital, and might like to minimize large deviations from this goal in either the positive or the negative direction.

It would be possible to solve the first difficulty by including the effect on profitability of investment in the various current assets in the objective function of the LP model. However, in an LP model the liquidity objective must still be expressed as a constraint with deviation from the objective possible in only one direction and with the amount of the deviation being of no consequence. In addition, all sacrifice in the model must be in the reduction of the level of achievement of the profitability objective, for the liquidity objective is treated as an inviolable constraint.

Lee [8] and Mao [9] have discussed the use of goal programming (GP), a relatively unexplored mathematical programming method developed by Charnes and Cooper [2] and Ijiri [5] in determining the optimal level of profit. Mao has suggested using GP to incorporate the liquidity and profitability objectives as goals for the model. However, he does not include the effects of investment in current assets on profitability.

MATHEMATICAL PROGRAMMING TECHNIQUES

LP is a technique used to allocated scarce resources in order to maximize or minimize some mathematical function. This function usually represents either profit or cost in a financial decision context. The general LP problem with n variables and m constraints is stated mathematically as

(1a) maximize $C_1X_1 + C_2X_2 + \ldots + C_nX_n$

(1b) subject to $A_{j1}X_1 + A_{j2}X_2 + \ldots + A_{jn}X_n \leq b_j,\ j = 1, \ldots, m$

(1c) $X_i \geq 0,\ i = 1, \ldots, n,$

where (1a) represents the objective function, with $X_1, \ldots, X_n$, representing levels of each of n decision variables and $C_1, \ldots, C_n$, representing per-unit contributions for each decision variable; where (1b) represents the constraint matrix, with $b_1, \ldots, b_m$, representing levels of available scarce resources and with the A_{ji}'s representing technology coefficients; and where (1c) represents the non-negativity restrictions.

The standard method of solving a problem of this form is the simplex method (see Dantzig [3]).

In contrast to LP, GP does not use only one goal or measure of performance (e.g., profit or cost) which is optimized subject to a set of constraints. Rather, use of GP assumes there are multiple goals (e.g., attaining a certain level of profitability *and* attaining a certain level of utilization of a scarce resource). Then, rather than maximizing or minimizing, an objective function is formulated which measures the absolute deviations from desired goals: this objective function is then minimized. In an LP formulation the value of the objective function is found and may be reduced so that the minimum or maximum values of the constraints are not violated. In a GP formulation priorities are established for each of the goals explicitly by the penalties assigned to violations of the goal, and goals are satisfied in a manner than results in a minimum penalty.

Krouse [7] has suggested a somewhat different multiple objective programming technique for working capital management. His procedure utilizes a hierarchical ordering of objectives and requires that they be satisfied sequentially in the implied order. First, the optimal solution is obtained with only the objective having the highest priority being considered. Since it is generally not possible for the other objectives to be satisfied when the first objective is at this optimum level, it is necessary to determine some acceptable suboptimal level. Next, a solution is obtained with consideration begin given to the second objective and with the additional requirement that the first objective at least achieve this suboptimal level. If an acceptable solution is not obtainable for both objectives, it is necessary to revise the initial constraining level for the first objective and resolve the problem. When an acceptable solution is obtained for both objectives, an acceptable suboptimal value is specified for the second objective and the solution proceeds to the third objective. This procedure continues until all objectives are considered. In a goal programming formulation priority weights establish the importance of the various goals rather than the order in which they must be satisfied; thus, a tradeoff between violations of the different objectives is automatically allowed in the solution.

Perhaps an example will best illustrate the concepts of GP. Consider a new company which produces 2 products, X and Y. The company has a total of 15 production hours available; each unit of product X requires 3 hours of production time, while each unit of product Y requires 1 hour. The company will allow the use of overtime, but prefers to use at most 15 hours of production time. The company's marketing department has determined that the company could sell, at most, 10 units of product X and, at most, 6 units of product Y. Since one goal of the new company is market penetration, the company would like to sell as close to the maximum number of units of each product as possible. Finally, each unit of product X generates a revenue of \$10, while each unit of product Y generates a revenue of \$8. The goal that the company's stockholders consider most important is net revenue. In fact, they expect a revenue of \$75 and are averse to any less.

Three goals can be distinguished: (1) minimizing the amount of overtime; (2) maximizing market penetration; and (3) attaining a revenue as close as possible to \$75. In terms of importance to the company, goal 3 is more important than goal 2, which is more important than goal 1.

Let d_i^+ represent an upside deviation from goal i and d_i^- a downside deviation, where both d_i^+ and d_i^- are non-negative numbers. Let the P_1, P_2, and P_3 multipliers in the objective function express the priority relationship described in the preceding paragraph, where $P_3 >>> P_2 >>> P_1$. (The P values allow us to treat incommensurable goals, that is, those which cannot be compared directly. For a more complete discussion of this, see Lee [8].) With these definitions the model for our problem is

(2a) minimize $P_1 d_1^+ + P_2 d_2^- + P_2 d_3^- + P_3 d_4^-$

(2b) subject to $3X + Y + d_1^+ = 15$ (hours)

(2c) $X + d_2^- = 10$ (units of product X)

(2d) $Y + d_3^- = 6$ (units of product Y)

(2e) $10X + 8Y + d_4^- = 75$ (revenue)

(2f) $X, Y, d_1^+, d_2^-, d_3^-, d_4^- \geq 0.$

This problem can now be solved using the ordinary simplex method for solving LP problems. It should be noted that the $d_i^{\pm}$ are not slack variables in the usual LP sense since their coefficients in the objective function are non-zero. The implication is that all constraints in the program are equality constraints, and there is a penalty if the constraints are not met exactly.

APPLICATION OF GP TO WORKING CAPITAL MANAGEMENT

The following illustration uses LP and GP together to develop a one-period financial decision model that includes both the profitability and liquidity objectives. One of the goals used in the GP formulation will be derived from a standard linear programming model used to maximize net present value of the firm subject only to technical constraints.

The ABC Company manufactures two products, Y and Z, which can be sold either for cash or on credit. The sales can be made either from production during the period or from beginning inventory. See Exhibit 1 for information on costs, demand, inventory, etc.

The firm has available a maximum of 1000 hours for production. The company incurs a carrying cost of 10% of the value of the ending inventory. ABC can obtain a loan secured by the ending inventory which has a cost of 5% for the period and which can have a maximum value of 75% of the ending inventory. The sale of one unit for cash creates a net cash inflow equal to the profit on the sale, while a sale of one unit on credit creates a net cash outflow equal to the production costs plus the credit costs. The carrying cost for the ending inventory is a cash drain for the period. An additional cash inflow of 95% of the value of the loan (the value of the loan minus the 5% interest cost) can also be obtained.

ABC managers would like to obtain as much profit during the period as possible. However, they also want an ending cash balance of $75 with downside deviations from this amount being less desirable than upside deviations. At the same time they feel than an opportunity cost of 5% exists for carrying an ending cash balance. In addition, the management would like to obtain an end-of-period current ratio of 2:1 and a quick ratio of 1:1, with either upside or downside deviations from these goals being possible but undesirable. For simplicity only, the firm presently has $150 in current liabilities, not expected to change throughout the period unless the firm obtains an inventory loan.

Before this set of goals can be incorporated in a GP formulation, it is necessary to specify some quantified goal for profit. The managers could choose some arbitrary profit figure as their goal, but this would not be consistent with the actual goal of maximum possible profit. A method of quantifying the profit goal is first to determine the maximum profit that could be obtained if the working capital goals were not present. An LP formulation is particularly appropriate for this purpose.

For the above illustration the objective function for the LP formulation would be

max profits = revenue for the period less any costs charged to the period.

max profits = \$5 (units Y sold for cash) + \$4.5 (units Y sold for credit)

+\$7.5 (units Z sold for cash) + \$6.5 (units Z sold for credit)

-(.1) (\$35) (ending inventory of Y)-(.1)(\$45) (ending inventory of Z)

-(.05)(value of loan) - (.05)(ending cash balance)

This objective function is to be maximized subject to the following constraints: sales ≤ production capacity plus beginning inventory; sales ≤ maximum demand; ending cash balance ≥ 0; value of the loan ≤ (.75) (value of

EXHIBIT 1. Data for ABC Company

Product	Maximum sales (units) Cash	Maximum sales (units) Credit	Price per unit ($)	Cost/unit ($) Production cost	Cost/unit ($) Credit cost	Cost/unit ($) Cash	Cost/unit ($) Credit	Beginning Inventory (units)	Hours used per unit produced
Y	150	100	40	35	0.50	5	4.5	60	2
Z	175	250	52.50	45	1.00	7.5	6.5	30	4

ending inventory); and number of units withdrawn from inventory must be less than or equal to number of units sold.

Solution of this LP problem resulted in a profit of $2,698.94 for the period, obtained by selling 150 units of Y for cash, 175 units of Z for cash, and 44.8 units of Z on credit. The ending inventory, cash balance, and loan are all zero. Since the inventory is zero, the current ratio and the quick ratio are equal at a value of 15.69. The maximum profit of $2,698.94 physically possible for the firm results, and thus becomes the profit goal for the GP formulation.

We are now ready to use GP to incorporate into the decision process the conflicting goals specified by ABC management. The firm's goals are (1) the maximum possible profit of $2,698.94, (2) an ending cash balance of $75, (3) an ending current ratio of 2:1, and (4) an ending quick ratio of 1:1. As explained earlier, these goals are incorporated in the model by creation of variables representing deviations from the goal and use of the simplex method to minimize these deviations. For illustration we used three possible sets of priorities: (1) the profit goal has a much higher priority than any of the working capital goals; (2) the working capital goals have a much higher priority than the profit goal; and (3) all goals have relatively similar priorities. (See the appendix for a mathematical formulation of the GP problem for this illustration.)

It should be noted here that in actual practice ABC managers may or may not have a feel for the priority of each goal. If they do have this feel, they could simply assign coefficients for the deviation variables based on these priorities. However, if these priorities do not clearly exist in the mind of the managers, the goal programming approach is still extremely useful. In a very short period of time, with the aid of a computer, the managers can see an entire range of possible priority situations and associated goal trade offs. By selecting the solution that best meets their needs they are implicitly establishing a set of priorities after the fact. Whether before or after the fact, the optimal solution for the managers, determined after examining a set of alternatives and associated goal trade offs, is useful. Thus, the method can be used for situations where the manager knows the exact weights to be placed on deviation variables, where he knows only relative priorities, and finally, where he knows nothing about his priorities. The three sets of priorities chosen to illustrate the method should adequately represent a series of alternatives that would be presented to management.

To show the effects of these three sets of priorities on the profitability and liquidity goals, arbitrary values were assigned to the coefficients of the variables representing deviations from the goals. See Exhibit 2 for the values for the coefficients that were used.

EXHIBIT 2. Coefficients for Deviation Variables Associated with Three Sets of Priorities in GP

Deviation variable	Coefficient Value		
	Set 1*	Set 2**	Set 3***
Downside Profit	999.0	0.05	6.0
Downside Cash	4.0	999.0	5.0
Upside Cash	3.5	999.0	2.5
Downside current ratio	40.0	999.0	5.0
Upside current ratio	40.0	999.0	5.0
Downside quick ratio	40.0	999.0	5.0
Upside quick ratio	40.0	999.0	5.0

*Profit has a much higher priority than the working capital goal.

**The working capital goals have a much higher priority than the profit goal.

***The priorities for all goals are similar.

The effects of the three different sets of priorities are given in Exhibit 3. For set 1, where profit has highest priority, results are identical to the LP solutions. In effect, the priority of the profit goal is so high in relation to the working capital goals that these lower priority goals are ignored in practical effect. When the liquidity goals have much higher priorities than the profit goal, the cash and the quick ratio are at their desired values, while the current ratio is 10% higher and profit is only $491.25 (see Exhibit 3). When the priorities are similar for all goals, the cash balance is equal to the goal of $75, the quick current ratios have risen

EXHIBIT 3. Results of the Goal Programming Solution Using Three Sets of Priorities

Goal	Actual Value		
	Set 1	Set 2	Set 3
Profit = $2,698.94	$2,698.94	$491.25	$857.84
Cash = $75	$0	$75	$75
Current Ratio = 2:1	15.7:1	2.2:1	3.4:1
Quick Ratio = 1:1	15.7:1	1:1	3.4:1

to 3.4:1, and the profit is $857.84 (see Exhibit 3).

Exhibit 4 gives the sales and end-of-period balances resulting from use of the three different sets of priorities in the GP problem. Results generated with the second set of priorities indicate that to approach the desired values of the current and quick ratios, it is necessary to increase the level of current liabilities. This necessitated some ending inventory to support the inventory loan.

EXHIBIT 4. Sales and End-of-Period Balances Associated With the Three Sets of Priorities Used in the Goal Programs

Item	Value		
	Set 1	Set 2	Set 3
Cash sales Y (units)	150.00	40.52	60.00
Credit sales Y (units)	----	19.48	----
Cash sales Z (units)	175.00	----	21.59
Credit sales Z (units)	44.84	3.56	8.41
Ending Inventory Y (units)	----	----	----
Ending Inventory Z (units)	----	26.42	----
Cash Balance ($)	----	75.00	75.00
Loan Outstanding ($)	----	891.83	----

A comparison of the results for Set 2 and Set 3 indicates that when the priority on the working capital goals is high, the penalty for upside deviations forces the current and quick ratios down, but it also reduces the profit. At this point the management of ABC might want to reconsider specification of their set goals with particular attention to the undesirability of too high a current and quick ratio.

SUMMARY

For illustration, we have used different sets of priorities to demonstrate their effect on the attainment of profitability and liquidity goals. In a practical application of this technique, managers presumably would have some subjective priorities they would attach to their goals. However, while their priorities might not be so concretely formed that they could specify absolute weights, they would probably be able to specify some relative priorities, such as upside deviations from cash being 1/2 to 1/3 as bothersome as downside deviations from the current ratio, and downside deviations from the current ratio being only 1/2 as important as the downside deviations from profit. The use of relative priorities allows the problem of meeting profitability and liquidity goals to be approached simultaneously in a manner similar to that employed in this paper. In other words, managers choose some arbitrary set of values that approximate the importance of various goals, and observe the result when these values are used as coefficients in the objective function of the GP. Then the managers allow these values to change and determine the sensitivity of the final result. The managers can then choose the particular mix they feel best achieves their desired goals. This approach may help managers understand which of their specified goals are hardest to attain and may even cause them to reassess goals and/or priorities.

A logical extension of the simplified model utilized here, but by no means a simple one, would be to make it a multiperiod model incorporating discounting for the time value of money. Since a realistic model must deal with uncertainty, it would be necessary to adjust for varying degrees of risk. A possible, but to our knowledge yet unexplored, extension would be for different aspects of risk to be employed in a goal framework.

APPENDIX

Following is a list of definitions of all variables used in the GP formulation of the working capital problem:

X_1 = unit sales of Y for cash

X_2 = unit sales of Y on credit

X_3 = unit sales of Z for cash

X_4 = unit sales of Z on credit

X_5 = unit sales of Y from inventory

X_6 = unit sales of Z from inventory

X_7 = dollar value of loan secured by inventory

X_8 = ending cash balance

X_9 = downside difference from profit goal

X_{10} = downside difference from cash goal

X_{11} = upside difference from cash goal

X_{12} = function of downside difference in current ratio

X_{13} = function of upside difference in current ratio

X_{14} = function of downside difference in quick ratio

X_{15} = function of upside difference in quick ratio

P_i, $i = 1,\ldots,7$ = weights on the deviations from goals. These weights are defined in Exhibit 2 for each of the three sets of priorities.

Using these definitions, the GP problem is formulated as follows:

minimize: $P_1X_9 + P_2X_{10} + P_3X_{11} + P_4X_{12} + P_5X_{13} + P_6X_{14} + P_7X_{15}$

subject to:

$$5X_1 + 4.5X_2 + 7.5X_3 + 6.5X_4 + 3.5X_5 + 4.5X_6 - .05X_7 - .05X_8 + X_9 = 2698.94$$

$$2X_1 + 2X_2 + 4X_3 + 4X_4 - 2X_5 - 4X_6 - \quad \leq 1000.00$$

$$X_5 \leq 60$$

$$X_6 \leq 30$$

$$X_1 \leq 150$$

$$X_2 \leq 100$$

$$X_3 \leq 175$$

$$X_4 \leq 250$$

$$5X_1 - 35.5X_2 + 7.5X_3 - 46X_4 + 3.5X_5 + 4.5X_6 + .95X_7 + X_{10} - X_{11} = 420$$

$$26.25X_5 + 33.75X_6 + X_7 \leq 2587.50$$

$$-40X_2 - 52.5X_4 + 35X_5 + 45X_6 + 2X_7 - X_8 + X_{12} + X_{13} = 3150$$

$$40X_2 + 52.5X_4 - X_7 + X_8 - X_{14} - X_{15} = 150$$

$$5X_1 - 35.5X_2 + 7.5X_3 - 46X_4 + 3.5X_5 + 4.5X_6 + .95X_7 - X_8 = 345$$

$$-X_1 \quad X_2 + X_5 \leq 0$$

$$-X_3 - X_4 + X_6 \leq 0$$

$$X_i \geq 0, \; i = 1, \ldots, 15$$

The following list defines the constraint given by each row in the constraint matrix:

Row 1 - profit plus downside deviation = \$2698.94

Row 2 - time used in production at most 1000 hours

Row 3 - at most 60 units of Y drawn from inventory

Row 4 - at most 30 units of Z drawn from inventory

Row 5 - at most 150 units of Y sold for cash

Row 6 - at most 100 units of Y sold on credit

Row 7 - at most 175 units of Z sold for cash

Row 8 - at most 250 units of Z sold on credit

Row 9 - total cash goals*

Row 10 - inventory loan constraint*

Row 11 - current ratio goal*,**

Row 12 - quick ratio goal*,**

Row 13 - constraint requiring cash to be non-negative

Row 14 - sales of Y for cash plus sales of Y for credit must be greater than or equal to Y drawn from inventory

Row 15 - sales of Z for cash plus sales of Z for credit must be greater than or equal to Z drawn from inventory

Finally, the following equations represent the goals prior to their being put into appropriate format for the goal program:

1) Cash: $X_8 = 5X_1 - 36X_2 + 7.5X_3 - 47X_4 - 3.5(60 - X_5) - 4.5(30 - X_6) + .95X_7 = 75$

2) Current ratio: $$\frac{X_8 + 40X_2 + 52.5X_4 + 35(60 - X_5) + 45(30 - X_6)}{150 + X_7} = 2$$

3) Quick ratio: $$\frac{X_8 + 40X_2 + 52.5X_4}{150 + X_7} = 1.$$

*The numbers of the right-hand side include not only the goal but also constants carried to right-hand side of the equality from left-hand side.
**Both ratio goals have been linearized by multiplying right-hand side by denominator of ratio.

REFERENCES

1. W. Beranek, *Analysis for Financial Decisions*, Homewood, Illinois, Richard D. Irwin, Inc., 1963.

2. A. Charnes and W. W. Cooper, *Management Models and Industrial Applications of Linear Programming*, Vols. I, II, New York, John Wiley & Sons, 1961.

3. G. B. Dantzig, *Linear Programming and Extension*, Princeton University Press, 1963.

4. G. Hadley and T. M. Whitin, *Analysis of Inventory Systems*, Englewood Cliffs, New Jersey, Prentice-Hall, Inc., 1963.

5. Y. Ijiri, *Management Goals and Accounting for Control*, Chicago, Illinois, Rand McNally & Co., 1965.

6. W. D. Knight, Working Capital Management--Satisficing Versus Optimization, *Financial Management*, (Spring 1972), p. 33.

7. C. G. Krouse, Programming Working Capital Management, in *Management of Working Capital*, ed. by K. V. Smith, St. Paul, Minnesota, West Publishing Company, 1974.

8. Sang Lee, Decision Analysis Through Goal Programming, *Decision Sciences*, (April, 1971), p. 172.

9. J. C. T. Mao, *Quantitative Analysis of Financial Decisions*, New York, The Macmillan Company, 1969.

10. C. D. Quirin, *The Capital Expenditure Decision,* Richard D. Irwin Inc., Homewood, Illinois, 1967.

11. William L. Sartoris and Ronda S. Paul, Lease Evaluation--Another Capital Budgeting Decision, *Financial Management* (Summer 1973), p. 46.

12. R. M. Soldofsky, A Model for Accounts Receivable Management, *Management Accounting* (January, 1966), p. 55.

13. H. M. Weingartner, *Mathematical Programming and the Analysis of Capital Budgeting Problems,* Chicago, Illinois, Markham Publishing Company, 1967.

READING 44

Programming Working Capital Management

Clement G. Krouse
University of California, Santa Barbara

I. INTRODUCTION

A variety of techniques have been used in the analysis of the firm's working capital management problem. Theoretical models of optimal capital structure lie at one extreme. Quite properly these assume the minimization of operating costs as a single criterion, simplified intertemporal dynamics, a restricted set of financial variables, and a limited parameter set.[1] It is the nature of these abstractions that such studies, while important conceptually, become of limited operational use.

At the opposite end of the continuum are the very positive simulation studies of the corporate financial process. At the kernel of these is a simultaneous-equation econometric model employing both accounting identities and behavioral relationships.[2] By specifically distinguishing instrument or decision variables from not-directly-controllable variables, forward recursion of the equations is used to project the firm's entire short and long-term financial structure under alternative decision strategies. Significantly, such recursion models, either deterministic or stochastic, do not involve any specification of a financial performance criterion nor, concomitantly, do they identify working capital strategies which are optimal nor, as an even lesser requirement, do they provide any algorithmic means for improving a benchmark strategy when specific single or multiple objectives are exogeneously supplied.

Thus, attempts in these two directions aimed at dealing with the working capital concerns of corporate financial managers have either been mechanical and terminated short of sufficient effort to analytically treat multiple financial goals and the derivation of optimal decision strategies, or they have been somewhat detached formalisms with abstract content lacking practical relevance. In view of these limitations, there remains an open middle ground for an operational approach to financial planning models.

[1] Cf., Baumol (1952), White-Norman (1965), Miller-Orr (1966), and Eppen-Fama (1968).

[2] Cf., Robichek-Meyers (1965), Peterson (1969), and Warren-Shelton (1971).

This paper has not been published previously. Reprinted by permission of author.

Models are required which are more descriptive than existing theoretical formulations and more directed to systematic optimization than extant simulations.

II. PLANNING WORKING CAPITAL WITH MULTIPLE OBJECTIVES IN A PROGRAMMING STRUCTURE

Only a few models which employ a programming (and hence systematic optimization) framework have been developed for short-term financial planning. The most detailed of these are linear programming formulations by Robichek *et al* (1966) and Carleton (1970) and a quadratic-linear programming formulation by Krouse (1969).[3] The approach in each of these three studies stems basically from Tinbergen's (1952) framework for quantitative macroeconomic policy. Thus, in general form these models can be summarized in discrete-time as

$$\text{(1a)} \quad \max_{\underline{d}.} \{G(\underline{x}_T) + \sum_{t=0}^{T-1} L^t(\underline{x}_t, \underline{d}_t)\}$$

subject to:

$$\left.\begin{aligned} &\text{(1b)} \quad \underline{x}_{t+1} = g^t(\underline{x}_t, \underline{d}_t) \\ &\text{(1c)} \quad f^t(\underline{x}_t, \underline{d}_t) \geq 0 \end{aligned}\right\} t = 0,1,2,\cdots,T-1$$

where $\underline{x}_t$ and $\underline{d}_t$ are respectively, column vectors of not-directly-controllable (state) and instrument (decision) variables, G and L^t are suitable *scalar-valued* functions determining the firm's performance criterion, difference equations (1b) represents the (reduced-form) econometric submodel setting forth the firm's financial process, the inequalities (1c) are a vector of technical constraints giving admissible state-decision combinations at all periods of time (e.g., as might arise from loan indenture or pension fund management agreements), and T is the firm's planning horizon.

While the mathematical techniques available for the solution of such models have rapidly advanced, it is all too clear that a crucial difficulty with these formulations lie in suitable specifying the performance functional. For, with models in this form the criterion is required to reflect analytically and with scalar value the proper proportion (total and marginal) of all the financial variables held vital to the corporations; e.g., profitability, liquidity, capital structure, and stability.

A first-level approach to this objectives problem in working capital management has been to simply circumvent it and rely on theoretical arguments that cost minimization is the firm's single relevant objective. Specifying linear financial process equations concerned with both short and long-term financing, Carleton (1970) has employed this approach. He further gives a time-block linear programming structure to the firm's planning problem and directly derives financial decision strategies which are "optimal." The central operational difficulty with such a formulation is that optimality is defined in the sense that it means maximum discounted dividends to the exclusion of other important financial considerations. It might be argued, as Carleton (p. 305) incidentally does, that the technical constraints (1c) could be formed to require other financial variables to lie in a "satisfactory" region; but this being the case, systematic attention must be given the vital question of what constitutes a satisfactory region. Clearly all financial variables have preferred exchange rates and satisfaction levels according to the values finally assigned it and every other variable by the mathematical program. And, dual variable evaluations to ascertain the "sensitivity" of such constraints are of limited use both because they are highly local measures

[3] This, of course, does not include the numerous programming formulations of the firm's capital budget problem, which models have a restricted scope.

and thus dependent on the, perhaps arbitrary, prevailing values of all model variables, and because they lose precise interpretation when variations in more than one constraint are considered.[4]

A more sophisticated and direct approach to specifying the performance functional, when multiple objectives are explicitly recognized, has been to distinguish the several arguments of the criterion and sum them in a linear or quadratic form.[5] Different weights are applied to each term, if not explicitly, then simply by the scale-dimension of the factor.[6] But since the numerical values, or even the form, of an optimal financial policy derived from such a model can change significantly as the weighting coefficients vary, and since the financial analyst typically has little *a priori* notion about what weights are appropriate, the conceded technique for employing these programming models is to solve them for a large number of weighting coefficient values and, subsequently, choose from these cases the one that is "best" according to an unspecified criterion, subjective or objective. This procedure therefore involves a certain amount of circularity and is in reality partly an art and partly objective.[7]

III. THE FINANCIAL UTILITY VECTOR

With these difficulties of extant programming formulations of the working capital management problem somewhat in mind, the intent of this section is to set forth, as the basis for an extended and revised model-form, a positive description of the firm's goal-directed financial behavior. An important, underlying observation that has already been noted in this regard is that firms have not a single goal, but a specific hierarchy of objectives. For example, the Lanzilotti (1958, p. 939) study of the behavior of large firms lead him to conclude that corporations adopt decisions policies "... that represent an order of priorities and choice among competing objectives rather than policies treated by any simple concept of profit maximization." Similarly, Lintner's (1956) observation that firms act to maintain some dividend payout target providing it meets *prior* constraints, and Cooper's (1949) early arguments for liquidity, control retention, and profits as distinct, *sequentially* attended-to elements of the firm's objective are also indicative of a hierarchy or priority ranking of financial objectives. Further supportive evidence of an ordered vector of financial goals can be found in the empirical evidence of Cyert-March (1963, Chaps. 3 and 8), Carter-Williams (1958, Chap. 4), Solomon (1963, Chap. 11), and Weston (1966, esp. p. 84). These writers imply that the firm hierarchically orders elements of a financial utility *vector*.

To help fix this goal concept formally, consider the definition of correspondent variable, x_j, for each of the firm's N financial objectives. Say, for example, the firm's profitability objective might have the associated variable of discounted net earnings. By appropriate definitions it is convenient to require higher

[4] After some background developments in the next section it will be easier to comment on the limitations of single-objective-variable-subject-to-side-constraint models and the fundamental ways in which they differ from the current formulation.

[5] The Robichek et.al. (1966) study is representative of those employing a linear criterion. The Krouse (1969) financial planning model employs a quadratic criterion. Importantly, the familiar certainty-equivalence theorem holds when the objective function is quadratic and the financial process equations are linear.

[6] In the case of the Krouse (1969, pp. 63-69) formulation a successive comparison and correlation procedure was proposed to estimate weighting coefficients in the quadratic criterion functional.

[7] A similar problem also arises in the specification of a welfare criterion in macroeconomic programming models. The apparent lack of system and consistency there has lead Fox, Segupta, and Thorbecke (1966, p. 463) to cite the formulation of objective functionals as one of the most fruitful areas for extending the scope and accuracy of optimal macrodynamic models.

values of such variables to be (weakly) preferred to lesser values. Further, construct an indexing of these financial variables $\underline{X} = \{x_1, x_2, \cdots, x_N\}$ where the lower-numbered variables are stipulated as being of a "higher priority" than higher numbered ones.[8] $\underline{X}$ is referred to as the firm's ordered, financial utility vector.

With regard to the properties of the several objectives of the utility vector, a range of evidence indicates that the dominance of precedent variables is subject to target or satisficing levels: one need only think of the familiar succession of empirical studies which have indicated that the decisions of corporate financial managements are with regard to target or satisficing values of current and quick ratios, debt-equity ratio, relative size and efficiency of capital budgets, rates of earnings and revenues growth, etc.[9] Thus, as a positive matter it further seems appropriate to admit an acceptable or satisficing level for each of the objective variables, x_j^*, such that

$$u_j(x_j \geq x_j^*) = u_j(x_j^*)$$

for all $j = 1, 2, \cdots, N$

where u_j is a monotonic nondecreasing utility function defined over an ordinal ranking of values for the firm's jth variable, x_j. The above Eq. implies that all satisficing and "extra-satisficing" states with respect to each financial objective are considered to be held indifferent and thus assigned the same utility index $u_j(x_j^*)$.

Encarnacion (1964) and Shubik (1961) specifically interpret the hierarchical listing of corporate objectives as a "starred" lexicographic ordering and further argue that it is rational for the firm to implement a financial policy over time which causes this utility *vector* to appropriately *dominate* all other admissible utility vectors.[10] Their specific meaning of vector dominance with a starred lexicographic ordering can be explained by the following paradigm:

Consider any two alternative vectors $\underline{X}^*$ and $\underline{\hat{X}}^*$.

$$\underline{X}^*: \{\min(x_1, x_1^*), \min(x_2, x_2^*), \cdots, \min(x_N, x_N^*)\}$$

$$\underline{\hat{X}}^*: \{\min(\hat{x}_1, x_1^*), \min(\hat{x}_2, x_2^*), \cdots, \min(\hat{x}_3, x_3^*)\}$$

Dominance is established by successive comparison of the corresponding components in the two vectors. If $\min(x_1, x_1^*) > \min(\hat{x}_1, x_1^*)$ then the financial policy leading to utility vector $\underline{X}^*$ is preferred by the firm, and conversely if the inequality is reversed. If, however, $\min(x_1, x_1^*) = \min(\hat{x}_1, x_1^*)$ --as, for example, would

[8] Specifically, a "starred" lexicographic ordering of variables is meant. This notion of "higher priority" is fully developed in the sequel.

[9] See for example, Simon (1952), Lintner (1956), Solomon (1963, Chap. 11), Granger (1964), and Weston (1966, p. 84). The Weston discussion on this issue is especially clear as he illustratively refers to an ordered list of "financial policy objectives":
1. growth in sales of 8% per annum
2. growth in earnings per share of 10% per annum
3. growth in common share price of 12% per annum
4. price-earnings ratio of over 20

Additionally, he cites targets for the firm's current ratio, quick ratio, debt/equity, and dividend payout as pertinent. The significant attributes of Weston's characterization of the firm's financial behavior is that (1) it is directed by multiple goals, and (2) each goal has an explicit satisficing target associated with it.

[10] Perhaps the most well known hypothesis of a corporate lexicographic utility vector with satisficing levels is that given by Baumol (1958, pp. 187-188), "... once (the businessman's) profit exceeds some vaguely defined minimum level, he is prepared to sacrifice further increments in profits if he can thereby obtain large revenues." Baumol thus postulates to two element, lexicographically-ordered utility vector with a starred level for the *precedent* profit constraint.

occur if both $x_1 \geq x_1^*$ and $\hat{x}_1 \geq x_1^*$ -- then comparison with regard to the second component would be required. Assuming the comparison reverted to the second vector component, $\underline{X}^*$ would be preferred to $\hat{\underline{X}}^*$ if $\min(x_2, x_2^*) \geq \min(\hat{x}_2, x_2^*)$, and conversely for the opposite inequality. Again, the comparison would succeed to the third vector component if equality held. And so forth in this fashion. It is of especial significance that (1) the lexicographic ordering with satisficing levels defines the preference of the firm for various financial alternatives on the basis of a *vector-valued* criterion, and (2) the hierarchical optimization procedure involves no requirement to directly compare different vector components.

In summary, it is argued that *multiple* financial objectives, formed to constitute a hierarchy of maximands, obtain for the firm. Further, these objectives appear to be pursued with a clear system of priorities; in the current notation with lower-indexed variables taking precedence over higher-indexed ones. At the point where a specified satisficing level of a financial objective is achieved, the next precedent variable becomes dominant and must then be maximized (subject, of course, to the requirement that the process does not cause lower-indexed variables to fall below thier satisficing levels). This specific hierarchical optimization procedure we symbolically represent as

$$(2)\ \text{opt}\ \{\underline{X}\} = \{\min(x_1, x_1^*), \min(x_2, x_2^*), \cdots, \min(x_N, x_N^*)\}$$

subject, of course, to both static and dynamic technical constraints. The financial decision strategy which yields the best obtainable, lexicographically ordered utility vector in this fashion is called optimal.

IV. HIERARCHICAL OPTIMIZATION FOR FINANCIAL PLANNING

In application to the planning of working capital, the sequential optimization procedure implied by equation (2) seems relatively straightforward; and, it would be if the satisficing levels of the objective variables were somehow given exogenously (as the Carleton programming model using a single objective with various side constraints alludes). Typically, however, what constitutes a satisfactory value of an objective variable for the firm will be dependent on the maximum feasible value (in the sense that technical and precedent-goal constraints are observed) and its marginal rate of substitution with the goal next in priority. Thus, in practice a procedure which explicitly develops such information to facilitate selection of satisficing (starred) levels is required. (It is to be noted that the three prior attempts at programming formulations in financial planning have not addressed these information requirements, although parametric sensitivity analyses was briefly suggested by Carleton, and the Robichek *et al* and Krouse multiple-argument criterion formulations noted iterative means for selecting weighting coefficients of the several objectives.)

In distinction to prior attempts, a hierarchical optimization approach specifically following the statement of equation (2) can be used to formulate and specify a working capital management model. An especially attractive feature of this approach is that it *directly* provides information as a basis for establishing satisficing goal levels. As a given, financial variables entering the performance criterion are considered to be ranked in order of importance as being primary, secondary, tertiary, etc. Additionally it is assumed that the firm's financial process equations are specified by an econometric model--as, for example, in the simulation models of Peterson (1969) or Warren-Shelton (1971). The basic hierarchical optimization procedure is then simply this:

An optimal program of policy instruments is derived with respect only to a primary criterion and its optimum valued obtained. A second optimization problem is then formed employing only the secondary criterion as the objective, where now the set of admissible policies is defined as those which cause the primary criterion to be within some satisficing level vis-a-vis both its optimum and subsequently its rate of technical substitution with the second precedent goal. This restriction takes the form of inequality bounds on the instrument or state variables in the second problem. Now the policy leading to an optimal value of the secondary criterion is developed over this restricted set. The rate of technical substitution between primary and secondary objectives is noted, along with the absolute values of the variables, and any desired adjustments made by changing the satisficing level of the primary goal. Next, the tertiary criterion is used where the admissible policies are given by the satisficing limits of both prior problems. The procedure is followed until the list of variables entering the performance functional are exhausted. The optimal decision policy for the last of these problems is then the final optimum optimorum.

Unlike the Robichek *et al* and Krouse multiple-goal planning models, specifying weights for the criterion functional at each stage of the analysis is not a problem in this hierarchical procedure, for as long as definitions of factors are made such that more of each is preferred to less it is entirely sufficient to directly optimize the value of the relevant financial variable (investment, sales, discounted dividends, growth, earnings, etc.) at its appropriate stage. However in the scheme the choice of satisficing level will of course depend on the nature of the model, the particular firm under question, and the subjective estimates of the financial planners. It is of importance to note that the hierarchical technique does *not* eliminate the subjectivity of optimizing approaches based on either a multiple argument criterion or a single variable criterion with side constraints, *but* it does present explicit and systematic procedures for its treatment (in developing the initial ranking of financial factors and in establishing suitable tolerances). Further, important indications of the technical substitution rates of the various objective variables to relevant-sized changes (as distinct from relying on local dual-variable interpretations) in admissible financial strategies are directly developed.

V. ILLUSTRATIVE EXAMPLE

A simplified example will help fix the manner by which working capital management might proceed using the hierarchical optimization procedure. As a basis for illustrative analysis, Table I lists a simple dynamic financial process and defines eleven state and four decision variables. For ease in the current exposition the process is considered linear and many interaction complexities are removed, but these are not a general limitation.

The first two equations of the financial process are behavioral relations, the first of which is a revenue function describing revenues as dependent on assets, an "effective" expenditure level, and revenues lagged one period. The second equation relates profits to revenues, variable production and distribution expenses, assets, and the level of debt outstanding. Equations (1-3) and (1-4) are behavior relations between inventory and accounts receivable, respectively, and revenues. For simplification, values of the state variables are assumed to be measured at the beginning of a period on the basis of the prior periods data (e.g., as might be derived from a balance sheet or income statement after the operating

Table I

STATE-TRANSITION EQUATIONS AND DEFINITIONS

Behavioral Equations:

(1-1) $R(t+1) = k_1 R(t) + k_2\ FA(t+1) + k_3\ C(t+1)$

(1-2) $P(t+1) = R(t+1) - a(t) - k_4\ FA(t+1) - k_5\ D(t+1)$

(1-3) $IN(t+1) = k_6\ R(t+1) + k_7\ [R(t+1) - R(t)]$

(1-4) $AR(t+1) = k_8\ R(t+1) - k_9\ R(t)$

Accounting Identities:

(1-5) $CA(t+1) + FA(t+1) = (1 - k_4)\ FA(t) + k_{10} P(t) + b(t) - d(t)$

(1-6) $D(t+1) = D(t) + b(t)$

(1-7) $E(t+1) = E(t) + k_{10} P(t) - d(t)$

(1-8) $CL(t+1) = D(t+1) + E(t+1) - FA(t+1) - CA(t+1)$

(1-9) $CA(t+1) = CA(t) + c(t)$

(1-10) $SC(t+1) = CA(t+1) - AR(t+1) - IN(t+1)$

Definitional Equation:

(1-11) $C(t+1) = k_{11}\ D(t) + (1 - k_{11})\ a(T)$

State Variables:

R = Revenues
FA = Fixed Assets
CA = Current Assets
C = "Effective" Cost Level
SC = Marketable Sec. and Cash
CL = Current Liabilities
D = Long-Term Debt
E = Equity
P = Net Profit
IN = Inventory
AR = Accounts Receivable

Decision Variables:

a = Period Variable Costs
b = New Debt (Incurred or Retired)
d = Dividends Paid
e = Change in Current Assets

Constants:

k_1, k_2, k_3 Regressors of the revenue behavioral equation
k_4 Overall depreciation rate on assets
k_5 Rate of interest on debt
k_6, k_7 Regressors of the inventory behavioral equation
k_8, k_9 Regressors of the accounts receivable behavioral equation
k_{10} One minus the corporate income tax rate
k_{11} Smoothing constant

year). Decision variables are dated to be executed with knowledge of the state variables having the same date.

Equations (1-3) through (1-10) are basic accounting identities requiring asset-liability and sources-uses equality over time. Accounts payable are for simplicity taken to be the only current liability. Equation (1-11) defines an "effective" level of corporate demand increasing expenditures (product quality, advertising, etc.). Being the current value of an exponentially smoothed series, effective expenditures implies a periodwise carry over effect. This realistically means, for example, that outlays on advertising and product quality in prior periods have an impact in the prevailing period.

These eleven equations of the firm's financial process serve to describe at any point in time, eleven jointly dependent state variables in terms of prior states of the firm and the financial manager's available decision instruments. Table II gives assumed values for the constants k_1 through k_{12}, initial values for state variables (all state variables are constrained to be nonnegative for all periods), and select feasibility and technical bounds for decisions. The decision complexity even in this very simple planning problem is obvious from these equations, for an optimal value assignment to a single decision variable is seen to depend on all other decisions, the initial state conditions, the state-transition equations, and all current and future expressed preferences of the firm's management. This is nothing more than recognizing that the optimality conditions of a dynamic financial process must be dependent on the interaction of many variables in a circularly causal relationship.

With regard to a performance criterion, for illustrative purposes take the firm's financial managers to have profitability, retention, and liquidity objectives, which they lexicographically order in precedence as

Primary criterion $\max \sum_{t=0}^{4} d(t)r(t)$

Secondary criterion $\max -[D(5) - sE(5)]^2$

Tertiary criterion $\max \{- \sum_{t=1}^{5} [uCA(t) - CL(t)]^2\}$

Where u is a target level for the firm's current ratio, s is a target level for debt/equity ratio, and $r(t)$ is the period t discount factor. Thus, of primary concern to the firm's financial managers is the discounted sum of dividends over the 4 period planning horizon, of secondary importance is a final period capital structure, and of tertiary importance is maintaining a target current ratio over time. For concreteness in the sequel choose $u = 1.5$ and $s = 2$, which implies a target current ratio of 1.5 and a debt/equity ratio target of 1/2. Additionally, the market discount factor is based on a 10% annual rate.

In view of the hierarchical fashion in which the financial performance criterion are ranked, we derive an optimal overall decision strategy as follows:

Stage 1. Maximization with respect to primary criterion only.

$$\max \sum_{t=0}^{4} d(t)r(t)$$

subject to: (δ)

where (δ) represents the firm's financial process given by equations (1-1) through (1-11). Solution for the discounted dividends extremal yields the optimal policy as given in Table III. Subsequently, the maximum value of discounted dividends ($141), the associated terminal debt/equity ratio, $D(5)/E(5) = 2.3$, and the current ratio sequence

$$\frac{CA}{CL} = \{1.67, 1.38, 1.22, 1.12, 1.07\}$$

Table II

INITIALIZING AND CONSTANT VALUES

State Variables:

$R(1) = \$225\ M$	$SC(1) = \$\ 32\ M$
$P(1) = 30\ M$	$D(1) = 50\ M$
$FA(1) = 100\ M$	$E(1) = 90\ M$
$CA(1) = 100\ M$	$C(1) = 160\ M$
$IN(1) = 30\ M$	$CL(1) = 60\ M$
$AR(1) = 38\ M$	

Constants:

$k_1 = 0.40$	$k_7 = 0.02$
$k_2 = 0.25$	$k_8 = 0.16$
$k_3 = 0.65$	$k_9 = 0.01$
$k_4 = 0.10$	$k_{10} = 0.50$
$k_5 = 0.08$	$k_{11} = 0.40$
$k_6 = 0.13$	

Technical Constraints:

$$0 \leq a(t) \leq R(t)$$
$$-D(t) \leq b(t) \leq 0.5D(t)$$
$$0 \leq d(t) \leq 0.5P(t)$$
$$-CA(t) \leq e(t) \leq CA(t)$$

Table III

OPTIMAL FIRST STAGE DECISIONS

Decision	Period 1	2	3	4
$a(t)$	100	110	125	140
$b(t)$	5	5	6	7
$d(t)$	29	63	42	27
$e(t)$	80	144	259	466

Table IV

OPTIMAL SECOND STAGE DECISIONS

Decision	Period 1	2	3	4
$a(t)$	100	115	128	136
$b(t)$	-10	- 8	- 6	- 5
$d(t)$	29	63	39	22
$e(t)$	60	96	154	246

over periods $t = 1,2,3,4,5$ can be determined by forward recursion of (δ).

With knowledge of this maximum potential discounted dividends it is considered that the firm's financial managers form a *tentative* satisficing level. For concreteness in this simple example assume this level to be benchmarked 5% below the maximum value of the primary criterion. Thus, at the second optimization stage it is to be required that the inequality constraints on dividend policy

$$\sum_{t=0}^{4} d(t)r(t) \geq 134$$

must obtain.

Stage 2. Maximization with respect to the secondary criterion.

$$\max -[D(5) - 2E(5)]^2$$

subject to: (δ)

$$\sum_{t=0}^{4} d(t)r(t) \geq 134$$

Solution for the optimal financial decision implied by this second-stage problem yields the results of Table IV. Again, by forward recursion of the financial process equations the firm's debt/equity ratio in year 5, constrained to yield discounted dividends above the satisficing level, can be derived as $D/E = 0.57$; the debt/equity ratio in year 5 now essentially attains its target. It is of especial interest to note that the hierarchical optimization procedure (through two stages) has resulted in a substitution of 5% discounted dividends for a significant improvement in the attained terminal value of debt/equity. The current ratio sequence becomes $CA/CL = \{1.67, 1.45, 1.29, 1.17, 1.10\}$. In view of the absolute levels of these variables, if this rate of technical substitution between discounted dividends and capital structure were thought inappropriate by the corporate planners, an adjusted satisficing level for discounted dividends could be considered. For the current illustration take this to be a fully suitable trade-off.

Proceeding again as at the end of Stage 1, if now a satisficing level for terminal period debt/equity is provisionally selected at, say, 15% of its constrained optimum, then $0.49 \leq D(5)/E(5) \leq 0.66$ must be an operative constraint during the Stage 3 optimization.

Stage 3. Maximization with respect to tertiary criterion only.

$$\max \{- \sum_{t=1}^{5} [1.5\, CA(t) - CL(t)]^2\}$$

subject to: (δ)

$$\sum_{t=0}^{4} d(t)r(t) \geq 136$$

$$D(5)/E(5) \geq 0.49$$

$$-D(5)/E(5) \geq -0.66$$

For this problem the firm optimally selects the financial decision strategy given by Table V. Accordingly, the firm's current ratio over the five periods becomes

$$CA/CL = \{1.67, 1.71, 1.65, 1.53, 1.45\}$$

Although these do not exactly attain the desired ratio of 1.5 in the five period horizon, they are a distinct improvement over those obtaining when only the two prior goals are considered. And, the minimal substitution in terminal debt/equity ratio for the noted improvement is explicit.

At this point in an operational implementation of the optimization procedure, the firm would have two courses of action. First, on the basis of the indicated substitution rates among the several objectives and their absolute values the financial planners might choose to reiterate the optimization

Table V

OPTIMAL THIRD STAGE DECISIONS

Decision	Period 1	2	3	4
$a(t)$	90	100	120	140
$b(t)$	-10	- 8	- 6	- 5
$d(t)$	29	63	39	22
$e(t)$	20	24	29	35

procedure. Alternatively, the prescribed decision strategy given in Table V might be directly adopted as the final optimum optimorum.

VI. SUMMARY AND CONCLUSIONS

From the very simple illustrative example it is clear that the proposed hierarchical optimization procedure causes the precedent criterion of one stage to become an inequality constraint at the next. In view of this one might simply ask the need for the sequential procedure, especially since the final problem is merely one in which the precedent criterion are written appropriately as constraints. But this is the essence of the step-by-step hierarchy: until prior problems are fully worked no generally acceptable benchmark of what constitutes satisficing levels of those objectives and, consequently, appropriate numerical value for the constraining inequalities, is available.

An especially important second distinction between the final problem of the hierarchical optimization procedure and the direct single-objective subject-to-side-constraint techniques is the specification of objective variable. In the former the lowest priority goal is the final maximand, while in the latter the "primary" criterion is maximand and "secondary" criteria are constraints. Thus the hierarchical procedure gives cognizance to the not always appreciated fact that to enter a variable as a constraint is to *elevate* its role in a programming model. For, the maximand is required to be compromised to absolutely meet any constraining conditions. This is a crucial distinction arising explicitly from the equation (2) statement of the firm's planning problem; quite clearly it will lead the models to different "optimal" financial strategies.

Finally, by the sequential nature of the hierarchical procedure the constraint set of the final problem is always feasible, whereas in the direct single-objective-with-side-constraint formulation infeasibility is a recurring problem both in initial specification and iterative parametric analysis, see Carleton (1970, footnote 18, p. 308).

The hierarchical optimization procedure, when the financial managers' objectives can be lexicographically ordered, yields a basis for informed economic judgment at each stage, as well as an indication of the sensitivity of various financial objectives to changes in the constraints. The subjectivity of earlier approaches to specifying the welfare criterion is not (and never will be) eliminated from the programming formulation, but the proposed analysis plan does have a theoretical basis and does treat the problem in a systematic and consistent structure, both by requiring the hierarchical ranking of the separate objectives and by the process of setting the satisficing levels used.

REFERENCES

Baumol, W., "On the Theory of Oligopoly," *Economica*, 25 (aug. 1958).

Baumol, W., "The Transaction Demand for Cash: An Inventory Theoretic Approach," *Quarterly Journal of Economics*, 66 (nov. 1952).

Carleton, W., "An Analytical Model for Long-Range Financial Planning," *Journal of Finance*, 25 (May 1970).

Carter, C., and B. Williams, *Investment in Innovation*, (London, 1958).

Cyert, R., and J. March, *A Behavioral Theory of the Firm*, (Englewood Cliffs: Prentice-Hall, 1963).

Cooper, W., "Theory of the Firm: Some Suggestions for Revision," *American Economic Review*, 34 (Dec. 1949).

Encarnacion, J., "Constraints and the Firm's Utility Function," *Review of Economic Studies*, 11 (April 1964).

Eppen, G., and E. Fama, "Solutions for Cash-Balance and Simple Dynamic-Portfolio Problems," *Journal of Business*, 1 (Jan. 1968).

Fox, K., J. Sengupta, and E. Thorbecke, *The Theory of Quantitative Economic Policy*, (Amsterdam: North-Holland Publishing Co., 1966).

Gordon, M., "Optimal Investment and Financing Policy," *Journal of Finance*, 18 (May 1963).

Granger, C., "The Hierarchy of Objectives," *Harvard Business Review*, 43 (May-June 1964).

Krouse, C., *Financial Planning: A Dynamic, Multiobjective Framework*, Ph. D. dissertation (Los Angeles: University of California, 1969).

Lanzillotti, R., "Pricing Objectives in Large Companies," *American Economic Review*, 48 (Dec. 1958).

Lintner, J., "The Cost of Capital and Optimal Financing of Corporate Growth," *Journal of Finance*, 18 (May 1963).

Marris, R., *The Economic Theory of Managerial Capitalism*, (New York: Free Press of Glencoe, 1964).

Miller, M., and F. Modigliani, "Dividend Policy, Growth, and the Valuation of Shares," *Journal of Business*, 34 (Oct. 1961).

Miller, M., and D. Orr, *An Application of Control Limit Models to the Management of Corporate Cash Balances*, Proceedings of the Conference on Financial Research and Its Implications for Management, A.A. Robichek, ed. (New York: Wiley, 1967).

Peterson, D., *A Quantitative Framework for Financial Management*, (Homewood, Ill.: Irwin, 1969).

Robichek, A. and S. Myers, *Optimal Financing Decisions*, (Englewood Cliffs: Prentice-Hall, 1965).

Robichek, A., D. Teichroew, and J. Jones, "Optimal Short-Term Financing Decisions," *Management Science*, (Sept. 1965).

Shubik, M., "Objective Functions and Models of Corporate Optimization," *Quarterly Journal of Economics*, 75 (Aug. 1961).

Simon, H., "A Behavioral Model of Rational Choice," *Quarterly Journal of Economics*, 65 (June 1952).

Solomon, E., *The Theory of Financial Management*, (New York: Columbia University Press, 1963).

Tinbergen, J., *On the Theory of Economic Policy*, (Amsterdam: North-Holland Publishing Co. 1952).

Warren, J., and J. Shelton, "A Simultaneous Equation Approach to Financial Planning," *Journal of Finance*, 18 (Sept. 1971).

Weston, J., *The Scope and Methodology of Finance*, (Englewood Cliffs: Prentice-Hall, 1966).

White, D. and J. Norman, "Control of Cash Reserves," *Operations Research Quarterly*, 3 (Sept. 1965).

READING 45

Integrating Working Capital and Capital Investment Processes

James A. Gentry
University of Illinois, Urbana-Champaign

Capital investment creates the need for additional investment in inventory, accounts receivable and cash throughout the life of the plant and equipment. It is normally assumed that an investment in working capital assets also causes a comparable expansion in current liabilities. The theoretical models for evaluating capital investment alternatives implicitly assume the costs resulting from changes in the working capital components or the cash benefits flowing from these components are imbedded in the cash flow of the investment, e.g., Bogue and Roll [8], Hertz [21, 22], Hespos and Strassman [23], Myers [40], Van Horne [57, Chapters 5-7, 13], Weingartner [59], and Weston and Brigham [61, Chapters 10, 11]. The implicit inclusion of working capital components in the capital investment model is correct theoretically, but having the capability to measure the explicit contribution of working capital components to cash inflows and outflows provides a powerful tool for management.

There are several reasons for identifying the costs and benefits created by the working capital components and linking them explicitly into the total investment planning process. More-than-likely, in the early life of an investment it is operating below capacity; while later in the life cycle, there is often an increase in operating capacity. Thus, throughout the life of an investment there is often a continuing growth of investment in working capital. Furthermore, the discounted cash outflows related to cash, receivables and inventories can range from a modest to a major proportion of the total cost of an investment. Also the source of financing for these current assets, either long or short-term, can affect the cash flow patterns of an investment. The need for additional investment in working capital is dependent on the type and size of investment, the size and growth of the market, the growth of the relative market share and length of the planning horizon. Additionally,

This paper was presented at the conference "Financial Management of Corporate Resource Allocations," the Netherland School of Business, Breukelen, Netherlands, August 1979. Reprinted by permission of the author.

the impact of inflation can create a drag on cash flows if the price increases related to labor and materials are always leading the price increase for the products sold by a significant margin. Finally, within many corporations, the managment of the working capital components is usually separate from the capital investment and long-run financial planning systems. Continuous communications between operating and strategic management are vital to the long-run success of a firm, but communications are often infrequent or nonexistent. These observations indicate the need for a planning model that explicitly integrates the working capital components into the capital investment decision-making process. That is an objective of this article.

There have been many valuable theoretical and operational contributions in managing cash [1, 2, 4, 17, 19, 25, 32, 39, 42, 43, 52, 53, 54, 55], measuring liquidity [6, 12, 29, 33, 56], managing receivables and credit selection [3, 4, 7, 24, 30, 31, 34, 35, 36, 60, 63], and controlling inventory [5]. Several authors have linked trade credit policy and inventory management [18, 37, 46, 47, 50]. Linear programming (LP) models were used to introduce the dynamic features of the working capital process. Two large scale LP models were designed to link the sources of short term credit to short term uses [44] and to integrate the variables involved in managing short term cash flow [42]. Sartoris and Spruill [45] used goal programming as a tool for the management of working capital. Gentry [14] and Gentry, Mehta, et al. [16] evaluated management perceptions of the working capital process. Walker [58, Chapters 7, 8] and Van Horne [57, Chapter 13] developed general working capital models. Several observations emerge from the preceeding set of articles. Each focused on specific segments of working capital management and each developed sets of relationships among the WC variables. Many of the models did not incorporate the dynamics of uncertainty involved in the short-run investment and financing processes and none of these models were integrated into the capital investment and long-run financing processes of the firm.

The need for integrating the working capital processes into the long-run financial planning processes has been recognized by several authors. A variety of theoretical linkages have been suggested [9, 10, 11, 15, 20, 26, 27, 28, 38, 48, 49, 54, 64]. The primary objective of this article is to offer an integrated model designed for management decision making and to provide a model for testing "what if" policy questions concerning the impact of working capital variables on the total profitability of a capital investment alternative.

The model is divided into two parts. The capital investment (CI) module will be presented first followed by the working capital (WC) module.

CAPITAL INVESTMENT MODULE

The financial planning process is composed of many variables and occurs in an uncertain and dynamic environment, therefore, this model will use simulation techniques to represent the interactions among the capital investment and working capital variables. The Hertz model [21, 22] is revised to simulate the capital investment process. The variables are divided into three major categories--market, investment and cost. The market analysis variables are market size, growth rate of market size related to the life cycle of the product, and market share related to the price of the product. The investment analysis variables are life of the investment, on line time, initial and future investment costs excluding working capital costs. The cost analysis variables are the variable and fixed costs. Each variable is assumed to be stochastic and independent. However, it is assumed the parameters specified for each variable by the decision makers reflects their perception of the interrelationships among the variables. If there are well established relationships among variables, these functional relationships can be easily inserted into the model. The variables involved in the capital investment module are presented in Figure 1 and the actual operation of the CI module is presented later.

The program randomly selects in a sequential order a value from the specified distribution for each variable. The uncertain and dynamic characteristics of the CI process are reflected in this random interaction of the variables. The selected values are used in the calculation of a net present value (NPV), internal rate of return (IRR), and a benefit/cost ratio (B/C) for each simulation. This process including the working capital module is repeated 100 times and the final outcomes are profitability profiles or cumulative frequency distributions of NPV, IRR, and B/C.

WORKING CAPITAL MODULE

An Overview

The module simulates the integration of working capital components into the capital investment (CI) process. Forecasting errors and inflation are introduced into the total investment planning process because they are the primary causes of working capital management problems. The objectives of the module are (1) to identify and measure the benefits and costs of investments in working capital components; (2) to identify the impact of forecasting errors and inflation on cash, inventory, receivables, payables and short-term borrowing; and (3) to measure the sensitivity of net present value (NPV) and internal rate of return (IRR) profiles to changes in WC strategies designed to offset forecasting errors and inflationary conditions.

Historically, WC activities are frequently revised, relatively routine and occur in a relatively short time period. Also the WC process is usually considered to be independent of the CI planning process. The management of short-run cash flows is a continuous and dynamic process occurring in an uncertain environment. However, because the CI model operates on an annual basis it is assumed, for convenience, that the strategic planning of the WC cycle also operates on a one year horizon. This assumption was made to simplify the calculation of monthly financial statements and hold down the size of an already complex computer program. A shorter time period could be programmed to accommodate the needs of decision makers.

Cash Flow Crises

A cash flow crises often occurs when unexpected events arise, e.g., actual short-run expenditures being greater than forecasted and/or actual short-run cash inflows being less than forecasted. Surprise outflows can be related to a large price increase for raw materials. An unexpected decline in inflows arises when actual sales are less than forecasted or if there is an extension of the normal trade credit payment pattern. In both cases total cash outflows are frequently greater than total cash inflows plus existing cash items.

The standard approach to investment planning is to assume that the forecasted cash flows actually occur. For example, in solving for the NPV or IRR of an investment it is assumed the forecasted distributions of revenues and costs actually occurred. By assuming the profitability profiles generated from the forecasted inputs actually happen, the analysis misses the affect a

FIGURE 1. Simulation of the Working Capital--Capital Investment Process

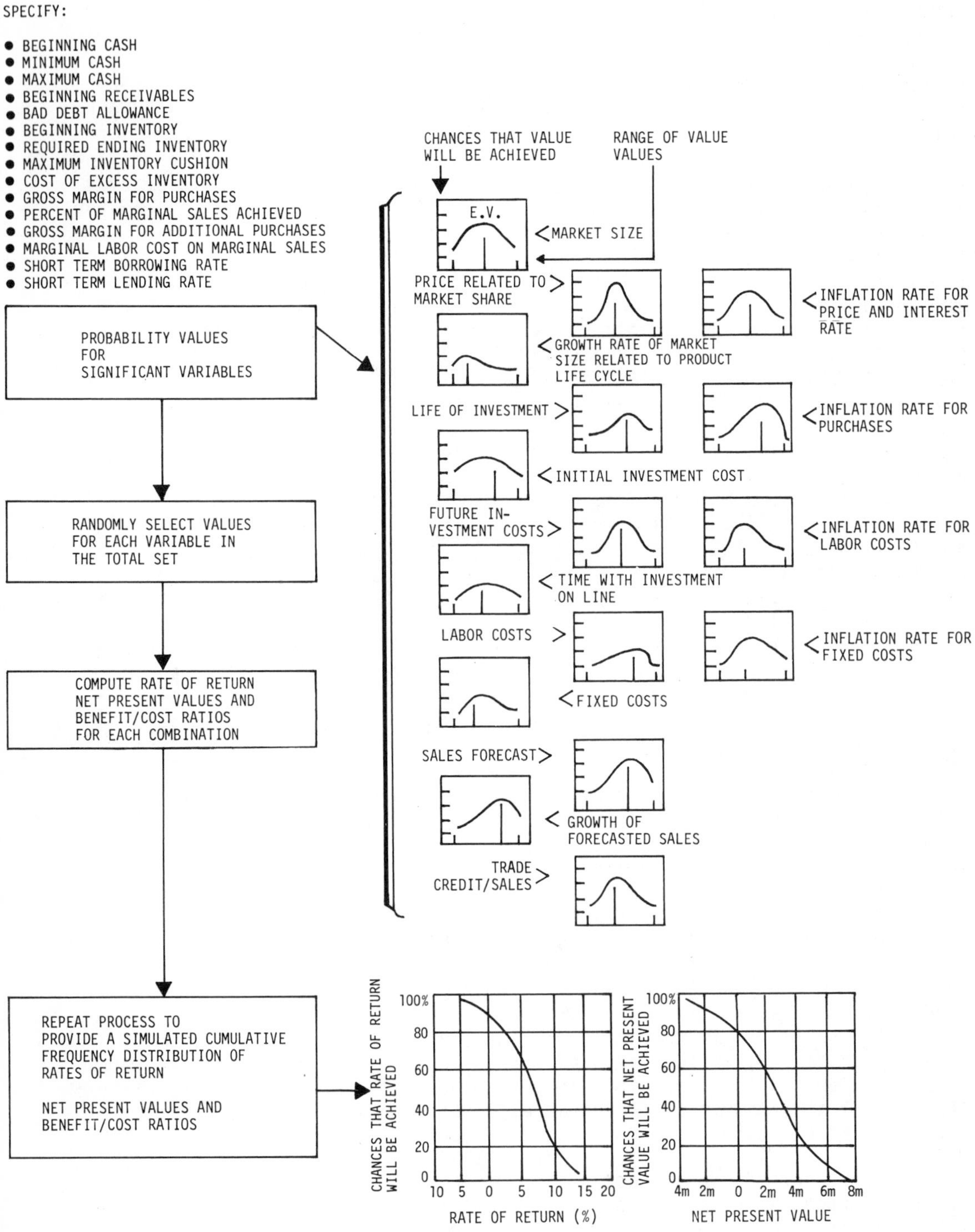

short-run financial crises has on cash flows. Because cash flow crises often arise when forecasting errors occur, the analysis of investment opportunities requires an additional step. A dual simulation process is introduced with one assumed to represent the *forecasted* results and the other the *actual* outcomes. In simulating these two sets of conditions, the model assumes sales are the key mechanism. It is assumed that the actual sales (S) are generated by the CI program and a separate forecast of sales (SF) is produced by the WC module. Simulating sales conditions where the actual sales are randomly different from forecasted sales captures the essence of forecasting errors, which incorporates the major cause of WC problems.

If the *forecasted* sales exceed *actual* sales there will be a cash flow shortfall. To offset the shortfall, current asset and current liability components are adjusted by management. The cash flow shortfall is the heart of the problem related to a WC crisis. The model provides management a variety of short-run policy alternatives to offset the cash flow shortfall.

New Variables

In the WC module two new sets of probabilistic variables are introduced and combined with the variables in the CI model. One set represents three WC variables. These variables inject the uncertainty existing in the WC system into the total financial planning process. The three probabilistic variables are sales forecast ($\tilde{SF}$) in year 1, an annual growth rate of forecasted sales ($\tilde{G}$) related to the life cycle of the product, and trade credit/sales ($\tilde{TC}$) ratio that is related to the quantity of production. These variables are presented in Figure 1.

The second set of probabilistic variables represent the inflation dimension as it impacts on the firm. There are four separate rates of inflation. The stochastic inflationary variables serve as an adjustment to the values selected for price (P), interest (i_b, i_L), total purchases (PUR), total labor costs (LC), and fixed costs (FC). These four stochastic variables are presented in Figure 1.

Additionally, management determines a single value for each of the following variables:

<u>cash</u>

- beginning cash
- minimum cash
- maximum cash (minimum cash plus marketable securities)

<u>receivables</u>

- beginning receivables
- bad debt allowance

<u>inventory</u>

- beginning inventory
- required ending inventory
- maximum inventory cushion
- cost of excess inventory

<u>operating</u>

- gross margin for purchases
- percent of marginal sales achieved
- gross margin for additional purchases
- marginal labor cost on marginal sales

<u>interest rates</u>

- short term borrowing rate
- short term lending rate

Each of these values are portrayed in Figure 1.

The working capital module is divided into three additional parts beyond the investment information presented in the CI module. The first module comprises the cost and income components. Also, inflation adjustments occur in this module. The second module involves the processes related to production and inventory. Finally, the module that links the total process together is the cash and trade credit system.

OPERATION OF THE WC MODULE

The objectives of each module and an explanation of its operation are presented in the following sections. A numerical example with accompanying comments concerning the operation of the module are found in Table 1. The example of the model in Table 1 integrates all of the modules in the total working capital-capital investment process (WC-CI). The following presentation is an explanation of the sequential operation of the WC module and is based on the data in Table 1.

Investment Information

The first operation of the model is the determination of *actual* and *forecasted* sales in both dollars and units. The initial price is provided by the user, which is $12.50 in our example in Table 1. A random market size of 4.54 million units is selected for year 1. Also, a market share of 17.92 percent is selected at random. Sales demand_1 is 862,219 units and is determined by multiplying the random market size_1 times the market share_1. Sales in dollars, $10.77 million, are calculated by multiplying price times sales demanded in units. Sales forecast_1 in dollars is randomly drawn from a distribution and sales forecast_1 in units is calculated by dividing by price.

The difference between sales demand (S) and sales forecast (SF) reflects the forecasting error and is a critical value in the working capital management process. If forecasted sales are greater than the actual sales ($SF_t > S_t$), the firm did not achieve its sales forecast. Therefore, the sales demanded (Q) become the actual sales (AS). However, if sales demand is greater than forecasted sales ($S_t > SF_t$), unforecasted or potential sales arise and it is assumed management will try to produce as much as possible to close this gap and meet these potential marginal sales. In the example in Table 1 management assumed 40 percent of potential marginal sales would be produced. Whenever $S_t > SF_t$, the marginal sales achieved are added to the sales demand to give actual sales (AS). The final operation of this module is the calculation of forecasted production (FPQ). Table 1 shows FPQ is calculated by adding the change in the amount of required ending inventory (units) to the sales forecast in units.

Each of the variables in this module make an important contribution to the total model. It is apparent the gap between S_t and SF_t is the primary reason for financial planning. The gap between S and SF introduces uncertainty into the investment planning process.

Previously capital investment theory has assumed that $S_t = SF_t$. A small contribution of the WC-CI model is to include a sales forecast variable and build in the assumptions that (1) $S_t \neq SF_t$, for $t = 1,\ldots n$, (2) if $S_t > SF$ all marginal sales may not be achievable and there might be a cost premium for marginal sales that should be added to total costs of the investment, (3) also, when marginal sales are achieved, they generate cash inflows that were not anticipated when it was assumed $S_t = SF_t$, (4) if $SF_t > S_t$, there can be a cost of carrying additional inventory that should be added to the total cost of the investment, and cash inflows will be smaller than planned under conditions when $S_t = SF_t$.

Costs and Income Module

There are several key operations involved in the costs and income module. The three primary operating costs are purchases (PUR), labor (LC) and fixed (FC). It is assumed these variables are closely related to the forecasted production, i.e., quantity of goods produced. When $S_t > SF_t$, it is possible to have marginal production above the original forecasted level. When this condition occurs, the marginal cost of purchases and labor are calculated separately and added to their respective forecasted costs for purchase and labor.

Increases in cost as a result of inflationary conditions are introduced in this module. The program randomly selects an inflation rate for purchases and this rate is applied to total purchases. The model also randomly selects and applies an adjustment to labor and fixed costs. Additionally, a random inflationary rate is injected into the price of the product. Thus, as shown in Table 1, *actual* sales are computed by multiplying the production quantity times the price which has been adjusted for inflationary pressures. When *actual* sales and costs are calculated, the model calculates the remaining components of the income statement.

The major cost items are calculated in this module and Table 1 provides an example of these calculations. First, for period 1, labor cost per unit of 2.52 was randomly chosen, and multiplied times forecasted production. The labor costs are increased for inflation, which was 5.35 percent in year 1. In this model inflation is assumed to be a random variable. When marginal sales are achieved, marginal labor costs are calculated in units of marginal sales. In Table 1, the marginal labor costs (MLCX) are 10 percent. Thus on the additional marginal sales achieved, the cost of labor was 10 percent higher than under normal operating conditions.

Fixed costs are assumed to be a random variable that is related to the sales demanded. The fixed $costs_1$ are also increased by a separate inflation rate, 4.45 percent, that was selected randomly.

Purchase costs are calculated by multiplying the gross margin (.5) times the dollar value of forecasted production. The gross margin is a key input variable determined by the user. When $S_t > SF_t$, there are marginal purchases made to accomodate the marginal sales determined earlier. Normally, the gross margin for marginal sales (GMMP) should be greater than the gross margin. It is .6 in Table 1. Additionally all purchase $costs_1$ are adjusted by a randomly selected inflation value of 5.35 percent.

In year 1 the initial investment cost of $7.72 million is randomly selected, and an annual straight line depreciation schedule of $857,778 is determined for nine year horizon. With all receipts and costs determined, earnings before interest and taxes (EBIT) of $758,065 are calculated. Next it is assumed the interest cost on short-term debt is paid the following year. Thus, in year 1, there is no interest cost, and earnings before taxes (EBT) equal EBIT. The assumed tax rate is 40 percent. Table 1 shows after the calculation of $303,226 in taxes, net $income_1$ equals $454,839.

Production-Inventory System

This module focuses on the production-inventory process. Management has at its discretion a set of variables that may be used for controlling inventory limits. In this module management establishes single point estimates for each of the following production-inventory decision variables. (1) An estimate of the beginning inventory quality (BIQ); (2) A required ending inventory (REI) value which is an estimate of management's desired ratio of ending inventory (units)/ sales forecast (units). The level of REI is related to the units of production in period t. (3) A maximum inventory cushion (MIC) that management expresses as a percent above the required ending inventory quantity (REI). If the *actual* ending inventory ($AEIO_t$) is greater than the maximum ending inventory ($MEIQ_t$), there is excess inventory (EXINV). (4) The cost of carrying excess inventory is a cost that arises when SF > S thereby causing a cash cost for holding inventory in excess of the forecasted inventory needs. The cost of carrying excess inventory is assumed to be the cost of capital. As shown in Table 1 it is multiplied times the dollar cost of excess inventory to determine the cost of holding excess inventory.

Cash-Trade Credit System

This module ties together receivables and the cash operations, including short-term borrowing or investing in marketable securities. The module collects all of the cash inflows and outflows which serve as inputs for calculating the net present value of the investment.

The primary decision variables available to management in controlling levels of cash and accounts receivable are: (1) The beginning value of cash (BC) and accounts receivable (AR); (2) A minimum cash level (CLOW) is determined as a ratio of cash/sales forecast (CMIN), which depends on the levels of production; (3) A maximum cash level (MAXCASH) that is expressed as a percent above the minimum cash balance (CLOW). MAXCASH is a discretionary variable that can range from zero to a large whole number. If ending cash (EC) falls between $CLOW_t$ and $MAXCASH_t$, the difference between EC_t and $CLOW_t$ is invested in marketable securities (MS_t). (4) The sum of minimum cash balances ($CLOW_t$) and marketable securities (MS_t) equals the maximum cash position in a specific time period (CMAX). There are three interest rate variables in the model: (5) Interest rate on short term borrow funds (i_b); (6) Interest rate on lending (i_L); (7) Cost of capital (k). The cost of capital is the discount rate in the present value equation.

The model assumes there is a controlled stochastic relationship between receivables and sales and between payables and sales. The ratios of receivables/sales (AR/S) and payables/sales (AP/S) serve as proxies for these two relationships. These two distributions are crucial management inputs in establishing trade credit policy. It is assumed management perceives a probability distribution of AR/S and AP/S ratios, and it wishes to control the level of each one within a specified range of sales. The difference between these two trade credit variables (AR/S - AP/S) is the input used to calculate the net for accounts receivable. In Table 1 a trade credit/sales (TC/S) ratio of .3535 was randomly chosen for year 1. Multiplying it times actual sales (AS_1) gives accounts $receivable_1$ of \$3.7 million. After deducting for bad $debts_{t-1}$ cash receipts (CR) are determined by adding to actual $sales_t$ the change in accounts receivable between period t and t-1. CR_1 equal \$6.78 million.

In Table 1 cash equals zero at the beginning of year 1. For subsequent years beginning $cash_t$ equals ending $cash_{t-1}$, which includes cash plus marketable securities. The total cash $available_t$ for meeting the cash $payments_t$ equals cash receipts (CR_t) plus beginning $cash_t$ (BC_t) plus interest earned on marketable securities (INT) minus any capital investment $costs_t$ (FUTCOST).

Total cash payments equals the sum of all cash outflows which are shown in Table 1. All outflows occur in the year the cost was incurred except for interest costs which are assumed to be paid in the next period after the borrowing occurred. If cash $payments_t$ are greater than cash $available_t$, the company will have to borrow short-term to meet the total cash payment. Under these conditions, ending cash equals the lower boundary (CLOW) prescribed by management. Table 1 shows this was the case in year 1. Ending cash is a complex variable that is explored further in the next few paragraphs.

If cash $payments_1$ ($CPAY_1$) were greater than cash $available_1$ ($CBAL_1$), it is necessary to borrow enough short-term funds to cover the cash shortfall plus maintaining the minimum level of cash. In the case where $CBAL_t > CPAY_t$, and there is short term (S/T) debt outstanding, the difference between $CBAL_t - CPAY_t$ is used to retire debt and also maintain the minimum cash balance. The model will continue to retire debt in future years when CBAL > CPAY. Once the S/T debt is retired and $CBAL_t > CPAY_t$, the model will invest the idle cash balances that exist above the cash lower boundary. Thus, the model assumes the investment is either borrowing or lending in any given period. Of course, it is possible that neither could occur, but it is highly unlikely. The model will invest up to CMAX in any year. Any cash above CMAX is included in cash receipts and is assumed to be earning the cost of capital.

When there is cumulative S/T debt outstanding, an interest cost is incurred at the short term rate (i_b). The interest costs became a cash outflow the following period. If there are investments in marketable securities, they earn at the lending rate (i_L). Any cash earned on marketable securities becomes cash available in the following period. Traditional analysis assumes investment is financed by long term sources and, furthermore, it assumes the debt/equity max is relatively stable in the long-run. It does not explicitly allow for a cash flow shortfall which results in an increase in short term debt. If a prolonged working capital crisis was financed by short-run financing, one serious outcome could be a radical change in a company's debt/equity mix. The chances of a short-term debt surge is quite plausible in an inflationary environment or a period of high interest rates. Finally the traditional approach does not consider a cash flow overflow, where liquid assets would earn less than the cost of capital. Thus explicitly introducing interest cost on short term borrowing and interest earned on marketable securities is an addition to traditional investment analysis.

PRESENT VALUE MODULE

Traditional Analysis

In traditional analysis cash receipts were equal to the inflow of funds from *actual* sales, and cash payments included initial and future investment costs, price adjusted labor cost, total purchases and fixed costs, plus taxes. In equation form, the net present value (NPV) of investment proposal A was:

$$(1) \quad NPV_A = -IC_0 + \frac{AS_1 - TCO_1}{(1+k)^1} + \frac{AS_2 - TCO_2}{(1+k)^2} + \ldots + \frac{AS_N - TCO_N + SV_N}{(1+k)^N}$$

Where

IC_0 = investment cost at the beginning of the period;

AS_t = total cash inflow from *actual* sales or cash inflow in each period

TCO_t = total cash outlows in each period which included the following:

TLC_t = total price adjusted labor costs, or $PALC_t + PAMLC_t$

TPC_t = total price adjusted purchases, or $PAPUR_t + PAMPUR_t$

$PAFC_t$ = price adjusted fixed costs;

T_t = taxes;

$FUTCOST_t$ = future investment costs;

Other variables included are:

SV_N = salvage value of the investment

k = cost of capital

Revised Analysis

An objective of this model is to provide a more comprehensive investment analysis framework by explicitly integrating the working capital operations into the capital investment process. Forecasting errors and inflation may cause cash flows from the revised model to vary markedly from flows generated by the traditional model. Short-term borrowing and/or the sale of marketable securities are used to offset a cash flow shortfall or the retirement of debt. Marketable securities absorb an overflow of cash above the minimum level but below the maximum level. Also changing required inventory levels, minimum cash levels or payment patterns of receivables and payables can alter shortfalls or overflows. Thus an objective of the revised model is to measure the size and sign of the cash flows and thereby make it possible to highlight the cost and benefits related to the working capital strategies. The significance of these working capital strategies on the net present value of an investment are explored in the following paragraphs.

First, declining business conditions and/or a prolonged inflationary environment can change payment behavior and dramatically alter the inflow of funds from receivables. Thus a lengthening of payments on receivables that was not forecast can result in a significant cumulative shortfall in the *actual* cash inflows from an investment. During this period if the delays in receivable payments are not offset by a stretching of payables, the net cash flows will be further reduced. If cash flows are negative short-term borrowing will occur after cash and marketable securities are reduced to their minimums. The borrowing costs are determined in the revised model and are reflected as a cash outflow. Alternatively, an acceleration of receivable inflows without a change in the payment of payables can expand the net cash flow during that period. Excess idle cash balances are invested and generate cash benefits for the investment.

Second, an adjustment in taxes is required because in the traditional models, short-term interests cost or benefits were not permitted. Thus, EBIT is increased when interest income is received which makes EBT higher than in the traditional case. Also, in the revised model, interest costs cause EBT to be lower than in the traditional model. Thus, tax outflows in the revised model differ from taxes in the traditional model.

Third, carrying excess inventory produces a holding cost. This cost enters the revised NPV equation as a cash outflow. This cost only occurs when inventory exceeds the upper control limit.

Fourth, another big actor in the revised model relates to cash management policies and operations. The change in the *ending cash account* (EC_t) between period t and t-1, can produce a substantive change in cash inflow or outflow. When $EC_t > EC_{t-1}$, it indicates an increase in the level of cash held and a reduction in cash available for meeting cash payments, which results in a lower net cash flow. The opposite effect occurs if $EC_t < EC_{t-1}$. There are several refinements related to ending cash and they are presented in Appendix 1.

Finally, positive cash $flows_t$ are used to retire accumulated short-term $borrowing_t$ ($SUMCX_t$), thereby reducing cash flows available for reinvestment, as shown in Appendix 1. When negative cash $flows_t$ happen, short-term borrowing will occur after liquid assets are reduced to a minimum. The result is $SUMCX_t > SUMCX_{t-1}$. Appendix 1 presents the logic of these two cases.

In comparing the revised cash flow (RCF) model to the traditional cash flow (CF) approach, it is necessary to refer to the equation for each one on the last page of Table 1. The RCFs differ from the CFs for the following reasons. First, the contribution of trade credit policies and bad debts are reflected in cash receipts (CR). Additionally, forecasting errors and inflation cause changes in the level of cash ($EC_t - EC_{t-1}$) and short-term borrowing ($SUMCX_t - SUMCX_{t-1}$). These two terms are algebraically added to the revised cash flows. Also the cost of carrying excess inventory because of forecasting errors enter the NPV equation as an outflow. The interest return from marketable securities and the interest cost of short-run borrowing are appropriately included in the revised cash flows.

If the sum of the $costs_t$ are greater than the $receipts_t$, and liquid assets are at a minimum, short term borrowing is employed to offset the amount of the negative cash flow. The rationale for this modeling assumption is that after the initial investment costs (IC) are incurred, any additional costs are related to an investment in working capital components or delayed capital expenditures ($FUTCOST_t$); in the event of a shortfall, short-term borrowing (STD) makes up this exact difference. Increases in the level of short-term borrowing ($SUMCX_t - SUMCX_{t-1}$) to offset a shortfall are included in the RCF equation as an inflow, therefore when $outflow_t > inflow_t$ additions to STD_t equal the shortfall and the RCF is recorded as a zero. Table 1 illustrates this concept. In the traditional model a cash flow (CF) shortfall is recorded as a negative value, e.g., year 1 in Table 1.

By making the working capital components explicit and introducing forecasting errors, the revised model can identify and measure the cost of the shortfall, which was not previously accomplished. When a positive cash flow exists, short-term borrowing is paid off before any positive cash flows are available for discounting. Thus, when borrowing occurs the RCFs are limited on the down side to zero and when positive flows occur the RCFs are limited on the top side by the retirement of debt, an increase in the level of cash or an increase in other working capital components. In conclusion, the RCFs will operate in a more narrow band than the CF from the traditional model.

For comparative purposes the model calculates the traditional (CF_t) and revised cash flows (RCF_t) for each period in the life of the investment. This provides management an invaluable source of information to compare the CF_t to the RCF_t. Because of the large number of possible combinations and permutations, interpretation of these data should be done with care. The size of the gap between CF_t and RCF_t profiles reflects the affect working capital components and strategies have on the profitability of an investment. For example, when the CF profile is positive and greater than the RCF profile, a narrow gap shows working capital components have a limited affect on the value of the investment. However, a large gap indicates the importance of working capital components and strategies in determining the value of the investment. An analysis of these wide differences can aid management in reevaluating the forecasted inputs, the forecasting errors and the working capital strategy that is creating the gap. There are many possible combinations of inputs that cause a gap. The model produces the necessary data to identify the variable(s) causing the problem.

Cost of Capital

In this model it is assumed management provides a single value it prefers to use as the initial cost of capital (k_0). However, the impact of inflation must be included in the cost of capital, k_t [41]. The cash inflows and outflows in the numerator of the NPV equation are adjusted for inflation. The price of the goods sold in period 2 (P_2) is calculated in the following manner as shown in Table 1: $P_2 = P_1(L + \tilde{PA}_2)$, where $\tilde{PA}$ is a randomly selected value for inflation drawn from a distribution established by managment. The inflation adjustment to the cost of capital is the *change in the perceived rate of inflation* between the current and most recent time periods, $\tilde{PA}_t - \tilde{PA}_{t-1}$. This adjustment for inflation is presented below in equation form, which reflects the real cost of capital_t:

$$(2)\quad (1 + k) = (1 + k_t)(1 + IF)$$

$$\text{where } IF = \tilde{PA}_t - \tilde{PA}_{t-1}$$

The $\tilde{PA}$ are price adjustment coefficients randomly selected from a distribution created by management. Using the change in the perceived rate of inflation between periods more closely approximates the behavior of financial markets [14, pp. 411-414], than an expected rate of inflation for a long time horizon [41]. The essence of the adjustment assumes a positive change in the rate of inflation will increase the cost of capital from the preceding period; however, if the rate of inflation decreases, the cost of capital will subsequently decrease. This would not occur if the adjustment process assumed a constant rising mean perceived rate of inflation as suggested by Nelson [41].

By allowing the cost of capital to change each year, the inflation adjusted net cash flows in the numerator are discounted with a different k in each period. In this simulation model the cost of capital is a probability distribution, and a cost of capital profile is created. The task of evaluating the profile of NPVs of an investment is complicated by not having a common cost of capital. Management must interpret the statistical properties of the NPVs, especially the mean, standard deviation, skewness and kurtosis when comparing separate simulations of the same alternatives or different alternatives. Furthermore, there is no longer a single cost of capital to serve as a benchmark for which the internal rates of return (IRR) can be compared. Previously if $IRR \geq k$ the investment was acceptable or rejected if $IRR < k$. In this simulation model, the profile of 100 IRR's are compared to the profile of the 100 k's and the judgment of the user is needed to determine if the investment is acceptable.

CONCLUSION

The WC-CI model extends the traditional capital investment model and provides management a tool to test the sensitivity of an investment's profitability to changes in working capital strategies. Forecasting errors and inflationary conditions are shown to be the primary causes of working capital problems. These working capital strategies are designed to offset forecasting errors and inflation. The model aids management in finding the best possible mix of strategies to generate the highest possible values of an investment.

TABLE 1. AN EXAMPLE OF THE WORKING CAPITAL-CAPITAL INVESTMENT MODEL

INVESTMENT MODULE

VARIABLES		YEAR 1	YEAR 2	COMMENTS
Price (P)	($)	12.50	13.44	P_1 is an initial input; $P_2 = P_1(1 + P\tilde{A}_2)$; $P\tilde{A}_2 = .0750$
Market Size (MSIZE)	(u)	4,811,491	5,105,954	$\widetilde{M}SIZE_0$ is a randomly selected variable = 4540000; $MSIZE_1 = \widetilde{M}SIZE_0(1 + \widetilde{M}SIZE_1)$; $GMSIZE_1 = .0598$ $GMSIZE_2 = .0612$.
Market Share (MSHR)	(%)	.179200	.220267	Randomly selected.
Sales Demand* (Q)	(u)	862,219	1,124,671	$Q_t = MSIZE_t(\widetilde{M}SHR_t)$
Sales Demand (S)	($)	10,777,737	15,115,577	$S_t = P_t \times Q_t$
Sales Forecast* (SFQ)	(u)	823,750	921,711	$\tilde{S}FQ_1$ is a randomly selected value. $SFQ_2 = Q_1(1 + \tilde{g}_2)$ where $\tilde{g}_2 = .0690$; $g_2, \ldots, g_n$ are randomly selected variables.
Sales Forecast (SF)	($)	10,296,875	12,387,798	$SF_t = SFQ_t(P_t)$
Pot Marg Sales (PS)	($)	480,860	3,727,779	$PS_t = (S_t - SF_t)$; if $SF_t > S_t$: $PS_t = 0$.
Marg Sales Achiev (MSA)	($)	193,344	1,091,111	If $SF > S$: $MSA = 0$; If $S > SF$: $MSA = PS_t(PSA_t)$; $PSA_2 = .4$, PSA = Potential Sales Achieved.

VARIABLES		YEAR 1	YEAR 2	COMMENTS
Marg Sales Achiev* (MSAQ)	($)	15,388	81,184	$MSAQ_t = MSA_t/P_t$
Actual Sales (AS)	($)	10,489,218	13,478,909	If $SF > S$: $AS_t = S_t$; If $S_t > SF_t$; $AS_t = (SFQ_t + MSAQ_t)P_t$
Actual Sales* (ASQ)	(u)	839,137	1,002,985	$ASQ_t = AS_t/P_t$
Forecast Prod (FPQ)	(u)	922,600	822,861	$FPQ_t = SFQ_t + (REIQ_t - AEIQ_{t-1})$; where REIQ is required ending inventory and $AEIQ_{t-1}$ is actual required ending inventory given below. These concepts are presented in the inventory module.

COST AND INCOME MODULE

VARIABLES		YEAR 1	YEAR 2	COMMENTS
Labor Cost (LC)	($)	2,324,951	1,876,123	$LC_1 = \tilde{LC}_1$ per unit (FPQ_1); where $\tilde{LC}_1 = 2.52$; where $\tilde{LC}_2 = 2.2799$ and BIQ = beginning inventory = 98,850 (u); LC_t for future years follows the second equation.
--Infl Adj Lab Cost (PALC)	($)	2,449,334	1,990,566	$PALC_t = LC_t(1 + PAL_t)$; where PAL is inflation rate for labor costs; $\tilde{PAL}_1 = .0535$; $\tilde{PAL}_2 = .061$.
Marg Labor Cost (MLC)	($)	42,654	203,609	If $S_t > SF_t$: $MLC_t = MSAQ_t(\tilde{LC}_t$ per unit x 1 + MLCX); MLCX = Marginal labor cost per unit above $\tilde{LC}$ per unit. MLCX = .10. If $S_t > SF_t$: MLC = 0.

VARIABLES		YEAR 1	YEAR 2	COMMENTS
--Infl Adjust (PAMLC)	($)	44,936	216,029	If $S_t < SF_t$: $PAMLC_t = 0$; If $S_t > SF_t$: $PAMLC = MLC_t(1 + \tilde{P}AL_t)$
Fixed Cost (FC)	($)	175,000	215,000	FC_t = related to SF_t.
--Infl Adjust (PAFC)	($)	182,787	216,029	$PAFC_t = FC_t(1 + \tilde{P}AF_t)$; where $\tilde{P}AF_t$ is inflation rate for fixed cost. $\tilde{P}AF_1 = .0445$; $\tilde{P}AF_2 = .064$.
Purchase Cost (PUR)	($)	5,766,248	5,576,087	$PUR_t = GM(FPQ_t \times P_t)$ where GM is gross margin. $GM = .5$.
--Infl Adjust (PAPUR)	($)	6,074,737	6,019,381	$PAPUR_t = PUR_t(1 + \tilde{P}AP_t)$; where $\tilde{P}AP_t$ is inflation rate for purchases. $\tilde{P}AP_1 = .0535$; $\tilde{P}AP_2 = .0795$.
Marg Purch Cost (MPUR)	($)	115,406	654,667	If $S_t > SF_t$: $MPUR = (MSAQ_t \times P_t)GMMP$; $GMMP = .6$, Gross margin for marginal purchases. If $SF_t > S_t$: $MPUR = 0$.
--Infl Adj (PAMPUR)	($)	121,580	7,076,712	$PAMPUR_t = MPUR_t \times (1 + \tilde{P}AP)$.
Operating Income (OI)	($)	1,615,843	4,317,355	$OI_t = AS_t - PALC_t - PAMLC_t - PAFC_t - PAPUR_t - PAMPUR_t$.
Investment Cost (IC)	($)	7,720,000	0	$\tilde{I}C_0$ is a randomly selected variable.
Deprec (DEP)	($)	857,778	857,778	DEP_1 is straight line depreciation; $DEP_t = IC_t/N$; where $N = 9$ years.
Book Value (BV)	($)	6,862,222	6,004,444	$BV_1 = IC_0 - DEP_1$; $BV_2 = BV_1 = DEP_2$.

VARIABLES		YEAR 1	YEAR 2	COMMENTS
EBIT	($)	758,065	3,459,477	$EBIT_t = OI_t - DEP_t$.
Interest (INT)	($)	0	241,050	$INT_t = i_b$ (cumulative S/T borrowing$_{t-1}$); i_b is borrowing rate of interest, $i_{b_1} = .08$; For $t_2, \ldots, t_n$, $i_{b_t} = i_{b_{t-1}}(PA_t)$; cumulative S/T borrowing$_{t-1}$ given on last page.
EBT	($)	758,065	3,218,526	$EBT_t = EBIT_t - INT_t$
Taxes (T)	($)	303,226	1,287,410	$T_t = TR(EBT)$; where TR is tax rate. $TR = .4$.
Net Income (NI)	($)	454,839	1,531,116	$NI_t = EBT_t - T_t$

PRODUCTION-INVENTORY MODULE

VARIABLES		YEAR 1	YEAR 2	COMMENTS
Required Ending Inventory (REIQ)	(u)	98,850	92,171	$REIQ_t = REI_t(SRF)$; $REI_1 = .12$; $REI_2 = .10$.
Begin Inventory (BIQ)	(u)	0	98,850	$BIQ_1 = 0$; $BIQ_t = AEIQ_{t-1}$ for $t_2, \ldots, t_n$
Actual Production (PRODQ)	(u)	937,987	996,266	$PRODQ_t = SFQ_t - BIQ_t + MSAQ_t + REIQ_t$
Actual Ending Inv (AEIQ)	(u)	98,850	92,171	If $S_t > SF_t$; $AEIQ_t = REIQ_t$; If $SF_t > S_t$: $AEIQ_t = PRODQ_t - ASQ_t + BI_t$
MAX Ending Inv (MEIQ)	(u)	118,620	110,605	$MEIQ_t = REIQ_t(1 + MIC)$; $MIC = .2$
Excess Inv (ExINVQ)	(u)	0	0	If $MEIQ_t > AEIQ_t$: $ExINVQ_t = 0$; If $AIEQ_t > MEIQ_t$: $ExINVQ_t = AEIQ_t - MEIQ_t$

VARIABLES		YEAR 1	YEAR 2	COMMENTS
--Carrying Cost (CEXINV)	($)	0	0	$CEXINV_t = ExINVQ_t(GM)(k)$, GM = Gross Margin = .5; k = cost of carrying inventory = .1
CASH-TRADE CREDIT SYSTEM				
Trade Credit/Sales ($\tilde{T}C$)	(%)	.3535	.331	$\tilde{T}C_t$ is a random variable and proxies for $(AR/S_t - AP/S_t)$.
Net Act. Rec. Bal. (AR)	($)	3,707,937	4,461,517	$AR_t = AS_t(\tilde{T}C_t)$
Bad Debt Allowance (BAD)	($)	370,794	446,152	$BAD_t = AR_t(BDA)$; BDA = .1
Cash Receipts (CR)	($)	6,781,281	12,354,531	$CR_t = AS_t + AR_{t-1} - BAD_{t-1} - AR_t$
Begin Cash + MS Bal (BC)	($)	0	617,812	$BC_1 = 0$; $BC_t = EC_{t-1}$, for $t_2, \ldots, t_n$
Cash Available (CBAL)	($)	6,781,281	12,972,343	$CBAL_t = CR_t + BC_t + BEXC_{t-1} - FUTCOST_t$, BECX is interest from S/T investment and is zero in years 1 and 2. FUTCOST = 0 future investment cost.
Total Cash Pay (CPAY)	($)	9,176,000	11,224,972	$CPAY_t = PALC_t + PAMLC_t + PAFC_t + PAPUR_t + PAMPUR_t + T_t + CEXINV_t + INT_{t-1}$
End Cash + MS Bal (EC)	($)	617,812	619,390	$EC_t = SF_t(CMIN_t) + MS_t$; $CMIN_1 = .06$; $CMIN_2 = .05$.
Cash Lower Bound (CLOW)	($)	617,812	619,390	$CLOW_t = SF_t(CMIN_t)$
MAX Cash + MS Level (CMAX)	($)	741,374	743,268	$CMAX_t = CLOW_t(1 + MAXCASH)$; MAXCASH = .2

VARIABLES		YEAR 1	YEAR 2	COMMENTS
Short Term Debt (STD)	($)	3,013,131	0	If $(CBAL_t - CPAY_t) > CLOW_t$; $STD_t = 0$; IF $(CBAL_t - CPAY_t) < CLOW$: $STD_t = (CPAY_t - CBAL_t) + CLOW$. See Appendix 1 for additional conditions.
Payment S/T Debt (PAY)	($)	0	1,127,981	If $(CBAL_t - CPAY_t) > CLOW_t$: $PAY_t = (CBAL_t - CPAY_t) - CLOW_t$. If $(CBAL_t - CPAY_t) < CLOW_t$: $PAY_t = 0$. See Appendix 1.
Cum S/T Debt (SUMCX)	($)	3,013,131	1,885,150	$SUMCX_t = SUMCX_{t-1} - PAY_t + STD_t$
--Interest Cost (INT)	($)	241,050	161,180	$INT_t = SUMCX_t(i_b)$; i_b = borrowing rate = .08
S/T LEND (Mkt Sec) (MS)	($)	0	0	If $SUMCX_t > 1$, MS = 0. See Appendix 1.
--Interest Benefits (BEXC)	($)	0	0	$BEXC_t = MS_t(i_L)$; i_L = lending rate = .07
Cash CT MAX Cash + MS (CEX)	($)	0	0	$CEX_t = CBAL_t - CPAY_t - SUMCX_t - CMAX_t$
Cash Flow (CF)	($)	2,395,320	1,274,186	$CF_t = CR_t - PALC_t - PAMLC_t - PAPUR_t - PAMPUR_t - PAFC_t - T_t^*$
Revised Cash Flow (RCF)	($)	0	0	$RCF_t = CF_t + T_t^* - T_t + BEXC_{t-1} - INT_{t-1} - (EC_t - EC_{t-1}) + (SUMCX_t - SUMCX_{t-1}) - CEXINV_t$
Cost of Capital (k)	(%)	.10	.1055	$k_t = k_{t-1} + (\tilde{P}A_t - \tilde{P}A_{t-1})$

* = T* is taxes on EBIT and arises in the traditional model. It is assumed there is no short-term debt to meet a cash flow shortfall, thus no interest costs (INT). Also in the traditional model it is assumed there is no short-term investment in marketable securities to accomodate a cash flow overflow, thus no income from short-term lending (MS).

APPENDIX 1. Determining Net Cash Flow From Investment After Adjusting For Ending Cash and S/T Debt Retirement or Addition

Legend

CBAL = Total cash inflow

CPAY = Total cash outflow

CEX = Net cash flow in excess of cash minimums

UNDISX = Net cash flow from investment after adjusting for ending cash and s/t debt retirement or addition

EC = Ending cash plus m.s. balance

BEXC = Interest benefit from s/t investment

INT = Interest cost on s/t debt

CMAX = Minimum level of cash plus m.s. in $

CMAX = CMINX * (1.0 + MAXCASH)

CR = Cash receipts

FUTCOST = Any future investment cost

CEINV = Cost of excess inventory

CLOW = Minimum cash balance

SUMCX = Cumulative s/t debt

$$CBAL_t = CR_t - FUTCOST_t + EC_{t-1} + BEXC_{t-1}$$

$$CPAY_t = \text{fixed cost}_t + \text{labor cost}_t + \text{purchase cost}_t + Taxes_t + CEINV_t + INT_{t-1}$$

$$CEX_t = CBAL_t - CPAY_t - CMAX_t$$

If $CBAL_t - CPAY_t \leq CMAX_t$, $CEX = 0$

When $CBAL_t - CPAY_t \leq CMAX_t$, $UNDISX_t = 0$

$$UNDISX_t = CBAL_t - CPAY_t - (EC_t + SUMCX_{t-1} - SUMCX_t)$$

Case 1. When $CBAL_t - CPAY_t < CLOW_t$

$$EC_t = CLOW_t$$

$$SUMCX_t = SUMCX_{t-1} + CLOW_t - (CBAL_t - CPAY_t)$$

$EC_t + SUMCX_{t-1} - SUMCX_t = CBAL_t - CPAY_t$

Therefore $UNDISX_t = 0$

Case 2. When $CLOW_t < (CBAL_t - CPAY_t) < CMAX_t$

and $CBAL_t - CPAY_t < SUMCX_{t-1}$

$EC = CLOW_t$

$SUMCX_t = SUMCX_{t-1} - (CBAL_t - CPAY_t - CLOW_t)$

$SUMCX_{t-1} - SUMCX_t = CBAL_t - CPAY_t - CLOW_t$

$EC_t + SUMCX_{t-1} - SUMCX_t = CBAL_t - CPAY_t$

Therefore $UNDISX_t = 0$

Case 3. When $CLOW_t < (CBAL_t - CPAY_t) < CMAX_t$

and $SUMCX_{t-1} < CBAL_t - CPAY_t$

$SUMCX_t = 0$

$EC_t = CBAL_t - CPAY_t - SUMCX_{t-1}$

$EC_t + SUMCX_{t-1} - SUMCX_t = CBAL_t - CPAY_t$

Therefore $UNDISX_t = 0$

Case 4. When $CMAX_t < CBAL_t - CPAY_t$,

$UNDISX_t = CBAL_t - CPAY_t - CMAX_t = CEX_t$, and

when $CMAX < CBAL_t - CPAY_t$ and $SUMCX_{t-1} < CBAL_t - CPAY_t$:

$EC_t = CMAX_t \quad SUMCX_t = 0 \quad SUMCX_{t-1} = 0$

$EC_t + SUMCX_{t-1} - SUMCX_t = EC_t$

Therefore $UNDISX_t = CBAL_t - CPAY_t - CMAX_t = CEX_t$

REFERENCES

1. Stephen H. Archer, "A Model for the Determination of Firm Cash Balances," *Journal of Financial and Quantitative Analysis*, Vol. 1 (March 1966), pp. 1-11.

2. William J. Baumol, "The Transactions Demand for Cash: An Inventory Theoretic Approach," *The Quarterly Journal of Economics*, Vol. 66 (November 1952), pp. 545-556.

3. Haskel Benishay, "Managerial Control of Accounts Receivable," *Journal of Accounting Research*, Vol. 3 (Spring 1965), pp. 114-132.

4. William Beranek, *Analysis For Financial Decisions*, Homewood, Richard D. Irwin, Inc., 1963.

5. William Beranek, "Financial Implication of Lot-Size Inventory Models," *Management Science*, Vol. 17 (April, 1967), pp. B401-B408.

6. Harold Bierman, Jr., "Measuring Financial Liquidity," *Accounting Review*, Vol. 35 (October, 1960), pp. 628-632.

7. William P. Boggess, "Screen-Test Your Credit Risks," *Harvard Business Review*, Vol. 45 (November-December, 1967), pp. 113-122.

8. Marcus Bogue and Richard Roll, "Capital Budgeting for Risky Projects with 'Imperfect' Markets for Physical Capital," *Journal of Finance*, Vol. 29 (May, 1974), pp. 601-613.

9. Willard T. Carleton, "An Agenda for More Effective Research in Corporate Finance," *Financial Management*, Vol. 7 (Winter, 1978), pp. 7-9.

10. Jack Francis Clark and Dexter R. Powell, "A Simultaneous Equation Model of the Firm for Financial Analysis and Planning," *Financial Management*, Vol. 7 (Spring, 1978), pp. 29-44.

11. Richard A. Cohn and John J. Pringle, "Steps Toward an Integration of Corporate Financial Theory," *Management of Working Capital*, ed. Keith V. Smith, St. Paul, West Publishing Co., 1974.

12. Gordon Donaldson, *Strategy for Financial Mobility*, Homewood, Richard D. Irwin, Inc., 1971.

13. Gary W. Emery, "A Stochastic Process Approach to the Investment in Liquid Assets," Ph.D. Dissertation, University of Kansas, 1978.

14. Irving Fisher, *The Theory of Interest*, New York, The MacMillan Company, 1971.

15. James A. Gentry and Stephen A. Pyhrr, "Simulating an EPS Growth Model," *Financial Management*, Vol. 2 (Summer 1973), pp. 68-75.

16. James A. Gentry, Dileep R. Mehta, S. K. Bhattacharyya, Robert Cobbaut and Jean Louis Scaringella, "An International Study of Management Perception of the Working Control Process," *Journal of International Business Studies* (JIBS), forthcoming.

17. Laurence Gitman, Jr., D. Keith Forrester and John R. Forrester, "Maximizing Cash Disbursement Float," *Financial Management*, Vol. 5 (Summer, 1976), pp. 15-24.

18. Charles W. Haley and Robert C. Higgins, "Inventory Control Theory and Trade Credit Financing," *Management Science*, Vol. 19 (December 1973), pp. 446-471.

19. C. L. F. Harley, *Cash: Planning, Forecasting and Control*, Business Books Limited, London, 1976.

20. Erich A. Helfert, *Techniques of Financial Analysis*, 6th Edition, Prentice-Hall, Inc., Englewood Cliffs, New Jersey, 1977.

21. David B. Hertz, "Risk Analysis in Capital Investment," *Harvard Business Review*, Vol. 42 (January-February 1964), pp. 95-106.

22. David B. Hertz, "Investment Policies that Payoff," *Harvard Business Review*, Vol. 46 (January-February 1968), pp. 96-108.

23. Richard F. Hespos and Paul A. Strassmann, "Stochastic Decision Trees for the Analysis of Investment Decisions," *Management Science*, Vol. 11 (August 1965), B244-B259.

24. Ned C. Hill, "Structuring the Cash Discount Decision on the Firm's Credit Policy," *Financial Management*, forthcoming.

25. Richard Homonoff and David Wiley Mullins, Jr., *Cash Management*, Lexington Books, Lexington, Massachusetts, 1975.

26. Moon K. Kim, "A Two-Stage Financing Approach to Long-Range Financial Planning Under Uncertainty: A Dynamic Programming Model," (Unpublished Ph.D. Dissertation, Department of Finance, University of Illinois, 1974).

27. W. D. Knight, "Working Capital Management--Satisficing Versus Optimization," *Financial Management*, Vol. 1 (Summer 1972), pp. 33-40.

28. Clement G. Krouse, "Programming Working Capital Management," *Management of Working Capital*, ed. Keith V. Smith, St. Paul, West Publishing Co., 1974.

29. Kenneth W. Lemke, "The Evaluation of Liquidity: An Analytical Study," *Journal of Accounting Research*, Vol. 8 (Spring 1970), pp. 47-77.

30. Wilbur B. Lewellen and Robert O. Edmister, "A General Model for Accounts Receivable Analysis and Control," *Journal of Financial and Quantitative Analysis*, Vol. 8 (March 1973), pp. 195-206.

31. Wilbur S. Lewellen and Robert W. Johnson, "Better Way to Monitor Accounts Receivable," *Harvard Business Review*, Vol. 50 (May-June 1973), pp. 101-109.

32. Eugene M. Lerner, "Simulating A Cash Budget," *California Management Review*, (Winter 1968), pp. 79-86.

33. Ungki Lim, "Corporate Liquidity Management in Relation to Dividend and Other Working Control Policy Decisions: A Time Series Empirical Study," Ph.D. Dissertation, University of Illinois, 1979.

34. George L. Marrah, "Managing Receivables," *Financial Executive*, (July 1970), pp. 40-44.

35. Dileep Mehta, "The Formulation of Credit Policy Models," *Management Science*, Vol. 14 (October 1968), pp. B-30-B-50.

36. Dileep Mehta, "Optimal Credit Policy Selection: A Dynamic Approach," *Journal of Financial and Quantitative Analysis*, Vol. 5 (December 1970), pp. 421-444.

37. L. J. Merville and L. A. Tavis, "Optimal Working Capital Policies: A Chance-Constrained Programming Approach," *Journal of Financial and Quantitative Analysis*, Vol. 8 (January 1973), pp. 47-59.

38. L. J. Merville and L. A. Tavis, "A Total Real Asset Planning System," *Journal of Financial and Quantitative Analysis*, Vol. 9 (January 1974), pp. 107-115.

39. Merton H. Miller and Daniel Orr, "A Model of the Demand for Money by Firms," *The Quarterly Journal of Economics*, Vol. 80 (August 1966), pp. 413-435.

40. Stewart C. Myers, "Interactions of Corporate Financing and Investment Decision-Implications for Capital Budgeting," *Journal of Finance*, Vol. 29 (March 1974), pp. 1-25.

41. Charles R. Nelson, "Inflation and Capital Budgeting," *Journal of Finance*, Vol. 31 (June 1976), pp. 923-932.

42. Y. E. Orgler, *Cash Management*, Belmont, Wadsworth Publishing Company, Inc., 1970.

43. Gerald A. Pogue, Russel B. Faucett, and Ralph N. Bussard, "Cash Management: A Systems Approach," *Industrial Management Review*, (Winter 1970), pp. 55-74.

44. Alexander A. Robichek, Daniel Teichroew, and J. Morgan Jones, "Optimal Short Term Financing Decision," Vol. 11, *Management Science*, (September 1965), pp. 1-36.

45. William L. Sartoris and Lynn M. Spruill, "Good Programming and Working Capital Management," *Finance Management*, Vol. 3 (Spring 1974), pp. 67-76.

46. Michael Schiff, "Credit and Inventory Management--Separate or Together?" *Financial Executive*, (November 1972), pp. 28-33.

47. Michael Schiff, and Zvi Lieber, "A Model for the Integration of Credit and Inventory Management," *Journal of Finance*, Vol. 29 (March 1974), pp. 133-140.

48. Keith V. Smith, "An Overview of Working Capital Management," *Management of Working Capital*, ed. Keith V. Smith, St. Paul, West Publishing Co., 1974.

49. Keith V. Smith, "Profitability Versus Liquidity Tradeoffs in Working Capital Management," *Management of Working Capital*, ed. Keith V. Smith, St. Paul, West Publishing Co., 1974.

50. Alan Shapiro, "Optimal Inventory and Credit-Granting Strategies Under Inflation and Devaluation," *Journal of Financial and Quantitative Analysis*, Vol. 8 (January 1973), pp. 37-46.

51. James McN. Stancil, *The Management of Working Capital*, Scranton, Intex Educational Publishers, 1971.

52. Bernell K. Stone, "The Use of Forecasts and Smoothing in Control-Limit Models for Cash Management," *Financial Management*, Vol. 1 (Spring 1972), pp. 72-84.

53. Bernell K. Stone, "The Payment-Pattern Approach of the Forecasting and Control of Accounts Receivable," *Financial Management*, Vol. 5 (Autumn 1976), pp. 65-72.

54. Bernell K. Stone, "Cash Planning and Credit-Line Determination with a Financial Statement Simulator: A Cash Report on Short-Term Financial Planning," *Journal of Financial and Quantitative Analysis,* Vol. 8, (December 1973), pp. 711-729.

55. Bernell K. Stone and Robert A. Wood, "Daily Cash Forecasting: A Simple Method for Implementing the Distribution Approach," *Financial Management*, Vol. 6 (Fall 1977), pp. 40-50.

56. James E. Townsend, "Abstract--A Multivariate Analysis of Relationship Between Liquidity Position and Common Stock Price," *Journal of Financial and Quantitative Analysis,* Vol. 7 (November 1975), p. 657.

57. James C. Van Horne, *Financial Management and Policy,* 4th Edition, Englewood Cliffs, Prentice-Hall, Inc., 1977.

58. Ernest Walker, *Essentials of Financial Management*, Englewood Cliffs, Prentice-Hall, Inc., 1971.

59. Martin H. Weingartner, *Mathematical Programming and the Analysis of Capital Budgeting Problems,* Englewood Cliffs, Prentice-Hall, Inc., 1963.

60. Merle T. Welshans, "Using Credit for Profit Making," *Harvard Business Review,* Vol. 45 (January-February 1967), pp. 141-156.

61. Fred J. Weston and Eugene F. Brigham, *Managerial Finance,* Hinsdale, Illinois, The Dryden Press, 1975.

62. T. M. Whitin, *The Theory of Inventory Management*, Princeton, Princeton University Press, 1953.

63. Dwayne Wrightsman, "Optimal Credit Terms for Accounts Receivable," *Quarterly Review of Economics and Business,* Vol. 9 (Summer 1969), pp. 59-66.

64. James M. Warren and John P. Shelton, "A Simultaneous Equation Approach to Financial Planning," Vol. 26, *Journal of Finance,* (May 1971), pp. 1123-1142.

READING 46

On Working Capital as an Investment by the Firm

Keith V. Smith
Purdue University

INTRODUCTION

Working capital is well recognized as an important decision area within the firm. Yet working capital does not seem to occupy a very prominent place within the academic field of finance. While a gap between theory and practice persists in many areas of management decision making, it would seem especially so for working capital management.

This paper suggests that the gap between theory and practice may not be so serious if working capital is given an appropriate decision-making context. Specifically, it is argued that working capital ought to be viewed as an investment, and that changes in working capital policies ought to be included in the capital budgeting process of the firm. Section II is an overall review of the working capital literature, while Section III focuses on the standard theoretical development. The results of a recent survey of working capital practices are presented in Section IV, together with some aggregate statistics on working capital investments. The major arguments of the paper are presented in Sections V and VI, followed by a numerical illustration in Section VIII. Brief implications are offered in Section VIII.

II. REVIEW OF LITERATURE

Much of the literature on working capital can be categorized in terms of the balance sheet of the firm. The following representation of a typical balance sheet will be helpful in briefly reviewing the literature. Using this representation, working capital is given by a, net working capital by $a - \ell$, while the balance sheet equation is $a + A = \ell + L + E$.

One plausible reason why developments in working capital management have seemed to lag that of other areas of finance is that the subject has emerged as a series of independent technologies rather than

This paper was presented at the conference "Financial Management of Corporate Resource Allocations," the Netherland School of Business, Breukelen, Netherlands, August 1979.

Current assets	$a = \sum_j a_j$	Current Liabilities	$\ell = \sum_j \ell_j$
Fixed assets	$A = \sum_j A_j$	Long-term debt	$L = \sum_j L_j$
		Equity	$E = \sum_j E_j$
Total assets	$a + A$	Total Sources	$\ell + L + E$

as a comprehensive subject. In introductory finance textbooks such as Weston and Brigham [32] and Van Horne [28], the unifying treatment for working capital is aggregate guidelines--that is, marketable securities a_j^* for investing surplus funds, and short-term borrowing ℓ_j^* for covering fund deficits. More detailed treatment in these and other introductory textbooks, however, is to discuss and illustrate individual technologies such as credit scoring, lockboxes, economic order quantities, etc., for managing individual current assets a_j and current liabilities ℓ_j.

In contrast, the more advanced finance textbooks hardly mention working capital at all. In the preface to their book, Fama and Miller [8] admit that they pass over some of the standard topics such as cash flow forecasting, cash budgeting, and credit management in developing a theory of finance. Haley and Schall [12] do not even mention that working capital management is excluded from their theoretical development. Mao [17] talks about the investment which a firm makes in cash, accounts receivable, and inventory--but more as a springboard for his discussion of how quantitative approaches can be used in those decisions.

Within the professional journals, there has been considerable treatment of the individual technologies--that is, of how individual current assets or current liabilities should be managed. Examples include Searby [25] on float management, Mehta [18] on credit analysis, Gitman, et.al [10] on cash disbursements, Magee [15] on inventory control, and Conover [6] on short-term bank borrowing.

At the same time, there have been attempts to discuss the interrelationships or linkages between certain working capital accounts. For example, Miller and Orr [19] treat cash and marketable securities, Schiff [24] considers accounts receivable and inventory, Beranek [2] examines inventory and bank credit, Haley and Higgins [11] focus on inventory and trade credit, and Maier and Vander Weide [16] interrelate cash collections with cash disbursements.

Mathematical programming models also have been useful in capturing some of the linkages between working capital accounts. Examples include the paper by Pogue, et. al. [22] which focuses on cash management, Orgler [21] whose perspective extends to other working capital accounts, and Robichek, et. al. [23] which centers on the short-term financing decisions of the firm.

There have been varying--albeit less satisfying--attempts to integrate working capital into the mainstream theory of finance. An earlier, introductory text by Walker [30] presents four principles that constitute a theoretical basis for working capital management. Walker focuses on the risk-return tradeoffs in each working capital account a_j, and how the firm ought to view each account as an investment. Friedland [9] suggests a portfolio theoretic approach to managing the firm's portfolio of asset accounts. In so doing, he examines the covariance $cov(a_i,a_j)$ between each pair of asset accounts. The popular capital asset pricing model has been applied to accounts receivable by Copeland and Khoury [7], to linking working capital with financial structure by Bierman, et. al [3], and to overall consideration of working capital management by Cohn and Pringle [5]. More recently, option pricing theory has been used by Levasseur [14] to develop a concept of firm liquidity.

III. THEORETICAL ANTECEDENTS

Both the theory of the firm and the theory of finance have had something to say about working capital. We begin with the theory of the firm. Following Vickers [29], we recall the profit maximizing decision for an all equity firm as

(1) Maximize $\Pi = P(Q)f(X,Y) - \gamma_1 X - \gamma_2 Y - b$

(2) Subject to: $\alpha X + \beta Y + a(Q) \leq E$

where:

Π = profit

P = price

Q = quantity

X,Y = input factors of production

$f(X,Y)$ = production function

γ_1,γ_2 = units cost of X and Y, respectively

b = fixed cost of production

α,β = capital requirement coefficient of factors X and Y, respectively

$a(Q)$ = working capital requirement

E = total equity

The appropriate Lagrangian function for this formulation is

(3) $$L(X,Y,\mu) \equiv P(Q)f(X,Y) - \gamma_1 X - \gamma_2 Y - b + \mu[E - \alpha X - \beta Y - a(Q)]$$

where μ is the Lagrangian multiplier. The first order condition is given by

(4) $$\frac{\partial L}{\partial X} = (P + Q\frac{dP}{dQ})f_X - \gamma_1 - \mu\alpha - \mu a'(Q)f_X$$

where f_X is the marginal physical product of input X, and $a'(Q)$ is the rate of change of the firm's working capital requirement. Setting expression (4) equal to zero leads to

(5) $$[P + Q\frac{dP}{dQ} - \mu a'(Q)]f_X = \gamma_1 + \mu\alpha$$

The bracketed quantity is marginal revenue net of the cost of working capital, while the righthand side is marginal resource cost. Note that working capital is costed at the firm's rate of return on equity, i.e., $\mu = \frac{d\pi}{dE}$. Using expression (5) plus a comparable relationship for input Y, one obtains the familiar result

(6) $$\frac{f_X}{f_Y} = \frac{\gamma_1 + \mu\alpha}{\gamma_2 + \mu\beta}$$

Although this is the same result that is obtained without consideration of working capital, the solution for each input does depend on working capital as seen in the bracketed quanitity in expression (5).

The theory of finance provides further perspective. In particular, we consider net present value, the accepted criterion for evaluating long-term investment projects of the firm. For a given project, net present value is given by

(7) $$\text{NPV(project)} = -C_o + \sum_{t=1}^{n} \frac{B_t - C_t}{(1+k)^t}$$

where C_o = initial cash outlay

C_t = additional cash outlay in period $t = 1,\ldots,n$

B_t = cash inflow in period t

k = the firm's average cost of capital

Many authors, particularly Bierman and Smidt [4], carefully point out the cash inflows and outlays should reflect working capital (wc). That is, both initial and subsequent cash outlays should include necessary investments in current assets a_t, while the final cash inflow B_n should include recovery of working capital at the end of the project. For the simplest case where $a_o = a_n = a$, and there are no interim adjustments to working capital, we can write an expression for the project plus its working capital implications as follows

$$(8)\quad NPV(\text{project} + wc) = -(C_o + a) + \sum_{t=1}^{n} \frac{B_t - C_t}{(1+k)^t} + \frac{a}{(1+k)^n}$$

For this case, the total project can be broken down into two major components

$$(9)\quad NPV(\text{project} + wc) = NPV(\text{project}) + NPV(wc)$$

Hence, for just the working capital investment, we have

$$(10)\quad NPV(wc) = -a + \frac{a}{(1+k)^n} = -a\left[1 - \frac{1}{(1+k)^n}\right]$$

Alternatively, if the firm makes adjustments (i.e., $\pm a_t$) to the working capital associated with a given project in each year of the project horizon, then the working capital investment would be given by

$$(11)\quad NPV(wc) = -a_o + \sum_{t=1}^{n} \frac{a_t}{(1+k)^t}$$

which is seen to be analogous to expression (7), the standard formulation for a capital budgeting project without explicit consideration of working capital. In other words, working capital can be logically viewed as a separate project.

IV. FURTHER PERSPECTIVE

The foregoing review demonstrates that working capital can be viewed in a variety of different ways. From a theoretical standpoint, it is clear that working capital is a variable that should be considered by financial managers, as well as from the perspective of the entire firm. In order to provide additional perspective on working capital as an investment, we provide two additional, though independent, viewpoints.

First, it is helpful to see how changes in working capital accounts compare to long-run investment projects made by the firm. One way to make that comparison is to examine year-to-year changes in certain balance sheet accounts. Using data from the Standard and Poor's COMPUSTAT tapes, it was possible to calculate the absolute changes in accounts receivable, inventory, and gross plant as a percentage of total firm assets. Absolute changes were measured since some changes in working capital policies (e.g., a tighter credit policy) may result in lower investment levels. Exhibit 1 presents the average changes of a sample of 2,000 firms for each year 1968-1977. The findings demonstrate that changes in both receivables and inventory have been substantial relative to changes in gross plant. Moreover, the total change in receivables and inventory exceeded the change in gross plant for each year.

Second, it also is helpful to see if financial managers view working capital as an investment. A recent survey by Smith and Sell [27] investigated current practices in

EXHIBIT 1. Average Absolute Changes in Selected Assets as a Percentage of Change in Total Assets, Annually 1968-1977

YEAR	RECEIVABLES	INVENTORY	RECEIVABLES PLUS INVENTORY	GROSS PLANT
1968	28.1%	31.2%	59.3%	58.0%
1969	31.1	33.9	65.0	60.6
1970	31.7	37.7	69.4	63.8
1971	30.8	35.4	66.2	57.9
1972	35.6	34.7	70.3	54.9
1973	31.5	41.4	72.9	50.6
1974	29.9	48.4	78.3	50.4
1975	32.5	44.0	76.5	57.2
1976	32.5	39.6	72.1	54.8
1977	34.1	36.7	70.8	60.1

NOTE: Calculations are based on the first 2,000 firms for which complete data was available on the Standard and Poor's COMPUSTAT annual industrial tape.

the management of working capital by America's largest industrial firms. Questionnaires were sent to a population of 653 firms, selected on the basis of both size and profitability, from the annual FORTUNE listing of industrial corporations. Completed questionnaires were returned by 210 firms, or a response rate of 32.2%. The survey instrument included both single-answer and ranked-response questions. Certain of the findings are pertinent here.

Two ranked-response questions focused on the criteria used in managing individual working capital accounts. With respect to criteria used in evaluating proposed changes in credit terms (Exhibit 2), "return-on-investment" (i.e., ROI) received fewer responses than that for the other possible answers. In terms of a weighted-rank response (which infers a cardinality scale on the part of the financial manager), ROI was ranked below firm profits and firm sales. With respect to criteria used in evaluating changes in inventory policy (Exhibit 3), ROI received slightly fewer responses than either inventory level or firm profits as a criterion. For the weighted-rank response, however the ROI response was second only to firm profits. Clearly, return-on-investment is a prominent concept in the minds of managers responsible for both receivables and inventory.

Three single-answer questions probed further on the issue of working capital as an investment. The authors asked financial managers if they use an ROI criterion in evaluating proposed changes in working capital components (Exhibit 4). Almost 90% of those responding indicated that they sometimes or always use ROI. The percentage response to "always use ROI" was slightly higher for the larger size and more profitable subsamples.[1] When asked if

[1]The "larger size" subsample consisted of 73 firms having an average sales of $4.7 billion, while the "smaller size" subsample included 53 firms with an average sales of $130 million. The "more profitable" subsample consisted of 63 firms with an average five year return-on-equity of 11.6%; the "less profitable" subsample included 72 firms with an average return-on-equity of -4.8%.

EXHIBIT 2. Ranking of Criteria Used in Evaluating Credit Term Changes

CRITERION	NUMBER OF RESPONSES	NUMBER ASSIGNING RANK 1	2	3	4	WEIGHTED RESPONSE
Effect on firm sales	161	53	50	43	15	2.12
Effect on level of receivables	147	29	36	39	43	2.65
Effect on firm profits	159	71	49	31	8	1.85
Effect on return on investment	139	36	36	29	35	2.46

EXHIBIT 3. Ranking of Criteria Used in Evaluating Inventory Policy Changes

CRITERION	NUMBER OF RESPONSES	NUMBER ASSIGNING RANK 1	2	3	4	WEIGHTED RESPONSE
Effect on inventory costs	139	24	39	51	25	2.55
Effect on level of inventory	148	43	34	36	35	2.42
Effect on firm profits	154	68	54	27	5	1.79
Effect on return on investment	142	50	43	17	32	2.22

EXHIBIT 4. The Use of Return-On-Investment Criterion in Evaluating Possible Changes in Working Capital Components (in percentage)

USAGE	TOTAL SAMPLE	LARGER SIZE	SMALLER SIZE	MORE PROFITABLE	MORE PROFITABLE
Never	12.5%	12.5%	19.2%	14.5%	11.1%
Sometimes	51.0	54.2	50.0	45.2	51.4
Always	36.5	33.3	30.8	40.3	37.5

working capital implications are included in the evaluation of capital budgeting projects (Exhibit 5), two-thirds of the responding firms indicated that they always do so, while only 5.7% never do so. A greater proportion of the larger size firms, as well as the less profitable firms, "always" reflect the working capital implications of capital projects.

Finally, and most apropos to this paper, we asked if changes in working capital components (e.g., easier credit terms, lower inventory levels) are considered <u>along</u> with other projects in the firm's capital budgeting process (Exhibit 6). Less than 20% of the total sample "never" do so, while 33% "always" do so. As for the subsample comparisons, a smaller fraction of both the larger and the less profitable firms do not consider working capital changes as investment projects.

V. FINANCIAL CONTROL

In view of the relative size of working capital changes, and also the

EXHIBIT 5. Working Capital Implications in Capital Budgeting Decisions (in percentage)

	TOTAL SAMPLE	LARGER SIZE	SMALLER SIZE	MORE PROFITABLE	LESS PROFITABLE
Never	5.7%	2.7%	11.3%	12.7%	1.4%
Sometimes	27.6	27.4	32.1	25.4	33.3
Always	66.7	69.9	56.6	61.9	65.3

EXHIBIT 6. Changes in Working Capital Components as Projects in Capital Budgeting Decisions (in percentage)

USAGE	TOTAL SAMPLE	LARGER SIZE	SMALLER SIZE	MORE PROFITABLE	LESS PROFITABLE
Never	19.1%	12.5%	20.8%	47.5%	30.0%
Sometimes	47.8	55.6	47.2	39.7	46.5
Always	33.0	31.9	32.1	30.2	36.6

finding that many firms do indeed view such changes as investment projects, it is well to consider more closely the relationship of working capital decisions to other financial decisions made by the firm. In my opinion, the relationship is found in financial control. While control is well known to be one of the key functions of management, it would appear to have received considerably less treatment than planning, at least in the financial literature. But just as control without adequate planning will likely be futile, planning without follow-up control will prove frustrating.

A first dimension of financial control that has been well documented is to monitor the financial progress of the firm over time. This usually takes the form of tracking selected financial ratios, and thereby assessing both the current status and likely future prospects of the organization. If attention is limited to single ratios for just profitability and liquidity, then financial control is relatively straightforward. If, instead, management tracks a larger number of financial ratios, then financial control is more complex as tradeoffs must be made. In general, if there are N measures being tracked, any investment project or change in policy will result in 2^N possible changes in the status of the firm: one change favorable for all N measures, one change unfavorable for all N measures, and 2^N-2 changes involving tradeoffs. Obviously, the number 2^N-2 quickly gets large as N is increased. One way to handle the complexity of multiple ratios is with composite measures such as the DuPont System [13] or the Altman bankruptcy test [1].

A second dimension of financial control is to consider corrective actions that can be taken when firm progress departs from firm plans. For example, if the liquidity position of the organization appears to be worsening, management may decide to issue either bonds or stocks in order to reduce short-term financial obligations. Alternatively, management may decide to reduce inventory levels and/or expand credit if the probability goal of the firm is not being achieved. Many possible corrective actions pertain to the current assets and current liabilities of the firm, and thus working capital adjustments can be an important part of overall financial control within the organization.

VI. WORKING CAPITAL INVESTMENTS

A logical extension of this idea is to view corrective actions as investments made by the firm. Just as investments are routinely made by the firm in capital projects, so too should the firm routinely consider changes in working capital accounts as investment projects. Viewed in this way, each investment in working capital is an attempt to move the firm closer to its expressed goals. This view, it should be noted, is different than just including working capital implications with each capital project being considered. It is also a view that is consistent, with the theory of the firm, the theory of finance, and apparently the current practices of many large industrial firms.

A list of possible corrective actions having to do with working capital is presented in Exhibit 7. The list, which is representative rather than exhaustive, is organized into six groups that correspond to certain current assets and current liabilities normally found on the balance sheet. Some of the changes result from internal decisions by firm management, while the effect of other changes depend on the actions of external constituencies, such as customers or suppliers. Certain changes reflect management's willingness to assume risk. Other changes are an attempt to influence float.

Not all of the corrective actions in Exhibit 7 would be feasible, let along desirable, for a given firm at a particular point in time. For each corrective action that is feasible, financial managers should identify the expected benefits and costs toward evaluating whether it would help the firm move toward its expressed goals. Corrective action #7, for example, is a change in the cash discounts which the firm offers to its credit customers. A cash discount is tantamount to a reduction in price. Suppose the discount is increased. To the extent that customers take advantage of the larger discount by paying their bills sooner, the firm's investment in accounts receivable is reduced. The expected dollar benefit of corrective action #7, therefore, should reflect the extent of the discount that is offered, the proportion of credit customers that are expected to take the discount, and the resulting decrease in the receivables investment. The expected dollar cost of corrective action #7 is the reduced profit to the firm as a result of credit customers that avail themselves of the larger discount.

Based on past experience with customer response to changing credit terms, the credit manager ought to be able to make reasonable estimates of the expected benefit and cost to the firm of offering customers a larger cash discount. Expected benefit and cost can then be combined in order to calculate a "return-on-investment" for the proposed corrective action. If a similar procedure is also followed for each corrective action being considered (such as those in Exhibit 7), then each corrective action can be viewed as a proposed investment project by the firm--and evaluated within the context of the capital budgeting process. Again, this would seem to be consistent with both received theory and current management practice.

EXHIBIT 7. Possible Corrective Actions Involving Working Capital

CASH

1. Change collection network
2. Change disbursement network
3. Change size of operating cash balance

MARKETABLE SECURITIES

4. Change method of investing surplus cash
5. Change method of transferring funds between cash account and marketable securities portfolio.

ACCOUNTS RECEIVABLE

6. Change cutoff score for credit applications
7. Change discounts offered customers
8. Change frequency of follow-up payment notices

INVENTORY

9. Change inventory valuation methods
10. Change inventory order quantities
11. Change inventory safety stocks
12. Change distribution network

PAYABLES AND ACCRUALS

13. Change suppliers used
14. Change response to supplier discounts
15. Change payroll procedures

SHORT-TERM BORROWING

16. Change lenders used
17. Change payment methods
18. Change collateral arrangements

VII. AN ILLUSTRATION

Using an illustration,[2] we complete the suggestion of evaluating working capital changes as investment projects. Suppose that financial executives for a particular firm are considering four corrective actions that involve working capital from the previous list (#1, 4, 6, and 10). Exhibit 8 includes for each change a brief description, a qualitative assessment and quantitative estimates of both its benefits and costs, and the calculation of a return-on-investment.

Before looking at the investment decision to be made, it is useful to

[2]An earlier version of this illustration appeared in Smith [26].

EXHIBIT 8. Illustration of four proposed changes in working capital

CHANGE	DESCRIPTION	ESTIMATED BENEFIT	ESTIMATED COST	RETURN-ON-INVESTMENT
#1	CHANGE COLLECTION NETWORK: Implement lockbox collection system in five metropolitan areas.	Reduced average collection time of one week. $50,000 lower investment in negative float.	Service fees to five banks for managing lockboxes. $7,000 annual fee.	$\frac{(\$7,000)}{(\$50,000)} = 14\%$*
#4	CHANGE METHOD OF INVESTING SURPLUS CASH: Hire manager for firm's portfolio of marketable securities.	Increased average yield on surplus cash balances. (1.5%)($2,400,000)=$36,000 annually	Total compensation package of added manager. $30,000 annually.	$\frac{\$36,000-30,000}{\$30,000} = 20\%$
#6	CHANGE CUTOFF SCORE FOR CREDIT APPLICATIONS: Relax credit by decreasing credit cutoff score.	Increased profit from added sales, net of likely increased bad debts. $54,000 annually.	Added investment in accounts receivable and inventory. $300,000.	$\frac{\$54,000}{\$300,000} = 18\%$
#10	CHANGE INVENTORY ORDER QUANTITY: Increase purchase quantities for parts used in manufacturing in response to supplier quantity discounts.	Increased profits (decreased total costs) associated with acquiring the parts. $13,000 annually.	Increased average inventory and hence investment in inventory. $100,000.	$\frac{\$13,000}{\$100,000} = 13\%$

*When both numerator and denominator are negative, a lower ratio is preferable to a higher ratio.

point certain features of the changes summarized in Exhibit 8. Changes #6 and #10 are relatively straightforward in that additional investments in current assets are expected to lead to increased annual profits (i.e., cash flows) to the firm. In addition, change #6 reflects an important linkage in that the estimated cost includes additional investment in both accounts receivable and inventory. For change #1, a reduced investment in a current asset (i.e., cash) is made possible through an annual expense and hence a reduced profit to the firm. For "reduced investments" of this sort, the associated return-on-investment must be less than the firm's cost-of-capital in order to be attractive to the firm. For change #4, an annual compensation expense leads to an annual expected increase in additional revenue (i.e., yield) to the firm. Since the firm must make an advance commitment for the new position, it is appropriate to think of the $30,000 salary as an annual "investment," just as with the other three proposed changes.

Suppose that the firm's cost-of-capital is estimated to be 15%. If the four proposed corrective actions are judged to be independent, and if no investment constraint is imposed by the firm, then changes #1, 4, and 6 would be acceptable according to the usual criterion of return-on-investment exceeding cost-of-capital. However, if management imposes a dollar investment constraint on the changes which can be made, then the projects must be considered in combination.

Exhibit 9 is a complete enumeration of all combinations of the four proposed changes for the illustration. For five proposed projects, there are $2^5 = 16$ combinations reflected in Exhibit 9. Without any changes, the firm is expected to earn 15% on its investment (i.e., total assets) of $1 million. The optimal choice of projects is indicated for each of several selected investment constraints. For investment constraints of $1,050,000 (5% growth in firm size) and $1,150,000 (15% growth), changes #1 and 4 should be implemented. For a constraint of $1,250,000 (25% growth), the combination of changes #1 and 6 is optimal. For a constraint of $1,350,000 (35% growth), the combination of changes #1, 4, and 6 is optimal. If there is no investment constraint imposed by management, then changes #1, 4, and 6 should all be implemented. The aggregate result of those three changes in working capital would be to increase the return-on-investment of the firm from 15.00% to 15.86%.

But what if working capital changes were evaluated alongside of the long-term capital projects of the firm? Would it change the optimal solution available to management? To answer these questions, suppose that financial executives also are asked to consider a single capital budgeting project--namely, the introduction of a new product for the firm. It is described as a twenty-year project for which the immediate investment of $200,000 is expected to increase after-tax cash flows by $36,500 per year. The internal-rate-of-return for that twenty-year project is approximately 17%, and thus the project would be acceptable given the firm's 15% cost of capital.

Again assuming independent projects, Exhibit 10 shows how the optimal solution would change for each level of investment constraint. For simplicity, the twenty-year project is referred to as project #20. There are now six projects being evaluated, and hence there are $2^6 = 32$ combinations under consideration. Exhibit 10 indicates that the optimal choice among the 32 combinations is different for a growth constraint of 15%, and also if there is no investment constraint. It is also seen that without a capital constraint, the optimal choice (projects #1, 4, 6, and 20) increases the total firm return from 15.86% to 16.18%. Though clearly

EXHIBIT 9. Optimal Choice of Working Capital Projects for Selected Capital Constraints

PROJECTS	RETURN*	INVESTMENT*	RETURN ON INVESTMENT	INVESTMENT CONSTRAINT*				
				1,050	1,150	1,250	1,350	Unlimited
none	150	1,000	15.00 %					
1	143	950	15.05					
4	156	1,030	15.15					
6	204	1,300	15.69	no	no	no		
10	163	1,100	14.82	no				
1,4	149	980	15.20	optimal	optimal			
1,6	197	1,250	15.76	no	no	optimal		
1,10	156	1,050	14.86					
4,6	210	1,330	15.79	no	no	no		
4,10	169	1,130	14.96	no				
6,10	217	1,400	15.50	no	no	no	no	
1,4,6	203	1,280	15.86	no	no	no	optimal	optimal
1,4,10	162	1,080	15.00	no				
1,6,10	210	1,350	15.56	no	no	no		
4,6,10	223	1,430	15.59	no	no	no	no	
1,4,6,10	216	1,380	15.65	no	no	no	no	

*In thousands of dollars.

no = project combination not feasible under constraint.

EXHIBIT 10. Optimal Choice of Working Capital and Capital Budgeting Projects for Selected Capital Constraints

INVESTMENT CONSTRAINT*	WORKING CAPITAL PROJECTS ONLY	WORKING CAPITAL AND CAPITAL PROJECTS	COMPARISON OF SOLUTION
1,050	1, 4 (15.20%)	1, 4 (15.20%)	same
1,150	1, 4 (15.20%)	1, 20 (15.61%)	different
1,250	1, 6 (15.76%)	1, 6 (15.76%)	same
1,350	1, 4, 6 (15.86%)	1, 4, 6 (15.86%)	same
Unlimited	1, 4, 6 (15.86%)	1, 4, 6, 20 (16.18%)	different

*In thousands of dollars.

NOTE: The value in parentheses for each case is the overall rate-of-return to the firm for that combination of accepted projects.

simplistic, the illustration demonstrates that management is led to different solutions when working capital changes are considered alongside of capital projects. To do otherwise is to suboptimize--especially if investment constraints are imposed by management.

VIII. IMPLICATIONS

This paper has dealt with working capital as an investment. Investigation included a brief review of the literature, a special focus on how working capital is treated in the theory of the firm and the theory of finance, empirical evidence on how annual changes in receivables and inventory have exceeded annual changes in gross plant for a large sample of industrial firms, and a look at current management practices with regard to working capital.

This led to a suggestion that working capital should not be treated as just a set of independent topics--as often is done in introductory textbooks--but rather as a set of investment projects. As part of overall financial control, each working capital project should be viewed as a corrective action in helping move the firm toward its expressed goals. Emphasis should be on relative changes--instead of absolute levels--for each working capital investment.

Furthermore, working capital projects should be evaluated alongside of long-term investment projects as part of the firm's capital budgeting process. Each working capital project should reflect, where appropriate, linkage to other working capital accounts, just as the projected cash flows for a long-term investment project should reflect necessary changes in receivables, inventory, etc.

Two limitations to these suggestions should be mentioned. First, the illustration assumed that all projects being considered were independent. Such an assumption is at odds with one observation made repeatedly in the paper, that all relevant linkages between working capital accounts should be considered. While some attention was given to the importance of linkages--especially for corrective action #6 in the illustration--we really did not come to grips with possible interrelationships. For example, in the second part of the illustration, we did not consider how the working capital implications of the capital project #20 might impact on the benefits and costs of the other four working capital projects being considered. In pursuing such interrelationships between projects, discussion comes full circle to the gap between theory and practice--since a portfolio view of financial management has been suggested in the literature [9], though probably not incorporated by very many firms.

Second, many readers probably observed that liquidity and risk were conspicuously absent from the illustration. The usual caveat, that the firm's cost-of-capital ought to reflect the relative risk of the projects being considered is not very satisfying. Still, if risk and liquidity can somehow be formulated as further constraints to the investment decision problem of the firm, the suggestions of this paper would still hold. That is, an investment framework should be appropriate for evaluating both the proposed working capital and investment projects of the firm, subject to all constraints that are identified. That decision problem, of course, has been well developed by several authors, especially Weingartner [31].

If an investment view of working capital is taken, then working capital becomes a more logical part of finance--rather than just a subsidiary topic. Moreover, it can be argued that an investment view of working capital provides a useful framework for integrating the seemingly disparate literature. Among the current assets and liabilities of the firm, only accounts receivable has consistently been viewed from an investment perspective.[3] Cash has tended to be viewed mainly from the perspective of reducing float, while inventory has been largely approached via a square root formula. Accounts payable has centered on the percentage cost of not taking cash discounts offered by suppliers, while discussions of short-term borrowing often have been examined from the viewpoint of how compensating balances and/or commitment fees on credit lines effectively increase the annual percentage cost of the borrowing. By looking at each working capital account as an investment--and, in particular, at relative changes in the investment level of each--it would seem that working capital begins to come together as a more coherent subject.

This paper began with an observation that there is a gap between the theory and practice of working capital. While academicians typically believe that their work is in advance of what occurs in practice, working capital may well be a decision area where practice has tended to lead theory. For we have seen that many firms do think of working capital as an investment, and many do evaluate working capital changes in a capital budgeting context. Hopefully, the suggestion of working capital as an investment by the firm--developed and illustrated here--will help to redirect the thrust of subsequent research on working capital management to be even more relevant to those who deal with working capital decisions in practice.

[3]For example, see Oh [20].

REFERENCES

1. E. I. Altman, "Financial Ratios, Discriminant Analysis, and the Prediction of Corporate Bankruptcy," *Journal of Finance*, September 1968, pp. 589-609.

2. W. Beranek, "Financial Implications of Lot-Size Inventory Models," *Management Science*, April 1967, pp. 28-33.

3. H. Bierman, K. Chopra, and J. Thomas, "Ruin Considerations: Optimal Working Capital and Captial Structure," *Journal of Financial and Quantitative Analysis*, March 1975, pp. 119-128.

4. H. Bierman and S. Smidt, *The Capital Budgeting Decision*, New York: Macmillan Publishing Company, fourth edition, 1975, p. 137.

5. R. Cohn and J. J. Pringle, "Steps Toward an Integration of Corporate Financial Theory," see Reading #3.

6. C. T. Conover, "The Case of the Costly Credit Agreement," *Financial Executive*, September 1971, pp. 40-48.

7. T. E. Copeland and Nabil T. Khoury, "Analysis Credit Extensions in a World of Uncertainty," see Reading # 24 in this book.

8. E. F. Fama and M. H. Miller, *The Theory of Finance*, New York: Holt, Rinehart & Winston, Inc., 1972, preface.

9. S. Friedland, *The Economics of Corporate Finance*, Englewood Cliffs, N. J.: Prentice-Hall, 1966.

10. L. J. Gitman, D. K. Forrester, and and J. R. Forrester, Jr., "Maximizing Cash Disbursement Float," *Financial Management*, Summer 1976, pp. 15-24.

11. C. Haley and R. C. Higgins, "Inventory Control Theory and Trade Credit Financing," *Management Science*, Dec. 1973, Parts I and II, pp. 464-471.

12. C. Haley and L. D. Schall, *The Theory of Financial Decisions*, New York: McGraw-Hill Book Co., 1973.

13. E. A. Helfert, *Techniques of Financial Analysis*, Homewood, Illinois: Richard D. Irwin, fourth edition, 1977, chapter 2.

14. M. G. Levasseur, "An Option Model Approach to Firm Liquidity Management," *Journal of Banking and Finance*, 1977, pp. 13-28.

15. J. F. Magee, "Guides to Inventory Policy: Problems of Uncertainty," *Harvard Business Review*, March-April 1956, pp. 103-116.

16. S. F. Maier and J. H. Vanderweide, "A Unified Location Model for Cash Disbursements and Lock-Box Collections, Summer 1976, pp. 166-172.

17. J. C. T. Mao, *Quantitative Analysis Of Financial Decisions*, New York: MacMillan Publishing Company, 1969, Chapter 13.

18. D. Mehta, "The Formulation of Credit Policy Models," *Management Science*, October 1968, pp. B-30-B-50.

19. M. Miller and D. Orr, "Mathematical Models for Financial Management," Selected Paper #23, Graduate School of Business, University of Chicago, pp. 1-20.

20. J. S. Oh, "Opportunity Cost in the Evaluation of Investment in Accounts Receivable," *Financial Management*, Summer 1976, pp. 32-36.

21. Y. E. Orgler, "An Unequal-Period Model for Cash Managment Decisions," *Management Science*, October 1969, pp. B-77-B-92.

22. G. Pogue, R. Faucett, and R. Bussard, "Cash Management: A Systems Approach," *Industrial Management Review*, Winter 1970, pp. 55-74.

23. A. Robicheck, D. Teichroew, and J. M. Jones, "Optimal Short Term Financing Decision," *Management Science*, September 1965, pp. 1-36.

24. M. Schiff, "Credit and Inventory Management--Separate or Together," *Financial Executive*, November 1972, pp. 28-33.

25. F. W. Searby, "Use Your Hidden Cash Resources," *Harvard Business Review*, March-April 1968, pp. 71-80.

26. K. V. Smith, *Guide To Working Capital Management*, New York: McGraw-Hill Book Co., 1979, Chapter 9.

27. K. V. Smith and S. B. Sell, "Working Capital Management in Practice," see Reading #5 in this book.

28. J. C. Van Horne, *Financial Management And Policy*, Englewood Cliffs, N. J.: Prentice-Hall, fourth edition, 1977.

29. D. Vickers, *The Theory Of The Firm: Production, Captial, And Finance*, New York: McGraw-Hill Book Co., 1968.

30. E. W. Walker, *Essentials Of Financial Management*, Englewood Cliffs, N. J.: Prentice-Hall, second edition, 1971, Chapter 7.

31. H. M. Weingartner, *Mathematical Programming And The Analysis Of Capital Budgeting Problems*, Chicago, Illinois: Markham Publishing Company, 1967.

32. J. F. Weston and E. F. Brigham, *Managerial Finance*, Hinsdale, Illinois: Dryden Press, sixth edition, 1978, Chapter 6.

0-8299-0296-1